# LAL BAHADUR SHASTRI

## A Life of Truth in Politics

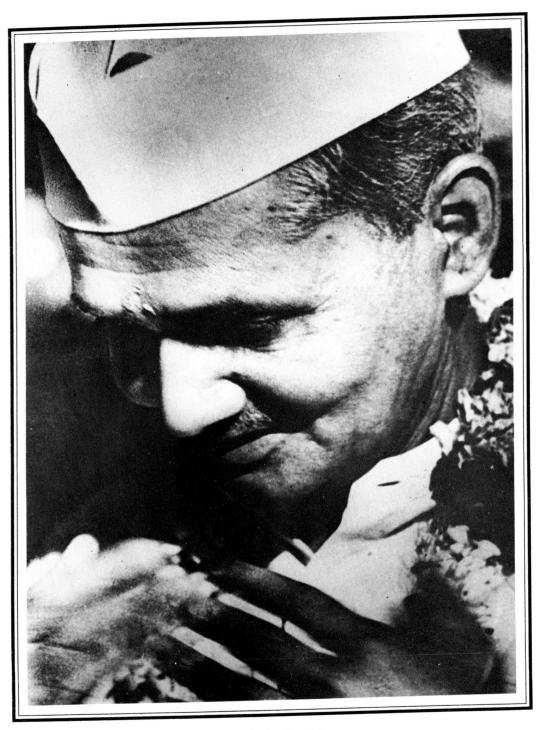

Lal Bahadur Shastri

# LAL BAHADUR SHASTRI

## PRIME MINISTER OF INDIA

9 June 1964 – 11 January 1966

## A Life of Truth in Politics

C. P. SRIVASTAVA

DELHI
OXFORD UNIVERSITY PRESS
OXFORD    NEW YORK
1995

*Oxford University Press, Walton Street, Oxford* OX2 6DP

*Oxford New York*
*Athens Auckland Bangkok Bombay*
*Calcutta Cape Town Dar es Salaam Delhi*
*Florence Hong Kong Istanbul Karachi*
*Kuala Lumpur Madras Madrid Melbourne*
*Mexico City Nairobi Paris Singapore*
*Taipei Tokyo Toronto*
*and associates in*
*Berlin Ibadan*

*ISBN 0 19 563499 3*

*Typeset by Rastrixi, New Delhi 110070*
*Printed in India at Pauls Press, New Delhi 110020*
*and published by Neil O'Brien, Oxford University Press*
*YMCA Library Building, Jai Singh Road, New Delhi 110001*

*This book is
dedicated to my dear wife*
NIRMALA
*who has been a profound source of
affection, encouragement, support and inspiration
ever since our marriage in 1947*

# Acknowledgements

I have gathered documentary material and photographs for this biography from a number of libraries and institutions. To all of them, particularly the following, I wish to express my profound gratitude: Nehru Memorial Museum and Library, New Delhi: Professor Ravinder Kumar, Director, Dr Hari Dev Sharma, deputy director, and librarian and staff. The library of the Ministry of Information and Broadcasting, Government of India, New Delhi: the librarian and staff of the library. All India Radio, New Delhi: the director-general and his staff. The Centre for Policy Research, New Delhi: Dr V.A. Pai Panandiker, director, and his staff. The Servants of the People Society, New Delhi: Shri Satya Pal. *The Hindustan Times*, New Delhi: I have quoted extensively from this newspaper and am deeply grateful. Also to Mr N. Thiagarajan, former chief photographer, Hindustan Times Group, who has provided the cover photograph and other photographs. The Films Division, Government of India, Bombay: the director and his staff. The Lyndon Baines Johnson Library, Austin, Texas, USA: David Humphrey, supervising archivist; John Wilson, archivist; Irene Parra, archivist; Linda Hanson, archivist; Regina Greenwell, archivist; Claudia Anderson, archivist; and Jeremy Duval, staff member. Yale University Library, Connecticut, USA: the librarian and staff of the library. The British Library, London: the librarian and staff of the library. The British Library, Newspaper Library, Colindale, London: the librarian and staff of the library.

I am immensely grateful to His Excellency Mr William Clark, Jr., the former United States ambassador to India, and to Mr John Walsh, former counsellor, US embassy in New Delhi, who introduced me to the above-named libraries in the United States.

I acknowledge an enormous debt of gratitude to the following who have helped me in my research in a variety of ways or have read parts of this biography and provided invaluable comments:

Paul Ellis and Victoria Zbylut of Washington; Gregoire and Catherine de Kalbermatten, Caroline Vance, Christine Egan, Manoj Kumar, Gagan Ahluwalia and Michael F. Foselli of New York; Capt Mangal Singh Dhillon of Fort Worth, Texas; Dr David Spiro, Dr Brian Wells, John

Glover, Ian Paradine, Dr R.N. Burjorjee, Lucinda Coleman, Paul Wynter, Bill Hansell, Chris Marlow, Chris Flatman and John Brooke of the United Kingdom; His Excellency Mr Leonid M. Zamiatin and Dr Bohdan M. Shehovych of Moscow; Jagdish Kudesia, Dr Deepak Chugh, Dr S.C. Nigam, Shyam Gupta, Dr U.C. Rai, Rajiv Kumar, Vijay Nalgirkar, Kiran Walia, Nirmal Kanta and Hari Kishan Khurana of New Delhi; Rajesh Shah, Bhagwan Kotak, Naresh Kotak and Krishna Kotak of Bombay; Yogi Mahajan, Prem Vaidya and Jagdish Srivastava of Pune.

In order to gather authentic information about Lal Bahadur Shastri's childhood, I met his relatives in Ramnagar and Mirzapur and am grateful to them for their ready assistance. I also met the family of Mr Nishkameshwar Misra in Varanasi. Mishraji had played an important role in helping and guiding Lal Bahadur during his school days.

A detailed account of the crucially important formative years of Shastri's life, spent in Harish Chandra High School and in Kashi Vidya Peeth, Varanasi, was provided to me by his classmate and lifelong friend Pandit Raja Ram Shastri, who rose to be vice-chancellor of the Kashi Vidya Peeth. He was a Member of Parliament and was decorated with one of the highest national awards — Padma Vibhushan. Pandit Raja Ram Shastri received me at his residence in Varanasi with overwhelming kindness. Every day for a whole week he talked to me about his many years with Shastri, recalling in detail specific events and anecdotes, delineating different facets of Shastriji's character and personality. Sadly, Pandit Raja Ram Shastri passed away on 21 August 1991 in New Delhi.

Another friend of Shastri in Varanasi, who provided information from personal knowledge about Shastriji's early life, was Shri Brij Nandan Prasad, nextdoor neighbour of Mr Raghunath Prasad, Shastri's maternal uncle, with whom Shastri stayed for about eight years.

In New Delhi I met Pandit Bishambar Nath Pande, Member of Parliament, a close personal friend and colleague of Shastri. I am most grateful to Pandeji for the information he provided from personal knowledge about Shastri's years in Allahabad from 1929 when he came in close touch with Jawaharlal Nehru and Purshottam Das Tandon.

I have benefited greatly from my talks with civil servants who worked closely with Shastri. Among them were Mr Dharma Vira, then cabinet secretary, Mr C.S. Jha, then foreign secretary, Mr L.P. Singh, then home secretary, Mr K.B. Lall, then India's ambassador to the European Economic Community and to Belgium, and Mr Govind Narain who was home secretary to the UP government when Shastri was UP's home and transport minister. I received a great deal of help in my research work from Dr Abid Hussain, former member, Planning Commission and ambassador to the United States of America, Mr Prakash Narain, former chairman, Railway Board, and principal secretary to the Government of India, Mr Naresh Chandra, former cabinet secretary, Mr Muchkund Dubey, former foreign secretary, Mr Mahesh Prasad, former secretary, Ministry of Information and Broadcasting, and Mr A.R. Bandyopadhyaya, former additional secretary, Department of Administrative Reforms and Public Grievances. To all of them I am immensely grateful.

In order to discuss some important matters relating to the Indo–Pak War of 1965, I met Air Chief Marshal Arjan Singh, then chief of the air staff, General P.P. Kumaramangalam, then vice-chief and later chief of the army staff, Lt-Gen. Harbaksh Singh, then army commander, Western Command and Wing Cdr Trevor Keelor who, among others, were the heroes of the war. They provided invaluable information and comments based on their personal knowledge and experience.

I have had the good fortune of meeting and talking with three renowned personalities of Indian journalism — Mr Prem Bhatia, Mr Kuldip Nayar and Mr Inder Malhotra, who knew Shastri well. I am most grateful for their perceptive comments about different aspects of Shastri's prime ministership.

I wish to express my deep gratitude to Dr Iain West, head of the Department of Forensic Medicine, Guy's Hospital, London, for his kindness in giving so much of his precious time to a consideration of the circumstances of Prime Minister Shastri's death.

Sqn Ldr R.K. Pal has helped greatly in my research work and also spent an immense amount of his time scrutinizing, with utmost thoroughness, the entire text of this work. He has made an invaluable contribution to the preparation of this biography.

To Commander H.S. Sharma I am grateful for his enormous help in arranging for the entire text to be put on computer, and for providing excellent secretarial assistance.

I acknowledge the many-faceted help which I have received from Mr P.C. Tandon, whose experience as a former deputy secretary, Bureau of Indian Standards, Ministry of Food and Civil Supplies, Government of India, was of great benefit to me in the typing of the text of this book and its revision. Mr Tandon went through the manuscript and made excellent suggestions for improvement.

Mr Derek Lee of the School of Languages, Anglia Polytechnic University, Cambridge, UK, has gone through the entire text with meticulous care and has made numerous suggestions for improvement.

In the concluding stage of the preparation of this book, Mr and Mrs Beaven of the United Kingdom provided invaluable help in entering the revised text on new diskettes and in printing the text for submission to the publishers.

I am also extremely grateful to Mr Alan Wherry, marketing director, Bloomsbury Publishing Limited, London, who, besides providing invaluable suggestions for improvement in the text, also introduced me to my publishers, Oxford University Press.

No one has helped me more than my editor at Oxford University Press; he has invested a great deal of his time in editing and improving the text of this book.

Finally, my wife Nirmala has fully shared my inner urge to write this biography and has extended every possible help. My elder daughter Kalpana and her husband Prabhat Kumar Srivastava have searched for and obtained several important photographs which have been included in this book. And my younger daughter Sadhana and her husband Rommel Varma, who are the joint authors of an acclaimed publication, *The Himalayas*, have taken great pains to enhance the text by careful in-house editing.

While acknowledging the debt of gratitude which I owe to all those who have been mentioned earlier by name and to those others who have helped in a variety of ways, I take full responsibility for the contents of this biography and am solely responsible for all the views and comments within it.

# Contents

# List of Illustrations

Frontispiece

*(between pp. 304 and 305)*

1. Three teachers and five students of the Shastri degree course in philosophy, Kashi Vidya Peeth, Benares. Left to right: Janardan Pati Tripathy, Dularey Sahai, Pandit Gopal Shastri, Ram Sakhe Singh, Dr Bhagwan Das, Pandit Raja Ram Shastri, Dr Sampurnanand, Lal Bahadur Shastri (the photo was taken in 1925).

2. UP leaders' camp, Allahabad, 1939. Shastri is second from left in the first standing row. On the chairs, Nehru is third from right, Abul Kalam Azad is fifth from left, and Purshottam Das Tandon is fifth from right.

3. President Radhakrishnan, Prime Minister Nehru, Minister Shastri.

4. Being sworn-in as prime minister.

5. The new prime minister being embraced by Congress President Kamaraj. President Radhakrishnan looks on.

6. With his wife, Lalita Shastri.

7. With his mother, wife, and youngest son Ashok.

8. With his family.

9. With his daughter Suman (to his right) and two grandchildren. The author, his wife Nirmala (to Shastri's left), and his daughters Kalpana (extreme left) and Sadhana (extreme right) are calling on the Shastris on the occasion of Diwali.

10. At a function in Bombay. The author's wife Nirmala introduces some guests to Shastri.

11. Being received by Wilson, London, December 1964.

12. With Nasser of Egypt, in Cairo.

13. With Tito of Yugoslavia and Makarios of Cyprus.

14. In conversation with the Canadian prime minister, Lester Pearson, Ottawa, 11 June 1965.

# Introduction

I first met Mr Lal Bahadur Shastri in June 1950. A few weeks earlier, I had been appointed as the city magistrate of Lucknow.* My immediate superior, the district magistrate of Lucknow, had asked me to meet Mr Shastri who was then UP's home and transport minister, to receive any guidance that the minister might wish to provide with regard to the discharge of my responsibilities.

I sought an appointment and was informed that the minister would meet me at 6 p.m. the next day at his official residence. I arrived there five minutes ahead of the appointed time and noticed that the minister's car was parked at the entrance to the bungalow, with a rear door open, indicating that he was about to go somewhere. His personal assistant appeared at the door and told me that the minister had been suddenly called to a meeting convened by the chief minister and that another appointment would be fixed for me soon. He gave the same message to another visitor who had also just arrived.

The next moment Mr Shastri emerged from his house. I had never seen him before and was struck by his small height and extremely neat appearance. He was wearing a well-pressed and spotlessly clean kurta and dhoti, and a Gandhi cap, all of home-spun cotton. He greeted the other visitor with folded hands in the traditional Indian style, with a kind smile on his face, and began to talk with him in a strikingly polite manner. After a couple of minutes the visitor handed some papers to Mr Shastri and moved away after exchanging the usual greetings. The P.A. then went up to the minister and, pointing to me, whispered a few words. I remained standing at some distance in order not to force myself on the minister's attention. What Mr Shastri did next left a deep impression on me. He moved a number of paces towards me and, looking up, greeted me with folded hands in a very kind manner. I was dumbfounded: a cabinet minister taking the initiative in greeting with folded hands a junior civil servant! This was a new experience and a lesson to me. I tried to retrieve the situation by responding promptly with great respect, but I knew within myself that

---

* Lucknow is the capital of Uttar Pradesh (UP), India's most populous state.

I had been remiss. The minister put me at ease by inviting me to join him in his drawing room. Being aware of his important engagement, I pleaded with him not to delay: I could come another day. But he insisted that I sit and talk awhile. In an unhurried manner, he enquired whether I had been allotted a residence and whether I had settled down. I replied in the affirmative, and then I asked whether he had any special instructions for me. He thought for a moment and said: 'Lucknow, being the capital of the state, is the centre of a great deal of political and other activities. Clean and efficient administration is of vital importance. There is also the need for constant vigilance about the law and order situation. The relations between the police and the people must be based on mutual regard and respect. Your district magistrate is an extremely able and experienced officer and he would be the best person to guide you.' When he had finished I stood up and apologized for delaying him. He smiled and asked me to see him again, later. We came out of his house together. He paused for a moment and asked if I had transport. I had. He then moved towards his car and bade me goodbye. As his car slowly moved away, I folded my hands and he smiled.

After he had gone I stood in the driveway, reflecting on the experience. An important political leader and busy cabinet minister had gone much out of his way to be overwhelmingly kind and gentle to a junior civil servant. I had known some ministers in New Delhi: their response to juniors was a cursory and rather busy nod of the head. I learnt later that Mr Shastri extended the same courtesy, consideration and kindness to all he met, regardless of their station in life.

After a few months I was promoted and transferred to Meerut as additional district magistrate. There was no particular need for me to meet the minister again and I left Lucknow. That, I thought, was the end of my brief acquaintance with Mr Shastri. Fortunately for me, it was not.

Two years later, in 1952, I happened to go from Meerut to Delhi's railway station to meet my wife Nirmala and my daughters Kalpana and Sadhana, who were due in from Nagpur. Their train steamed in and I received my family. The platform was now crowded with disembarking passengers, all jostling to get away as quickly as possible. Nirmala and I decided to stay back, holding on to our two children who were then four and two years old. At this time another train arrived on the other side of the platform, from Lucknow. A large number of railway officials had arrived earlier and were obviously waiting to receive some very important person. All at once I saw Mr Shastri emerge from one of the compartments and be welcomed by the awaiting railway officials. Mr Shastri had by that time moved to New Delhi and was then the cabinet minister for railways and transport in the government of Pandit Jawaharlal Nehru. Accompanied by these officials, Mr Shastri began to move away. My family and I remained standing on the other side of the platform. Suddenly, Mr Shastri happened to glance in my direction; but the next moment he looked away as someone in his group began to talk to him. I was hesitant to push my way through to greet him, for I was more or less sure he would have forgotten me. We had met in Lucknow two years earlier, for barely three or four minutes. As this thought passed through my mind, Mr Shastri looked again in my direction. I wondered who he might be looking for. I looked on either side. What happened next put me to shame. Minister Shastri left his group, walked towards me and, just as he had done two years earlier, raised both his hands to greet me, saying: 'Srivastava saheb, namaste. Aapne mujhe pahchana nahin. Main Lal Bahadur hoon.' (Srivastava saheb, namaste. You did not recognize me. I am Lal Bahadur.)

I was understandably stunned and lost for words. Recovering my wits, I responded respectfully, saying that everyone recognized him, and so of course did I, but I did not know how he could be so gracious as to remember me after all this time. Smiling benignly, Mr Shastri recalled our meeting in Lucknow and said he knew of my posting to Meerut. He enquired after my welfare and my family's; I murmured in answer and, smiling broadly again, he went back to resume his departure.

After this chance second meeting in 1952, I had no occasion to meet Mr Shastri until 1957. That year he became the union cabinet minister for transport and communications. By this time I had been transferred back to the Government of India: in 1957 I was posted as deputy director general of shipping in Bombay.

As minister for transport, Mr Shastri was responsible for shipping. He asked the director general of shipping, Dr Nagendra Singh, who was stationed in New Delhi, whether he could recommend an officer of the Indian Administrative Service for the post of his private secretary. Dr Nagendra Singh suggested my name. I was summoned to New Delhi and was asked to see the minister immediately. I entered his room in the secretariat building and succeeded in greeting him first. Apparently the minister had already seen my confidential *curriculum vitae* and was satisfied as to my suitability. Therefore, after welcoming me with his usual kindness, he asked whether I would like to assist him. I expressed my extreme gratitude to him for his confidence in me and added that it would be a great privilege to serve him. Within a few days I joined the minister's office as his private secretary.

With each passing day I got to know his requirements with regard to official work better and better. He wanted everything done on the basis of absolute integrity and complete truth. For me there could be nothing more congenial and, indeed, elevating. He worked for long hours and so did I, happily, along with him.

All was going well when, one day, the occasion arose for yet another lesson — my third from Mr Shastri. One afternoon, when I was with him in his office discussing official matters, Prime Minister Jawaharlal Nehru telephoned, inviting Mr Shastri to join him next morning at 9 a.m. for a flight in a new Fokker Friendship plane which the Dutch ambassador wanted to show the prime minister. I offered to ask the personal assistant dealing with the minister's appointments to make the necessary arrangements for Minister Shastri to get to the airport a few minutes before the prime minister. On leaving the minister's office, I spoke with the personal assistant, who got busy with the necessary enquiries and arrangements.

Next morning I reached Mr Shastri's residence at 9.30 a.m. and, to my consternation, learnt that the minister had missed his appointment with the prime minister, because he had been driven to the wrong airport. Now, in India more than anywhere else, ministers do not take chances with their prime ministerial engagements. I was deeply distressed at letting down Mr Shastri in this rather crucial and delicate matter. I did not know how Mr Shastri had reacted, but I was ready for the dressing down of my life.

Someone went into the house and informed the minister that I had arrived. Almost immediately he came out of his residence and we exchanged silent greetings. To my utter surprise he wore his usual smile, as if nothing untoward had happened. My face, which always mirrors my feelings, showed how very upset I was. The minister looked at me for a moment and then enquired: 'You are not looking too well. Are you alright?' All I could do was offer unconditional apologies: 'I am awfully sorry, sir, that I did not ensure proper arrangements.' Without a moment's pause, the minister responded with soothing words: 'There is nothing to worry about.' Then, with an even broader smile, he added: 'I sent a message to the prime minister well in time and he took off with the Dutch ambassador. I will have a look at the plane some other day.'

'It is most kind of you, to say so sir,' I said, 'but I still feel very unhappy with myself. This should never have happened.'

Mr Shastri said, with his usual immense kindness, 'Please remember that I have asked you to join me for assistance in my official work. It is not your responsibility to look after my appointments at all. There are personal assistants for that purpose. You must not feel that you were in any way responsible for the mishap today. So, please, just give no further thought to this matter.' After a moment's pause he added: 'Also, I request you not to say anything to the P.A. As it is, he is very upset. He is a very conscientious worker and he did his best to ascertain all the facts. Really, there was no carelessness at all. Sometimes things go wrong despite all the care that we take. Let us get on with our work. I will take a few minutes to get ready, then we will go to the office together.'

Mr Shastri never demonstrated his feelings by gestures of the hand. He expressed himself through the way he looked, and his look was one of soothing kindness and benevolence, which were expressions of an unusually deep magnanimity of soul. I saw with complete clarity Mr Shastri's ethical stature, his warm humanity, his extreme decency, his capacity for understanding and forgiveness.

The cumulative effect on me of the three incidents I have described was enormous. It set the tone for the whole of my working life. I continued to work for Mr Shastri with complete devotion. In discussions, he seemed to appreciate my views and comments, which were based, to the best of my ability, on objective criteria. He began to place great confidence in me, and soon I became a sort of personal advisor to the minister.

When in 1959 Mr Shastri assumed the portfolios of commerce and industry, he took me to that ministry as his private secretary. This was a heavy charge and our working day seldom, if ever, finished before 10 p.m. Life went on like this for a few months. Unfortunately, my health suffered. The extreme climate of Delhi, particularly its heat and dust, caused me problems. The seaside climate of Bombay had suited me better. By chance, the ministry of transport were very keen to get me back to the directorate general of shipping in Bombay, to deal with certain urgent and complex issues. Accordingly the director general of shipping, Dr Nagendra Singh, prevailed upon Mr Shastri to release me.

It was with some emotion that I took leave of Mr Shastri. He had remarkable control over his feelings and was never demonstrative. But he expressed his affection and regard by telling me that this was not the end of our relationship, and that I should keep in close touch with him. Thereafter, whenever I went to New Delhi or whenever Mr Shastri came to Bombay, we always met for a brief while, and the personal bond between us remained strong.

Then suddenly in the month of October 1959 came the upsetting news that Mr Shastri had suffered a heart attack and been hospitalized in Allahabad. I felt deeply distressed and concerned. My friends in New Delhi who were in touch with the hospital in Allahabad told me Mr Shastri's condition had stabilized and that there was no cause for anxiety. This was most gratifying. I felt, nevertheless, that I should go to Allahabad. Within a few days I arrived there and, with feelings of trepidation, entered Mr Shastri's room in the hospital. He was resting in bed and his face wore his usual smile. We exchanged greetings, as we had always done. He was obviously pleased to see me and said he was feeling better. His voice was firm and clear and he showed no anxiety whatsoever. I stayed a few minutes and came away, greatly relieved. After about three weeks, Mr Shastri returned to New Delhi and resumed his responsibilities.

During the years between 1959 and 1963 I met Mr Shastri off and on. In April 1961 he had become minister of home affairs with a much enhanced stature in the political life of the country. In 1963 the Congress Party's highest executive body — the Congress Working Committee — invited senior cabinet ministers in the central government and chief ministers in the state governments to relinquish their positions in government to work among the people in order to strengthen the party. Six senior cabinet ministers were to leave the Nehru cabinet. Prime Minister Nehru was most unwilling to let Mr Shastri go under this scheme, which came to be known as the Kamaraj Plan, but eventually agreed on Shastri's insistence. Thus, along with the others, Shastri left the cabinet. But only a few months later, in January 1964, he was recalled to the cabinet by Jawaharlal Nehru who had become indisposed and wanted Shastri to help him discharge his responsibilities.

Pandit Jawaharlal Nehru passed away on 27 May 1964. At that time I was in the United Kingdom, attending a shipping conference. Pandit Nehru had been my hero, as he had been of the entire Indian nation, and his death grieved me deeply. One could not think of India without Nehru, but the unthinkable had come to pass. There was grave anxiety about the future of the country. However, the news from India was reassuring. Efforts were being made by the ruling Congress Party to elect a successor quickly and preferably by unanimity, in order to ensure an orderly transition. On 2 June 1964 came the news that Lal Bahadur Shastri had been elected as the new leader of the Congress Parliamentary Party and that he would soon be sworn in as the next prime minister.

The news of Mr Shastri's election naturally delighted and thrilled me. However, on my return to Bombay, I read in the newspapers that the prime minister had been taken ill and that his doctors had advised a period of bed-rest. The rumour was that he had suffered another heart attack, though fortunately a mild one this time. My wife and I were both concerned, and she urged me to go to New Delhi immediately to offer my services to the new prime minister. She felt strongly that, as Mr Shastri had confidence in me, it was my duty to assist him in whatever way I could. Being a civil servant I was most reluctant to take any such initiative, for the prime minister might be embarrassed if, for whatever reason, he did not wish to include me in his team.

A few days later, however, I *had* to go to New Delhi to attend a meeting and I judged that I could, without putting the prime minister to any awkwardness, avail myself of the opportunity to visit his residence with a view to enquiring about his health. In fact, as my personal relationship had been maintained over the years, I should be quite remiss if, having come to New Delhi, I failed to ask to meet him, especially at a time when he was unwell.

And so I went to the prime minister's residence. The personal assistant on duty told me the attending physicians had advised against too many visitors, but he would still mention my arrival. He soon returned saying the prime minister had agreed to my seeing him, adding that I should not stay more than a minute or two. I went in. Mr Shastri was lying in his bed. He looked alright and responded to my greetings in his usual way, with a smile. I offered my respectful felicitations on his assumption of the leadership of the government and the country and wished him a speedy recovery.

Two personal assistants were in the room, listening to the conversation and, conscious of their responsibility no doubt, wanted to make sure, that I did not stay over long. I myself was anxious not to put pressure on the prime minister by further talk. After a few seconds of silence, I folded my hands and asked permission to leave. The two personal assistants nodded approval. But Prime Minister Shastri had other ideas in his mind. To my surprise and even more to the surprise of the personal assistants, he asked me to stay on and requested the others to retire from the room. I sensed that there might be something momentous in store for me. When only the two of us were left, Mr Shastri said: '*Aap ko to Bambai bahut pasand hai. Abhi wahan kab tak rahene ka irada hai?*' (I know you like Bombay. How much longer do you intend to stay there?) '*Ji, aap jab tak munasib samjhen.*' (Sir, only as long as you consider it appropriate.)

Mr Shastri looked momentarily at me and then said: '*Main sochta hoon ki ab aap yahan aa jaiye aur meri madad kariye.*' (I think you should now come to New Delhi and help me.)

I responded promptly: '*Ji, achcha.*' (Yes, sir.)

Mr Shastri was pleased. He said my transfer would be arranged immediately.

I then took leave of the prime minister and returned with the glad tidings to Bombay. Nirmala was delighted. I was equally happy that things had turned out well for me without, in any way, a violation of propriety or norms of service conduct.

Shortly thereafter my transfer orders were received and I left Bombay for New Delhi, where I reported to the prime minister. My official designation was joint secretary to the prime minister of India; my specific duties were to be assigned by the prime minister himself. I was shown into his chambers and, after the customary salutation, I said: 'I am profoundly grateful to you, sir, for this renewal of confidence in me. I would like to know what my duties will be.'

I asked this because two outstanding officers of India's top civil service cadre — L.K. Jha and Rajeshwar Prasad — had already been appointed in the prime minister's secretariat as secretary and joint secretary, respectively, and I wanted to discover my specific responsibilities. 'You have to work for me and assist me as you used to do when you were my private secretary,' replied Mr Shastri.

What he conveyed to me in effect was that he wanted me to work with him closely as his personal aide, in accordance with his wishes and requirements. I was well aware that the responsibilities of a prime minister were vastly different from those of a cabinet minister and was anxious to know if the prime minister had any specific instructions for me in that context. On this count he said: 'You have to be available to me all the working time, as before. Please set up an office for yourself at each of the three places where I have to work — Parliament House, the Secretariat Buildings and the Official Residence. I will ask for your help in any matter I need to. You should also feel free to advise me or give me your comments on any matter under my consideration. As you know already, in my statements and letters I do not want to express even one word more than can be actually achieved. We must say less and perform more.' He added as an afterthought: 'The job of a prime minister is difficult, but not impossible. Let us try. If we succeed, well and good. If I fail, I will resign and go.'

Those words rang out clearly and firmly and I hear them even now. For me, they were the most succinct expression, the most apt symbol of his total integrity of character: mark the words — 'If *we* succeed' and 'If *I* fail'. He was prepared to share the credit for success with those who worked with him; but in the event of failure he wanted the entire blame. Thus began a working relationship between the prime minister and myself which was to become closer with each passing day.

My daily routine was to arrive at No 10 Janpath, the prime minister's official residence, in the morning, and thereafter to move with him when he went to Parliament House or the Secretariat Buildings. When he went to the Lok Sabha or the Rajya Sabha,* I would invariably sit in the official gallery to be available in case he needed additional information at short notice. In the evenings the prime minister worked in his office at 10 Janpath

---

* India's two Houses of Parliament.

until very late. During the days of the Indo-Pakistan war the working day never ended before midnight, and sometimes went on even until the early hours of the next day. I was in my office nearby, or with him, during all this time.

We developed a close working relationship based upon his complete confidence in me and my total loyalty to him. He felt assured that he could discuss any official matter with me, however sensitive or delicate it might be, without running the slightest risk of leak or betrayal. Further, over a period of time, he judged that if he asked for my comments or advice he would receive from me a response which would strain towards the objective and the truthful. He knew also that I said nothing only to please him: he had asked me to be honest and frank whenever he consulted me, which accorded entirely with my own inclination. While he listened to my views and took into account what I had to say, he would make up his mind on every issue entirely according to his own judgment, after careful and deep thought. It was on this understanding that, late in the evening each day before finishing work, we would discuss the day's main events and the programme for the next day. It was thus that I had the great advantage of knowing his mind on most issues. This helped me enormously in preparing draft letters or speeches in consonance with his thinking.

I knew also that he was not fond of the usual secretariat officialese. He was extremely careful and precise about what he said and what he wrote. Hyperbole was anathema to him. He wanted crisp drafts, written in clear, direct and wholly unequivocal language. He said precisely what he meant and he meant precisely what he said. He had the courage of his convictions and he never prevaricated. No one working with him could get anything past him by pretence or flattery: he had an exceptional capacity to see through people in no time. He was always prepared to overlook or forgive unintentional or bona fide mistakes, but anyone who attempted the slightest dishonesty or trickery was off his list.

To work with him was easy and difficult at the same time. It was easy because all one had to do was be totally honest, straightforward and courteous. It was difficult because one had to dedicate oneself heart and soul to one's duties. For both himself and for those who worked with him, there was no time for friends or personal interests, and very little time even for the family. The closer one was to the prime minister, the more demanding was the relationship. He devoted almost every moment of his time and indeed his whole being to his public responsibilities, and anyone who worked with him closely had to do the same. But this did not come in any sense as a compulsion from him. Not at all. It was one's own inner compulsion, clearly fired by Mr Shastri's selfless example.

My duties included the drafting of such letters and statements as he wanted me to, and the pursuit of such matters as he entrusted to me from time to time. He asked me to give particular attention to work relating to Parliament and the press. I accompanied him on most of his foreign missions, including the final one to Tashkent. During those days of the historic peace conference I spent nearly all my time in the prime minister's villa, frequently talking about the developing situation. Late in the evening we would review the day's deliberations and talk about the next day. He narrated to me in great detail his conversations with President Ayub Khan of Pakistan and Premier Kosygin of the USSR. Our attention was totally riveted on the matter at hand. For me the memory of those days, some of the most precious of all my life, will never fade.

During the two spells that I worked with Mr Shastri (1957–9 and 1964–6), my whole family came close to him and his family. We were frequently invited to his residence at festivals, or for dinner. Mr Shastri and his family had developed great regard and respect for my wife Nirmala on account of her nationalism, patriotism and spirituality. She had participated in Mahatma Gandhi's 1942 Quit India movement and her father, P.K. Salve, was an important Congress leader of Madhya Pradesh. He had sacrificed much for nationalism and suffered imprisonment, and Nirmala had imbibed his spirit. When we visited Mr Shastri, he talked to her about saints and sages and about religion and spirituality, fields in which she had great knowledge. He would also talk to her about other subjects, ranging from home economics to political affairs, and, in 1965, he even wanted Nirmala to join the Congress Party. However, Nirmala was more inclined towards spirituality and not attracted to politics.

During all those days, the members of the prime minister's family were extremely considerate to my family and me. We addressed Mrs Lalita Shastri, Mr Shastri's wife, as 'Mataji' (respected mother). Mr Shastri's sons, Hari Krishna Shastri, Anil Shastri, Sunil Shastri and Ashok Shastri always treated me as a brother, and I reciprocated their feelings. Mr Shastri's sons-in-law, Kaushal Kumar and V.N. Singh, showed us the same affection and regard. Despite our close personal relationship, never did any of them intervene in the slightest degree in any official matter within my sphere of work.

Such then was the happy situation when we went to Tashkent on 3 January 1966. There Pime Minister Shastri created history by signing the peace agreement — the Tashkent Declaration — with Pakistan at 4 p.m. on 10 January 1966. As we all know, within a few hours of that historic moment Mr Shastri passed away. On that day of triumph and tragedy I promised myself that I would, after retirement from public service, write

Prime Minister Shastri's biography. This book has been written in fulfilment of that promise.

While this biography covers the entire span of Mr Shastri's life, the main focus is on the period of his prime ministership. This was a momentous period, full of crises, of historic war and then peace. It was over this time that India and the world saw Mr Shastri in his real stature, as a great leader and world statesman.

To perform my task properly as a biographer, I am advised to disclose Mr Shastri's weaknesses and deficiencies alongside his achievements. Weaknesses of character or integrity? I am afraid I could not discover any. The truth is that, early in his life, he adopted an unwritten but comprehensive moral code to which he firmly adhered all his life. He had no passion for power, no greed for money, no lust for women. That is the reason why, during the long period since Mr Shastri's death on 11 January 1966, no person and no forum has ever suggested that there were skeletons in his cupboard. Had there been such revelations to be made, they would undoubtedly have been made by vigilantes in the political arena: witness the ongoing reappraisal of President Kennedy who was, in his day, the hero of an admiring world.

What then of Mr Shastri's deficiencies? Yes, indeed, he had some. He was barely 5 feet 2 inches tall and caused a lot of amusement in the first few months of his prime ministership, when he stood by the side of the high and mighty figure of President Nasser of Egypt. And though Mr Shastri's mild personality had a charm of its own, it was by no means as charismatic as Mr Nehru's. Mr Shastri was no great orator either, nor wrote Nehru's beautiful English prose. Whereas Jawaharlal Nehru was aristocratic and had all the high-society graces that go with riches, Mr Shastri's background was one of poverty, and in his early years he had had to struggle hard even to survive. But none of this created complexes in Mr Shastri. He was always self-possessed, confident and dignified, steeped in the best traditions of India's many-splendoured culture. Despite the god-given 'deficiency' of a small physical frame and the other 'deficiencies' caused by poverty in his early years, Mr Shastri was a political meteor who, on the strength of his character, integrity and truthfulness, fulfilled in an uniquely modest and yet unshakeably courageous way the great demands that history placed upon him.

This book narrates the uncommon life-story of this common man of India. In the prevailing mist of political and social cynicism that seems to characterize our own day, I dare to hope that this biography will provide a luminous and inspiring model.

# Chapter 1

# Birth, Childhood and Education

Lal Bahadur Shastri was born on 2 October 1904, at Moghalsarai, close to the holy Indian city of Benares. He died on 11 January 1966 at Tashkent, Uzbekistan, then a part of the USSR. His life-span of sixty-one years coincided with one of the most momentous and decisive periods of Indian history. In 1904, the year Shastri was born, India was in bondage to the British, whose power was total and unchallenged. And yet that very year circumstances arose which were to result in the commencement the following year, 1905, in something like a revolution. A political movement was launched for swaraj—self-government. The Indian National Congress, established in 1885 by the determined efforts of an Englishman, Allan Octavian Hume, became after 1905 the medium for the advancement of this new movement. In 1920 Mahatma Gandhi took over the leadership of the Indian National Congress. He travelled incessantly through the country, carrying his new message of satyagraha and non-violence. India rallied round the Mahatma, who launched a mass movement for freedom. Lal Bahadur was a child of this revolutionary age.

By a remarkable coincidence Shastri's birth date—2 October—was the same as that of Mahatma Gandhi, who was born thirty-five years earlier. Lal Bahadur's father, Sharda Prasad, was a schoolteacher in Allahabad. His mother, Ram Dulari Devi, was the daughter of Munshi Hazari Lal, who was headmaster and English teacher in a railway school at Moghalsarai, the large railway junction near Benares. Lal Bahadur was born in the house of his maternal grandfather, Munshi Hazari Lal. He was Ram Dulari Devi's second child; the first was a daughter, Kailashi Devi, who was about four years old at that time.

Sharda Prasad's father (Lal Bahadur's grandfather), Babu Nandan Lal, was a sub-postmaster. Lal Bahadur's forebears on the paternal side were employed in the service of Ramnagar estate in Benares district. There is a small ancestral house in Ramnagar where some of his relations still live. Lal Bahadur Shastri thus belonged to a lower-middle-class family whose members depended for their livelihood on employment as schoolteachers, sub-postmasters and similar positions.

A few days after Lal Bahadur's birth his mother returned with both her children to her husband's home in Allahabad. One day, when Lal Bahadur was just a month old, his mother, went to a *mela*—a fair on the banks of the Ganga (Ganges). She was carrying the child in her arms when she was suddenly pushed by the surging crowd, and Lal Bahadur fell out of her hands, disappearing in the confusion and bustle. She tried her best to find the child but did not succeed. The loss was reported to the police and, as if by a miracle, Lal Bahadur was shortly recovered from the hut of a cowherd in a neighbouring village and restored to his distraught parents. Lal Bahadur had fallen into the basket of a cowherd who had believed that the Almighty and the sacred river, Mother Ganga, had granted his fervent prayers for a son. When the police explained the facts, the cowherd and his wife readily, though sadly, agreed to part with the child.

In 1906, when Lal Bahadur was just eighteen months old, his father suddenly died of the plague. The breadwinner of the family was gone, leaving a young widow of twenty-three with two small children, one eighteen months old and the other five. Sharda Prasad, whose selection for the post of naib tahsildar, a subordinate executive position, had just been announced, left neither money nor property. It was a disastrous situation for Ram Dulari Devi and her two children. Normally, in keeping with the traditions of Hindu families, Sharda Prasad's father, Babu Nandan Lal, should have immediately gone to Allahabad and brought the distressed family to his house. But that did not happen. Babu Nandan Lal's second wife was Sharda Prasad's stepmother. She had no love for Sharda Prasad or his family and firmly declined to provide any succour whatsoever.

Providentially, Munshi Hazari Lal, who greatly loved his daughter Ram Dulari Devi, brought her and his grandchildren to his house in Moghalsarai. At this time Ram Dulari Devi was carrying her third child. A girl was delivered three months later and named Sundari Devi.

But soon the benefactor too suffered a paralytic stroke and passed away, in 1908, barely two years after his daughter became a widow. With these successive tragedies, Ram Dulari Devi, Lal Bahadur and his two sisters faced a very difficult situation. But providential assistance came to their rescue once again.

Munshi Hazari Lal had a brother, Munshi Darbari Lal, who was a head clerk in the opium department of the government at Ghazipur in Uttar Pradesh. He, like his brother, was humane, warm-hearted and generous. Immediately, he assumed financial responsibility for the entire family in Moghalsarai and averted possible disaster. At this time, Lal Bahadur was only three and not yet grown-up enough to understand the gravity of their situation. His mother, then a young woman of twenty-five, faced her misfortunes with great courage. She was determined to prevent

Lal Bahadur being scarred by these experiences. Munshi Darbari Lal regularly sent money for the family's maintenance to his son, Bindeshwari Prasad, who became the family's local guardian. By this time Bindeshwari Prasad had also become a schoolteacher in Moghalsarai. In this way stability was restored to the unfortunate family.

As the youngest son of the family, Lal Bahadur enjoyed everyone's affection and his mother's constant care. Bindeshwari Prasad was generous-hearted and kindly and he too took good care of Lal Bahadur. There was another person in the family who became very fond of the child. This was Purshottam Lal, son of the late Munshi Hazari Lal and younger brother of Ram Dulari Devi (and thus maternal uncle or 'mama' to Lal Bahadur). Purshottam Lal's pet name in the family was Lallan. He was just seven years at the time. To Lal Bahadur he was both mama and friend. This relationship gave a measure of security to the young Lal Bahadur, though in actual fact his life was full of uncertainty.

In the family of Munshi Hazari Lal and Munshi Darbari Lal, it was customary to initiate the education of a child under the personal charge and care of a *maulvi*, a learned man of the Muslim faith. Initially, children had to learn Urdu, and the initiation into learning was quite a ceremony in itself. When Lal Bahadur was four years of age his initiation—or, as it was called then, his Bismillah ceremony—was performed by Maulvi Budhan Mian of the neighbouring village of Padhza. Under Maulvi Saheb's tutelage, Lal Bahadur learnt not only Urdu but also *tahzeeb*, a combination of social etiquette and cosmopolitan culture. This was the first external formative influence on him and he imbibed everything that was given to him assiduously. He developed a great interest in Urdu literature, especially Urdu poetry. As we shall see later, one of Mirza Ghalib's poems became his lifetime favourite. Maulvi Budhan Mian was a respected teacher in the Railway Boys' School, Moghalsarai, where Lal Bahadur studied up to Class VI.

Lal Bahadur's childhood until the age of twelve was spent in Moghalsarai, with occasional visits to Mirzapur. During this period the care and affection from his mother and his maternal family—grandmother, grandfather and uncles—allowed him to pursue his education much as any other child of the family would have done. The passing away of his father did not therefore seriously affect his development, nor cause him serious mental stress.

There are three incidents from this period of his childhood which bring out certain innate qualities in Lal Bahadur's character. One summer evening, Lal Bahadur and his maternal uncle Lallan Mama went out for a stroll in Mirzapur. Near the bank of the Ganga they saw an old man with a loaded basket on his head, passing by. Lal Bahadur asked the old man what he was carrying in his basket. The old man stopped, put down the basket and answered the question: 'I have very nice mangoes. Here is one for you and another for your companion. Taste it. You will like it. Since it is evening time and I would like to sell some of these before getting home, I'll sell you a hundred mangoes for just one anna.' *

Lal Bahadur and Lallan Mama tasted the mango: it was delicious. Lal Bahadur looked at Lallan Mama, who nodded approval. They pooled their resources, two paisas each, and Lal Bahadur gave the money to the old man, who began to set apart and count the mangoes. When he reached fifty, Lal Bahadur intervened and told the man not to take out more. The old man was puzzled. He said: 'My boy, you've given me an anna and I have to give you another fifty mangoes to make up the hundred.' Lal Bahadur replied: 'The money is yours. Actually we don't need more than fifty mangoes. Thank you very much.' The old man looked at Lal Bahadur in disbelief, put the basket with the remaining mangoes on his head, and slowly walked away. All this time Lallan Mama, himself a little boy of about ten and only four years senior to Lal Bahadur, was watching the proceedings without intervening. When the old man was gone, he said: 'That was very foolish of you. We paid for a hundred mangoes but you've taken only fifty.' Lal Bahadur explained: 'You remember the old man saying he was prepared to sell a hundred mangoes for just one anna? It was a distress sale. Why take advantage of such a situation? In any case, we don't really need more than fifty mangoes for the family.' For all his youth, Lal Bahadur's innocent conviction was persuasive. What was it that impelled a six-year-old child to act as he did? He had not received lessons to infuse in him this exceptional sense of fair play. It is a reasonable inference that Lal Bahadur had a highly developed conscience nurtured in invisible ways by a moral family environment, which had manifested itself spontaneously on this occasion.

The second incident is an even better indication of that innate strength of moral will. Lal Bahadur's maternal uncle, Bindeshwari Prasad, the head of the family, was very fond of good food. He was especially fond of pigeon meat, and to ensure ready availability, he had reared a number of birds in his Moghalsarai house. At his sweet will he would select one, have it killed, cooked and served up for dinner. One day the particular pigeon selected by him flew off and hid itself on the tiles of the roof. Bindeshwari Prasad asked Lal Bahadur to climb the rooftop and report on the pigeon. Lal Bahadur obeyed and, having sighted the pigeon, reported accordingly to

* One anna was then one-sixteenth of a rupee. It consisted of four paisas.

Bindeshwari Prasad. Bindeshwari Prasad asked the boy to catch the pigeon and bring it down. Lal Bahadur remained sitting, quite downcast, and did not move: he was a strict vegetarian. The conversation between them then proceeded on the following lines:

| | |
|---|---|
| BINDESHWARI PRASAD | Nanku, go and get the pigeon at once. |
| LAL BAHADUR | No, I won't. |
| BINDESHWARI PRASAD | Why not |
| LAL BAHADUR | Because I know you will kill the pigeon and eat it up. |
| BINDESHWARI PRASAD | That's what pigeons are for. Now go quick and get it. |
| LAL BAHADUR | No, I won't. You will kill it. |
| BINDESHWARI PRASAD | Alright, go and get it. I won't kill it. |

Lal Bahadur, still a child, thought he had won over Mama Bindeshwari Prasad. He jumped up, caught the pigeon and brought it down. But of course Bindeshwari Prasad did not keep his word. He had the pigeon killed and prepared for the pot. Lal Bahadur was doubly aghast. His Mama had broken his pledged word, and 'his' pigeon had lost its life. His conscience was up in revolt. What could he do? Bindeshwari Prasad was a strong-willed man and head of the family. Little Lal Bahadur could not carry on arguing. But he would not give up either. Even at that tender age, he did not act hastily or impulsively. After due thought, he decided to do what Mahatma Gandhi was to do years later when seeking redress for grave injustice. He went on a hunger strike and abstained from food all day, resisting all persuasion by his mother and the others in the household. Lal Bahadur, being much loved by all the ladies of the family, was joined in his brave protest and they too refused to eat. Next morning Bindeshwari Prasad found himself facing the combined remonstrations of all the ladies of the house. When they had had their say, Bindeshwari Prasad summoned Lal Bahadur and addressed him firmly: 'You ate nothing yesterday. I'm sure you are very hungry. You will certainly eat something today.' Lal Bahadur looked at his uncle respectfully and responded without giving in: 'No I won't', he said. 'Why did you kill the pigeon when you told me you wouldn't?'

Bindeshwari Prasad had no answer. 'Nanku, you are right', he said finally. 'I should not have done what I did. I promise you I will not kill pigeons any more. In fact I won't eat pigeons ever again. In fact, I promise I'll become a vegetarian.' Bindeshwari Prasad kept his word. This was Lal Bahadur's first exercise in satyagraha.

These two events were obviously of no public importance, they were mere happenings within a family. And yet they indicate a nascent moral will and an extraordinarily lively conscience which were to manifest themselves more remarkably in Shastri's public and political life.

The third incident was of a different kind. Lal Bahadur, while a student of Class VI in the school at Moghalsarai, noticed that he was registered in the school as Lal Bahadur Varma. He was twelve at the time. He told his mother and family that he did not wish to keep the caste surname 'Varma': he did not like caste differences. Munshi Darbari Lal was not amused, but he raised no serious objection. His son Bindeshwari Prasad, who had no caste surname, liked Lal Bahadur's idea. They joined hands and made an application to the headmaster for the deletion of the surname 'Varma' in Lal Bahadur's school records. A delicate situation arose because the headmaster was himself a Varma—Basant Lal Varma. Sensibly, he did not take umbrage and approved the proposal. Lal Bahadur Varma thus became just Lal Bahadur. 'Shastri' was added to his name in 1925, after he acquired the degree of 'Shastri' (one who knows the Shastras) from the Kashi Vidyapeeth in Benares.

In 1917 Lal Bahadur had to leave Moghalsarai because, consequent upon the transfer of Bindeshwari Prasad, the whole family had to move. Most members of the family went to their ancestral home in Mirzapur. Lal Bahadur went to Benares for further education. Thus in 1917 ended the first and most delicate phase of his life.

From Moghalsarai Ram Dulari Devi took her three children to Benares, where the two married daughters of her uncle were living. They first stayed in the house of one of these relatives, and Lal Bahadur joined Dayanand High School. The atmosphere in this family was not congenial and Ram Dulari Devi shifted with her children to the house of her other cousin whose husband, Raghunath Prasad, was an employee of the Benares municipality. They were not closely related to each other but Raghunath Prasad accepted the new arrivals and willingly provided them food and shelter. Lal Bahadur stayed in this house from 1917 until 1925, when he completed his education.

Having joined Class VII in Harish Chandra High School, he continued his education in this institution until Class X. These four years, from 1917 to 1921, constituted a crucial period in his life for the formation of his character, the nurturing of inner qualities and his evolution into a staunch young patriot.

Benares is a holy city of antiquity. The Vishwanath temple, the Buddhist shrine at Sarnath, the holy Ganga, the ever-shuffling gathering of sages, various places of learning, the Centre of the Theosophical Society, and the pervasive culture and heritage of India all combine to give Benares its unrivalled pre-eminence and sanctity. To all this, a political dimension was added when the Indian National Congress held its twenty-first session in Benares in December 1905, under the presidentship of Gopal Krishna Gokhale. This session marked a turning point in the history of the Congress. The partition of Bengal, brought into effect in October 1905, had created unprecedented emotional upheaval. Gokhale condemned the partition as a 'cruel wrong' and reiterated the anger and resentment of the whole country on this issue.[1] He urged the people of India to promote political struggle through the Swadeshi Movement in particular, and initiated a debate within which the powerful voices of leading nationalists and patriots—Lala Lajpat Rai, Bal Gangadhar Tilak and Bipin Chandra Pal—were heard with rapt attention and much enthusiasm. From about this time Benares became an important centre of political activity in the country.

It was in this atmosphere that Lal Bahadur began his education. When he arrived there he was a self-possessed, well-behaved, quiet and intelligent young boy of thirteen, a keen and attentive student. Soon he came to the notice of one of the most respected teachers of the school, Nishkameshwar Misra, who took the gifted little boy to his heart.

Misra was a remarkable person. Besides being a good teacher he was humane and extremely patriotic, taking great interest in his students. He organised special outdoor excursions on Sundays and holidays for the benefit of his pupils:  these were voluntary, and those who participated had to pay an anna each to cover expenses on transport and food. Misra's purpose was to inculcate a wider interest in surroundings—in architecture, especially historic monuments, and in flowers and gardens—as well as generate a spirit of comradeship and fellow feeling amongst them.

Misra found Lal Bahadur the most intent, devoted and disciplined student in his class, and so appointed him class monitor. In this capacity, it was one of Lal Bahadur's duties to prepare a list of volunteers for the next picnic and collect the requisite contributions. On one such occasion Misra noticed that Lal Bahadur had not included his own name on the list. Taking the boy discreetly aside he asked why. Lal Bahadur replied with candour: 'Because I cannot pay the contribution, sir. I need the money for essentials in the house.' 'Include your name on the list', said Misra, 'I will pay the anna for you.' Misra had understood Lal Bahadur's financial situation:  he was living with his *mausa* (maternal uncle), in whose house he was provided with meals as a part of the family but no regular cash allowance.

That evening, after the picnic tour, Misra took Lal Bahadur to his house, introduced him to his wife and asked her to treat the new arrival as another son. At first the lady protested, saying they had enough children in the house already. But she soon took to him and bestowed upon him unstinting affection and hospitality. Lal Bahadur became a regular visitor to the house and almost a part of Misra's family. In return he asked to be tutor to one of the small children in the house. Misra was well pleased with this arrangement. Being sensitive, noble-minded and magnanimous, he decided that Lal Bahadur's work as a tutor needed to be recompensed not merely by kind words, affection and the occasional meal but also by regular remuneration. Knowing that Lal Bahadur would not accept cash payments, he found a way out. Every month he put some money in a savings box earmarked for Lal Bahadur. Years later, when Lal Bahadur's sister was about to get married, Misra gave the whole sum which he had thus accumulated to Lal Bahadur's mother, saying the money was Lal Bahadur's hard earned wages. The money was accepted and Misra's insistence proved useful in financing marriage expenditures.

The years 1917 to 1921, when Lal Bahadur was at Harish Chandra High School in Benares, saw several major political changes. Mahatma Gandhi, who had arrived in India in 1915, began to participate in political activities from 1917 and launched the massive Non-Cooperation Movement early in 1921.

Nishkameshwar Misra, who was immensely patriotic, undertook now to instil in some of his chosen pupils deep feelings of love and devotion for the motherland. After the regular classes he held a special class each day to talk about India's ancient heritage and fabulous prosperity before the British invasion. He would recall in detail how the British subjugated India, how they decimated its flourishing industries, and how ruthlessly they exploited the peasantry. He would enthral his pupils by recalling Maharana Pratap and Chhatrapati Shivaji, and describe in detail the endeavours of Gokhale, Surendranath Bannerji, Bal Gangadhar Tilak, Lala Lajpat Rai, Bipin Chandra Pal, Aurobindo Ghose and others who had promoted India's recent political renaissance. He told his students of the role of Indian newspapers in building up a sense of nationalism among the educated classes, and of the nobility and courage of those who had worked to establish the Indian National Congress as a forum for India's political advancement towards swaraj. Mother India, he would say, needed new young soldiers for the ongoing freedom struggle.

Lal Bahadur, who was born and brought up in a family which had no nationalistic background or leaning, listened avidly to every word of Misra's special discourses on the plight of India and the duty of Indians to join the battle for freedom. He devoted himself to a detailed study of India's recent history, especially the Indian National Congress. He also read the teachings of Swami Dayanand on social reform and of Swami Vivekanand who had recently taken Vedanta to America, thereby attempting to open a channel through which the ancient wisdom of India would reach popular audiences in the West. Bankim Chandra Chatterji's novel *Anandmath* was another of Lal Bahadur's favourites. He also studied and was influenced by Annie Besant's discourses on Theosophy, the other significant vehicle for Indian ideas in the West.

He imbibed the best of what he read and by persistent effort made it a part of his character and personality, practising in everyday life what he learnt from teachers and mentors. All this set into motion a process of continuous inner evolution and transformation. From history he learnt how foreigners had subjugated India and became convinced early of how essential it was to create a united will among all of India. The quintessential message of the great political leaders of that time, whether moderates like Gokhale and Ranade or extremists such as Tilak and Aurobindo Ghose, was the same: it was his duty to prepare himself for the service of his country. That was his first and essential duty, his dharma. For this purpose he had to instil in himself an unbounded love for his motherland, which meant unselfish patriotism and nationalism. He had also to develop an invincible moral character and be prepared for sacrifice in the country's cause.

Lal Bahadur accepted this message as if sent by divine providence through the medium of his teacher Misra. He assimilated it in all aspects into his mind and heart. What Lala Lajpat Rai said about himself might have been said in these years by Lal Bahadur: 'To amass wealth was not the object of my life. To enjoy luxury was not my goal. To win official honours was not my ambition. My spirit yearned for things quite different from these. I wanted to sacrifice myself for my people and for my country, as the moth burns itself on the candle flame.'

In 1919 came the Rowlatt Act, curbing freedom of expression, and the Jallianwalla Bagh massacre. Both led to immense anguish and distress in Lal Bahadur, now fifteen years old. Having become deeply interested in political activities, he followed events day by day. Mahatma Gandhi's emergence in 1920 as leader of a resurgent India, and his message of a non-violent and nationwide movemement for swaraj, further steeled Lal Bahadur's resolve to join the patriots. He did not yet know how this would come about; he wanted to finish school before engaging in politics.

In January 1921, then a student of Class X, he was preparing for the final school examination, scheduled three months later. The school leaving certificate would qualify him for employment in a subordinate position in government service, or as a teacher in a school. The expectation of his family was that Lal Bahadur would pass the exam and find a suitable salaried job. For his mother and unmarried sister, as well as for himself, the days of financial stringency and indeed of misery would then be over. Destiny intervened once again, beckoning him along another path.

After the conclusion of the Nagpur session of the Indian National Congress in December 1920, Mahatma Gandhi resumed a tour of different centres in the country in order to explain the momentous decisions taken at that session and to seek the support of the people for the Non-Coopera-tion Movement. At Pandit Madan Mohan Malaviya's invitation, Gandhi came to Benares in January 1921. A public meeting was organised on this occasion and Lal Bahadur, together with his friends Tribhuvan Narain Singh, Raja Ram and Algu Rai, went to the meeting. It was a large gathering and everyone was anxious to see and hear Mahatma Gandhi, now the acknowledged leader of Congress and indeed the country.

To his expectant audience Gandhi explained the reasons for the de-cision of Congress to launch a non-violent national movement; he called upon all Indians to join his movement; he addressed young students in particular and asked all those who were sixteen or more (Lal Bahadur had just completed sixteen) to withdraw forthwith from government-aided or government-controlled institutions, 'regardless of the consequences'. This was the duty, the dharma of every boy and girl. It seemed a moment in the life of a nation which came but once in any age or yuga. 'What you must do now is a matter of historical necessity—your yuga dharma', said Mahatma Gandhi, and added: 'You have to do your duty, even if this means disregarding the views of your elders. Mother India needs you today. Do not fail her.'

Pandit Madan Mohan Malaviya, who was presiding over the meeting, spoke after Mahatma Gandhi and made his own powerful and unequivocal appeal. With evident feelings of anxiety and concern, Malaviya said: 'I fully support the Non-Cooperation Movement and I join Mahatma Gandhi in urging you to participate in this historic movement. We all have to be together in the struggle for freedom. But I do not agree that you young students should disobey your elders. You will have to keep in mind the interests of your mother and father.'

Lal Bahadur listened to Gandhi and Malaviya with great attention. After the meeting he and his friends went to Misra's house, where there was considerable discussion. Lal Bahadur, deep in thought, wanted to act according to Mahatma Gandhi's advice, but he had noted the caution administered by Malaviya. There were some in the group who wanted to complete the course, secure the school leaving certificate, and then volun-teer for the movement. All this could be done within the next three months which, after all, was not a long way off. Others, a smaller number, were for joining immediately, 'regardless of the consequences'.

Lal Bahadur went home and explained to his uncle Raghunath Prasad and other elders in the family what had happened at the meeting, and indicated his intention to respond immediately to the call of Congress and Mahatma Gandhi by withdrawing from Harish Chandra High School, a government-aided institution. Furthermore, he wanted to become a Congress volunteer for national service. The news was received in the family with utter bewilderment. With the exception of his mother, all were furious. They told Lal Bahadur in no uncertain terms to behave with a sense of responsibility. He had a duty to look after his mother. If he discontinued his education at this stage, without obtaining even the first recognized qualification easily achievable within the next few months, how would he find work? What would become of his mother and unmarried sister? Was it not his prime dharma to look after his mother? He was reminded that after his father's death his mother had brought him up with love and care, while herself suffering all the rigours of penury. It was now his turn to behave as a dutiful son. Lal Bahadur listened to all this unperturbed. He then turned questioningly to his mother, Ram Dulari Devi, to whom he was greatly devoted. Her advice was generous and clear. 'Son,' she said, 'think deeply about the right course of action, then make up your mind and hold firmly to your decision.'

Lal Bahadur followed his mother's words and they were to become the abiding principle of his life. He thought deeply that night, listened to his own inner voice and made up his mind. At that moment, he concluded, his supreme loyalty was to Mother India, his higher dharma was to serve his country, regardless of the sacrifice involved. It was a decision which added one more to the many qualities he already possessed, namely the will to make a sacrifice, however large, in order to pursue what he had clearly perceived as the right course of action. Next morning he withdrew his name from Harish Chandra High School and joined the Congress Party as a volunteer. From that day on he became a devoted follower of Mahatma Gandhi and dedicated himself to the Mahatma's ethical principles of truth and non-violence.

After leaving Harish Chandra High School, Lal Bahadur joined the local Congress Party in Benares as a volunteer and began to participate in non-co-operation activities such as picketing and demonstrations. He was arrested by the government authorities and sent to prison but was soon released. This was his first imprisonment, and, though very brief, it set him firmly at the age of sixteen on his new course—that of a soldier in the battle for freedom.

As a Congress volunteer, Lal Bahadur worked under Acharya J.B. Kripalani, who was renowned for his interest in national education and who had resigned from Benares Hindu University in response to the call of Congress for the boycott of government-aided institutions. Acharya Kripalani pioneered the establishment of a Gandhi Ashram in Benares, mainly for the propagation of the use of khadi, which Gandhi saw as a simple yet effective method of emphasizing the value of self-reliance and promoting a national cottage industry. Khadi, the simple homespun cotton cloth, became a symbol of national pride and of economic as well as political resurgence. Lal Bahadur and his close friends Tribhuvan Narain Singh, Algu Rai and Raja Ram became Acharya Kripalani's assistants in this task.

These young boys thus became enthusiastic salesmen for khadi. However, Acharya Kripalani decided to help them resume their studies, though this was to be *rashtriya shiksha*—nationalist education—which would concentrate on the history of India's freedom movement and on the qualities of nationalism and patriotism, besides the usual subjects. Within the Gandhi Ashram, functioning in a rented building, an informal school was organised by Kripalani and his friend Vichitra Narayan Sharma who, like Kripalani, had left Benares Hindu University to join the Congress. During the day they and their group of young boys worked in the Gandhi Ashram, selling khadi. In the evenings they organised classes in national education. The objective was to build up a cadre of dedicated and informed freedom fighters. For this purpose lectures were delivered on the lives of the Italian nationalist Mazzini (1805–72) and Garibaldi (1807–82). De Valera of Ireland was another hero. Lala Hardayal, a friend of Lala Lajpat Rai, sent published material on the lives of these and other freedom fighters from England.

In asking young boys and girls of sixteen and above to discontinue their education in government-aided institutions, Gandhi had undertaken a heavy moral responsibility—that of promoting the establishment of national educational institutions unaided by the government of the day. For this urgent purpose he found immediate assistance from a leading philanthropist and educationist of Benares, Shiv Prasad Gupta, who came of a rich family. Deeply steeped in Indian culture and tradition, Gupta was an active participant in the Congress movement, having joined the organisation in 1904.[2] He was entirely opposed to the continuance of government-aided educational institutions, which, in his view, served no purpose but to create a body of clerks for the government's administrative machine. What the country needed was a large number of educated Indians who would fight for India's freedom. In order to make a personal study of the system of education in independent democratic countries, Gupta had travelled extensively, visiting Oxford and Cambridge to see what happened there. He had returned to India with the conviction that his country needed similar institutions for the advancement of excellence in education.

At the Congress sessions in September 1920 in Calcutta and December 1920 in Nagpur, national education was one of the important subjects on the agenda. Gupta, who participated in both sessions, had prepared a plan for the establishment of a national institution to provide university-level education using Hindi as the medium of instruction. He discussed his ideas with Mahatma Gandhi at the Nagpur session in December 1920. The Mahatma was delighted and blessed the proposal, promising his wholehearted support.

Gupta returned to Benares from Nagpur after the conclusion of the Congress session on 30 December 1920 with full determination to establish a new national institution of higher education in Benares within the following few weeks. This required substantial monetary support; Gupta himself provided the necessary resources and did so in an uniquely humble manner. After the early death of his only brother Har Prasad, Shiv Prasad Gupta had become the sole owner of his father's former estate, which was then valued at Rs 2,000,000 (two million). Shiv Prasad announced that he had no moral right to his deceased younger brother's share and donated half his property to a trust named after this younger brother. The trust income, estimated at Rs 40,000 per annum, was to be utilized solely for the maintenance of the new national institution. This donation enabled the establishment of the Kashi Vidya Peeth, the first national university in India with Hindi as the medium of instruction. Shiv Prasad Gupta was thus regarded in his time as the inspirer and supporter of rashtriya education and other rashtriya activities in Benares.

The Kashi Vidya Peeth was inaugurated as a national institution of higher education by Mahatma Gandhi on 10 February 1921 in a rented building in Benares, in the presence of a number of national leaders, including Jawaharlal Nehru and Abul Kalam Azad. The Mahatma made an impassioned inaugural address. 'This Vidya Peeth,' he said, 'has no large building—only a small place like a hut. But it is national. It is a symbol of the nation's determination to pursue non-cooperation. It is a place where you will not feel any subservience to a foreign flag. Here education will be provided in national language, in the national interest.' Addressing young boys and girls, he urged: 'Leave government-aided institutions . . . Come and join the Vidya Peeth.'[3] Lal Bahadur was present at this inaugural function and was among the first to join the Kashi Vidya Peeth, along with his friends T.N. Singh, Raja Ram and Algu Rai. This group was given a special entrance examination and then admitted to a four-year course, leading to the Shastri degree, later recognized as equivalent to a Bachelor of Arts.

The Kashi Vidya Peeth had an extremely eminent, learned and distinguished faculty, headed by Dr Bhagwan Das, who was posthumously awarded the Bharat Ratna (the highest national honour) and who was regarded as an illustrious and profound scholar, a great exponent of Indian philosophy. Among others in the faculty were Yagya Narayan Upadhyaya (Sanskrit), Jag Mohan Varma (Hindi), Dr Sampurnanand (Western Philosophy and International Law), and Dr Gopal Shastri (Eastern Philosophy).[4] Lal Bahadur joined the Philosophy course. The subject which interested him most was Ethics. The four years he spent studying at the Kashi Vidya Peeth (1921–5) constituted the third formative period of his life.*

While studying for his degree in the Kashi Vidya Peeth, Lal Bahadur was deeply influenced by Dr Bhagwan Das, a teacher who possessed an engaging freshness of approach and seemed a great model. Das had studied in great depth all the major religions of the world and presented an integrated picture of them in his treatise *The Essential Unity of All Religions*. He also propounded a philosophy of his own called *samanvay vad* or 'the integration of different points of view'. By this he meant that within diverging views on a subject there was always an element of truth in each. A genuine endeavour to see that element of truth would result in a positive, noncombative approach to life, from which in turn an 'integrated point of view' could be synthesized, a viewpoint more broadly acceptable to combatants. He asked his students to say *yeh baat bhi theek hai* (this is also right) and not *yeh baat hi theek hai* (only this is right). In this way, no one would feel defeated or humiliated. Lal Bahadur accepted and implemented this *samanvay vad*, this philosophy of integration, with disarming transparency and sincerity.

While applying himself to the study of his core subjects for the Shastri degree, Lal Bahadur took special interest in literature—English, Hindi and Urdu. His early education had been in Urdu. So he was already profoundly

---

* Fortunately, I was able to get detailed and authentic information about this period from one of Shastri's closest friends, Pandit Raja Ram Shastri, who was Lal Bahadur's classmate both in Harish Chandra High School and in the Kashi Vidya Peeth. I spent seven days with Pandit Raja Ram Shastri in Benares, during which he recalled for me the events of those times and related various anecdotes. My narration of Lal Bahadur's early life is based primarily on the information I obtained from Pandit Raja Ram Shastri and from some of his other friends and relations in Benares, Ramnagar and Mirzapur.

in tune with the philosophical poetry of Ghalib, the greatest poet in the Urdu language. The *Diwan-e-Ghalib*, a compendium of Ghalib's poetry, was his constant companion and he was often heard reciting to himself the following poem by Ghalib:

> *Rahiye abb aisi jagah chal kar jahaan koi na ho;*
> *Hum sukhhan koi na ho aur hum zabaan koi na ho;*
> *Bay dar-o-deewaar sa ek ghar banaya chahiyay;*
> *Koi hamsaaya na ho aur passbaan koi na ho;*
> *Pariyay gar beemaar to koi na ho teemaardaar;*
> *Aur agar mar jaiyay to noha-khwaan koi na ho.*

(I want to go away to a place where I can live in solitude; where there is none to converse with me; none to speak my language. I want to build a house without walls or doors. I want to be where there are no neighbours; none to comfort me; none to care for me if I fall ill; none to mourn if I pass away.)

Once, when Raja Ram Shastri heard Lal Bahadur recite this, he asked: *'Yeh kya bat hai? Yehi nazm kyon baar baar dohrate ho?'* (What's this? Why do you repeat this poem again and again?) Lal Bahadur replied: *'Jo Ghalib ne likha hai, wahi main apne liye chaahta hoon. Antim vairagya yehi to asli cheez hai.'* (What Ghalib has written is exactly what I want for myself: a totally detached life and ultimately renunciation. That's the real thing.)

Even at eighteen, Lal Bahadur was attracted to the idea of detachment: as time passed, renunciation was to become an integral part of his being.

It is generally believed that Lal Bahadur spent his childhood in abject poverty. Fanciful stories are told about his having to swim across the Ganga every day, books tied on his head, because he did not have money to pay the boat fare. This daily swimming acrobatics is hardly within the realm of possibility. Nor was it necessary. Lal Bahadur lived close to his school and, as it happened, on the same side of the river, a few hundred yards from the school. He personally told me he had only once swum across the Ganga. That was when he wanted to get to Ramnagar to see his ailing mother and had no money for the boat fare. 'Poverty is not an ornament to be exhibited,' his headmaster had once said. Lal Bahadur accepted it as good advice. He neither demonstrated his poverty nor talked about it. During the entire period I worked with him, only once did I hear him refer to the subject. Addressing a massive public meeting in Calcutta in October 1965 he told his audience: 'No one knows more about the pangs of poverty than I do.' That was all he said.

Poverty did not embitter him. In fact the straitened circumstances of his early years created a powerful and lifelong asset. At an early age he decided to keep his wants to the very minimum and adhered firmly to this decision all his life. Apart from his morning and afternoon tea and frugal meals, he had almost no other wants. He accepted and implemented faithfully Mahatma Gandhi's concept of *asangraha*, i.e. non-acquisition. The Mahatma's precept was: 'Acquire nothing which is not essential to life itself. If you have no unnecessary wants, you need have no fears.' Non-acquisition led to *aparigraha* or 'non-covetousness', and this could take interesting forms. At the home of his uncle Raghunath Prasad, where he was living at the time, the ladies of the house prepared delicious vegetarian food which Lal Bahadur enjoyed very much. But as time passed he began to be unhappy about this Epicureanism, and one day he came up to Raja Ram Shastri and expressed annoyance on this weakness for tasty food. The following conversation was narrated to me by Raja Ram Shastri:

| | |
|---|---|
| LAL BAHADUR | I'm very fond of tasty food. It is a bad habit. This is not suited to a Congress volunteer. We have to be ready to travel to villages and eat whatever food is available and enjoy it. |
| RAJA RAM SHASTRI | I see no problem. Eat tasty food when you get it. Otherwise eat whatever you get. You don't have to deny yourself tasty food all the time. |
| LAL BAHADUR | I have this bad habit. I have to conquer it. |
| RAJA RAM SHASTRI | Very well. But how will you do it? |
| LAL BAHADUR | I'll find a way. |

After about a month Raja Ram Shastri reverted, a little humorously, to the matter: 'How are you getting along with your taste-for-good-food problem?' he asked. 'Oh, I've succeeded,' said Lal Bahadur. 'One evening I poured a whole *lota* [tumbler] of water all over the *thali* [tray] in which my food was served. Then I mixed up everything so it became a sort of thick cold tasteless soup, which I swallowed. I have since repeated the experiment and my taste buds now give me no problem.' Raja Ram, rather aghast, said: 'You could have asked your family to cook plain, bland food.' To which Lal Bahadur's answer was: 'No, I could not do that, because this would have forced tasteless food on all the others. For them it was unnecessary. They are not Congress volunteers.'

Mahatma Gandhi had practised *aswaad*, the ascetic freedom from bondage to taste, and regarded it as an attribute of those who wanted to face the rough and tumble of everyday political life. Those who had the privilege of staying in the Gandhi Ashram at Wardha recall that food prepared in the ashram was tasteless and intended only to provide sustenance for keeping body and soul together. Arming himself with this new attribute of aswaad, Lal Bahadur had taken one more step towards becoming a determined follower of Mahatma Gandhi.

Raja Ram Shastri emphasized that this anecdote brought out two important traits in Lal Bahadur: first, his determination to eliminate even the slightest weakness in his mental make-up or character, and second, a deep and genuine concern for the feelings of others.

Debates and group discussions were an important feature of life and study in the Kashi Vidya Peeth. The educational atmosphere was that of a *gurukul*, an ancient Indian university, where teachers were meant to be men of immense learning and wisdom as well as the highest moral character. The number of students in each class was relatively small and teachers were able to give them individual attention. The subjects chosen for debate or discussion were not limited to the curriculum for the Shastri degree. Often, discussions focused on political issues. The principal objective was the creation of an educated and dedicated cadre of freedom fighters. Lal Bahadur participated actively in these debates and discussions. His views were, by all accounts, expressed in clear, simple and well thought out sentences. His reasoning was unemotional; his effort was to be persuasive without dogmatism and to gain the support of all his listeners. At the end of the debate or discussion he would usually provide a summary of conclusions which invariably found broad acceptance. When he asked questions, he would do so in a mild manner, with a sincere effort to understand the other's point of view. When he provided answers to questions, his manner was gentle and disarming. He generally shunned all vehemence in speech.

Lal Bahadur was not a lonely, self-righteous moral recluse: far from it; he was the life and soul of a small group of friends which included Algu Rai, Tribhuvan Naryan Singh and Raja Ram. He was jovial, but his jokes were mostly at his own expense. His joviality was also limited to this small circle of friends. Outside, he was somewhat reserved, quiet and dignified. Although poor and with very few clothes, he was always neatly attired. He had two sets of kurta and dhoti, of which he wore one and the other he washed for the next day. Lal Bahadur was keen on personal cleanliness and neatness; there was nothing slipshod about him.

He had a well developed and informed aesthetic sense and he was especially interested in architecture. Raja Ram Shastri recalled that during visits to Allahabad he and Lal Bahadur would always look at the statue of Queen Victoria. The canopy over this statue was a beautiful piece of architecture and they would sit opposite the statue, admiring it. During visits to Lucknow they would visit the famous Imambaras. Beautiful monuments, said Lal Bahadur, brought him a sense of peace and inner order.

Lal Bahadur was also fond of Indian music and occasionally sang. Raja Ram Shastri said that though he had no opportunity to learn classical music, Shastri would sometimes try to mimic the *ustaads* and *pandits* (experts). It seems he did this rather well.

Towards the end of this period Shastri wrote a thesis on 'The Philosophy of Dr Bhagwan Das' for his Shastri degree. He passed the Shastri degree examination in 1925, in the first division. His friend Raja Ram Shastri achieved the same distinction. On the basis of this degree, 'Shastri' was added to his name. It was an educational suffix which, in course of time, became assimilated to his name. He now came to be known to the world at large as Lal Bahadur Shastri, or just Shastri.

# Chapter 2

# Member, The Servants of the People Society

'It was due to my life-membership of the Society that I got an opportunity to serve my country the most. The Society has been instrumental in inculcating in me the true meaning of the term—servants of the people!'[1]

—Lal Bahadur Shastri

In 1925, after his education in the Kashi Vidya Peeth, Shastri was ready as a Congress volunteer to dedicate himself to the service of the country. By this time he had developed himself into a *karma yogi* and was now looking for his *kshetra*, his arena. He did not have to wait long. His close friend Algu Rai Shastri invited him to Lahore in order to present him to Lala Lajpat Rai, who had conceived and become founder president of The Servants of the People Society. This Society was formally inaugurated by Mahatma Gandhi on 9 November 1921; the inspiration for this initiative had come to Lajpat Rai by the example of Gokhale, who had founded the Servants of India Society in Poona in 1905. The objective of both was much the same and spelt out by Lala Lajpat Rai:

> The idea, from the very first, has been to produce a kind of national missionaries whose sole object would be to devote the whole of their time to national work, in a spirit of service, without hankering for promotion or for furthering their worldly interests. They are contented with the allowances given to them by the Society, and they live a life of comparative poverty, which is a noble ideal by itself. They do their work in a spirit of sacrifice and service and in their own way, they are a kind of beacon light and example to others.[2]

Algu Rai Shastri who had graduated from the Kashi Vidya Peeth the year before Shastri, had already joined the Society. In response to his invitation Lal Bahadur set out for Lahore and upon arrival was lodged in the headquarters of the Society.

Next day came the moment he had been waiting for with great expectation. Lala Lajpat Rai's life and writings had inspired Lal Bahadur since his school days. Even to be in his presence was an elevating experience.

As was his custom, Lajpat Rai had a detailed talk with the new arrival in order to make a personal assessment. This was no routine exercise: Lajpat Rai insisted on the highest possible standards, both in regard to dedication and personal character. The number of persons accepted for membership of the Society was no more than four or five per year. Lala Lajpat Rai found in Shastri the kind of dedicated missionary he was looking for. Soon thereafter Shastri, who at that time was twenty-one, was assigned to Muzaffarnagar district in Uttar Pradesh (then the United Provinces) for fieldwork. He was given charge of the Achhut Uddhar Centre of the Servants of the People Society. This was Shastri's first opportunity to put into practice the various qualities which he had already acquired—chiefly a capacity for hard, selfless, dedicated work. Lala Lajpat Rai was so pleased with Shastri's work that he admitted him as a Probationary Member of the Society early in 1927. Considering that Shastri was still only twenty-two, this was prophetic recognition of his calibre by a national leader of eminence. Later, in 1930, Shastri was confirmed as a life member of the Society at which time he took an oath:

> I agree to work for the Society for at least twenty years commencing from the date of confirmation as life member. During this period I shall be bound by the rules and discipline of the Society and will further the interest of the Society with zeal and will do nothing that goes against its objects and interests.
>
> It shall always be my endeavour to lead a pure personal life.
>
> The service of the country will occupy first place in my thoughts and in serving the country I shall not be actuated by motives of personal advancement.
>
> I shall work for the advancement of the people of my country, without distinction of caste and creed.
>
> I shall be content with such allowances for myself and my family, as the Society may fix or permit and shall take no part in any activity with the object of earning more money for myself or my family.
>
> I shall declare my assets in writing before the President at the time of joining, and after every five years.

In Muzaffarnagar district the Society had established a centre for social work among the Untouchables. Shastri devoted himself heart and soul to this work, which involved living in the midst of the deprived. Welfare programmes for children and women in particular, and literacy programmes for adults, had to be organized with only limited local help. During 1926 Shastri made ceaseless efforts to accomplish the tasks he had been allotted. His life was hard and close to poverty on account of a very meagre allowance. This did not worry him; on the contrary he was grateful to

Lajpat Rai and Algu Rai Shastri for the opportunity to begin his working life in a challenging area of social activity.

Lajpat Rai was a hard taskmaster. He believed in the dignity of labour and regarded all work as important. He set the highest standards for himself and for those who wanted to be associated with him or with the Servants of the People Society. He watched Shastri's work with keen interest and by the end of 1926 was completely satisfied. In 1927, as I said, he accepted him as a probationary member of the Society.

This marked an important event in Shastri's life. It meant public recognition of his abilities, dedication, and reliability by an eminent national leader: he had passed his first 'field test' with distinction. Second, as a probationary member Shastri was entitled to a monthly allowance of Rs 50, later raised to Rs 60, per month. For the first time, he became financially self-reliant. To express gratitude to his uncle Raghunath Prasad, in whose house he had found shelter over his years of education in Benares, Shastri sent the whole of his first salary. Prasad was deeply touched; he retained only a rupee and returned the balance.

Shastri continued to work in Muzaffarnagar during 1927 and 1928. In November 1928 Lala Lajpat Rai died as a result of injuries inflicted on him by the police during a lathi-charge (baton-attack) on demonstrators he was leading during Non-Cooperation activities. This only strengthened Shastri's resolve to dedicate himself to national service.

Lajpat Rai's sudden demise created a void in the Servants of the People Society. Lalaji was not just the Society's founder, he was also its principal benefactor. He had donated his property, a substantial part of his financial resources and his library to the Society. Who was then to succeed Lala Lajpat Rai as president and leader of the Society? Senior members of the Society turned to Mahatma Gandhi for guidance. Gandhi suggested Purshottam Das Tandon. Tandon was a close associate of Lalaji in the political arena. Like Lalaji, he was an ardent patriot with strong and uninhibited views who had given up highly-paid positions in order to serve his country. To many he was a *rishi*, a sage unattached to material possessions. Purshottam Das Tandon was then invited to assume the office of President and and this he did on 1 January 1929.

Tandon was most frequently in Lahore, but he decided that he would function as president of the Society from Allahabad. To assist him, Shastri was posted to Allahabad, and this marked the commencement of yet another chapter in his life.

While in Allahabad Shastri was elected a member of the local municipal board and this, alongside other facets of his activities (the principal one being his service to The Servants of the People Society) provided him with opportunities for a much broader exposure of his capabilities, in particular his capacity to handle complex situations. Tandon, under whose guidance Shastri functioned at Allahabad and who may well be said to have been Shastri's political guru, spoke of him as a genius at striking the right balance, at handling difficult situations, at achieving successful compromises, and as a rock of toughness behind his humility.

After Tandon and Balvantray Mehta, who served the Society as its presidents from 1929 to 1962, and 1962 to 1965 respectively, Shastri was elected as its president and, in succession to Jawaharlal Nehru, also as president of the Lajpat Rai Centenary Committee. In this dual capacity Shastri strengthened the Society's financial base.*

## MARRIAGE

Shastri's monthly allowance being adequate for the upkeep of a single person and even of a young couple, in October 1927, at the age of twenty-four, he was considered 'marriageable'. Early in 1928, when Shastri's mother was visiting her father's house in Mohalla Ganeshganj, Mirzapur, a proposal came up for the marriage of her son with Kumari Lalita Devi, daughter of Sita Ram, who was then holding the post of Deputy Inspector of Schools. He was also a resident of Mirzapur and had a house in Mohalla Chetganj. Sita Ram's social status and financial circumstances were of a good middle-class family. He owned two houses and a carriage and was financially well off. So, when Lalita Devi's father proposed his daughter's marriage with Shastri, it was accepted. As an obedient son, Shastri accepted his mother's decision. Among Lalita Devi's relations there was some concern that she was being married to a person who was financially not-so-well established. This did not, however, influence the course of events. Shastri's marriage with Lalita Devi was solemnized on 16 May 1928. At that time, Lalita Devi was seventeen. Shastri declined to accept any dowry or even presents, except for a *charkha* (a spinning wheel) and a piece of khadi cloth.

During a conversation with Shrimati Lalita Shastri, whom I respectfully addressed as Mataji, I asked whether she recalled any incidents of that time. She reminisced for a moment and then recalled certain words which Shastri spoke to her when they found themselves alone after their marriage: 'You belong to a well-to-do family and you could have married a more

---

* The Society continues to render useful service through its various centres all over the country, in fields such as medical relief, education, the improvement of conditions for women and Harijans, marriage information, health, relief and rehabilitation in the event of natural disasters, the removal of untouchability, legal aid, and so on.

prosperous person. Now that you have married me, I would suggest that for your future happiness and contentment, you should look at those who are even less favoured by fortune than ourselves.' Lalita Devi was nearly seven years younger than Shastri. Even so, she was mature and knew the background of the person she had married. She accepted her bridegroom's advice cheerfully. She also recalled that the same day, when she was inside the house, he sent her a message asking her to give away all her silk sarees and to wear only the khadi cotton sarees which he had bought for her. Thereafter Lalita Devi wore only khadi sarees all her life.

After their marriage the couple lived for several years in Allahabad before moving to Lucknow and then to New Delhi. Lalita Devi recalled that throughout her married life they lived with deep mutual regard. She respected and adored him as her idol, and he gave her all his affection as well as immense personal consideration. Ordinarily, he would address her as *tum* (the affectionate form of 'you'). But if he ever felt upset about a household matter, he would address her with the more formal *aap*. The change from *tum* to *aap* was the only indication to her that something had gone wrong, for Shastri never expressed in words any displeasure or annoyance. Both of them shared cheerfully the trials and tribulations of life. Shastri spent about nine years of his life in jail. During these spells his wife looked after the children and the household. She was the perfect, devoted Hindu wife.

In later years, when Shastri had become prime minister, his wife accompanied her husband during his state visits to the USSR and Yugoslavia. Although she did not speak English, she got on well both with Mrs Kosygin (wife of the prime minister of the USSR) and with Madame Tito (wife of the Yugoslav president); indeed they became friends.

Lalita Devi's large vermilion mark on her forehead, the *tika* or *bindu* (the sign of a married woman in Hindu society), her benign smile and profound courtesy, won her respect and admiration. She passed away on 13 April 1993. While she lived she seemed to embody the goodness of her husband, and this was most comforting to all who knew her and her husband. Her body was cremated in New Delhi's Vijay Ghat, by the side of her husband's *samadhi*.

# Chapter 3

## From Village-level Worker to Provincial Leader

Early in January 1929 Shastri, still a probationary member of The Servants of the People Society, presented himself to the new president, Purshottam Das Tandon, in Allahabad. Tandon was a respected Congress leader and also president of the Allahabad District Congress Committee. His political beliefs were much the same as those of Lala Lajpat Rai. A fearless patriot, he was an ascetic of the highest integrity. Deeply religious, he conformed to the ideals and values of Hinduism without being communal or sectarian. Indeed, he pleaded for Hindu–Muslim unity and was critical of casteism. He was dedicated to the spread of Hindi but at the same time was a scholar of Urdu and Persian. He laid great emphasis on moral character. As regards education, he believed firmly that knowledge of India's ancient cultural heritage should be an essential part of all syllabi.

Shastri could not have hoped for a better person to work with. Tandon was very nearly a replica of Lala Lajpat Rai—the same burning patriotism, the same resoluteness, the same belief in moral values, and the same dedication to hard work in the service of the country. Shastri was in the same mould, except that, unlike Tandon and Rai, he believed in moderation and reconciliation rather than in the strong expression of views which might seem partisan. This aspect of Tandon's style did not worry Shastri unduly; he knew how far to adopt the qualities of his leader and where to be guided by his own convictions.

Tandon entrusted Shastri with tasks involving work in the rural areas of Allahabad district, which Shastri accomplished to Tandon's satisfaction. As time passed, Tandon discovered many of Shastri's virtues, in particular his capacity for incessant work to tight schedules. Soon Tandon developed a great liking, indeed affection, for Shastri. On his part, Shastri regarded Tandon with immense respect and admiration. As was to be expected, within a few months Tandon also began to assign Congress Party tasks to Shastri. Here again, Shastri's persuasive, non-combative approach yielded the desired results.

It was at this point that Shastri came in touch with the Nehru family. The office of the All India Congress Committee was functioning then in Swaraj Bhawan, a building donated to the Congress Party by the Nehru family. For some time, Shastri worked as a staff member in the All India Congress Committee office. Nehru noticed the young man with the dignified and unobtrusive manner. Nehru was then president of the City Congress Committee and in need of some assistance himself. He gave a number of assignments to Shastri which were completed with the usual thoroughness and expedition, and the reports on these were presented in a neat and methodical way. Nehru was much impressed.

When Nehru became Congress president in 1929 he had to undertake a great deal of correspondence. He would often ask Shastri and B.N. Pande (presently a Member of Parliament) to help him. B.N. Pande remembers Nehru's appreciation of these drafts in Shastri's lovely handwriting in Hindi, Urdu or English, as required.

As is well known, Nehru was not interested in listening to excuses. He wanted results and was pleased with Shastri's total dedication of mind and heart. If there was ever a difficult or complicated problem, Nehru looked to Shastri to find a generally acceptable solution unobtrusively. Shastri soon developed into a confidant and trusted aide of Nehru.

While assisting Nehru, Shastri maintained his close association with Tandon. They used to meet almost every day and Shastri attended now to work relating to the Society as well as to the Congress Party. Tandon was a hard taskmaster. He maintained the highest standards himself and expected the same of his associates. Not surprisingly, he and Shastri developed the special relationship of *guru* and *chela*; in course of time Shastri became Tandon's confidant as well.

Nehru and Tandon, however, did not get on well with each other. In fact they were poles apart on crucial political and social matters. Nehru, who had studied at Harrow and Cambridge, was very much the westernized secularist who saw independent India as a socialist state. He wanted Indian education to be based on modern science and technology and did not like the idea of mixing politics with religion. Tandon on the other hand was immersed in Indian tradition and culture. He was an ascetic and believed deeply in the values of pristine Hinduism; he did not believe in any concept of secularism which might deprive India of its ancient Hindu moral base.

To serve both Nehru and Tandon at the same time, to secure and keep their trust, was a difficult task. Nehru and Tandon both had strong views, both were men of strong likes and dislikes, both were unwilling to make compromises on what they regarded as essential. And both were deeply involved in the civic and political life of Allahabad, the focal point of the

Congress Party. The situation seemed almost created for Shastri to put into practice his chosen philosophy of samanvay vad. Could he serve as a bridge between the two?

Nehru knew well that Shastri was very close to Tandon, and Tandon knew equally well that his protégé was equally Nehru's. But because both had complete confidence in the loyalty and objectivity of Shastri, neither ever suggested that he should distance himself from the other. In fact both felt that a person like Shastri could serve as an invaluable asset and mediator.

It often happens that when two strong-willed persons, convinced of the eternal validity of their own point of view, become adversaries, they go on talking without listening. Shastri felt that as both Nehru and Tandon were fiercely patriotic and full of idealism, there was a distinct possibility of finding some points on which both could agree without giving up their basic philosophies. Nehru and Tandon were involved in the affairs of the Congress and in matters relating to civic services in Allahabad as well as the district; there was always something within Tandon's area of responsibility where Nehru wanted some particular action to be taken, and vice versa. In such situations Nehru would ask Shastri to draft a letter from him to Tandon. As Shastri was well aware of Tandon's thinking, he would prepare a draft which would seem reasonable and acceptable to Tandon, and almost always, Nehru would write to Tandon as proposed by Shastri. On receiving the letter, Tandon on his part would ask Shastri to draft a suitable reply: in this way, Shastri became draftsman for both. Thanks to his particular skills, the tone of the letters was friendly on both sides and numerous tasks were happily accomplished to the satisfaction of all parties.

As time passed, the trust and confidence placed by Nehru and Tandon in Shastri grew stronger and eventually unshakeable. Indeed both showered affection in abundance on the young man, now just over twenty-five. From the level of an assistant he was elevated by both, within the span of a year, to the level of an advisor. Together, these contrasting nationalists propelled Shastri ahead into Indian politics.

Nehru, steeped in Western thought and culture, found in Shastri, the homespun Indian, an invaluable complement. Shastri never wanted anything for himself. This, Nehru knew, was not a posture. Renunciation and selfless service were his most evident hallmarks. Gradually, Nehru began to consult Shastri even on family matters. Bishambhar Nath Pande remembers that, once Shastri had been given this sort of confidence by Nehru, Shastri endeavoured to bring about a reconciliation between Nehru's sister Vijay Lakshmi and Nehru's daughter Indira. Nehru loved his daughter immensely: she was his very special weakness. Vijay Lakshmi was a very close second. The two women never got on together. With Nehru's tacit approval, Shastri tried to promote a certain mutual understanding between them. Thus, in a variety of ways, Shastri's role in Nehru's life deepened and widened. Shastri certainly retained the complete trust and confidence of Nehru till the end.

Similar developments marked Shastri's relations with Tandon. In values and background, Shastri was nearer Tandon than Nehru. Both were ascetic: Tandon overtly, Shastri inwardly. Shastri regarded Tandon as his first political guru. There was, all the same, one fundamental difference. Tandon could speak out strongly, and his words could be abrasive. Shastri had developed an emotional balance and never in his life did he utter an impolite word. The guru liked his disciple all the more for this difference.

The year 1929 was important in Shastri's life. In the beginning of that year, when he arrived at Allahabad to report to Tandon, he was no more than a social worker; by the end of it he had become the close advisor of two of India's powerful leaders. The year ended with the historic session of the Indian National Congress in Lahore under the presidentship of Nehru. Shastri was present at this session and witnessed the unforgettable spectacle of Nehru unfurling the Congress flag and declaring that freedom from foreign rule was now the clear objective of the Congress. This was a thrilling and elevating experience: the course was now clearly set.

In 1930 Nehru, although president of the Indian National Congress, continued to hold the offices of president of the Allahabad City Congress Committee and vice-president of the Allahabad District Congress Committee. Nehru was entirely the luminous rising star in the Congress firmament. Tandon was president of The Servants of the People Society and president of the Allahabad District Congress Committee. Both came to the conclusion, independently, that Shastri should be entrusted with specific organisational responsibilities. Accordingly, Shastri was appointed secretary of the Allahabad District Congress Committee. This enhanced his responsibilities and raised him from the level of a worker to a district-level leader. The propagation of the new message of the Indian National Congress which he had brought from the Lahore session of the Congress was now largely his responsibility.

At this point in time, events began to move rapidly ahead. Mahatma Gandhi decided to follow up the decisions of the Lahore session by launching the Civil Disobedience Movement on 12 March 1930, when he undertook his historic march to Dandi for the salt satyagraha. This created a new spirit of defiance. In Allahabad district Shastri, with the authorization of Nehru and Tandon, organised a 'no-rent' campaign as part of the movement. Congress workers went round to villages, urging peasants to refuse to pay rent. The government took immediate steps to thwart this movement. Shastri, its principal organizer in Allahabad, was arrested soon after he had delivered his first speech in support of the campaign. He was sentenced to two and a half years' imprisonment, though, on account of subsequent political developments, he was released after about a year.

The viceroy, Lord Irwin, initiated discussions with Gandhi to defuse the situation and arrange for an exchange of political views between Indian leaders and the British government. The Gandhi–Irwin Pact was signed, following which a Round Table Conference was convened in 1931 by the British government in London, to which Indian leaders were invited. At this conference Gandhi was forthright:

> I am here very respectfully, to claim, on behalf of the Congress, complete control over the defence forces and over the foreign affairs of India. The alien rulers might be able to hold India by the sword for some time. But that would be no more than a passing phase and even during that transitional period, it would be a disgruntled, rebellious and inflammable India, ready to rise any moment to overthrow the foreign yoke . . . [1]

The British government was not willing to concede this demand. The Hindu–Muslim problem, aggravated by the British, was used as a convenient excuse. Indeed the situation was worsened by the Communal Award, announced by the British prime minister, Ramsay MacDonald. This forced another wedge between the two largest communities in India.

When Gandhi returned to India in December 1932 without any tangible results, there was great disappointment in the country. Gandhi sought an interview with the viceroy to discuss the prevailing situation, but this was refused. The Congress Working Committee met on 1 January 1931 and decided to resume the Civil Disobedience Movement and organize a boycott of foreign goods. Once again there was national upheaval. Gandhi and other Congress leaders were arrested, and their party was declared an unlawful organization. Shastri too was arrested and sentenced to a term in jail.

Between 1930 and 1945 Shastri was imprisoned seven times for his participation in the freedom struggle. The nine years of Shastri's life spent in confinement constituted an important and meaningful portion of his life. In jail, as when free, Shastri was a model of good behaviour. He asked no concessions or favours for himself. He was helpful to fellow Congressmen imprisoned with him in whatever way he could. 'My jail life', he said, 'was interesting from more than one point of view. I used to do a lot of reading every time I went to jail.'[2]

While Shastri was in jail his family naturally suffered great distress.

Once his eldest daughter, Manju, fell ill rather seriously. According to the jail rules, Shastri could be released on parole for a short period, provided he signed a declaration that he would not engage in political activity during that period. Shastri held the view that it was not proper for a freedom fighter to sign any such declaration. The jail superintendent, who had some discretion in the matter and who had great regard for Shastri, allowed him to leave the jail on parole for fifteen days without signing the usual declaration. The jail superintendent took the risk because he was confident Shastri would adhere to the rules. The day Shastri reached home his ailing daughter, tragically, passed away. He performed the last rites and immediately thereafter went back to jail, not utilizing the fifteen days' parole granted to him.

On another occasion Shastri's eldest son, Hari Krishna, only four years old at the time, was laid up with typhoid. He was running a high fever of 104°F, and his condition was not improving. Shastri was allowed a week's parole on this occasion, again without conditions. He went home and nursed his ailing son for the whole of that week. Hari's condition got worse; the fever rose to 105°F and he was growing weaker day by day. When the parole period was about to end, the jail superintendent made it known that parole could be extended, but Shastri would now have to give a written undertaking promising dissociation from political activity. Shastri declined this conditional offer. Neither circumstance nor even emergency, leave alone expediency, could shake his hold over moral principle.

Hari wanted his father by his side, and Shastri was not bereft of emotion. But he steeled himself and opted for the moral course. He went back to jail in time. On these occasions, as on many others in his life, Shastri had to choose between family and country.

Between 1930 and 1935 Shastri participated vigorously in various facets of the Civil Disobedience Movement and was imprisoned for different terms in 1930, 1932 and 1934. He played a leading role in the no-rent campaign and the salt satyagraha. By the end of 1934, he had acquired a key position in the Congress Party organisation in Allahabad, the focal point of the activities of the Indian National Congress at that time. His reputation was of a person possessing high ethical qualities, a huge capacity for work, and a unique talent for reconciling different points of view by promoting a generally acceptable consensus. He had succeeded remarkably as secretary of the Allahabad District Congress Committee and demonstrated exceptional organizational abilities. He was ready for higher responsibilities and a larger arena. He did not have to wait very long.

In 1935 Nehru became president of the UP Provincial Congress Committee (UPCC) whose head office was located in Lucknow. This involved meeting a lot of people, listening to their points of view, resolving problems and making important decisions. By this time Nehru was deeply immersed in national affairs and could not find time to deal with the nitty-gritty of provincial Congress Party matters. He needed someone competent and trustworthy to assist him and share his responsibilities. He chose Shastri, appointing him general secretary of the UPCC. With this appointment Shastri moved up the political ladder from district to provincial level. However, as was the general practice at that time, he retained his political base in Allahabad. In 1936 he was elected president of the Allahabad District Congress Committee and as member of the Allahabad Municipal Board, on which he served for seven years. Amongst his colleagues on the Municipal Board was Nehru's sister, Vijay Lakshmi. Shastri was also a member of the Allahabad Improvement Trust for four years. 'That is,' says D.R. Mankekar, 'where his gift for committee work was cultivated.'[3]

The centre of Shastri's political activities now clearly shifted to Lucknow. In his new capacity he began to deal with Congress Party affairs of the entire province and interact with leaders of District Congress committees, as well as with provincial political leaders, some of whom had already acquired national repute. Among these were Govind Ballabh Pant, Sampurnanand and C.B. Gupta, all of whom were to become chief ministers of UP in later years. There were other important personalities as well—Rafi Ahmad Kidwai, Syed Ali Zaheer and Hafiz Mohammad Ibrahim, who later became cabinet ministers.

The sudden elevation of Shastri, who was then a young man of thirty, could well have caused the ruffling of some feathers. There were several others with longer periods of service to the Party who had aspirations to positions of responsibility. In the event, no problems arose. Shastri had arrived with a high reputation and the known support of Nehru. That gave him a good start. He had to win general goodwill as well, and began to attend to his responsibilities with his usual dedication. He met people who wanted to meet him. He listened with patience and full attention. He kept brief notes of each meeting and followed them up with such action as was required. He was very careful about promises and fulfilled whatever he undertook to do. He did all this with transparent sincerity and with evident respect for every person he met, regardless of their status or position. The word soon spread; within weeks, Shastri had won general acclaim as well as the trust and affection of his seniors in the party.

Earlier, in Allahabad, Shastri had played a leading role in Congress Party affairs, but the field was limited. There, it had been largely the carrying out of the wishes and mandates of Nehru and Tandon. In Luck-

now the field was the whole of UP, India's largest province and the fore-
front of the freedom struggle. Shastri now had to assume much greater
responsibility in dealing with Party matters and in reconciling different
points of view, while keeping Nehru well informed. As general secretary
of the UP Congress, he had to ensure that in all districts Congress Party
workers and leaders maintained close contact with village people to spread
the message of the Congress. 'If in Uttar Pradesh, every village was
Congress-minded', says D.R. Mankekar, 'the credit must be shared between Jawaharlal Nehru, Purshottam Das Tandon and Lal Bahadur.'[4]

In the next year, 1936, Shastri was entrusted with an important new
responsibility which brought him to the centrestage of UP's political affairs.
In going to the rural masses for support the Congress Party had committed
itself to a major reform in the prevailing feudal zamindari system, under
which agricultural land was owned by zamindars who paid land revenue
to the government of the province. These zamindars collected rent from
cultivators, whose status was that of tenants. Many others did not enjoy
even such rights and were treated as landless labourers, employed on meagre
wages. The system was unfair and riddled with abuses but it had the
backing of the law. Reforms could be brought about only by new legislation. This matter was one of the most urgent and important items on the
agenda of the Congress Party. To study this problem in detail and make
suitable recommendations for reform, the UP Congress appointed a non-
official committee of which Shastri was made convener. This was a matter
of all-India interest because land reforms were needed not just in UP but
in the other provinces as well.

Shastri devoted himself to this complex and politically vital problem.
He studied the available documentation, as well as the relevant provisions
of the existing law. He noted in detail the evils of zamindari. The more
important and indeed crucial task of the committee was to formulate clear
and specific recommendations for reform. This required innovative thinking. Within a matter of weeks, Shastri produced a report with detailed and
practicable recommendations for land reforms. His report was acclaimed
by Congress leaders in UP as a work of monumental importance for the
welfare of the peasantry who, after many decades of exploitation, were now
hoping for a new deal. As we shall see later, when the Congress Party
assumed governmental responsibility in 1937, one of its first decisions was
to redeem its pledge to the people on land reforms by enacting new
legislation based largely on the recommendations of the Lal Bahadur
Shastri Report. In later years this report was used as a model in other
provinces for the implementation of land reforms.

At this time, under the pressure of the Civil Disobedience Movement, the British government came to the conclusion that some constitutional reforms, involving a considerable transfer of power to Indians in the governance of their own country, were essential. Accordingly, the British parliament passed the Government of India Act, 1935, which provided for elected provincial legislatures and responsible provincial governments subject to some special responsibilities vested in the British governors. After being assured of the genuineness of the autonomy provided in the 1935 Act, the Congress Party accepted the reforms and agreed to participate in elections to the provincial legislatures. These elections were held in 1937 and Shastri was elected to the UP assembly from one of the Allahabad constituencies. He thus secured, for the first time, the mandate of the people. His political base in Allahabad was further strengthened by the election.

Having secured a large majority in the UP assembly in the 1937 elections, the Congress Party formed the government. But its tenure lasted only for about two years. In 1939, when the Second World War broke out, Congress resigned office in all provinces where it was in power to protest against the British decision to commit India to the war in Europe. While India was against the Nazis in Germany and the Fascists in Italy, Indian leaders were firmly of the view that the decision to join the war ought to have been taken by Indians themselves, not by the foreign ruling power. To deal with the resulting situation the British government vested the viceroy, Lord Linlithgow, with extraordinary powers to carry on the administration of the country as well as maintain and strengthen the war effort. The viceroy declined to deal with Congress any further. The old imperialist card of setting one community against another was played again. The Muslim League was encouraged to present its own charter of demands.

After the resignation of the provincial government and the dissolution of the provincial assembly, there was an interregnum in political affairs. Shastri returned to Allahabad and began work on the reorganization of the Congress Party machinery in the district. But his health was in poor condition at this time. 'Frequent jail terms', says D.R. Mankekar, 'lack of nutritive food even when he was outside jail, and continuous hard work, were beginning to tell on Shastri's health. His physique had never been very strong anyway. And he failed to pay much attention to the poor state of his health until a serious illness laid him up.' In Benares for some work, he decided to go across the river to Ramnagar, to meet his relatives. When he reached the ghat to take a boat, 'he felt a severe pain in his chest. The pain was so overpowering that he fainted. People there removed him to hospital and informed the Benares Congress office about his condition.'[5]

Shastri's mother was immediately taken to Benares by a family friend.

His wife, Lalita, could not reach him immediately because there was no money to pay for the fare. Purshottam Das Tandon came to her help: he arranged the tickets for her and her children. By the time Lalita reached Benares, Shastri had been shifted to the house of Kamlapati Tripathi, a local Congress Party leader, to ensure proper treatment and attention. Lalita found her husband's condition grave. According to D.R. Mankekar, Shastri had had a severe attack of pleurisy; it was so virulent that for the first three days he even lost his speech.

Lalita gave all her attention to her husband, Yet it took him a month to recover. Thereafter Shastri and his family returned to Allahabad. With the summer, the heat began to affect Shastri's health again. The attending doctor advised a cool place, preferably a hill station. This suggestion could not be ignored, but the besetting problem once again was money. Lalita was insistent that money be borrowed for the trip. On this occasion Shastri, finding his health failing again, accepted his wife's suggestion. Some funds were arranged and a friend found cheap accommodation for their stay. They went to Ranikhet where, after a month, Shastri's health improved rapidly.*

In 1941 Congress launched a new, carefully planned political movement. Especially selected members of the Party were asked to offer 'individual satyagraha', making a public declaration of their opposition to the war effort and demanding independence for India. Shastri was one of them. He offered satyagraha and was arrested. On 19 August 1941 he was imprisoned for a term of five months. He was released from prison on 14 December.

At this time the war was going badly for the Allies. Practically the whole of Western Europe had been conquered by the Nazis, and Great Britain itself was under the threat of invasion. The British government decided to explore the possibility of some political settlement in India and sent a high-powered mission under the leadership of Sir Stafford Cripps. Congress wanted a responsible government at the centre, with real power vested in a cabinet consisting only of Indians, with the viceroy as a titular head. The Cripps Mission had no authority to discuss these Congress proposals. What the Mission offered was dubbed by Mahatma Gandhi as 'a post-dated cheque on a crashing bank'. The Cripps Mission did not succeed.

Congress then decided to convene a meeting of the All India Congress Committee (AICC) in the first week of August 1942 to decide upon their future course of action. The meeting commenced as planned, with the

---

* Ranikhet is a small hill resort in UP.

entire Party leadership present. The session was attended by delegates from all parts of the country. All who participated in the debate were of one view: India must launch a massive movement for freedom. On 8 August 1942 the AICC adopted the Quit India resolution, demanding that the British should leave India to Indians. Government authorities, who were monitoring the situation from moment to moment, acted swiftly. At 4 a.m. on 9 August 1942, Gandhi was arrested. Jawaharlal Nehru, Abul Kalam Azad, Vallabhbhai Patel and Rajendra Prasad were among hundreds of other leaders arrested at the same time.

The demand of Congress that the British should 'quit India' immediately electrified the country. News of the arrest of Gandhi and the others enraged the people. In Bombay and other cities people came out onto the streets to demonstrate their support for the call. In Bombay, now the centre of this national resurgence, the government tried to restrict the movement of people by imposing a curfew in a number of localities. The police used tear gas to disperse crowds, and when this did not succeed they resorted to firing. The brutality of the police added fuel to the fire. Similar incidents took place in different places all over the country. This did not quell nationalism: on the contrary, thousands of men and women, young and old, joined this virtual war of independence, in dealing with whom the police were ruthless.

According to a statement made by Sir Reginald Maxwell, member for home affairs in the viceroy's executive council, the police resorted to firing on 538 occasions in different parts of the country, killing 940 and injuring 1630 persons. By the end of 1942 as many as 60,229 people had been arrested. The British government announced that the revolt had been crushed. Prime Minister Churchill made his pompous declaration: 'Let me make it very clear, in case there should be any mistake or any doubt about it in any quarter. We mean to hold our own. I have not become the King's First Minister in order to preside over the liquidation of the British Empire.' India became free within less than five years of Churchill's declamation.

Despite the assertions of Maxwell and Churchill, the Quit India movement was by no means dead. While many Congress leaders and workers were arrested and imprisoned, a large number quickly went underground to continue the campaign.

Shastri had quietly left Bombay on 9 August 1942. Being aware that he would be arrested if he went to the main station at Allahabad, he alighted at a small suburban stop to dodge the police. After daylight, he went to the Congress Party office in Anand Bhawan, where he organized an underground information centre. News-sheets were prepared, giving information about the national movement, police atrocities and the bravery of men and women who were carrying on the struggle. The people were asked to continue their resistance in whatever way they could.

In this way an underground network of clandestine centres was established with code numbers and fake names. As was bound to happen, in many places people resorted to violence, cutting telegraph and telephone lines, disrupting railway transport, burning government property, etc. It became a hit-and-run guerilla campaign. However, Shastri continued to organize peaceful agitations. Whenever possible, he would go out in disguise, meet people in villages, explain the Congress call for independence, and urge them to join the movement.

One day, when he was hiding in an upper-floor room at Anand Bhawan, the police suddenly arrived. They located Vijay Lakshmi on the ground floor and arrested her. They did not make a thorough search and Shastri was able to keep himself in hiding. But within a matter of days he too was arrested, on 19 August 1942, and held in prison for three years, until August 1945.

During these three years Shastri's family went through immense suffering. Their only income was a small allowance of Rs 100 per month, granted to Shastri by The Servants of the People Society, of which he was a life member. This was just about enough to keep the family going. Extra expenditures caused them serious problems. Over illnesses, it was difficult and often impossible to find the money for doctors and medicines.

During these three years of Shastri's imprisonment the situation was much worse in all sorts of other ways too. The government had outlawed the Indian National Congress, banning all its activities. Even the work of The Servants of the People Society had come to a stop. With large-scale arrests, hardly anyone was left to conduct normal activities or pay out funds. In these circumstances the allowance of Rs 100 per month to Shastri could not be disbursed. Lalita had, in fact, to go away to her parental house in Mirzapur, where she managed somehow to keep body and soul together and feed her children. But anxiety for her husband and malnutrition made her health fail. Eventually, she contracted tuberculosis.[6] She did her best to keep the news from her husband, but he got to know and felt greatly perturbed. He had then to request a fellow Congress worker, Purnima Banerji, the sister of Aruna Asaf Ali, for help. Lalita was brought to Allahabad and Purnima Banerji took charge of her treatment. Within a few months Lalita recovered. With some help from friends, she continued to live in Allahabad with her children. A Muslim family in the neighbourhood, learning of their poverty, arranged for provisions and fuelwood to be supplied to Lalita's house. When Lalita protested, the Muslim family insisted, saying it was small recompense for her husband's sacrifices for their country.[7]

# Chapter 4

## Parliamentary Secretary and Cabinet Minister

When the Second World War ended the question of India once again became one of the important items on the British agenda. The Quit India movement, even if crushed at the time by the might of the state, had nevertheless convinced the British that it was no longer profitable or even feasible to hold India in bondage for much longer by repression. The viceroy, Lord Wavell, went to London for talks to secure Churchill's agreement to the release of Mahatma Gandhi and other Congress leaders from detention, and to commence a political dialogue.

The world had just gone through the holocaust of a global war and there was a new determination and a new idealism to promote a more just world order. The United Nations was established to ensure peace and security around the world. Even Winston Churchill, who had not forgotten his avowed refusal to preside over the liquidation of the British empire, had begun to accept that in a postwar world India would have to be free: the United States of America had clearly encouraged him to think on those lines. Not that he envisaged this possibility with any pleasure. He made the viceroy wait in London for four weeks and then, during the course of a talk lasting forty minutes, indicated his view that India might have to be divided into three parts—Hindustan, Pakistan, and Princestan.[1] However, he accepted Wavell's proposals for the release of political detainees, and for negotiations with the Congress Working Committee.

Wavell released the Congress leaders on 15 June 1945 and invited them to Simla for talks at the end of the same month. Jinnah and Liaquat Ali of the Muslim League were also invited, as were other important national leaders. The viceroy offered to constitute a new representative executive council, composed of an equal number of caste Hindus and Muslims, together with one Hindu scheduled caste member and possibly a few belonging to other minorities. Wavell indicated further that his veto would not be unreasonably used.

Congress accepted the proposals despite its known dislike for the parity formula. Jinnah, however, rejected them. He wanted the absolute right to nominate all Muslim members of the council. Wavell did not agree; he wanted to nominate one Muslim from the Unionist Party in Punjab, which had helped greatly in the war effort. The talks broke down.

Just about a month later there was a general election in Britain. The British people surprised the world by voting Labour into power, in preference to the Tories led by Winston Churchill. The new British government led by Clement Attlee decided that fresh elections to the central and provincial assemblies should be held in India as soon as possible. This decision was implemented expeditiously. The election results revealed that the Muslim League had become the most important representative body of the Muslim community. The non-Muslim vote went to Congress. It was now abundantly clear that no political settlement was possible which was unacceptable to the Muslim League. Having demonstrated its strength, the League staked strongly its claim to be the sole representative body of the Muslims of India. As was to be expected, there was a sharper cleavage now between the aspirations of the Congress Party and those of the Muslim League.

Attlee's government once again took the initiative in resuming political contacts through the viceroy. Towards the end of January 1946 a Cabinet Mission came to India, determined to find a solution. Essentially, it made proposals which at one stage both Congress and Muslim League accepted but then turned down.

The British government, now determined to transfer power to India within months, made it known that if there was no agreement between Congress and the League, power would be transferred to a partitioned India, with the Muslim-majority areas of British India constituting Pakistan, and the rest of the country retaining the name 'India' (or any other name that it chose). On this basis the viceroy invited Congress and the League to join an interim government with equal representation for caste Hindus and Muslims, with some additional members to represent the scheduled castes and other minorities. The Congress Party accepted the invitation, but the Muslim League laid down conditions unacceptable to the viceroy. All the same, an interim government was formed with Jawaharlal Nehru as vice-president of the executive council. A little later the Muslim League had second thoughts and decided to come in. But they disrupted the functioning of the government as one collective entity. It was almost like two antagonistic governments functioning under the viceroy.

The appalling difficulties experienced in trying to make the interim central government work, composed as it was of the nominees of Congress, the Muslim League, and the minorities, finally convinced Congress and other small constituent units that the communal monster would never allow smooth functioning of such a composite government even after the transfer of power. Independence would have little meaning if the goverment was to be thwarted at every step.

Lord Louis Mountbatten was sworn in on 24 March 1947 as the new viceroy of India. He had come with ideas of his own which would have balkanized the Indian subcontinent. But finding strong resistance from Nehru, he gave up his ideas quickly. From then on it was a question of proceeding with the partition plan. Muslim majority areas were to be demarcated and any disputes were to be settled by a boundary commission. There was to be a referendum in the North West Frontier Province. Action on all fronts was speeded up and Mountbatten announced that British power could be withdrawn by the middle of August 1947. And so it was. After the secession of Muslim majority areas on 14 August to form Pakistan, India became independent at the midnight hour between 14 and 15 August 1947. There was great rejoicing when the Union Jack was hauled down and the national flag of India unfurled.

But soon came the shattering news of a holocaust. What followed the partition of the country was a massive migration of populations in both directions, the like of which is rare in human history. Indescribable brutalities were inflicted upon innocent human beings; those who escaped lost all that they had. But life had to go on. Nehru had become free India's first prime minister. He was Gandhi's choice: 'Pandit Jawaharlal and I have had differences from the moment we became co-workers, yet I have said for some years and say it now that not Rajaji, not Sardar Vallabhbhai, but Jawaharlal will be my successor. You cannot divide water by repeatedly striking it with a stick. It is just as difficult to divide us . . . When I am gone, he will speak my language.'[2]

While the historic events of 1945–7 were taking place in New Delhi, Shastri was still a Congress Party leader in UP. He was busy in Lucknow with the responsibilities assigned to him by the party, and yet he was a distant observer of the great happenings in the capital. The news came from there, in 1945, that elections would be held in the provinces. Especially selected persons were appointed to organize all aspects of these elections on behalf of the Congress Party. In UP this responsibility was entrusted to Shastri, who was appointed as secretary of the parliamentary board of Congress. This was a large task, involving the organization of a province-wide election campaign, the establishment of fair and objective procedures for the selection of candidates, meeting a large number of party workers and aspirants, maintaining constant contact with Congress Party leaders in UP, and running the office of the UP parliamentary board more or less twenty-four hours a day.

This was the most important and politically sensitive assignment entrusted to Shastri thus far. In the organization of elections, the most difficult aspect is the reconciliation of rival claims made by applicants for the party ticket. The person selected is pleased; the rest fester and turn on the chief selector. What made Shastri's task even more daunting was the enormous size of UP and the large number of seats in the assembly. In 1946, UP's population was in excess of 50 million—the size of a major country in Europe.

Shastri assumed his responsibilities with equanimity. He both lived and worked in the office of the UP Provincial Congress Committee and was available at any hour of night or day, on the telephone, as well as personally, to all Congress Party leaders, candidates and workers. The mammoth task of selecting party candidates, the conduct of the party's political campaign, the elections themselves, scrutiny during the counting of votes, and the declaration of results were all accomplished satisfactorily. The Congress Party won a resounding victory in UP. Shastri was himself elected to the assembly, once again from an Allahabad constituency. He had also won wide acclaim for fair play and impartiality; even those who lost did not seem to blame him. This in itself was an exceptional achievement. But on this occasion, and thereafter throughout his life, he showed that he possessed other qualities, namely humility, integrity, and a phenomenal memory.

Shastri's humility was distinctive; it was fundamentally different from the humility one encounters in everyday life. It had no relation to Churchill's sarcasm that 'a humble politician must have much to be humble about.' Shastri's humility was neither an expedient nor a cultivated posture for effect. It was not induced by any feeling of deficiency either. It was the spontaneous outer expression of innate virtue. He genuinely believed that all human beings who are created by the same Almighty God should be treated with consideration and respect, regardless of their station in life, their power or their wealth. He was full of concern for the common man and his feelings. Most people who met him cherished the memory of that meeting. Shastri had a way, all his own, of receiving and talking with visitors. Invariably, he got up from his chair and folded his hands in salutation, welcoming the visitor with a smile. He put the visitor at ease by making enquiries about his welfare and paying him undivided personal attention. He listened well and made brief notes of points requiring action. If necessary, he asked questions and sought clarifications, which indicated and indeed meant that he was sincerely interested in what the visitor had to say. He never diminished the importance of visitors by looking at papers or files. He never diverted attention by suddenly making a telephone call. He never showed haste nor gave the impression that he was anxious to get rid of his visitor. In short, in every way his manner was polite and respectful. He was, of course, the soul of discretion and never let out secrets. The conversation over, Shastri would again get up from his chair and bid goodbye with folded hands. Not surprisingly, Shastri made a vast number of friends, for he gave to the common man the same consideration he gave to cabinet colleagues.

Shastri's integrity, too, was absolute and all-pervading. From 1946 he was called upon to assume governmental responsibilities, first as parliamentary secretary to the chief minister of UP, later as cabinet minister of home and transport in the state. In 1951 Nehru asked him to move to New Delhi, where he became general secretary of the Congress Party. In that capacity he took charge of the Congress campaign for India's first general election in 1951–2. Working closely with Nehru, Shastri had, for all practical purposes, prime responsibility for the initial selection of party candidates (though the final decision was taken by the Congress Party parliamentary board). After 1952 he was, in succession, the central government cabinet minister for railways and transport, for transport and communications, for commerce and industry, and for home affairs. In 1964 he became prime minister. Nehru excepted, no Indian had till then exercised as much power over Congress Party and government affairs. Yet, unlike most politicians, Shastri remained untainted by power. All his life he limited his expenses to the salary he was paid. His own wants were always limited, but his family, too, always lived unlavishly. On three occasions, in 1951, 1956 and 1963, when he resigned from the position of cabinet minister, Shastri's income fell and his family cut out expensive vegetables from their meals in order to live within the available means. When one of his sons needed a tutor, Shastri agreed on condition that the tutor's remuneration be found by reducing expenditure on the washing of clothes; he showed the way by washing his clothes himself. There was always a struggle, but this was a price he cheerfully paid in order to live a life of absolute purity. When Prime Minister Shastri died in 1966, he left behind no house, no land, no money. In fact, far from a positive bank balance, he still owed a small debt to the government, this being part of a loan which he had taken for a jeep for the use of the family, and which he was repaying by monthly instalments. As we shall see, financial propriety was only a part of Shastri's integrity.

These assets were supplemented by an unusually good memory. Shastri never forgot a name or a face. Dr K.M. Zararia, who now lives in Baroda, remembers that he first met Shastri for a few minutes in Tibia College, New Delhi, in 1959. Zararia saw Shastri again six years later at the Niagara Falls, when Shastri was visiting Canada, in 1965. To Zararia's amazement and delight Shastri recognized him immediately and talked for quite a few minutes. A large number of people recount the same experience.

It only remains to be stated that Shastri's life was an open book. In the mould of Mahatma Gandhi, he was a moral colossus in Indian politics.

The elections to the provincial assemblies, held towards the end of 1945, had given the Congress Party an overwhelming majority in UP. Govind Ballabh Pant, a politician of national stature, was unanimously elected as leader of the Congress Party in the legislature and became chief minister. Pant was a member of the Congress Working Committee, the highest decision-making body in the organization. He was renowned for his political sagacity and his counsel was sought by Jawaharlal Nehru on important national affairs.

Pant needed a parliamentary secretary who was both able and trustworthy. He selected Shastri. As the chief minister's parliamentary secretary, Shastri had to assist Pant primarily in his legislative responsibilities. During this period of ministerial apprenticeship, Shastri came into close contact with most members of the state legislature, including those of the opposition, and gained their esteem. Pant was much impressed and assigned to Shastri specific tasks outside the legislature as well. According to D.R. Mankekar, Pant described Shastri as 'likeable, hard-working, devoted, trustworthy and noncontroversial.'[3] Mankekar adds:

> Pant was in the habit of working late in the office, and so was Lal Bahadur, whereas the other ministers and Parliamentary secretaries preferred to knock off for the day at a decent hour of the evening. It thus happened that the Chief and his young and late-working Parliamentary Secretary began to go home together every evening in the former's car. That brought the two frequently together and the 'Tiger of Kumaon'[4] thus came to study Lal Bahadur from close quarters and developed a great affection for him, which the latter fully reciprocated.[5]

The events of 1929 in Allahabad were repeating themselves in Lucknow in 1946; then, Shastri had won the confidence and affection of Nehru and Tandon. Now he had won the trust and affection of Pant, an astute administrator and a great judge of men. Neither in 1929 nor in 1946 did Shastri tailor his image to suit the perceived likes and requirements of these senior leaders. He remained strictly as he was, nothing was put on. By the end of 1946 Chief Minister Pant had formed the judgment that Shastri was ripe for advancement and in 1947, appointed him cabinet minister for home and transport.

This was Shastri's first ministerial appointment, which carried a relatively decent salary. His family was now able to live in reasonable comfort. His own lifestyle, of course, never changed to the end of his life.

As home and transport minister, Shastri put into practice some of his own ideas about the welfare of the common man. He was responsible for the police force in the state. During the British days, the police was seen by common people as an instrument of repression. Shastri knew that the police would need to use the baton. He was firm that they must discharge their law-and-order role effectively, but also that this should be done as humanely as possible. He conveyed this through the inspector-general of police. He also evolved a new method for the dispersal of unlawful mobs. Instead of lathis (batons), the police was asked to use water-hoses in the first instance. Lathis were to be used only as a last resort. In some situations when he was present himself, he advised the police to show restraint even when they had suffered injury. He would then personally visit each injured policeman and explain the reason behind his policy. Further, in order to improve the public image of the police, he recruited into its upper cadres a large number of young men who had suffered imprisonment during the Quit India movement. These were now trained for service in the police force, which was subject to strict discipline. Shastri's approach tried to impart, to the new style of policemen, feelings of national pride and a determination to be fair and understanding without undermining their effectiveness.

Shastri's own moral credibility and sense of humour helped him defuse difficult situations, particularly volatile communal situations. Under him the police was encouraged to become, if only for a duration, less violent than it was used to being.

Shastri also organized a semi-official civil defence force called Prantiya Raksha Dal. This was a voluntary organization which recruited and trained young persons for civil defence duties in emergency situations.

In the transport sector, Shastri found the existing bus services unreliable and inefficient. Rural areas were poorly served. He responded by establishing a wholly state-owned and state-run bus service covering the entire province. This was seen as a great boon by the public.

When dealing with senior civil servants and departmental heads, he encouraged them to state their point of view clearly and objectively, reading what they wrote on files and listening to them patiently. His decisions were impartial and he took full responsibility for what he decided. No extraneous considerations or pressures worked with him.

Within three years, by 1950, Shastri had grown further in political stature. It was now time for him to move to the national stage in New Delhi.

# Chapter 5

# National Leader and Central Cabinet Minister

In 1950 there was a titanic contest for election to the office of president of the Indian National Congress. Nehru, as prime minister, gave strong public support to the candidature of veteran Congress leader J.B. Kripalani. Sardar Vallabhbhai Patel, the deputy prime minister, gave equally strong and open support to another candidate, Purshottam Das Tandon. The election was thus virtually a contest between Nehru and Patel. Nehru was a socialist; Sardar Patel, who had a vast following in the party, was seen by Nehru as a conservative. The two pillars of the Congress Party never got on together. So, besides supporting Kripalani, Nehru made it known that he was firmly opposed to Tandon, and that if Tandon were elected he would treat it as a vote of no-confidence in himself by the Congress Party and resign as prime minister. The polling took place on 29 August 1950, the result was announced on 1 September. Despite Nehru's strong opposition and threat of resignation, Tandon secured an absolute majority of votes and was declared elected. Nehru was furious. He announced that he would not join the Congress Working Committee. Without the prime minister, who was the leader of the Congress Parliamentary Party, the Working Committee could not possibly function smoothly or effectively. Though Nehru did not resign as prime minister, a political crisis was developing.

Shastri, who was then home minister in UP, was naturally distressed by this situation. He was perhaps the only person in the country who had equal access to both Nehru and Tandon, and who could at least endeavour to reconcile their differences. Though the task was daunting, Shastri decided to act. 'I came all the way from Lucknow to New Delhi to speak to Panditji,' he told his biographer, D.R. Mankekar.

> I had three meetings with him, one in the morning, the other in the afternoon, and the third at night. We had prolonged talks and I suggested to Pandit Nehru that some way should be found out to avoid further widening of the rift. It did have some effect on Pandit Nehru. Ultimately,

however, Tandonji himself resolved the deadlock by resigning from the Congress Presidentship.[1]

Tandon gave up presidentship of Congress with a view to maintaining harmony within the party, to which he had devoted his whole life. Nehru then assumed the office of Congress Party president. He was now in full control both of government and the party. Patel, who had been ailing for some time, passed away on 15 December 1950. With Patel gone, the Nehru era assumed full force in 1951.

Nehru invited Shastri to move to New Delhi and take over as general secretary of the Indian National Congress. Shastri resigned as home minister of UP and took charge of his new responsibilities. He was now entered upon the national stage, the whole country was henceforth his political arena.

The general secretary was probably the most important and prestigious assignment in the Congress Party, next only to that of the Congress president. As Nehru was preoccupied with prime ministerial responsibilities, he relied heavily on Shastri, whose loyalty was total.

Shastri's most important responsibility as general secretary of the Congress Party was to organize the first general election under the new constitution, scheduled to be held in 1952 on the basis of universal adult suffrage and a secret ballot. This was a large task. Shastri had to tour the country intensively to meet and address party workers, chalk out the party's strategy, and help state Congress committees in their preparation of lists of candidates for state assemblies as well as for the central parliament. He spent long hours listening to people and reconciling their differences as best he could.

The general election was held early in 1952 and the Congress Party won resounding victories. 'A great part of the credit,' says D.R. Mankekar, 'for the landslide victory won by the Congress in those elections must go to Lal Bahadur.'[2]

At the end of the elections Shastri certainly emerged a respected and admired national leader in the party. He had established personal acquaintance with Congress Party chief ministers and cabinet ministers in various states. Though it was well known that he was Nehru's most trusted colleague in the party, he did not throw his weight about. Quite the contrary, he seemed to most people a rarity: a genuinely humble politician.

Soon after the general elections the newly elected parliament was convened for its inaugural session. The president of India, Rajendra Prasad, invited Nehru to assume the office of prime minister and form the new government.

Nehru decided to include Shastri in his cabinet. Although Shastri had organized the election campaign, characteristically he had not sought to be a candidate and was therefore not a member of the new parliament. It being necessary for a minister to be a member of either of the two houses of parliament or to become one within six months of his appointment, Nehru arranged for Shastri to be elected to the Rajya Sabha. On 13 May 1952 Shastri took oath of office as minister of railways and transport.

Since he had already functioned as a cabinet minister in UP, Shastri did not find it difficult to get into stride. He worked long hours and studied his briefs, as usual. His interactions were now with a very large number of bureaucrats, press people and politicians. Above all, he had to keep in close touch with Nehru, both as regards governmental responsibilities as well as party affairs. He evolved certain guidelines for himself to which he adhered.

First, as a minister of government he would confine himself strictly to his own sphere of responsibilities and not comment, except at cabinet meetings, on matters within the jurisdiction of other ministers. This precluded him treading on other ministers' toes, as well as in controversies with his colleagues. But it also created the false impression that Shastri did not have any views on major national issues of the day, such as planning for development, general economic policy, foreign affairs, etc. Obviously he had, but he consciously and wisely decided to keep them to himself.

Second, he devoted special attention to members of parliament, not only those of his own party but also all others. Most MPs he met felt unusual respect towards Shastri. This stood him in very good stead in later years, especially when the question of a possible successor to Nehru began to arise.

Third, as he had already done in the UP government, Shastri established his usual friendly relations with civil servants with whom he had to interact every day. He encouraged them to express their views openly.

Fourth, Shastri gave high priority to the promotion of common welfare and made this known to his officials from the very beginning.

Finally, and above all, he wanted to make every effort to promote integrity in administration. He had cordial relations with the press and spoke to reporters and editors with disarming frankness and truthfulness.

At this point in time the railways were endeavouring to get over the organisational problems caused by Partition. A programme for the renovation and augmentation of passenger and cargo capacity was under way. In formulating his policies and programmes, Shastri had to reckon with considerable financial constraints. He would have liked much larger investments in the country's infrastructure—railways, roads and communications—than was provided at that time, because it was evident to him that the success and efficiency of the ministries in his charge held the key to accelerated economic development. Shastri did ask the Planning Commission for a higher allocation for railways and transport, but in the end had to make do with whatever was available.

He gave full encouragement and support to the implementation of plans for the rehabilitation of the railways and the improvement of the rolling stock and tracks. He also tried new ideas, introducing sleeping accommodation for long-distance third-class passengers. This was a major reform and a significant improvement in the amenities for the common people. He also introduced a 'Janta' corridor train with a well-equipped dining car and conductor. Over his tenure the railways also introduced carriages with seating accommodation for short-distance first-class passengers, and vestibuled air-conditioned fast trains between Delhi and Bombay, Calcutta and Madras. He announced plans to abolish the third class and to have only two classes—first and second—in addition to air-conditioned carriages. He secured improvements in the quality of food served on trains by introducing departmental catering, organized and managed by the railway administration.

The research section of the Central Standards Office was reorganized and upgraded into a directorate of research, with its headquarters at Lucknow, and two sub-centres—one at Chittaranjan for chemical and metallurgical research and the other at Lonavla for research in building materials. Shastri appointed a committee under the chairmanship of Dr A. Ramaswami Mudaliar for a review of the existing rate structure on the railways and related matters. Recommendations made by the Ramaswami Mudaliar Committee were then implemented. Shastri also established an efficiency bureau in the Railway Board whose work resulted in visible improvements in railway performance.

In order to increase security on railway property and goods in transit, he appointed a security adviser to the Railway Board and, on the recommendation of this adviser, the Watch and Ward Organisation was converted into a statutory force called the Railway Protection Force. This new force, working in co-operation with the state police, secured a major improvement in the protection of railway property and goods. It was Shastri also who approved the Ganga Bridge Project which has provided a direct and fast link between north and south Bihar. Another achievement of the railways during his term of office was a substantial increase in the output of the Chittaranjan Locomotive Works, from 120 to 200 engines per year. The production of railway carriages at the Integral Coach Factory was also speeded up.

While the railways were making steady progress and the rehabilitation programme was proceeding apace, repeated accidents were causing anxiety to the people and government. A serious accident occurred in August 1956 at Mehboobnagar, in which 112 lives were lost. Shastri, as minister of railways and transport, was deeply distressed. He owned responsibility for the accident and submitted his resignation to the prime minister. The PM did not accept the resignation. Unfortunately, another disastrous accident took place in November 1956, at Ariyalour in south India, in which as many as 144 passengers were killed. Shastri resigned again, accepting moral responsibility. On this occasion he was so insistent that Nehru felt obliged to accept his resignation. This was the first instance of a cabinet minister accepting moral responsibility for a mishap within his ministry and resigning from government, though he had nothing to do with it directly. While announcing in the Lok Sabha his acceptance of Shastri's resignation, Nehru paid his tributes:

> I should like to say that it has been not only in the Government, but in the Congress, my good fortune and privilege to have him as a comrade and colleague, and no man can wish for a better comrade and better colleague in any undertaking—a man of highest integrity, loyalty, devoted to ideals, a man of conscience and a man of hard work. We can expect no better. And it is because he is such a man of conscience, that he has felt deeply whenever there is any failing in the work entrusted to his charge . . . I have the highest regard for him and I am quite sure that in one capacity or another, we shall be comrades in the future and will work together.

Shastri's resignation increased his moral stature nationally. He had set a new precedent for political conduct. And, paradoxically, by giving up high office he had moved even closer to Nehru.

In 1957, as India's second general election hove in sight, Nehru appointed Shastri as the chief organiser of the Congress Party campaign. This was a repetition of the 1952 exercise. Once again, Shastri was occupied night and day with election work. On this occasion he was asked by Nehru to seek election to the Lok Sabha from an Allahabad constituency. As Shastri gave nearly all his time to the election campaign of the party, he was able to visit his own constituency only very briefly. All the same he was elected by a large majority, as was Congress. At the end of the election Shastri was more firmly in control of Congress Party affairs than ever before. It was no surprise that when Nehru formed his new cabinet after this second general election, he included Shastri as a cabinet minister. The portfolio allocated was transport and communications. Shastri took oath of office on 17 April 1957.*

* Soon thereafter I joined him as his Private Secretary.

Shastri gave a great deal of attention to the development of Indian shipping and shipbuilding. With the consent of Finance Minister T.T. Krishnamachari, he established a 'revolving' Shipping Development Fund for the grant of loans to shipping companies at a low rate of interest for the acquisition of ships. This enabled shipping companies to get over their financial constraints. Loan repayments were ploughed back into the fund and utilised to grant new loans.

The establishment of appropriate training facilities, in which too he was instrumental, was acknowledged when the Nautical and Engineering College in Bombay was renamed the Lal Bahadur Shastri Nautical and Engineering College.

Shastri's tenure in the ministry of transport and communications was rather short—less than one year. Early in 1958 T.T. Krishnamachari resigned from the government because of the Mundra affair. Morarji Desai, then minister of commerce and industry, was appointed as the new finance minister and Shastri was made the minister of commerce and industry (28 March 1958). Shastri's elevation to this important portfolio made him one of the key ministers in Nehru's cabinet. The pressure was on for India to build up a self-reliant industrial base and to forge a modern and efficient economy. It was Shastri's job now to guide this effort.

Now, his working day in the secretariat seldom ended before 10 p.m. Nehru got to know of this. Late one evening he rang up Shastri and, finding him still in office, admonished him in a most caring way, telling him not to work such long hours. That day Shastri went off home, but his work habits did not change. He looked in quite good health, but the truth was that the privations of his early life and the almost round-the-clock work for many years took their toll. In October 1958 he had a heart attack while on tour in Allahabad and was confined to bed in a hospital there. Fortunately he recovered within a few weeks and resumed normal duties in New Delhi.

Shastri was at this time much involved in the problems of foreign trade, especially the promotion of exports and the establisment of new industrial projects. When examining new proposals, he would, as K.B. Lall (then additional secretary in the commerce and industry ministry) put it, invariably want to know what their effect would be on the welfare of the common man.

D.R. Mankekar describes Shastri's performance as minister of commerce and industry in considerable detail:

> At this controversial Ministry, Lal Bahadur achieved the unique feat of remaining persona grata with the business community, while resolutely pursuing the Nehru Government's industrial policy with its bias in favour

of the socialist pattern of society. The tiding over of a major foreign exchange crisis about this time also fell to his lot. His decisions over the Company Law were unpalatable to the business community. But with all that, Lal Bahadur retained their respect as a man of integrity and sincerity.

In the public sector, the most significant development during the tenure was the formation of a Heavy Engineering Corporation, with the help of the Soviet Union and Czechoslovakia . . . Hindustan Machine Tools, Bangalore, began its expansion programme for doubling its output to 2000 machines annually. The Nangal Fertilizer Factory went into production and the watch factory in the public sector at Bangalore, an Indo-Japanese venture, put on sale its first consignment of low-cost quality watches assembled there. The Heavy Electricals Ltd., at Bhopal, started production of heavy electrical machinery.

A record rise of 14 to 15 per cent in industrial output, exceeding the Plan targets in many fields, was the highlight of the year 1960 . . .

Lal Bahadur also prepared a scheme for agro-industrial integration. The combination of industry with agriculture, he concluded, would solve the problem of unemployment in rural areas. He wanted village industries to be converted into small-scale industries over a period of 20 to 30 years. This scheme became the basis of subsequent progress in the field.'[3]

The ministry of commerce and industry was also a testing ground for integrity: the minister had enormous powers. He could approve or reject applications from private sector industrialists and businessmen for the grant of licences to establish new projects or import goods, involving vast sums of money. All that Shastri made for himself in this position was an enhanced reputation for impeccable integrity.

Early in 1961 Govind Ballabh Pant, the home minister, fell seriously ill. On 25 February 1961 Nehru asked Shastri to assume responsibility for the ministry of home affairs in addition to his functions as minister of commerce and industry. Pant did not survive his illness and passed away early in April 1961. Nehru appointed Shastri as the new home minister.

Destiny was now carrying Shastri rapidly ahead of his cabinet colleagues. Shastri was now responsible for the central government's relations with the states in the Indian federation, and therefore in close touch with the state governors and chief ministers. The civil service and the overall administration of the country also fell under him. Shastri had the double advantage of being Nehru's closest colleague. The new ministry suited Shastri's particular genius and he was now in full flow.

Soon after he became home minister, Shastri had to deal with the language issue in Assam, which was assuming ugly proportions. Assam has a large Assamese-speaking majority but there is a considerable minority of

Bengali-speaking persons. Assamese, Bengali and English had all been used for many years for official purposes. But in 1959 the Assam Sahitya Sabha put forward its demand that Assamese be declared the official language of the state. Soon this resulted in a campaign against Bengalis. Serious language riots erupted in April 1960, and by July 1960 a number of casualties had been reported. In October 1960 the state legislature of Assam enacted an Official Language Act declaring Assamese the official language of the state. Now the Bengalis, who were mainly concentrated in Cachar district, began to agitate for the recognition of Bengali as an additional language. In May 1961 language riots erupted again.

Shastri, who had become minister of home affairs barely a month earlier, decided to proceed to Assam immediately to find a generally acceptable solution. With passions running high, reconciling the differences among antagonistic groups was not going to be easy. On the question of the official language or languages of a state, the States Reorganisation Commission had proposed that if 70 per cent or more of the population comprised one language group, that state could be unilingual. Where this was not the case, the state should be bilingual or multilingual, as appropriate. According to the 1951 census, the Assamese-speaking population in Assam was less than 70 per cent

On 31 May 1961 Shastri flew to Assam. First he consulted the state authorities and soon thereafter began a series of talks with representatives of the two rival groups, one speaking for the Assamese and the other for the Bengalis. From these meetings the members of the two groups went back satisfied that the home minister had listened carefully. Shastri then evolved a package of proposals which came to be known as 'the Shastri formula'. It comprised the following:

(1) The provision of the Official Language Act of 1960, empowering local government bodies in Cachar to substitute Assamese for Bengali as the language of the administration, would be repealed.

(2) The state government would use English in correspondence with Cachar and Hill districts until it was replaced by Hindi.

(3) At the state level, English would be used exclusively for the present and later would continue to be used along with Assamese.

(4) The safeguards for linguistic minorities in regard to education and employment, provided in the Constitution and accepted by the Central Government following the States Reorganisation Commission's recommendations, would be fully implemented.

(5) All Acts, Ordinances, Regulations, Orders, etc., would continue to be published in English as well as Assamese.

The implication was that the English, Assamese and Bengali languages would all be used in future, according to the Shastri formula. In particular, correspondence between Cachar district (which had a concentration of Bengalis), and the headquarters of the Assam government would be conducted in English. Further, both Assamese and Bengali could be used in the Cachar district office and schools, though in practice Bengali, being the language of the majority of the people of Cachar district, would receive preference. Despite the preceding bitterness, Shastri's formula, which he took much personal pains to work out, was acceptable to both sides. Consensus had been wrested out of apparently irreconcilable antagonisms.

Another challenging situation arose when Master Tara Singh of the Akali Dal launched an agitation in August 1961 for a new Sikh-majority state called 'Punjabi Suba' on the grounds that Sikhs had been discriminated against by the government. Shastri appointed a commission of enquiry under the chairmanship of a former chief justice of India, S.R. Das. The other members of the commission were C.P. Ramaswamy Iyer and M.C. Chagla. The commission made a thorough study of the situation, reporting categorically that 'on the material before it, no discrimination against the Sikhs in the Punjab has been made out.' The commission added that Sikhs 'in and outside the Punjab are an honoured part of Indian society.' After this clear verdict the much publicized fast of Master Tara Singh, which went on for forty-eight days, eventually petered out. Shastri managed this problem with a combination of reasonableness and firmness.

Shastri was deeply concerned about what he saw as his responsibility to promote the concept that India was not just a conglomeration of religious and linguistic communities, but a single united nation of Indians. He wanted to counter fissiparous tendencies in different parts of the country by bringing people together on a common platform devoted to national integration. With this end in view he convened a National Integration Conference of all parties in New Delhi from 28 September to 1 October 1961. The conference, which was presided over by Nehru, adopted a code of conduct for all political parties which called upon them to refrain from aggravating differences and tensions, from inciting people to violence, and from resorting to agitations likely to disturb the peace and create inter-community strife and bitterness. The conference also dealt with the language problem and, while recognizing that Hindi must ultimately develop as the national link language, accepted unequivocally that English must continue as the medium.

The states of southern India did not feel satisfied with these conclusions of the National Integration Conference, and another potentially dangerous language problem began to loom on the national horizon. People in the southern states were not ready for a change-over to Hindi from January

1965, as envisaged by the provisions of article 341 of the Constitution. They wanted to be assured that there would be no effort to impose Hindi on them against their will. More specifically, they wanted action to be taken well in time under article 341(3) (a), for an indefinite extension of the period for the continued use of the English language, as heretofore. In order to allay these legitimate apprehensions, Shastri, while addressing an audience at the Fifth All-India Youth Conference in Tirupati in September 1962, made a declaration of the central government's policy in this regard: 'Unless Hindi is sufficiently developed and the people of our country have learnt it well, there is no other medium of speaking or, if I may say so, a medium which could be used in the commercial world or the administration, especially between State and State, except English. English is the common language spoken in all the States of our country.' D.R. Mankekar believes that with this Shastri

> won the confidence of the South by his ready recognition of the Southerners' genuine difficulties in agreeing to the displacement of English in favour of Hindi as the medium of official communication in the Central Government. This gesture, coming as it did from the heartland of Hindi chauvinism, won him a lasting and grateful allegiance from the South. That stood him in good stead later when the country had to choose a successor to Nehru.[4]

The assurances given by Shastri, confirmed by Nehru later, were then incorporated in the Official Languages Act 1963, which was steered through parliament by Shastri.

All this paled into insignificance when in October 1962 India was suddenly attacked by its powerful and expansionist neighbour in the north, China. The Chinese invasion and its rapid advance into Indian territory created a state of emergency. The Government of India assumed draconian powers to deal with the situation. As minister of home affairs it was Shastri's responsibility to administer this emergency. He managed it with great restraint, being careful to maintain liberty: action was taken only against a limited number of extreme Communists. Although the Chinese withdrew their forces in December 1962, the state of emergency continued for some time because of the continuing threat. A great deal of Shastri's time was taken up by this issue.

Despite these preoccupations Shastri began to pursue some matters of long-term importance which were close to his heart. One of his responsibilities was to ensure integrity and efficiency in the administrative machinery. With both political and economic power concentrated in the hands of a few politicians and bureaucrats, the corrosive effect of power had began to take its toll in the years after independence. Civil servants, even of senior rank, had began to seek favourable postings or early promotions by playing up to the wishes of their political bosses, with scant regard for the merits of a matter under consideration. Distressed by this, on 28 June 1963 Shastri put forward his thoughts on some fundamental administrative issues in a detailed minute:

> There are some important problems facing us at the present moment. I would especially like to refer to certain tendencies in the country with which the administration is closely connected.
>
> A number of discussions have taken place on the streamlining of the administration. The Committee of Secretaries has also given thought to the matter. An O & M organisation has been set up. There has been some improvement and yet red-tape, as it is said, still continues. There are delays and prompt action is yet to be achieved. Sometime back in the United States of America a Committee was appointed with ex-President Hoover as its Chairman. The purpose seemed to be to make it a high-powered Committee, so that it could carry weight with the Government as well as the public. I also sometimes think that a similar high-powered Commission should be appointed by us which should study all the important aspects of this problem. Terms of reference will also have to be carefully drawn up and personnel also discreetly chosen. The important selection will be that of the Chairman. I shall be thankful if this matter is given further thought in the Ministry and a note put up along with tentative terms of reference. Otherwise precise terms of reference could be drawn up later on the basis of the note. I would then like to discuss it with the Prime Minister and, if necessary, place it before the Cabinet, which to my mind perhaps is not absolutely essential.
>
> I do not know if the District Administration could also form part of the terms of reference of the Commission I have suggested above. The District Administration in many of the States has gone weaker, resulting in much dissatisfaction amongst the people. It is true that most of the work of the departments has considerably increased, for example, Irrigation Department, Co-operative Community Development, and Agriculture, which is of vital importance to us. I am not sure if their organization and working are up to the mark. However, for the limited purpose I have in view at the present moment, I would like to lay stress on the civil and police administration. What are its shortcomings and how could they be rectified? How far have the recommendations of V.T. Krishnamachariji been implemented and what has been the impact?
>
> There are certain points in connection with the staff. Discipline amongst the staff is on the wane and it would be wrong if we cannot put a check to it. I do not want to confine myself merely to taking effective and strong action against the staff. This is not the real solution. It is important that there should be a forum for discussion and talks

between the officers and the staff. We have recently taken certain decisions in consultation with Labour and Defence Ministries. Railways and P & T are also agreeable. As soon as the Cabinet clears it, positive steps will have to be taken which may remove some of the irritations felt by the staff. The second point we have to consider is what are the other reasons for the indiscipline amongst the staff. This deserves careful study and we should try to go to the root of the problem.

It is also essential that there should be greater restraint shown by the officers. It is unfortunate that even the senior officers of the Government of India sometimes go about canvassing themselves either for their promotion or for some small benefits. It is bound to have an adverse effect not only on their morale but on the morale of others who are serving under them. This is a matter on which some effective action is called for. Home Secretary and Special Secretary might like to think over it.

There is the problem of Ministers and services. There also the relationship between the two is not what it should be. It should be possible to prescribe some concrete principles to govern this relationship. If the officers have merely to function throughout under a fear complex it would not be good for the administration. The officers should be free to express their views but ultimately agree to implement the orders of the Ministers. It would be unfortunate if we have some kind of a personal rule in our country. There should be a code which the Ministers should also accept. Oral orders and instructions should be avoided and the officers should not involve themselves in group politics in any way. The officers should also have a code of conduct and they must not directly ask for any favours from the Ministers. Their cases must go up to the Ministers through [the] proper channel. If there is any injustice done in any specific case, formal representations should be made to the Minister. Their representations by and large should not be withheld and should be sent to the Ministers.

These are only a few points.

H. Secretary and Special Secretary can think of many others. The important thing is that while we streamline the administration at all levels, we should clarify the relationship between Ministers, Officers and non-officials. I would very much like that the different aspects of these problems are gone into.[5]

An excellent administrative set-up had been established by the British. This had served India well in the years immediately following independence, but it was designed primarily to maintain the status quo. What the country needed now was an administration which was development oriented and which could make well-considered but quick decisions to advance economic development. The pace of decision-making in government was much too slow and bred corruption. Shastri found the civil services excellent in ability and patriotic in outlook, but in need of reform. The cumbersome administrative structure, the plethora of rules, the outdated and dilatory procedures, the over-cautiousness amounting almost to obstructiveness—all needed decisive intervention. Shastri intended to appoint a high-powered body to perform this, but his sudden resignation under the Kamaraj Plan prevented this from happening. Subsequently, however, as prime minister, he revived the matter, and on 5 January 1966 he appointed an Administrative Reforms Commission under the chairmanship of Morarji Desai.

Shastri also applied his mind to the growing corruption in governmental administration. Government officials were already subject to stringent rules of conduct. A Central Bureau of Investigation was established in February 1963 to pursue breaches of these rules. Shastri further appointed the Santhanam Committee to examine corruption at the administrative and political levels and make suitable recommendations. As a result, a code of conduct for ministers was evolved.

Thus far, Shastri had never ventured into foreign affairs. Even as minister of commerce and industry he had not been abroad. In March 1963 Nehru asked Shastri to visit Nepal to smoothen India's relations with its neighbour. Kathmandu appeared to be getting closer to Peking and Rawalpindi. Hostility towards India was evident in the columns of the Nepali press and in the political pronouncements of Nepali leaders. The home minister's visit to Kathmandu was initially greeted with distrust by that country's press. But once he arrived in the Nepali capital, his disarming charm won them over.

Shastri was received by King Mahendra, who warmed to his visitor after their first meeting, and they met twice more. Shastri had meetings also with Tulsi Giri, chairman of the council of ministers, and Vishwabandhu Thapa, the Nepali home minister. His main mission was to dispel the impression in Nepal that India was trying to behave like a 'big brother', not showing proper respect for the sovereign independence of its smaller neighbour. He succeeded in this mission to a considerable extent. The joint communique issued at the end of the visit referred to the 'unbreakable ties of geography, culture and traditions' between India and Nepal. When a press correspondent asked Shastri whether, in his view, Nepal was unduly inclined towards China, he answered with characteristic straightforwardness: 'It is entirely for Nepal to decide its policy and course of action.' Nepal was pleased. Cordial relations were restored. Shastri's first diplomatic mission was acclaimed a success.

While the country was gradually recovering from the Chinese invasion, senior leaders of the Congress Party were becoming increasingly concerned about the deterioration in people's perception of Congress as an organization unselfishly devoted to the service of the country. It was beginning to be felt that the mass appeal of Congress was on the wane. Top ranking leaders had assumed governmental responsibilities and the organizational work of the party had been left to men who did not always have the required high standing and stature.

It was in this context that K. Kamaraj, then chief minister of Tamil Nadu, submitted a proposal to the Congress Working Committee, suggesting that some chief ministers in the states and a few senior cabinet ministers at the centre should relinquish their offices and devote themselves to organizational work. The Congress Working Committee welcomed this proposal and it was approved unanimously by the All-India Congress Committee at its session in New Delhi on 10 August 1963.

On 24 August 1963 the Congress Working Committee, on the re-commendation of Nehru, approved a list of six central cabinet ministers and chief ministers of six states for organizational work. Their resignations from office were approved. The central ministers whose resignations were accepted were: Morarji Desai (Finance), Jagjiwan Ram (Transport and Communications), Lal Bahadur Shastri (Home), S.K. Patil (Food and Agriculture), B. Gopala Reddi (Information and Broadcasting), and K.L. Shrimali (Education).

Nehru had not initially included Shastri in his list, but Shastri himself prevailed upon Nehru to include him.

After independence, this was the biggest shake-up in Congress. Its scale surprised and thrilled the country. In his note to the Congress Working Committee Nehru had justified his proposals by saying: 'If the AICC resolution is accepted in all earnestness, it follows that the action taken should be big enough to be important and striking. That means that the top personalities in the Congress who are now in high office should retire and devote themselves to organizational and other forms of service to the people.'

On relinquishing office as home minister, Shastri was appointed as a member of the two most important organizational bodies of Congress, namely the Parliamentary Board and the Organizational Committee. He now began to devote his time to the work of the Indian National Congress.

While the country at large welcomed the Kamaraj Plan, some critics felt that there was more to the plan than met the eye. It was even suggested that the plan had been designed primarily to eliminate from high office those ministers who had proved inconvenient. This was certainly not true in respect to Shastri, who told me it was only at his repeated insistence that Nehru agreed to his resignation.

During the months following his resignation Shastri travelled to different parts of India on behalf of the Congress Party. Once during this period he passed through Bombay on his way south. I went to the airport to meet him, as I always did when he visited Bombay. His connecting flight was delayed by a few hours, so I invited him to my residence. He readily agreed. My wife Nirmala was not in Bombay at the time, else she would have prepared a meal. All I could do was offer fruit and tea as refreshment. As usual, he was the picture of kindness. I asked him how he foresaw future developments. His reply was unemphatic. 'At present I have the opportunity once again to work for Congress,' he said. 'There is a lot of work to be done in the field. Beyond that I do not know.' He rested quietly for a while and then we went back to the airport.

In view of decisions on the revitalization of Congress, the question of the next president of the party, in succession to D. Sanjivayya, had become a matter of great importance. Party leaders in different states were in consultation with each other and Nehru. As a result, a consensus emerged in favour of K. Kamaraj, who was considered the best choice in those tumultuous days. Kamaraj was a man of the highest integrity; selfless, patriotic, wise, objective and decisive. At the meeting of the Congress Working Committee on 9 October an informal decision was taken, on the proposal of the West Bengal leader Atulya Ghosh, that the Congress high command should itself sponsor the name of K. Kamaraj. The election procedure was set in motion. As Kamaraj was the only candidate in the field, he was declared elected as Congress president on 27 November 1963. He took over from D. Sanjivayya in January 1964, at the 68th annual session of the Indian National Congress at Bhubaneshwar. Although the plenary sessions of the Congress were to be held on 9 and 10 January, delegates started arriving earlier to participate in preparatory meetings of the Subjects Committee and other bodies.

Suddenly the sky fell upon the session. News broke out that Nehru, who had arrived on 6 January, had suffered a stroke the next day, on 7 January 1964. Shastri was asked by the Congress president to break the news of Nehru's illness to the Subjects Committee, which was then in session. Shastri informed the committee that Nehru was indisposed and had therefore not come to the session. He then read out a medical bulletin issued by doctors attending the prime minister which concluded: 'The prime minister is cheerful and in good spirits.' Shastri then said: 'I might also add that Panditji is anxious to come here, but we all have requested him not to do so.'

All at once, an unthinkable question was now becoming open and urgent—After Nehru, Who?

The Subjects Committee proceeded with the business on the agenda. 'Then the Congress rank and file also noted,' says D.R. Mankekar, 'that the honour and responsibility of moving the most important resolution before the Subjects Committee of the session—on Democracy and Socialism—fell upon not Gulzarilal Nanda, nor on Morarji Desai, a leader next only to Nehru in national stature, but on Lal Bahadur who had ceased to be a minister five months earlier and whose very claim to be a socialist was questioned by leftists like Krishna Menon and Keshav Dev Malaviya.'[6]

Shastri piloted the resolution on democracy and socialism with consummate political skill. He made it clear that democratic socialism to him meant a polity dedicated to the welfare of the common man, and that to achieve concrete results idealism had to be tempered with realism. About state trading, he left no one in any doubt about his position: 'We should be very careful in resorting to state trading, particularly in foodgrains. Until the government is ready to cope with the enormity of the problem, state trading would not only increase corruption but might add to the difficulties of the people.'

The debate on this resolution, in which seventy speakers participated, showed all the hues of the Congress spectrum, from the extreme right to the extreme left. At the end of the debate the resolution, which had been drafted under the personal guidance of Nehru, was adopted unanimously on 10 January 1964. It gave highest priority to assuring a national minimum of essential requirements to every citizen in respect of food, clothing, housing, eduction and health. It laid stress on reducing the 'vast disparities in income and wealth which exist now.' The objective of attaining the national minimum was expected to be realized by the end of the Fifth Plan. 'Otherwise,' the resolution warned, 'planning and progress will become devoid of meaning for the common man.' A day earlier, on 9 January 1964, Congress had adopted an amendment to its constitution to the effect that the objective of the party in future shall be 'the establishment in India, by peaceful and constitutional means, of a Socialist State based on parliamentary democracy.'

On 11 January Kamaraj nominated members to the Congress Working Committee, the highest executive body of the party, popularly known as the Congress high command. These were Shastri, Morarji Desai, Jagjivan Ram, S.K. Patil, D. Sanjivayya, N. Sanjiva Reddy, Atulya Ghosh, Fakhruddin Ali Ahmad, S. Nijalingappa and Gulzarilal Nanda.

So, at the end of this session, which was the last attended by Nehru, Shastri had emerged, with the evident support of both Prime Minister Nehru and Congress President Kamaraj, as the person most likely to succeed Nehru as India's prime minister. Soon events began to point even more clearly in that direction.

While still in Bhubaneshwar, Nehru told Shastri that he would like him to return to the cabinet as soon as possible to help him. Given the situation, Shastri agreed. He told me that a brief but significant conversation took place between him and Nehru:

SHASTRI :    *Mujhe kya kaam karna hoga?* (What work will I be doing?)
NEHRU:       *Tumhen mera sab kaam karna hoga.* (You will have to do all my work.)

On 22 January a communiqué from Rashtrapati Bhavan announced the appointment of Shastri to the cabinet as a minister without portfolio, to 'carry out functions entrusted to him by the Prime Minister in relation to the Ministry of External Affairs and the Departments of the Cabinet Secretariat and Atomic Energy.' Under this presidential order, the prime minister issued a directive stating that 'the Minister Without Portfolio sees and deals with the papers that come to the Prime Minister from the Ministry of External Affairs, the Department of Atomic Energy and the Cabinet Secretariat. He obtains the Prime Minister's specific orders whenever necessary.'

Shastri was allotted an office in the South Block of the secretariat buildings, close to the prime minister's suite. The actual arrangements for the conduct of business and disposal of files were rather amorphous. Some files and papers were sent to Shastri, others were sent to the prime minister directly, bypassing Shastri. Political circles noted that the functions of the minister without portfolio were rather restricted, giving him no room for initiative. Shastri did not find himself fully occupied, let alone challenged by the new assignment. In fact the arrangement did not conform to what the prime minister had told Shastri in Bhubaneshwar. But Shastri did not feel anything could be done to rectify the situation. He said nothing about it to the prime minister, who was still unwell. However, he did not have to wait long for a challenging task.

A sacred hair of the Prophet Mohammed, preserved for 300 years at the Hazratbal shrine in Srinagar, was removed by miscreants on 26 December 1963. This holy relic had been handed down from father to son from the time of the Prophet until it reached Sayyid Abdullah, the Mutawalli (administrator) of the Prophet's shrine in Medina. In 1634 Sayyid Abdullah arrived at Bijapur in India, carrying the holy relic with him. From his descendants, the relic was seized by Emperor Aurangzeb at the end of the seventeenth century. Following a dream, the emperor sent the relic to Kashmir according to the wishes of its last keeper, where it was finally lodged in the Hazratbal mosque, which developed into an important centre of pilgrimage.[7] The people of Srinagar and Kashmir were incensed. Hindus and Sikhs joined Muslims in angry demonstrations. Pakistan, always ready to foment communal trouble in India, began its usual role again. The Central Bureau of Investigation of the ministry of home affairs was asked to investigate the theft and make every possible endeavour to find the sacred relic as soon as possible.

The loss of the sacred relic gave Nehru much sleeplessness. Fortunately, eight days after the theft the relic was mysteriously found in the shrine on 4 January 1964. V. Vishwanathan, the home secretary who had gone to Srinagar for consultations with the state government, said on 5 January that the relic had been 'surreptitiously' placed back in the shrine by the 'culprits' amid hot pursuit by men of the Central Bureau of Investigation. Nehru was much relieved.

Unfortunately, the hope that the situation would now cool down was belied. Though Home Secretary Vishwanathan contended that almost all persons in a position to identify the relic had accepted its genuineness, members of a local action committee were not satisfied. They were pressing for a special *deedar* (viewing) by their members and by divines for a verdict on the genuineness of the relic. The state government regarded this request as a move by agitationists to excite the people against the government, and opposed its acceptance. So did Home Secretary Vishwanathan. The agitation was gaining momentum. *The Times* of London reported on 27 January 1964 —

> renewed disturbances in Srinagar this weekend and yesterday police fired on mobs on several occasions, killing four people, according to the official account. It appears that the demonstrations expressed the continuing public suspicion in Kashmir that the true relic of the Prophet has not been recovered since its theft last month and that the hair now in Hazratbal shrine is not the one that was stolen . . . The first target of this agitation, which is reported to amount in Srinagar to a continuing hartal (a closing of all shops and services), has been Bakshi Ghulam Mohammad, the previous Prime Minister of the State. But this has been extended to include his successor, Shamsuddin, and the whole National Conference Party. There must be a danger, at least, that the continuing movement will aim at the Indian Government, which has far so long upheld Bakshi Ghulam Mohammad and his party.

In this explosive situation Nehru turned to Shastri. Nehru gave him a free hand, asking him to deal with the situation as he thought best. As it was freezing cold in Srinagar, Nehru gave Shastri his own overcoat. Wearing this 'mantle of Nehru', Shastri flew to Srinagar in an Indian air force plane on 30 January 1964. *The Times* now noted, in its issue of 1 February 1964: 'This sudden move shows the seriousness with which the Government of India views the continued unsettled conditions here, the realization that any solution will have to be imposed from Delhi—and dramatically confirms Shastri's return to the centre of affairs.'

In Srinagar Shastri's discussions showed that the leaders of the agitation were insisting that the relic be vouched for by a panel of devotees free of political ties. Failing this, riots seemed imminent.

Home Secretary Vishwanathan, an able and strong-willed administrator, advised Shastri against accepting this request of the agitators who constituted the action committee. State government officials were in agreement with Vishwanathan. Shastri listened patiently, but indicated he would decide after his own consultations with members of the action committee. He held direct talks with the action committee, particularly Maulana Mohammad Saeed Masoodi, whom he found a responsible and respectable leader. The key issue for judgment was whether the members of the action committee were genuinely seeking to verify the relic, or whether they were bent upon creating a dangerous situation by rejecting the relic for political reasons. Officials led by Vishwanathan feared the latter and therefore strongly opposed any special deedar.

Shastri came to the conclusion that, in all probability, the relic was genuine. He then concluded that, in regard to such a holy relic, no Muslim divine or devotee would risk rejecting its sanctity for political reasons. Shastri therefore ruled out the possibility of a mischievous verdict. Even so, there was always an element of risk—grave risk, for passions had been roused. But Shastri had been assured by Maulana Masoodi and others that 'politics' would be kept out of this sacred matter.

Having thought the matter through, Shastri firmly overruled Home Secretary Vishwanathan. He announced that a special deedar would be held on 3 February, and he agreed to the inclusion of representatives of the action committee on the panel of maulvis who would inspect the relic.

The deedar was held on 3 February 1964. Rawle Knox, special correspondent of London's *Daily Telegraph*, sent this report on the event:

> Amid mounting tension, venerable priests meeting in the historic Hazratbal Mosque outside Srinagar . . . agreed today that the lost and now recovered hair of the Prophet Mohammed was genuine.
>
> Soldiers, priests, divines and the general public milled around in the lakeside mosque, while in the background stood the insignificant figure

of Shastri, India's new Minister Without Portfolio. He had gambled on this inspection against the advice of his officials.

The three-inch-long hair, in a silver-capped glass phial, was missed from the mosque on Dec. 26. Two people were killed in riots before it was found again in the mosque eight days later.

Troops and police patrolled almost every street today as the population waited in sullen silence for the public showing of the restored relic on Thursday.

In the mosque, when the moment came to open the casket containing the relic, the chief priest's hands trembled so violently, he had to call a colleague to complete the task. The continuous chanting of prayers turned into wailing and sobbing.

Then a green velvet bag was extracted from the casket, and the phial containing the hair was taken from the bag. One by one the leading priests bent their turbaned heads over the phial, straightened to hold it against the light, then nodded their acceptance.

A wave of incredulous relief swept through the crowds in and around the mosque. On Thursday the public showing of the sacred hair should be a joyous formality.[8]

Shastri was literally mobbed by the crowd. He had become the hero of the day. Many of the gathered divines expressed their satisfaction and gratitude. Shastri congratulated them and made a personal offer of Rs 101 to the Hazratbal shrine, a gesture much appreciated.

Shastri returned to New Delhi the same evening and immediately drove to the prime minister's house to report on his mission. Later that evening Shastri received the Sadar-i-Riyasat of Jammu and Kashmir, Karan Singh, and had a detailed talk with him about the political situation in Kashmir.

Shastri's success was hailed by parliament and press. His perceptive judgment, strong will and firm resolve in handling a delicate political situation were much lauded. One of the leading political commentators of the time, K. Rangaswami, said:

Lal Bahadur Shastri has become the successful troubleshooter of the Congress Party. It was given to him to solve the Punjab and Assam language controversies some years ago. Now the Prime Minister sent him to deal with the Kashmir crisis following the disappearance of the holy relic of the Prophet. Lal Bahadur Shastri has returned to the capital adding another laurel to his credit in the public and political life of India. His asset is his basic nature to deal justly and with tolerance and understanding even towards opponents. It is this quality which won him the affection and the confidence of all groups in Kashmir and which gave him courage to take a calculated risk which the Home Minister and his advisors had earlier thought it safe to avoid.[9] . . . Lal Bahadur's risk paid dividends and the Muslim divines unanimously acclaimed the holy relic as the genuine one. Thus the purely religious aspect of the controversy ended, and by so doing, Lal Bahadur succeeded in separating it from the political issue, a task which the Central Home Ministry has been endeavouring to accomplish.[10]

While the religious issue had thus been settled, there was an underlying political problem which also needed to be resolved. Shastri had come back from Kashmir totally convinced that the state premier, Shamsuddin, a protégé of Bakshi Ghulam Mohammed, had lost the confidence of the people and that drastic change was necessary. Shastri wanted to achieve this not by central diktat but by persuasion and consensus—no easy task, given the prevailing bitterness among different groups in the ruling National Conference. To pursue this he went to Jammu on 20 February, where he had prolonged consultations with Karan Singh, Shamsuddin, G.M. Sadiq and Mir Qasim. According to D.R. Mankekar,

> after he had held parleys with them for a couple of days, Shamsuddin appeared to be ready to eat out of Lal Bahadur's hand, while Bakshi went all out loudly to offer his co-operation to the Union Minister Without Portfolio in his efforts to bring peace and normalcy to Srinagar and stability to the State's Government . . . On February 27, Shamsuddin announced to a meeting of the National Conference Legislature Party his decision to resign from the Prime Ministership of the State 'in deference to the wishes of Bakshi Ghulam Mahommed'. The next day, G.M. Sadiq was elected leader of the party, with Bakshi himself proposing his name.
>
> Releasing Bakshi's grip on the affairs of Kashmir was a consummation long devoutly wished for by many in New Delhi. But even Nehru did not find the gumption to set about it. And thus Bakshi ruled in Srinagar like an absolute despot, his right none to dispute and his misrule none to question. Now this little man from New Delhi had done the trick with the ease of a David felling a Goliath.[11]

Comment in the Indian press was equally appreciative. In its editorial comment on 25 February 1964 the *Hindustan Times* said: 'Lal Bahadur Shastri has been able to achieve another notable success in clearing up the mess in Kashmir, so fully exposed in the episode of the missing relic from Hazratbal. For this his clarity of purpose was as much responsible as his negotiating skill.'

With a new ministry installed in Srinagar under G.M. Sadiq, a political leader known for his integrity and sagacity, Shastri proceeded next to deal with yet another delicate issue. Sheikh Mohammed Abdullah had long been in detention. There was a general demand among the Kashmiri people that he should be released. Shastri persuaded Nehru to agree to this. The new state premier, G.M. Sadiq, accepted this suggestion and Sheikh Abdullah was released on 8 April 1964. This decision was made on political grounds: Sheikh Abdullah, the Lion of Kashmir, could not be kept in detention any more without causing a deterioration in the Kashmir situation. The new government was confident of handling the consequences of his release, which, to say the least, were unpredictable. Indeed, after his release Sheikh Abdullah first made volatile statements about the right of Kashmiri people to determine their own future. A few days later he sobered down and expressed a wish to bring India and Pakistan together on the question of Kashmir. Then he got busy in that endeavour.

On the broad political front, while the impression was gaining ground that Shastri was Nehru's heir apparent, the question 'After Nehru, Who?' had by no means been firmly answered. At the time that Shastri was busy with the Kashmir problem some people in Delhi were promoting the idea that Indira Gandhi should be inducted into the cabinet as quickly as possible. K. Rangaswami, the well-informed correspondent of *The Hindu* of Madras, wrote in an article published on 9 February 1964:

> Strangely enough, one finds in this rapidly changing situation a sudden spurt of organised pressure to get Indira Gandhi included in the Cabinet. Lal Bahadur's influence, as for that matter anyone else's, is dependent on the extent of his nearness to the Prime Minister. But if Indira Gandhi came on the scene in an official capacity, it is natural to expect that she would be nearer the Prime Minister than anyone else. There is open canvassing that Indira Gandhi is the ideal person to be made the Foreign Minister. When Lal Bahadur was away in Kashmir, an official communique was issued defining his functions as a Minister Without Portfolio. Many leaders feel that the communique was very unhappily worded, as it gave the impression of restricting the scope for any initiative on the part of Lal Bahadur.

Who the protagonists of this move were was not stated and it is very doubtful if Nehru knew anything at all about it. He was a sick man, now functioning at a fraction of his former capacity. The general impression was that the governance of the country was now effectively vested in a triumvirate comprising Home Minister Gulzarilal Nanda, Finance Minister T.T. Krishnamachari, and Minister Without Portfolio Lal Bahadur Shastri.

After Bhubaneshwar, Nehru had gradually recovered and was able to attend parliament off and on. On 22 April 1964 he made a brief statement in the Lok Sabha: 'Mr Speaker, Sir, I have to inform the House that it is proposed to hold a meeting of the Commonwealth Prime Ministers in London in July next. The dates proposed are 8th to 15th July though these are not quite certain yet. I have accepted the invitation and I hope to attend this Conference.'

Nath Pai, a leading member of the Lok Sabha, then asked: 'May I know, when he is going on a long journey, whether he is going to contemplate who will be looking after the very important matters of State as officially designated Deputy Prime Minister?'

The whole house waited expectantly, but Nehru gave no specific answer to the loaded question. Side-stepping the implied reference to his possible successor, Nehru simply replied: 'I do not remember any previous occasion when any special arrangements had to be made or were made.'

Shastri himself did not quite know where he stood in this uncertain political situation. His responsibilities as minister without portfolio were nebulous. At about this time I happened to meet him in New Delhi, and hoping for some indication of his position I came straight to the point: 'There is a general feeling that you will be the next prime minister.'

Shastri looked into space in silence, then replied: 'Some people do say that, but nothing is clear about the future.' He did not exude his usual confidence. Certainly his own disposition and the country's future seemed in the balance.

# Chapter 6

# India's Prime Minister

## AFTER NEHRU, WHO?

During the first decade after Independence, Nehru's wish was the will of the people of India. After the death of Sardar Patel in December 1950 the Nehru era was in full force: India loved Nehru, Nehru loved India, and no one could even think of an end to this idyllic situation. Then all of a sudden on 4 April 1958, at a press conference in New Delhi, Nehru jolted the nation with a hint of profound changes to come, declaring that he was feeling rather 'flat and stale' and in need of some 'freshening up'.

> I have said that I feel stale. My body is healthy, as it normally is. But I do feel rather flat and stale and I do not think it is right for a person to feel that way and I have to deal with vital and very important problems. I am not fresh enough. There has to be some creativeness of the mind. I have had eleven and a half years of office continuously without a day's respite. I think I may have some further years of effective service because I am bodily fit and, although I cannot judge my own mind, I do not think that it is slipping. But it is, I think, stale and requires freshening up.[1]

The remarks sent shock waves across the country. The thought germinated that if Nehru was tired today, he might not be at the helm sooner than anybody thought. What then of India?

The first person to raise this question in public was Jaya Prakash Narayan. In a statement issued on 27 April 1958 Narayan made, in his own words, 'a straight suggestion that Nehru should step aside and place somebody of his own choice in his seat [as Prime Minister] and help him from outside.' Narayan expressed the view that such a step by Nehru would be good, not only for the prime minister but for the country. 'This should be done now,' Narayan said, 'when Nehru is in full command of the situation.' He also made it clear that he was not making this suggestion merely because the prime minister was feeling tired or stale. For some time now fears had begun to be expressed in several quarters about what would happen after Nehru. 'I think in the peculiar conditions existing in our country, this is a very important question,' Narayan said.[2]

On 29 April the bombshell came. Nehru told a meeting of the Congress Parliamentary Party that he wanted to quit office. He explained: 'I feel now that I must have a period when I can free myself from this daily burden and think of myself as an individual citizen of India and not as prime minister.'

A virtual storm broke out in the party, which refused to entertain the idea of Nehru's resignation even for a short period. By 3 May Nehru was prevailed upon to give up any thought of retirement. At a meeting of the Congress Parliamentary Party that day he said: 'in all humility and with my deep feelings for what you have said, I shall not proceed to take this step that I suggested [last Tuesday].' Nehru explained that he had thought of this grave step out of 'a feeling that a certain vulgarity and coarseness were creeping into Indian public life, not in the Congress only but in the whole country.'[3]

Having shaken the nation, Nehru began once again to go about his tasks with dynamism.

But though the crisis had passed, the question remained. Nehru had greatly enhanced the office of prime minister; he was now looked upon as both head of government and also as leader of the nation. He had enormous powers—powers which could corrupt a lesser man. While India was at this time a reasonably well established parliamentary democracy, its delicately balanced political set-up needed to be nurtured and sustained. In whose hands would this responsibility be placed? The question began to be debated publicly.

In his book *India Today*, published in 1960, Frank Moraes, one of the most respected personalities of the Indian press at the time, discussed this question at length. He first assessed the possibility of Nehru's successor being found from amongst three leading political figures of the day— Rajendra Prasad (then president of India), Govind Ballabh Pant (home minister), and Morarji Desai (finance minister). Finding each of them had problems relating to health or personality which might militate against their general acceptability, Moraes made a prophetic observation:

> There is therefore the possibility of a comparative dark horse emerging as Nehru's successor, and many see him in the person of the present minister for commerce and industry, fifty-five-year-old Lal Bahadur Shastri, who also comes from Uttar Pradesh. Politically and personally Shastri is very close to Nehru, but he lacks an assertive personality, being of diminutive stature and a retiring disposition. He remains, however, the best compromise choice, particularly if one or other of the contending trio chooses to exercise more decisive political direction as the president.
>
> If on Nehru's demission the Congress rightists succeed in controlling

the Party machine, the dominant group will probably comprise Prasad, Pant and Morarji Desai, with S.K. Patil and the fifty-nine-year-old minister for parliamentary affairs, Dr Satya Narain Sinha, who hails from Bihar and is very much to the right, in close tow. Lal Bahadur Shastri, despite his present leftist leanings, would probably work in conjunction with this group. A government inclined right of centre would then emerge.[4]

Moraes did not know then that he was hitting the bull's eye firmly in the centre.

A masterly analysis of the succession question was also made by Welles Hangen in his book, *After Nehru, Who?* (1963). He listed eight possible successors—Morarji Desai, V.K. Krishna Menon, Lal Bahadur Shastri, Y.B. Chavan, Indira Gandhi, Jaya Prakash Narayan, S.K. Patil and Brij Mohan Kaul. After examining each, Hangen came to the conclusion that Lal Bahadur Shastri was the person most likely to succeed Nehru, though he warned that Shastri's health might cut short his tenure:

> Shastri is the most authentically Indian of the personalities described in this book. He is nearest the mind and soil of India. He reflects the strengths and weaknesses of the Indian villager. If he is to enter history as the second prime minister of independent India, he must do so with the mandate of the Party bosses, including Nehru. If he is to be more than a footnote to history, the mandate must be upheld against all challenges by the overwhelming will of the Indian people. Armed with the Party mandate and sustained by the popular will, Lal Bahadur Shastri could take his place with vastly magnified stature on the world stage.[5]

In the concluding chapter of his book Hangen observed: 'There is something typically Indian in the fact that Lal Bahadur Shastri, who insists that he could never fill the prime minister's shoes, will probably be the first person asked to do so.'[6] But Hangen added a prophetic warning: 'Shastri's most serious handicap, besides his unassertive personality, is probably his health. A former colleague in the Union Cabinet says that his first heart attack caused no lesion but a second or third attack could be crippling.'[7]

By early 1964 the question of a successor to Nehru became urgent, after Nehru suffered a stroke on 7 January in Bhubaneshwar. Shastri's reappointment to the cabinet on 24 January 1964 as minister without portfolio to assist the prime minister was generally seen as a step in the direction of prime ministership. In its issue of 23 January 1964 the reputed British daily, *The Guardian*, welcomed this appointment:

> It looks as if Lal Bahadur Shastri is being 'evolved' as the next Indian Prime Minister. Yesterday it was announced that he is rejoining the

Cabinet which he left in August under the Kamaraj Plan. The news is welcome for two reasons, first that the problem of the succession is at last being tackled, and secondly, that Shastri is the man in view.

There was sense in Nehru's remaining in office as long as his health allowed. For his value to India did not merely reside in the 'leadership' looked for in any head of Government: others might have provided that.

More important, his primacy was taken for granted by almost all like that of a monarch; here was stability at least at the top in a rapidly changing nation. But now, cruelly, these assets for India have been cancelled by his ill-health. For a time at any rate—a time when India urgently needs leadership—he is not able to provide it except at risk of his life; and his continuation in office without a clear successor stimulates rather than assuages factional struggle.

Shastri's name, until recently, has rarely been in Western headlines, but in India for several years he has been talked about by those to whom none of the more publicised candidates appealed as the best Prime Minster-designate they had. He is still a man of the centre, a compromise candidate—more acceptable to the left wing of Congress than Morarji Desai, and more acceptable to right than Krishna Menon.

But (like Attlee in similar circumstances) he has much more to him than the quality of not being someone else more disliked, he has personal characteristics that might make him a most effective Prime Minister in a divided Party and country.

On 30 March 1964 Nehru was asked by H.V. Kamath in the Lok Sabha whether the appointment of a minister without portfolio was only a step towards advising the president to appoint a deputy prime minister. The prime minister again sidestepped the issue and replied: 'I do not think it has arisen and therefore there is nothing for me to answer.' At the same time, he praised Shastri for discharging many duties efficiently.

In a television interview recorded in New Delhi a few weeks earlier and shown in New York on 18 May 1964 the interviewer, Arnold Michaelis, asked Nehru about the problem of succession and the reports circulating about Indira Gandhi 'being groomed as your successor', which, Michaelis added, was 'a fascinating thought'. Nehru said in reply that it was very unlikely that his daughter would succeed him, and he was 'certainly not grooming her for anything.' The interviewer later conveyed these remarks to Indira Gandhi during an interview with her, and quoted her as having said: 'I think he is right in what he has said in that I have no such idea. I would not call it ambition because to me it does not seem a good thing. Different types of people want different things—and it just is not what I want for myself.'

The next question put to Indira Gandhi was: 'Would it not be a question of who had the necessary equipment to carry the tremendous burden. I am sure you have.' Indira Gandhi answered: 'Well, I am not conceited enough to think that I am the only person who has it—even if I do. But a lot of other things depend on who will succeed. I know that I will not enter into this at all.'[8]

Nehru made some general comments also, in his interview, indicating his mind on the manner in which a successor should be found. He said that the choice of his successor would be best left to the people. 'Somebody would come on to take the job of prime minister,' he said and added: 'If I nominated somebody, as people seem to expect, that is the surest way of his not becoming the prime minister. People would be jealous of him, dislike him. Winston Churchill nominated Anthony Eden but he didn't last long.'

Nehru addressed a press conference on 22 May 1964, when he was asked again if he had considered grooming a successor during his lifetime. The prime minister responded: 'My lifetime is not ending soon.' In fact, it ended five days later.

Clearly, then, Nehru's public position was that the people, which really meant the Congress Party, should be free to choose the next prime minister, which was entirely correct. The question generally asked is whether he had any preferences. It is easier to state what he did not want. He did *not* want the stigma of promoting dynastic rule by grooming Indira Gandhi for the post. Had he wanted to perpetuate his dynasty, he could easily have appointed Indira Gandhi as a cabinet minister, and she could then have succeeded her father as prime minister. Some people believe that at heart Nehru devoutly wished his daughter to succeed him, this being only natural for a father; he just did not wish to be seen as propelling her, because history would have accused him of perpetuating his dynasty in practice while declaring in public that he had no such wish. On this question Dharma Vira, who worked directly and closely with three prime ministers—with Nehru as his principal private secretary and with Shastri and Indira as cabinet secretary—told me that Nehru *was* building up Indira Gandhi for the position of prime minister but thought in 1963–4 that she was not ready for the job. Nehru had the greatest faith in Shastri and had promoted him in the expectation that he would be a 'stopgap' prime minister who would be fair to Indira Gandhi when the time came.

Among other possible candidates for the prime minister's post were Morarji Desai, Jagjivan Ram, Y.B. Chavan, and Gulzarilal Nanda. But for all practical purposes only Lal Bahadur Shastri and Morarji Desai were regarded the most likely successors, especially as Indira Gandhi had declared she would not enter the contest.

## THE END OF AN ERA

On 23 May 1964 Nehru went to Dehradun for a brief three-day holiday. He was accompanied by his daughter. On 26 May he returned to New Delhi. Upon arrival he looked fresh and relaxed. Shastri, who received Nehru at the airport, drove along with him to the prime minister's house.

On 27 May 1964, what the country dreaded came to pass. Nehru suffered a heart attack at about 6.30 a.m. His life gradually ebbed away and he died just before 2 p.m. Present by his bedside at that time, besides Indira Gandhi, were Gulzarilal Nanda, T.T. Krishnamachari and Lal Bahadur Shastri. The news of Nehru's death plunged the entire nation into deep gloom. It was the severest blow to India after the assassination of Mahatma Gandhi on 30 January 1948. Nehru's body was cremated on 28 May 1964, near Mahatma Gandhi's *samadhi* in Rajghat. The Nehru era had ended.

Next only to Mahatma Gandhi, Jawaharlal Nehru had dominated the Indian political scene for nearly three decades before independence. After independence, he was the leader and architect of modern India. His patriotism, his love for the people of India, his dynamism, his vision of a vibrant, prosperous India, his dedication to human liberties assured by a democracy based on universal adult suffrage and the secret ballot, his respect for the great institutions of a free and well-ordered society, his secularism and deep concern for the welfare of the minorities, his modern and scientific mind, his urbanity and warmth—all these were unparalleled. The people of India loved him beyond measure and gave him their unquestioning confidence. Nehru could have been a monarch or a dictator if he had wished. But he was a democrat to whom a free society functioning under the rule of law was the *sine qua non* of civilized existence.

*Now Who?* and *Now What?* were, consequently, the dominant questions in the mind of every Indian. The answer to the first question, as we shall see, was found by the political leaders of the Congress Party within a few days. The answer to the second question took much longer.

## SHASTRI'S ELECTION

The Congress Party was faced with an unprecedented task: there was no set procedure for the election of prime minister. The holder of this office is not just head of central government in the Indian federation, Nehru having invested the office with vast attributes. The prime minister was in a very real sense the ultimate repository of the power of governance within the country. He had to hold the country together and determine the path of its development. So his election was not just a party matter, nor just a matter for the chief ministers of states. In a real sense, it was a matter for the people of India.

It was the country's great good fortune that at this moment of crisis a man of the highest political calibre and integrity was president of the Congress Party. K. Kamaraj Nadar, who had gained national reputation as chief minister of Madras, had resigned from that office in 1963 under the plan which carried his own name. He had presided with dignity and ability at the annual session of the Indian National Congress in Bhubaneshwar in January 1964 and was now in full control of the party. He was known for his clarity and decisiveness. As Congress president, Kamaraj set about the task of the election of a new prime minister with alacrity.

Some people on the left wing of the party wanted the election to be postponed on the grounds that the people were much too grief-stricken and unprepared for this crucial decision. This argument did not find favour with Kamaraj. On 28 May informal discussions took place in the capital among different political groups. On 29 May a major effort was made to avoid a contest. The Congress President held a series of meetings with senior Congress Party leaders, among them Lal Bahadur Shastri, Gulzarilal Nanda, T.T. Krishnamachari, Morarji Desai, Jagjivan Ram, Y.B. Chavan and some state chief ministers.

According to press reports there was considerable canvassing, but it centred principally around two persons—Lal Bahadur Shastri and Morarji Desai. A former Congress MP, K. Santhanam, issued a statement suggesting that the Congress Working Committee, which was due to meet the next day, should set an appropriate convention by leaving the Congress Parliamentary Party unfettered to choose its new leader, who would then become prime minister.

The Congress Working Committee met on 30 May and adopted a resolution of condolence on the death of Nehru. It decided to meet again the next day to fix a date for the election of a new leader by the Congress Parliamentary Party. The executive of the Congress Parliamentary Party also met on 30 May and decided to fix a date for the election of its new leader in consultation with the Congress President. The same day, eighteen MPs belonging to the Scheduled Castes and Backward Classes decided that Jagjivan Ram should contest the election for party leader. Morarji Desai had a long talk late in the evening of 30 May with Kamaraj. Later, Desai told newsmen that he would not shy away from contesting the leadership election 'if people find me fit for the job'. He added, however, that efforts were being made by 'everyone' to bring about a unanimous choice. The Congress president, questioned by the press representatives about his efforts to secure this unanimous choice, advised them to 'wait till tomorrow when the Working Committee announces its decision.'

Some time on 30 May Shastri met Indira Gandhi and suggested to her that she should assume the leadership of the country. The precise words he used on that occasion, which he recalled to me later, were: '*ab aap mulk ko sambhal leejiye.*' (You should now assume responsibility for the country.) Indira Gandhi declined the invitation, saying she was then in such grief and pain that she just could not think of contesting the election. Shastri wanted to be quite clear about her position.

On 31 May the Congress Working Committee had a long session. No names for the leadership of the Congress Parliamentary Party were discussed. There was a wide consensus in the Working Committee that every effort should be made to find a unanimous choice. Towards this end the Working Committee unanimously authorized Kamaraj to hold further consultations with members of the committee, state chief ministers and senior members of parliament, and 'make his recommendation accordingly'. The Congress Working Committee also decided that the Congress Parliamentary Party should meet in the morning of Tuesday, 2 June 1964, to elect its new leader. All the possible contenders for this office were present at the Working Committee meeting, and were thus in agreement with the decision to seek unanimity through the efforts of Kamaraj. There was agreement that the verdict of Kamaraj would be accepted and that there would be no contest.

Behind the scenes, hectic canvassing was still going on. Leftists, centrists and rightists in the Congress Party were trying to gather support, but with decency and decorum. A proposal was floated at this stage by the leftist group that Gulzarilal Nanda, who was serving as stopgap prime minister, continue in this station for a few months, so that the Congress Parliamentary Party might consider a long-term arrangement after it had got over the trauma of Nehru's passing away. This was a clever and pregnant suggestion. After a few months the period of grief would have been over for the Congress Parliamentary Party and, more significantly, also for Indira Gandhi. But this fascinating move did not find much favour. Later in the day, when it appeared that only two contestants were left in the field, i.e. Lal Bahadur Shastri and Morarji Desai, Krishna Menon, the leader of a leftist group, tried to commit the support of this group to Morarji Desai, who was described as a rightist. But the laity refused to be led by the high priest of leftism on this occasion. Jagjivan Ram, the Harijan leader who was at one time a candidate himself, switched his support to Morarji Desai. The southern and eastern states strongly supported Shastri, who was himself a northerner. Elsewhere, the support was divided. But overall it had become clear, by the evening of 31 May, that Lal Bahadur Shastri had wide support among MPs, state chief ministers, and the members of the Congress Working Committee.

1 June 1964 was the day for a historic decision, and India's man of destiny for this purpose was Kamaraj. There was no better person to handle the assignment: Kamaraj was totally honest and selfless. In the course of the day he consulted about 150 members of parliament individually, state chief ministers, and other senior leaders. He ended his consultations late in the evening. His finding, which was to be formally conveyed next morning to the Congress Parliamentary Party, was that Lal Bahadur Shastri commanded wide support in the party. Shastri's election on 2 June as the new leader of the Congress Parliamentary Party and his appointment as the new prime minister were now regarded as certain.

After completing his consultations, Kamaraj called on Lal Bahadur Shastri and Morarji Desai and conveyed to them the consensus of opinion which had emerged. Shastri later called on Desai and was with him for more than an hour.

On 2 June 1964 India displayed to the world its political maturity. At the meeting of the Congress Parliamentary Party, Gulzarilal Nanda proposed the name of Lal Bahadur Shastri. The proposal was seconded by Morarji Desai. As there was no other nomination, Shastri was declared elected as the new leader of the Congress Parliamentary Party by unanimity and acclamation. All the leaders who spoke on this historic occasion promised full support to the new leader, through 'thick and thin'. The transition had happened swiftly and without acrimony, demonstrating a democratic strength of which people had often been sceptical.

Shastri was deeply moved but he maintained his poise and dignity. His message on the momentous occasion was brief and from the heart:

> I have now been entrusted with a very heavy responsibility, with the highest charge. I tremble when I am reminded of the fact that this country and Parliament have been led by no less a person than Jawaharlal Nehru, a hero and fighter for the independence of our country . . . I can assure you I will try to discharge my responsibility with utmost humility. And may I beseech you for your help, support and co-operation and above all a sense of understanding . . . You should try to appreciate my difficulties and see the other side of the medal on any issue which confronts us. If you do it, you will add to my strength and make my efforts fully successful.
>
> My wish and desire is that we should stand as one people and tackle our problems as effectively and as quickly as we can. I would very much like that. Those who are in power have to realize fully the great respon-

sibilities we have been charged with after the departure of the late Prime Minister. We must work hard and try to co-operate with each other.

I am sure that our countrymen will rise to the occasion. I have full faith in the people. There have been difficult situations. Sometimes we, those who are called leaders, might have failed. They [the people] have not.[9]

This was a moment of glory. A man from amongst the masses of India had been elected to lead the country. The day belonged to two heroes—the one who had been elected—Shastri; and the other who had wrought consensus in a complex situation—Kamaraj. In answer to a question about a successor, Nehru had once referred to the possibility of collective leadership in his talks with R.K. Karanjia in 1963–4, mentioning precisely these two names. Karanjia had asked: 'You mentioned a collective leadership by way of a successor government. Has any such group emerged from the Kamaraj Plan?' Nehru had answered:

Of course; it is there. It has always been there. What else are we running the Government and Congress with? We have men of considerable ability of whom any nation can be proud. There is Kamaraj himself, a leader of the masses in every sense of the word, truly imbued with the Gandhian spirit, who is dedicated to our ideology. Shastri is another person after Gandhiji's own model: simple, modest and gentle with nothing authoritarian about him and therefore well suited to the task of reconciling different groups to our middle way.

In the same talk with Karanjia, Nehru had underlined the significance of this attribute: 'The important thing in our democratic set-up is to avoid any authoritarian tendency.'[10] These two—Shastri and Kamaraj—were the names uppermost in Nehru's mind for government and Congress.

Shastri and Kamaraj were not only great personal friends, they also had similar backgrounds. Kamaraj was born on 15 July 1903 and was therefore only about a year older than Shastri. Kamaraj, like Shastri, lost his father, Kumaraswamy Nadar, when still a child. Kamaraj joined Mahatma Gandhi's Non-Co-operation Movement in 1920 when he became a Congress Volunteer. Shastri did the same early in 1921. Both were selfless patriots and men of the highest integrity.

After the election process was over, Shastri and Kamaraj both went straight from Parliament House to call on Indira Gandhi. From there, they went to the samadhi of Mahatma Gandhi and Jawaharlal Nehru to pay homage. A white lotus for Mahatma Gandhi and red roses for Nehru—and a few tears—were the reverential offering made by Shastri to his mentors. He then went back home to his mother who had brought him up and to his wife and children who had stood by him through years of hardship. The mother blessed the son and asked him to serve India well and look after the common people in particular. Shastri's work was cut out for him. His mother's desire echoed his own and the country's as a whole.

# Chapter 7

# India at the Time of Succession

The sense of transition from nationalism-and-independence to in-dependence-and-democracy that India experienced during Nehru's time was given fine utterance towards the close of his career by Nehru himself. He referred to the fading away of a sense of mission. 'After all', he said, 'many of us came to politics, not for the normal reason of coming to politics—to find a career, to get a job, and all that. We came because it was part of a mission that we had undertaken— a part of it, not the whole of it. Now I realized more and more that that "mission part" was disappearing as a whole.' Nehru then spoke about the race for posts and a deterioration in standards. On these he was equally forthright: 'And so, while I was disturbed at things that happened in the Congress organisation all over the country, the disruptive tendencies, the rather unseemly race for office or for posts, the bitterness that is generated amongst comrades and Congressmen and all that, I was really thinking not so much of the Congress, but of what was happening in the country as a whole: deterioration of our standards, a certain coarseness into our public life, a certain vulgarity coming into it.' The question, he went on

> is not of any kind of very high standards, the question becomes one of common decency. The ordinary standards of a human being are not high moral standards. I have often said that we in India suffer from a split personality—a real split personality. One part of us is of the highest moral standard. We talk about it and we believe in it—not that we do not believe in it—and yet another part of it forgets that completely and functions, well, very far removed from that standard. And so this other part seems to be coming up more and more, the allegations and pulling of each other down, knocking each other down. It has really been an extraordinarily painful thing.[1]

Nehru had diagnosed the disease extremely well. But what was the root cause of this disease, and what the treatment? These fundamental questions needed to be asked and answered. Nehru idealistically believed that by laying bare the malady he would induce at least Congressmen to begin some introspection. What actually happened was different. One part—the moral part—of those who were present listened intently to

Nehru's words of pain, but the other part forgot all about it as soon as they went back home. And at the grassroots things went on as before.

As time passed, the situation got worse. The infrastructure was poor, retarding the pace of economic development. Food production gradually fell below the requirements of a growing population, necessitating massive imports and resulting in dependence upon foreign countries. And then came the disastrous Chinese invasion in October 1962. The Indian armed forces were inadequately prepared, the country deeply humiliated. On 18 February 1964, during a debate in the Lok Sabha, Acharya J.B. Kripalani summed it all up in an agonized statement:

> Our people feel that now for some years after Independence the health of our nation has been fast deteriorating.
>
> Our economy is in such doldrums, that it is impossible for millions of our people to keep body and soul together, in spite of the promises made at the beginning of every Five Year Plan that the people would not only live but also live well. Our public life is riddled with corruption, nepotism, graft, inefficiency, indifference, and these have sapped the moral fibre of the nation. No learned statistics are required to prove all this to the people, whether they be given by Dr Lohia or Dr Nanda. Our people feel these conditions within the marrow of their bones, if any marrow is left in their bones.
>
> Our foreign policy too has miserably failed. We have no real friend left in the world—'none so poor as would do us reverence'. Even our great friend Russia, as evidenced in the UN discussion on Kashmir, is more concerned with the susceptibilities of Pakistan and the Western block, than with our rights which she proclaimed loudly from the housetops.
>
> How has all this happened? Why is the national health in such condition. Is it due to natural causes of decay and decline, is it due to acts of God? I believe that it is not due to the decay and the decline of a nation, as was evidenced when there was a universal uprising on the invasion by China of our territories in the Himalayas. It was not the people that failed. It is my opinion, shared by the bulk of my people, the intelligentsia and the common people, that the condition we find ourselves in has been brought about by the acts of commission and omission of our leaders, especially the leaders who are in charge of our Government.

Kripalani was acerbic. But on 19 February 1964, in the same debate in the Lok Sabha, an Opposition spokesman, Nath Pai, who was regarded as a balanced politician and not usually given to intemperance in his speeches, said much the same:

This seems to be a country under the present Government which is politically confused, militarily unprepared, economically stagnant and administratively disorganised and demoralised. They have brought us to such a sad state of affairs. We have come to such a pass today under the present leadership, that we are without an effective leader at home, without a dependable friend abroad . . .

In contrast to the general mood of despair, the state of the polity was reassuring. Parliamentary democracy had been well established. Three general elections had been held in an atmosphere of freedom. Parliamentary government had functioned successfully, in accordance with the best traditions of well-established democracies. Nehru had greatly succeeded in encouraging the Opposition to perform its watchdog functions. The federal constitution was well safeguarded by a competent, independent and respected judiciary. The freedom of the press was regarded as sacrosanct. The general law-and-order situation all over the country was satisfactory. The political parties were well organised and lawful association was unhampered. Politically then, the ship of state was on even keel.

Defence, however, was in need of urgent action. The Chinese invasion shattered the illusion that India was guarded by the Himalayas. The Indian army was routed for no lack of bravery, but more because, as General P.P. Kumaramangalam told me, the defence minister had played havoc with the armed forces. The General added acidly: 'Krishna Menon believed that he could defeat the Chinese by a volley of words.'

The menace now seemed to lie more on the flanks. Pakistan had acquired Patton Tanks, Sabre Jets and Star Fighters, India had no matching capability. During the two years following the Chinese invasion, the new defence minister, Y.B. Chavan, gave a great deal of attention to the enhancement and modernization of India's defence capability. President Kennedy of the USA agreed to provide some assistance for India's Mountain Divisions, but procuring high-performance aircraft proved a problem. In brief, the Indian army and air force both had vintage equipment, and a great deal needed to be done to enhance their capability to combat aggression.

The state of the national economy was also cause for anxiety. The third Five Year Plan covering the period 1961–2 to 1965–6 was then under implementation and the fourth Five Year Plan was being formulated. During the first half of 1964, the most serious problem facing the economy was rising prices, caused mainly by a decline in agricultural production, which in 1962–3 was 3.3 per cent lower than in 1961–2. The gap between planning and implementation had also widened during the preceding years, the rate of actual growth being considerably lower than the 5 per cent per annum which was the Plan objective. The infrastructure was inadequate and inefficient, handicapping development efforts. After the Chinese invasion in 1962, it had become necessary to increase the outlay on defence, and this affected the resources available for development.

The performance of the public sector generally was not particularly edifying. The 'commanding heights of the economy' had been entrusted to the public sector but not much pragmatic thought had been given to ensuring efficient and businesslike management. Although in theory each enterprise was autonomous, working under a board of directors, in reality these enterprises were often treated as subordinate offices of the ministries under which they came. This curbed initiative and innovative management. The secretariat culture began to descend upon public enterprises, a tendency which only a few strong chief executives managed to resist. The most serious problem facing the government was the relative incapacity of its administrative machinery to ensure efficient implementation. And while even existing responsibilities could not be discharged, the Planning Commission, in its memorandum on the fourth Five Year Plan, envisaged an increasing role for the government and the public sector, extending it even to the realm of consumer goods industries! The following excerpt shows the prevailing air of unrealism among doctrinaire planners:

> As in the past, a large part of the responsibility for promoting development in the agricultural, industrial and services sectors will fall on the public sector. Apart from this, the State will have to move towards attaining a commanding position in the distribution of essential consumption goods. These tasks will impose a heavy burden on the administrative machinery at all levels. These responsibilities have to be accepted, and suitable organisations built for their efficient discharge if the goal of raising the standards of living of the people within the framework of democratic socialism is to be attained within a reasonable period.[2]

At the time of independence, the Indian Civil Service constituted the apex of the administrative apparatus of the country. Indian members of this service were people of high ability, imbued with patriotism and a desire to serve their country. But their number was limited and an enormous burden was placed upon them. After independence a successor cadre, the Indian Administrative Service, had come into being. Members of this proved extremely capable, but also came to be known for care, caution and prudence—essential for integrity in administration. But they were hemmed in by the old structures which left little room for the boldness or innovation so vital for development. The pace of decision-making was slow, not only because of the prevailing mental habit of overcautiousness but also because of the growing plethora of rules and regulations. Other services involved in the development effort were also bogged down for the same reasons. No serious effort had been made by the government to introduce administrative reforms with a view to cutting red tape.

In world affairs, India was at this time in something of a limbo between the USA and the Soviet Union. The efforts of the Soviet Union at this stage were to mend its fences with Pakistan, even though India had been assured that this would not be done at the expense of Indo-Soviet friendship. Yet it caused the feeling in India's political circles that an 'everlasting' Indo-Soviet friendship had been dented. Pakistan, meanwhile, was much closer to the Western Alliance than India. Some began to feel that India had become almost friendless in the world. It was not a happy situation.

# Chapter 8

# The Task for Prime Minister Shastri

To succeed an outstanding person is difficult enough; to succeed a legend, a phenomenon, a beloved national hero, an admired statesman and a charismatic leader who had enchanted a country is impossible. Shastri wisely decided to declare that he did not regard himself as Nehru's successor, for, as he said, there was no one in India who could fit his shoes.

Yet Shastri had to function as an effective prime minister and establish his own leadership, with a manner and style all his own. While he was a cabinet minister under Nehru, he had established the fact that power in his hands was safe, that it would be exercised in the national interest and for the common people. He had also demonstrated an inexhaustible capacity to listen to people with attention and humility and then come to his own decisions, taking into account all that he had heard. Now the country was his responsibility. He would be looked up to not merely for reliability but for leadership, and the question in many minds was whether he had the inner resources necessary to meet the challenges which were bound to face him in this new, exalted position. 'The capacity to listen patiently and to act decisively,' said an editorial in *The Indian Express*, written in all probability by Frank Moraes himself, 'is the hallmark of democratic leadership. It is in the latter capacity that Shastri has still to be tested, and it is the ability to act decisively after due deliberation and consultation, which India expects to discover in her new Prime Minister.'[1]

Srinagar had shown Shastri's capacity to act decisively in a crisis, but one swallow does not a summer make. Shastri knew well that he had still to strengthen and enlarge the confidence of the people. While this was Shastri's most important task, he was in no hurry to demonstrate decisiveness. He knew that in the normal course situations were bound to arise which would test his mettle. He knew also that he had the capacity to judge a situation and decide whether to act cautiously or boldly or as the situation demanded. There was, however, a continuing question mark against Shastri, at this stage, in the minds of many people on this account. For him it was now essential to establish a direct nexus with the people, because the power of the prime minister must come directly from the people if he has to function effectively and decisively. Without this broad base of popular support, Shastri knew he would be vulnerable to the debilitating effects of groupism.

There was also the ever-present danger of communal strife. Shastri did not believe in the divisive concept of majority and minority religious communities. To him religion was a personal matter, and it could not be the basis of political activity. For all that, he did not believe in amoral politics. According to him, politics had to be founded on those clear moral and ethical principles which are the fundamental elements of *all* faiths. He wanted every citizen of the country to feel emotionally and intellectually as an Indian first and last, with pride in the country. It was therefore one of his primary aims to foster nationalism, patriotism and secularism, and to promote a national unity which was perpetually threatened by communal undercurrents, as he had seen closely when a cabinet minister.

As home minister when the Chinese had invaded India in October 1962, Shastri had seen how ill-prepared the Indian army was to defend the country. The Pakistani threat, too, was ever present. It was therefore a matter of the highest priority to build up the defence capability of the country and restore the morale of the armed forces.

Inadequate attention to agriculture in governmental planning meant that food production had fallen below the country's essential requirements. Vast quantities of foodgrains had to be imported. Shastri knew rural India and saw that if better care were given to agriculture, with practical programmes initiated to provide seeds, fertilizers and a more efficient water supply along with incentive prices for farm products, India could become self-sufficient. Politically, this was extremely necessary to avoid dependence on foreign countries.

The implementation of the third Five Year Plan was not proceeding apace. In any case—and this was of particular concern to Shastri—the benefit of economic advancement had not yet reached the common man, especially in rural India. He believed that the existing generation of people could not and must not be asked to continue in misery so that long-gestation projects might be implemented to benefit future generations. Shastri was firmly of the view that those who were alive now must be provided with the basic necessities of life: adequate food, essential clothing, drinking water. This could be done only by taking practical steps to accelerate economic growth. As prime minister and as chairman of the Planning Commission, as also of the National Development Council, he would have all the opportunity.

As minister of home affairs he had given personal attention to the improvement of Indian administration. Drastic change was required in procedures, rules, regulations and mental attitudes. He wanted the administrative machinery, right down to the district level, to become development oriented. For this he had made up his mind to appoint a high-powered commission on the model of the Hoover Commission of the USA.

One of the biggest challenges facing Shastri was ensuring honesty in government administration. Corruption was spreading and he wanted to make a determined effort to stem the tide. He had set the highest standards in integrity for himself and had thus the moral right to expect the same of his colleagues. Shastri believed that the only effective way to fight corruption was to begin at the very top; if ministers were honest, they would promote integrity in their ministries. Today this might seem impractical idealism, but at that time the floodgates of corruption had not been opened, and it was not running the risk of being termed starry-eyed to hope that corruption might be controlled. In any case, this matter was an article of faith with Shastri and he was determined to make the necessary effort. He believed completely that if the evil was not fought with determination, it would engulf the entire administration of the country—as it has now more or less done.

As home minister, Shastri had visited Nepal and the visit was a significant contribution to improved Indo-Nepalese relations. As prime minister, Shastri wanted to continue the process and improve relations with Pakistan, Burma and Ceylon. It was his view that India, being the largest country in the South Asian region, should take the initiative in allaying the apprehensions of its smaller neighbours. He wanted also to strengthen relations with the USSR and develop equally close bonds with the USA, Japan, Britain, and Europe.

The challenges, thus arrayed, demanded a response at once firm, flexible and clear. As India began to look for her way beyond Nehru, Shastri began to realize what it really meant to be at the helm so hot on the heels of that subcontinental Colossus.

# Chapter 9

# Shastri's Approach

Before recounting the story of Shastri's career as Nehru's successor and as a successful premier in his own right, an overview of his philosophy and moral credo will be in order.

One of Shastri's principal objectives was to ensure institutional control of power for the governance of India. He believed that in a democratic set-up, which embodied the essential mechanism of checks and balances to prevent the concentration of power in any one centre and its abuse, each institution must play its own appointed role, that being the only way to ensure that democracy took root. For the achievement of this objective, his career shows that he displayed enormous respect for the great institutions of the republic, namely the president, parliament, the cabinet, the judiciary, the civil service and the press. Shastri gave much respect to the president of India, on whom he called regularly to keep him well posted on developments in government. It is a well-known fact—as the history of India since the promulgation of its constitution in 1950 has shown—that problems arise in the delicate relationship between the president and the prime minister, involving sometimes a clash of wills or personalities. President Radhakrishnan never had any such problems with Nehru. The two got on famously. Shastri too listened to Radhakrishnan with respect, as was his wont, but in matters which fell within his own jurisdiction Shastri made his own decisions.

By far the most important of the great institutions was of course parliament. During his tenure Shastri, made frequent and detailed reports to parliament on important matters affecting the country's internal administration or foreign relations. He also used the forum of parliament, through his statements, supplemented by broadcasts to the nation, to promote and inspire unity, national pride, loyalty. He also made much effort with Opposition MPs in parliament, believing that they, like Congress MPs, were representatives of a segment of the country.

He met leaders of the Opposition parties regularly. At these meetings, he was disarmingly straightforward in placing before them all the facts as they were. He would then explain his policies and decisions on the basis of those facts. Members of Parliament found this a happy experience and felt that they were participating in the national decision-making process. Strong criticism *was* voiced on various issues, and several no-confidence motions *were* moved to censure the government, but it would be correct to say that MPs generally were convinced that power in the hands of Shastri would never be abused, that the highest level of integrity would be maintained. Congress, as much as the Opposition, knew that Shastri was always ready to resign in order to maintain his high standards and ideals, and never compromise for personal gain.

Regarding the day-to-day functioning of parliament, he had one great ambition. He wanted the proceedings to be conducted in accordance with the highest principles and practices of parliamentary democracy. He wanted decorum and orderliness. He was against attempts to shout down or disturb speakers. As far as he was concerned, he listened with patience to every speaker, making his own notes, never interrupting, speaking later and to the purpose. I recall several occasions when he was interrupted by vociferous members of the Opposition. He would on such occasions yield place, but would on resuming urge members to listen patiently. Once or twice he expressed anguish over noisy scenes, saying that if these practices were continued, parliamentary democracy would be in danger. He therefore gave a great deal of his time to the preparation of his statements in parliament. He would not approve drafts until fully satisfied. He insisted on the use of simple, clear and direct language. His statements came from a clear mind and from the heart.

During his first year in office Shastri faced many ups and downs in parliamentary debates, but later, especially after the Indo-Pak War began, he became beloved of the entire house. This gives the measure of his success as a parliamentarian in troubled times.

As for the cabinet structure, Shastri maintained it entirely as he had found it. In addition to the cabinet itself, there were several cabinet committees such as the Emergency Committee and the Defence Committee. All these were maintained as the essential forum for collective decision-making.

In Nehru's days the debate in the cabinet on each agenda item generally comprised a dialogue between the minister concerned, who explained the case, and the prime minister who gave his reactions. The rest of the cabinet usually nodded assent. In exceptional situations a debate did ensue. Nehru eventually summed up the proceedings and the consensus as he saw it. And that was the decision.

When Shastri became prime minister, the scene in the cabinet changed. In the absence of the towering, if not dominating, personality of Nehru, and with a new prime minister in the chair whose main assets were his humility and patience to listen, ministers participated freely in the debate, expressing their points of view. Taking into account the comments made by different ministers, Shastri would then indicate the lines of decision. His decision was nearly always acceptable to the whole cabinet.

Every important issue came up before the cabinet or the Emergency Committee or the other cabinet committees. Thus the cabinet system of government and the concept of collective responsibility were in full force during the prime ministership of Shastri. According to the cabinet secretary, Dharma Vira, decisions were made on time and with despatch and efficiency. Shastri did not form any inner group or 'kitchen' cabinet; he did not encourage extra-constitutional centres of power. His whole style of government conformed strictly and reassuringly to the letter and spirit of the constitution.

In similar spirit, Shastri stood for the independence of the judiciary. He was against the executive branch of government interfering directly or indirectly with the judicial process. He wanted the judiciary to be committed, not to his views or to those of government, but to the constitution and laws of the land. He had a friendly but deferential relationship with the chief justice of India, P.B. Gajendragadkar.

As regards the civil service, one foreign writer expressed the view that in the post-Nehru era senior civil servants assumed a far more powerful role than before, and that Shastri was much too deferential and even respectful to secretaries to government. I put this view to L.P. Singh who, both in his capacity as home secretary, and personally, was very close to Shastri. L.P. Singh simply said: 'Shastri was respectful to every human being.' He went on:

> Shastri regarded civil servants as colleagues. He extended great courtesy to them. If we made a proposal and Shastri did not positively accept it, we knew that he had disapproved. He listened to us very attentively but all his decisions were his own. He always had the last word. There was no question of any civil servant having undue or excessive influence on him.

Once, Shastri asked L.P. Singh: 'Why are civil servants not more expressive? Why this excessive caution?' The questions were clearly meant to encourage civil servants to be more forthcoming.

I asked Dharma Vira, who had worked closely with both Nehru and Shastri, about their respective attitudes towards civil servants. I asked particularly if civil servants had become more powerful and influential under Shastri than they were under Nehru. Dharma Vira answered:

> Nehru and Shastri both showed the same respect and consideration to

civil servants, but each had a different style. Nehru usually talked briefly—in the shape of a pill. Once I sent a note to Nehru about a proposal, saying that I would like to explain it in detail personally. Nehru sent for me and then we had a conversation. Nehru said: 'You think you are very able, but in my view you are not quite as able you believe you are.' I replied, 'If I am not good enough, why is the government wasting four thousand rupees per month on me. While I hold this post, I have a right to express my views to you. After listening to me, you may make any decision you like and I will implement it fully.' So he said, 'Go ahead and tell me what you want to.'

Dharma Vira said he then explained the case. After listening to him, Nehru smiled and said: 'Do what you want.' The entire conversation was conducted in good humour, as between friends.

Shastri, said Dharma Vira, had a different style. To illustrate this, he recalled:

Once I sent a note to Shastri on some urgent matter. He sent for me and then we had a conversation. I said, 'This is an extremely important and urgent matter. I would like to have your decision now.' And Shastri said, 'I agree that the matter is very important and urgent. Do you think any great harm will be caused if I took time till tomorrow morning to think it over?' I replied, 'Not really.' To which he said, 'Then do please wait for just one day.'

Shastri gave his decision next morning.
According to Dharma Vira, who summed it up—

Both prime ministers gave full freedom and encouragement to civil servants to function objectively and independently. Nehru occasionally lost his temper, but he regained it the next moment. To make amends quickly, he would offer a cigarette. Shastri was different. He gave a lot of time, made one feel at ease, listened patiently, encouraged objective opinion on the merits of a matter, but always made up his mind after deep thought. Civil servants were equally effective in both regimes. Both prime ministers recognized that civil servants had an important role to play in government and that they had the duty and responsibility to advise, to execute and to provide stability to administration.

I myself was only a joint secretary when I was working with Shastri, and I was with him for several hours a day. And yet there was no question of his taking me for granted. When in his office tea was served in a tray, he would insist on pouring a cup for me himself, because it was his room and he was the host. During the course of a talk or discussion with me in his office, Shastri would sometimes leave his chair and walk a few paces up and down, while still continuing the conversation. Since at that time all the lights were not required—no paper was being read—he would himself switch off some of the lights to avoid waste of public money. He would not have thought of asking me to switch off the lights.

As regards the press, Shastri did not seek publicity, but when he became prime minister he considered it essential that his message should get through to the people. He maintained a close and open relationship with the editors and political commentators of leading newspapers. Barring those of the extreme left, the others were usually appreciative and supportive of Shastri's endeavours. Amongst those with whom Shastri maintained fairly regular contact were Frank Moraes, editor of *The Indian Express*, S. Mulgaonkar, editor of *The Hindustan Times*, and Pran Chopra, editor of *The Statesman*. As regards state chief ministers, since Shastri valued the autonomy of the states of the union, he did not see the prime minister as an all-powerful potentate whose personal writ must run everywhere. In contrast to some of his successors, he saw very clearly that an excess of central rule would prove institutionally infructuous and eventually disastrous because it would debilitate chief ministers, sap local initiative, discourage innovation and encourage groupism. Shastri once expressed his clear perception of the integrative rather than dominating role of the centre in its relations with individul states in a succinct comment to L.P. Singh, who was then home secretary: 'We need a wise central government, a government which could harmonize differences, which could function as a conciliator.'

Shastri did not forget that his mandate to be prime minister had, initially, come from the Congress Party. He was acknowledged as one of the national leaders, but at the same time he was not yet a leader of the masses. Over the years, especially since his appointment by Nehru as the general secretary of the Indian National Congress in 1951, Shastri had developed close personal relations with Congress Party leaders at various levels. He had friendly relations also with members of the Congress Working Committee and the All-India Congress Committee. Because of Shastri's particular friendship with Congress President Kamaraj, whom he met frequently, some got the impression that, in the initial months of Shastri's prime ministership, a two-horse team was running the government. Shastri soon dispelled this impression. He made it clear that in regard to his responsibilities as prime minister, he made his own decisions. Thus, with Mahatma Gandhi as his guide, with an adherence to the moral values of the *Ramayana* and the *Gita*, with his own ideas about the governance of the country, and with a style of government based on respect for all, Shastri embarked upon his task as India's second prime minister.

# Chapter 10

# The First Year in Office

## THE FORMATION OF THE CABINET

With his deep concern for stability and a smooth transition, it was apparent that in essence the new Prime Minister would wish for continuity in government rather than drastic change. At the same time, it was necessary to bring some new faces into the cabinet, some new talent. Shastri had also to make some critical decisions. The first and the most delicate related to Indira Gandhi. He considered it necessary to include her in the cabinet, because she was Nehru's daughter and her presence in government would provide a visible symbol of continuity. Indira Gandhi agreed but asked for a light portfolio —the Ministry of Information and Broadcasting. Shastri agreed readily.

The next and perhaps equally important question was Morarji Desai, who had acted with exceptional dignity and discipline in connection with the election of the new prime minister. Shastri had great personal regard for Desai and wanted to include him in the cabinet, but an acutely difficult problem arose about his rank in the cabinet. Desai wanted to be placed in the number two position, next to the prime minister. Gulzarilal Nanda, who had occupied the number two position in Nehru's cabinet and who had functioned, albeit only for a few days, as prime minister, staked his claim for the same slot. Nanda's claim was strongly backed by Indira Gandhi and the left wing of the Congress Party. Kamaraj was also inclined the same way. In the circumstances, Shastri felt rather hemmed in. After some excruciating thought, he offered the next position, number three in the cabinet, to Desai. Shastri had an hour-long talk with Desai, but the latter did not accept this offer and preferred to stay out of the cabinet. It is to Desai's eternal credit that he did not show any resentment in public. In fact, he maintained a very dignified stance and indirectly supported Shastri wherever he could. Desai's nobility is demonstrated by a remark he once reportedly made about Shastri: *'Main to ek purush hoon. Lal Bahadur mahapurush hain.'* (I am just a person. Lal Bahadur is a truly great person.)

The third crucial question in Shastri's mind pertained to finding a talented minister for food and agriculture. Shastri was determined to promote measures for increased food production within the country and to reduce, indeed eliminate, the country's dependence on food imports. He wanted an able and dynamic minister who could be trusted to push ahead a well-conceived and result-oriented programme in this regard. Shastri decided the right person was C. Subramaniam. He had handled the portfolio of steel, heavy engineering and mines with great ability and could be expected to use his considerable talents to produce results in the ministry of food and agriculture. Shastri took the unusual step of going personally to Subramaniam's residence to ask him to join the cabinet. Subramaniam himself relates what happened then:

> After Nehru, Lal Bahadur Shastri became prime minister and, immediately after assuming office, visited me at my residence in Delhi—a rare gesture by a Prime Minister. Lal Bahadurji requested—he termed it a request—that I should be a member of his cabinet.
>
> We discussed the portfolio, and I told him that I would like to continue with my present assignment, because I was in the midst of reorganising the Steel Plants and other heavy industries and had achieved a fair amount of success in that field. He said he would consider my request.

Shastri did not make the proposal he had in mind because he wanted to consider Subramaniam's request earnestly. During the day, he looked around for some other suitable person for the portfolio of food and agriculture, but by the evening he decided to put his suggestion to Subramaniam because he still appeared to be the best choice. Shastri had a further talk with him, this time on the telephone, and asked him to take over food and agriculture. Subramaniam's response and his further conversation with Shastri were as follows:

> I exclaimed—'why this change?' and he replied, 'No other senior Minister is prepared to take up this portfolio because it has been the Waterloo of many former ministers'. He thought it was a challenging job and that I should take over. Put that way, I could not refuse.[1]

Next, foreign affairs. As prime minister, Nehru had handled this portfolio himself and he was indeed the best person to formulate independent India's foreign policy. Shastri perceived that it was now a matter essentially of pursuing the same policy of non-alignment and peaceful relations with a view to winning as many friends for India as possible. This would obviously involve a great deal of travel, of which Shastri was not particularly fond. He appreciated that India's foreign relations were in any case his special responsibility as head of government, but he preferred the usual arrangement in most countries: a foreign minister of cabinet rank who performs his duties in close consultation with the head of government. But Shastri's problem was that no clear suitable and obvious cabinet-rank candidate for the job was at hand. So he decided to retain the foreign affairs portfolio in his own hands for a while and to divest himself of this charge as soon as he was able to find a suitable foreign minister.[2]

On 9 June 1964 the cabinet was sworn in:

| | |
|---|---|
| Lal Bahadur Shastri | Prime Minister, External Affairs and Atomic Energy |
| Gulzarilal Nanda | Home Affairs |
| T.T. Krishnamachari | Finance |
| Indira Gandhi | Information and Broadcasting |
| Sardar Swaran Singh | Industry (including Heavy Engineering and Technical Development) |
| S.K. Patil | Railways |
| Ashok Kumar Sen | Law and Social Security |
| Y.B. Chavan | Defence |
| N. Sanjiva Reddy | Steel and Mines |
| C. Subramaniam | Food and Agriculture |
| Humayun Kabir | Petroleum and Chemicals |
| Satya Narayan Sinha | Parliamentary Affairs and Communications |
| H.C. Dasappa | Irrigation and Power |
| M.C. Chagla | Education |
| D. Sanjivayya | Labour and Employment |
| Mahavir Tyagi | Rehabilitation |

Fifteen ministers of state and twenty deputy ministers were also appointed the same day.

## THE PRIME MINISTER'S RESIDENCE

Nehru had designated the house that, under the Raj, had been the commander-in-chief's residence, as the official residence of the prime minister. This was the most prestigious residence in New Delhi, next only to that of the viceroy (which had become the official residence of the president of India). Nehru had lived in this official residence, renamed Teen Murti House, throughout his tenure.

In the normal course, the new prime minister should have moved into the official residence already established. I have no doubt that Nehru himself would have wished his successor to stay in that house. The minister of works and housing urged Shastri to move into this official residence, which had all the facilities for efficient functioning and which was appropriate from the point of view of the dignity of his office as well as the requirements of security. This, the minister said, was essential in the public interest, because any new arrangement would mean wasteful public expenditure. It was a powerful argument.

However, soon after Nehru's death, some of his close relatives expressed the wish that Teen Murti House be dedicated to Nehru's memory by being converted into a museum and a library. Nehru's sister Krishna Huthee Singh, wrote to Shastri, pressing this proposal which, Shastri was informed, had the support of Indira Gandhi. Shastri could not possibly reject the proposal and, within days, it was officially accepted. And so the decision was taken to dedicate the official residence of the prime minister to Nehru's memory. Shastri was criticized by those who were of the view that he should have proposed instead the construction of a new Nehru Memorial, retaining Teen Murti House as the official residence of the prime minister. But those who knew Shastri well understood why he had acted in this delicate matter as he did.

As Number 1 Motilal Nehru Place, where Shastri was living at that time, did not have adequate facilities for the reception and hospitality of official visitors, it became necessary to consider alternative arrangements. In the situation which had emerged, Shastri was not inclined to shift to a large residence. However, at the insistence of the minister of works and housing, Shastri, accompanied by members of his family, visited two other buildings—Hyderabad House and Jaipur House. After these visits, the family gathered to discuss the issue. Shastri's younger daughter, Mrs Suman Singh, told me that on being asked by one of his children which of the two places he wanted, Shastri's prompt answer was 'neither'. He told his family he did not wish to move to either of these palatial buildings. He wanted to live unostentatiously and was quite happy where he was. And so, in order to provide additional space for the prime minister's office and for the reception of visitors, an adjacent house at Number 10 Janpath was selected and linked to Number 1 Motilal Nehru Place. It became Prime Minister Shastri's official residence.

## THE PRIME MINISTER'S SECRETARIAT

Nehru had appointed a principal private secretary of the rank of secretary to the Government of India as official head of the prime minister's secretariat. Shastri decided to change the designation of the official head of the prime minister's secretariat from principal private secretary to secretary to the prime minister of India. Basically it was a change in nomenclature, but it made the status of the official concerned visibly equal to that of all other secretaries to the Government of India. This facilitated the work of consultation and co-ordination with other ministries, which was the main responsibility of the secretary to the prime minister, apart from assistance to the prime minister on important matters. One post of joint secretary to the prime minister was also created initially. L.K. Jha, an outstanding member of the Indian Civil Service, who was economic affairs secretary in the ministry of finance at that time, was specially selected by the prime minister and appointed on 12 July 1964 as the official head of the prime minister's secretariat and designated secretary to the prime minister. Shastri made this selection because of Jha's expertise in economic and financial matters—areas in which Shastri had not had much exposure in his former assignments. For the post of joint secretary, he selected another brilliant officer—Rajeshwar Prasad of the Indian Administrative Service. Both Jha and Rajeshwar Prasad had worked with Shastri when he was a cabinet minister and were therefore well known to him personally. My appointment as joint secretary to the prime minister was made a little later and, as I said, my duties as decided by the prime minister were those of a private secretary and an aide, working closely and directly with the prime minister.

The strengthening of the prime minister's secretariat was seen as an innovation which could lead to some overlap with the functions of the cabinet secretariat headed by the cabinet secretary. But no serious problem arose as L.K. Jha and Cabinet Secretary Dharma Vira were personal friends.

How important was the role of the prime minister's secretariat and particularly of L.K. Jha? Michael Brecher, in his book *Nehru's Mantle—The Politics of Succession in India*, has suggested that Shastri was working under the overweening influence of L.K. Jha. Brecher apparently made his judgment on the basis of some casual remarks made by Jha in what Brecher calls 'a candid and revealing interview' on 26 September 1964—barely two months after Jha had been appointed secretary to the prime minister. If Brecher had met Jha again one year later, say on 26 September 1965, Jha is likely to have given a different assessment. As it is, Brecher's comments on this issue are fanciful and even amusing. Let me quote the following:

> The main function of the Secretariat, in Jha's words, is 'to prepare drafts of important speeches, statements and letters'. But this seemingly innocuous role—which Nehru could dispense with because of an extraordinary capacity for work and superb drafting ability—carries with it the seed of influence, especially when the prime minister relies heavily on advice; the line between articulating someone else's ideas and intruding one's own is a very thin one.

According to Brecher, Jha had mentioned particularly in his interview that he had prepared, within the first few weeks of his appointment, drafts of several important letters and speeches. Brecher went on: 'Since Jha acknow-ledged that the prime minister consults him regularly on high policy matters, it is reasonable to conclude that he is not merely a Secretary of a Ministry.'[3] Later, Brecher reconfirmed his judgement on the pivotal role of L.K. Jha: 'Indeed, there is ample evidence to indicate that the Prime Minister's Secretariat, through the forceful personality of L.K. Jha, has become a major power centre in all-India politics, an interest group in its own right. It has exerted pressure on many issues, notably in the vital spheres of economic policy and foreign affairs.'[4]

What Brecher did not know, but what the reader will now be familiar with, was that Shastri listened to all advice given to him, yet always made his own decisions. No one ever successfully used pressure on Shastri to get things done. If L.K. Jha prepared drafts for the consideration of the prime minister, that was one of his duties; and not all drafts were prepared by L.K. Jha. The truth is that most of the drafts of speeches and letters were, as I know personally, prepared by various officials, depending upon the subject. What is more relevant and important is the fact that Shastri unhesitatingly rejected drafts if he did not like them or he corrected and improved them to suit his own style and purpose.

To suggest, as Brecher also does, that Shastri gave primacy to agricul-ture because of Jha's views is to miss the vital point of Shastri's deep concern for the common people. On 9 June 1964 Shastri had appointed C. Subra-maniam cabinet minister of food and agriculture because he had already decided to give the highest priority to agriculture. L.K. Jha had nothing to do with this decision: he had not yet joined the prime minister's secretariat. Shastri's views on economic planning, especially his concern for the welfare of the common man, were entirely his own and, as we shall note later, Shastri had already addressed the Planning Commission, in-dicating his new approach and priorities, before L.K. Jha had begun to function as his secretary.

## MILD HEART ATTACK AND RESUMPTION OF DUTIES

Soon after Prime Minister Shastri had formed his ministry on 9 June 1964, he suffered a mild heart attack—the second of his life in public office—and was advised rest in bed. As it was generally known that the illness was not serious, it was not seen as a danger signal. After a few days, Shastri began to receive visitors and among the first who came to convey their good wishes for a speedy recovery were Congress President Kamaraj and Morarji Desai.

However, on medical advice, the prime minister decided to cancel his

planned visit to London in July to attend the Commonwealth Prime
Ministers' Conference. He deputed instead a team of two cabinet ministers—T.T. Krishnamachari and Indira Gandhi—to represent him at the
conference. Shastri's absence caused disappointment in London, but everyone concerned understood the situation.

On 5 July 1964 the attending physicians issued a statement, saying
that as the prime minister was recovering well there was no need to issue
any further bulletins on his health. Soon Shastri recovered completely and
got busy with the responsibilities of office.

The ministry announced by Shastri was generally welcomed as indicating his desire for continuity. Ministers got busy, there was an atmosphere
of confidence. The world was impressed by the maturity of India's political
leaders and by the remarkably quick, efficient and constitutional manner
in which India had completed the first stage of transition from Jawaharlal
Nehru to Lal Bahadur Shastri.

The new prime minister began to give attention to urgent policy issues.
The implementation of the third Five Year Plan had run into difficulties
and the fourth Five Year Plan was under preparation. There was also the
issue of rising prices, especially of food, which Shastri regarded as the most
serious problem facing the new government.

Shastri had understood that India's economic problems were caused
by a concentration of ownership in the hands of the state without the
requisite means of ensuring efficient implementation. Coupled with this
was a strangulating web of rules and regulations which frustrated even the
private sector. Both these factors resulted in delays, wastage and huge cost
overruns, as well as rapidly growing corruption. Shastri favoured a lib-
eralization of the economy. He wanted a fundamental change in priorities,
and above all he wanted to give special attention to the needs of the poor
who were still not being provided with basic food, clothing and shelter.
'No doubt,' he said,

> we have to have bigger projects, bigger industries, basic industries, but
> it is a matter of the highest importance that we look to the common
> man, the weaker element of the society. When we think in terms of the
> common man, we have to think of his food, his clothing, his shelter,
> medical facilities, recreation for the children. These are some of the basic
> necessities of life which everyone needs, and more so in the rural areas.
> We cannot ignore this fact in whatever we may plan, and howsoever big
> our plan might be. We cannot go on doing things which do not touch
> the common man, which do not touch the weaker element in our
> society.[5]

For this reason, in part, Shastri repeatedly emphasized efficient implementation according to a strict time-schedule. 'Our plans are sound,' he observed, 'our policies are correct, our programmes are practical, but the important point is how they are implemented.'[6] On another occasion he said: 'What is most important is the implementation of our programmes and policies . . . I would therefore beg of you, as I said especially to those who are connected with the government, to see to it that our implementation is sufficient and effective.'[7]

As regards priorities, Shastri wanted the Planning Commission to develop an integrated plan for accelerated agricultural development with a view to attaining self-sufficiency in food as soon as possible. In his view, the requirements of such a plan should be the first charge on available resources. In respect of industries, the Mahalanobis model, inspired by the Soviet example, had concentrated to a large extent on heavy industry. Projects in the heavy industry sector usually had long gestation periods, causing inflationary pressures. As a result, the prices of basic commodities had escalated rapidly. In an address early in July 1964 Shastri made it known to the Planning Commission that emphasis should be laid on quick yielding projects. The impact this had on the Planning Commission was brought out in the following news item in *The Hindustan Times* of 13 July 1964:

> Prime Minister Lal Bahadur Shastri's remark that emphasis should be laid on quick-yielding projects seems to have set a new line of thinking in the Planning Commission. The Commission is understood to have decided that the strategy of development during the Fourth Plan should be re-oriented.
>
> The Third Plan is also likely to be pruned with a view to concentrating more on projects yielding quick results. The scope of the new quick-yielding projects which could be taken up in the Third Plan period is, however, not yet clear.
>
> Projects with long gestation periods, whose construction has not yet begun, might be put off till the Fourth Plan. Bokaro [Steel Plant] and the fertilizer projects will, however, be exceptions.
>
> Three major reasons have called for this modification of the Third Plan. First, the rate of growth in the first three years has been only 2.5 per cent as against 5 per cent envisaged. Secondly, there has been a steep rise in defence expenditure, which has caused additional strains on the economy. Thirdly, the price situation is threatening to go out of control.

Shastri emphasized some other points as well. He wanted plans for rural development, particularly rural industrialization, in order to carry, within a reasonable time frame, the benefit of planned economic development to the masses by the creation of many more jobs. He laid emphasis on the development of consumer goods industries. Shastri had also cautioned the Planning Commission against large deficit financing.

This was new thinking to which the Planning Commission was unaccustomed. The press welcomed this breath of fresh air. *The Hindustan Times* (14 July 1964) commented editorially:

> Even as the conventional exercise of target setting for the next Plan is being gone through, there is evidence, as yet somewhat fugitive, of an unfreezing of some old habits of thought on planning. The emphasis on employment and concentration on quick-yielding projects in the prime minister's recent address to the Planning Commission could hardly be construed as inconsequential obiter dictum leaving intact the very different orientation of the present plan. On the contrary the altered priorities may well be his considered reaction to the manifestations of an over-extended economy that have recently become distinctly alarming. While these have to be combated in the short run as best as we may, rethinking of a more fundamental kind is inescapable. The implied advocacy of a pause for consolidation of earlier gains and pursuit of ends comparatively neglected so far is not tantamount to a recommendation of a state of suspended animation. Though these suggestions have their obvious relevance in the present context of inflationary pressures, the larger compulsions behind them are equally unevadable. For example certain obvious limitations to the scale of possible investment cannot be wished away. This fact, often shirked in formal contexts and documents in the past, should be faced squarely in the formulation of the Fourth Plan if the kind of disillusionment with the Third Plan that currently plays havoc with public morale is to be avoided. Apart from the size of the Plan, there is the even more difficult question of reordering priorities and rearranging sectoral divisions of responsibilities. Here the exercise in rethinking will be more agonising; but in terms of the basic requirements spelt out by the prime minister, the emphasis on a rapid expansion of consumer goods production (including, of course, basic articles of consumption like food and clothing) will become inevitable. This will in turn involve the shedding of hoary prejudices about the quantum of investment to be allowed in the private sector.
>
> Agriculture's primacy in the Fourth Plan hardly needs any special avowal, though the entire approach to its practical tasks will have to be transformed if the present stagnation is to end . . .

## LEFTIST ATTACKS

Shastri's pragmatic views on economic planning and development priorities riled and then angered leftists and radicals. The new prime minister, they said, was departing from the Nehruvian policy of planned development on the Mahalanobis model. On 7 September 1964 the Lok Sabha commenced its first session with a new leader of the house and a new prime minister. The session began dramatically as the opposition groups, with the exception of the Swatantra Party, lost no time in tabling a motion of no-confidence, and since this was supported by more than fifty members, it got admitted, according to the applicable rules, for debate in the house. The Swatantra Party, representing the rightists and conservatives, did not support this motion because it felt that Shastri's government, which had been in office no more than three months, should be given more time to formulate its policies and programmes. The speaker decided that the no-confidence motion would be taken up for debate on 11 September 1964. Thus, at the very start of his ministry, Shastri found himself in troubled waters.

Meanwhile the Lok Sabha began a debate on the worsening food situation. The government was severely criticized for inadequate food production within the country and for its inability to keep prices in check. The government was even accused of shielding the hoarders and speculators. On the other hand A.B. Vajpayee, the Jan Sangh leader, attacked the government from a different angle, contending that the alarming rise in prices was due mainly to large-scale deficit financing and ever-increasing non-Plan expenditure. All this criticism was justified, but the blame for this long-festering malaise fell unjustifiably at Shastri's ministry which had assumed power only three months earlier. In his spirited response to the debate, the food and agriculture minister asked the Opposition not to play politics with food. He accepted that the larger producers and hoarders were colluding with each other and explained the steps which the government was taking to set up a Foodgrains Trading Corporation to fight hoarding. He referred to the impracticability of police action against hoarders at the village level. In the short term, there was no alternative to substantial food imports and he expressed gratitude to the US government for its large assistance in this regard. In the longer term, the country had to produce adequate food and the Shastri government was initiating a new policy for achieving this objective. The main elements of this policy were a scientific approach to agricultural production, ensuring the availability of high quality seeds, a soil survey, making available of suitable fertilizers in adequate quantities and fixing remunerative prices for producers. After listening to the minister's statement, the Lok Sabha felt satisfied that the country was on the right track and approved the government's food policy by an overwhelming majority.

Then, on 11 September, N.C. Chatterjee (Independent) moved a censure motion expressing lack of confidence in the government. He accused the government of failure on every front. A large number of members from every section of the house participated in the ensuing debate, some supporting and others opposing the motion, according to their party affiliation.

On 14 September the proceedings were enlivened by a sharp personal attack on Prime Minister Shastri by Hiren Mukherjee of the Communist Party. Mukherjee expressed concern that in the name of giving 'new direction' to the country's economic policies, Nehru's policy of concentration on the development of heavy industries was being given a 'go-by' in the interests of developing agriculture. He charged the Shastri government of discarding the policies of Nehru in the domestic and foreign spheres. Mukherjee then attacked Shastri directly by describing him as a man with a 'split personality', who, while professing to follow the policies of Nehru, was incoherent. The gravamen of Mukherjee's charge against Shastri was 'deviation' from the Nehruvian line.

On 18 September 1964 Shastri replied in a two-hour address to the marathon five-day debate in the Lok Sabha on the no-confidence motion. First, in his lucid and persuasive style, he gave a detailed explanation of his approach to the many issues which had been raised by the various speakers. This exposition displayed his grasp of detail and excellent memory. Shastri then turned to Hiren Mukherjee's remarks. He first took exception to Mukherjee's personal attack on him and said the Communist leader's remark characterizing him as a split personality was highly objectionable. He added that it did not lie in the mouth of Communists to make such an accusation against him when they were still in doubt as to whether China had committed aggression against India or not. Congress Party members applauded vigorously at this.

Shastri then referred to the charge of deviation from Nehru's policies and said he wanted to be 'brutally frank' on this question. In an uncharacteristically uninhibited and hard-hitting rejoinder, which laid the ghost of deviation forever, Shastri said:

> Now I would like to refer to what Hiren Mukherjee said the other day. He suggested that I had deviated from Nehru's policies. If he will permit me to say so, it should not be difficult for a professor to know the correct position. But since he happens to be a Communist, it is difficult for him to think outside the framework of the Communist idea. May I tell him that in a democracy there is nothing like 'deviation' or 'deviationist'? It does not find a place in the dictionary of a democracy. In a democracy there is every opportunity for re-thinking and freedom of the formation of new schemes and policies.
>
> I said on the very first day of my election, and on more than one occasion later, that the Government of India will continue to follow the

policy of Nehru in international matters and democratic socialism will continue to be our objective in our domestic policy. May I also remind him of what happened during our freedom struggle days? I know it personally at least for the last forty or forty-two years. What happened when Mahatma Gandhi took over the leadership? There was a complete overhaul, complete change in philosophy, policy, technique and programmes. Mahatma Gandhi completely 'deviated' from Lokmanya Tilak, Aurobindo Ghose and Lala Lajpat Rai. Will you condemn Gandhiji for this? I hope Professor Mukherjee will be good enough at least to excuse Gandhiji if not me.

And what happened in the case of Jawaharlal Nehru himself? In a way, Gandhiji was his preceptor, the guru in a sense. But did he entirely agree with Gandhiji? No. And yet could you find a more loyal and devoted person to Gandhiji than Jawaharlal? I say, he loved Gandhiji immensely and he gave his fullest loyalty to Gandhiji; yet, he had his own way of thinking, an independent way of thinking. When he joined the government, it was not possible for him to put into effect each and every idea of Gandhiji.

Why restrict ourselves to India? When the first Communist Government was formed, Lenin tried to put into effect fully all the policies enunciated by Marx in *Das Kapital*. Lenin found after some time that it was impossible to work some of them. So he announced a new economic policy (NEP) and it was put into effect. It was a departure from what Marx had actually said in his book.

Now, Lenin goes and Stalin comes. What does he do? I need not tell the House—everyone of you is aware—as to what Stalin did. In fact, he was totally different from Lenin. I consider Lenin to be one of the greatest revolutionaries of the world. But if I might say—I hope, I would be excused—I consider Stalin not to be revolutionary at all. Whether one agrees with it or not is a different matter, but Stalin used the government machine for continuing his reign over the Soviet land till he lived. For him it was just a struggle for power throughout his life.

Now, let us consider the policy Premier Khrushchev is pursuing. He has censured Stalin—and his policies also—in the strongest terms possible. The basic ideology is wholly acceptable to Premier Khrushchev —in fact, he is the greatest exponent of this theory in modern times—but he has flatly refused to tread the beaten track and he has adopted a new programme and technique. I consider Premier Khrushchev to be one of the most distinguished leaders of the world, because he refuses to walk on the beaten track. In the political field situations change, men change, conditions change, environments change and the real leader must respond to these changing conditions.

We do not want to drag in the name of Jawaharlalji for covering our lapses and inefficiencies. We cannot forget our great leader Jawaharlalji—our prime minister, our hero, with whom we worked for forty years, for about half a century.

But I would like to say that it is clear that we have followed a well-set course for a number of years in international matters. We believe in non-alignment and in the pursuit of peaceful methods for the settlement of international disputes. We are equally clear that colonies should not exist and that racialism should be resisted. Coexistence is a wholesome and absolutely sound policy which was initiated and strengthened by our late Prime Minister Jawaharlalji. We wholeheartedly endorse it and it is a great achievement of the policy of coexistence that in certain matters even the biggest powers are coming closer to each other. Any threat or danger of war would be ruinous for the world, especially for countries like India who are engaged in fighting an exceedingly difficult problem—that of poverty and unemployment.

I must say that I do not fancy the idea of keeping in complete isolation and not talking or discussing with others. We have always tolerated differences of opinion, and I feel pained when I see an exhibition occasionally of intolerance. I would like to recall what the late President Kennedy said in his inaugural address: 'Let us never negotiate out of fear, but let us never fear to negotiate.' I think that is the best principle which should be accepted by us in this country.

Shastri completed his demolition of the Opposition with a characteristic and stirring reminder of the central concerns of his social and economic thinking:

I would like to conclude by affirming our firm faith in democracy and socialism. To my mind, socialism in India must mean a better deal for the great mass of our people who are engaged in agriculture, the large number of workers who are engaged in the various factories and the middle classes who have suffered much during the period of rising prices. These are what I call the common men of my country. As the head of the government, it would be my continuous endeavour to see that these objectives are realized and that a social and economic order is established in which the welfare of our people is assured.

This robust reply in which the prime minister asserted his right to take new initiatives delighted the Congress Parliamentary Party. The non-Communist Opposition had been disarmed by a frank and sincere reply and the Communists had been put in their place. Shastri had stood his ground and spoken with authority. The no-confidence motion was defeated by an overwhelming majority. The executive of the Congress Parliamentary Party, which met later the same day, felicitated Shastri for his outstanding speech in the Lok Sabha. Members of the executive expressed the view that Shastri's reply was 'a landmark in the annals of Parliament'. This was his first speech as prime minister enunciating his government's policy, and it established his reputation as a leader of the house.

## DEFENCE OF THE COUNTRY

Ever since the Chinese invasion in October 1962, the Government of India had begun to take steps for the modernization of the defence forces. Shastri accorded the highest priority to defence alongside agriculture. This was epitomized by the slogan he later gave the country—'*Jai Jawan Jai Kisan*' (Praise to the Soldier and to the Cultivator).

The defence minister, Y.B. Chavan, had visited the USA in May 1964. His discussions there with Secretary of Defence Robert S. McNamara, Secretary of State Dean Rusk, and Governor Averell Harriman had been extremely useful. The US government had agreed to provide assistance:

(1) An immediate credit of US $ 10 million for the purchase of defence articles and equipment from the United States which was intended to be used for the modernization of plant and equipment in ordnance factories.

(2) Military grant assistance was to be continued during the fiscal year 1965 at the same level as in 1964. This would cover items for the support of Indian Mountain Divisions, air defence communication equipment, transport aircraft, and support and road-building equipment for the Border Roads Organisation.

(3) Further credit to the extent of US $ 50 million was to be made available during the fiscal year 1965, intended to be used, among other things, to meet the requirements of the Artillery Shell Plant to be set up at Ambajhari.

Y.B. Chavan had been due to meet President Lyndon B. Johnson on 28 May but this engagement was cancelled because the defence minister had to rush back to India on 27 May 1964, on hearing of the sudden passing away of Jawaharlal Nehru.

In further pursuit of the twin objectives of securing military hardware and technical assistance for enhancing national defence production capability, Y.B. Chavan made a special visit to the Soviet Union. He reached Moscow on 28 August 1964 and had discussions with Defence Minister Marshal Malinovsky and senior members of the State Committee for Foreign Economic Relations. Chavan had discussions also with the chairman of the USSR council of ministers, Nikita Khruschev. The discussions were extremely cordial and fruitful, and produced the following positive results:

(1) The Soviet government would provide plant and machinery, jigs and tools etc. of Soviet manufacture to facilitate the early establishment

of the MiG complex of factories. They agreed also that Soviet technical teams would be associated closely with the preparation of detailed working projects and production schedules. Arrangements for the supply of major assemblies, sub-assemblies and raw materials from the Soviet Union for the production of initial batches of MiG-21 aircraft were also finalized.

(2)    Agreement was concluded for the purchase of a certain number of MiG-21 aircraft and associated equipment.

(3)    The Soviet government agreed also to supply a certain number of light tanks and associated equipment.

The Soviet government agreed to receive payments for all these items in Indian rupees, which could be utilized by them for the purchase of goods from India under the existing arrangements.

In an important policy statement made in Parliament on 21 September 1964, Defence Minister Chavan announced the decision of the Shastri government to implement a five-year defence plan for enhancing the strength of India's defence forces by March 1969 to: (1) an army of 825,000 men, and (2) an air force of 45 squadrons of modern fighter aircraft.

The defence minister also gave details of the agreements which had been reached already with the governments of the United States of America and the Soviet Union for assistance to India's defence requirements. He emphasized on this occasion that both these governments had expressed great appreciation for India's foreign policy of non-alignment.

All this was very reassuring. The country was now moving towards requisite levels of defence capability.

## ADMINISTRATION

Shastri wanted a clean administration and honesty among ministers of government. On 15 September 1964 a comprehensive code of conduct for ministers was adopted by the union cabinet. The authority to enquire into allegations against central ministers was vested in the prime minister and similar authority in respect of ministers in the states was vested in the chief minister concerned. A Central Vigilance Commission was appointed to deal with allegations of corruption in the administrative machinery. These decisions were taken by the central government after considering the recommendations of the Santhanam Committee, which had been appointed by Shastri when he was the minister of home affairs.

Shastri was of the view also that the pace of decision-making in the governmental machinery needed to be quickened. There was need for a major operation to cut down red tape. Accordingly, he established an Administrative Reforms Commission to undertake this task.

Shastri had noticed that senior civil servants were engaged in too many meetings, with the result that even urgent decisions were delayed. Telephone any senior officer and the response usually was: 'He is in a meeting.' Accordingly he decided that on one day in a week there should be no meetings, so that all the time of the civil servants that day could be used for dealing with pending files and taking decisions. He decided that Wednesdays should be 'meeting-less' days.

Shastri also decided that anonymous complaints, which were usually sent by unscrupulous people or disgruntled officials to harass senior officers, should not be taken notice of. Dharma Vira, the cabinet secretary, issued circular instructions to this effect.

## THE FOOD CRISIS

Unbelievable though it may seem now, India's planners had not initially given agriculture the high priority which it deserved and, as events were soon to prove, desperately needed. The focus in the first two Plans, according to the Soviet model, was heavy industry. Gradually, food shortages began to develop, compounded by a rising population, and it became necessary for India—basically an agricultural country—to import foodgrains, mainly from the USA under Public Law 480 and the AID Programme. While the volume of food imports in 1956 was less than a quarter million tonnes, it began to escalate rapidly from next year as shown by the following figures:

| Year | Total imports from the USA (in metric tons) |
|------|---------------------------------------------|
| 1956 | 236,358 |
| 1957 | 2,200,534 |
| 1958 | 2,227,386 |
| 1959 | 3,676,859 |
| 1960 | 3,529,792 |
| 1961 | 3,950,108 |
| 1962 | 2,682,938 |
| 1963 | 4,058,510 |

When Shastri became prime minister in June 1964 the country was in the grip of a food crisis. Shortages had led to hoarding and a sharp increase in prices. The new food and agriculture minister, C. Subramaniam, grappled with this as well as he could. An unfortunate failure of the monsoon that year exacerbated the situation, which began to assume alarming proportions. The inability or unwillingness of the central and state governments to crack down on grain hoarders in the cities and villages worsened the situation and created the general impression that the Shastri government was dithering. Shastri was constantly in touch with chief ministers, who were invited to New Delhi for urgent discussions and for the consideration of issues such as rationing in major cities and the organization of food zones.

Shastri and the chief ministers were inundated with advice on firm and drastic action to deal with hoarders and black-marketeers. But while they took some action here and there, they were aware that wholesale arrests might lead to a situation which could get out of control. Shastri came to the conclusion that the only way to get over the immediate crisis was to make every effort to import larger quantities. At the same time, signals from the United States indicated that President Johnson wanted to assure himself personally that India was doing all that it could to enhance food production at home. In fact, the US agriculture secretary, Orville L. Freeman, had clearly advised the Indian government during his visit to India in April 1964 that the only possible means of satisfying India's rapidly increasing food needs was for Indians to invest more of their own resources in agriculture.

Shastri knew this was true: he had made the decision to give the highest priority to agriculture in the fourth Five-Year Plan, then under preparation. But some concrete new initiatives were necessary to satisfy President Johnson that India now meant business on this account. There is no evidence to suggest that Johnson was using India's vulnerability on the food issue to pressurize her politically. In my view, Johnson was doing India a great service, even if his methods were rather unsophisticated, by insisting that India take steps to help herself by producing more food at home.

While endeavouring to import a large quantity of foodgrains from the USA, Canada, Australia and other countries, Shastri asked Subramaniam to develop a new strategy for enhancing food production within the country. In order to get a first-hand impression of how he went about this task, I met C. Subramaniam, then governor of Maharashtra, on 11 December 1991 in Bombay. He first recalled the complacency of the planners with regard to agriculture during the first two Five Year Plans. It was this, he insisted, which had led to a national crisis. He personally made a thorough examination of the agricultural scene by talking, not just with those who, as he said, had only 'file' experience, but also with those who had 'field' experience in agricultural matters.

His first conclusion was that the procurement price for foodgrains was far too low. In order to provide an incentive to farmers to produce more per acre by investing in better seeds and fertilizers, it would be necessary to pay them a higher price for their produce. Accordingly, he presented a paper to the cabinet with this recommendation. Subramaniam recalled that in the cabinet Finance Minister T.T. Krishnamachari opposed the suggestion on the ground that this would cause further inflation. Shastri, however, overruled the finance minister and decided in favour of an adequate price increase. A committee later recommended an increase of 16 per cent as an 'inducement' to food producers. Shastri approved of this recommendation. Subramaniam recalled further that a food purchasing organization, the Food Corporation of India, was established to ensure that the producer actually received the benefit of this new policy. An Agricultural Prices Commission was established to fix prices in the future.

Subramaniam next turned to agricultural scientists for help, because it was they who could best strengthen the faith of agriculturists in new methods based on science and technology. Subramaniam found that agricultural scientists were paid poorly and hence government jobs in this sector were not attracting the best talent. He therefore proposed a reorganization of the Indian Council of Agricultural Research and better scales of pay for agricultural scientists. Shastri welcomed these proposals and got them approved in the cabinet.

In order to enhance the effectiveness of the ministry of food and agriculture, Subramaniam wanted a secretary who had had field experience in this sector at the state level. He selected B. Sivaraman who was then serving in Orissa. The chief minister of Orissa, B. Patnaik, opposed the transfer of as competent a civil servant as Sivaraman from the state to the central government. This matter also was taken to Shastri who spoke personally to Chief Minister Patnaik and secured Sivaraman's release from the service of the Orissa government. Sivaraman transformed the functioning of the food and agriculture ministry and gave it a more practical orientation.

In order to secure a higher yield per acre, it was essential to import better seeds and large quantities of appropriate fertilizers. For the import of seeds and fertilizers, foreign exchange had to be released by the finance minister. On this question also there was a battle royal in the cabinet. The finance minister opposed the proposal. The finance ministry, said Subramaniam, favoured the easy way of supporting PL 480 imports from USA, for which payment was made in Indian rupees. Shastri again backed the food and agriculture minister and his request for adequate foreign exchange to import high-yield seeds and requisite fertilizers was approved.

Innovative steps were still necessary to persuade the traditional farmers to change over to new methods of farming. In their case, said Subramaniam, only 'seeing' would lead to 'believing'. To provide practical demonstration of improved results, about 1000 plots of 5 acres each were taken from farmers in wheat-growing areas, and these were used for the demonstration of the benefits of new scientific methods. This was extended later to rice-growing areas as well.

All these measures put together constituted a new and effective agricultural strategy for substantially higher production. Shastri's decision to appoint C. Subramaniam had proved good, and the two together thus launched the Green Revolution which has since made India self-sufficient in food despite an increasing population. This new strategy also convinced the United States government and Johnson personally that India under Shastri was giving the highest priority to agriculture.

But even these measures could not produce more food overnight. The results would surely come, as they did in later years, but at that time the food situation was getting more and more dire. The United States' ambassador in New Delhi, Chester Bowles, was constantly urging his government to rush more food supplies to India. In 1965 the situation had assumed emergency proportions and the requirement of imported food had gone up to about 1 million tonnes per month. The question then was whether the ports and infrastructure in India could cope with such a vast quantity of imports. Fortunately, the port and dock workers, led by S.R. Kulkarni, co-operated fully and, happily, the country was able to handle much larger imports.

In December 1965 Shastri sent Subramaniam on a mission to the United States to negotiate with the US administration a substantial increase in food shipments to India in its hour of need. Shastri requested Johnson to receive Subramaniam for a personal discussion and this was arranged. Subramaniam also addressed a gathering of US senators and congressmen: all were impressed by Subramaniam. Johnson too was pleased with his personal discussions with Subramaniam. On 17 December 1965 Johnson issued National Security Action Memorandum No. 339, which is reproduced below in full:

THE WHITE HOUSE
WASHINGTON
December 17, 1965
NATIONAL SECURITY ACTION MEMORANDUM NO. 339
MEMORANDUM FOR THE SECRETARY OF AGRICULTURE

SUBJECT: *Critical Indian Food Situation*

I am deeply concerned on humanitarian grounds with the near famine conditions which are developing in India, and which may require a dramatic rescue operation on the part of those nations able to assist. As you know, I have already announced that the United States would participate in such an effort.

I further understand from my discussions with you that the key bottleneck may be less the availability of sufficient foodgrains from abroad than lack of available shipping, inadequate Indian port facilities within India. These factors could critically hamper any international effort to get enough food to India's hungry.

Therefore, I request that you establish a special committee, including representation from the Departments of State, Defence, Commerce, the Agency for International Development, and such other Departments and Agencies as you deem necessary, to examine urgently how to cope with the looming Indian famine problem. I want you to regard all available resources of the US Government as being at your disposal in planning for such an effort. After assessing the likely dimensions of the crisis and what would be required to meet it, you and your group should recommend whatever imaginative emergency techniques and devices which may be necessary to help prevent mass starvation in India.

I would like personally to review your recommendations as soon as they can be made available, before deciding what action I will take along with other interested governments.

Signed
(Lyndon B. Johnson)
cc: The Secretary of State
The Secretary of Defence
The Secretary of Commerce
The Director, Bureau of the Budget
The Administrator, Agency for International Development
Special Assistant to the President for Science and Technology.[8]

In accordance with this Orville L. Freeman, the USA's agriculture secretary, organised a mammoth effort in subsequent months to ensure the regular despatch of substantially enhanced quantities of food to India. He assigned a personal representative, Horace Davis, to the Indian food ministry, to keep him informed of the Indian situation. Canada and Australia also helped by supplying substantial quantities of food. As an Indian and as a person who was a part of the Indian government machinery at that time, I recall those days with feelings of profound gratitude to the government and people of the United States of America, Canada and Australia. Their humanity and generosity saved many thousand Indians.

## THE LANGUAGE CRISIS

While the critical food situation was causing immense anxiety, the language issue erupted in the south, suddenly, like a volcano.

As we have seen, the constitution of India had provided that 'the official language of the Union shall be Hindi in Devanagari script'. This provision had, however, been qualified by the proviso that 'for a period of fifteen years from the commencement of this Constitution, the English language shall continue to be used for all the official purpose of the Union for which it was being used immediately before such commencement . . . '.

As the constitution of India had commenced on 26 January 1950, the period of fifteen years, during which English was officially to be used, was to come to an end on 25 January 1965. The framers of the constitution had been aware that the whole country might not be ready for a change-over to Hindi on this date and had therefore wisely provided that:

> Notwithstanding anything in this article, Parliament may by law provide for the use, after the said period of fifteen years, of—
> (a) the English language..........
> for such purpose as may be specified in the law.

People in the south Indian states were not ready for a changeover to Hindi from 26 January 1965; they wanted the necessary legislation to be enacted by parliament well before that date for an indefinite extension of English. To meet this demand, parliament passed the Official Languages Act in 1963 which provided, inter alia, that as from 26 January 1965 the English language may continue to be used, in addition to Hindi, for all official purposes of the union and for the transaction of business in parliament. This legislation had been piloted through parliament by Shastri who was then the home minister in Nehru's cabinet. Nehru had also given the assurance that Hindi would never be imposed on any part of the country and that English would continue to be used as long as the non-Hindi speaking states wanted it. The Official Languages Act 1963, together with Nehru's unequivocal assurances, had seemingly settled this vexed question.

Time passed and January 1965 dawned. During this month—on the 26th day—India was to pass through a moment of immense psychological importance. From this date, Hindi was to acquire the constitutional status of the official language of the union, displacing English from its primacy in governmental affairs. In practical terms, however, no great change was to be effected, because under the Official Languages Act of 1963 the use of English was to be continued as before. Normally, this should have been a moment of rejoicing because a national language was replacing a foreign language. Unfortunately, this was not so because people in the south, especially students, were apprehensive that they would be disadvantaged by this change.

Shastri did not receive reports either from intelligence agencies or from the chief minister of Tamil Nadu or from the Congress president, K. Kamaraj (who was in close touch with the political situation in Tamil Nadu), that there were any signs of a re-emergence of anti-Hindi feelings. Life was proceeding normally and very possibly nothing untoward might have happened in the south on 26 January, if it had not been for thoughtless exuberance on the part of some officials in New Delhi.

On 24 January the ministry of home affairs provided a fairly detailed briefing to the press, referring to the likely enhanced use of Hindi in administrative matters from 26 January, when Hindi would become the official language of the union. Some caution was, however, shown in this briefing by an indication that the change would be gradual. This story was carried by the Press Trust of India and published in the newspapers of 25 January. This, together with the rumoured issue of a circular by the ministry of home affairs about the new status and role of Hindi, caused a sudden eruption of feelings in Madras. Young people in the south had not forgotten that a decision was reported to have been made in July 1964 to allow Hindi as an alternative medium in the Union Public Service Commission Examinations for recruitment to the All-India Services, subject to the development of an approved moderation scheme to ensure fairplay. Although this proposal had not been implemented, it had caused misgivings. Whether because of the newspaper reports on 25 January about the new status and role of Hindi or because of some secret preparations by the DMK, the opposition party in Tamil Nadu, on that day students all over Tamil Nadu held demonstrations, protesting against the introduction of Hindi as the official language of the union from 26 January. It was alleged by some that the DMK had falsely propagated that English was to be replaced by Hindi, just to cause anger and alarm. These student demonstrations on 25 January provided the first clear danger signal.

On 26 January *The Hindustan Times* carried the following story with the dateline of 25 January:

> From tomorrow, Hindi will be India's official language. English, which enjoyed unchallenged primacy for a century, will have a secondary status.
>
> The 15-year deadline envisaged in the Constitution for the gradual switch-over ends today. It has been a period of tumultuous debates —intense championing by Hindi enthusiasts, matched by equally deep fears, suspicions and hostility by its opponents. Hindi now steps out of

the realm of sentiment into the world of reality—heralded by a few symbolic gestures. The Central Gazette, announcing the Republic Day Awards by the President, today appears for the first time as 'Bharat ka Raj Patra'.

Since English will continue to be used for all practical purposes—as an additional official language—tomorrow's change may not give the appearance of a turning point. However, it is significant as the start of a process to which Government is committed under the Constitution. Moreover, it is a definite psychological break with the past.

On 26 January the ministry of information and broadcasting, without the approval of the minister, Indira Gandhi, issued instructions about some circulars being sent out in Hindi only. This added fuel to the fire.

On 27 January there were further demonstrations in Tamil Nadu and one student was killed while another was injured in police firing in the town of Chidambaram, 140 miles south of Madras. The DMK was now spearheading a violent protest movement. Two DMK supporters burnt themselves to death in Madras city. At least 1000 DMK leaders and workers were arrested under the orders of the Congress Party government then in power in that state.

On 28 January Madras was quiet. In New Delhi Shastri, who was deeply perturbed over the self-immolations, appealed to the people to give up violent agitation. 'I cannot understand,' he said, 'why people should kill themselves for something which should pose no problem at all. We do not want to impose any language on any part of the country.'

On 31 January Shastri, speaking at a function in Trivandrum, re-iterated that the changeover to Hindi as the official language of the union would have no adverse effect on non-Hindi speaking persons, as under the Official Languages Act 1963 the use of English would be continued. On his way back to New Delhi, Shastri made a stopover in Bangalore, where he had a talk with Kamaraj about the situation in Madras. The impression which the prime minister carried back was that the DMK's efforts to mis-lead the people would soon peter out. The same assessment was conveyed to the prime minister by the chief minister of Tamil Nadu. This, as events proved later, was a misjudgment of the situation. For the truth was, and this should have been evident by this time to the local leadership, that even though the DMK was exploiting the anger of the students, there was genuine apprehension and suspicion in the minds of the people of Tamil Nadu. New steps to allay these apprehensions were needed.

On 7 February Subramaniam stated at a press conference in Madras that an 'all-India' solution based on Nehru's assurances would have to be evolved, so that every aspect of those assurances was kept both in the spirit and the letter. Suddenly, on 10 February, the agitation in Tamil Nadu took an extremely violent turn in several parts of the state. The police fired on unruly mobs in several places and nineteen people were killed. Troops had to be called out to control the situation. The prime minister held immediate talks with his colleagues, especially Home Minister Nanda, Finance Minister Krishnamachari and Food Minister Subramaniam. Such was the seriousness of the situation that Shastri decided to address the nation on the subject the very next day. 11 February was a day of immense tension and high drama. Violence continued unabated throughout Tamil Nadu and a further six persons were killed in police firing. A cabinet meeting was held. At this meeting Subramaniam fought for 'a statutory basis' for the implementation of Nehru's assurances. While everyone agreed that these assurances must be honoured fully in letter and spirit, several ministers felt that a decision at this stage to incorporate Nehru's assurances in an act of parliament without prior consultation with the Hindi region might harden attitudes and make a final agreed solution much more difficult. There seemed to be a consensus that the next immediate step should be a proposed broadcast to the nation by Shastri, reaffirming unconditional adherence to Nehru's assurances.

Shastri returned from the cabinet meeting to his official residence and began immediately to work on the text of his broadcast. He improved the official text considerably in order to convey clearly that he would ensure full implementation of Nehru's assurances in letter and spirit, without any qualification whatsoever. He then got ready to leave for Broadcasting House and, as he was about to board the waiting car, a letter addressed to the prime minister and marked 'immediate' was delivered by a special messenger. The prime minister read the letter, thought for a moment, and then passed it on to me, saying he would like to see it again after returning to his residence. He looked grim and, as I soon discovered, with good reason. The crisis had taken a new dimension for the government. Subramaniam had sent in his resignation. I went with the prime minister to Broadcasting House. On the way, he did not utter a word. He had obviously not expected this shocking development. Casting aside his anxiety for the moment, he delivered his address to the nation with his usual confidence and persuasiveness. This is what he said to urge that nothing should be done which might affect the unity of the country:

> I am speaking to you tonight with a deep sense of distress and shock over what has happened in Madras state on account of apprehensions which seem to have been aroused on the language question. I cannot adequately express my sorrow at the loss of life and my thoughts and sympathies are with those who have suffered so grievously.

The strong emotions which have found expression in tragic events are apparently based on a feeling that assurances given earlier on the question of language have not been fully observed; there also seems to be a misunderstanding of the constitutional and legal position and of the policy decision taken by the Government of India. I honestly and sincerely believe that these apprehensions are based on an unfortunate misunderstanding of the factual position. I propose therefore to place before you as clearly as possible the facts as they are and then ask you to bestow upon them your dispassionate consideration.

In the course of speeches in Parliament in August and September 1959, Jawaharlal Nehru gave certain assurances to the non-Hindi-speaking people, and the assurances gave great satisfaction. What exactly were those assurances? Let me quote the key sentences from his two speeches. 'English,' he said, 'can be used by any State in writing to the Government'—the reference obviously was to the Central Government—'or in writing to each other.' He went on to explain that while for internal State work presumably the State language would be used, there would be no limitation on the use of English in dealings on the all-India scale between States. Continuing he said: 'There is no limitation of time even to that, except when people generally agree—and I had said that these very people in the non-Hindi speaking areas who might be affected should agree.'

In another speech he said:

I believe also two things . . . There must be no imposition. Secondly, for an indefinite period—I do not know how long—I should have, I would have, English as an associate language . . . because I do not wish the people of the non-Hindi areas to feel that certain doors of advance are closed to them . . . So, I would have it as an alternative language as long as people require it and the decision for that I would leave not to the Hindi-knowing people but to the non-Hindi knowing people.

Amplifying his remarks he added:

Hindi progressively develops, I would try for that. I love English to come into the picture to be used as long as people require it. Some states have followed it, they can go on using it and gradually allow languages to develop and to replace English.

These were the assurances given by Nehru and I wish to reiterate that we stand by them fully and solemnly. They will be honoured both in letter and in spirit without any qualification or reservation. In order to remove all doubts, I would like to state what the policy decisions are:

First, every state will have complete and unfettered freedom to continue to transact its own business in the language of its own choice, which may be the regional language or English.

Secondly, communications from one State to another will either be in English or will be accompanied by an authentic English translation.

This is based on the unanimous decision of state chief ministers. Similarly, English translations will be available of Hindi communications addressed to the centre by any state or the public.

Thirdly, the non-Hindi States will be free to correspond with the Central Government in English and no change will be made in this arrangement without the consent of the non-Hindi States.

Fourthly, in the transaction of business at the Central level English will continue to be used.

It should be quite clear from what I have just said that there is no question whatsoever of Hindi being imposed on the non-Hindi States for as long as the people consider such use to be necessary.

I would now like to talk about recruitment to the services. It is on this question that serious apprehensions have apparently been caused in the minds of the student community. So far English has been the only medium for the examinees sitting for the Union Public Service Commission examinations. Even now English will continue as a medium and its use will not be discontinued unless the people from non-Hindi speaking areas themselves ask for it.

It is quite true that in accordance with the provisions of our Constitution adopted in 1950, Hindi has become the official language of the Union with effect from January 26, 1965. Ordinarily English would have ceased to have any official status with effect from that date, but two years before the crucial date, the central government enacted legislation to provide for the continuance of English. Thus it is by law that English continues to be an associate language and thus also a medium for examinations. It was decided in 1960 that Hindi might be permitted as an alternative medium after some time. This question was placed before the chief ministers of all the states and it was decided in consultation with them that effective arrangements for moderation must be made before Hindi was used as an alternative medium. But this will be allowed only when a satisfactory moderation scheme has been evolved. For this purpose the Government of India will consult all the chief ministers and eminent educationists from different parts of the country. This may well take time. We shall make sure that the method eventually to be adopted for moderation is considered to be satisfactory by the chief ministers. The scheme of moderation has to be such that it leaves no ground for any genuine apprehension that the use of one medium or another would bestow advantages or give a handicap to any group of candidates. May I assure the student community that every care will be taken to ensure that their employment prospects are not adversely affected?

I do hope that, from what I have said about our decision and our policies, it will be clear that we are most anxious to safeguard the interests of non-Hindi speaking people to the fullest extent and to avoid any inconvenience to the non-Hindi speaking states. These will be our guiding considerations throughout. We shall consider, in consultation with the chief ministers, measures to implement these assurances.

What disturbs and distresses me is the fact that an agitation has been launched without any attempt to discuss. This, I want to say in all humility, is not the way in which grievances should be ventilated or differences voiced in a great democracy like ours. In this vast country of ours, people profess different religions, speak different languages, dress differently and observe different customs; but we are one nation; the history of our struggle for independence and our faith in our future development are our common bonds.

I want to appeal to you to pause and ponder over the whole situation. What is involved is the very unity of the country. Whatever the area to which we belong, whatever the language we speak, we must consider what is best for the country as a whole. Mahatma Gandhi, Jawaharlal Nehru and so many other national leaders and the framers of our Constitution, who were men of wisdom and foresight, decided that there should be a common language to forge all the people of India into a well-knit nation. The objective is desirable, indeed noble. But our methods have to be such as to inspire confidence all round. I ask you, all my countrymen, to lift this issue to a higher plane and to bestow upon it the most rational consideration. If some of you still feel that there are any legitimate grievances or that some administrative or executive action has been taken which should not have been taken, I and my colleagues are ready immediately to listen and to discuss in a sincere endeavour to remove all genuine misapprehensions. I do hope that my talk with you tonight will provide enough assurance to enable the present agitation to be withdrawn.

This was a reassuring and stirring statement and would have had an immediate impact. But the resignation of C. Subramaniam, who himself came from Tamil Nadu, had complicated the situation. The gravity of the situation was heightened by another resignation the same evening—that of minister of state O.V. Alagesan, who also came from Tamil Nadu, which, as we have seen, was the centre of the anti-Hindi agitation.

Shastri had a talk with Subramaniam and asked him to stay in the cabinet. The prime minister told the press that he was trying to persuade Subramaniam not to leave the cabinet. 'But it all depends on him,' said the prime minister.

The next morning—on 12 February—the newspapers gave prominence to the resignation of two southern ministers from Shastri's government. The prime minister's address was overshadowed by these resignations. In Tamil Nadu, the state-wide disturbances continued unabated and a further twenty-four persons were killed as a result of police firing on violent crowds. Another two burnt themselves to death.

Shastri announced early in the day that he had convened a two-day conference of chief ministers in New Delhi on 23 and 24 February to work out steps for the implementation of Nehru's assurances. The prime minister spoke on the telephone personally with all the chief ministers and impressed upon them the importance of these consultations. This was his first step towards a decision to provide a statutory basis to these assurances, but typically he wanted this decision to be based on the unanimous support of the chief ministers of all states. The resignations of Subramaniam and Alagesan were kept pending. The prime minister did not accept them and the ministers concerned did not withdraw them. Indira Gandhi and D. Sanjivayya left for Madras in an effort to mollify the states of the south.

While Shastri's broadcast did not satisfy the people in Tamil Nadu, who wanted Nehru's assurances to be incorporated in an act of parliament, the West Bengal chief minister, P.C. Sen, found the broadcast fully satisfactory. Sen's opinion was important because he spoke for a non-Hindi state.

By 13 February the situation in Tamil Nadu had returned more or less to normal and, at a meeting of the Congress Parliamentary Party convened by Shastri to discuss the situation on the language question, the party endorsed the policy enunciated by the prime minister in his broadcast on 11 February. But the prime minister went further and said that while there was no need to amend the constitution to give effect to Nehru's assurances, the party must be ready to endorse any steps which the chief ministers might recommend after their deliberations at the forthcoming conference on 23 and 24 February. He was thus already preparing the party for a possible amendment of the Official Languages Act 1963.

C. Subramaniam and O.V. Alagesan arrived in Madras on 13 February and went straight to the residence of Kamaraj, where they discussed their future course of action. When asked about his resignation, Subramaniam replied that his letter was still with the prime minister and that he did not wish to say anything more. On the same day, N. Sanjiva Reddy, union minister of steel and leader of Andhra Pradesh, issued a statement supporting the demand for new legislation.

On 14 February, the union cabinet considered two alternative solutions—one, a formal resolution by Parliament incorporating Nehru's assurances; and the other, a modification of the Official Languages Act of 1963. Amendment of the constitution was completely ruled out.

By 16 February the political crisis began to abate. Kamaraj, who had so far refrained from public statement, had a long talk with the prime minister. Later in the day he announced his support for new legislation. C. Subramaniam met the prime minister, who explained his difficulties as well as his ideas for solving the language issue. The talk satisfied Subramaniam and he withdrew his resignation. Alagesan did the same. The withdrawal of these two resignations marked the end of the most dangerous crisis which the Shastri government had faced since its inception. The whole country heaved a sigh of relief.

The policy of the Shastri government as now evolved was enunciated in the statement which was prepared and approved by the cabinet and which was delivered by President Radhakrishnan on 17 February at a joint session of the two houses of parliament. In this statement, there was a clear reiteration of Shastri's assurance that English would continue as an associate official language as long as the non-Hindi speaking people wanted it. It was stated in addition that parliament would consider the language policy in all its aspects —'legal, executive and administrative'. Meanwhile, the union law ministry, under instructions from the prime minister, had prepared a draft amendment to the Official Languages Act 1963 to incorporate 'the assurances' on the Hindi question into this parliamentary statute.

Minutes after the conclusion of the joint session of parliament on 17 February, Shastri addressed the general body of the Congress Parliamentary Party and gave an exposition of the language problem as he saw it, and the party decided to conduct a detailed debate on this question. Shastri also announced that he would soon call a conference of the leaders of all parties in parliament so that he might benefit from their views. Thus the prime minister was now well on his way to promoting what, in that surcharged atmosphere, only he could—a reconciliation and national consensus in order to strengthen the forces of integration. The path was by no means clear. There were still strong divergences between different stalwarts of the Congress Party. At a meeting of the Congress Working Committee held on 21 February, sharp differences emerged on the nature of the solution. Looking at this picture, everyone agreed that government should not act in haste.

How strong the feelings were on the other side was shown by the remarks of two Congress Party leaders of national stature. Harekrishna Mahtab, MP, former chief minister of Orissa, acidly observed in New Delhi on 22 February that 'an atmosphere of downright hypocrisy was being created in a vital national matter if the Congress leadership intention is to use Nehru's assurances on the continued use of English as a cover to postpone Hindi till eternity.' Speaking in Ahmedabad the same day, Morarji Desai said that 'we should immediately switch over to Hindi in the Central administration and the regional languages in the States.'[9]

This was the atmosphere in which the chief ministers met in New Delhi on 22 February under the chairmanship of Prime Minister Shastri. In his thirty-minute address, the prime minister urged the chief ministers to rise above local political considerations and to speak fearlessly. This reminder of the key issue of national unity set the tone of the whole debate. The statements made by the chief ministers were free from acrimony and the plea of the chief ministers of non-Hindi speaking states for an amendment of the Official Languages Act was not seriously challenged by the other chief ministers.

The debate in the Congress Working Committee and at the conference of chief ministers continued on 23 February. The debate in the Congress Working Committee was still heated. Morarji Desai, Jagjivan Ram and Ram Subhag Singh were, even at this stage, opposed to any amendment of the law. An unscheduled additional session of the Congress Working Committee had to be convened to reach some broad conclusions. By late evening the Congress Working Committee and the chief ministers accepted the need for an amendment to the Official Languages Act and to the conduct of examinations for the all-India services not only in English and Hindi but also in all the other principal languages, the choice of specific language being left to each candidate. A proposal for the establishment of a quota system based on population, to ensure an equitable share in the services, was also accepted. (This dangerous and divisive proposal was eventually dropped.)

After the conclusion of the meeting of the Congress Working Committee and the chief ministers' conference, the chief minister of Tamil Nadu, M. Bhaktavatsalam, a key figure in this emotional issue, declared while still in New Delhi that the decisions which had been reached by consensus on the language question 'satisfy our requirements'. He added that the extremists on both sides would not be pleased but, as he said, 'extremists are hard to satisfy'.

Shastri made a report to parliament on 24 February on the decisions of the chief ministers' conference, in which he committed the government to a consideration of all 'practical issues' relating to the effective implementation of Nehru's assurances, including the amendment of the Official Languages Act. This was Shastri's first policy statement on the language question after the eruption of disturbances in the south. He had prepared his statement with very great care, knowing well how raw the nerves were on all sides. He made carefully balanced observations and, while clearly promising necessary action to remove the 'genuine difficulties' of the non-Hindi areas, asserted unequivocally that 'Hindi is the official language of the Union and English is to continue as an associate language.' There was no question of making any modifications in these basic decisions, on which alone a sound policy could be evolved.

Events thereafter proceeded without further ado. Parliament endorsed

the course of action proposed by Shastri and in due course a draft amendment to the Official Languages Act was prepared to give statutory basis to
Nehru's assurances. This was processed and the amendment was passed by
parliament in 1966. The English–Hindi controversy thus finally came to
be settled in this manner.

During the stormy days of the language crisis, the political pundits of
the English newspapers were forever commenting adversely on what they
considered to be the 'silence' of Shastri on the burning issue of the day.
They were suggesting an immediate announcement by the prime minister
proposing an amendment to the Official Languages Act in order to give
legal force to the previous prime minister's assurances. It did not occur to
these pundits that any such announcement by Shastri, without consultation with and getting the agreement of all sections of the people, was
certain to cause a backlash in the Hindi areas. Shastri was not a person to
be hustled. He maintained constant contact with local leaders who advised
restraint in the interest of national unity. His balanced intervention
produced the right result. Shastri's reputation as a sagacious and unflap-
pable leader now stood considerably enhanced.

### Vijay Lakshmi Pandit and Shastri

Though Shastri had come out of the language crisis with his reputation
unscathed, his detractors, most of them in the opposition, thought that
the beleaguered prime minister was now fair game. There were still food
shortages. Prices had not been controlled. The language problem had not
been dealt with decisively at its early stage. This is what the critics said,
and this was material enough for them. There was a certain feeling of
unease about the general situation in the country, and on this Shastri's
opponents built up their anti-government case.

To the surprise of many, the most piercing attack came not from the
opposition but from an important member of the Congress Party itself—
Nehru's sister, Vijay Lakshmi Pandit. She had just been elected to the Lok
Sabha from Nehru's constituency in Allahabad district. In her maiden
speech in parliament on 24 March 1965, she strove to make a deep impact.
Intervening in the general debate on the budget which had been presented
to the house by the finance minister, she said: 'In spite of Finance Minister's
attempts, wealth is accumulating in the wrong hands. Men are deteriorating and society has become decadent.' This, according to her, was 'the root
cause of more than half the problems that we face.' She had a medicine
for this disease. 'We have to do something about lifting up the individual,
we have to do something about re-imposing standards by which individuals

and events could be judged and we must stop this canker that is growing up in our midst.' Quite a few nodded assent. She was encouraged and delivered some more homilies. Then she declared: 'What is needed is that spark which has not been given us yet. Today we are waiting for the Government to ignite that spark.' She gave her own analysis of the prevailing situation. 'One reason for this is a sense of indecision that has crept into this country. People are not making firm decisions anywhere.' At this point she paused for a moment, glanced at the prime minister who was sitting in the house listening to her speech impassively, and calling up some well-coined and quotable phrases, continued: 'What do we see? Nothing but rocks ahead . . . The road ahead of us is strewn with rocks. From Kerala to Kashmir, from Sheikh Abdullah to Vietnam, there are no decisions. We are becoming the prisoners of our indecision.'

Vijay Lakshmi Pandit was not just being critical. She offered a solution: 'I believe that socialism is the only road that can take India out of this situation into the promised land.' For this she did not get the kind of applause she might have expected, because her credentials to being a true socialist were not quite impeccable. Undaunted, she returned to the charge. 'Why is the government afraid?' she asked. 'What is the government afraid of?' Finally, she offered support to the prime minister with a small 'but' thrown in: 'I would end', she said, 'with the plea to the prime minister and his colleagues that they should move forward with resolution to the completion of that task and assure them that we would walk behind them with faith and with loyalty. But—and there is a 'but'—there must be no compromise with principles, for only in this way shall we see the dawn of a new day.'

Vijay Lakshmi Pandit's attack was aimed clearly at Shastri personally. From my seat in the official gallery, I was looking alternately at the prime minister and at Vijay Lakshmi Pandit. The lady spoke with relish and members of the opposition were particularly delighted that an important Congress Party member was attacking, on the floor of the house, the prime minister. Vijay Lakshmi Pandit was obviously disappointed by Shastri's nine months in office.

Shastri, who had listened to the entire speech without the slightest expression of annoyance or disapproval, went back to his office in Parliament House after Vijay Lakshmi Pandit had finished. She followed him and went into his office. After a few minutes, she came out and went away. I then entered the prime minister's office and saw him looking at some files. I did not distract him with questions. But the prime minister guessed what was going through my mind. He said: 'She came to ask whether she had said anything which she should not have. I told her that this was a matter for her own judgment. *Aap ne jo theek samjha woh kaha.'* (You said what you thought was right.) I was struck again by Shastri's quiet but formidable self-possession. He had just faced a public onslaught on his credibility from an unexpected quarter; yet he had taken the incident with his usual equanimity.

Later, after the Indo-Pak war, when Shastri became a national hero, Vijay Lakshmi Pandit graciously changed her opinion and praised Shastri's decisive leadership.

### FOREIGN AFFAIRS

Apart from his visit to Nepal, Shastri's experience in foreign affairs had been small. But it was not as if he had no views of his own. He had frequently listened to Nehru's masterly enunciation of foreign policy issues and had kept himself abreast of developments. As minister without portfolio he had been formally in charge of the work of the external affairs ministry, as a part of his responsibilities to assist Nehru. Thus he was by no means a greenhorn in foreign affairs when he became prime minister. Initially, he retained the external affairs portfolio, and although after a few weeks he appointed Sardar Swaran Singh as external affairs minister, Shastri continued to maintain close personal touch with foreign affairs.

The fundamental tenets of India's foreign policy—non-alignment and peaceful coexistence—had been laid by Nehru and had received enthusiastic national support as well as international acclaim. This policy was in complete accord with Shastri's own view and temperament.

In Shastri's implementation of this policy there was, however, a distinct shift in emphasis. During Nehru's days, India's foreign policy had four principal components: (i) non-involvement in any military bloc or alliance with a view to maintaining total independence of approach to international issues; (ii) full solidarity with dependent peoples and newly emerging developing countries; (iii) strong friendship with the Soviet Union; and (iv) an attitude towards the Western countries which oscillated between occasional warmth based on common adherence to democratic values and frequent criticism of policies and actions which were seen as being hostile to the aspirations of the poor nations.

The result was that in the West India was seen as 'nonaligned and neutral on the other side'. Shastri was in full support of the first three components but as regards the fourth he wanted to develop closer relations with the West in the larger interests of India, without diluting India's friendship with the Soviet Union. This was noted in the West and had an effect on the approach of Western countries, especially the USA. For example when, at a later date, Shastri intervened in the global debate on Vietnam and supported certain proposals formulated by some non-aligned countries for the stoppage of US bombing as well as other steps towards a peaceful resolution of this conflict, President Johnson, who had a very raw nerve on the Vietnam question, welcomed India's role and conveyed a request through Governor Harriman to Shastri to intercede with Prime Minister Kosygin of the USSR on this issue in Tashkent. The following two letters, one dated 4 January 1968 from President Johnson to Prime Minister Shastri and the other dated 6 January 1968, written by Prime Minister Shastri from Tashkent to President Johnson, bring out clearly the relationship which had developed between the US president and the Indian prime minister.

THE WHITE HOUSE, WASHINGTON
January 4, 1966

Dear Mr Prime Minister:

I am very pleased that you and Mrs Shastri will visit Washington early in February and am looking forward with much anticipation to meeting you both then. Your visit comes at a most appropriate moment in the history of our two countries and will give us a valuable opportunity to get to know each other and learn more about the problems we both face. Our two countries have much in common, and we shall have much to discuss.

Secretary Freeman and I were pleased with our discussions about your short and long term agricultural problems with Food Minister Subramaniam. While firm commitments were neither asked nor given, he has enhanced our confidence in your determination to cope not only with India's grave agricultural difficulties but with its larger development needs. We are glad that you sent him here.

I should also like to take this occasion to thank you for your thoughtful message at the time of my recent illness. I do appreciate your kind wishes and warm expression of concern.

Mrs Johnson joins me in sending season's greetings to you and Mrs Shastri.

Sincerely,
Signed (Lyndon B. Johnson)


His Excellency
Lal Bahadur Shastri
Prime Minister of India,
New Delhi, India.

Tashkent,
January 6, 1966

Dear Mr President,

1) I was happy to get your message which was conveyed to me by your Embassy in New Delhi just after Christmas. Minister Subramaniam told me about the warmth of the reception he had in Washington and of the generous offer of additional help to meet the critical shortage of foodgrains which we in India are facing due to the extremely poor monsoons that we had last year. We are doing everything possible to mobilize whatever assistance we can get from other countries, so that the entire burden does not fall upon you.

2) Ambassador Harriman saw me in Delhi on the eve of my departure for Tashkent. I am greatly impressed by the determined effort which you are making to bring about peace in Vietnam. Ambassador Harriman recognized that our own relationship with Hanoi was not such as to enable us to make a positive contribution by making any direct approaches to the Government of North Vietnam. He was, however, anxious that I could speak to Mr Kosygin and I had a talk with him on the subject last night.

3) Mr Kosygin's attitude was not negative. He emphasized, however, that the important thing was to find a basis for talks which was acceptable to Hanoi also and he welcomed the approach which Ambassador Harriman had made to the Government of Poland. He also indicated that the visit of Shelepin to Hanoi was intended to help the cause of peace.

4) My talks with President AYUB have just started. We are facing many difficult issues. I am hoping that both of us would subscribe to the principle of not having recourse to force for resolving them and I feel that once this has come about, there will be a different atmosphere in which it will be easier to resolve and reconcile our differences.

5) My wife and I are looking forward to our visit to the USA. I hope that even before that, there will be substantial progress towards lowering of tensions in Asia.

6) May I once again express my deep appreciation for the timely and generous help you have offered in dealing with our food problem? With warm personal regards,

Yours sincerely
LAL BAHADUR

The President
The White House,
Washington DC.[10]

This was the last letter signed by Lal Bahadur Shastri as prime minister of India. Johnson was impressed by Shastri's intervening personally with Kosygin about Vietnam and writing about it from Tashkent, despite his preoccupations with the conference. Apparently Johnson kept this letter on his table in the White House for some time and showed it to visitors.

Chronologically, Shastri began his engagement in world affairs when he stepped out of India on 2 October 1964 to attend a conference of heads of state and government of non-aligned countries in Cairo. There he was received by President Nasser of Egypt. In his address at the conference, Shastri paid tribute to his predecessor, Nehru, one of the founding fathers of the non-aligned movement, and recalled Mahatma Gandhi's role as the leader of India's freedom struggle. He proposed a positive programme for the furtherance of peace, comprising the following five elements: (i) nuclear disarmament; (ii) peaceful settlement of border disputes; (iii) freedom from foreign domination, aggression, subversion and racial discrimination; (iv) acceleration of economic development through international co-operation; and (v) full support for the United Nations and its programme for peace and development. Shastri's proposals were welcomed and supported.

It was at this conference that he made his first acquaintance with numerous world leaders, particularly Nasser of Egypt, Tito of Yugoslavia, Soekarno of Indonesia, and Mrs Sirimavo Bandaranaike, of Ceylon. His humility and dignity won him respect. But it was after the conference was over that he was to have a significant meeting.

It was Shastri himself who had taken the initiative of proposing that he meet President Ayub in Pakistan on his way back from Cairo. Ayub had readily agreed and invited Shastri to visit Karachi. They met on 12 October 1964 for luncheon and discussions. This was their first meeting and each was sizing up the other. After the meeting, Shastri decided to pursue the path of peace. Ayub—or more specifically Pakistan's Foreign Minister Bhutto—had however decided to plan an invasion of India. But of that later.

Meanwhile, to improve India's relations with neighbouring countries, Shastri deputed his foreign minister, Sardar Swaran Singh, to visit Afghanistan, Nepal, Burma and Ceylon. Relations between India and Ceylon had not been on an even keel because of the problem of 975,000 stateless persons of Indian origin living in Ceylon. Despite sporadic efforts during the preceding twenty-five years, no solution had been found to this major irritant in Indo-Ceylonese relations. Shastri decided that a new effort should be made to find a just and equitable solution. He discussed the matter briefly with Mrs Bandaranaike when he met her in Cairo, followed this up by asking Swaran Singh to visit Ceylon, and on receiving a positive report from Swaran Singh invited the Ceylonese prime minister to visit India. She accepted this invitation and arrived in New Delhi on 22 October 1964. After a week of discussions an agreement was reached on 29 October, bringing to a happy conclusion an old problem. The two prime ministers agreed that out of the 975,000 persons involved, Ceylon would accept 300,000 as citizens of Ceylon and India would accept 525,000 as Indian citizens. The status of the remaining 150,000 was to be determined later. It was agreed further that the admission of 300,000 to Ceylonese citizenship and the repatriation of 525,000 to India should be spread over a period of fifteen years and that the two processes should keep pace with one another.

Shastri's first visit to the Western world took place early in December 1964. At the invitation of Prime Minister Harold Wilson of the United Kingdom, Shastri arrived in London on a cold winter day, 3 December, wearing his usual winter dress—dhoti, kurta, button-up coat and cap—all in khadi. The government, the people and the press were all keen to see and hear India's new prime minister. To Shastri the audience did not require any change in style or approach. He was self-confident, dignified and unassuming in London, as in India. His first exposure to the British took place on 4 December, when he met leaders of business and industry at a reception organised by the British Federation of Industries. In his address, Shastri explained India's economic problems and outlined the policies which his government was following to deal with them. Later he answered questions put to him by industrialists and bankers. At the end, Sir Peter Runge, president of the British Federation of Industries, observed that a remarkable performance by Shastri in clearing the doubts of Britain's top industrialists had won India and its government 'devoted and long-life' friends among bankers, investors and giants of business and industry in the United Kingdom. 'It was not any extraordinary eloquence or brilliance which won the top industrial brass of Britain,' commented V.R. Bhatt, correspondent of *The Hindustan Times*. 'It was Shastri's directness, frankness and pragmatism. He spoke the language which they understood and appreciated. He did not expound the philosophy or the theory of Indian socialistic approach or ideals. He spoke of India's problems of food, foreign exchange and population and her plans to surmount them by proper priorities and practical methods.' Refusing to be flapped by probing questions about India's apparently desperate food situation, Shastri reassuringly outlined the measures he was implementing to deal with the problem. Shastri also assured the audience that there would be no change in the Indian patent law. For possible British investors, this was good news.

Only one personal question was asked, and this related to the story that as a boy he swam the Ganga every day on his way to school. He was clearly amused by this reference to a popular fable about him, and with a smile replied that he had swum the Ganga only once because he had no money to pay for the ferry, and that this had not been a habit.

In his concluding remarks Shastri expressed his appreciation for British technology and investments, which had gone into the steel plant at Durgapur, the heavy electrical project at Bhopal, and into oil refineries and heavy engineering works in various places. These, he said, were the symbols of a new and enduring relationship between the United Kingdom and India.

Shastri's talks with Harold Wilson and other ministers, which concluded on 5 December, were equally successful. Shastri had come to the United Kingdom to get acquainted with the country and its political and industrial leaders. He had not come to ask for any specific aid. But as a result of his discussions, and in response no doubt to his pragmatism and to the confidence he generated, it became apparent that Britain felt interested in playing a greater role in India's development plans.

An important question which came up was India's nuclear policy. Shastri explained that India's policy of limiting nuclear energy to peaceful purposes only was under intense public pressure, especially after the Chinese nuclear explosion. India would stick to that policy, he said, adding a significant qualification—'just at present'. When pressed for his support to the policy of non-proliferation Shastri countered by suggesting to Prime Minister Wilson that the big nuclear powers—the USA, the USSR, the UK, and France—should give the highest priority to total nuclear disarmament. While this was being pursued, Shastri suggested, these nuclear powers should together try to work out, through the forum of the United Nations, a global nuclear guarantee for all non-nuclear countries, whether they were non-aligned like India, neutral like Sweden, or allied like Canada. If this were done, he said, it might be possible to end nuclear proliferation. This was not a request for a nuclear umbrella for India. Wilson welcomed the idea and indicated that he might talk it over during his forthcoming meeting with Johnson.

The British press hailed Shastri's visit as an unqualified success. *The Observer* printed a large photograph of Shastri dressed in white dhoti and kurta, describing him 'neat as a snowdrop'. There was only one thing that Shastri, characteristically, did not 'achieve' in London: he visited no shops and bought nothing.

The next foreign mission came in May 1965. This was a visit to the Soviet Union, then one of the two superpowers and a close friend of India. Politically this was an extremely important visit. The left wing in India had already grown apprehensive that Shastri's 'middle of the road' stance might dilute the warmth of Indo-Soviet friendship, which had been built up to ecstatic heights by Nehru. Other sections of political leadership in India were concerned about the rapprochement between the Soviet Union and Pakistan which had begun to take shape even during the final two years of Nehru's life. India-Pakistan-USSR relations had become even more important because of the recent Pakistani incursion into the Rann of Kutch. Shastri's visit to the USSR was watched with keen interest also by non-aligned countries, who were interested in India remaining a pillar of the non-aligned movement. Western countries were anxious to see whether the close Indo-Soviet friendship of the Nehru era would continue unabated or whether India under Shastri would take a more evenly non-aligned position between the two power blocs.

When Shastri arrived in Moscow on 12 May 1965 he was received by the prime minister of the USSR, A. Kosygin. But the welcome accorded him was not effusive. At the banquet in the evening both prime ministers reiterated their well-known positions on world affairs and both referred to the warmth of Indo-Soviet friendship. The policy of non-alignment was especially praised by Kosygin.

Formal talks between Shastri and Kosygin began at the Kremlin in the morning of 13 May. The talks were amiable and there was an identity of views on almost all issues. But there was nothing in the talks to set Moscow on fire. At the luncheon at the Indian embassy which followed the talks, the USSR prime minister was accompanied by Alexander Shelepin, deputy chairman of the USSR council of ministers, a senior party leader Polyansky, and the deputy prime minister K.T. Mazurov. The respective speeches at the luncheon more or less followed the lines of the speeches at the banquet the previous evening. There was, however, a noticeable difference in the nuances the two sides used in their diplomatically worded references to China and Pakistan. The USSR did not express direct criticism of either of the two countries.

After this initial round of talks, the overall impression was that the Soviet side was being diplomatically correct, and to a certain extent friendly, but the kind of warmth which might normally have been expected at a summit meeting between India and the USSR was not noticeable. Possibly there was some question in the mind of Russian leaders about the new prime minister of India to which they had not yet found an answer.

And then came the evening of 13 May, which changed the entire atmosphere as if by magic to visible warmth and effusive cordiality. Shastri and his party were invited to a Soviet ballet at the Bolshoi Theatre. When Shastri, accompanied by Kosygin, entered the special box for state guests, the entire audience accorded a standing ovation to Shastri: this was the usual custom to welcome heads of government.

While Shastri was watching the ballet, his mind was riveted on the ongoing talks which, to say the least, had not yet 'taken off'. He felt that he himself had to take some new initiative and decided he should now do what he was best at—one-to-one conversation with Kosygin, without aides. As soon as the recess commenced, he suggested to Kosygin that they might use the time for personal talks (with the assistance of interpreters). Kosygin agreed and their conversation stretched beyond the recess. This dialogue seemed to work a complete transformation in Kosygin. On emerging from his private talk, he was perceptibly cheerful and even deferential to Shastri.

I had accompanied the prime minister to the ballet and witnessed from a distance the two leaders talking to each other with evident sincerity. When, after the performance, Shastri returned to his dacha in the outskirts of Moscow, I asked him how things had gone. He replied that he had explained to Kosygin that the fundamental objective of his economic policy was to promote the welfare of the masses in India by taking practical steps to meet their basic needs for food, clothing and shelter. Shastri had expressed anguish about India's dependence on foreign countries for substantial quantities of foodgrains. It was essential, he had told Kosygin, that India should become self-sufficient in food as soon as possible and that, with this end in view, agriculture had to be given the highest priority, even ahead of heavy industry. Shastri had added that he wanted to encourage quick-yielding projects, including consumer industries, so that the life of the current generation be lifted above the prevailing level of abysmal and degrading poverty. This to him was the essence of socialism, Indian in conception. Shastri also stated that he was neither a leftist nor a rightist, that he was not doctrinaire, that his approach was entirely pragmatic. The frankness, as usual, struck a chord in the listener.

On foreign policy, Shastri said unambiguously that he stood firmly for non-alignment. He expressed his gratitude for the support which had been extended to India by the Soviet Union through thick and thin. The continuing help of the Soviet Union was especially important for India's accelerated economic development and for the enhancement of India's defence capability. Shastri had added that he wanted to promote friendly relations with all countries including Pakistan. He had also indicated that he would endeavour to seek friendly ties with the USA, but that there was no question of India departing from independence in foreign policy matters. It seemed that as a result of this personal talk the doubts aroused in the Soviet government by tendentious signals from the extreme left in India had been dispelled. From this time Shastri and Kosygin became close personal friends, and their friendship lasted till the final moment of Shastri's life.

Shastri's talks the following day with Leonid Brezhnev, first secretary of the Soviet Communist Party, went extremely well, and so did Shastri's visit to Leningrad, Kiev and Tashkent. Shastri visited Lenin's mausoleum, and he went on to visit Lenin's apartment in the Kremlin. I noticed that on entering he removed his cap from his head as a mark of respect to Lenin, whom he regarded as the greatest revolutionary the world had ever known. Kosygin accompanied Shastri everywhere and, as a touching gesture of respect, ate vegetarian food when sitting next to him at lunch or dinner. So, in the end, Shastri's visit to the Soviet Union, which had begun with a question mark, ended with triumph.

In his report to parliament on 16 August 1965 Shastri spoke in terms of complete agreement with the Soviet Union on most of the important international issues of the day. The Soviet leaders had appreciated India's position on the question of Kutch but had urged a peaceful solution; they had reaffirmed their traditional stand on Kashmir. 'My visit to the Soviet Union,' concluded Shastri, 'has surely deepened the friendship and co-operation between India and the Soviet Union.'

The visit to the USSR on a note of unexpectedly high success, coupled with similar success in the United Kingdom, added an international dimension to the growing image of Shastri. He now began to be seen as a political leader in the international arena, equally acceptable to the West and the East, and as a person with whom (to use a famous phrase by Margaret Thatcher) both power blocs 'could do business.'

Shastri visited Nepal from 23 to 25 April 1965. He had already established warm relations with the king of Nepal, as well as with the prime minister of that country, during his first visit to Nepal. This second visit, now as prime minister, went off well. Then, Shastri visited Canada from 10 to 14 June 1965. This visit, especially his personal talks with Prime Minister Lester Pearson, renewed and strengthened ties. Shastri's visit to Yugoslavia in July 1965 was pleasant and memorable. President Josip Broz Tito received Shastri with warmth and effusion. Cordial talks in Belgrade were followed by a trip to Tito's island resort in Brioni. Tito was a world statesman, renowned for his fearless independence and wisdom. He agreed with Shastri that India should seek equally close and friendly relations with both superpowers. While their lifestyles were different, Shastri and Tito became good friends.

Shastri met several foreign heads of state and heads of government during their visits to India. Among these dignitaries were the prime minister of Mauritius S. Ramgoolam; the prime minister of Afghanistan Mohammad Yusuf; the chairman of the Revolutionary Council of the Union of Burma General Ne Win; the president of the Republic of Finland Urho Kaleva Kekkonen; the prime minister of France M. Pompidou; the prime minister of the Czechoslovak Socialist Republic, Jozef Lenart; the prime minister of Uganda, A. Milton Obote; and the king of Nepal.

There remained only Pakistan.

# Chapter 11

# India's Relations with Pakistan

Ever since Partition in 1947 India and Pakistan have had a hostile relationship. They have fought three wars, the first in 1947–8, the second in 1965, and the third in 1971; and no one knows when another war will break out. Reason and wisdom demand that these two neighbouring countries live together peacefully. But that millennium is nowhere in sight. The fundamental problem between them is deeply rooted and it is necessary to explain how this problem is seen by Pakistan and by India.

Pakistan asserts that there is only one problem—Kashmir—which bedevils the relations between India and Pakistan. Once this problem has been resolved to Pakistan's satisfaction, all will be well. And the only solution to this problem is a plebiscite in Kashmir to enable the people of that state to decide whether they wish to be with Pakistan or with India. Pakistan's faith in the democratic process of plebiscite is buttressed by the belief that by appealing in the name of Islam, Pakistan will win the vote because the majority in Kashmir consists of Muslims.

The fact that the princely state of Jammu and Kashmir acceded to India in conformity with a constitutional process enacted by the British parliament on the basis of a prior acceptance by both sides, and that as a result the state of Jammu and Kashmir became a part of India, is in Pakistan's opinion no more than a legal quibble. India had in any case offered a plebiscite to ascertain the wishes of the people on the question of accession and therefore India must fulfil its commitment. The fact that (i) India had made this offer in 1948 conditional upon the vacation of aggression by Pakistan, who had without legal right occupied a large part of the territory of this state, and (ii) that this aggression has not been ended to this day despite an injunction to the same effect from the United Nations Security Council, is dismissed by Pakistan as irrelevant. According to Pakistan, peace between India and Pakistan can be secured only after a 'satisfactory' solution of the Kashmir question.

India believes that the real problem is the 'two nation' theory propounded by Mohammad Ali Jinnah, which eventually formed the basis for the partition of India and the establishment of Pakistan. Jinnah contended that Hindus and Muslims constituted two different nations. To him all talk of the essential unity of various religions was hypocritical nonsense. According to him, what existed in real life was 'antagonism', not 'unity'. The idea that Muslims had not merely a separate religious identity but also a corresponding political identity had been accepted and indeed promoted by the British when they introduced a communal electorate in India under the Minto-Morley Reforms of 1909. At that time separate voting lists were established for Muslim voters, who alone could vote in the constituencies reserved for Muslim candidates. From then on the concept of Muslims constituting a separate political group gained strength in the minds of Muslims, with the active encouragement of the ruling power. When, after the end of the Second World War in 1945, the transfer of power to Indians became a near possibility, Jinnah pursued his 'two nation' theory with unremitting passion. Pakistan was thus founded on the basis of Jinnah's 'two nation' theory, in which antagonism between Muslims and Hindus was inherent.

India did not accept the 'two nation' theory. It accepted Partition as a political necessity to gain freedom. Whereas Pakistan became a Muslim theocracy, India continued as a secular democracy. It does not suit Pakistan's purpose to acknowledge that India has a larger Muslim population than the total Muslim population of Pakistan and that this large Muslim population (more than 100 million) has the same rights of citizenship as all other Indians.

During the years since Partition, India has settled down as a functioning secular democracy. No elective office in India is reserved for a specific community. India has gone through nine general elections on the basis of universal suffrage. India has established the rule of law with an independent judiciary. India has a free and vibrant press.

Let us now consider the case of Kashmir in the political context just described. Prior to the British withdrawal from India, there were two distinct categories of political entities. The first were the provinces of what was called British India with a central government in New Delhi functioning under the Government of India Act of 1935, enacted by the British parliament, delegating considerable powers of self-governance to Indians. The second category of political entities comprised the princely states over which the British Crown exercised 'suzerainty' under past agreements and treaties.

Under The Indian Independence Act 1947, enacted by the British parliament, all power for the governance of the territories of British India was transferred from 15 August 1947 to the two succeeding dominions namely India and Pakistan.

Under Section 7(i)(b) of the same act, the 'suzerainty' of the British Crown over the princely Indian states and all treaty obligations, lapsed with effect from the same appointed date, namely 15 August 1947. The complete power of governance in each princely state reverted solely to the ruler of that state. The right of each princely state to accede to India or to Pakistan or to remain unattached to either also became vested solely in the ruler of each state. This arrangement was explicitly accepted by the leaders of India and Pakistan and had the same legal and constitutional backing as the dominions of India and Pakistan had for their establishment and future governance, namely The Indian Independence Act 1947 read with the Government of India Act, 1935.

Many rulers of Indian states decided to accede to the dominions of their choice by executing an Instrument of Accession. There was no clause for 'temporary' or 'provisional' accession. If a ruler decided to accede, the accession of his state to the dominion of his choice was to be final and irrevocable after the Instrument of Accession had been accepted by the governor-general. And there was no clause for any 'provisional' acceptance of an Instrument of Accession. The governor-general could accept or reject, but if he accepted an Instrument of Accession, the accession of the state was full and final as from the moment of such acceptance. And from that moment, the territory of the acceding princely state became an integral and constitutional part of the dominion concerned for ever and ever. There was no legal provision for a ruler to take his state out of the state of the dominion concerned. The procedure for the separation of the territory of an 'acceded' state would be the same as for the cession of any other part of the territory of the dominion. In the case of India which has a written constitution, such cession can be given effect to only by an amendment of the constitution by parliament.

As regards Kashmir, on 15 August 1947 the ruler of Jammu and Kashmir, the maharaja, became free to make a decision about the future of his state. He decided to wait for some time. The Government of India kept clearly away from the maharaja, leaving him free to decide for himself. The maharaja was a Hindu and the majority of the population of his state was Muslim. This caused the maharaja to think carefully about the future and to make no hasty decision. Pakistan made overtures but the maharaja stood still, pondering the situation. Suddenly, in October 1947, Pakistan let loose a large number of armed raiders, including regular soldiers in plain clothes, into the territory of the state. These pillaged and plundered at will. Even the maharaja's life was threatened, but he managed to escape to a safe resort. Jinnah's purpose was to browbeat him into accession to Pakistan, but he failed. The maharaja turned to India for help in dealing with the armed raiders.

The following is an excerpt from the letter dated 26 October 1947 which Maharaja Hari Singh, ruler of the state of Jammu and Kashmir, addressed to the governor-general of India, Lord Mountbatten:

> Afridis, soldiers in plain clothes, and desperadoes with modern weapons have been allowed to infiltrate into the State, at first in the Poonch area, then from Sialkot and finally in a mass in the area adjoining Hazara District on the Ramkote side. The result has been that the limited number of troops at the disposal of the State had to be dispersed and thus had to face the enemy at several points simultaneously, so that it has become difficult to stop the wanton destruction of life and property and the looting of the Mahura Power House, which supplies electric current to the whole of Srinagar and which has been burnt. The number of women who have been kidnapped and raped makes my heart bleed. The wild forces thus let loose on the State are marching on with the aim of capturing Srinagar, the summer capital of my Government, as a first step to overrunning the whole State. The mass infiltration of tribesmen drawn from distant areas of the North-West Frontier Province, coming regularly in motor trucks, using the Mansehra Muzaffarabad road and fully armed with up-to-date weapons, cannot possibly be done without the knowledge of the Provincial Government of the North-West Frontier Province and the Government of Pakistan. In spite of repeated appeals made by my government, no attempt has been made to check these raiders or to stop them from coming into my State. In fact, both the radio and the press of Pakistan have reported these occurrences. The Pakistan Radio even put out the story that a provisional government has been set up in Kashmir. The people of my state, both Muslims and non-Muslims, generally have taken no part at all.
>
> With the conditions obtaining at present in my state and the great emergency of the situation as it exists, I have no option but to ask for help from the Indian Dominion. Naturally they cannot send the help asked for by me without my state acceding to the Dominion of India. I have accordingly decided to do so, and I attach the instrument of accession for acceptance by your government. The other alternative is to leave my state and the people to freebooters. On this basis no civilised government can exist or be maintained. This alternative I will never allow to happen so long as I am the ruler of the state and I have life to defend my country.[1]

The Instrument of Accession, dated 26 October 1947,[2] sent by the maharaja was in proper form and style. This was an instrument of final accession to the Dominion of India and there was nothing provisional about it.

The Instrument of Accession was accepted clearly and unconditionally by the governor-general of India on 27 October 1947. The complete text of this Instrument of Acceptance is reproduced below:

ACCEPTANCE OF INSTRUMENT OF ACCESSION OF JAMMU AND KASHMIR STATE BY THE GOVERNOR-GENERAL OF INDIA

I do hereby accept this Instrument of Accession.
Dated this twenty-seventh day of October, nineteen hundred and forty-seven.

Mountbatten of Burma
Governor-General of India.

Thus on the twenty-seventh day of October, nineteen hundred and forty-seven, in complete accordance and conformity with the applicable statutory provisions of the British parliamentary enactments transferring power to India, namely The Indian Independence Act 1947 and the Government of India Act 1935, as adapted by the governor-general in exercise of his powers under Section 9 of The Indian Independence Act 1947, the state of Jammu and Kashmir became irrevocably an integral and constitutional part of India.

This is not 'legalistic quibbling', but a statement of the constitutional status of Jammu and Kashmir which is described in the Constitution of India as a state of the Union of India. This position can be altered only by an amendment of the Indian constitution by the Indian parliament in accordance with prescribed procedure. No subsequent comment or 'offer' by an officer of the executive branch of the government can detract from the binding constitutional position described.

Why then did Nehru refer this matter to the United Nations? In view of the emergency in Kashmir, he had accepted the immediate accession of Jammu and Kashmir to India. But he had made up his mind to seek a reaffirmation of this accession by a reference to the people. This was mentioned in Lord Mountbatten's letter of 27 October 1947, addressed to the maharaja in the following words:

In the circumstances mentioned by Your Highness, my government have decided to accept the accession of Kashmir State to the Dominion of India. In consistence with their policy that in the case of any state where the issue of accession has been the subject of dispute, the question of accession should be decided in accordance with the wishes of the people of the state, it is my government's wish that, as soon as law and order have been restored in Kashmir and its soil cleared of the invader, the question of the State's accession should be settled by a reference to the people.

The language and import of this letter are somewhat confusing. The first sentence affirms the acceptance of accession which had already been 'settled' in accordance with the applicable statutes. How could it be said in the same letter that 'the question of the State's accession should be settled by a reference to the people.' It would be reasonable to assume that what Lord Mountbatten wanted to convey was the wish of the government to seek 'reaffirmation' by a reference to the people. The implication would then have been that if such 'reaffirmation' were available, this subject would then call for no further action. If, however, such were not the case, the government would then, in exercise of its sovereign authority, consider what further steps should be taken.

Mountbatten persuaded Nehru to refer the matter to the United Nations 'by arguing that the only alternative was a full-scale war.'[3] Vallabhbhai Patel was against this referral.[4] Mahatma Gandhi was also reluctant. But Nehru decided to follow the advice of Mountbatten. A comprehensive memorandum entitled 'Indian Complaint to the Security Council' was prepared and submitted by the permanent representative of India to the president of the Security Council on 1 January 1948. In this memorandum, full details were provided about the activities of the raiders, the devastation caused by them and the complicity of Pakistan. It was specifically mentioned that:

(1)  the invaders were being allowed transit through Pakistan territory
(2)  they were being allowed to use Pakistan territory as a base of operations
(3)  they included Pakistani nationals
(4)  they were drawing much of their military equipment, transportation and supplies (including petrol) from Pakistan, and
(5)  Pakistan's officers were training, guiding, and otherwise actively helping them.

The memorandum then conveyed the request of the Government of India to the Security Council 'to call upon Pakistan to put an end immediately to the giving of such assistance which is an act of aggression against India.'

The circumstances in which the accession of the state of Jammu and Kashmir was accepted by the Government of India were fully explained and it was emphasized that not only the ruler of the state but also Sheikh Mohammad Abdullah, the leader of the largest political organization of the people of the state, had strongly pressed the request. As a result of this accession, the state of Jammu and Kashmir had become an integral part of India.

Thereafter the following significant declaration was made in the memorandum:

> But, in order to avoid any possible suggestion that India had utilised the State's immediate peril for her own political advantage, the Government of India made it clear that once the soil of the State had been cleared of the invader and normal conditions restored, its people would be free to decide their future by the recognized democratic method of a plebiscite or referendum which, in order to ensure complete impartiality, might be held under international auspices.

The long memorandum of the Government of India was true and sincere in detail and demonstrated the straightforwardness of Jawaharlal Nehru. He meant what he had said, and if Pakistan had vacated the territory which it had unlawfully occupied and normal conditions had been restored, he would, without doubt, have gone through the procedure of a plebiscite or a referendum in Kashmir at that time. For this he had the backing and support of Sardar Patel.

Why then did the plebiscite openly pledged by India not take place? In making its pledge, India had stated that a plebiscite would be held as soon as the soil of the state had been cleared of the invader. The UN had also laid down that the first step was the withdrawal of Pakistani forces from the state of Jammu and Kashmir.

The resolution of the United Nations Commission for India and Pakistan (UNCIP) dated 13 August 1948 included the following specific provisions in this regard:

> A.1.  As the presence of troops of Pakistan in the territory of the State of Jammu and Kashmir constitutes a material change in the situation since it was represented by the Government of Pakistan before the Security Council, the Government of Pakistan agrees to withdraw its troops from that State.
>
> 2.  The Government of Pakistan will use its best endeavours to secure the withdrawal from the State of Jammu and Kashmir of tribesmen and Pakistan nationals not normally resident therein who have entered the State for the purpose of fighting.

Pakistan accepted this resolution but never complied with it. It was only after compliance with the preceding resolution by Pakistan that steps for the organization of a plebiscite under the supervision of a UN nominated plebiscite administrator were to be taken by India.

The key to the commencement of the plebiscite process was therefore in Pakistan's hands. All that Pakistan had to do was to withdraw its invading forces. It did not do so and thus frustrated the entire scheme. Pakistan was probably unsure of the result of the people's vote at that time.

Sheikh Abdullah was openly and firmly for secular India. So, on one pretext or another, Pakistan did not comply with the UN Security Council resolution. One third of the territory of the state of Jammu and Kashmir is still under Pakistan's unlawful occupation.

But the question was asked then and continues to be asked: was it wise or even necessary to go to the Security Council of the United Nations? The Security Council is not a supreme court of justice to give a verdict objectively and strictly on the merits of the case. It is a political body—an association of governments who are necessarily guided by their national interests, group loyalties, predilections and prejudices. To rush to such a world body with a matter of immense national importance which was totally within the jurisdiction of the country itself and within the competence of the national government and armed forces was, according to Nehru's critics, like extending an open invitation to powerful outside interests to meddle in India's affairs.

In the Security Council, the petitioner became virtually the accused. The representative of Pakistan solemnly denied any involvement with the raiders. Having absolved themselves in the Security Council of any blame, the Pakistanis went on the offensive, accusing India of aggressive designs on Pakistan.

After the first meeting of the Security Council convened to discuss India's complaint, the Pakistanis found themselves accepted in the UN forum as interested parties. Their involvement in the fighting in Kashmir gradually became more open. But as a result of the intervention of the Security Council, 'cease-fire' was secured with effect from 1 January 1949. A ceasefire line was also established in July 1949, which was meant to be respected by both sides.

From then on, the Security Council met on several occasions, passed several resolutions and sent several missions, but the position of both sides remained the same. Pakistan continued to insist on a plebiscite without taking the first step towards the plebiscite process, namely the vacation of invaded territories. Pakistan's intransigence on this question sounded, with the passage of time, the death-knell of the plebiscite idea. India continued to maintain that Jammu and Kashmir was an integral part of India and that India's sovereignty over that state was not negotiable. Thereafter, relations between the two neighbouring countries were continuously in a state of tension, just below boiling point, always threatening to explode. This was the situation when Shastri became prime minister in June 1964.

# Chapter 12

# India's Relations with the USA

While fighting the scourge of Nazism, the Allies, led by the United States of America, had declared their vision of a new world free from want and fear, founded on the concepts of liberty and justice. The withdrawal of British power from India in August 1947 was in consonance with that idealism. It would have been reasonable to expect that free India, wedded to Mahatma Gandhi's principles of truth and nonviolence and to Jawaharlal Nehru's vision of social justice and rule of law, would become the brightest jewel in the crown of this brave new world, supported and encouraged by democratic nations, especially the United States of America. And so it might well have been but for the emergence of two factors, one global, namely superpower rivalry, and the other related specifically to India, namely Kashmir.

Although the Allies had fought alongside the Soviet Union to defeat Hitler, the Soviet Union soon became a Communist empire under the ruthless dictatorship of Stalin. To the United States of America this meant a defeat of freedom and the spread of darkness. The Cold War soon developed between these two countries.

On Kashmir the USA took the view in the Security Council that 'the basic issue before the UN was the disposition of Kashmir, which was interwoven with a complex of religious feelings, national prestige, legal subtleties, and economic pressures.'[1] The legal aspect was important, but in the US view an 'agreement between the two nations for an enduring settlement of the dispute must be reached on broad political grounds.'[2]

The United States representative to the General Assembly, Ernest A. Gross,[3] suggested that India and Pakistan, both friends of the USA, should consider a settlement on the basis of the following principles:

> In the first place, a lasting political settlement must be an agreed settlement.
>
> Secondly, the Security Council will always welcome agreement of the parties which they themselves can reach on any theory that will settle the dispute which is consistent with the principles of the Charter.
>
> Thirdly, it is the role of the Security Council to assist the parties in seeking to reach agreement.

Fourthly, agreement most frequently is reached step by step through negotiation, and negotiation involves an element of compromise.

Finally, the Security Council should consider with care the views and the recommendations of its representative and indicate to him and the parties its views on the positions he has taken.[4]

These were unexceptionable principles in theory, but the practical problem was that the dispute which India had brought to the UN Security Council was not that of accession of Kashmir to India, which had been accomplished already, but that of invasion of Kashmir by tribesmen who had come through Pakistan territory. India found that while it had gone to the UN in good faith, it had not received fair treatment. The USA and UK representatives had, for all practical purposes, disregarded India's complaint. They had lost sight of the fact that India need not have come at all to the United Nations, as the country was powerful enough to defend the state and drive away the tribesmen. Pakistan denied any involvement, and any action which India might then have taken would have been against the invading tribesmen who, in any case, had no *locus standi* at all. They were freebooters, killing and raping like men from the wild.

The question might be asked as to why India proposed a plebiscite to ascertain the wishes of the people. Was it not self-evident that the majority Muslim population would opt for Pakistan? The answer is that the most important leader of the people of the state, Sheikh Mohammad Abdullah, a Muslim himself, was secular in outlook and was in favour of accession to India. In fact it was he who had decisively influenced the acceptance of Kashmir's accession to India by Mountbatten and Nehru. That would itself have been enough evidence of popular will for Kashmir's accession to India, but India wanted to be above suspicion. Hence the announcement of a plebiscite or referendum under international auspices.

The USA and the UK played a leading role in making Pakistan a partner in this enterprise, although Pakistan had no legal position *vis-à-vis* Kashmir. According to its own affirmation in the Security Council when the initial complaint by India was considered, Pakistan had no physical involvement or presence in Kashmir either. In these circumstances, by accepting Pakistan's contention that it had a part in the plebiscite process, the Security Council made it an India *versus* Pakistan question, with all its consequences.

If the USA and the UK had accepted the good faith of India and asked the Pakistan government not to meddle, there is not the slightest doubt that Nehru would, after the clearance of tribesmen, have conducted a free plebiscite under international auspices and implemented its result. At that point of time, the vote, in all probability, would have reaffirmed Kashmir's accession to India. But even if the vote had gone in favour of Pakistan, Nehru and Patel would have carried the country with them in parting with the state. What the Security Council did was to make Pakistan an aggrieved party and Kashmir an issue between the two countries, appointing itself as umpire. India took this as an unwarranted, unfair and hostile decision in which the USA and the UK had taken the leading part.

The role played by the United States in the Security Council had soured India's feelings and created a distance between the two countries. From time to time, the Security Council or a commission appointed by the council or a mediator dealt with the Kashmir question, but no acceptable solution was found.

In order to break the deadlock, Nehru offered directly to the then prime minister of Pakistan, Mohammad Ali, during the latter's visit to New Delhi in 1953, a plebiscite for the entire state of Jammu and Kashmir to be conducted under a plebiscite administrator to be appointed by the end of April 1954.[5]

While negotiations were under way between Nehru and Mohammad Ali, Pakistan turned to the United States for military alliance. The United States was looking for allies in Asia who could provide military bases and political support for the USA in its efforts to combat the expansion of Communism. The membership of such an anti-communist alliance carried with it the benefit of military assistance under the Military Alliance Programme (MAP) approved by the Congress as a part of its Mutual Security Legislation. Pakistan saw in this a great opportunity for realizing its ambition to neutralize India's relatively larger military power. Pakistan could join the Western alliance and then secure arms aid, which would in any case help by reducing the military imbalance between Pakistan and India. On 12 June 1952, Pakistan's ambassador to the United States declared publicly that his country was positively with the West: 'Do not count Pakistan as a neutralist nation of Asia. Our basic sympathies are strongly with the West.'[6]

In 1953, Dwight Eisenhower of the Republican Party became the thirty-fourth president of the United States. He appointed John Foster Dulles as his secretary of state. Both gave the highest priority in foreign policy to the containment of Communism. Military alliance with Pakistan was now a matter of urgency. In February 1954, a decision for the conclusion of such an alliance between the United States and Pakistan was announced in both countries.

Eisenhower took the precaution of writing to Nehru on 24 February 1954, assuring him that 'the action is not directed in any way against India.' Eisenhower assured Nehru that military aid given to Pakistan would not be used against India. He added further that this development did not in any way affect US relations with India and that he was recommending to the Congress the continuance of US economic and technical aid to India.[7]

The Pakistanis were jubilant. This was their master stroke. As far as they were concerned, US military aid would place them in a much better military position to deal with India. Eisenhower had assured Nehru that if India decided to ask for military aid under US mutual security legislation, India's request would receive the most sympathetic consideration. But there was no question of India joining any 'mutual security' arrangement and the question of seeking military aid on this basis just did not arise.

This development created a new situation. The Cold War between the two superpowers was now on India's doorstep. With Pakistan within the Western military alliance, the possibility of a peaceful resolution of mutual problems between India and Pakistan was now jeopardized. On 1 March 1954 Nehru announced in parliament:

> The military aid being given by the United States to Pakistan is a form of intervention in these problems which is likely to have more far-reaching results than the previous types of intervention.[8]

In the United States many people understood that Pakistan had joined the military alliance to fight India and not Communism. Senator William J. Fulbright of Arkansas made his views clear:

> I think the decision to supply arms to Pakistan is an unfortunate mistake. I have the greatest respect for the people of Pakistan, as I do for the people of India. Their mutual difficulties have threatened war, so we are not unaware of the tension between them and therefore should have been extremely careful in our relations with them . . . I disapprove of this move and I wish the record to show clearly my disapproval, because in the future when the results of this policy are evident to all I want to be clear where the responsibility rests.[9]

Somewhat later an American correspondent, A.T. Steele, after a visit to Pakistan, wrote the following in the *New York Herald Tribune* (7 June 1956): 'The average Pakistani thinks very little about the Communist threat, if he thinks at all. His hostility is towards India, rather than the Soviet Union. And he assumes that in the event of a show-down with India, the American supplies will be drawn upon.' Democratic Congressman Cellar from New York was equally forthright. He disagreed with the US defence department assessment that 'a militarized Pakistan is essential in view of India's neutrality in the event of any Soviet invasion of South-East Asia.' After visiting India and Pakistan, Congressman Cellar expressed his impressions and views clearly: 'The Russian and/or Chinese Communists would cut through Pakistan like a hot knife through butter. Nehru and his Cabinet felt that in the event of that aid, they would have to match Pakistan's new military strength by an expansion of the Indian Army. This would greatly impede the social and economic programme that Nehru has in mind to advance the living standards of 400 million Indians. American aid of this character would be grist to the Communist propaganda mill.' Cellar was not against assistance to Pakistan but he believed that the US should provide economic rather than military aid. He added: 'We should maintain the friendship of both countries—Pakistan and India. We should help each country in every possible way. They are indeed worthy of our assistance but we should not help one at the expense of the other.'[10]

Ambassador Chester Bowles was equally direct in his opposition to the military pact with Pakistan: 'It is bad arithmetic to alienate 360 million Indians in order to aid 80 million Pakistanis who are split in two sections, divided by 1000 miles of Indian territory. Instead of adding to the stability of the subcontinent, this will create new tensions and suspicions and thus further contribute to insecurity.'[11]

The Press in India was also perturbed and incensed. *The Hindustan Times*, a strong supporter of the 'free world', expressed the feelings of the people of India: 'To drag Pakistan into the Middle East Defence Organisation will be to drag the whole of the Indian subcontinent into a war and no one can say that this is a matter which does not concern India. Any part of the territory of the Indo-Pakistan subcontinent cannot be dragged into military commitments elsewhere without India also being drawn into it.'[12] In an editorial in its issue dated 12 December 1953, the same paper commented: 'We cannot believe that the object of Washington is to alienate India from the US and weaken the forces of democracy in Asia . . . We cannot conceive of a more unfriendly act toward India than the conclusion of the proposed agreement by the US.'

Despite the well known strength of India's views, there were many political leaders, especially in the Republican Party, who favoured the pact with Pakistan. They were led by Vice-President Richard Nixon and the Senate Republican leader William Knowland. Senator Knowland advised Eisenhower to go ahead with the pact and not to worry unduly about India's objections. 'To withhold American aid because of the protest of neutralist India,' said the Senator, 'would be discouraging to those nations willing to stand up and be counted on the side of the free world . . . These nations might then think that it was better to play the game of Indian neutralism than to throw in their lot with the free nations.'[13]

The views of Vice-President Richard Nixon, Senator Knowland and others of the same mind prevailed, and the Mutual Defence Assistance Pact between the USA and Pakistan was signed in Karachi on 19 May 1954.

This then was the burning debate on the question of the US-Pakistan Military Alliance—an event which greatly affected the future conduct of India's foreign policy. Until that time, India was neutral and non-aligned. The arming of Pakistan, ostensibly for the purpose of combatting the spread of Communism in Asia, created in reality an enhanced threat to India from Pakistan. Surely what was evident to so many Americans would have been evident to Eisenhower also. Why then did he, an outstanding military leader himself, wedded to the freedom and stability of democratic nations such as India, approve this proposal? There was no feeling in India then, and there is none in retrospect even now, that Eisenhower was in any way hostile to India. His Vice-President Nixon was, but in the United States government it is the president who personally makes important decisions with the assistance of his White House staff. Eisenhower must therefore have felt convinced of the essential need for this step. Was he being advised by some foreign powers as well? The famous American political commentator Selig S. Harrison had a theory of his own:

> In a series of three articles published on August 10, August 24, and September 7, 1959, in the 'New Republic', Selig S. Harrison rightly narrated how and why the United States came to take the decision of granting military aid to Pakistan and later to set up the South East Asia Treaty Organisation which Pakistan joined as a member. According to him, the United States in taking up this policy decision was influenced by the opinion of certain prominent British officials that Pakistan should be groomed to fill the vacuum created by Britain's withdrawal from the subcontinent of India. Apart from the British influence, the desire of some influential Republicans to get tough with Nehru played an important role in shaping the policy. Selig S. Harrison concluded by saying that Vice-President Nixon 'urged this alliance (with Pakistan) not for its purported defence value against aggression but for the very reason Pakistan had sought the aid—as a counter force to the confirmed neutralism of Jawaharlal Nehru's India'. No wonder, if many Indians suspected as such.[14]

From 1954 onwards, during the entire period of General Eisenhower's presidency (upto 1961), Pakistan continued to receive substantial military aid in the shape of modern armour and aircraft for land and air warfare. Although Eisenhower had personally assured Nehru that no military aid supplied under the mutual security Military Assistance Programme could or would be used against India and that the US would ensure compliance with this condition, India knew that Pakistan did not worry about such niceties. India had therefore to prepare itself for the probability of Pakistan using its newly acquired military muscle against India. Thus the conclusion of the US–Pakistan Pact in 1954 compelled India to review its national priorities and to make a much bigger effort to augment the country's defence capability.

This was the moment when the USSR warmed up to India. While in the earlier period the representatives of the USSR took a detached view in the Security Council debates on the Kashmir issue, hereafter they began to give open support to India's point of view. The result was a growing India–USSR friendship based on principles of mutual benefit, coexistence and non-interference in each other's internal affairs. The USSR began to support openly India's position that Kashmir was a national problem of India as the state of Jammu and Kashmir was an integral part of India. During their visit to India in December 1955, Soviet Premier Bulganin and the first secretary of the Communist Party of the Soviet Union, Khrushchev, affirmed this unequivocal support publicly. The USSR's veto was available and was used to ensure that the Security Council did not pass any further resolutions on Kashmir which were unacceptable to India.

Nehru now launched himself on the world stage as the promoter and leader of non-alignment. Meetings of non-aligned nations, however, became a platform for diatribes against the imperialist West, and the impression grew that some members of this group were pro-Soviet 'surrogates' who were promoting the Soviet view of the world and hostility towards the West. Nehru was now playing the leading role on the world stage. With Nasser of Egypt and Tito of Yugoslavia, he formed the leading triumvirate of third world countries. During the Suez crisis of 1956 Nehru gave strong support to Egypt, and this resulted in a further alienation from the Western countries. In the Korean, Cambodian and Vietnam crises India played what some countries thought was a 'larger than life' role.

The USA, though irritated by India, recognized that despite the differences it was necessary to extend economic aid to India, so that the process of democratic development might continue apace. After all, India had a government elected by the vote of the people. India had an independent judiciary, rule of law, guaranteed human rights and a free press. And India, which was a part of the free world, provided one fifth of the world population. So, throughout this period, India continued to receive generous economic and technical assistance from the USA. In fact, in absolute terms, India was the recipient of the largest segment of US economic assistance every year.

In 1961, John F. Kennedy became the thirty-fifth president of the

United States of America. He was forty-four years old. A new generation had taken over in America. Attitudes in the White House towards India changed dramatically. The 'Nixon effect' disappeared and was replaced by the influence of friends of India such as ambassadors Galbraith and Chester Bowles. In the White House, two of the new top presidential aides, McGeorge Bundy and R.W. Komer, were also sympathetic to India.

On the question of Kashmir, Kennedy decided upon a policy of abstention and made it known that in his view this problem could be resolved only by negotiation and agreement between the two parties. While the previous administration had accepted the Nixon–Pakistan thesis that India constituted a perennial threat to the very existence of Pakistan, Kennedy refused to go along with this assessment. Kennedy also agreed with the views of ambassadors Galbraith and Bowles that it was in the interest of the United States to provide assistance to India. Thus in 1961–2 things were moving ahead well for India.

The new policy approach to India was reflected in the following excerpt from a White House memorandum dated 11 January 1962, prepared by R.W. Komer,[15] commenting on a state department 'Briefing Paper on US Relations with South Asia':

> While agreeing with state that we should not accede to offensive Pak suggestions on how US should run its policies, I think we should go further and use opportunity to impress upon Ayub that [while we will protect him against India], we cannot back his ambitions vis-à-vis India, e.g. Kashmir. We are running into so many differences with Ayub that I question whether we should wait much longer before explaining to him the limitations as well as the advantage of our support.
>
> As State memo points out, if we must choose between Pakistan and India, the latter is far more important . . . [16]

The same memorandum contains the following further comment:

> Sooner or later, if Sino-Indian border dispute gets worse, we'll have to face up to major military sales to India, probably at a discount. Ayub will raise hob about this unless Kashmir is already settled and unless he already knows that we are determined on this course.

In June 1962 there was a hiccup in the growing Indo–US relations on the question of MiG aircraft purchases from the Soviet Union. While Kennedy understood India's need to acquire supersonic military aircraft, he was anxious that the West should meet this requirement, for obvious political reasons. This matter was discussed by Kennedy at a meeting in the White House on 14 June 1962, when Defence Secretary Robert McNamara, Under-Secretary George Ball, Ambassador Galbraith, Ambassador

McConaughy, McGeorge Bundy and R.W. Komer, along with others, were present. At this meeting Kennedy decided to send a full statement on this matter to Nehru through Ambassador Galbraith, explaining the president's approach. From the available records it seems that Kennedy had asked the British government to offer Lightning supersonic aircraft to India. In addition, Kennedy approved a simultaneous US offer to sell India nine C-130 transport aircraft against rupees. All this was an alternative to the MiG deal which was then under consideration. In this connection, Kennedy sent the following letter to Nehru:

> Dear Mr Prime Minister,
> I know you are considering the important question of placing an order for supersonic aircraft. In recent days I have been reviewing with care those aspects of this matter which relate to our own problems and purposes; I have talked at length with Ambassador Galbraith and I am asking him to bring you a full statement of our thoughts when he returns to New Delhi next Monday. Meanwhile I send this interim message simply to indicate that we do have a real and serious interest in helping to work out an answer to this question which will serve our common interests.
>
> Sincerely,
> John F. Kennedy

As mentioned earlier, the White House was anticipating already the likelihood of a worsening of Sino–Indian relations and the need then of immediate military assistance from the USA to fight the possible Chinese aggression. Keeping this in view, and also the imperative need of the president to have Congressional and public opinion on his side, he felt that the MiG deal might create problems which might hamper a swift response. Nevertheless, he was aware how essential was India's need of supersonic aircraft at that time, in view of the twin menace from Pakistan and China.

On 20 June 1962 President Kennedy held another meeting on India–Pakistan problems when Ambassador McConaughy (the US ambassador to Pakistan), McGeorge Bundy and R.W. Komer were present. At this meeting Kennedy instructed Ambassador McConaughy to tell President Ayub that the US counter-offer was in the best interests of Pakistan as well as the USA because a western-controlled supply of jets to India was infinitely preferable to uncontrolled reliance on Soviet sources. If, however, the MiG deal went through, President Ayub should be told that 'it didn't change the military balance much (as a hedge against new Pakistani requests for jets) . . . ' Further, the president was dubious about giving more jets to the Pakistanis regardless of what happened to the MiG deal.

McGhee, one of the participants at this meeting, noted 'the Pakistani desire for a public US guarantee of Pakistan's security against Indian aggression. He felt that reiteration of the Pak guarantee in some form might be essential to mollify Ayub if we and the UK supplied planes to India. The President said he was extremely reluctant to give any new commitments to the Pakistanis; he queried why we got into such commitments in the first place.'[17]

As it happened, Indian Defence Minister Krishna Menon rejected the British proposal to supply Lightning supersonic aircraft which, he thought, were expensive, and went ahead with the MiG deal. This must have caused disappointment to Kennedy but, as we shall see later, he did not hold this matter against India when, barely four months later, India had to turn to him for immediate military aid, including aircraft.

On 20 October 1962 the Peoples Republic of China launched a massive invasion of India and inflicted a crushing defeat upon the Indian army. For Nehru, this was by far the most traumatic experience of his life. He had, in earlier years, made every possible effort to befriend China. India was amongst the first countries to recognize the new Communist regime in China and to promote friendly relations between the peoples of the two countries. In 1954, Premier Chou En-lai of China visited India and reportedly assured Nehru that there were hardly any major boundary problems between the two countries. But within a few years the Chinese began to nibble at India's frontiers and when in October 1962 India took action to stop the Chinese intrusions into Indian territory, the Chinese army invaded India in strength. The Indian army, wholly unprepared and unequipped, was routed. The northern plains of India were now at the mercy of the Chinese forces. An extremely precarious situation arose for the country. The Soviet Union could not come to India's aid despite Indo–Soviet friendship. China and the USSR had not yet completely broken off relations with each other and, of course, both were Communist countries.

Nehru's China policy, his defence policy and his non-alignment policy, all seemed to have collapsed. He was compelled in the national interest to turn to the United States of America for immediate military help.

It was fortunate for India that a statesman of vision and decisiveness like Kennedy was president of the United States at that time. The news of the Chinese attack worried him deeply and he was ready to hear from Nehru on what the USA could do for India.

On 26 October 1962 Ambassador B.K. Nehru saw President Kennedy and delivered to him Nehru's letter asking for immediate military assistance. By that time, the Indian army had been forced to retreat along a wide area of India's border with China in both the north-west and the north-east. The Chinese had occupied some inhabited places and had even gone beyond the territory they formerly claimed. The aggressors offered a ceasefire and mutual retreat of twenty kilometres from the line of battle, but this offer had been rejected by the Government of India. *Pravda*, which was the voice of the government of the USSR, had characterized the Chinese offer as reasonable and urged its acceptance.

Kennedy responded immediately and sent Nehru the following letter:

Dear Mr Prime Minister,

Your Ambassador handed me your letter last night. The occasion of it is a difficult and painful one for you and a sad one for the whole world. Yet there is a sense in which I welcome your letter, because it permits me to say to you what has been in my mind since the Chinese Communists have begun to press their aggressive attack into Indian territory. I know I can speak for my whole country, when I say that our sympathy in this situation is wholeheartedly with you. You have displayed an impressive degree of forbearance and patience in dealing with the Chinese. You have put into practice what all great religious teachers have urged and so few of their followers have been able to do. Alas, this teaching seems to be effective only when it is shared by both sides in a dispute.

I want to give you support as well as sympathy. This is a practical matter and, if you wish, my ambassador in New Delhi can discuss with you and the officials of your government what we can do to translate our support into terms that are practically most useful to you as soon as possible.

With all sympathy for India and warmest personal good wishes;

Sincerely,
John F. Kennedy.[18]

On 28 October 1962 Kennedy wrote to Ayub, also assuring him that the USA would 'ensure, of course, that whatever help we give will be used only against the Chinese.'

Immediate practical steps were taken for the supply of military aid to India. In this effort, Kennedy and Harold Macmillan were working closely together. In his letter dated 19 November 1962 Nehru asked, among other things, for '12 all-weather fighter squadrons to be manned by Americans for operations over India and two B-47 squadrons to be manned by Indians.'

Requests from India were given urgent consideration. Kennedy himself was convening meetings in the White House frequently and making decisions as necessary.

As was to be expected, Ayub lodged a strong protest, expressing his opposition to any military aid to India which, he apprehended, would further endanger the security of his country. Ayub added that, in any case, military aid to India must be made conditional upon a prior settlement of the Kashmir question. On 17 December 1962 Ayub wrote on these lines to Kennedy. On 22 December 1962 Kennedy sent the following reply:

Dear President Ayub,

Thank you for your two letters of December 17. I will answer you separately on the matter of the Tarbela Dam after I have had a chance to hear the views of my advisors on this difficult and complex problem.

I have reviewed your other letter with Prime Minister Macmillan at Nassau. After a full discussion of the problems created by the Chinese Communist aggression against India, we have come to what seems to us a prudent course of action at this time to meet the challenge—a course of action which is in the best interests of the Free World. We agreed on a reasonable and frugal programme of military assistance designed solely to enable India to defend itself better should Chinese Communists renew their attacks at an early date.

To deny India the minimum requirements of defense would only encourage further Chinese Communist aggression, an aggression which we both see as posing as grave an ultimate threat to Pakistan as to India. Therefore, the supply of arms for this purpose would not be made contingent on a Kashmir settlement. Beyond this stage, however, we will certainly take any one-sided intransigence on Kashmir into account as a factor in determining the extent and pace of our assistance.

The Prime Minister and I are fully conscious of the great opportunity that now exists for the settlement of this major issue within the Free World. As you know, our primary concern is the long-range defense of the subcontinent within the context of our global strategy. No single step could contribute as much to the security of the subcontinent as the resolution of the Kashmir problem. Despite the probably painful and time consuming process required, we look forward with confidence to real progress in the ministerial discussions which lie ahead.

Ambassador McConaughy, who participated in all of our deliberations, will give you a full account of the meetings in Washington and Nassau.

With warm personal regards,

Sincerely,
John F. Kennedy.[19]

Ayub was not convinced. He and his foreign minister Bhutto continued their opposition, expressing the view that India should not be given military assistance because in their view the Chinese would not attack India again. Kennedy noted the Pakistani protests but maintained his policy of continuing military assistance to India. Immediately after sending his letter dated 22 December 1962 to Ayub, he began to pursue further the question of enhanced military aid to India, including 'an air defense' component, and made the following proposal to Macmillan:

> Now that the Indians have let us know that they would welcome the visit of a Joint UK/US Air Defence Team, we are ready to move ahead and get our experts on the ground. In his last letter to me, Prime Minister Nehru said, 'the earlier it comes the better.'
>
> The small group of officers which we are selecting for the Team can come over to London around January 15 if this is convenient. After several days work with your officers, the Joint Team could then go to India.[20]

Further action was taken on the basis of the above proposals. On 9 May 1963 the sensitive question of 'Air Defense for India' was discussed at a meeting of the National Security Council when President Kennedy 'Approved going forward with the arrangement on air defense for India recommended in the Secretary of State's memorandum to the President of May 8, 1963', and 'Asked the Secretaries of State and Defense to recommend how we can best proceed unilaterally should the United Kingdom prove reluctant to commit itself to joint arrangements for the air defense of India.'[21]

Although Kennedy was prepared to go ahead unilaterally with the air defence programme, he was able to secure British support as well. By this time, Kennedy and Macmillan had formed a common policy which they announced in a joint communique issued on 30 June 1963: they would continue to help India by providing further military aid to strengthen her defences against the threat of renewed Chinese Communist attack. Pakistan characterized this as an 'unwritten alliance' between the Anglo-American bloc and 'uncommitted India' and contended: 'Without entering into a formal alliance with the Nehru Administration, President Kennedy and Premier Macmillan have now decided to bestow upon India many of the "benefits" and security normally accruing to members of a military alliance.'[22]

These comments and insinuations did not deflect the USA, but Kennedy decided it would be worthwhile sending his envoy to Pakistan to explain US policy and seek some clarifications and affirmations from the Pakistan president. Under-Secretary Ball of the state department undertook the mission in September 1963. This mission was in effect a continuation of the earlier conversations which Governor Harriman and the secretary of state, Dean Rusk, had had with Ayub in November 1962 and April 1963, respectively.

Besides explaining policy, Ball was asked to try to obtain:

(1)  A clearly stated definition of Pakistan policy towards the Chinese Communists and an assurance that the Government of Pakistan will not adopt a posture towards or extend further its involvement with the Chinese Communists to the detriment of the alliance relationship

(2)  Recognition that public attacks on US and alliance relationship have gone too far and that he must take steps to reverse this trend

(3)  A statement by President Ayub that he is willing to live with a version of the US–Pakistan alliance relationship compatible with continued Western military assistance to India designed to increase India's capacity to resist Chinese Communist pressure

(4)  An understanding that Kashmir is a subcontinental problem, not a US problem. His moves towards Communist China and his refusal to recognize the Chinese threat to the subcontinent have reduced sharply our ability to help in the resolution of this problem. More specific instructions on the line you should take on the Kashmir mediation proposal will be sent to you in time for your talks with Ayub.[23]

In addition Ball was asked—if the conversation went well and he considered it necessary—to assure Ayub that the United States would come to his assistance if Pakistan were subjected to aggression from any source. Ball was also authorized to offer a joint US–Pakistan military study of the Sino–Soviet threat to Pakistan.

This tough, clear and yet friendly message was delivered. It is important to note that Kennedy had conveyed to Ayub firmly that military aid to India would continue and that the US–India relationship would have to be lived with. The message also went loud and clear that Kashmir was a 'subcontinental problem', not a US problem, and further that while the USA would promote efforts to find a mutually acceptable solution, military aid to India could not be made conditional upon a resolution of the Kashmir problem.

Much the same message was conveyed by US Defence Secretary Robert McNamara to the House Foreign Affairs Committee:

Our military assistance to India has deeply troubled Pakistan, as you are well aware. Nevertheless, it is important to the entire free world, including Pakistan, that India be able to defend itself against Chinese communist aggression. The United States has taken great pains to assure the Government of Pakistan that our aid to India will not be at the expense of Pakistan's security to which we are committed under our mutual defence agreements.[24]

India–US relations had now become much closer. In an uninhibited manner, India began to discuss its defence plans with the defence authorities of the USA. A five-year plan for military assistance, as recommended by Ambassador Chester Bowles, which included the supply of high performance aircraft for the Indian air force, was prepared and was about to be approved, when on 22 November 1963, Kennedy was assassinated. For India this was a grave misfortune.

In India, Kennedy was looked upon as a special friend. He was the author of the Indian Resolution in Congress and had frequently spoken in support of aid to India. He had singled out India as a great experiment in democracy. When he had assumed office in 1961, Indo–US relations were at a low ebb. The US government's attitude to 'neutralist' India had oscillated between ambivalence and muted hostility. Under Kennedy, all this changed dramatically. To him, a free, strong and prosperous India was the most effective counter to Communist China. Hence economic and military assistance was fully justified. The 'neutralism' of India was not seen as an irritant but as an expression of the dignified reassurance of a country which had thrown off foreign rule and was anxious to preserve its independence. On the question of Kashmir, Kennedy had decided upon a policy of abstention. This meant that he did not wish to push any particular solution.

The most significant development of the Kennedy presidency was a thorough review of relations with Pakistan. The president personally rejected Pakistan's contention that its existence was endangered by an aggressive India. He followed this up by making it known to Pakistan that the US–Pakistan alliance did not give any veto to Pakistan on US relations with India, and that the alliance would have to accept and live with America's new policy of a close relationship with democratic India.

Kennedy was succeeded in the White House by his vice-president, Lyndon Baines Johnson. Although they belonged to the same political party and had been elected together as a team, Johnson was an entirely different personality. The atmosphere in the White House once again changed dramatically. There was still a great deal of continuity in the examination of issues and in the 'coaching' of the new president, as top staff in the White House were left unchanged. McGeorge Bundy and R.W. Komer continued in their key positions. Johnson also requested Chester Bowles to continue in New Delhi and reassured Nehru that Bowles, an old friend of his, had the new president's full confidence.

The sanitized record of meetings in the White House at that time, of memos sent up to President Johnson by Secretary of State Dean Rusk, of letters and messages sent by Ambassador Chester Bowles from New Delhi and by Ambassador McConaughy from Karachi, as well as of comments

presented by McGeorge Bundy and R.W. Komer, of the remarks of the
Defence Secretary Robert McNamara and the Director of the Central
Intelligence Agency, all make fascinating reading and demonstrate how
Indo–US relations were inextricably intertwined with US–Pakistan, India–
Pakistan, Pakistan–China and India–China relations.[25]

In trying to build new bridges with the Johnson administration, Pakistan was immediately off the mark. Ayub sent a personal letter to his old
friend Johnson, through Foreign Minister Bhutto, offering his felicitations.
Ayub must have now hoped for a US swing towards Pakistan and away
from India. Johnson agreed to receive Bhutto on 29 November 1963. In
order to brief the new president on India–Pakistan relations, R.W. Komer
sent a memorandum to the president for his attention prior to his meeting
with Bhutto. Here are some extracts which clearly reiterate the Kennedy
line:

> The Bhutto session may be tricky. Pakistanis and Indians both regarded
> President Kennedy as pro-Indian; both seem to think you may now be
> pro-Pakistani. So you'd want to be wary of any special Bhutto appeal.
>
> But we have done very well by our Pak allies (over $ three billion
> in aid since 1955). We have also told them that . . . we must just agree
> to disagree about India.
>
> US stands fully behind its Pak ally, provided Pakistan stays faithful
> to alliance obligations too (and doesn't lean too far toward Chicoms).
>
> But we are in the business of defending the Free World against
> Communist aggression. As President Kennedy made clear, we intend to
> help any free country like India which is seeking to defend itself.
>
> US/Pak alliances are against Communists, not India. We do not
> agree India will just acquire US arms then turn on Pakistan.
>
> As President Kennedy made clear to Bhutto last month, we are going
> ahead with India but stand ready to do what we can to ease Pakistan's
> fears. General Taylor will continue discussions of military aspects of this
> problem.[26]

As regards Pakistan, Johnson's feelings constituted an amalgam of love
and irritation. Since Ayub's visit in 1961 to Johnson's personal ranch—he
was then vice-president—both had become bosom friends. When Johnson
later paid a return visit to Pakistan, he befriended a camel driver, Bashir
Ahmed, as a token of his love for the people of Pakistan, and subsequently
invited Bashir Ahmed to pay a visit to the United States of America as his
guest. Ayub was a cultured, decent, pleasant, plausible and warm-hearted
person. Johnson had taken to this 'truly great' man with all his heart. But
Johnson was a staunch opponent of Communism and was unhappy that
Ayub was now in the arms of an enemy—Communist China. And Johnson

knew that Foreign Minister Bhutto was the principal architect of the Pakistan–China relationship. The meeting he had with Bhutto on 29 November 1963 was therefore pretty stormy.

Bhutto handed over to Johnson, Ayub's personal message of warm friendship. After the exchange of courtesies, Johnson thanked Bhutto for the latter's statements that despite some difficulties 'the association between the people of Pakistan and the US was fundamentally strong and that the US still had a true friend in Pakistan.' But significantly and pointedly Johnson added that 'he was indeed a friend of Pakistan and would continue to be one if Pakistan would let him.' He amplified his comment by saying that whereas 'the American people and the Congressional leaders had known Pakistan as resolutely strong against Communists,' he now understood that 'Pakistan was going to have a state visit by the leaders of Communist China.' Johnson told Bhutto in unmistakable language that 'there would be a serious public relations problem here if Pakistan should build up its relations with Communist Chinese.' Johnson added that 'he was not pro-Pakistani or pro-Indian but pro Free World.'

Bhutto then played his favourite card—the Indian threat. 'He could not describe the intensity of Pakistani feeling about India. India was bigger and stronger and Pakistan could never forget Indian antagonism.' Johnson then gave the assurance that the US would live up to its commitments to Pakistan and that America would do nothing to hurt Pakistan. Bhutto probably felt encouraged enough to justify the growing Pak–China friendship. He said that—

> Pakistan being an ideological state itself, understood the strength of other ideological states such as the Communist ones. There were dangers, but Pakistan could be trusted to handle them. US actions which contribute to the growing power of India were driving Pakistan to the wall. Ayub Khan had the strength to stand against this trend. Pakistan did not want to end its relations with the US. Yet everything since the Chinese attack on India had confirmed Pakistan's views that South East Asia, not India, was the object of Chinese appetite.

At this point the president interjected acidly: 'It is you who are going to sit down to eat with the Chinese Communists.' Johnson then left Bhutto in no doubt that the Pak–China friendship and the planned state visit of Chinese leaders to Pakistan would have an adverse effect at a time when he was trying to keep up the alliance and to secure Congressional approval for aid. He emphasized that the strongest men in the Congress for Pakistan were also the strongest men against Communist China. The implication was obvious. Bhutto tried again to justify Pakistan's policy by referring to the difficulties which were being caused to Pakistan by US actions *vis-à-vis*

India, but evidently this did not create a dent in Johnson's thinking. At the end of the meeting, Johnson reiterated his friendship for Pakistan and his warm wishes to Ayub.[27]

This meeting, at the very commencement of the Johnson presidency, was of considerable significance. Johnson understood that Pakistan would not retract from friendship with China, and Bhutto understood equally clearly that, despite a change from 'pro-India' Kennedy to what Bhutto must have regarded as 'pro-Pakistan' Johnson, there was to be no swing in US policy to an anti-India stance.

As the record shows, Bhutto was upset by this conversation. He carried Johnson's rather sombre message to Ayub. In order to make sure that his message got through to Ayub in the clearest possible terms, Johnson sent a letter dated 9 December 1963. The following portions are relevant to our story:

> We here have always seen in Pakistan a warm and staunch friend of the United States, resolutely strong against Communist aim. Yet, over the last several months your Government has taken several actions which redound to the advantage of Communist China. The State visit which is planned for February is particularly unfortunate. Regardless of Pakistan's motivations, which I understand but frankly cannot agree with, these actions undermine our efforts to uphold our common security interests in the face of an aggressive nation which has clearly and most explicitly announced its unswerving hostility to the Free World.
>
> I am greatly concerned about the public and congressional relations problem that this visit and the other steps will create here. From long experience, I know that the people in Congress who are most friendly to Pakistan are also the strongest against the Chinese Communists. The latter sentiments have, if anything, increased in the last few weeks. The Chinese Communists expressed no sorrow at President Kennedy's death; rather they mocked it.
>
> During recent months, I have followed closely the talks between our two governments and I know of your concerns about the effect of our actions toward India upon your security. Although we do not see great cause for worry, we are aware of the intensity of your feelings. We believe we have looked after Pakistan's security interests as we have moved to strengthen Free World defenses in the area. To have done otherwise would have been unthinkable . . . I am glad that you and General Taylor will shortly have a good talk on the full range of these matters.
>
> I am strongly persuaded that Pakistan's interests are best served by doing everything possible to strengthen, not weaken, its ties with the Free World; to improve and not make matters worse with its Free World neighbours; and to refrain from actions which impede the efforts of its friends to be helpful.
>
> It is on these premises that we continue to hold unshakably to our

alliance. I know that our personal friendship and the friendship between our two peoples will become even stronger as we work together in the months ahead.

With warm regards and best wishes,

Sincerely,
Lyndon B. Johnson.[28]


Johnson's view at this time was that the US should 'embrace' both India and Pakistan.[29] He also thought privately that Ayub was not really serious about the Chicoms, and that he had been pressurized by his advisors into conducting a campaign, counting on US vulnerability on the Chicom issue. This, of course, demonstrates that Ayub was an extremely able persuader. He had managed to convince Johnson that the Pakistan–China friendship had been spearheaded by Bhutto and that, willy nilly, he had gone along with it because of the situation created by Kennedy's military assistance to India. It is, of course, possible that in fact Ayub was pushed by the dynamism and fanatical extremism of Bhutto.

For India, Johnson's feelings, in the early days of his presidency, comprised a bundle of irritation covered translucently by a thin veil of neutralism on the conflict between Pakistan and India. To Indians, he seemed at that time to be pro-Pakistan or at least a 'neutral on the other side.' Almost immediately after assuming office, he made it known that he wanted to feel assured personally about the soundness of the Kennedy policy of substantial economic and military aid to India. He wanted a thorough reappraisal of aid to India and, of course, to Pakistan as well, to demonstrate his neutralism. In accordance with this new approach, the following announcement was made on 12 December 1963 by Secretary of State Dean Rusk. This was meant only for the US ambassadors in New Delhi, Karachi and Paris, and General Taylor: 'Decision has been made to defer further consideration of long run military assistance for India and Pakistan until General Taylor has reported on his trip to subcontinent and until there is clearer picture of Congressional action on MAP appropriations.'[30]

As a result, there was now a presidential question mark about the five-year plan for military assistance to India, which included an air defence component, and which, after going through the various processes of examination, had received all-round approval just prior to Kennedy's assassination, awaiting only the final presidential nod. Now this was in the melting pot.

Johnson's lack of enthusiasm for India in the early days of his presidency was expressed in other ways as well. Soon after Kennedy's assassination,

Nehru wrote a letter to Johnson on 29 November 1963, conveying India's feelings of deep sorrow and at the same time expressing the wish that the existing close relationship between the two countries would continue. Nehru had asked Ambassador B.K. Nehru to deliver this letter personally to Johnson, with his best wishes for the new president's success. The ambassador asked for an appointment but was informed that owing to the president's preoccupations it would be some time before it would be possible for the president to receive him.[31] This was the usual diplomatic way of saying 'no'. Nehru's letter had to be despatched by post.

Two weeks later Ambassador Nehru again asked for an appointment to see the president. This request was forwarded by the acting secretary of state, George Ball, to the president with the following comments:

> The Indian Ambassador has requested an appointment with you some-time between December 18 and December 23, prior to his departure for consultation in India before the end of December. I recommend that you give an appointment to Ambassador Nehru before his departure if your schedule permits.
>
> Ambassador Nehru believes his government will expect him to have talked with you about the general state of United States–Indian relations before he returns to India. As indicated in Prime Minister Nehru's letter of November 29, the Indians desire to continue the type of relationship with you they had with President Kennedy. It seems important that you reinforce in a talk with Ambassador Nehru what you said on this subject in your letters to President Radhakrishnan and Mr Nehru. Ambassador Nehru, under instructions from his Government, earlier asked to deliver Prime Minister Nehru's letter of November 29 to you personally, but no appointment could be arranged at that time.
>
> George Ball
> Acting Secretary.[32]

The president's answer once again was that he could not fit this request into his schedule.[33]

During the same period, Johnson had received Bhutto and had a long talk with him. It is, of course, possible that Johnson was more worried at that time about US–Pakistan–China triangle than about US–India relations, which were then on an even keel. The department of state, however, reviewed Indo–Pakistan relations and submitted a paper to the White House on 18 December 1963. While the paper itself is not available, the memorandum forwarding that paper observes as follows:

> In view of the major decisions presently pending concerning military assistance to India, we thought you would be interested in an assessment

of current Indo-Pakistan relations. The paper, which is enclosed, con-
centrates on the developments since October. We have concluded that
in the future Indo-Pakistan relations will be tense but, at this stage,
serious hostilities appear unlikely. We have also concluded that the most
that the United States can do in the present atmosphere is to try to exercise a moderating influence and that no initiative on Kashmir is possible
at this time.[34]

Chester Bowles resumed the thread some time later, and Johnson
decided to send General Maxwell Taylor to India and Pakistan for local
discussions and subsequent recommendations. General Taylor made both
these visits and, on his return, made his recommendations to the secretary
of defence in a memorandum dated 23 December 1963. Taylor expressed
his agreement that a five-year military assistance plan should be approved
for India and a parallel five-year plan also for Pakistan.

On the basis of recommendations from the secretary of state, Johnson
gave his approval to 'exploratory approaches looking toward possible five-
year MAP programs for India and Pakistan', subject to certain conditions.[35]
The important point was that a programme for military assistance to India
(and Pakistan also) which had been stalled earlier was now moving ahead
again, though hedged in by a number of conditions.

Meanwhile, Ayub wrote to Johnson, informing him that Pakistan had
asked for a Security Council meeting to discuss the Kashmir question. The
opinion in the White House and the state department was that Pakistan
should not take this step. This was expressed in the draft reply prepared
by the department of state for consideration of the president. This draft
contained the following paragraph which stated the US government's
policy on Kashmir at that time:

> The position of the United States on the problem of Kashmir has been
> and remains quite clear. It is an issue in dispute between Pakistan and
> India. It cannot be settled unilaterally. Neither can it be settled except
> by agreement between you. A solution cannot be imposed from outside.
> We are as desirous as ever of being of whatever help we can, but the
> principal responsibility for solving the issue lies with Pakistan and India.
> It requires a realization that a solution is essential to your common
> security interests.[36]

This draft was not approved by the president and R.W. Komer
prepared another draft, as desired by the president. Here is an excerpt from
this draft:

> Our correspondence and our own personal friendship, which I so value,
> is best served by mutual candor and straight from the shoulder talk. So
> I will express privately to you my real doubts that the build-up of tensions

between India and Pakistan provides a very fruitful setting for the compromise settlement which is the only way Kashmir will be resolved. Nor do I see the Indian government, at the moment of Nehru's illness, being in much of position to do other than stonewall. So I personally doubt that recourse to the Security Council, with the inevitable exchange of recriminations, will bring you much satisfaction. Disputes like Kashmir are only going to be resolved by creating the kind of atmosphere in which mutual give and take can take place.[37]

However, before any reply could be sent, the Security Council was convened and a debate took place at several sessions in which India was represented by M.C. Chagla and Pakistan by Bhutto. Chagla presented India's case brilliantly. The US representative, Adlai Stevenson, played a low-key role, reiterating the past US government position. The leading role in support of Pakistan was played by the British delegate, Sir Patrick Dean. In his statement giving total support to Pakistan, Sir Patrick, while reiterating support for self-determination, made the following comment on the question of Kashmir's accession to India: 'We consider it unrealistic to consider the status of Kashmir purely in terms of the legal effect of the Maharaja's Instrument of Accession.'[38]

No statement in all the debates in the Security Council has caused greater resentment in India than the one quoted above. That the British delegate should so downgrade the effect of an act of parliament of his own country, which provided the legal basis not only for Kashmir's accession to India but also for the establishment of the new states of Pakistan and of India, was naive in the extreme. In fact what has bedevilled most the Kashmir debates in the Security Council is the refusal of the British government representatives to explain to the Security Council that the accession of Kashmir to India had become constitutionally binding because of the supremacy on this question of the Indian Independence Act 1947 and the Government of India Act 1935 of the British parliament. It was wholly unrealistic to entertain the belief that the sovereignty of India over Kashmir would somehow disappear because of debates in the Security Council.

But to revert to the US–India–China–Pakistan question: despite Johnson, Ayub took further steps to strengthen the Pakistan–China friendship. In February 1964 Premier Chou En-lai and Vice-Premier Marshal Chen Yi (who was also the foreign minister), made a well publicized state visit to Pakistan. It was no coincidence that immediately after this visit a Kashmir Cell was established in the Pakistani foreign ministry, under the chairmanship of Foreign Secretary Aziz Ahmad, to prepare a plan for the 'defreezing' of the Kashmir question and for waging a war against India.

This was the state of Indo–US relations when Shastri became prime minister of India. It was a difficult situation for India and for her new prime minister. There was a serious food shortage and prices were rising sharply. Wheat supplies from the United States, which had been coming in earlier under PL 480, were suddenly held up on the personal orders of the president. The available papers in the Lyndon B. Johnson Library do not show that he did this out of pique or hostility towards India. Nor is there an iota of evidence to suggest he wanted to pressurize India on Kashmir by withholding food supplies. He merely noted that there was an alarming increase in the Indian demand for wheat, from about three million tonnes in 1960 to about six million tonnes in 1964. He felt that if this situation was not corrected, India would require about the whole of the US wheat crop in another decade. It was clearly a worrying prospect and Johnson felt strongly that the Indians had not done enough to enhance their own food production. In forming this opinion he was entirely correct. He wanted it to be known that aid from the United States, even of food, could not be taken for granted. India, he said, must take practical measures, such as ensuring supplies of better seed to farmers, the production of more fertilizers, improving irrigation, and paying higher prices to farmers. In particular, he wanted special steps to be taken for enhancing fertilizer production in India, if necessary by involving the private sector. In thinking along these lines, he was behaving as a friend of India because he wanted India to become self-reliant.

Unfortunately, even though friendly, Johnson acted in a brash manner. Despite urgent pleas from Chester Bowles and recommendations from his own White House staff, he withheld his approval for each shipment to India till almost the eleventh hour. Regular food shipments were eventually resumed, but not before unhappy feelings had been roused within India. And there was always the suspicion, though unfounded, that India was being squeezed on food so as to force concessions on Kashmir.

The question of the visit of Shastri to the United States was also handled by Johnson in what must be seen as an insensitive manner. An invitation was extended to Shastri, first through Bowles and later through a personal letter dated 23 March 1965, for a visit during the first week of June 1965. Shastri accepted this invitation by his letter dated 14 April 1965, addressed to Johnson. Then came the bombshell. No sooner had Shastri's letter of acceptance left New Delhi when the news came, via an announcement by Radio Pakistan, that Johnson had postponed the visits to the United States of both Ayub and Shastri. Naturally, there was a furore in India. No one, not even the American ambassador, knew what had happened. When Chester Bowles checked with official sources in Washington, he was advised that the news was true. The facts which emerged subsequently were that Johnson, who was essentially a politician steeped in the ways of Capitol Hill and had been fortuitously catapulted into the White House, was still listening constantly and closely to the noises from the Senate and the House of Representatives. In the very beginning of April 1965, he formed the view, on the basis of what he had heard from his friends and erstwhile colleagues, that if Ayub came to Washington at that time (Ayub's visit was scheduled to take place later that month), the question of the growing Pakistan–China friendship would erupt in the press and in Congressional circles, endangering the passage of aid legislation which was then under consideration. He was also extremely preoccupied with the Vietnam situation. On 5 April 1965 he made a snap decision to postpone the visit of Ayub and made it known to his staff on 7 April. An afterthought within a day or two was—and again this was Johnson's own—that the arrival of Shastri would also throw up the India–Pakistan problem over Kashmir, which again might be seized upon by opponents of the aid programme. Once again, on his own initiative and without consultation, Johnson decided that the visit of Shastri should also be postponed. If the White House had taken the necessary step of informing the respective ambassadors first, diplomatic reason and language could certainly have been found to portray the postponement of the visits as mutually agreed. But Secretary of State Dean Rusk was away from Washington and the processing of the president's decision was bungled in an unbelievable manner.

Shastri was naturally upset. He could not understand how and why Johnson had sent an official invitation on 23 March and then decided, barely a fortnight later, to postpone the visit unilaterally and in cavalier fashion. He therefore announced in parliament that he had decided to cancel the visit. This was greeted with thunderous applause in the house. In India, Johnson now appeared to be unfriendly. Taking into account this inexcusable *faux pas* and Johnson's position on the question of food shipments, economic and military aid, etc., the press in India was bitter in its denunciation of the US president. The angry comments were duly reported to the White House and aggravated the situation further. But it must be emphasized that this unpleasant situation was entirely of Johnson's making. Equally, the available record of events shows clearly that not one element of this depressing situation was the result of any hostility towards India or towards Shastri personally. It was simply the result of the particular style of the new president, who did not possess sufficient sensitiveness towards the feelings of the leaders and peoples of other countries. Shastri, who felt discomfited initially, soon erased the hiccup from his memory; a few months later he accepted another invitation from Johnson. The visit was to have taken place from 31 January to 5 February 1966, just three weeks after the scheduled conclusion of the Tashkent Conference.

As mentioned, the last letter Shastri wrote from Tashkent was to Johnson, giving news of the talks with Kosygin on Vietnam, which Shastri had undertaken in a spirit of friendship and understanding for the USA. The fact that Johnson kept this letter for a long time on his desk indicates that, even though the two leaders had not met, they had begun to understand each other. And the Tashkent Accord, which had been strongly supported by Johnson, would certainly have brought them close together if the programmed visit had taken place, very probably opening a new chapter of friendship between India and the USA. But this was not to be.

# Chapter 13

# India's Relations with the USSR

Friendly contacts between India and Russia are rooted in past centuries, as this fragment of a poem from a Russian book of the twelfth–thirteenth centuries, called 'The Story of India the Rich', indicates:

> They thought 'India is burning';
> But no. Behold! India was not on fire;
> India lies there before them all shining in gold;
> Here they have palaces made of white marble;
> Here they have columns cast out of metal,
> And the roofs are gilded with gold . . . [1]

Lenin took a keen interest in the political situation in India and supported India's struggle for independence. The strength of his feeling for the downtrodden in India, and indeed in Eastern countries, is shown by a message which he sent in May 1910 to the Indian Revolutionary Association of Kabul (headed by Raja Mahendra Pratap):

> The toiling masses of Russia follow the awakening of the Indian worker and peasant with unabating attention. The organisation and discipline of the working people and their perseverance and solidarity with the workers of the world are an earnest of ultimate success. We welcome the close alliance of Moslem and non-Moslem elements. We sincerely want to see this alliance extended to all the toilers of the East. For only when the Indian, Chinese, Korean, Japanese, Persian, Turkish workers and peasants join hands and march together in the common cause of liberation, only then will decisive victory over the exploiters be ensured. Long live free Asia. [2]

In an article published in *Pravda* (4 March 1923), Lenin again referred to India in the context of the struggle between socialism and imperialism:

> In the last analysis, the outcome of the struggle will be determined by the fact that Russia, India, China . . . account for the overwhelming majority of the population of the globe. And during the last few years it is the majority that has been drawn into the struggle for emancipation with extraordinary rapidity, so that in this respect there cannot be the slightest doubt what the final outcome of the world struggle will be. In

this sense, the complete victory of socialism is fully and absolutely assured.[3]

It was only natural that the socialists in the Indian freedom movement should be deeply attracted to this new anti-imperialist force. The most important among them, Jawaharlal Nehru, expressed the following views about Russia in a speech in 1928:

> And Russia, what of her? An outcast like us from nations and much slandered and often erring . . . But in spite of her many mistakes she stands today as the greatest opponent of imperialism and her record with the nations of the East has been just and generous. In China, Turkey and Persia of her own free will she gave up her valuable rights and concessions, whilst the British bombarded crowded Chinese cities and killed the Chinese by the hundreds. In the city of Tabriz in Persia, when the Russian Ambassador first came, he called the populace together and on behalf of the Russian nation tendered formal apology for the sins of the Tsars. Russia goes to the East as an equal, not as a conqueror or a race-proud superior. Is it any wonder that she is welcomed.[4]

In his presidential address to the annual session of the Indian National Congress in 1936, Nehru observed:

> Some glimpse we can have of this new civilisation in the territories of the USSR. Much has happened there which has pained me greatly and with which I disagree, but I look upon that great and fascinating unfolding of a new order and a new civilisation as the most promising feature of our dismal age. If the future is full of hope it is largely because of Soviet Russia and what it has done, and I am convinced that if some world catastrophe does not intervene, this new civilisation will spread to other lands and put an end to the wars and conflicts on which capitalism feeds.[5]

When, prior to India's independence, Nehru became head of the interim government in September 1946, one of his first initiatives in the realm of foreign affairs was to propose the establishment of direct diplomatic relations between India and the USSR. The leaders of the USSR welcomed this proposal, even though India had not yet become independent, indicating their interest in developing friendly relations with a country which was on the verge of success in its efforts to throw off the yoke of imperialism. With the agreement of both sides, an announcement was made on 13 April 1947 that the two countries had agreed to establish diplomatic relations.

Ever since then, the Russians stood by India. Nehru was attracted not by the political but by the economic model which the Soviet Union provided. In this model he saw the promise of a new economic order in which the state commanded the resources and utilized them for the benefit of the masses. This was an idealist's vision and at that time the inherent but latent dangers of corruption and inefficiency could not be foreseen. Free India under Nehru's leadership moved ahead with economic planning, mainly though not wholly on the Russian model.

During the nineteen fifties, Indo–Soviet co-operation and friendship acquired a major economic as well as a political content. On the economic side, a comprehensive trade agreement between India and the Soviet Union was signed in December 1953. This agreement had some novel features of great benefit to India: the agreement was to last for five years, trade was to be conducted on the basis of the rupee, there was to be two-way traffic in an endeavour to balance the trade, and the cargoes were to be carried in Indian and Soviet shipping on the basis of equal shares.

During the years of foreign rule, India was a source of raw materials and a market mainly for British manufactured goods. Independent India wanted to move ahead with industrialization. The Soviet Union agreed to assist India in the development of her own heavy industries in the public sector. An event that thrilled the people of India was the India–Soviet Steel Agreement signed in February 1955. Under this the Soviet Union agreed to help India in setting up its own iron and steel plant at Bhilai, with a production capacity of one million tonnes of steel per year. As Nehru said, 'Bhilai is embedded in the national consciousness of the people of India as the symbol of a new era . . . '[6] The Bhilai steel plant was the precursor of several other similar projects, such as the Heavy Engineering Complex in Ranchi, and the large steel plant in Bokaro.

On the political side, what brought India close to the USSR was that country's role in the debate on the Kashmir question at the United Nations. The Soviet Union gave full support to India's case and went to the extent of using its veto power in the Security Council, where necessary. Indo–Soviet relations were greatly enhanced and strengthened by the visit of Jawaharlal Nehru to the Soviet Union and the return visit of the prime minister of the USSR, N.A. Bulganin, both in 1955. Nehru's visit to the USSR in June extended over two weeks, during which he travelled some 13,000 kilometres and visited many places of political, industrial or cultural importance. At the end of visit Nehru said in Moscow: 'We believe in democracy and in equality and in the removal of special privileges and we have set ourselves the goal of developing a socialistic pattern of society in our country through peaceful methods. Whatever shape that pattern or democracy might take it must lead to open access to knowledge and equal opportunity to all.'[7]

Later, in the early sixties, when the West was dithering over the supply of high performance aircraft to the Indian air force, the Soviet Union agreed to the supply of an advanced MiG aircraft and to collaboration for its manufacture in India.

On the question of Kashmir, the support of the USSR for India was, of course, extremely significant. Ever since India made a complaint to the United Nations Security Council in 1948 against Pakistan regarding the latter's aggression in Kashmir, the Western powers in the Security Council had taken an unfavourable stance towards India. The public declaration made by Pakistan in 1952 of its allegiance to the West and Pakistan's decision in 1953 to join Western military alliances formed to combat Communism led to an intensified interest by the USSR in Indo–Pak relations generally and in the Kashmir question in particular. The USSR also began to express its admiration for India's independent and non-aligned foreign policy, which was clearly expressed on the question of the Korean war. So, on Kashmir the USSR began to give full public support to India's position, to the effect that the state of Jammu and Kashmir was an integral part of India and that any problems in this regard between India and Pakistan should be resolved peacefully by mutual consultations, without any outside interference.

In 1957 the Soviet delegate to the Security Council commented on the role of the Western powers who were trying to reopen discussion on the Kashmir question:

> It would seem to have been no mere coincidence that the resumption of the discussion of the Kashmir problem at the beginning of 1957 occurred at the very time when certain Western powers were expressing open dissatisfaction with the foreign policy of India, which had taken a stand in favour of the peaceful coexistence of States and the settlement of outstanding international problems by negotiation. Having artificially created the unhealthy atmosphere which surrounds the Kashmir problem, the Western powers are seeking to use it as a means of applying political pressure on India. The Security Council, however, cannot and must not be a Party to, much less an instrument of, such pressure. It is quite obvious that any sort of proposal to send international troops into Kashmir or to refer the question for consideration to various arbiters and mediators, primarily represents a blatant attempt to exert pressure on India. Furthermore, the purpose of such proposals is to cover up and justify foreign intervention in the Kashmir problem and the domestic affairs of India to the detriment of its national sovereignty. For that reason, the objections voiced here by the Indian representative to the proposal to institute a special arbitration procedure for investigating the facts of the Kashmir problem are fully justified. The Council cannot disregard those objections.

In concluding his remarks, the Soviet delegate asked the Security

Council not to impose the will of others on the people of Kashmir, but to bring about the cessation of activities which were increasing tension in the relations between two Asian countries: 'If the Security Council follows this course,' said the Soviet delegate, 'it will win the support and understanding of the forces of peace everywhere, and will help to restore the situation in the Kashmir area to normal and to strengthen peace and security in South-East Asia, and, consequently, throughout the world.'[8]

Over the years, India's relations with the USSR became more extensive. A comprehensive Indo–Soviet trade agreement was signed on 16 November 1958 which came into effect on 1 January 1959 and remained in force for a period of five years. The highest state dignitaries of the USSR visited India and these visits were reciprocated by India's president and prime minister: Khrushchev, chairman of the council of ministers of the USSR, paid a visit to India from 11 to 16 February 1960. In June 1960, Dr Rajendra Prasad visited the Soviet Union at the invitation of President Brezhnev. This was followed the next year by the visit of Nehru to the USSR from 6 to 11 September 1961.

When the Chinese invaded India, the USSR government was put on the horns of a dilemma. The combatants were the fraternal Chinese Communists on one side and democratic, friendly India on the other. The USSR decided upon a tightrope walk with as much dexterity as possible. Through an editorial comment on 25 October 1962 in *Pravda*, the Russians decried the McMahon line as 'notorious' and expressed the specious view that this line had been 'imposed on the Chinese and Indian peoples.' *Pravda* neatly overlooked the fact that the Indian side relied upon the McMahon line as delineating its border with China in the north-eastern sector. However, on the other hand, *Pravda* did not support the Chinese contention that India had provoked the conflict by taking armed action first. In this way the Soviet Union sought to demonstrate its solidarity with both China and India. *Pravda's* main emphasis was on an immediate ceasefire and a resolution of the India–China dispute by peaceful means. The plea was repeated in another *Pravda* editorial on 5 November 1962 which made no reference to the McMahon line. This episode caused no more than a hiccup in Indo–Soviet relations, which soon resumed their friendly course.

There was, however, one other off-shoot which became a new element in India–USSR relations. On the basis of the age-old principle that the enemy's enemy is your friend, the Pakistanis began to warm up to the Chinese, who had just succeeded in humiliating India. The prospect of a Pakistan–China axis caused concern both to the USA and the USSR. US–Pakistan relations began to deteriorate thereafter. On the other hand, the Soviet Union decided to commence a diplomatic effort to mend its fences with Pakistan, while making it clear at the same time that there would be no change in its policy of friendship towards India. It was obvious that the Soviet Union wanted to wean Pakistan away from China as much as possible.

The prospect of a rapprochement between the USSR and Pakistan caused some apprehension in India, especially in relation to the Kashmir question. How could the USSR befriend Pakistan without modifying in some material respect its position on Kashmir? The answer was provided by the Soviet delegate to the Security Council in his statement before the Council on 14 February 1964. 'The position of the Soviet Union,' he said unambiguously, 'is that the question of Kashmir's belonging to India has already been decided by the Kashmiri people.'* The Soviet delegate further reiterated the view that the differences between India and Pakistan on the Kashmir issue should be settled by them through bilateral negotiations and entirely by peaceful means.[9]

Was there any new element in the USSR's approach to the Kashmir question at this time? The answer must be in the affirmative. Having watched how warmly Chou En-lai and Marshal Chen Yi of the People's Republic of China had been received in Pakistan early in 1964, the Soviet Union at about this time or soon thereafter came to the conclusion that, in order to prevent Pakistan from falling irretrievably into the lap of China, the USSR should adopt a less strident posture in support of India and begin to use some phraseology in relation to Kashmir which might encourage Pakistan to believe that an improvement in its relations with the USSR was desirable in its own interest. Thus, hereafter, there was to be a new emphasis in Soviet utterances on the need for India and Pakistan to find an agreed peaceful solution to the Kashmir problem. And while there was to be no departure from the firm Soviet position that Kashmir was part of India, there was now to be a more pressing and neutralist plea by the Soviet Union that both sides should come together and resolve the Kashmir question by peaceful means. I would describe this not as a change, but as an evolution of the Soviet Union's perception of the priorities of the Kashmir problem. And I would add that, by this time, the Soviet Union had also come to the conclusion that it should in future play a more active role in bringing India and Pakistan together by maintaining friendly relations with both countries, and by engendering confidence in Pakistan

---

* By the general elections of February 1954 and the subsequent ratification by the constituent assembly of the accession of Kashmir as a self-governing state within the Republic of India.

that the Soviet Union would in future look at India–Pakistan issues in a more balanced way from Pakistan's point of view.

Clearly, this was a change more in form than in substance. But there was a shift in emphasis. In terms of international diplomacy, however, this was a developing situation in India–USSR relations which needed to be handled by India's new prime minister, Lal Bahadur Shastri.

# Chapter 14

# Peace and War

The most important and immediate objective of Shastri's foreign policy was to improve India's relations with Pakistan so that the two countries could live as peaceful neighbours. Given the past history, this task was bristling with difficulties. But it was essential to make the best possible endeavour and the prime minister decided to do so personally. Shastri's credentials for this were impeccable. He had no communal bias. He believed in the fundamental unity of all religions. Thus he saw no dichotomy in being a pure Hindu himself and at the same time holding Islam in the highest regard. One of his close friends, B.N. Pande, Member of Parliament, recalled that while Shastri was imprisoned in the Naini jail, he sat late in the evenings with a co-prisoner, Maulana Hussain Ahmad Madani, to study the fundamental teachings of the Holy Quran.

The broadcast by Mohammad Ayub Khan of Pakistan, made after Shastri's election as prime minister, had been conciliatory in tone, but that could be beguiling propaganda. Realistically, the chances of securing genuine and dependable reciprocation were very poor indeed, considering that Pakistan's claim on Kashmir was based on the concept of a fundamental cleavage between the followers of Hinduism and Islam. Even so, Shastri wanted to make a sincere effort, and to him such an effort was well worth while as it would demonstrate that there was no substance in the ceaseless propaganda by Pakistan that 'Hindu India' was intent upon destroying 'Muslim Pakistan'.

In his first broadcast to the nation on 11 June 1964, after being sworn in as prime minister, Shastri included the following message about relations with Pakistan:

India and Pakistan are two great countries linked together by common history and tradition. It is their natural destiny to be friends with each other and to enter into close co-operation in many fields. Goodwill and friendship and mutual co-operation between these countries will not only be of immense benefit to them but will make a great contribution to peace and prosperity in Asia.

Far too long have India and Pakistan been at odds with each other. The unfortunate relations between the two countries have somehow had their repercussions on the relations between communities in the two countries, giving rise to tragic human problems. We must reverse the tide. This will require determination and good sense on the part of the governments and peoples of both India and Pakistan. President Ayub Khan's recent broadcast showed both wisdom and understanding and it has come just at the appropriate time. However, a great deal of patience will still be necessary.

Soon thereafter preparations began to be made for India's participation in the Non-aligned Summit Conference, scheduled to be held in Cairo during October 1964. Pakistan was not a member of the Non-aligned Conference and there was therefore no possibility of Shastri meeting Ayub in Cairo. But Shastri took the initiative of suggesting that he would welcome an opportunity to meet Ayub on his way back from Cairo. Ayub invited Shastri to make a stopover in Karachi, and, as we have seen, this invitation was accepted.

In Karachi on 12 October 1964 Ayub and Shastri drove together to the president's house and en route they were cheered by friendly crowds. After luncheon they had talks for about ninety minutes and in all they spent five hours together. They talked about world affairs and Indo–Pakistan relations. Both agreed that the two neighbours needed to improve their relations and expressed their readiness to try. Underneath the geniality, this was essentially a probing exercise. Shastri formed the impression that Ayub had a 'practical approach' which could help in the resolution of India–Pakistan problems in a peaceful manner. He did not form the same impression about Bhutto who could, Shastri felt, throw a spanner in the works at any time. Nevertheless, a follow-up meeting at the home minister's level was agreed to discuss the question of ceasefire violations in Kashmir. Foreign ministers might meet later and, somewhat further in time, another summit might be held. On returning to India the same evening, Shastri, while talking to the press at the airport, expressed his happiness at meeting Ayub. 'The two sides are prepared to show a spirit of conciliation,' he said, but cautioned that 'one should not expect too much.'[1]

On the Pakistani side, an assessment was being made of Shastri by Ayub and, more significantly, by Bhutto. In the foreign ministry of Pakistan there was a Kashmir Cell working under Foreign Secretary Aziz Ahmad. On the basis of an assessment of India under the leadership of Shastri, the Kashmir Cell was to formulate a new strategy for dealing with the Kashmir question.

On returning to the capital, Shastri briefed his cabinet colleagues and senior officials on his talks with Ayub. He was determined to pursue the path of peace and he would personally endeavour to convince President Ayub that:

(1)   India had no desire whatsoever to acquire even one square inch of Pakistani territory

(2)   India genuinely wished Pakistan well and would be delighted to see Pakistan progress and prosper

(3)   India would never allow any interference by Pakistan in Kashmir which was an integral part of India, and

(4)   India and Pakistan had to live together in peace and harmony as they were then constituted without either side trying to do anything to destabilize the other.


## PAKISTAN PREPARES FOR WAR

Meanwhile in Pakistan, after his meeting with Shastri, Ayub went back to Rawalpindi, leaving it to Bhutto to formulate Pakistan's policy towards India. For Pakistan, and for Bhutto in particular, the main issue was Kashmir. Important and authentic information about the manner in which Bhutto proceeded with the development of his new strategy is provided in a revealing book, *My Version*, by General Mohammad Musa, who was commander-in-chief of the Pakistan army in 1965.

According to General Musa the Kashmir Cell was established early in 1964 under the chairmanship of Aziz Ahmad.[2] This Kashmir Cell

> met, off and on, to review the developments in occupied Kashmir and the strategy we might adopt to exploit them. GHQ was associated with it and was represented by the General Staff Branch. Normally, the Defence Secretary, the Director of Intelligence Bureau, the Chief of the General Staff or the Director of Military Operations attended its meetings. Sometimes, Secretary to the President and other senior officers were also invited. It had no terms of reference, nor a proper agenda for discussions, nor the power to make any decision. Its deliberations were not recorded, on the plea that the Cell was merely a 'loud-thinking' body and that, in view of their highly sensitive nature, it would not be advisable to put on paper anything about the issues it considered. We were told that the Chairman himself apprised the President, verbally, of the proceedings of the meetings.[3]

It seems that soon after Shastri's personal meeting with Ayub on 12 October 1964, the Kashmir Cell came to the conclusion that even the new Indian prime minister was unlikely to loosen India's links with Kashmir and that it was time for Pakistan to take some overt action for 'reviving' the Kashmir issue and 'defreezing' what, from Pakistan's point of view, was a dishearteningly quiet and stable political situation in Kashmir.[4] 'In one of its sessions in December 1964, as far as I recollect,' says General Musa, which was also attended by me at the request of the Chief of the General Staff, Aziz Ahmad told us that he had discussed with the President, that morning, the Foreign Office view that the time had come for GHQ to play a positive part in Kashmir and launch the raids they had proposed and that Field Marshal Mohammad Ayub Khan had approved it. I enquired whether the President's decision was meant to be physically implemented by us or was it to be merely considered by the Cell. To us there was a world of difference between its implementation and discussion. The Foreign Secretary said that the President would have no objection if the matter was discussed, even at that late stage. His reply caused more confusion, because we could not make out what purpose would be served by just exchanging ideas on an affair about which, according to the Chairman, the Head of the State had already given his blessing. Anyhow, I pressed that our views be recorded and submitted to the President for his consideration, as we firmly believed that we should not stick out our neck too far until we had built up our military potential to a level that would enable us, not only to keep up the momentum of the guerilla operations but also to deal effectively with an external threat to Pakistan.[5]

To make doubly sure that Ayub knew General Musa's view, the latter submitted a note to the president explaining his reluctance to mount the proposed clandestine operations in Kashmir at that time and reiterating his caution against hasty action there. Following this, General Musa continues:

I personally discussed with the President the concept and timing of launching raids in Kashmir and the dangers inherent in the Foreign Office proposal. He assured me that he would put his foot down to discourage such moves. It was therefore not only surprising but also distressing that, despite the Supreme Commander's concurrence with us, it was decided in May 1965 that GHQ should plan and execute them. The sponsors and supporters of the raids had at last succeeded in persuading the President to take the plunge that led to an all-out armed conflict with India, which, I feel, he himself wanted to avoid and which the armed forces had to face under strategic limitations and when there was a great quantitative imbalance in the defence services and resources of the two countries.[6]

General Musa was then directed to prepare two plans of action in Kashmir—'an all-out one and another, in a lower key.' 'The latter', according to General Musa, 'was abandoned, most probably because of the favourable outcome of the Rann of Kutch encounter, and GHQ was asked to go ahead with the other.'[7]

This then was the genesis of the 1965 war which Pakistan launched against India to capture Kashmir by force. As General Musa's book makes clear, the mastermind behind this decision was Foreign Minister Zulfikar Ali Bhutto, working through Foreign Secretary Aziz Ahmad. Ayub is delineated as a reluctant partner in this enterprise, who was persuaded by a persistent and unscrupulous Bhutto. Bhutto even tried to brainwash some of his commanders in order to secure an acceptance of his own point of view as against that of General Musa. By the end of 1964 then, Pakistan's hawks, led by Bhutto, had developed their strategy for a war with India which was to have four phases:

(1)  A 'probing' encounter in some place of Pakistan's choosing
(2)  An 'all-out' but disguised invasion of Kashmir by the Pakistan army for 'guerilla warfare', camouflaged, according to plan, by the Pakistani propaganda machine, as a 'revolt' by the local population
(3)  A full-scale army assault by the Pakistan army in the Chhamb area in Kashmir to capture Akhnoor bridge and cut off the Indian supply route, and
(4)  A massive and lightning armoured attack to capture Amritsar, the important religious and commercial centre, about sixteen miles inside Indian territory, and as much of other Indian territory as possible, to be exchanged eventually for Kashmir when defeated India begged for peace.

I find it difficult to believe that such an audacious plan, exposing the country to the danger of counterattack by India, could have been developed without frequent consultations with the president himself. And the president could not possibly have been persuaded to approve and adopt such a plan unless he was reasonably assured of success. It is apparent that Bhutto and Aziz Ahmad had succeeded in convincing Ayub that it was time to strike and wrest Kashmir from India because of a combination of factors favourable to Pakistan:

(1)  India had a new prime minister who was still finding his feet
(2)  India was facing enormous economic difficulties, including a serious shortage of food
(3)  After the humiliating defeat at Chinese hands in 1962, the morale of the Indian people and of the Indian armed forces was low
(4)  Pakistan had far superior armour for both land and aerial warfare —India had no match for Patton Tanks and Sabre Jets
(5)  The Indian army was numerically much larger but a considerable part was bottled up on the border with China and the rest could be easily defeated by the skill and valour of the superior Pakistani soldier
(6)  China was a powerful friend of Pakistan and an enemy of India and the continuing Chinese threat would prevent India from

diverting its forces from the Chinese to the Pakistani border; and, finally

(7) India was building up its defence capability. After a few years the balance might tilt decisively in favour of India. The present opportunity when (because of the high quality of Pakistani armour) the balance was in favour of Pakistan, should not be lost.

These, from the Pakistani viewpoint, were convincing reasons in themselves. And the president had some additional reasons of his own. In the international arena, he had assiduously built up a high standing for himself. He had done much to improve Pakistan's relations with the Soviet Union, so that in the event of a war the Soviet Union was unlikely to side with India automatically. Ayub was greatly liked by the Western military top brass. Here is an interesting assessment of Ayub by Ambassador Chester Bowles:

> The Pakistanis are very able people; they're good people. Most of their leaders act more like Westerners than almost anybody in Asia. Here's Ayub Khan with his British Army methods speaking excellent English, arguing with his western counterparts whether you ought to put an olive or an onion in a martini. And our people say, 'Well, there's one Asian I understand; he speaks my language.'[8]

Ayub had a close personal friendship of this kind with many of the leading figures in the Pentagon and in the UK and would therefore have felt reasonably assured of a sympathetic understanding of his position in those influential circles. He had also successfully created the impression in the minds of many foreigners that 'Muslim Pakistan' was under constant threat from the much larger 'Hindu India'.

Incredibly, no one ever asked for evidence that India was clandestinely planning an invasion of Pakistan. No one has been able to point to any evidence that India ever prepared a covert plan for attacking Pakistan in order to destroy it. No one ever asked what advantage India might gain by such an invasion. The fact that Indian leaders had repeatedly assured Pakistan of their goodwill and of their wish for Pakistan's prosperity was always suppressed. No one was ever told that India had actually neglected its defence requirements so badly as to be humiliated by the Chinese in 1962 and that it was only after this debacle that India had woken up to the need for a better defence capability. Kennedy was one of the few who was not taken in, and began eventually to ask questions. This subject came up for discussion at a meeting convened by the president in the White House on 12 August 1963, which was attended by Secretary of State Dean Rusk, Under-Secretary Ball, Governor A. Harriman, Assistant Secretary

Talbot, Administrator Bell, AID, Turner Cameron, NEA, William Bundy, Brigadier General Charles Johnson, CIA Director John McCone, James Critchfield, and McG. Bundy and R.W. Komer of the White House.

The meeting had been convened to discuss instructions to be given by the president to Under-Secretary Ball, who was being sent to Pakistan on an important mission. As we have seen the Americans were concerned that Pakistan was getting much too close to China. The following excerpts from the 'sanitized' record of proceedings of the meeting show that while several participants contended that Ayub was genuinely worried about an 'Indian threat', Kennedy did not accept this thesis:

> Secretary Ball described his mission as being to tell Ayub where we are going and to find out where he is going. The core of the problem is that Ayub can't defend himself against India, so has to rely on us. Our problem is to reassure him that our commitment to defend him is credible. The question is what we can do to make our assurances more credible.
>
> Harriman thought the real problem was that Ayub wants to take care of the Indian threat himself. We have got to convince him he can't but must depend on us. This is why credible assurances are necessary. In fact, the Indians are now fearful that the Paks will attack them, so India wants reassurances too. Thus the hub of the problem is how to convince Ayub we mean what we say. If we demand that Ayub stop his flirtation with China, we must give him confidence we will protect him.
>
> *The president queried whether Ayub was really trying to use us to solve Kashmir. What could Ball say to him that would be helpful.*
>
> Harriman's answer was to tell Ayub he couldn't get along without us. While we can't go to joint planning against India, we can give credible evidence of our ability to support Pakistan.
>
> Talbot said that Ball's job was not just to reassure Ayub against Indian aggression but to stress our primary interest in the threat to the north, which demanded Pak/Indian reconciliation if it was to be met effectively.
>
> McCone thought it would be difficult to keep Ayub off the track of worrying about India.
>
> *The president doubted that Ayub was worried militarily about the Indians. He wanted to use us against the Indians on Kashmir and we couldn't give this to him. So what could we offer him? There wasn't much for Ball to say except to repeat our position.*
>
> *The president reverted to what Ball could say that would convince Ayub.*
>
> Ball replied we could warn him about coming trouble on the Hill, citing the Broomfield Amendment which almost passed.
>
> Harriman adverted to the thought that the Paks were genuinely worried about an Indian attack, so we should study how we could reassure them.

Rusk proposed the tactic of asking Ayub some direct questions. For example, did he want US military aid to continue? Did he want US support in event of an Indian attack? We should try and put the monkey on Ayub's back.

Komer added that what Ball didn't say would be just as important as what he did. The Paks were mounting a pressure campaign on us, and to the extent that Ball did not respond by promising them additional aid, it would be a warning that such tactics wouldn't work.

*The president seemed unsatisfied by these rejoinders and again asked 'what precisely do we want to get from Ayub.' We know each other's arguments, so the best we can do is remind them we don't like the Chicoms, get them to call off their distasteful press campaign and tell them that if they don't play ball, we will give our aid to someone else. The president said he understood Ayub's arguments and could see his point of view. As seen by the Pakistanis, India was a threat to their interests. However we were right too in our position, so the best we could get was a standoff.*

Ball rejoined that the Paks needed us more than we needed them. Ayub would pull back from his China gambit if we pressed him hard enough.

*The president still didn't think that Ayub was really scared of India. What would the Indians get out of attacking Pakistan? They'd lose a billion dollars in western aid. What Ayub was really worried about was that he was losing the capability to attack India successfully or at least to get his way vis-a-vis India.*[9]

Kennedy's successor Johnson was, as we saw, a different kettle of fish. Johnson once asked Chester Bowles: 'Why in the world don't they have a plebiscite, just decide it that way?' Ambassador Chester Bowles replied: 'Let me ask you a question. Suppose an American President about 1875 received a letter from the President of Mexico saying, 'we'd like to have a plebiscite in Texas, to see whether it wants to come back to Mexico or remain as part of the United States'. If you were President of the United States, what would you do?' 'I would think he was out of his mind,' Lyndon Johnson replied.[10]

Within a few months, Johnson too understood Ayub's game and made it known he was not prepared to waste money supporting Pakistan against India. By the end of 1964, Ayub had begun to realize that he could not hope to augment his military strength further by securing American assistance for his anti-India plans. Time, he felt, was not on his side. If he had to act against India, he had to act now. He accordingly directed, early in 1965, that the first phase of the master plan for an assault on India be implemented. This was the beginning of the war between India and Pakistan.

# Chapter 15

# Operation Desert Hawk

By the end of 1964 Pakistan had finalized its plan for the invasion of India with a view to seizing Kashmir by force. The heavy defeat of the Indian army by the Chinese in 1962 had given the Pakistanis the comforting impression that India was vulnerable. The date and the location of the probing operation which would mark the first stage had to be decided by the president of Pakistan.

Early in January 1965 Field Marshal Mohammad Ayub Khan, who had assumed power by a coup on 7 October 1958, was declared elected as president of Pakistan for a term of five years under a system of 'Basic Democracy'. Ayub had legitimized his rule and was in full command. He chose the Rann of Kutch as the area in which the Pakistan army might conduct a trial operation against the Indians. He raised a claim to about 3500 square miles of territory in this area which, according to Bhutto, was in the 'adverse possession' of India. He followed up this specious claim by police and later military action.

The facts about the location of the Rann of Kutch were stated by Shastri in a statement made by him in parliament on 3 May 1965. The relevant extracts are quoted below:

> The Kutch–Sind border is a well-defined, well-known and well-established border which is clearly marked in the various editions of the Survey of India maps ever since 1871. A large part of the boundary is not demarcated on the ground. This is so, however, because there was no disputed boundary between the Province of Sind and the Kutch Durbar, and it was not customary to demarcate with pillars the boundary between provinces and states of British India as they were not international boundaries.
>
> On 15 August 1947, Pakistan was carved out of India as an independent state. Under the Independence Act, the territories of Pakistan were enumerated and these included the province of Sind. The boundary between Sind and Kutch thus became an international boundary. Pakistan is precluded from claiming any more territory than was included in the province of Sind on 15 August 1947. No part of the territory south of the Kutch–Sind border which is shown in the map as situated north of Kanjarkot, and which is thus clearly Indian territory, could conceivably

be a part of Pakistan. In fact this area was under the jurisdiction and authority of the Ruler of Kutch which had extended at all times both in law and in fact right up to the border between Sind and Kutch as shown in the Survey of India maps of 1871, 1886, 1943, and 1946 which was the last map before the date of independence.

Shastri referred also to other official documents of the British period, in which the boundary between Kutch and Sind was described in detail, all being categorical about the Rann of Kutch being outside the province of Sind. Among these were the official Gazetteer of Sind published in Karachi in 1907, the Gazetteer of India of the Bombay Presidency published in 1909, and the Imperial Gazetteer of India published by the British secretary of state for India in 1908. In all the documents of the political department of the British Government of India pertaining to the years 1937, 1939 and 1942 defining the political charges of the various officials, the Rann of Kutch was invariably shown as falling within the Western India States Agency and never as falling within the province of Sind. And the entire Western India States Agency had become a part of India as a result of accession. Accordingly, observed Shastri, the Rann of Kutch was entirely Indian territory.

However, as Shastri knew only too well, the India–Pakistan border in this sector had not been demarcated on the ground. But as the boundary itself was well established by survey records of the British period, there should ordinarily have been no problem in demarcating the international boundary. But when there is a hostile neighbour, a problem can be created at any time. India had neglected this on the India–China border with disastrous results; a similar problem was imminent with Pakistan.

In 1962 Pakistan conveyed to India its reservations about Kanjarkot, a place inside India, about three miles from the Gujarat–Pakistan border.[1] In 1963 the Pakistan–Rajasthan boundary was established and demarcated but the Pakistan–Gujarat border was still left undemarcated on the ground. In May 1964 the local police commander noticed three Pakistanis near Kanjarkot. He accepted their plea that they had lost their way and allowed them to return across the border. As subsequent events showed, these three intruders were probably men of the Indus Rangers of Pakistan who had started patrolling a portion of Indian territory. Since the three were not detained for questioning, the incident was forgotten and no action was taken to strengthen Indian presence in that area, nor was any post established at Kanjarkot.

Then suddenly on 20 January 1965 the Indian police patrol noticed that an eighteen-mile track running within the Indian territory and connecting Ding with Surai, both of which were situated just on the other side of the India–Pakistan border, was being patrolled by Pakistanis. They also found that Pakistani border guards had been patrolling for some time along this track on the plea that this area lay within the Pakistani side of the border.[2] The Indian police expelled the Pakistani guards and then erected outposts to secure the area. The Pakistanis soon returned and there were skirmishes. A further incident of violation of Indian territory by Pakistani patrols took place on 18 February 1965. When the Indian government lodged a protest, the Pakistan foreign office denied any such violation and claimed that the area in proximity to Kanjarkot had been in the 'continued possession' of Pakistan since August 1947. Simultaneously, the Pakistan authorities established a checkpost at Kanjarkot. They did not, however, occupy Kanjarkot Fort.

It seems that about this time Ayub directed that the 'probing exercise' against India should be undertaken. Pakistan decided to escalate the tension and began to amass substantial force in proximity to this area at Maro, Bedin and Rahim Ki Bazar.

Shastri, who had gone out of his way to improve relations with Pakistan, was now concerned at the turn of events. But he still wanted to do all he could to urge Pakistan not to give up the path of peace. At a public meeting in Hyderabad on 21 March 1965, Shastri 'appealed to the Pakistan government not to resort to the use of force to resolve minor disputes over demarcation of the India–Pakistan border involving a few acres of land.' He added: 'These issues could be solved by the officials of the two governments sitting together.' But he also said that if Pakistan did not pay heed, 'then we will have to act as the situation demands.'[3]

On returning to New Delhi, Shastri had a talk with the army chief, General J.N. Chaudhuri. He then called a meeting of the executive of the Congress Parliamentary Party and informed them about the Rann of Kutch situation. On 7 April 1965 the prime minister convened a meeting of opposition leaders also to apprise them of the latest developments. This meeting was attended by the Home Minister Nanda, Defence Minister Chavan, External Affairs Minister Swaran Singh, Parliamentary Affairs Minister Satya Narain Sinha, the Minister of State in the Home Ministry, J.L. Hathi, and the Chief of the Army Staff General J.N. Chaudhuri.

From the opposition, N.G. Ranga (Swatantra), Surendra Dwivedy (Praja Socialist Party), Hiren Mukherjee and Bhupesh Gupta (Communist Party of India), Atal Behari Vajpayee and U.M. Trivedi (Jan Sangh), Maniram Bagri (Samyukta Socialist Party), K. Manoharan (Dravida Munnetra Kazhagam), D.P. Maurya (Republican), and Prakash Vir Shastri, Indulal Yagnik, N.C. Chatterji and Frank Anthony (Independents) attended the meeting. From this point on Shastri frequently invited members of the executive of the Congress Parliamentary Party as well as leaders of the opposition to meetings in his chamber in Parliament House, to give them up-to-date information on important developments, with a view to building up a strong national consensus behind the policy he was now evolving to meet the Pakistani challenge. Barring matters in respect of which secrecy had to be maintained, the prime minister gave information.

On 9 April 1965 Pakistani troops launched an attack in brigade strength on Sardar Post near the small town of Vigokot, supported by artillery, heavy mortars and MMGs. The policemen, who were the only defence force at this point, fought bravely, inflicted heavy casualties on the invaders and beat them back. A second attack was launched by about 3500 Pakistani troops armed with 25-pounder guns and heavy mortars and artillery. The defenders then had to withdraw to Vigokot. By the afternoon on this date, the Indian army took over from the police and reoccupied Sardar Post.

Pakistani prisoners who were captured in the engagement provided information that the 51st Infantry Brigade of the Pakistan army had moved in from Karachi cantonment to the Kanjarkot area 'several days ago'. Orders to attack were issued on 7 April, the troops took up their position on 8 April and the attack was launched on 9 April. It was a premeditated and well planned attack. After Sardar Post had been retaken by the Indian army, Pakistan made a proposal for talks but India insisted on the vacation of Kanjarkot by the occupying Pakistani forces before any talks could be held. Rawalpindi would not agree to the vacation of Kanjarkot and no talks were therefore held.

During the second week of April, Pakistan's Infantry Division,[4] stationed in Quetta (Baluchistan), was moved to the Kutch–Sind border in preparation for yet another major assault. On 24 April Pakistan simultaneously attacked four Indian positions—Sardar Post, Biar Bet, Vigokot and 'Pt. 84', using Patton tanks and 100-pound guns for the first time. Fierce fighting continued till 30 April, when Indian army artillery caused heavy damage to Pakistani ammunition dumps. The Pakistani attack then faded away. At the end of this week-long fierce engagement, India was still in possession of Sardar Post, Vigokot and the southern tip of Biar Bet, but had lost its hold on 'Pt. 84'.

The situation was still grim and it was by no means clear what the Pakistanis would do next. Meanwhile British Prime Minister Harold Wilson had made some proposals for a ceasefire and parliament was anxious to know what these proposals were. Shastri made a statement in the Lok Sabha on 28 April 1965, in which he stated that India would be prepared for a peaceful settlement in regard to Kutch provided the status quo ante was restored. He also warned that 'if Pakistan discards reason and persists in its aggressive activities, the Indian army will defend the country and it will decide its own strategy and the employment of its own manpower and equipment in the manner it deems best.'

On 30 April there was persistent demand in the Lok Sabha for some clear information about the peace proposals put forward by British Prime Minister Harold Wilson. There were noisy scenes in the house. Shastri listened patiently to the excited outbursts of his critics. When they had finished he rose to inform the house that the main initiative about the ceasefire had come from the British prime minister, who had addressed simultaneously a message to him and to Ayub. 'While these discussions are taking place between the United Kingdom on the one side and Pakistan and India on the other,' Shastri said firmly, 'it will not be in public interest to spell out details of the British proposals. I would, however, assure the House that we shall not accept anything which is not consistent with what I had stated and which this House generously approved.'[5] He was referring to his assurance that the status quo ante would have to be restored as an essential prerequisite to ceasefire. Then, raising his voice (a rare phenomenon), he declared:

> I want members of the opposition to remember that we on this side also know something of the national honour and how to protect it. Just four or five people alone cannot claim to be its sole custodians. Dr Lohia has displayed much heat today. He used the strongest language possible. I am not bothered about it. It is for him to choose his words.
>
> But I want to make it absolutely clear that to run the government is our responsibility and we are going to discharge it. We do take broad guidance from this honourable house on matters of policy. But we cannot be given executive directions every day. It would be an impossible situation and I cannot accept it.

The prime minister had spoken with authority and had brought good order back into the proceedings. Shastri paused and went on to stress in a persuasive way that while members had every right to ask questions or come forward with adjournment motions, a minimum of restraint and decorum had to be maintained. And in a firm tone he cautioned: 'If we generate so much heat day after day, this house would lose its respect and place the whole future of parliamentary democracy in jeopardy.'[6]

Shortly after the debate, *The Hindustan Times* (3 May 1965) reported that Sir Morrice James, British high commissioner in Pakistan, and John Freeman, British high commissioner in India, were persevering in their peace efforts under the direction of Harold Wilson, who had provided some fresh guidance. On 2 May 1965 Sir Morrice had returned to Pakistan from New Delhi after consultations with John Freeman and had later seen President Ayub in Rawalpindi, to whom India's comments on the British proposals had been conveyed. In the fighting, there was some sort of a lull, barring occasional gunfire.

On 3 May 1965, during a five-hour debate in the Rajya Sabha, Shastri declared categorically that the Government of India did not recognize that there was any territorial dispute over the Rann of Kutch, and further that the threat of total war held out by Ayub 'will not deter us from performing our rightful duties.'[7] The prime minister's speech, as well as his reply, were marked by frequent cheers from all sections of the Upper House.

There was no major engagement thereafter, except that on 25 May and again on 15 June 1965 Pakistan took some further aggressive action, but without success. Harold Wilson and the British high commissioners in India and Pakistan continued their efforts to secure the agreement of both Shastri and Ayub to Wilson's proposals. After an immense amount of perseverance and diplomatic activity, Wilson succeeded and a ceasefire became effective on 1 July 1965. As a part of this arrangement the status quo ante as on 1 January 1965 was fully restored, as demanded by Shastri. But Pakistan retained the right to patrol the eighteen-mile track between Ding and Surai because it was established that Pakistan used to patrol that stretch prior to 1 January 1965.

It was agreed further that the border in this sector would be demarcated by a three-man tribunal, one to be nominated by India, one by Pakistan, and the third, who would be the chairman, jointly by India and Pakistan or, in the event of a failure of agreement on this issue, by the United Nations secretary-general. Eventually, India nominated a Yugoslav, Pakistan an Irani, and the UN secretary-general nominated a Swedish national as chairman. As regards this tribunal, it was clarified by Shastri that its sole task was to demarcate the boundary between the province of Sind and Kutch according to the relevant records. There was no question of any territorial dispute.

During the period of this conflict, Shastri had maintained close contact with the army chief, General Chaudhuri, who had explained to the prime minister early in April that the Rann of Kutch terrain on the Indian side was unsuitable for major warfare. It was therefore better from the army point of view to contain the Pakistani attack and not to allow it to escalate. If Pakistan persisted in belligerence, there were other areas where India could fight on even terms. Shastri had accepted this advice. From the Indian side, the effort was rightly limited to beating back the invader.

At that time, it was not quite clear why the Pakistanis had used so much force in terms of men and armour, including Patton tanks, to gain very little advantage, if any. In a subsequent book, *The Indo-Pakistan Conflict* by Russell Brines, the motive became apparent: 'This was a military decision that, it would appear, could only have been valid if further military action were already contemplated.'[8] And so it was. This initial incursion, Operation Desert Hawk as it was soon to be revealed, was the first of a four-phase plan of Pakistan's meticulously prepared war against India.

On the political side, Shastri was in control of the situation and never allowed it to get out of hand. He had shown firmness, self-confidence, self-restraint, wisdom and flexibility. He was in favour of peace, but not peace at any cost. He had laid down clear conditions which had been accepted as a part of the ceasefire arrangement. At the back of his mind was always the firm advice of the army chief that an escalation of fighting in the Rann of Kutch area was, tactically, not in the country's interest and that if there had to be a trial of strength between India and Pakistan, it should be elsewhere.

On 12 July 1965 the Congress Parliamentary Party executive, after a close scrutiny of the Kutch agreement, 'endorsed the action taken by the government'. The executive also agreed with the broad analysis of the situation that Shastri delivered. The prime minister made it clear that the agreement could not and would not set a precedent in regard to the settlement of other points at issue between India and Pakistan. 'Each dispute,' he observed, 'has a history of its own and is a separate matter.'

Shastri was aware that the Jan Sangh and the Praja Socialist Party were not pleased with the agreement. There was also some doubt even within a section of the Congress party about the role of a boundary tribunal. Where sovereignty was involved, there should be no question of arbitration by a tribunal, they said. But the prime minister was clear and categorical: the tribunal had only a clearly defined and limited role and it had no jurisdiction to entertain any claims to territory. It had one single purpose, namely to demarcate the boundary between Kutch and the erstwhile province of Sind as it existed on 15 August 1947. This position was in accord with and a sequel to the 1959 agreement between India and Pakistan which was entered into when Nehru was prime minister. This agreement included the following provision:

> Both governments reaffirmed their determination to resolve border dis-
> putes by negotiation and agreed that all outstanding boundary disputes
> on the East Pakistan–India border and the West Pakistan–India border,
> raised so far by either party, should, if not settled by negotiation, be
> referred to an impartial tribunal for settlement and implementation of
> that settlement by demarcation on the ground and by exchange of
> territorial jurisdiction if any.[9]

If the demarcation of the boundary, strictly on the basis of historical evidence, resulted in some exchange of territorial jurisdiction, that would have to be accepted, otherwise there would be no meaning in the demarcation of the correct boundary.

The Pakistani incursion in the Rann of Kutch had roused the emotions of the people of India. They had vivid memories of the humiliation India had suffered in 1962. They were understandably apprehensive about the Kutch situation. Furthermore, whereas the people had confidence in Shastri's wisdom and integrity, they had still to be satisfied about the firmness of his leadership. There was also the possibility that the opposition parties, and some disgruntled elements within the Congress Party, might try to misinterpret the Kutch agreement to the people by creating the impression that the prime minister had not handled the situation with the requisite strength. It was therefore vital for Shastri to explain the Kutch agreement directly to the people and not leave the field uncovered. In any case, he had to establish a direct rapport with the people to strengthen his popular support. On the day when the ceasefire took effect, namely 1 July 1965, the prime minister made a detailed broadcast to the nation in which he explained the situation.[10] With characteristic understatement, Shastri summarized the success of his policy by declaring simply that 'a situation full of the gravest possible consequences for both India and Pakistan had not been allowed to get out of hand.'

Why was air power not deployed in the Rann of Kutch conflict? Air Chief Marshal Arjan Singh told me the reason. He said that soon after the commencement of hostilities in the Rann of Kutch region, he received a telephone call from Air Marshal Asghar Khan, his counterpart in Pakistan, suggesting an informal agreement that neither side should employ the air force in the conflict. Arjan Singh himself agreed on the wisdom of this proposal but he confirmed the arrangement after receiving political clearance from the defence minister and the prime minister. Arjan Singh was also of the opinion that the Rann of Kutch was not a suitable area for large-scale operations by India.

Furthermore, Shastri was a man of peace and he was still determined to go to the farthest extent possible consistent with national security and honour, to maintain peace with Pakistan. In his statement on 3 May 1965, in the Rajya Sabha, he made the following observations:

Mr Chairman, the Indian Government and the Indian people have no ill-will against the people of Pakistan. We wish them well and we would be happy to see them progress on the road to prosperity. We are aware that their prosperity as well as the prosperity of the people of India, of 600 million people who inhabit this subcontinent, depends upon the preservation of peace. It is for this reason that we have adhered fervently to the path of peace all these years. A war in the Indian subcontinent may well undo the massive efforts which have been made in both countries to secure an improvement in the living standards of the people. The march in this direction has only just begun and there is a long way yet to go. But President Ayub has talked of a total war between India and Pakistan. We on our part have been greatly restrained, not because we are unprepared to meet President Ayub's challenge, but because we feel that reason and sanity should prevail over aggression and bellicosity. President Ayub seems to suggest that whereas his country has the right to commit aggression on Indian territories at will and at a point of its own choice, India must not take effective countermeasures. This thesis is totally unacceptable to us. The pattern of Pakistan's activity is this. First raise a claim to neighbour's territory, suddenly mount an attack taking the neighbour by surprise and launch an ingenious propaganda campaign to suggest that action is only of a defensive character. I do want to urge President Ayub Khan to think a little more carefully of the consequences of the line of action that he has chosen to pursue. So far the Pakistani aggression on the Kutch border has been met only by local defensive action to protect our territory. From the Indian side there have been no countermeasures and the aggression has therefore been a totally one-sided affair. We have restrained ourselves, but if the Government of Pakistan persists in its present aggressive posture, the Government of India will be left with no alternative except to think how best to defend the territorial integrity of the motherland.

Shastri then made a plea to the nation:

I would not like to take much time of the House but I might say that if once we are fighting the aggressor, it is exceedingly important that we remain peaceful and united inside the country. Any talk of hatred or bitterness against any community would be most suicidal. I know that there has been a very great response. I have been receiving letters and telegrams from the minority communities that they are prepared to offer their services and they are prepared to sacrifice themselves for the security and the freedom of the country. In these circumstances, I would appeal that there should be complete unity and accord in our country between the different communities and we should all stand as one to fight the present difficult situation and come out of it successfully.

This showed great foresight: it showed the making of a sure foundation on which he was later to build with success the superstructure of national unity and common endeavour during the war with Pakistan, which came just a few months later, in September 1965.

Paradoxically, even Ayub did not want to intensify the Rann of Kutch conflict. He had launched that operation because he wanted to give his troops and armour a full dress rehearsal to prepare them for a full-scale invasion of India, first in Kashmir and immediately thereafter in East Punjab, bordering West Pakistan. He also wanted to assess the will and capability of Indian soldiers to fight a war. By the end of May 1965 the Pakistanis seemed to have completed their trial run, their probing operation, to their apparent satisfaction. As Russell Brines makes clear, Ayub and the Pakistani military top brass drew self-comforting and encouraging conclusions from the Rann of Kutch conflict:

> Pakistani officials were clearly encouraged by the tactical results in the Rann and by the international political climate. Their equipment had fulfilled their expectations. *Dawn* asserted on May 19 that Pakistani commanders,[11] both on the front and on the base, generally subscribed to /the view that the battles against the Indians by and large had been 'easy victories' for Pakistan. The trouble with the Indians was that they would hardly ever allow themselves to get too close to the Pakistanis. Even at the sight of the Pakistanis, they fled the field in much disorder. They 'vanished' without looking back. And later, in London, President Ayub told a group of his countrymen that a full Indian Division would have been destroyed in the Rann battle except for his express orders restraining pursuing Pakistani troops. 'We had to shake off the Indians somehow,' he added, 'But I did not want the rift to get wider. Even so, they are squealing like they did after their conflict with China. We want peaceful relations with India but we want peace with honour and do not want to be a satellite. In view of her chauvinistic attitude, we shall have to watch India. If war is forced on us, it will have to be one that seeks a decision. We shall go full out, and smaller though we are than India, we shall hurt India beyond repair'.[12] Pakistan was obviously encouraged also by the international political climate. The United States protested against the use of the American arms in violation of the mutual defence agreement, but was unable to prevent the fighting. The rest of the world was not unduly concerned.[13]

Not without reason, Ayub was ebullient. He had built up the armed forces of Pakistan, first as commander-in-chief of the Pakistani army from January 1951, later from October 1958 as chief martial law administrator and president. He had secured massive military aid from the USA, ostensibly for use against the Communists. Himself a former commander-in-chief and field marshal, he had now reached the firm conclusion that with the high quality of its armour and the prowess of its fighting men, the Pakistan army could 'hurt India beyond repair'. The prospect of snatching Kashmir from India by a blitzkrieg operation was now glittering.

By 26 May 1965, 30,000 armed men, constituting the so-called 'Gibraltar Forces',[14] had gathered in Murree, Pakistan, for the planned clandestine invasion of Kashmir. Major-General Akhtar Husain Malik, commander of Pakistan's 12th Division, was appointed by Ayub as the supreme commander of these 'Gibraltar Forces'. Pakistan's 'Operation Gibraltar' was ready to be launched, awaiting only the signal from President Ayub.

# Chapter 16

# Operation Gibraltar

The 470-mile-long Ceasefire Line in Kashmir, established in 1948, has been supervised ever since by the United Nations Military Observer Group in India and Pakistan. Across this line at numerous points, Indian and Pakistani soldiers face each other to prevent intrusions. The policy of the Government of India has been to respect this line and its armed personnel have instructions to follow the policy that the Ceasefire Line is inviolable.

The Government of Pakistan had also accepted the line in 1948, but its policy has been to keep the pot boiling in Kashmir by creating incidents on the line with unremitting frequency, in order to prevent its stabilization. This is the context in which the United Nations Observer Group in Kashmir has reported, ever since 1948, innumerable violations. Pakistanis have harassed Indian personnel and vehicles moving on the Srinagar–Leh road from their vantage points on their side of the line. Indians have occupied locations to stop intrusions by Pakistan. These have been invariably vacated on the intervention of the United Nations Observer Group. The temperature along the Ceasefire Line has mainly been raised or lowered at will by Pakistan. The Pakistanis have also, from time to time, sent emissaries in disguise to foment trouble and cause disruption in Kashmir.

In the month of May 1965 Ayub decided that the second phase of the invasion plan, comprising a massive invasion of Kashmir across the Line by disguised men armed for guerilla and sabotage activities, should be put into effect. Accordingly, 30,000 men comprising the so-called Gibraltar Forces were assembled in Murree and placed on 26 May 1965 under the command of Major General Akhtar Husain Malik of the Pakistan army's 12th Division. The component units of this large group, called forces with a specific name of their own, were commanded by officers of the regular Pakistan army.

> The group was composed of eight to ten 'Forces', each comprising six units of five companies (110 men to each company). Each company contained regular troops of the Azad Kashmir army, which was part of the Pakistan army, along with Mujahid and Razakar irregulars. The men were equipped with standard automatic weapons, including light

machine guns, as well as hand-grenades and other explosives. They were trained comprehensively for six weeks at four camps in Pakistan, learning guerrilla and sabotage techniques, as well as basic military conditioning.[1]

General Musa, commander-in-chief of the Pakistan army, was against this plan masterminded by Bhutto and Aziz Ahmad. There was, furthermore, a difference of opinion between General Musa and Bhutto about the strategy and the timing of this disguised invasion. Musa discussed with Ayub the concept and timing of launching raids in Kashmir and the dangers inherent in this foreign office proposal. The president assured him that he would put his foot down to discourage the plan. Musa was therefore greatly distressed to find later that, despite his objections, Ayub decided in May 1965 that GHQ should go ahead with the plan and execute the raids. Musa had been opposed to the raids primarily on the ground that there was no local support in the Kashmir valley for this activity and that for this reason the raiders would fail. He later commented:

> History has proved that the success of guerrilla warfare greatly depends on the co-operation of the people of the area where it is carried out. Professional assessment in this respect did not appear to have had the desired impact in this case. Historical lessons were ignored.[2]
>
> We hadn't even consulted the public leaders across the Cease-Fire Line about our aims and intention, let alone associating them with our planning for the clandestine war.[3]
>
> In the circumstances in which we went in, it was pure wishful thinking on anyone's part to expect them to risk their lives by trying to give us more than very limited support for a vague purpose in which they had practically no say.
>
> Because of the haste with which the operation was launched, even Azad Kashmir leaders were not taken into confidence by the advocates of guerrilla raids.[4]

The final go-ahead was given by Ayub when he visited Murree during the second week of July 1965 to address a special conference of the Force Commanders of Operation Gibraltar.[5] As events showed, the operation actually commenced on 5 August 1965.

On the Indian side, information about these large-scale preparations by Pakistan was extremely sketchy and in fact limited to an awareness that Pakistan was likely to step up guerrilla activities. However, until the disguised invasion actually began on 5 August 1965, Shastri was not provided with any clear intelligence about Pakistani plans. And there was no intelligence report whatsoever on the next phase of the invasion plan, namely Operation Grand Slam, which was to follow within less than a month, involving an open attack in strength by the Pakistan army.

Russell Brines delineates the relative state of the unpreparedness of India for imminent massive onslaught by its neighbour:

> Indian authorities were alert to the guerrilla threat, if incompletely prepared to meet it, but generally they were oblivious of the potentialities for conventional attack. In July, officials of the New Delhi Home Ministry met with State authorities in Srinagar and decided that guerrilla sabotage was possible but that Pakistan was unprepared for major conventional war against India.
>
> On August 2, a senior Indian army commander told officers in Srinagar that the next phase of the Kashmir struggle would not be overt organized power but murder and terrorism. On the other hand, a variety of intelligence agencies received solid information during this period about a build-up of conventional Pakistani power. In July, a European official of a specialized UN Agency returned from the Punjab with this information: 'The Pakistanis,' he said, 'are assembling a massive tank force in the Punjab. The Indians are asleep, and they won't know what hit them.' Some foreign observers with access to unpublished information had concluded at this time that Pakistan had decided to attack in a desperate attempt to change the course of history.[6]

General Musa, somewhat ingenuously, suggests that only the clandestine invasion Operation Gibraltar had been decided upon by Ayub initially, and that all other steps such as the open Pakistani attack on 1 September 1965 in the Chhamb area—Operation Grand Slam—were not preplanned but were undertaken as a reaction to India's measures. Yet his own statements belie that contention. General Musa first describes the tasks assigned to the Gibraltar Forces in the following words: 'Broadly, the plan envisaged, on a short-term basis, sabotage of military targets, disruption of communications, etc., and as a long-term measure, distribution of arms to the people . . . and initiation of a guerrilla movement there with a view to starting an uprising in the valley eventually. The push towards Akhnur was not part of it.' But in the very next sentence he adds: 'However, it was considered as one of the likely operations that we might have to undertake, as we felt our activities would have an escalating effect.'[7] He also says: 'To deal with any escalation, which, in our opinion, was inherent in the operation and had therefore been visualized by us as mentioned earlier, all the defence forces had their emergency plans up-to-date all the time . . . '[8]

Musa rightly anticipated that India would respond vigorously, and it follows that the massive Operation Grand Slam (the push to Akhnoor) had been conceived and meticulously prepared well in advance to contain the inevitable Indian reaction to the initial disguised invasion by Pakistan. As Musa says: 'We had also clearly appreciated that India would retaliate violently against Azad Kashmir territory and had therefore considered countermeasures in the shape of attacks in the Chhamb valley and else-where. And to face the very likely contingency of a general war, we kept the whole army in its forward concentration areas throughout the country . . . "[9]

The disclosures made recently by Altaf Gauhar, then information secretary of the Pakistan government, in his book *Ayub Khan,* also confirm that the attack on Akhnoor was not an improvised reaction to Indian thrust across the Ceasefire Line but a military assault which had been planned well in advance. The decision in this regard was taken by Ayub on 13 May 1965, a few weeks before the commencement of Operation Gibraltar:

> Ayub went to Murree on 13 May 1965, six weeks before the ceasefire in the Rann of Kutch became effective, to examine the plan that had been prepared by General Akhtar Malik, General Officer Commanding of 12 Division, to launch guerrilla operations in Kashmir. General Malik, a tall handsome officer, highly respected by his colleagues and popular among his men, explained the details of 'Operation Gibraltar on a sand-table. Bhutto, General Musa and some other senior army officers were present at the briefing which went on for over an hour. Toward the end Ayub put his finger on Akhnur, an important town of great strategic value, and asked, 'But why don't you go for the jugular?' 'That would require a lot more men and money', replied General Malik. After some discussion Ayub sanctioned additional funds and told the commander-in-chief to provide the necessary manpower. Thus was Akhnur intro-duced into the operation which was shown as a red flag in General Malik's plan. The assault on Akhnur was later given the code name Grand Slam. The timing of Grand Slam was not discussed but everyone admired Ayub for giving the operation a real edge and a new dimension.[10]

That Pakistan planned to capture Amritsar also is shown by the following statement of Musa, who naturally knew the facts:

> For reasons I have mentioned earlier, I Armoured Division was diverted to this sector from its forward concentration area, not very far from Kasur, with a view to capturing Amritsar in the event of an open war. It was to move through 11 Infantry Division bridgehead towards its objective when Khem Karan fell. To prepare him mentally, I spoke to the Divisional Commander myself on the telephone about the change in his mission a few days before GHQ written instructions were issued by the Chief of the General Staff on 26 or 27 August.[11]

Seven stages were envisioned by Pakistan:

*Stage 1*: Commence infiltration across the Ceasefire Line on 5 August 1965 by sending about sixty companies each consisting of 110 armed personnel, with instructions to move to sixty different locations throughout Kashmir and to launch at each such location an orgy of arson, murder, destruction of bridges, communications and other government properties, etc., by using hand grenades, explosives, sten guns, etc.

*Stage 2*: In the expectation that by 8 August 1965 large-scale damage would have been caused in Kashmir, announce on 8 August 1965 over a 'new' radio station called 'Sadai-Kashmir' (the voice of Kashmir), purported to be located within Kashmir (though actually located in Pakistan Occupied area), that, on the occasion of the anniversary of the arrest of Sheikh Mohammad Abdullah, the people of Kashmir had risen in revolt against the government, describing the terrorist activities of the infiltrators as 'peoples' uprisings'; announce also that a Revolutionary Council had been established by the people which had decided to cancel all agreements with India.

*Stage 3*: Announce over Sadai-Kashmir that the Revolutionary Council had taken over all authority in Kashmir, that it had set up a 'National Government' in Kashmir, and that 'patriots' were gaining resounding victories.

*Stage 4*: Repeated denials by Bhutto that Pakistan had sent in the infiltrators and reiteration by Bhutto that what was happening in Kashmir was a local uprising which had nothing to do with Pakistan at all.

*Stage 5*: The anticipated response by India against the 'infiltrators' to be described as 'futile attempts to suppress rebellion'; and steps taken by India across the Ceasefire Line to stop further infiltration to be described as 'aggression' by India into Pakistan Occupied Kashmir.

*Stage 6*: Pakistan army to launch massive attack across the Ceasefire Line and across the international frontier into the Chhamb area in Kashmir in order to capture Akhnoor; Pakistani propaganda machinery to describe this invasion as 'defensive action' forced on Pakistan by 'Indian aggression' across the Ceasefire Line.

*Stage 7*: Immediately after successful launch of 'defensive' action in Chhamb, Pakistan army to launch a massive attack with Patton Tanks on East Punjab in India with a view to capturing Amritsar.

The execution of this operation commenced on 5 August 1965 as planned. 'Operation Gibraltar,' says Altaf Gauhar, 'was entrusted to five forces, Tariq, Qasim, Khalid, Salahuddin and Ghaznavi, all named after legendary Muslim conquerors.'[12] Altogether about sixty companies of the Pakistani armed personnel in disguise, armed with modern weapons and explosives, infiltrated across the Ceasefire Line in Kashmir to various locations, as shown in Map 1. They had been assigned the task of blowing up strategic bridges, raiding supply dumps, destroying places of strategic importance, causing arson by incendiary bombs and killing VIPs.

This highly secret plan did not remain secret for long. On 5 August, says Altaf Gauhar, 'a shepherd boy, Muhammad Din, reported to the police in Tungmarg the presence of "strangers" who had tried to bribe him to get information. The Indians reacted immediately.'[13] The first report on these raiders reached New Delhi on 7 August 1965. *The Hindustan Times* dated 8 August 1965 carried the following news:

> Six Pakistani raiders were killed in a clash with an Indian police patrol near the Cease-Fire Line in Jammu on August 5, according to a report received at the Defence Headquarters here.
>
> The clash occurred near Dhabrot village in the Mendhar Sector of the Cease-Fire Line. The Indian patrol suffered three casualties.
>
> On the same evening, there was a second clash between an Indian patrol and a Pakistani raiding gang near Buna Danwas village in the Uri Sector . . .
>
> Defence Headquarters described the clashes as a serious setback.

It was only on 8 August 1965 that more detailed information about 'extensive infiltration by armed men from Pakistan' was provided to Shastri, who immediately summoned a meeting of the Emergency Committee to consider the situation. The chief of the army staff attended this meeting and gave his assessment of the situation. By this time it was clear from the statements made by some Pakistanis who had already been captured that this was a large operation, planned, organized and equipped in Pakistan.

The Pakistani authorities had not anticipated these confessions. 'The first report,' says Altaf Gauhar

> came at 10 o'clock at night on 8 August, the day the operation commenced according to Brigadier Irshad. In its nine o'clock news, All India Radio claimed that four Pakistani soldiers had been captured by Indian troops in the news bulletin. Half an hour later the captives gave an account of what they called 'Operation Gibraltar', in which they were engaged, and provided details of their assignments. The Information Secretary immediately drove up to Muzaffarabad, the capital of Azad Kashmir, to ask Brigadier Irshad whether he had heard the interviews of the captured soldiers. He had not. When he was given a summary of what the soldiers had told their interviewer Irshad slumped into his chair: 'Oh my God, the . . . have spilt the beans.' In less than 24 hours the details of 'Operation Gibraltar', which had been kept secret even from those officials in Pakistan who were to be directly involved in its execution, were in possession of the enemy while the people of Pakistan were still in the dark.[14]

Map 1  Pakistani Infiltration in the Indian State of
Jammu and Kashmir

The chief of the army staff assured Shastri that the army and the police had full control over the situation and that the raiders were being rounded up, though some further acts of sabotage would undoubtedly be committed by raiders still at large. Shastri asked General Chaudhuri to take whatever action he considered necessary to prevent new infiltrations. The prime minister further asked the foreign minister to ensure that India's missions abroad were fully informed so that they could keep the governments to whom they were accredited well aware of the facts of the situation.

Until 8 August 1965 Pakistani newspapers had made no mention of the activities of the infiltrators, who were later to be described as local 'patriots' and 'freedom fighters'. But on the morning of 9 August 1965, coinciding with the anniversary of Sheikh Abdullah's arrest, the Pakistani press came out with screaming headlines about a rebellion in Kashmir, as conjured up by Bhutto, Aziz Ahmad and Altaf Gauhar. With a finesse which might now seem hilarious, this group had decided to ascribe this explosive information to a radio announcement said to have been made by a new secret station in Kashmir from which 'freedom fighters' were broadcasting 'news' of their 'heroic exploits'.

According to Pakistani propaganda, this non-existent radio station, the so-called Sadai-Kashmir, was supposed to be located in Kashmir and was said to be broadcasting under the authority of a Revolutionary Council. The Voice of Kashmir broadcasts were in fact being made by the so-called Azad Kashmir Radio in Muzaffarabad, under the control of the Pakistan government, as admitted by Altaf Gauhar: 'The Indians must have discovered the hoax within a few hours,' says Altaf Gauhar.[15] And indeed they had.

The Karachi newspaper *Dawn*, the principal mouthpiece of Bhutto and Company, came out on 9 August 1965 with the following full-length front-page headline followed by a detailed report:

REVOLUTIONARY COUNCIL IN HELD KASHMIR

Liberation War to be Waged

ANNOUNCEMENT BY SECRET RADIO

A REVOLUTIONARY COUNCIL HAS BEEN SET UP BY THE PEOPLE OF THE OCCUPIED PART OF KASHMIR TO CONDUCT AN ALL-OUT WAR OF LIBERATION AGAINST THE INDIAN IMPERIALISM.

THIS WAS ANNOUNCED BY A RADIO STATION DESCRIBING ITSELF AS 'SADAI KASHMIR' AS PICKED UP BY THE MONITORING DEPARTMENT OF THE AZAD KASHMIR RADIO LAST NIGHT.

The Revolutionary Radio Station also announced the termination of all so-called agreements with India and declared that Kashmiris 'must rise to a man to fight for their honour.'

On 10 August 1965, *Dawn* came out with another huge headline:

REVOLUTIONARY COUNCIL TAKES OVER ALL AUTHORITY IN HELD KASHMIR.

The fantasy had to be developed further. Using Chinese jargon, the newspaper described the lawfully established Government of Kashmir as a 'puppet' and conjured up 'collaborators' who had to be liquidated. So the paper, functioning as a mouthpiece of the imaginary Revolutionary Council, made the following 'announcement':

NO TAXES TO PUPPET REGIME. COLLABORATORS TO BE SHOT: HARTAL OBSERVED.

For the next three days, it continued with its massive propaganda and full-length headlines:

11 August 1965
PATRIOTS CUT SRINAGAR–JAMMU ROAD.

LIBERATION PLAN UNFOLDED/REVOLUTIONARY COUNCIL DECREE
MUZAFFARABAD, August 10: The Revolutionary Council set up in occupied Kashmir by the Freedom Fighters today announced the establishment of a National Government of the People of Jammu and Kashmir.

12 August 1965
BARAMULA BRIGADE HQ ATTACKED
Battalion wiped out nearly: big clash in Chhamb under way
SRINAGAR SEALED OFF: 12 ROADS,
COMMUNICATIONS CUT.

13 August 1965
HELD KASHMIR TOWNS UNDER CURFEW
SRINAGAR ISOLATED FROM BARAMULA, LEH/CONVOY AMBUSHED:
BRIDGES, ARMY CAMP DESTROYED
Patriots inflict heavy losses.

As far as the rest of the world was concerned, the truth was soon known remarkably accurately. Western press correspondents saw for themselves that there was no uprising in Kashmir nor any Revolutionary Council.

After 11 August 1965 the headlines in *The Dawn* about the 'uprising' in Kashmir became smaller by the day, and soon disappeared altogether. Pakistan had to accept the bitter truth that Bhutto's Operation Gibraltar had been a flop and a disastrous misadventure: Operation Gibraltar was on the rocks. As Musa acknowledges: 'Generally, although their performance was not altogether disappointing, the main aims for which the hazardous missions were entrusted to them were not accomplished. The freedom fighters returned to Azad Kashmir, mostly, after the cease-fire came into effect.'[16] Altaf Gauhar describes the result in much the same vein. 'By 16 August,' says Gauhar, 'the Indians had neutralized the infiltrators and started retaliatory operations' by occupying two important posts in Uri Sector.'[17] He blames the General Headquarters (GHQ) of the Pakistan army for the fabricated and atrociously false propaganda which was being put out by the Pakistani press:

> According to Gul Hasan some of the formations were sending highly dubious and exaggerated reports: 'Self-delusion had become a code with us replacing conscience.' The colonels would put an optimistic glow on the reports sent to them by their field officers and the brigadiers would remove any hint of failure and by the time the reports reached GHQ they read like an account of a triumphal procession.[18]

Gauhar adds the following on the same subject: 'Few people knew that GHQ had been feeding the press with highly exaggerated stories of imaginary victories against fictitious foes. Within the government there were no arrangements to check or verify these stories. Whether it was an advanced form of camouflage, self-delusion, or prevarication by common consent to boost one another's morale and prospects, conscience had certainly yielded place to wilful fabrication.'[19] What the propaganda chief of Pakistan's government now suggests is that he, as a part of that government, had no hand in putting out this false propaganda, and that only the generals were to blame!

Meanwhile, in India, as we saw, Shastri had convened a meeting of the emergency committee of the cabinet on 8 August 1965 and given instructions to the army chief, General Chaudhuri, to take firm measures to deal with the infiltrators. Shastri thereafter kept in close touch with the situation in Kashmir. He received reports over the telephone, both from the army chief as well as from the Kashmir chief minister G.M. Sadiq. In the evening of 9 August 1965, Sadiq broadcast a message over Radio Kashmir in which he said that, during the preceding few days, Pakistan had mounted a full-fledged attack on certain areas of Jammu and Kashmir and that the armed foreign intruders had killed and spread terror wherever they had gone. Sadiq then reassuringly said India's armed forces were defending the lives and honour of the people of Jammu and Kashmir, and that everything was being done to repel the marauders. Though there was no need for anxiety or alarm, he said, 'let us calmly prepare ourselves for giving Pakistan a final and crushing reply.'[20]

Clashes between the Indian security forces and the Pakistanis continued for several days. There can be no doubt about the potential seriousness of the situation: about 60 groups of trained infiltrators, each group comprising 110 persons armed with modern weapons, moved around in civilian clothes to attack roads, bridges, aerodromes and communications wherever they could, until they were killed or captured. Some of these groups penetrated as far as the outskirts of Srinagar city. Others were active in the Chhamb and Jaurian sectors. They were being encircled and mopped up.

The barrage of Pakistani propaganda campaign did not impress the West, and a United States spokesman went out of his way to state: 'We have noted reports that infiltrators from Pakistan have violated the cease-fire line in Kashmir.'[21] This was diplomatically worded, but nevertheless clear. In the UK newspapers, reports about Pakistani infiltration were published generally without comment. However, *The Telegraph* commented in an editorial that the truth might be somewhere between the two versions of the events, but India was responsible for the situation because no plebiscite had been organized. *The Guardian* asked pointedly whether the Pakistanis were attempting their Bay of Pigs in Kashmir.

By 11 August 1965 Shastri felt reasonably assured that the Indian security forces had full control over the situation. But in his own mind he was not certain at all that this was the end of the current confrontation. In fact he had the distinct feeling that Pakistan was probably up to serious mischief, and he therefore decided on precautionary policy decisions.

First, there would be no approach by India to the United Nations Security Council. The state of Jammu and Kashmir was part of India and therefore to defend the territorial integrity of the country the threat from Pakistan had to be met by India on its own strength.

Second, Pakistan must be clearly told that while India stood for peace, it would not tolerate interference with its sovereignty and territorial integrity.

Third, the full cabinet should now consider the implications of the situation and discuss Shastri's plans for dealing with all eventualities. There was the immediate threat from Pakistan but there was also the lurking threat from China.

Fourth, the nation should be informed of the facts of the current situation and of the policy which Shastri intended to pursue to deal with future developments.

In pursuance of the above, Shastri convened a meeting of the full cabinet on 12 August 1965. The highest civilian, military and police officers were also invited to the meeting to explain the situation in Kashmir. The cabinet endorsed the views of the prime minister.

Soon thereafter he came to his personal office at 10 Janpath and began to think of the lines on which he would address the nation. Shastri knew that people's morale was low, their anxieties high. Premier Chou En-lai had made a state visit to Pakistan in February 1964. He had visited Pakistan again in June 1965. In between, Ayub had made a state visit to China in March 1965, when he had met the highest dignitaries in that country, including Mao Tse-tung. These, as well as the numerous internal problems, weighed on the prime minister on the eve of his historic broadcast to the nation on 13 August 1965. Shastri spoke from his heart. His address marked a turning point, both for Shastri and for India, in as much as after suffering waves of invasion for centuries India had decided for the first time ever to fight the invader and drive him back.

> Friends, I want to speak to you tonight about the situation in Jammu and Kashmir. The events of the last few days have caused us all deep concern and great anxiety. I would like to tell you first what has actually happened and how things stand today.
>
> About a week ago, the Government received information that armed infiltrators from Pakistan and Pakistan-occupied Kashmir had crossed the cease-fire line in civilian disguise and that they were indulging in sabotage and destruction at a number of places. During these few days, the raiders have attacked strategic places, such as bridges, police stations and petrol depots, and they have obviously acted according to a plan prepared for them by those in Pakistan who are directing these operations. There is no doubt that this is a thinly disguised armed attack on our country organized by Pakistan and it has to be met as such. Our valiant security forces, both army and police, are meeting the situation firmly and effectively. Swift action has since been taken to locate the infiltrators. Several engagements have occurred at a number of places and heavy casualties have been inflicted. So far, 126 infiltrators have been killed. Our security forces have also captured 83 officers and men. Other groups have since been surrounded and are about to be apprehended. Mopping-up operations are now in progress and Pakistan's latest attempt at creating disorder in Kashmir is being crushed. No quarter will be given to the saboteurs. We have, of course, to be continuously vigilant in Kashmir because the possibility of attempts being made to create further trouble cannot be ruled out.
>
> Pakistan has, on the one hand, sought to deny its complicity and, on the other, she has put herself forward as the chief spokesman for the infiltrators. The world will recall that Pakistan had created a similar situation in 1947 and then also she had initially pleaded innocence. Later, she had to admit that her own regular forces were involved in the fighting.

Pakistan is trying to conjure up the spectre of some people in revolt; she is talking of some revolutionary council and of a lot of other things. All this is a mere figment of Pakistan's imagination. Pakistani propaganda is blatantly and completely untrue. The people of Jammu and Kashmir have shown remarkable fortitude. They still remember how the Pakistani raiders pillaged and plundered Kashmir on an earlier occasion. There is no revolution in Kashmir nor is there any revolutionary council. The people of Jammu and Kashmir have, in fact, themselves given the lie to Pakistan's propaganda.

The more important question before us now is not that of the infiltrators and their activities, because we are quite clear about what to do with them. The real question is that of our relations with Pakistan.

In April last, they committed naked aggression on our Kutch border. We acted with great restraint and forbearance despite serious provocation. We left them in no doubt, however, that if they did not vacate the aggression forthwith, we would have to take requisite military steps to get the aggression vacated. Eventually, the armed forces of Pakistan had to go back from Indian soil and it was reasonable to hope that our mutual relations might take a turn for the better.

In this context, it is amazing that Pakistan should have embarked upon yet another adventure. On this occasion, the method adopted and the strategy used show signs of a new tutelage, possibly a new conspiracy. Only one conclusion is now possible and it is this: Pakistan has probably taken a deliberate decision to keep up an atmosphere of tension. Peace apparently does not suit her intentions. We have therefore to reckon with this situation in a realistic manner.

We have to consider how best to deal with the dangers that threaten our country. We have also to state our views categorically, so that there are no miscalculations.

If Pakistan has any ideas of annexing any part of our territories by force, she should think afresh. I want to state categorically that force will be met with force and aggression against us will never be allowed to succeed. I want also to tell our brothers and sisters in Kashmir that the people of the entire country stand solidly with them, ready to make any sacrifice for the defence of our freedom. I know that every young man in our country is prepared today to make even the supreme sacrifice, so that India may continue to live with her head aloft and her banner high.

When freedom is threatened and territorial integrity is endangered, there is only one duty—the duty to meet the challenge with all our might. We must all fully realize that the country faces its severest trial today. At this hour, across our vast borders are massed forces which threaten our continuance as a free and independent country. We have all to stand together firmly and unitedly to make any sacrifice that may be necessary. *In normal times, we may well have our individual loyalties— loyalties to policies and programmes about which there can be genuine differences of opinion amongst different sections and groups. That is an essential part of our democratic set-up. But when our very freedom and sovereignty are threatened, all these loyalties have to be subordinated to that ultimate loyalty—loyalty to the Motherland.* I appeal to all my countrymen to ensure that our unity is strengthened and our internal peace and harmony are not disturbed in any manner. Anyone who acts to the contrary will be acting against the interests of the country. I want to make it known that we shall allow no quarter to anyone who indulges in any anti-national activities.

In another two days, we shall complete eighteen years of Independence after centuries of foreign rule. Each year shows a thinning out of the generation which strove, struggled and suffered in order that the generations to come may live in freedom. Each year sees a higher proportion of our people for whom foreign rule is something to be read about in history books and not a part and parcel of their own personal experience. This is particularly true of the student community in schools and colleges. They are fortunate that they live their lives in freedom; but it would be unfortunate if they take freedom for granted or forget that eternal vigilance is the price of liberty.

Undoubtedly, we are passing through perilous times. But these are also the times of great opportunities. With unity among ourselves, and with faith in our future, we should do all we can to preserve our freedom and sovereignty and should march ahead confidently towards the attainment of the national objectives which we have set for ourselves.

The statement announced in the clearest possible terms that, hereafter, 'force will be met with force.' As Shastri was known to be extremely careful about his spoken and written word, this warning to Pakistan was not mere rhetoric, but an unequivocal advance intimation of India's response to aggression. This also had the effect of reassuring those in India who had felt that there should have been a tougher response to Pakistan's aggression in the Rann of Kutch. The broadcast made it abundantly clear that Shastri was providing the firm leadership that India needed. Shastri re-emphasized the same points when, two days later, on the occasion of India's Independence Day, he addressed the nation again on 15 August 1965 from the ramparts of the Red Fort: 'I want to state categorically that Pakistan will not be allowed to take even an inch of our territory in Kashmir.'

Meanwhile a flurry of activity continued at the political level within and outside the country. On 14 August 1965, Shastri addressed the parliamentary executive as well as the general body of the Congress Party and gave a full account of developments and latest situation. He also stoutly defended the Kutch Agreement, under which India had achieved all its objectives. At these meetings Shastri made his assessment of Pakistani intentions, which at that time might have been taken as obiter dicta, but which in retrospect can be seen as prophetic. He said simply that Pakistan's definite objective in his view was to create a situation which would allow its regular army to follow the infiltrators into the Kashmir Valley.[22] He had no intelligence reports to this effect and was therefore making a judgment according to his own evaluation of events. As we shall see, the Pakistani army was to invade Kashmir in massive numbers seventeen days later.

At the global level, India's diplomatic missions were keeping foreign governments well posted from day to day on the developing situation. Ambassador B.K. Nehru met the United States Secretary of State Dean Rusk on 12 August 1965 and gave him full details of Operation Gibraltar. Ambassador Nehru told Rusk that while the Indian government had been showing great restraint despite grave provocation, it would have to discharge its responsibility to maintain India's territorial integrity and security.[23]

At the United Nations, the permanent representative of Pakistan, Ambassador Amjad Ali, called on the UN Secretary General U Thant, about the same time, and reportedly told him that Pakistani forces were not involved in infiltrations and denied Pakistani responsibility.[24] He was, of course, dutifully echoing the statements of his foreign minister, Bhutto.

In Kashmir, a number of raiding parties continued their sabotage activities, but they were pursued by the Indian security forces. From 15 August 1965 onwards the Pakistani army stepped up its violations of the Ceasefire Line. A series of attacks were launched by the Pakistanis at different points on the Srinagar–Leh road, the lifeline to Ladakh. This road runs close to the Ceasefire Line for a stretch of about fifteen miles in the Kargil area. India retaliated by capturing three Pakistani posts in this sector.

Of about 30,000 armed personnel who had been assembled in Murree in May 1965, about 7000 had been sent across in early August. Another wave of infiltrators could easily be launched. To prevent this, it was strategically necessary for the Indian security forces to move across the Ceasefire Line in order to seal off as many points of ingress as possible. Shastri had given instructions that any action which the army chief considered necessary for this purpose should be taken.

This was the situation when the New Delhi correspondent of *The New York Times* asked for an appointment to see the prime minister. This request was accepted. In the interview, Shastri was clear and categoric about the next step India would have to take: 'If Pakistan continues her aggression, India will not limit herself to defensive measures but will strike back.' India could not go on forever pushing Pakistan off her territory, said the prime minister, and added: 'If this continues, we will have to carry the fight to the other side. It all depends on what Pakistan does now. It is up to them.' It was clear to him that India and Pakistan were closer to war now than at any time since Partition. 'It is very bad,' he said.[25]

As the Pakistanis continued their attacks across the Ceasefire Line in the Kargil and Chhamb sectors, General Chaudhuri visited Srinagar on 22 August 1965 and met General Nimmo, the United Nations' chief military observer, and invited his attention to the continuing violations. He also mentioned to General Nimmo that since their meeting a few days earlier, the Pakistani regular troops had been firing across the Ceasefire Line with heavy artillery in an attempt to soften the pressure from Indian security forces on Pakistani infiltrators who had been surrounded and contained on the Indian side.[26]

The Pakistan army, finding that their Gibraltar Forces had failed to achieve their main purpose of fomenting a rebellion against the legitimate government, became more desperate, audacious and open in their attacks. On 23 August three companies of the Pakistan army comprising more than 300 men, armed with artillery, light machine guns and mortars penetrated into the Mendhar sector, near Poonch in Indian territory, in a bid to dislodge Indian forces from their posts. After fierce fighting which lasted several hours the Indians repulsed the attack, inflicting heavy casualties on the Pakistanis.

General Robert H. Nimmo (an Australian) sent regular reports to U Thant, in which he stated that a large number of raiders in disguise had crossed the Ceasefire Line from the Pakistan-occupied side into Kashmir. These reports from an independent UN observer established the veracity of Shastri's statement that Pakistan had launched a thinly disguised attack on Kashmir. On the basis of these reports, the UN secretary-general drafted a statement on Kashmir which would place responsibility on Pakistan for the disturbances in Kashmir. An advance copy of this statement was made available to the governments of India and Pakistan by the secretary-general of the United Nations. However, before the Security Council could approve the proposed statement, the government of Pakistan raised serious objections and, according to a press report, even threatened to resign from the United Nations if the intended statement was issued.[27] The secretary-general considered the situation, and with a view to preserving the possibility of playing a mediating role, decided not to issue the proposed statement.

While Secretary-General U Thant's motive for withholding his factual statement based upon General Nimmo's reports was well understood, some people have subsequently expressed the view that a disclosure of the established facts of the situation on or about 23/24 August 1965 might have built up a general pressure on Pakistan to desist from any further escalation. Ayub may then have reconsidered the wisdom of the massive army invasion which he had already planned to launch on 1 September 1965. And if this invasion had not been launched, the twenty-two day India-Pakistan war of 1965 may never have occurred. But all of this must remain in the realm of speculation. The United Nations was still finding its feet at that time. Those were the days of the Cold War, and any decisive action by the UN, such as is possible today, could not have been taken in the circumstances of that time. So, instead of issuing any statement, the UN secretary-general summoned General Nimmo to the UN headquarters in New York for consultations.

By now the truth was out anyway. A US daily, *Denver Post,* stated the feelings of many Americans, in an editorial which was reproduced in *The Hindustan Times* of 28 August 1965: 'The burden of border fighting in Kashmir', said the paper,

> must fall on the aggressor which appears to be Pakistan . . . The attack also raises major questions for the United States. We have given great quantities of military and economic aid to Pakistan. Now they have turned on us. It appears that President Ayub Khan of Pakistan has decided to play ball with Peking rather than the West. He has made pacts with the Chinese, established airline routes with the Chinese and cheered vociferously any Chinese border foray against India. He has, at the same time, criticized US actions in South Vietnam.
>
> Such things have led the US to withhold aid to Pakistan and cancel the scheduled State visit to Washington by President Ayub.
>
> What next? We probably cannot influence events of the next few days in Kashmir, but we need to keep a close eye on them. If there emerges a chance to mediate in the crisis to the advantage of the West, such a course should be explored.
>
> On the other hand, it may well be that President Ayub is betting on the take-over of all Asia by the Red Chinese and has totally committed himself to that proposition. If that becomes clear, the US must then take the other task of giving India all the help she needs in defending her borders.

The Soviet Union was following the events in Kashmir with deep interest. It maintained its traditional stand that Kashmir was part of India and accepted that the disturbances in Kashmir had been created by infiltrators from Pakistan. The best policy at the time, according to the USSR, was for both countries to resolve their dispute by peaceful means.

The Indian parliament was concerned about the external threat. Quite a lot of time in the Lok Sabha was taken up, during the second half of August 1965, in discussing a no-confidence motion tabled by the opposition against the government. One persistent demand from the opposition was that in view of the serious trouble the agreement on the Rann of Kutch border question should be scrapped. The other demand, of course, was for a much tougher attitude towards Pakistan. Shastri had by now the full backing of the Congress Party in parliament as regards his policy on both questions. The Kutch border had to be demarcated in accordance with the procedure which the Indian government and indeed the Indian parliament had specifically and clearly accepted in 1960. This in essence was the purport of the new 1965 agreement on the Kutch question and Shastri firmly declined the opposition demand for the unilateral cancellation of the 1965 Rann of Kutch agreement. For Shastri it was vital that India should not be seen to be going back on a clear international agreement. For him moral integrity was an absolute in national as well as international affairs. There could be no compromise on this vital issue, no half measures. He stood firm on this question and, eventually, the agreement was approved by parliament. On the subject of Pakistan's aggression, Shastri repeated in parliament the firm stand which he had already taken in his broadcast to the nation on 13 August 1965. The no-confidence motion was defeated and Shastri emerged stronger.

On 28 August 1965 Indian forces crossed the Ceasefire Line in the Uri sector to prevent a large concentration of armed Pakistani infiltrators from entering the Kashmir Valley via this route. This preventive action was taken because of reliable reports that a large number of infiltrators had been massed in that area, ready to penetrate into the valley. The Indian army continued its preventive operations and on 30 August drove out Pakistani army units and hordes of raiders from more than nine Pakistani bases in the big Uri-Poonch loop on the Ceasefire Line. It was during these operations that the strategically important Haji Pir Pass, located at a height of 8600 ft, was also captured. The other Pakistani posts which were occupied by the Indian army units in these operations were Sankridge, Burji, Pathra, Ledwali-gali, Kuthnar-ki gali, Sawan-Pathri and Jabbar.

At the United Nations, Secretary-General U Thant was continuing his personal consultations with General Nimmo, and it was understood on 30 August 1965 in UN circles in New York that Nimmo's report might after all be circulated to members of the Security Council, as demanded by India. Nimmo's presence in New York had provided the opportunity to several members of the Security Council to get a more detailed oral report. Evidently, Nimmo incurred the wrath of Pakistan, which had been anxious to suppress his report. It was stated at the United Nations head-quarters on 31 August 1965 that Secretary-General U Thant had completed his consultations with General Nimmo, who had left New York the

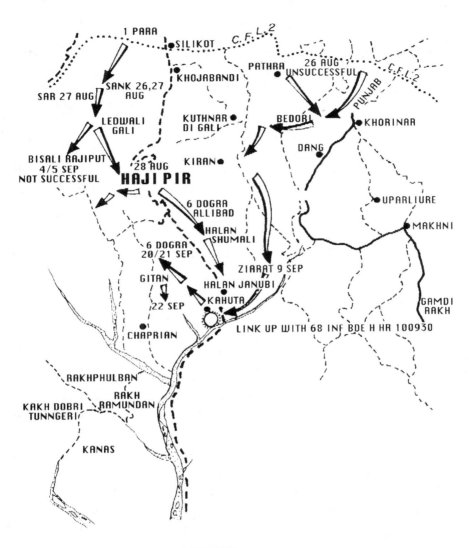

**LEGEND**

 PROGRESS OF THE TWO-PRONGED INDIAN
THRUST WITH DATES.

Not To Scale

Map 2   The Haji Pir Operation

previous night to return to his responsibilities in Kashmir. It was also stated that the secretary-general had in mind some proposals for easing the crisis between India and Pakistan, but no details were provided.

In Kashmir the Indian army consolidated its position in the Uri-Poonch loop on the Ceasefire Line by bringing in further reinforcements. Indian security forces in Kashmir were now in full command of the situation. Since 5 August, when the invasion began, Pakistan had lost 1100 armed personnel.

This was not a situation which Ayub or Bhutto had expected. Strange though it may seem, Ayub had gone away to the border state of Swat immediately after the commencement of Operation Gibraltar and had stayed there during these critical days, no doubt to demonstrate his detachment from and indeed his 'unawareness' of the activities of his infiltrators. Towards the end of August, both General Musa and General Malik found themselves in a desperate situation and began to insist that Operation Grand Slam now be launched immediately. 'The problem,' says Altaf Gauhar,

> was that the Grand Slam would require the Pakistani forces to move across a small section of the international frontier between Sialkot and Jammu. The Information Secretary was present at this meeting when General Musa was urging Bhutto to obtain Ayub's approval to launch Grand Slam. It was obvious that Bhutto and Aziz Ahmad were now in a hopeless situation; they knew that Gibraltar had collapsed and their whole plan had come apart. Akhnur looked like the proverbial last throw of a gambler but there was no other way to retrieve the situation. Perhaps the Indians would not notice the minor transgression of the international boundary. Bhutto decided it was a gamble worth taking.[28]

For this purpose Bhutto flew to Swat and came back with the 'directive' signed by Ayub on 29 August 1965. Gauhar gives a careful description of the contents of Ayub's directive and its implications:

> The directive was addressed to the Foreign Minister and the Commander-in-Chief and bore the title: 'Political aim for struggle in Kashmir.' The aim was 'to take such action that will defreeze the Kashmir problem, weaken Indian resolve, and bring her to the conference table *without* provoking a general war (emphasis added). However the element of escalation is always present in such struggles. So whilst confining our action to the Kashmir area we must not be unmindful that India may in desperation involve us in a general war or violate Pakistani territory where we are weak. We must therefore be prepared for such a contingency. To expect quick results in this struggle, when India has much larger forces than us, would be unrealistic. Therefore, our action should be such that can be sustained over a long period. As a general rule Hindu

morale would not stand more than a couple of hard blows at the right time and place. Such opportunities should therefore be sought and exploited.' This directive is the most revealing document of the war. It shows conclusively that Ayub did not know, even on 29 August, nine days before the war started, that Gibraltar had failed, that not one of its major objectives had been achieved, and that enemy forces were in a commanding position with Muzaffarabad, the capital of Azad Kashmir, within their reach.[29]

The directive also shows that Ayub's mind was still tuned to some pre-Gibraltar number. After having fired all his shots he was still living in a make-believe world dreaming about taking 'such action that will defreeze the Kashmir problem, weaken Indian resolve and bring her to the conference table without provoking a general war'. He did not 'expect quick results' and was thinking in terms of action 'that can be sustained over a long period' not knowing that his Foreign Office and GHQ had already taken all the action behind his back. He was still fantasizing about the general rule that 'Hindu morale would not stand more than a couple of hard blows at the right time and place'. That was why he did not give a clear directive to his forces to launch an offensive on Akhnur and left it to his Foreign Minister and his Commander-in-Chief to choose the right time and place to deliver a 'couple of hard blows' to the Hindu. Ayub Khan, the decision-maker, was acting like an adviser, whose responsibility did not go beyond suggesting the guide lines for action.

Bhutto could not have asked for a more helpful directive which put him in a pre-eminent position: no other minister could challenge his authority and the Commander-in-Chief had to rely on him to interpret the terms of the directive. Bhutto must have assured General Musa that Ayub had authorised the launching of Grand Slam in the full knowledge that the operation would involve the transgression of the international boundary.[30]

Ayub had thus accorded his approval to the launching of an attack on India. The die was now cast.

Ayub returned to Rawalpindi on 31 August for an emergency cabinet meeting. The same night Khwaja Shahabuddin, the Pakistani information minister, made the following ominous announcement: 'The time has come when Pakistanis will have to make sacrifices to liberate their Kashmiri brethren from Indian imperialism.'[31] He further warned that Pakistanis might be required for the assistance of 'freedom fighters' any moment now. Within a few hours of this announcement, the Pakistan army moved in strength to implement the next phase of its invasion plan—Operation Grand Slam.

# Chapter 17

# Operation Grand Slam

In the early hours of 1 September 1965 the Pakistan army launched an attack. The Bhimber–Chhamb area in Kashmir across the Ceasefire Line and also across the international frontier between West Pakistan and the state of Jammu and Kashmir was the target. At 0345 hours an intense artillery and mortar bombardment began.[1] After heavy preparatory artillery fire and three infantry probing attacks, Pakistani forces drove into Indian territory with a column of seventy tanks and two brigades of between 3000 and 4000 infantry troops.[2] The objective was to capture Akhnoor, particularly Akhnoor bridge, and the purpose was to cut off the link and supply route from East Punjab to Kashmir. The India–Pakistan war had now commenced. The Pakistani code name for this war was Operation Grand Slam.

Shastri received information about the Pakistani invasion by about midday over the telephone from J.N. Chaudhuri who was then in Srinagar, and immediately convened a meeting of the emergency committee of the cabinet. While the cabinet committee was considering the situation, General Chaudhuri reached New Delhi with the latest information and made an important proposal for the prime minister's approval. Chaudhuri reported that although the available Indian forces were putting up resistance, the Pakistan army, which had Patton tanks, was pushing ahead. Indian units did not have matching armour, and were thus not in a position to stop the invasion. The Indian army, said the general, would defend the Akhnoor bridge, but the situation was hazardous. Chaudhuri requested immediate support from the air force.

A similar situation had arisen in 1962 at the time of the Chinese invasion, when the question of the use of the air force had been considered in order to halt the forward rush of the Chinese army. At that time the government had decided against the use of the air force. On this occasion, however, Shastri decided that the air force should immediately go into action. He was conscious of the danger that the Pakistani air force might bomb Indian cities or vital installations but this was a danger which had to be faced. The cabinet committee concurred. Defence Minister Y.B. Chavan conveyed the decision to the chief of the air staff, Air Marshal

Arjan Singh, who replied that the Indian air force was ready. This was at about 4 p.m. The air force was on the job at 5.19 p.m.

After the cabinet meeting Shastri met press representatives who were waiting for news and told them: 'This is a regular attack and we will meet it.' Late in the evening Shastri returned from his office in Parliament House to his residence. He had telephone conversations with Chaudhuri and Arjan Singh to get the latest information.

As he had announced a fortnight earlier to the nation, force was now being met with force. But this was just the beginning of the open war. It was apparent from his talks that in the Chhamb area Pakistan had great logistical advantages. Supplies and munitions could be secured by the Pakistan army from across the nearby West Pakistan frontier, whereas the Indian sources of supply were far. In any case, the heavy Indian tanks could not reach the Chhamb area. The deployment of the air force had had the desired effect of halting the advance of the Pakistani army, but Pakistan would try to resume the advance with additional ground forces under the aerial protection of the Pakistani air force. Unless, therefore, military action were immediately taken by India elsewhere to put pressure on Pakistan, there was grave danger of the Akhnoor bridge falling, with disastrous consequences.

But attack elsewhere did not mean across the Ceasefire Line into Pakistan occupied Kashmir, because that could not achieve the purpose in view. It had to be an attack on Pakistan at a point strategically most suitable for the Indian army. Such a possibility was implied in Shastri's earlier declarations that if it became necessary the Indian army would determine where its men and equipment would be deployed. An attack on Pakistan would mean a general war between the two countries. This would widen the area of conflict, with international implications. First and foremost was the possibility of collusive military action by China. During the preceding weeks, China had issued several statements giving full support to Pakistan. The infiltration by Pakistan into Kashmir was based on the Chinese model. Chinese 'guerilla' experts were reported to be providing training to Pakistanis. Ayub and Chou En-lai had met several times and there was no doubt that Pakistan's bellicosity against India had been encouraged by China. It was, however, by no means clear whether the Chinese had secretly agreed to take overt military action against India to keep the Indian armed forces engaged on two fronts. The Chinese knew that their intervention would invite the intervention of the United States in support of India, and the war could thus become a global conflagration because the USSR, which was the most important border state in this strategic Punjab–Kashmir crucible, might then come in too. Furthermore, an Indian attack on

Pakistan, diversionary though in intent, would have to be an attack in strength.

Information was now available that a vast amount of artillery and a large number of tanks had been amassed by Pakistan on the West Pakistan–East Punjab border, ready to be rolled towards India as soon as Ayub's signal was given. India would have to attack to ensure that all this Pakistani armour could be engaged and damaged beyond repair. Pakistan would use its effective propaganda machinery to cry out for help. The West might then put immense pressure on India both directly, and indirectly through the Security Council, for a ceasefire, before India had time to deal with the threatening Pakistani armour.

One internal danger which had to be avoided was communal disturbances. On that very morning, 1 September 1965, serious communal rioting had broken out in Poona. The army had had to be called out and the situation had been controlled quickly. But a recurrence had to be avoided, because in the surcharged atmosphere of war with Pakistan the communal virus could spread rapidly. The situation was thus full of dangerous possibilities, both nationally and internationally. Shastri had now to make vital political decisions.

## COUNTERATTACK

I was with the prime minister at 10 Janpath throughout that evening when he had to make perhaps the most momentous decision of his life. In normal times he was a dedicated apostle of peace and of reconciliation. But now, like Arjuna at Kurukshetra, he was faced with the duty to fight. Shastri got up from his chair and began to pace from one end of his office room to the other, as he usually did when he wanted to think about the pros and cons of some important matter. All I heard him say was— 'ab to kuchch karna hi ho ga' (now something has to be done). I did not ask him what he had in mind nor did he tell me any more.

It was well past midnight when he left his office for his residence next door, for a brief spell of sleep. I could see from the expression on his face that he had made up his mind and, as we were soon to discover, the decision was that the Indian army should march towards Lahore as soon as possible. At that time, this was a secret which he kept to himself.

The news of the Pakistan army's invasion appeared in the newspapers on the morning of 2 September 1965. Along with that appeared a confident message from Shastri that the Pakistani attack would be met and that there was no cause for concern. Nevertheless, there was great excitement among the people.

Shastri received an urgent appeal from the secretary-general of the United Nations, asking for an immediate ceasefire. There was no question of India accepting this appeal while Pakistani forces were so dangerously close to Akhnoor bridge. The official response was, however, that the appeal would be considered.

In Kashmir, India's ground and air forces were making determined efforts to stop the advance and, despite the odds, were succeeding. Indian air force fighter planes fought a pitched battle against a number of Pakistani F-86 Sabre jets over the Chhamb area.

Shastri had a very heavy agenda for the day. Apart from his meetings with the chiefs of the army and air force, he had a long meeting with leaders of the opposition during which he gave them the latest available information about the battles in Kashmir. He could not of course tell them what his plans were. Throughout the period of the war, the prime minister convened frequent meetings with members of his party, as well as with leaders of the opposition to keep them informed.

After clearing the text with the prime minister, Defence Minister Y.B. Chavan made a statement in the Lok Sabha in which the likely course of future events was hinted at but not spelt out: 'The massive intervention of armour by Pakistan has escalated the conflict rapidly. We have to take an overall view of defence.' He went on to assure the house that 'our forces are confident to meet any situation.'

Shastri met the press and again expressed his determination to meet the situation. Later in the evening he convened a meeting of the emergency committee of the cabinet to consider the latest situation and discuss future strategy. Although he had formulated his own ideas clearly, it was essential to carry his colleagues with him in his decision. Now Shastri explained his view, which he had already discussed with Chaudhuri, that in order to defend Kashmir it was essential to make a diversionary attack on West Pakistan which would force the Pakistanis to give up their Kashmir venture in order to defend their own territories. He explained that the attack on West Pakistan would have to be made without delay. All members of the cabinet committee were invited to express their views: all present expressed their full support, except one, who referred to the likely adverse repercussions abroad, especially in the United Nations Security Council. This was debated at length, but as Cabinet Secretary Dharma Vira and Home Secretary L.P. Singh confirmed to me, the general view was that as Pakistan had now openly invaded Kashmir, it was entirely for India to decide how to defend itself. As the discussion was not completed, another meeting of the emergency committee of the cabinet was convened next morning when the proposal made by the prime minister was unanimously endorsed.

Thus, on 3 September 1965 Shastri gave the go-ahead to launch a counterattack. For the first time in recorded history India had decided to carry the fight into the invader's territory.

## WAR OBJECTIVES

Now Shastri turned his attention to defining the war objectives of the political leadership, leaving the details of the military strategy to the army and air force chiefs. Such a definition was essential particularly from the international point of view. Once India's counterattack was launched in substantial strength in three sectors—Lahore, Sialkot and Barmer (Rajasthan)—Pakistan would seek foreign intervention on the plea that it was about to be crushed by Indian invasion. China in particular might find in that situation an opportunity to take some limited overt military action on India's northern borders, enough to discomfit India without risking United States intervention. It was important for the world to know that India was not out to destroy or reabsorb Pakistan. In order to ensure that India's declared intentions gained credibility, the military operation would have to conform strictly to those intentions.

Shastri convened a meeting with the defence minister and the army and air force chiefs. Then he defined the country's war objectives:

(1)   To defeat the Pakistani attempts to seize Kashmir by force and to make it abundantly clear that Pakistan would never be allowed to wrest Kashmir from India
(2)   To destroy the offensive power of Pakistan's armed forces
(3)   To occupy only the minimum Pakistani territory necessary to achieve these purposes, which would be vacated after the satisfactory conclusion of the war

The prime minister requested Arjan Singh to ensure that there was no bombing of civilian areas in Pakistan. Foreign Minister Sardar Swaran Singh and Foreign Secretary C.S. Jha were told to ask all Indian diplomatic missions abroad to brief the governments of their accreditation.

Later, Shastri looked at the various messages which had been received from foreign governments urging restraint. Immense diplomatic pressure was building up to restrain India from countermeasures. The United Nations secretary-general's appeal was already before him. The British high commissioner, John Freeman, asked for an appointment to deliver an urgent message from Harold Wilson. Shastri received Freeman and had a fairly long talk with him. He requested Freeman to convey his thanks to

Wilson for his message and to explain to him the seriousness of the Pakistani invasion. In the evening of the same day, 3 September, Shastri delivered an address to the nation in a broadcast over All India Radio. He gave details of the Pakistani invasion, which included mention of Pakistani bombs killing many civilians as well as destroying a mosque, where fifty persons, who had gathered for prayers, had been killed. The following are some excerpts from the prime minister's address:

> In the Agreement between India and Pakistan in connection with the Gujarat–West Pakistan border, signed on June 30 this year, Pakistan solemnly affirmed its hope that the Agreement would result in better relations and easing of tensions between India and Pakistan. The conscience of the world would be shocked to know that even at the time this Agreement was being signed, Pakistan had already drawn up a plan of armed infiltration into Kashmir and was training its personnel in Murree for the operations which were undertaken just over a month later, even before the ink was dry on the Agreement of June 30. Such conduct speaks for itself.
>
> Let me add that our quarrel is not with the people of Pakistan. We wish them well; we want them to prosper and we want to live in peace and friendship with them.
>
> What is at stake in the present conflict is a point of principle. Has any country the right to send its armed personnel to another with the avowed object of overthrowing a democratically elected Government? I have received a communication from the Secretary-General of the United Nations containing an appeal to both sides to observe the Ceasefire Line. The Secretary-General has appealed both to Pakistan and to India for peace. We believe in peace. We have worked for it and we shall never cease to work for peace.
>
> Those who want peace will always have our support and co-operation, but they must face the realities of the situation. A ceasefire is not peace. We cannot simply go from one ceasefire to another and wait till Pakistan chooses to start hostilities again.
>
> What is the duty and responsibility of our citizens in this hour of serious crisis? Your foremost duty at the present moment is to do everything possible to ensure that peace is not disturbed and that communal harmony is maintained. There are no Hindus, no Muslims, no Christians, no Sikhs, but only Indians. I am confident that the people of this country, who have given proof of their patriotism and common sense on so many occasions in the past, will stand united as one man to defend their country.

Meanwhile in Kashmir there was some sort of a lull in the ground fighting but intense battles were being fought in the air. Squadron Leader Trevor Keelor, flying a light fighter-interceptor Gnat, shot down a Pakistani F-86

Sabre jet. The main effort of the Indian army and air force was to stop the advance of the Pakistani army towards the strategic Akhnoor bridge, and they had so far managed this.

Press comment in the West was beginning to be realistic though not entirely favourable to India. In a long and analytical editorial in its issue of 3 September 1965, *The Economist* of London warned Ayub that Pakistan could not win, however just he considered his cause. It advised him in effect to forget Kashmir if the problem could not be settled by 'a spontaneous burst of goodwill.' It added:

> They tried direct talks with India; they tried a flirtation with China and found that even when Indians were reeling from one Chinese attack and in deadly fear of another, Nehru was not going to safeguard his other frontiers by making concessions, however hard Duncan Sandys twisted his arms. They tried to use the popular appeal of Sheikh Abdullah for their own purposes which are not his and found him arrested. Last month they tried force.
>
> And again they will probably fail. The guerrillas from across the ceasefire line had taken a beating. Even if it now developed into an outright war, Pakistan would probably lose. Even if fighting halts short of that, the Indians are now totally determined not to negotiate, let alone compromise. Kashmir they say is Indian and that's that.[3]

On 4 September 1965 a detailed reply was sent by Shastri to Secretary-General U Thant. It made an unequivocal statement of India's position:

> There is no other name for the massive Pakistani infiltrations across the Ceasefire Line . . . that Pakistan has launched into our territory, but aggression. That aggression throws on us, a sovereign State, responsibilities for defence which it is our right and duty to discharge.
>
> To sum up, I have taken this opportunity of acquainting you with all the aspects of the complex and dangerous situation that has been brought about by Pakistani actions. We owe it to you and to the high office you occupy with such distinction, to leave you in no doubt as to our position.
>
> Mr Secretary-General, you have appealed for peace and we greatly appreciate your anxiety and the sincerity of your efforts. India has always stood firmly for peace and our position needs no reiteration. What is essential, however, today is that Pakistan should undertake forthwith to stop infiltrations across the Ceasefire Line and to withdraw the infiltrators and its armed forces from the Indian side of the Ceasefire Line and the international frontier between Jammu and Kashmir and West Pakistan.
>
> Furthermore, we would have to be satisfied that there will be no recurrence of such a situation . . . I trust that, in the first instance, you will ascertain from Pakistan if it will accept the responsibility for withdrawing not only its armed forces but also the infiltrators and for

preventing further infiltrations. This, in fact, we take it, is the basic assumption underlying your appeal.[4]

The prime minister was aware that the Security Council would soon meet at its own initiative to consider the Indo–Pakistani conflict, and would certainly meet again as soon as the news of India's planned counterattack was received at the UN headquarters in New York. In consultation with the emergency committee of the cabinet, he decided that Education Minister M.C. Chagla should lead the Indian delegation, and that he should be assisted by Foreign Secretary C.S. Jha. As Chagla was not able to proceed to New York immediately, the prime minister decided that C.S. Jha should in any case leave for New York at once, so as to be able to attend a likely meeting of the Security Council on 6 September, and explain India's counterattack. Shastri had full confidence in C.S. Jha, but even so he could not disclose to him the military secret about India's planned action on the West Pakistan frontier. When Shastri personally asked C.S. Jha to leave for New York immediately without telling him the real reason, Jha felt rather puzzled. As he says:

> Early on the morning of Saturday, 4 September 1965, Shastri sent for me in his residence at 1, Moti Lal Nehru Place and told me that he had decided to send M.C. Chagla, education minister, to represent India in the Security Council but that the latter would not be able to leave Delhi until the following week. Meanwhile, he wished me to proceed immediately to New York. I submitted to him that another meeting was unlikely to take place for a few days more. In that case I could perhaps go along with Chagla. Shastri gave me no reasons but said that he was clear in his mind that I should proceed to New York that very day. I could not quite understand then why the prime minister was so insistent on my leaving immediately. However, as directed by him, I left for New York in the early hours of the morning of 5 September 1965.
>
> It was only later that I understood the reason for my being despatched to New York post-haste.[5]

As the prime minister had anticipated, C.S. Jha's presence in New York and his participation in the Security Council debate ensured an effective presentation of India's position and the subsequent adoption of a resolution, on 6 September 1965, which took account of India's concerns.

In New Delhi, throughout the day on 4 September, there was a great deal of speculation in political circles as well as among foreign diplomats as to the next step which India might take. The decision which the prime minister had taken remained secret.

At about midday Shastri received Chester Bowles at the latter's urgent request. Ambassador Bowles made a persuasive plea for restraint and for a positive response to the UN appeal for peace. Shastri knew Bowles was a sincere friend and supporter of India, and therefore gave him patient hearing. He then responded more or less on the same lines as he had to the UN secretary-general. Bowles sent a detailed report to Washington. A sanitized and declassified version of this report is available in excerpts:

At 1215 hrs Saturday I called on Primin who was cool, collected, articulate and very clear in his views throughout conversation which lasted about 35 minutes. British Highcomm Freeman who saw him yesterday had similar impression.

At least it is clear that we are not dealing with a mad man who is about to fly off on an emotional tangent although it does not mean that Shastri will necessarily come up with wise decisions. This does mean he is unlikely to act in blind anger.

I stated I was speaking not only as American amb but as established friend of India who had watched her development over long period of time, who has been deeply encouraged in [past] months by positive factors which are now beginning to contribute to India's faster growth and who is looking forward with keen anticipation to major economic breakthrough here in India within next few years which could have tremendous implications for entire world.

. . . Primin is facing [kind] of fateful historic decision that had been faced by scores of other leaders in different parts of world in last several hundred years. Some had met challenge with courage and imagination, others under pressure had taken what turned out to be wrong path with heavy cost to every one involved. For instance in Europe in late July and early August 1914 leaders of key countries found themselves locked in by previous speeches and pronouncements and what they assumed were demands of public opinion, in spite of fact that each one recognized in his heart that the powers were on military collision course . . .

In present situation one point at least was clear. Regardless of what his govt did now, it may be that Paks themselves have decided to push situation into all-out war; if so, there is nothing he could do to stop them. But what he can do is to make a war-like course on part of Pakistan much more difficult by establishing a strong case for India before world opinion by his own restraint. If under those circumstances Paks should decide in favor of war, Shastri's own personal role and that of India would be clear beyond question and thoughtful men throughout world would support him.

. . . three points were in his opinion of utmost importance:

A. Nimmo report must be made public. UN border observers had no police power, i.e. no authority to stop fighting by physical means. Therefore it has been clear from outset that their role is to inform syg [secy-gen.] and world as whole what is actually going on in Kashmir so that there is no need to [depend] on conflicting propaganda claims of the two nations.

Most direct way to achieve this objective would be to have syg [secy-gen.] himself based on observer's report decide where blame should be placed and then publicly state his findings.

Since syg had decided to take neutral position in order to enhance his own peace making powers, it was essential that report at least should become public knowledge even though in some respects it was critical of India so that world opinion could be brought to bear. If UN observers could not fulfill this function, what was purpose of sending them to Kashmir?

B. Following publication of the report Pakistan must agree to withdraw remaining . . . infiltrators who had crossed border starting August 5. Until infiltrators are withdrawn by Pakistan, there can be no hope for peaceful solution.

C. In order to prevent repeat performance UN observer team's staff should be greatly expanded to give them effective coverage of whole area.

Bowles reported further that before the close of the meeting, Shastri referred to other important matters. First, he expressed the hope that the 'US and other nations would not assume that this was a good time to discuss long-term settlement of Kashmir problem.' 'At present,' the prime minister said, 'we are close to war brought on by Pak aggression.' If some day Ayub had a change of heart and got rid of Bhutto, there would be better hope for genuine peace. The second matter raised by the prime minister was the use of US tanks, planes and other weapons for aggression against India. Bowles responded by expressing the hope that all fighting would stop, but added that to prevent the aggressive use of US weapons and equipment, 'we would have to consider measures that might be taken.'

The concluding paragraphs of Bowles' report make interesting reading:

In final ten minutes of discussion we went over same points in various ways. I ended exchange by strong personal plea for moderate and affirmative response to syg's appeal and by expressing hope that Shastri would seize this historic opportunity to establish himself as man of peace in Nehru–Gandhi tradition and at same time to win respect of hundreds of millions of people throughout the world who had learned at heavy cost what destruction modern war could bring.

Shastri followed me to door and expressed his appreciation in warm, friendly and yet confident manner for what he described as helpful exchange.

Comment: I do not dare predict how Indians in last analysis will react. In spite of Shastri's calm appearance, mood here in Delhi is one of frustrated militance; there is strong feeling even among normally sober people that once new ceasefire is established, Paks will turn to some new form of military harassment and that process will go on indefinitely.

Faced with this situation Shastri has taken strong and not unreasonable position, i.e. that Pakistan's responsibility for training and sending in large guerilla unit should be made public and that based on facts established by this report, Paks should then agree to remove infiltrators from valley and from Jammu. Indian and Pak troops should at such stage be withdrawn to their own policing system involving adequate personnel and perhaps . . . mile wide neutral belt would be set up in place of present ineffective system.

However this combination is admittedly difficult for Paks to swallow since they have officially denied there are any infiltrators from Pakistan on Indian-held territory and are still insisting that whole valley is in wild revolt against Indians under leadership of nonexistent revolutionary govt.

I again suggest that if Indians come through with reasonable presentation at Security Council as I earnestly hope they will, Paks can be persuaded to agree to ceasefire only by application of some kind of sanctions by US, by US and UK or by UN generally.[6]

After these meetings with Freeman and Bowles neither Wilson nor Johnson could be left in any doubt as to who the aggressor was, what the serious consequences of such aggression had been to India, and why India had no real alternative but to counterattack. This precautionary action was all the more necessary because Pakistan was a military ally of these countries and likely to ask for their help as a part of the alliance obligation.

Later on 4 September Shastri met President Radhakrishnan and Congress Party President Kamaraj to discuss the current situation with them.

From the battle-front the news by the end of the day was mixed. A new thrust had been made by a Pakistani tank column across the Munawar Tawi river in the Chhamb–Jaurian area. This meant that the Pakistanis were continuing to make efforts to move eastwards. The Indian air force had been active throughout the day and news was received that the little Gnat had shot down another two Pakistani F-86 Sabre jets. In a dramatic five-minute air battle, Flt Lt V.S. Pathania, flying a Gnat, had got behind one of the Pakistani fighters. He had closed in at high speed and had shot down the Pakistani plane. Another three Gnats had destroyed the other Pakistani jet. The Indian ground and air forces had destroyed about thirty-three Patton tanks by now.

In Pakistan there was great jubilation because the Pakistanis had crossed the River Tawi and had pushed another five miles eastwards, according to their sources. *The Dawn* announced this by a banner headline across its front page in its issue of 5 September.

The Chinese vice-premier and Foreign Minister Marshal Chen Yi paid another visit to Pakistan on 4 September. He was welcomed by Bhutto. Their talks during the day lasted more than four hours. According to *The Dawn*, Marshal Chen Yi, while talking to newsmen a little before midnight at the Chinese embassy, had declared full support for Pakistan and for the struggle of 'freedom fighters' in Kashmir. Also on 4 September, the official newspaper of the Chinese government, *People's Daily*, reported that the tension in Kashmir had been caused by India alone. The Pakistan–China axis was well in exhibition.

On 5 September, a report was received in New Delhi that the United Nations secretary-general had finally submitted a report to the Security Council on developments in Kashmir. This report, dated 3 September 1965, 'on the current situation in Kashmir with particular reference to the Ceasefire Agreement, the Ceasefire Line and the functioning of UNMOGIP', in order to provide information for the use of the Council, had been considered by the Security Council at its session on 4 September.[7] It will be recalled that the UN secretary-general had prepared a report on Kashmir earlier which he had made available informally to UN Security Council members and also to India and Pakistan. Its publication was then strongly opposed by the Government of Pakistan and the secretary-general had consequently decided to withhold publication. But on 1 September, Ambassador Arthur Goldberg, the United States' permanent representative to the UN, had assumed the presidentship of the Security Council for the month of September. The first thing he did was to see U Thant to urge him to make public his unofficial report on Kashmir. He also suggested that 'U Thant call a session of the Council and indicated that the goal of the UNSC session would be a consensus or resolution along the lines of the secretary-general's recommendations.'[8] Significantly, by 2 September Johnson had decided that the United States would not pressurize either side directly but would instead place primary reliance on the United Nations for the time being.[9]

The presence of American-made tanks and planes in the Pakistani offensive in the Chhamb area had given rise to a great deal of resentment in India. Ambassador B.K. Nehru called on US Secretary of State Dean Rusk on 3 September 1965 to enquire where the United States stood on this question. He reminded him that Eisenhower and John Foster Dulles had given firm assurances to India in the 1950s that the United States would not permit this equipment to be used against India. Secretary Rusk responded that he had already discussed this problem with Johnson, but emphasized that the most important thing was to get peace and that he supported the UN appeal for ceasefire. This was the background in which, pressed by the president of the Security Council, Goldberg, U Thant submitted his report. Explaining the purpose of the report, the secretary-general said:

In the course of my recent consultations with members of the Council, a need for a report from me was generally expressed. The report will serve to inform the members of the grave situation that has developed in Kashmir, of my deep concern about it, and of the steps I have been taking in past weeks in seeking to avert further deterioration of that situation and to restore normal conditions in the area. For the same purpose, I presented to the Council members individually on 31 August an informal and confidential paper, which was made available also to India and Pakistan.

The secretary-general went on to provide the following comments and information on recent developments:

There can be little doubt that the Kashmir problem has again become acute and is now dangerously serious. Implicit in it, in my view, is a potential threat to peace not only between India and Pakistan, but to the broader peace.

General Nimmo has indicated to me that the series of violations that began on 5 August were to a considerable extent in subsequent days in the form of armed men, generally not in uniform, crossing the Ceasefire Line from the Pakistan side for the purpose of armed action on the Indian side.

UNMOGIP received an Indian complaint of Pakistan shelling, on 1 September, of pickets and a battalion Headquarters in the Chhamb area of the Jammu–Bhimber Sector of the Ceasefire Line. The complaint stated that at 0230 hours on that date, one and a half Pakistan tank squadrons crossed the Ceasefire Line in this area, supported by artillery. Pakistan artillery was also said to have fired on a battalion Headquarters near Punch from 1630 hours on 1 September and on an Indian battalion Headquarters in the Jangar area. The substance of these complaints was subsequently confirmed by United Nations Military Observers. A Pakistan complaint reported that Indian soldiers had crossed the Ceasefire Line in strength in the Kargil, Tithwal and Uri–Punch sectors, as reported above. Pakistan, in this complaint, also affirmed the crossing of the Ceasefire Line by Pakistani troops in the Bhimber area on 1 September, as a defensive measure to forestall Indian action, asserting also that in this Sector the Indian air force had taken offensive action against Pakistani troops.

He added the following information:

I have not obtained from the Government of Pakistan any assurance that the Ceasefire and the Ceasefire Line will be respected henceforth or that efforts would be exerted to restore conditions to normal along that Line. I did receive assurance from the Government of India, conveyed orally by their representative at the United Nations, that India would act with restraint with regard to any retaliatory acts and will respect the Ceasefire Agreement and the Ceasefire Line if Pakistan does likewise.

The report of the secretary-general had made it abundantly clear that the responsibility for causing the war in Kashmir was Pakistan's.

The Security Council met on 4 September under the presidentship of Goldberg to consider further action. By that time Shastri's letter dated 4 September 1965 in response to secretary-general's appeal of 1 September 1965 for a ceasefire had not been received by the secretary-general, but it was read into the record by the permanent representative of India to the UN, G. Parthasarathi, at the 1237th meeting of the Security Council, which was then in progress. During the debate Parthasarathi made it clear that while a ceasefire was desirable, it could not come until Pakistan was identified as the aggressor and asked to withdraw. It would also be essential for Pakistan to provide an acceptable guarantee that there would be no recurrence of such a situation.

Members of the Security Council who participated in the debate supported a draft resolution jointly sponsored by Bolivia, Ivory Coast, Jordan, Malaysia, Netherlands and Uruguay, and asked for an immediate ceasefire by India and Pakistan. Among others, the British representative Lord Caradon invited attention pointedly to that part of the secretary-general's report in which he confirmed that the initial crossing of the Ceasefire Line had commenced when armed men had gone across the line from the Pakistan side for armed action on the Indian side. From the Indian point of view, the importance of the debate in the UN Security Council on 4 September lay in the fact that every member had clearly noted, from the report of the UN secretary-general and from the debate in the Security Council, first that Pakistan had committed the aggression; second that Pakistan had violated the ceasefire terms; third that Pakistan was lying by disclaiming responsibility for the infiltrators; fourth that the Pakistan army had launched an open invasion on 1 September 1965. This background and context were invaluable assets to India when, as we shall see later, the Security Council met again, two days later, on 6 September 1965, to consider further developments, because they gave complete credence to India's assertion that her strike at West Pakistan on the morning of 6 September was a purely defensive measure.

At the conclusion of the debate the Security Council adopted the following resolution unanimously:

The Security Council

Noting the report of the Secretary-General (S/6651) dated 3 September, 1965

Having heard the statements of the representatives of India and Pakistan,

Concerned at the deteriorating situation along the Ceasefire Line in Kashmir,

(1) Calls upon the Governments of India and Pakistan to take forthwith all steps for an immediate ceasefire;

(2) Calls upon the two Governments to respect the Ceasefire Line and have all armed personnel of each party withdrawn to its own side of the line;

(3) Calls upon the two Governments to c-ooperate fully with the UNMOGIP in its task of supervising the observance of the ceasefire;

(4) Requests the secretary-general to report to the Council within three days on the implementation of this resolution.[10]

This resolution made no difference to India's position. As the prime minister had already conveyed to the secretary-general, the first step towards peace had to be Pakistan's acceptance of responsibility for the infiltrators and their immediate withdrawal. The prime minister, therefore requested the foreign minister to respond to the UN Security Council resolution by reiterating the same position.

On 5 September there was much public rejoicing in Pakistan because of the news given out by the government that the so-called 'Azad' and Pakistani armed forces had captured Jaurian, which was close to Akhnoor. The expectation was that in another day the advancing Pakistani columns would capture Akhnoor bridge and thus cut off the lifeline between Kashmir and the rest of India. Every person of any consequence in the Pakistan government sent congratulatory messages to the armed forces. Ayub congratulated the officers and soldiers on their commendable performance; Musa, declared that the fall of Jaurian was a severe blow to the Indian forces sending the following message to his men in the battlefield: 'You have got your teeth in him. Bite deeper and deeper till you destroy him, and destroy you will, God willing.'[11]

Pakistan now sent out its planes for an attack on an Indian air force base near Amritsar. An F-86 Pakistani Sabre jet fighter-bomber came low over the IAF unit close to Amritsar and attacked it with rockets but was driven away by Indian anti-aircraft guns. No damage of military significance was caused. Indian ground forces were engaged in fierce battles to hold their positions near Jaurian; the air force continued its operation against Pakistani columns pushing forward towards Akhnoor. Keelor and Pathania were awarded the Vir Chakra by the president of India. The news that Pakistani planes had bombed a mosque in Jaurian and killed fifty men who had gathered there for prayers had angered people everywhere. Meetings were held in all parts of the country and many Muslim organizations conveyed their full support to Shastri.

In an address on 5 September to a meeting of the National Development Council (the country's supreme body established for the consideration of national development plans and priorities), Shastri was resolute: 'We cannot allow this thing to continue. We do not want that there should be a continuous conflict forced on us by Pakistan, and that they should cross into our territory and then sue for peace, in the hope that we will agree to some kind of a ceasefire. This has become intolerable. We do not and cannot accept it. We have to bring this matter to an end.'[12]

On 5 September Shastri attended to official business till about midnight. I was with him in his office. We talked about a number of things, but not about the military action which he was about to launch. The prime minister then left for his residence for some rest. When a few hours, on the 6th, General Chaudhuri informed the prime minister that the Indian army had moved into Pakistan and that some of its units were at that very moment approaching the outskirts of Lahore. The Indian air force was supporting the ground forces and attacking important military targets inside Pakistan. The general war with Pakistan had begun. India under Shastri had crossed the Rubicon.

At about midday on 6 September, the defence minister, Y.B. Chavan, stated in the Lok Sabha:

> Hon. Members are aware that I have been keeping them apprised from time to time about the aggression being committed on our territory by the armed forces of Pakistan, clandestinely at first and openly thereafter. The first wave of aggression was through armed infiltrators constituted from regular and irregular soldiers of the Pakistani army, though Pakistan assumed a posture of innocence with regard to these happenings. On 1 September, the Government of Pakistan threw off this posture and put in its regular forces in the shape of a massive armed attack in the Chhamb Sector of our state of Jammu and Kashmir. This attack was mounted with a large force of infantry and tanks and accompanied by air cover. Naturally, we have had to repel all these attacks and our armed forces have been giving an exceedingly good account of themselves, notwithstanding the difficulties which they had to face.
>
> We have, as I informed Hon'ble members earlier, had to carefully watch the developing situation and have had to take an overall view of the defence of the country.
>
> On the afternoon of 5 September, Pakistani aircraft intruded across the international boundary at Wagah near Amritsar and fired rockets at an air force unit. Anti-aircraft action drove them away. This violation was reported but there were further violations over the same border by

the Pakistani air force and it was quite apparent that Pakistan's next move was to attack Punjab across the international border. The indication that this was going to happen was building up over some time. In order to forestall the opening of another front by Pakistan, our troops in the Punjab moved across the border in Lahore sector for the protection of the Indian border. Our aircraft carried out a number of sorties over West Pakistan this morning and attacked a number of military installations including a goods train carrying military stores and inflicted considerable damage. All our aircraft returned safely.

We have taken the decision to effectively repel Pakistani aggression in the full knowledge that the whole nation, irrespective of party alignments, is one with the Government in this matter. The Prime Minister has received the fullest assurance from all quarters in this regard.

At all meetings addressed by the prime minister during that day, complete support was expressed for his action by members of his own party as well as opposition leaders. Perhaps most significantly, Mohammad Ismail, president of the Muslim League, affirmed that the 'people will make all sacrifices in fighting the enemy.' The DMK chief, Annadurai, urged that there should be a moratorium on all controversies. It was heartening for Shastri to hear every opposition leader speaking with strong feelings of nationalism and patriotism.

News of Indian troops having reached the outskirts of Lahore and of Indian military planes bombing military targets in Pakistan electrified the nation. Special editions of newspapers were out everywhere. In a moment, India was transformed.

## THE WAR AND WORLD REACTION

The advance of Indian troops towards Lahore on 6 September had an immediate and dramatic effect, as described by Lt-General Harbaksh Singh:

> As the crisis in the CHHAMB Sector was rapidly slipping into disaster, recourse to force in a sector of our own choosing became inevitable to relieve the enemy pressure. This led to the mounting of full-fledged offensives in the LAHORE and SIALKOT Sectors by XI and I Corps respectively . . . The enemy reacted instantaneously. Within a few hours, the major portion of medium armour, artillery and a brigade of infantry were ordered to pull out of the CHHAMB Sector. PAK's ambitious thrust towards the AKHNUR Bridge was checkmated just in the nick of time.[13]

That the Pakistan army gave up its push towards Akhnoor bridge as a direct result of India's counterattack against West Pakistan is confirmed by General Mohammad Musa, in his book *My Version* :

Meanwhile, India invaded Pakistan on 6 September. From then onward, the country's security took precedence over other missions in Kashmir. Therefore, and in view of our limited resources and because the threat to Azad Kashmir had receded, I withdrew from Chhamb the additional artillery allocated to the counteroffensive force and an infantry brigade for deployment on the Sialkot front. These moves weakened our offensive power in the Chhamb Valley. Consequently, and after ascertaining the local commander's views on the assault on Akhnur with a depleted force, we decided to postpone it. He also showed reluctance in undertaking it in those circumstances.[14]

But the big battles on the India–West Pakistan borders were just being joined and there was now a state of general war. It was the gravest crisis in the subcontinent since the Second World War.

News of the war shook the world. Would China join the war against India? Would the USA feel compelled to go to India's help to prevent China from expanding over South Asia? And what of the Soviet Union? The battleground was far too close to its borders, and therefore to its interests. The Soviet Union was by now dead against Chinese expansionism. With two Commonwealth countries engaged in bitter fighting, the position of the United Kingdom was unenviable. Clearly, if the powers of the world did not act quickly and in concert, global peace might be imperilled.

It was soon apparent, however, that barring China no other country wanted the India–Pakistan war to continue, much less expand. By informal contacts among members of the Security Council, two conclusions quickly emerged early on 6 September in New York, first that a meeting of the Council be convened immediately, and second that firm signals be given to prevent any spread of a potentially global conflict.

Harold Wilson sent messages to Shastri and Ayub, urging them to order a ceasefire. He had intervened successfully in the Rann of Kutch dispute and it was perfectly understandable that he should wish to use his personal acquaintance with both to secure some quick and positive result.

I am horrified at the rapid escalation of fighting between Indian and Pakistani Forces culminating in the news that Indian forces have today attacked Pakistan territory across the common international frontier between India and Pakistan in the Punjab. This attack is a most regrettable response to the Resolution adopted by the Security Council on (4 September) for a ceasefire.

A most dangerous situation has been created which may have the gravest consequences not only for India and Pakistan but also for the peace of the world. War is a terrible and incalculable thing. The security of millions of members of minority communities in both India and

Pakistan has become dangerously at risk. Extensive fighting is bound to be destructive to the economic development of both countries in which, as you know, my government have taken a deep interest. There is a real risk of the conflict spreading and involving further countries.

It is not for me to distribute blame for the present situation between the governments of India and Pakistan. We made clear in the Security Council our view about the infiltration of armed men from Pakistan across the Ceasefire Line. But both governments bear responsibility for the steady escalation which has subsequently occurred, and today's attack in the Lahore area presents us with a completely new situation.

His message concluded:

I earnestly appeal to you even at this late hour to agree to an informal arrangement, provided that the Pakistan government similarly agree, under which all Indian and Pakistani forces now in contact with each other immediately stop fighting against each other and stand their ground. This would provide a pause for the negotiation of a formal ceasefire and a mutual withdrawal of all armed personnel to their own sides of the border and the Ceasefire Line in co-operation with the Secretary-General of the United Nations. I am making a similar appeal to President Ayub.[15]

Prime Minister Shastri was puzzled by Wilson's message. Indian political circles were incensed. India wondered why Wilson held India responsible for the new situation. Why had he ignored the established fact that Pakistan had committed aggression first? Why did he overlook the fact that the Pakistan army had invaded Kashmir with heavy tanks and was getting dangerously close to its objective—Akhnoor bridge. Why did he not see that militarily India had no choice except to counterattack? I do not believe that this was due to any bias against India. The clue may lie in Wilson's subsequent statements, in which he justified his message to Shastri by saying that the Indo-Pakistani situation called for an immediate statement from him, and that he issued his statement on the basis of such information as he had at that time about the Indian attack on West Pakistan. The information he was referring to was probably the Pakistani statement, issued early on 6 September, which read as follows:

CGS Pakistan Command: On 060500.
    September 1965, Indian troops have attacked across the West Pakis-tan border. Estimated strength whole Indian Army less four divisions.[16]

The truth was that a major part of the Indian army was tied up on the Indo–Chinese border and that smaller part was deployed on the Western border. In any case, the need of the moment was an immediate cessation of hostilities, and Wilson, in these circumstances, sent off his sharp message to Shastri without bothering overmuch about niceties. Wilson sent the following message to Ayub, in which also he blamed India for the dangerous situation:

> I am horrified at the rapid escalation of fighting between Pakistan and Indian forces, culminating in the attack today by Indian forces across the common international frontier between India and Pakistan in the Punjab.
>
> A most dangerous situation has been created which may have the gravest consequences not only for Pakistan and India but also for the peace of the world. War is a terrible and incalculable thing. The security of millions of members of minority communities in both Pakistan and India has become dangerously at risk. Extensive fighting is bound to be destructive to the economic development of both countries in which, as you know, my government have taken a deep interest.
>
> It is not for me to distribute the blame for the present situation between the governments of Pakistan and India. Both seem to me to be responsible for the steady escalation which has occurred.
>
> I earnestly appeal to you to . . . immediately stop fighting against each other and stand [your] ground. This would provide a pause for the negotiation of a formal cease-fire and a mutual withdrawal of all armed personnel to their own sides of the border and the Ceasefire Line in co-operation with the Secretary-General of the United Nations. I am making a similar appeal to Shastri.[17]

Wilson's message referred specifically only to the Indian attack on West Pakistan which had, according to him, created a dangerous situation. Therein lay the imbalance between the two messages, causing the impression of bias and partisanship. Within a week of receiving Wilson's message, Shastri sent back a brief reply asking Wilson to consult his own military advisors on the dangerous situation which had been created for India by the Pakistani attack in the Chhamb region on 1 September 1965.

President Johnson decided not to send any message directly to the combatants but to act through the Security Council to urge an immediate ceasefire. He was personally in close touch with his UN representative, Goldberg. Already involved heavily in the Vietnam situation, Johnson's anxieties were heightened by the possibility of Chinese intervention in the Indo–Pak war. But unlike Wilson he did not rush in with peremptory messages. From the available records it is clear that Johnson's main and immediate concerns on 6 September 1965 were a ceasefire, the prevention of offensive use of US supplied arms, and the prevention of Chinese intervention against India. Apparently, the detailed reports from New Delhi sent by Chester Bowles and the regular briefings provided on developments in the UN had provided Johnson with correct information.

On 4 September, coinciding with the first resolution of the Security Council on the Indo–Pak conflict, Kosygin of the USSR had written at length both to Shastri and Ayub, urging an immediate ceasefire and a return of the respective troops to positions behind the Ceasefire Line of 1949. In the same letter Kosygin had offered his country's good offices in future negotiations for the peaceful settlement of their differences if India and Pakistan considered this useful. Kosygin's letter of 4 September said: 'We should not be frank if we did not say that the military conflict in Kashmir arouses the concern of the Soviet Union also because it has occurred in an area adjacent to the borders of the Soviet Union.' It was equally clear that the USSR did not want either the Chinese or the US position in South Asia to strengthen. In 1962, when the Chinese had invaded India, the USSR had done nothing to help India despite the strong India–USSR friendship because the USSR had still not broken completely with China. The situation now was different. India was a friend of the USSR, China an enemy. Even so, it would have been extremely awkward for the USSR to help India, a non-communist country against China—a fellow communist country. The USSR did not want to be placed in that position. The only solution was an immediate cessation of hostilities.

This then was the state on the world political chessboard, with the danger of a global conflagration on the horizon, when the United Nations Security Council met on 6 September 1965. With the hindsight of history, it is clear that if the secretary-general had not presented his report, and if the Security Council had not met on 4 September for a detailed considera-tion of that report, the meeting on 6 September 1965 might well have been overwhelmed by India's march towards Lahore and the focus of blame could have shifted to India. As events actually unfolded, however, Pakistan's slate in the Security Council was by no means clean when the Security Council met on that day.

C.S. Jha had arrived in New York in the afternoon of 5 September, still unaware of the reason why he had been sent there in such haste. But he did not have to wait long, because overnight came the news of the Indian army's march towards Lahore. It also became known that a meeting of the Security Council had been convened at 3.00 p.m. New York time. This gave Jha time in the morning to establish informal contacts with members of the Security Council and explain why India had been forced to make a diversionary attack. Among those whom he met were Adlai Stevenson of the USA, Sir Patrick Dean of the UK, Federenko of the USSR, Ramani of Malaysia, Abdul Moneim Rifai of Jordan and Arsene Usher of the Ivory Coast. Most of them were his former colleagues at the United Nations and were, therefore, well known to him. 'I briefed them,' says Jha, 'on the sequence of events and urged them to view the Indian military action not as an aggressive act but as defensive military action forced on India by Pakistan's military action in Chhamb and the consequent threat to the territorial integrity of India and to the Indian lines of communication in Kashmir.'[18] C.S. Jha conveyed the same message to UN Secretary-General U Thant, and Under Secretary-General Ralph J. Bunche.

An important development took place early in the afternoon. Although the Security Council was scheduled to meet at 3.00 p.m., the meeting was shifted to a later hour the same day as members of the Security Council were still in consultation. During that period Ambassador P. Morozov, deputy permanent representative of the USSR, showed Jha and Partha-sarathi (India's permanent representative at New York), the draft of a resolution which had gained support as a result of consultations among the Security Council members. From India's point of view, the text was extremely unsatisfactory and needed to be amended in two important respects. Jha used his diplomatic abilities to secure the requisite improvements well in time. This is how he describes the problems and the manner in which he resolved them:

> The resolution sought to give precision to the 4 September resolution whose operative part was merely a demand for ceasefire and withdrawal of forces by both sides. However, there was a sting in the preamble to the draft resolution which had a short and seemingly innocuous phrase, 'regretting the crossing of the international frontier'— it was not stated precisely by whom, when and where. Furthermore, the draft resolution talked of withdrawal to positions prior to 1 September. I explained to Morozov the mischievous nature of the resolution. In the first place, since the 4 September resolution contained no such expression as 'regretting the crossing of the international frontier, the only inference could be that while Pakistan's crossing of the Ceasefire Line on 5 August and of the international frontier between (Punjab) Pakistan and the State of Jammu and Kashmir on 1 September was not a matter of regret and could be condoned, India's crossing of the international frontier towards Lahore was regrettable and, therefore, by implication amounted to aggression. The Government of India, I told Morozov, would never accept that position. Secondly, the demand for withdrawal of forces to positions prior to 1 September virtually amounted to an acceptance of Pakistan's plea that nothing had happened prior to 1 September, and a rejection of India's allegation of massive infiltrations by Pakistani armed forces across the Ceasefire Line beginning on 5 August 1965. It appeared that in private conversation among Council members, Morozov had signified his 'no objection' to the draft resolution. I stressed to Morozov that the withdrawals must be to pre-August 5 positions. I felt so strongly about

the iniquity of the draft resolution that I said that if it was introduced in the Council as an agreed resolution, I would have to dissociate myself from the proceedings and to leave the Council Chamber. This seemed to shake Morozov. When he asked whether I would go so far, I answered in the affirmative and added that I was sure that my government would approve of my action. Morozov admitted that our objections were well-founded and that he had not looked at the resolution in that light. He stated forthrightly that he would inform the sponsors of the resolution that he would have to oppose it in its present form.

Parthasarathi and I heaved a sigh of relief. Morozov went back to the members of the Council and threatened to vote against the resolution in the present form. The resolution as finally introduced in the Security Council and adopted unanimously, omitted the offending preamble and asked for the withdrawal of forces of both sides to positions before 5 August 1965, thus accepting by implication that Pakistan had violated the Ceasefire Line by sending armed infiltrators to J & K on and after 5 August 1965.[19]

Another member of the Security Council who helped India greatly was Ambassador Ramani of Malaysia.

During discussions in the Security Council, Ambassador Amjad Ali of Pakistan launched a tirade against India, but this was to be expected. Jha defended India's position with restraint and dignity. Ultimately the following resolution was unanimously adopted by the Security Council:

The Security Council . . . Noting with deep concern the extension of the fighting which adds immeasurably to the seriousness of the situation,

(1)  Calls upon the parties to cease hostilities in the entire area of conflict immediately, and promptly withdraw all armed personnel back to the positions held by them before 5 August 1965;

(2)  Requests the Secretary-General to exert every possible effort to give effect to this resolution and the resolution of 4 September 1965, to take all measures possible to strengthen the UNMOGIP, and to keep the Council promptly and currently informed on the implementation of the resolutions and on the situation in the area;

(3)  Decides to keep this issue under urgent and continuous review so that the Council may determine what further steps may be necessary to secure peace and security in the area.[20]

This resolution constituted a diplomatic and political triumph for India. By calling upon the parties to cease hostilities and promptly withdraw all armed personnel back to the position held by them before 5 August 1965, the Security Council had in effect identified Pakistan as the aggressor. Pakistan could no longer beguile the world with its distortions. Second, Pakistan could no longer seek military assistance from its alliance partners to defend itself against 'Indian aggression'. Third, the resolution and the proceedings of the Security Council conveyed that India had been attacked by Pakistan. Fourth, Pakistan's credibility in the United Nations Security Council plummeted.

After the meeting, U Thant announced that in pursuance of the wishes of the Security Council he would leave for Rawalpindi and New Delhi the following day, 7 September.

In most Western newspapers of 7 September, India's counterattack towards Lahore was the main front-page story. Some carried reports sent by their New Delhi correspondents, stressing India's precarious position in the Akhnoor region resulting from the advancing military units of the the Pakistan army. Others, however, ignored this and described India's act as 'invasion of Pakistan' pure and simple. *The New York Times* made the following editorial comment:

> India could not stop the column that Pakistan sent in toward Jammu in Kashmir because she has no armored force comparable to the Patton and Sherman tanks and the artillery that the United States furnished Pakistan as a member of the South-East Asia Treaty Organization. The obvious military strategy for India was to use her numerical superiority and her infantry to make a thrust at Lahore, the provincial capital of Pakistan's Punjab.

But what was obvious to *The New York Times* was not so visible to the New Delhi correspondent of *The Times* London. His report of 6 September appeared the next day under the heading INDIAN ARMY INVADES PAKISTAN:

> The Indian invasion of Pakistan seems to be meant as a quick and overwhelming blow to cripple Pakistan's military strength and to end once for all her sustained attempts to shake India's grip on Kashmir by diplomacy, subversion, or force.
>
> India has not declared war, and it was said for the Government in Delhi tonight that 'we are not at war with the State of Pakistan or with the people of Pakistan. All our operations are intended to destroy bases from which our territory has been attacked.'
>
> When Chavan, the Defence Minister informed Parliament today that Indian troops had crossed the border with Pakistan in the Lahore sector, he said that this had been done to forestall an attack on India by Pakistan.
>
> Whatever the reasons officially advanced here, India has attacked Pakistan in an act of war. In the Indian view this was no more than a continuation and an extension of the fighting that was already going on in Kashmir. The fact remains that today's invasion of West Punjab was something essentially different from the fighting in Kashmir.

The political indications are that the Pakistanis had no such purpose, their intention was to keep their fighting limited to Kashmir.

*The Washington Post* presented a balanced picture, summed up by two headlines:

5 September 1965
UN DEMANDS KASHMIR TRUCE
PAKISTAN BLAMED

7 September 1965
INDIA INVADES PAKISTAN AS WAR SPREADS

On the whole, in its reports and comments the Western press was not as hostile as it could have been if Pakistani propaganda against India had been believed. Generally, it was accepted that the Indian military action launched on 6 September was a response to earlier aggression by Pakistan. Nevertheless, the significant escalation by India was viewed with deep concern by the Western press mainly because of the apprehension that China might decide to fish in troubled waters and thus ignite a wider conflagration.

From 6 September onwards, with ferocious battles raging in the Lahore and Sialkot sectors, and under immense pressure from nearly all heads of government, Shastri stood his ground. His attitude was not one of defiance but of determination. I recall here that when Johnson wrote to Shastri sending his best wishes on the first anniversary of his assuming the office of prime minister, he had added: 'The year has been difficult one for both of us, but I know that our faith in the democratic way of doing things will bear fruit.'[21] Shastri had thanked Johnson for his good wishes and explained his approach to his responsibilities:

We have in the Hindu religion, Mr President, a doctrine known as 'Nishkama Karma' which enjoins the individual to perform whatever duties may be entrusted to him, having regard solely to what is right and not to what profit it may or may not bring to him. It is allegiance to such a principle that provides sustenance to our efforts.[22]

Shastri received Chaudhuri and Arjan Singh every day and sometimes every few hours to get first-hand information on the war situation. In parliament, the prime minister made frequent reports, either himself or through the defence minister. He convened meetings to pass on information on the ongoing battles. He kept in touch with the people of the country by national radio broadcasts, through statements in Parliament, and via personal contacts with the leading personalities of the press.

At the international level, the prime minister wrote a detailed letter to a large number of heads of state and of government on 7 September 1965, giving them complete background information about the aggression committed by Pakistán against India beginning on 5 August 1965 and vastly escalated on 1 September 1965 with the use of a large number of troops, heavy artillery, tanks and aircraft. In these circumstances, India had no alternative but to fight back. This was an extremely important letter, sent as it was, on the day immediately following the start of India's counter-attack. Shastri's timely letter defeated Pakistan's effort to mislead world opinion by painting India's response as 'naked aggression'. The prime minister's letter of 7 September 1965 addressed to Johnson (similar letters were sent to many other heads of government) is reproduced below:

New Delhi,
September 7, 1965.

Excellency:

You are doubtless aware that starting 5 August, 1965, armed personnel from the Pakistan side of the Ceasefire Line in Kashmir began massive infiltration across the Ceasefire Line. The whole world knows, and ample support to this has been given in reports of General Nimmo to the secretary-general, that these armed personnel were, in fact, not stray raiders, but had been trained and equipped in Pakistan to bring about a revolution in the Indian state of Jammu and Kashmir. The developments that have taken place since are doubtless known to you both through press reports, as well as information obtained through diplomatic channels. The conflict unleashed by Pakistan on 5 August 1965, has been escalating steadily. When the expectation that there would be some kind of internal unrest or rebellion which the infiltrators would lead and support was belied, further heavy reinforcements began coming in from the part of Kashmir under Pakistani occupation, supported by artillery fire across the Ceasefire Line. As the UN observers confessed their inability to stop the repeated violations of the Ceasefire Line, we had no option but to ask our armed forces to take up new positions even by going across the Ceasefire Line in order to seal the passes and put an end to the infiltration.

In order to prevent further escalation, we were anxious that the UN should assert itself to ensure that the Ceasefire Line was respected. We were, therefore, anxious that General Nimmo's reports to the secretary-general should be made public and that the secretary-general should himself issue a statement which would clear the air and disprove the claim of Pakistan that she had no responsibility in the matter. Eventually, on 31 August, the secretary-general did address an informal and confidential memorandum on the subject to members of the Security Council of which India and Pakistan were supplied copies. The very next day on 1 September, Pakistan launched a brigade strength attack supported by heavy artillery, heavy tanks and aircraft in the Chhamb sector of the state of Jammu & Kashmir. Apart from the fact that this was a massive attack by the regular forces of Pakistan without any attempt to disguise the fact, this particular invasion altered the whole area of the conflict, because the attack was launched not across the Ceasefire Line, but across the international boundary between the Indian state of Jammu & Kashmir and West Punjab in Pakistan. Our armed forces naturally fought back the invaders, but in any fighting in the Chhamb sector, our troops were severely handicapped. While the Pakistan forces were supported from bases in Pakistan only a little across the border, our troops were handicapped by a long line of communications which was not suitable for the transport of heavy tanks and artillery.

On 2 September, I received a message from the secretary-general of the UN. I replied to it on 4 September saying that India is not at all anxious for a military conflict and pointing out that the withdrawal of the infiltrators and armed forces that had come from Pakistan across the Ceasefire Line and the international frontier between Jammu & Kashmir and West Pakistan, should be the starting point for the restoration of peace. We should also be assured that there would be no repetition of such aggressive actions in the future. So far as we know, there was no response to the secretary-general's message from President Ayub.

On 4 September, the Security Council met and adopted a resolution. While we were still considering it, Pakistan's offensive in the Chhamb sector was further intensified. On the evening of 5 September, a Pakistani aircraft bombed an IAF Unit near Amritsar in Punjab. At about the same time, the Pakistan air force bombed Ranbirsinghpura and other places in Jammu & Kashmir well away from the Ceasefire Line. In these circumstances, our armed forces had no option but to take action against the bases in West Punjab from which the entire range of operations first across the Ceasefire Line, then across the international boundary with Jammu & Kashmir and finally, across the international boundary between India and Pakistan were mounted and assisted.

In acquainting you with these developments, I only want to emphasise to you that our action is purely defensive in character. All we are concerned with is preserving the integrity of our boundary with Pakistan.

Yours sincerely,
(Signed) Lal Bahadur


His Excellency
Lyndon Baines Johnson,
The President of the United States of America,
WASHINGTON, D.C. [23]


At this time, Ayub appealed to the USA for help. A recorded note of the US state department says:

President Ayub called in Ambassador McConaughy to inform him officially of the Indian attack. Ayub asked that the United States act immediately to 'suppress and vacate' the Indians under the terms of the 1959 agreement between the United States and Pakistan. Ayub admitted Pakistani complicity in the Kashmir infiltration and the use of MAP equipment. Nonetheless he asked whether US support would be forthcoming . . . The Secretary instructed our posts in New Delhi and Karachi to inform the highest levels of Government there of the great concern of the United States and the great danger of Chinese Communist involvement. In response to Ayub's appeal, the Secretary replied that the United States was deeply concerned but that our first objective was unstinting support for the United Nations action. Secretary Rusk noted that Pakistan had precipitated the crisis.[24]

Pakistan also made a special plea for help to the Shah of Iran and to the President of Turkey. Both wanted to respond positively but the military hardware they had was US MAP equipment which they could not send to Pakistan without United States concurrence. The Turkish ambassador in Washington met Ambassador Talbot of the US state department on 10 September and discussed the Indo–Pak conflict. The sanitized version of the record of this meeting, reproduced below, shows that the United States firmly refused to allow Turkey to send US supplied arms to Pakistan:

Ambassador Talbot described events leading to present stage in Indo-Pak conflict. Said we have great sympathy for both parties, whatever their share of blame. We have impression neither party is yet fully committed, but moment of irrevocable decision must be very close. In circumstances, arrival of U Thant seemed one factor that might arrest headlong plunge. Our thinking will be profoundly affected by SecGen's report. We would expect both parties to propose unacceptable conditions for cease-fire, and SecGen would need find mutually acceptable middle ground. (Turk Ambassador interjected he had news report that Paks refused talk to SecGen.)

In response to Ambassador's question, Talbot said we indeed aware long-term Kashmir problem must be solved, but our first concern was stop fighting. Until fighting stops, we won't know exact nature long-term problem, since it could broaden much beyond Kashmir and affect inter-communal relations both countries.

Talbot said we felt it prudent cease MAP deliveries when conflict started. US would regret seeing other countries send additional material, which would prolong struggle. However, aside from legal limitations MAP use, other countries must make own decision regarding providing material support to combatants. [Parts deleted during sanitisation.] Talbot said we disturbed at Ayub attitude this regard, and felt this possibility another reason quick ceasefire needed.[25]

This minor setback to Ayub was accompanied by a more major one. Johnson's letter to the Pakistan president of 4 September says:

> I am well aware that a restoration of normal conditions along the Ceasefire Line will not in itself bring an end to this dispute. And I know of the depth of feeling of your countrymen regarding Kashmir. But I am convinced that a real settlement of that difficult problem cannot be had by resort to force or unilateral action by either side. Whatever the merits of the dispute, there can be no real settlement except through peaceful means and through redoubled efforts by men of goodwill to reason together in both your country and India and to find a way, as you say, to settle this and other disputes in an honorable and mutually beneficial manner. It will continue to be the policy of my country to do whatever we can to encourage and support efforts toward that end.[26]

As regards Pakistan's appeal to Iran, a high-level meeting was held on 11 September in Tehran. This was convened personally by the Shah of Iran and was attended by the US ambassador and the British charge d'affaires. On the Iranian side, the Shah was assisted by Prime Minister Hoveyda and Acting Foreign Minister Miffenderski. The Shah said that he was planning a mission to Karachi to show true friendship to Pakistan. After some remarks about the importance of Pakistan's friendship for Iran, the Shah turned to the question of military aid which could be despatched to Pakistan if U Thant's efforts failed. 'To his inquiry', said the US ambassador,

> I reiterated, much to Shah's chagrin, our opposition to transfer of MAP-supplied equipment to Paks. I noted that like British USG has stopped arms supplies to both Paks and Indians, a move which would be pointless if Paks received supplies through back door. With deep bitterness Shah said there evidently no use sending Hoveyda to talk to Paks. Except for few rifles all of Iran's equipment is MAP supplied. Hoveyda would have no RPT no tangible help to discuss with Paks. I said on contrary there is much Iran is doing and can do to retain its friendly ties with Pakistan, but certainly at this stage field of effort should be non-military. Stressing support for UNSYG, I urged once again not to jog surgeon's arm.[27]

Pakistan expected help from SEATO (South-East Asia Treaty Organization) and CENTO (Central Treaty Organization) of which Pakistan was a member. But the secretary-general of SEATO, Jesus Vargas, declared in Bangkok on 6 September that the organization would not intervene in the Kashmir fighting because Kashmir was not within the treaty obligations.[28] On 7 September the British Commonwealth Secretary, Arthur Bottomley, announced in London that Britain would not help Pakistan against India under the terms of the CENTO Pact. Britain had always made it plain, said Bottomley, that CENTO could never be employed against a Commonwealth member.[29] It seemed that Pakistan had made a formal request for help only to CENTO, but withdrew it on being told that CENTO could not help against India. On 8 September the United States government announced the complete stoppage of all aid to India and Pakistan, military and economic. Britain had already announced the stoppage of military shipments to India. By 11 September the efforts of Pakistan to secure military equipment from foreign countries had been effectively checkmated, principally because of the efforts of the USA and the UK to prevent a widening of the conflict. But future developments were to depend upon the results of the efforts of the UN secretary-general to persuade India and Pakistan to agree to a ceasefire. But there was still the China factor.

China had repeatedly announced its full support for Pakistan. Chen Yi's declaration to this effect on 4 September in Karachi was followed by a statement issued by Chou En-lai on 9 September in Peking, branding India as the aggressor and warning India that it would be responsible for all the consequences.[30] It was, however, not clear at all as to what the Chinese would actually do to demonstrate their full support. There were various possibilities.

(1) Statements by the Chinese government supporting Pakistan and blaming only India for the conflict, which was already being done.

(2) Threats to India on some conjured-up charges such as border violations by Indian troops.

(3) An ultimatum to India for the redress of imaginary grievances, failing which threat of unspecified action by the Chinese forces.

(4) The supply of weapons of aggression to Pakistan for use against India.

(5) The invasion of India by Chinese forces in certain circumstances such as the spread of war to East Pakistan or serious military reverses for Pakistan in the Western sector.

(6) The invasion of India by Chinese forces to put military pressure on India and thereby to assist Pakistan in wresting Kashmir from India by force.

But the Chinese also knew that on this occasion both superpowers were strongly against the involvement of any other country in the India–Pakistan conflict. Sino–Pak friendship may not have been worth risking broad superpower intervention. But the situation nevertheless constituted the proverbial Chinese puzzle. Even Johnson did not quite know what the real intentions of the Chinese were.

Shastri was under no delusions about the complexity and importance of the Chinese element in the war situation and decided to handle the Chinese in accordance with a considered policy:

(1)  No military action was to be taken by the Indian army or air force in East Pakistan unless it became essential in order to repel aggression. Pakistan might well try to provoke India by deliberately creating some incident, but India would have to resist the urge to strike back unless it became unavoidable. The clear purpose was that no pretext should be provided for the Chinese to intervene in the conflict.

(2)  Great care would have to be exercised to ensure that there were no incidents on the India-China border which might be exploited by China to create tension.

(3)  There would be no official response to the routine Chinese press statements in support of Pakistan.

(4)  India's official response to Chinese 'notes of protest' about one imaginary grievance or another would have to be prepared with great care and circumspection. India's replies would have to be clear and firm, but the Chinese were to be given no opportunity to describe them as 'provocative'.

(5)  If, despite all precautions, the Chinese intervened aggressively with a military attack, India would have to fight back. But the world would then understand the Indian position.

A difficult situation arose on 7 September, when the Pakistan air force carried out an air attack on Kalaikunda in West Bengal. Pakistan also dropped some paratroopers between Gauhati and Shillong in Assam. Arjan Singh was naturally upset. He met Shastri to obtain permission for retaliatory strikes. The prime minister heard him patiently but said that while he fully understood and appreciated the feelings of the air force chief, he was of the view that, considering the world situation, it was necessary in India's national interest to exercise restraint and to confine the fighting to the India–West Pakistan sector. He wanted to keep clear of China. Moreover, West Bengal and East Pakistan were both heavily populated and many lives could be lost on both sides. No one would want that to happen. Air Marshal Arjan Singh found himself, perhaps to his own surprise in complete agreement. After a cup of tea and some more conversation, he thanked the prime minister and returned home, convinced that Shastri was right. As it happened, the US government was also deeply concerned about the danger of the war spreading to East Pakistan. Secretary of State Dean Rusk sent the following message on 8 September 1965 to Chester Bowles in New Delhi:

PERSONAL FOR THE AMBASSADOR FROM THE SECRETARY
As seen from here there are very urgent reasons why we should

attempt to prevent Indo–Pak fighting from expanding into the Bengal–
East Pakistan area. Quite apart from strong humanitarian reasons for
not extending ground and air operations in area of massed populations,
the military situation in the West still appears to be somewhat tentative
and possibilities of getting ceasefire and pull back still exist. Opening up
of front in the Eastern subcontinent would be further major inflamma-
tion and would substantially increase risks of Chinese involvement.
Surely, given threatening noises out of Peking, Indian authorities can
see the point of conserving their resources in the East to meet a possible
Chinese move rather than catch up East Pakistan in the step by step
escalation which becomes increasingly difficult for either of two governments or the UN to control.[31]

The ambassador was asked to take up this matter with the Indian
government at the highest level, with an indication that, if the response of
the government of India was positive, the US government would take up
the matter with the Government of Pakistan in an effort to ensure peace
in the East.

When, in pursuance to this, Bowles talked with Shastri, he was relieved
to be advised that the prime minister had already decided against the
extension of the war to the eastern region and that he hoped that Pakistan
would stop further provocative acts, such as the attempted bombing of
Kalaikunda and Barrackpore.

On 8 September and for some days after, Shastri met a large number
of envoys, explaining India's position. Then he awaited U Thant, who was
due to arrive in New Delhi on 12 September.

# Chapter 18

# U Thant Visits India and Pakistan

In pursuance of its resolution of 6 September the UN secretary-general, U Thant, decided to visit India and Pakistan immediately. He left New York on 7 September for Rawalpindi and was received at the airport by Bhutto. He went straight to the president's house where he had a working lunch with Ayub Khan.[1] Later he had a talk for about seventy minutes with Bhutto. In the evening he met Ayub for further talks and was with him for about ninety minutes. On 10 September he continued his talks with Bhutto. According to a report in *The Dawn* of 11 September, Ayub was understood to have told the secretary-general that a ceasefire agreement with India to end 'the present Indian aggression' must include a self-executing agreement guaranteeing the holding of a plebiscite in Kashmir.[2]

An official spokesman, giving details of U Thant's talks with Bhutto, said inter alia that the foreign minister had provided the secretary-general with a detailed background to the events leading to the 'massive uprising' in 'occupied Kashmir' where people had been 'groaning under Indian rule'.[3] Bhutto was reported to have added that the 'so-called infiltrators' were the 'sons of the soil' who, 'in utter desperation', had decided to strike the final blow against Indian imperialism in their homeland and make supreme sacrifices for it. While on 6 September Ayub had conveyed to Johnson through the US ambassador to Pakistan, McConaughy, that Pakistan had organized the infiltrators and sent them from the Pakistan side of the Ceasefire Line, Bhutto told the UN secretary-general on 9/10 September that Pakistan had nothing to do with these people, who were all local freedom-fighters.

Pakistan was not prepared to agree to a ceasefire in terms of the UN Security Council resolution of 6 September. This was the final message with which U Thant left Rawalpindi on the morning of 11 September for New Delhi, via Karachi and Bombay.

The two days which the secretary-general spent in Rawalpindi were critical days for the Indo–Pak war. Pakistan had launched a massive counterattack in Khem Karan in the Lahore sector, throwing into the battle its crack I Armoured Division, supported by an infantry division. On

9 September Ayub and his foreign minister must have had high hopes of a decisive breakthrough in the Indian defences, which did not have anything like matching armour. The capture of Amritsar must have seemed that day an immediate prospect.

By the time U Thant arrived in New Delhi on 12 September, the Indian armed forces had won two decisive battles, first in Assal Uttar near Khem Karan where the Pakistani armoured division had been virtually decimated, and second in Phillora in the Sialkot sector where again, despite inferior armour, the Indian forces had inflicted blows on the Pakistanis and destroyed a large number of their tanks. Thus the Pakistani war machine had already been badly crippled and rendered incapable of mounting thrusts against India in any sector. This was the assessment provided by General Chaudhuri and Air Marshal Arjan Singh. It could be reasonably said at this time that the main war objective of Shastri, namely the destruction of the offensive capability of the Pakistan army, had been largely achieved. Major battles were still being fought in the Sialkot sector, but the outcome was now in no doubt. In brief India had, for all practical purposes, accomplished the task which Shastri desired.

U Thant arrived in New Delhi on Sunday 12 September and was received at the airport by Foreign Minister Sardar Swaran Singh, the Burmese ambassador to India, and General Robert Nimmo. He was taken straight to Rashtrapati Bhawan, where he stayed for the duration of his visit. He had an informal lunch with President Radhakrishnan and, late in the same afternoon, had a talk for nearly two hours with Shastri. No other person was present at this meeting, which was held at the prime minister's official residence.

From the look of things it was evident that the two leaders, who in essence were much of the same mould, had taken well to each other. Shastri was deeply appreciative of the fact that it was primarily the secretary-general's report, based on Nimmo's on-the-spot observations, which had ensured a balanced approach by the Security Council at its meetings on 4 and 6 September.

During their discussion Shastri received from U Thant an account of his talks with Ayub and Bhutto, both of whom had made a ceasefire dependent upon an agreement on the holding of a plebiscite in Kashmir after the withdrawal of Indian and Pakistani forces from the state and the introduction of an Afro-Asian force to keep the peace. U Thant stressed the dangers of globalizing the conflict. This, according to him, was a certain prospect if the Indo–Pakistan war continued. He urged Shastri to accept the Security Council resolutions and agree to an unconditional ceasefire.

On his part Shastri gave a detailed account of the development of the conflict and drew attention in particular to the way in which Pakistan had planned and launched its aggression against Kashmir. India was not interested in a prolongation of the war because India did not covet Pakistani territory but simply wanted to safeguard her own territory. However, the prime minister made it clear that a ceasefire at that time would have no meaning unless Pakistan were specifically identified as the aggressor. This could be done on the basis of the secretary-general's own report. He added that India must have dependable assurances that Pakistan would not commit aggression against India again, open or disguised. His position was firm and clear. There could be no question of a plebiscite or any interference in India's internal affairs.

The secretary-general returned to Rashtrapati Bhawan, from where, the same evening, he sent an identical message to Shastri and Ayub. The message to Shastri, delivered at 8.30 p.m. concluded:

> In the light of the frank and useful talks I have had in Rawalpindi and New Delhi in last few days, I now request Your Excellency to order a ceasefire without condition, and a cessation of all hostilities in the entire area of the current conflict between India and Pakistan to take effect on Tuesday, 14 September 1965 at 1800 hours, Rawalpindi time (1830 hours New Delhi time). I assume, of course, that all of your commanding officers in the field would be given their orders by you considerably in advance of this time. I have heard and understand, in the course of my talks, the difficulties on both sides to a simple ceasefire, but I make this request to you, nevertheless, because of my strong conviction that it is just and right for your country and your people as well as for the world at large. I have no doubt that your positive response would win for you the gratitude of the world.
>
> As soon as this request has been acted upon positively, I am confident that the Security Council will wish to provide the necessary assistance in ensuring the supervision of the ceasefire and the withdrawal of all armed personnel on both sides back to the positions held by them before 5 August 1965, as called for by the Security Council resolution of 6 September.
>
> I am sure also that the Council will wish to explore, as a matter of urgency, methods for achieving enduring peace between India and Pakistan. On the basis of my talks with Your Excellency, I am confident that, with the well-being of your own country and the people at heart as well as the peace of the world, you will find it possible to respond favourably to this appeal to carry out the Security Council resolutions of 4 and 6 September. I would ask you to be good enough to communicate your response to me urgently, and in any case, not later than 0730 hours New Delhi time, 0700 hours Rawalpindi time, on Tuesday, 14 September 1965. This message will be held private and confidential until your reply has been received.

In conclusion, may I assure you of my earnest wish to be of continuing assistance in the solution of outstanding problems and of my warmest good wishes.

Shastri had already sounded General Chaudhuri and Air Marshal Arjan Singh, both of whom indicated their preference for compliance with the UN Security Council request provided Pakistan did the same. Y.B. Chavan had expressed the same views. The UN Security Council had asked both India and Pakistan to agree to ceasefire without conditions. If, therefore, India laid down preconditions, it would amount to a rejection of the UN appeal for ceasefire. Shastri had already been approached by many countries to accept the UN secretary-general's appeal: Johnson, Brezhnev, Kosygin, Wilson, Nasser and Tito had all formed a chorus. Not one country would be prepared to stand by India if India rejected the UN appeal.

But Shastri was not the man to give in to pressure or act with obstinacy. He came to the conclusion that, with a favourable military situation and with Pakistan's armour crippled, it would not be to India's disadvantage to accept a ceasefire unconditionally while reiterating India's position on the fundamental issues. It would enhance India's standing in the world and ensure her understanding and even support when India sat with Pakistan to negotiate a peace settlement. Shastri now convened meetings the next day for political consultations and governmental decisions. The emergency committee of the cabinet met in the morning to consider the UN secretary-general's letter. The prime minister also addressed the Congress Party's parliamentary executive committee. There was a consensus for a response on the lines indicated by the prime minister. On some aspects, however, the prime minister wanted further clarifications from the secretary-general. For this purpose, another meeting took place between the two.

By early afternoon on 13 September it was clear that it would be difficult to deliver a reply to the secretary-general by 0730 hours on 14 September, as requested by him. Accordingly, at 5 p.m. on 13 September, the secretary-general was informed that the Government of India needed more time to complete its consideration of the matter and accordingly asked to extend the time limit to a later hour on 14 September. The secretary-general agreed.

During the course of the afternoon a draft reply to the secretary-general was prepared. It was considered by the emergency committee of the cabinet late in the evening and approved, subject to some comments. The final version of the draft letter was delivered at the official residence of the prime minister at about 11.30 p.m. The prime minister had told me earlier that he would like to review the draft letter. He read it carefully but did not seem fully satisfied. As mentioned earlier, Shastri was extremely meticulous about his written or spoken words. The proposed letter was an important document in which India's position had to be stated carefully and in detail. Having reviewed the draft, the prime minister said it needed to be revised. He gave detailed instructions for a new draft, which he asked to be given to him before 8 o'clock the next morning. After considering the revised text he finally felt satisfied. However, as the previous draft had been approved by the emergency committee of the cabinet, he immediately convened another meeting at his residence. The cabinet committee also preferred the revised draft, subject to the addition of a sentence proposed by Finance Minister T.T. Krishnamachari. The letter was signed by the prime minister and delivered to the UN secretary-general at Rashtrapati Bhawan early in the afternoon on 14 September. The bulk of it repeated India's position *vis-à-vis* Pakistan and Kashmir. It concluded:

> I would not go further into this aspect of the matter, but must add that having been attacked by Pakistan, we had to take action to defend ourselves. I must also stress and I hope it will be appreciated that at every stage whatever action our armed forces took was directed solely by the requirements of self-defence to meet the aggression of Pakistan.
>
> Whatever may be the context, Mr Secretary-General, we greatly welcome your visit and we recognize the importance of your mission from the point of view of peace, not only in the Indian subcontinent, but indeed in the world as a whole. India has always believed in peace and her adherence to peaceful methods stands unshaken.
>
> In deference to the wishes of the Security Council and to the appeals which we have received from many friendly countries, we accept your proposal for an immediate ceasefire. We would, therefore, be prepared to order a ceasefire effective from 6.30 a.m. IST on Thursday, 16 September 1965, provided you confirm to me by 9 a.m. tomorrow that Pakistan is also agreeable to do so.
>
> In your letter, it has been suggested that the Governments of India and Pakistan should give the requisite orders to their field commanders with a view to ensuring an effective ceasefire from the appointed time and date. This will, however, be effective only in respect of the armed forces in uniform engaged in the present combat. The problem of thousands of armed infiltrators who have crossed over into our State of Jammu and Kashmir from the Pakistan side will, I am afraid, continue to remain on our hands. Armed as they are with dangerous weapons of destruction, such as machine-guns and hand-grenades, they do even now, as I write this letter, make sudden depredations in an effort to damage vital installations and other property and harass the people of the state of Jammu and Kashmir.

That this invasion by armed infiltrators in civilian disguise was conceived, planned and executed by Pakistan is now well established; your own report, Mr Secretary-General, brings this out clearly. And yet, as we understand from you, Pakistan continues to disclaim all responsibility. We are not surprised at this denial, because even on an earlier occasion when Pakistan had committed aggression by adopting similar methods, she had at first denied her complicity, although at a later date she had to admit her involvement. We must urge that Pakistan should be asked forthwith to withdraw these armed infiltrators. Until that is done, our security forces will have to deal with these raiders effectively . . .

In the light of our own experience during the last few months, we will have to insist that there must be no possibility of a recurrence of armed attacks on India, open or disguised. Let me make it perfectly clear, Mr Secretary-General, that when, consequent upon ceasefire becoming effective, further details are considered, we shall not agree to any disposition which will leave the door open for further infiltrations or prevent us from dealing with the infiltrations that have taken place. I would also like to state categorically that no pressures or attacks will deflect us from our firm resolve to maintain the sovereignty and territorial integrity of our country, of which the state of Jammu and Kashmir is an integral part.

In conclusion Mr Secretary-General, I must point out that the menacing forces of aggression are unfortunately at large in Asia, endangering the peace of the world. If the Security Council does not identify the aggressor and equates it with the victims of aggression, the chances of peace will fade out. The situation which the Security Council is being called upon to handle has grave and vital implications in respect of peace and political stability in Asia. What is involved is the welfare of millions of human beings who have suffered for long and who are now entitled to relief and to a better standard of living. If the forces of aggression are not checked effectively, the world may find itself embroiled in a conflict which may well annihilate mankind. We sincerely hope that the forces of peace will win and that humanity will go forward towards ever increasing progress and prosperity. It is in this spirit that we are agreeing to your proposal for a ceasefire.

However, Ayub sent a reply to the secretary-general's letter rejecting the ceasefire unless certain conditions regarding Kashmir were accepted at the same time. His letter dated 13 September was delivered to the UN secretary-general on 14 September, while he was still in New Delhi. After explaining Pakistan's case and branding India as the aggressor, Ayub Khan made the following comments on the subject of the ceasefire:

Nevertheless, Pakistan is not against a ceasefire as such. In fact, in order to save this subcontinent from being engulfed in what would clearly be

an appalling catastrophe, we would welcome a ceasefire. But it must be
a purposeful ceasefire: one that effectively precludes that catastrophe and
not merely postpones it. In other words, it should provide for a self-
executing arrangement for the final settlement of the Kashmir dispute
which is the root cause of the India–Pakistan conflict.

While you propose a 'ceasefire without condition', you go on to add
that the Security Council would, soon after the ceasefire, proceed to
implement its resolution of 6 September. The provisions of the Security
Council resolutions of 4 September and 6 September that the ceasefire
be followed immediately by withdrawal of all armed Pakistani personnel
to the Pakistan side of the Ceasefire Line and the consolidation of the
Ceasefire Line through the strengthening of the United Nations Observer
Group would result in restoring India's military grip over Kashmir. We
would thus merely revert to the same explosive position which triggered
the present conflict.

Moreover, India has committed wanton aggression against Pakistan.
The foregoing ceasefire proposals if implemented would in effect reward
the aggressor.

We would, therefore, urge that, if the conflict is to be resolved and
this subcontinent spared the horror of an even wider war, the ceasefire
must be accompanied by action which would resolve the real cause of
this conflict. This would be possible if the ceasefire is followed immediately by complete withdrawal of the Indian and Pakistani forces from
the State of Jammu and Kashmir, the induction of a United Nations
sponsored Afro-Asian Force to maintain order in the State and the
holding of a plebiscite in the State within three months.

The UN Secretary-general wanted the acceptance of a 'ceasefire without conditions'. He therefore immediately addressed another message
dated 14 September to Shastri and Ayub:

I have received Your Excellency's reply to my message of 12 September
in which, in pursuance of the mandate given to me by the Security
Council, I requested you to order a ceasefire without condition and a
cessation of all hostilities in the entire area of the current conflict. I
appreciate the positive attitude towards a ceasefire expressed in your
reply, an attitude which has also been expressed by President Ayub Khan.

I note, however, that both governments have added to their replies
to my request for an unconditional ceasefire conditions and qualifications
upon which I have no right under the Security Council resolutions to
give firm undertakings. These aspects of the replies of the two governments must be referred to the Security Council for its urgent consideration, and they will be so referred immediately by me.

Pending the Security Council consideration of the conditional parts
of the replies, I would again ask you in all sincerity, in the interests of

the two countries, and world peace, to order a ceasefire and cessation of all hostilities in the entire area of the current conflict.

Since again delays have transpired, I would set the effective time and date of such ceasefire for 0630 hours New Delhi time, 0600 hours Rawalpindi time, on Thursday 16 September 1965.

I would ask Your Excellency to be good enough to send me an immediate response to this message.

Shastri sent a reply to this message in the morning of 15 September. This communication, which was delivered to U Thant before his departure from New Delhi in the afternoon of 15 September, said:

Thank you for your message of 14 September which was conveyed to me late last night.

You have said that you cannot give any undertakings. I fully appreciate and understand this and in fact I did not ask you for any. It was, however, essential for us to state clearly our stand in regard to certain matters which are of vital importance to us.

I reaffirm my willingness, as communicated, to order a simple ceasefire and cessation of hostilities as proposed by you, as soon as you are able to confirm to me that the Government of Pakistan has agreed to do so as well. The actual time when the ceasefire would become effective would depend upon the time when you are able to convey to me the agreement of the Government of Pakistan to a ceasefire.

This reply was clear enough, but U Thant had not by that time received any response from Ayub. Before leaving New Delhi at 2.30 p.m. on 15 September, U Thant dispatched yet another message, the third in this series, reiterating his request for the acceptance of an unconditional cease-fire and making a new suggestion that the heads of government of the two countries might agree to meet for mutual negotiations. Ayub sent a further response to the secretary-general in New York on 16 September, maintaining his position that 'it would be necessary to evolve an effective machinery and procedure that would lead to a final settlement of the Kashmir dispute'.[4] Ayub knew by this time that Pakistan had lost the war and was trying desperately to salvage something either through the Security Council or through the mediation of Johnson, to whom he now had to turn for a lifeline. But Johnson was determined to act only through the Security Council and was awaiting the report of the UN secretary-general on the result of his visit to India and Pakistan, and his proposals for future action.

Meanwhile the Chinese decided to make their presence felt again by launching a personal attack on U Thant. On 14 September, the *People's Daily* of Peking asserted that 'the US is behind U Thant's current mission to India and Pakistan and the UN secretary-general is merely acting as Washington's political broker.' In an editorial under the headline 'the UN is serving as a sanctuary for the Indian aggressor', the paper claimed that U Thant in his report to the Security Council on 4 September had already taken India's side and that both resolutions passed by the Security Council were in favour of India. 'Under these circumstances, how can one expect U Thant to uphold justice?' the paper asked. 'Under the thumb of US imperialism, the UN, reversing right and wrong and calling black white, has always served the interests of the aggressor and branded his victim as the aggressor,' it alleged. The editorial concluded: 'It can be safely predicted that through the present Indian aggression against Pakistan, an increasing number of people will come to see even more clearly the true colours of the UN.'[5]

The UN secretary-general left New Delhi on 15 September and almost immediately thereafter, Prime Minister Shastri reviewed the entire situation in order to decide upon the future course of action. Having noted the conditions which President Ayub Khan had laid down for a ceasefire, the prime minister decided to leave no one in doubt about his total opposition to each and every one of those conditions. Accordingly, the next day he addressed another letter to President Johnson and to other heads of government explaining his position on Kashmir in clear yet firm language which left no room for doubt as to India's desire for peace on the one hand and determination to defend her sovereignty on the other. The text of this letter to Johnson is given below, in full:

New Delhi,
September 16, 1965

Dear Mr President:

Ambassador Nehru has reported to me the sympathetic hearing which you gave him when he delivered my last message to you regarding the present conflict between India and Pakistan. I am sending this further communication to you to keep you informed of subsequent developments and to share with you, on a personal level, my thoughts and concerns about the trend of events.

1) As you doubtless know by now, I indicated to the Secretary-General the willingness of my Government to agree to an immediate cease-fire without any preconditions, while acquainting him with our stand on certain issues. One of the features of the Pakistani invasion is that it includes large numbers of armed personnel who are not in uniform for whom Pakistan disowns responsibility, although there is unquestionable evidence to show that they have, in fact, been equipped, organized and directed by Pakistan. This is a new technique of aggression to deal with which no effective weapons have yet been designed by the

international community. Even so, as I have said, I was agreeable to a cease-fire if Pakistan also agreed to it. While I do not know the precise nature of President Ayub's reply to U Thant, the fact remains that there has been no cease-fire and the fighting continues.

2) I notice from President Ayub's press conference that he regards Pakistan to be engaged in a life and death struggle with India. All I can say is that so far as we are concerned, we consider it to be in our interests to see the people of Pakistan prosper and to live in friendship with India. We are not out to destroy Pakistan, but to protect our own territory from repeated attacks.

3) President Ayub, in his press conference, also stated that what he really wants the UN Security Council to do is not to deal with the issues raised by Pakistani invasion, overt and covert, but to lend support to Pakistan's fantastic claim over the State of Jammu and Kashmir. This claim is based on Pakistan's assertion that since the majority of inhabitants of the State of Jammu and Kashmir are Muslims, the State should have acceded to Pakistan and not to India.

4) The Indian nation consists of people who subscribe to different religious beliefs—Hindus, Muslims, Sikhs, Christians, Parsees, as well as tribal peoples living in this country from pre-historic times—who speak different languages, almost as many as are spoken on the continent of Europe. We have, in fact, as many Muslims in India as there are in West Pakistan. In India, as in the United States of America, people of different origins, different races, different colours and different religions, live together as citizens of a state in which, despite the stresses and strains which do develop in a mixed society, the Constitution and the laws guarantee equal rights to all citizens. You yourself, Mr. President, have made, in recent months, a tremendous contribution in your own country to the task of giving adequate legal protection to a racial minority. It is through national solidarity, rather than through the mischievous doctrine of self-determination, that the minorities can find their fulfilment.

5) The reason why, when in 1947, we first went to the Security Council with a complaint of aggression against Pakistan, we made a unilateral promise of having a plebiscite in the State of Jammu and Kashmir, was that, at that time, the State had no democracy, having been under the rule of a prince in the British days, and we were anxious ourselves to be satisfied that the people, as distinct from the ruler, genuinely favoured accession to India. Ever since the accession of the State, we have been building up democratic institutions. There have been three general elections in conditions of freedom. The results of these elections have demonstrated clearly that the people of Jammu and Kashmir have accepted their place in the Indian Union. I should like to state quite categorically that there can be no further question of any plebiscite to ascertain the wishes of the people of Jammu and Kashmir. Furthermore, I would assert that the relationship between a federal government and its constituent states is no matter for any other country or for the

Security Council. If President Ayub feels that by launching an invasion on the State of Jammu and Kashmir he will pressurise us into ceding any part of the State of Jammu and Kashmir, all I can say is that he is grievously mistaken. Much though we love peace, we shall not buy it by selling our territory.

6) The real question before the UN, the Security Council and the international community, as a whole, is not of the State of Jammu and Kashmir, but that of restoring peace which was broken once again by Pakistan, and of ensuring that the boundary line between India and Pakistan is not repeatedly violated either by regular troops or by those in disguise.

7) President Ayub has made an appeal to the United States to use its influence for the restoration of peace. I very much hope, Mr. President, that the United States will do so. I think the first essential for this is to prevent the conflict from spreading. Pakistan, as you know, has appealed to many nations for help: to western powers in the name of its alliance, to middle-east and Arab countries in the name of religion, as well as to Indonesia and China on the basis of the philosophy of which these two countries are the main exponents. I hope, Mr. President, you will find it possible to make it clear to Pakistan that the neutrality which you have, for understandable reasons, maintained in this conflict so far, will have to be modified if other powers begin to join it directly or indirectly. That Pakistan is anxious to spread the conflict is evident from the fact that despite further declaration that we do not want to see any fighting start in East Pakistan, it is making repeated air attacks from East Bengal on Indian air bases, particularly those which are vital for our defence against China.

8) Before leaving India, the Secretary-General left with me a letter throwing out various suggestions for the restoration of peace, his efforts to bring about a cease-fire having failed. One of them is a meeting between President Ayub and me. I do not see how, while the armies of the two countries are locked in combat, the heads of two governments could start a dialogue across the table. You can imagine the effect it would have on the morale of our troops and our people who are solidly behind them. Quite apart from that, I cannot quite see what such a meeting might possibly lead to. As you know, in 1962 there was a meeting between President Ayub Khan and Jawaharlal Nehru when it was agreed that there should be meetings between ministers followed by a summit. We did have a number of meetings between the foreign ministers of two countries, but their positions were so far apart that it became pointless to think of a meeting at the level of heads of government.

9) The Secretary-General has also put forward the idea of mediation by the Secretary-General himself, or by a power friendly to both countries. The difficulty about this too is that what Pakistan wants is not a mediation to bring about an end to fighting and to restore peace without

losing face, but mediation in respect of Pakistan's claim to the State of Jammu and Kashmir, which we cannot possibly accept.

10) I do not question that even after the present fighting has come to an end, there will remain many issues between the two countries which will continue to create ill-feeling and give rise to friction. We have always felt that this is an unfortunate state of affairs and with better relationship and greater cooperation between the two countries, their economic progress, which is the prime task before them, and in which your great country has been helping so much, will be accelerated. Such an improvement in the relationship between the two countries is eminently desirable, but it would need at least a couple of years of real peace on the borders and a willingness on the part of Pakistan not to align itself in any way with the main threat against India, namely China, before any efforts to improve overall relations between the two countries can really become fruitful.

Yours sincerely,
(Signed) Lal Bahadur[6]

The prime minister's initiative in sending this letter helped to ensure that India's case should be clearly understood at the White House and in the Security Council. Shastri wrote similar letters to other heads of government.

## PARLIAMENT

After sending off his letter to heads of governments on 16 September, Shastri proceeded to parliament to make a statement the same day on U Thant's visit and the current situation. He said:

As the Hon. Members are aware, the Secretary-General of the United Nations, U Thant, arrived in New Delhi on September 12, 1965 and, after staying here for three days, he left yesterday for New York. We welcomed him amongst us not only as a high dignitary, but also as a representative of the world organisation on which lies the heavy responsibility of preserving international peace. The Secretary-General and I had free and frank discussions. He met the Foreign Minister and also the Defence Minister.

During the discussions, the Secretary-General drew attention to the grave implications of the present conflict, especially in relation to the welfare of the 600 million people belonging to India and Pakistan. He referred to the Security Council resolutions of September 4 and 6 and appealed that a cease-fire should be ordered immediately by both countries.

I gave a factual narration of the events as they had taken place and pointed out that the present conflict was not of our seeking. It was started

by Pakistan when thousands of armed infiltrators invaded our State of
Jammu and Kashmir commencing from August 5, 1965, with the object
of destroying or capturing vital positions such as airports, police stations
and bridges, and ultimately of seizing power forcibly from the State
Government at Srinagar. Finding that its initial invasion had largely
failed, Pakistan had launched on September 1, 1965, a massive armed
attack not only across the Ceasefire Line but across the international
frontier as well. Pakistan had thus not only started the conflict, but had
further escalated it in such a manner as to leave India with no choice
except to take countermeasures in self-defence.

I explained all this to the Secretary-General and told him that the
present conflict had been forced upon us by Pakistani aggression. We
are determined, however, to preserve fully and completely the sovereignty
and territorial integrity of our country of which the State of Jammu and
Kashmir formed an integral part; nor could we accept a situation in
which Pakistan may continue to launch its armed aggression on India
time and again.

The Secretary-General was particularly anxious that, as a first step,
we should agree to the ceasefire and to the cessation of hostilities. I told
him that a ceasefire in regard to the fighting between the troops was
understandable, but the question of raiders would still remain on our
hands. I pointed out that we would have to continue to deal effectively
with these raiders, many of whom were still at large in the State of Jammu
and Kashmir, unless of course Pakistan undertook to withdraw them
from our territory.

We went into the pros and cons of the cease-fire in detail. Subsequently, I received a letter from the Secretary-General in which his
appeal for a ceasefire was reiterated. After full consideration of all aspects
we sent a reply. As the Hon'ble Members would see from a perusal of
this letter, we raised no objection to the Secretary-General's proposal for
the ceasefire. However, in regard to certain matters of vital importance
to India, we made our stand perfectly clear. For instance, as already
stated, we would have to deal with the raiders who were still sporadically
attacking public property or harassing the people in the State of Jammu
and Kashmir. Also, we could not possibly revert to a situation in which
we may find ourselves once again unable to prevent infiltrations or to
deal effectively with those who had already come in. In regard to the
political aspect of the question, we made it clear that we were fully
determined to maintain the sovereignty and territorial integrity of India
of which the State of Jammu and Kashmir was an integral part. From
this resolve we could never be deflected, no matter what the pressure or
the threat. These were not conditions attached to our acceptance of the
ceasefire, but were meant to be a clear and unequivocal reiteration of
our stand in regard to these vital matters.

Later in the evening of 14 September, I received a further letter from
the Secretary-General saying that he could not give any undertaking, to

which I sent a reply yesterday morning pointing out that as a matter of fact we had not asked him to give any undertaking to us. Our acceptance of the cease-fire proposal thus complied fully with the appeal of the Secretary-General.

The Secretary-General told me, prior to his departure from New Delhi, that if by the evening of 15 September, 1965, Pakistan did not give a reply agreeing to the cease-fire, we should take it that an agreement on this question had not been possible. Since no such acceptance was received by the stipulated time, an announcement was made that our defence forces will have to continue the operations with unabated vigour.

Although the Secretary-General's present effort to bring about a stoppage of hostilities in order to pave the way for peace has not been fruitful through no lack of cooperation from us, he intends, as he has announced, to pursue his efforts further, and just before leaving Delhi, he sent me a further letter.

As Hon. Members would see, we have made every effort to extend all cooperation to the United Nations in its efforts to restore peace and we accepted the Secretary-General's proposal for an immediate cease-fire. Pakistan, on the other hand, has given no such acceptance. In fact the indications are that she is intent upon continuing the fight, unless her own plan involving withdrawal of the armed forces of India and Pakistan from the entire State of Jammu and Kashmir, the induction of the United Nations Force and a plebiscite within three months thereafter is agreed to. Let me state on the floor of this House that not one of these conditions is acceptable to India. It is obvious now that Pakistan launched an aggression on India by 5 August, 1965, with a view to making an attempt to revive the settled issue of the State of Jammu and Kashmir. She wants to force a decision by naked aggression. This we cannot possibly allow. We have no alternative, therefore, but to carry on our struggle. We fully realise that the present armed conflict between India and Pakistan will cause untold hardships and misery to people in both countries. However, I am confident that our countrymen would cheerfully undergo those hardships but they would not allow an aggressor to endanger our freedom or to annex our territories.

I have seen some press reports of President Ayub Khan's press conference of yesterday. Among other things, he is reported to have observed that good sense required that India and Pakistan live together in peace. If this is a new and sincere thought, I would greatly welcome it, however belated it might be. But if past experience is any guide, these remarks would appear to be part of a propaganda to beguile the world. Previously also, President Ayub had talked of the virtue of peace and has followed it up by unprovoked aggression on India in Kutch and, subsequently, in Kashmir. President Ayub has I trust by now seen the result of Pakistan's policy of hate and hostility against India.

As the circumstances exist today, the nation has to be continuously alert and be ready for any sacrifice to preserve our freedom and integrity.

I am greatly beholden to Parliament, to all the political parties and, indeed, to the entire nation for their united stand against the aggressor. I want also to express once again the gratitude of the nation to the valiant armed forces who have already demonstrated that they are capable not only of defending our frontiers but also of delivering crushing blows to the invader. Their deeds of heroism will make a glorious chapter in the annals of India. This Parliament and the whole country is proud of them. I am confident that we will continue to meet this challenge with the same determination and courage.

Parliament listened to the prime minister with rapt attention and nodded approval. When he had finished, MPs from every section of the house rose to express their unreserved support and appreciation for the prime minister and his policy. This was an inspiring display of unanimity. Members spoke with dignity, poise and self-restraint. Not a single speech contained a hint of jingoism or expressions of enmity and bitterness. For Shastri this was a moment of glory, constituting the success of his leadership. Evidence of this is apparent from some of the things that various parliamentarians said:

> *N.G. Ranga* (Chittoor): Sir, it is a historic moment. The prime minister has made a very important and, if I may say so, a very worthy and inspiring statement on this occasion.
>
> I wish to associate myself, the group that I represent and the party for which we stand here, with the determination that the prime minister has expressed through his statement to resist aggression and to prevent any loss of either territory or any possession that has come to us by virtue of our constitution.
>
> I have only one thing more to say and that is that the government has presented the case of our country, as per the statement made by the prime minister, before the United Nations and its secretary-general in a worthy manner and has placed the case of our country in the right light before the whole of the world by offering to accept their proposals and showing to the whole of the world who really is keen on aggression.
>
> *H.N. Mukerjee* (Calcutta Central): Sir, the prime minister has spoken for the whole country . . .
>
> I would like, however, to tell the prime minister that since he has made every conceivable effort, in honour and in decency, to meet the requirements of peace in our part of the world and since Pakistan has in its characteristic fashion repulsed whatever steps we were proposing to take, it is our duty now, a more bounden duty, to take more energetic steps in all the capitals of the world and especially in the capitals of great powers to make clear of the endeavours we have pursued in the face of the utterest provocation to bring about peace in our part of the world. That is the request I shall make to the prime minister . . .
>
> *Surendranath Dwivedy*: I welcome this statement, which represents

not only the viewpoint of the government or Parliament, but this is the unanimous voice of the entire country. I wish and hope that we shall continue to fight the enemy till the end and shall continue in our resolve to see that the sovereignty of our country is maintained and that the prestige and honour of our jawans who are fighting in the front are completely vindicated by the actions that we countrymen do . . .

*Karni Singhji* (Bikaner): The statement made by the hon. prime minister is most welcome and has the entire support of the members of my parliamentary group. Knowing the prime minister as we do, we were certain that he would take a strong stand on the Kashmir issue. We would like to congratulate the hon. prime minister, the defence minister and the members of the cabinet on the strong stand taken as the country had expected from them. All of us in this country are proud of our jawans. All of us in this country expected from them that given the opportunity, our forces would show their worth and this was the opportunity and they proved their grit. I once again congratulate the hon. prime minister and say that the nation wholeheartedly stands by him in this hour of crisis.

*Dr M.S. Aney* : I am glad that the prime minister has made this statement and we are glad to find that he has made the statement which we expect from him on this occasion. We stand by it. The whole country stands by it, and the world will know that India would stand like one man so long as the obstinacy of Pakistan continues.

*K. Manoharan* (Madras South): On behalf of the DMK group in parliament, I congratulate the prime minister on the historic statement he has made and I welcome it wholeheartedly. On behalf of my party, here is my positive assurance that we will strengthen the hands of the prime minister in weeding out the aggressor from this country. I again assure you that we will do all that is necessary to see the aggression vacated completely, fully and eventually. To that extent, on behalf of my party, I once again give this assurance that we are with him in whatever he does towards this end.

*Mohammad Ismail* (Manjeri): Mr Deputy-Speaker, I wholeheartedly support and endorse every word of the statement made by the prime minister. I also endorse the determination which has been expressed that we will not rest until the last trace of Pakistani aggression is eliminated. I assure you we are at the back, solidly and determinedly at the back, of the prime minister in every step that he takes for liquidating that aggression.

I also endorse the words of other friends who have spoken on this matter showing their determination. I wish every success, glorious success, will attend the nation's endeavour in its efforts in this defensive war of ours.

*J.B. Kripalani* (Amroha): Mr Deputy-Speaker, Sir, I represent unfortunately no particular section of the Indian people, but as an old servant of the nation I hope I represent the whole of India.

I fully associate myself with what has been said by our prime minister and I congratulate him on the firm stand that he has taken at this time.

I also associate myself with all those sentiments that have been expressed here by the leaders of the different parties.

Shastri's satisfaction on this remarkable occasion was, however, brief. Awaiting him was an ultimatum of war from China.

# Chapter 19

# The Chinese Ultimatum

When Marshal Chen Yi visited Pakistan on 4 September he declared full support for Pakistan. In a press interview in Karachi that day, he said: 'We condemn Indian imperialism for violating the Ceasefire Line, promoting and enlarging the conflict in Kashmir. We support the just actions taken by the Government of Pakistan to repel India's armed provocations.'[1] On the same date, the official Chinese newspaper *The People's Daily* of Peking, accused India of aggression in Kashmir and held India responsible for the tension in Kashmir. It added that Pakistani troops had been forced to hit back in self-defence, after Indian troops had 'poured' across the Ceasefire Line and 'pushed deep' into Pakistan controlled area. On 5 September again *The People's Daily* published a long article attacking India and supporting the Pakistani line that there were no 'infiltrators' in Kashmir. In the same article, the Peking paper attacked 'US imperialists' and 'Khrushchev revisionists' for supporting 'Indian expansionism'. On 7 September, the Chinese government issued a statement which was reported by the New China News Agency. The relevant bit of it said:

> India is still entrenched on the Chinese territory on the Sino–Sikkim border and has not withdrawn. It is constantly probing furtively and making intrusions and harassment against the Chinese territory in the Western sector of the Sino-Indian border. Indian violations of the Chinese territory are far from coming to an end ... The Chinese government has served repeated warnings. And it is now closely following the development of India's acts of aggression and strengthening its defences and heightening its alertness along its borders.
>
> Aggression is aggression. India's aggression against any one of its neighbours concerns all of its neighbours.
>
> Since the Indian government has taken the first step in committing aggression against Pakistan, it cannot evade responsibility for the chain of consequences arising therefrom.[2]

The Indian government perceived this as a declaration of intent to take some action in support of Pakistan. For this the Chinese had, of course, to provide some additional justification, and to that end they resorted to the familiar charges of 'intrusions and provocations'.

Shastri was closely monitoring these utterances. He was not surprised by the tone of the Chinese government statement. It was the usual familiar stuff, though this time it did contain an implicit threat. On the other hand, it was a general statement, not specifically addressed to India. The Indian armed forces were 'on the alert', but with instructions to avoid falling into Chinese traps to provoke local skirmishes which could be worked up into 'incidents'.

The next day, on 8 September, the Chinese government heightened world tension with a further turn of the screw by sending a threatening note to India, protesting against 'successive serious violations of China's territory and sovereignty by Indian troops.' The Chinese note went on to demand that 'India dismantle all the aggressive military structures it has illegally built beyond or on the China-Sikkim border, withdraw its aggressive armed forces and stop all its acts of aggression and provocation against China in the western, middle and eastern sectors of the Sino–India border.' The note added that if this was not done, India would bear the responsibility for all consequences arising therefrom.

The note was not intended for the eyes of the Indian government alone and the Chinese felt some necessity to explain to the world why the Indian government had suddenly decided in August/September 1965, after a lull since the 1962 war, to become 'intrusive' and 'provocative' all along the Sino–Indian border, particularly when the Indians were engaged in a major conflict with Pakistan in the West and were therefore hardly likely to provoke the Chinese at the same time. To provide a credible reason for India's alleged aggression at that point in time, the Chinese government note added the following:

> The Indian provocations in August in the western sector of the Sino–Indian border cannot be regarded as isolated cases. They are by no means accidental, occurring as they did not at a time when the Indian Government was carrying out armed suppression against the people in Kashmir and unleashing and expanding its armed aggression against Pakistan. Facts have proved once again that India has not the slightest respect for its neighbours. But makes incursions, harassment and encroachments upon them whenever there is a chance.[3]

Clearly, the purpose of these words was to convey to the Pakistanis how strongly China was supporting them in the war.

This note of 8 September was followed by yet another blast, this one from Chou En-lai himself. Speaking at a Korean embassy reception in Peking on 9 September, the Chinese prime minister condemned India outright as the aggressor and added: 'If peace is to be safeguarded, aggression must be opposed. India's acts of aggression pose a threat to peace in this part of Asia, and China cannot but closely follow the development of the situation.'[4]

In Shastri's judgement, the Chinese could not take any overt action against India on the basis of allegations which, in the eyes of the world, were fictitious. The Chinese would obviously need something more credible as a basis for attacking India. No such basis was available to them yet. But the Chinese notes made him take stock. He reassessed the situation and his conclusion was that as long as India continued to adhere firmly to her word on not seizing Pakistani territory, most of the countries which mattered would continue to show understanding for India and the Chinese could be held at bay. If India went beyond its declared intentions in dealing with Pakistan in the current war, world opinion could shift against India, thus providing the Chinese with room for manoeuvre. He decided to continue to pursue the policy which he had formulated earlier, that India should continue to refute Chinese allegations. A reply from India on 12 September said:

> The Chinese protest is intended to malign India and to cause confusion in the international world and also to prepare a pretext for any illegal actions directed against India which the Chinese Government might be contemplating.
>
> On several occasions in the past, the Government of India have informed the Government of China that Indian troops have never crossed the Sikkim–Tibet boundary which has been formally delimited and is clearly distinguishable by well-marked natural features. Nor have Indian troops built any structures either on the Tibetan side of the border or on the border itself—there was indeed no need for India to do so. Therefore the demand of the Chinese government to dismantle the structures and to withdraw the troops is meaningless.

Nevertheless, the note added, India was willing to have the location inspected by an independent and neutral observer.

Shastri's assessment was that the Chinese would not launch a major attack as they had done in 1962 because they had no important and immediate objective of their own to achieve. Even the Pakistanis could not expect China to take on the wrath of the United States for the sake of its fortuitous friendship with Pakistan. As Senator Stuart Symington, a senior Democratic member of the Senate Foreign Relations and Armed Services Committee, had observed, if the US did not wish to intervene in Himalayan heights, they could do so on other fronts. He was possibly hinting at the known Pentagon interest in Chinese nuclear installations.[5] The Chinese were unlikely to expose themselves to such a risk.

On 13 September the Soviet Union also issued a warning to those powers which by their 'incendiary statements' or policy were trying to push India and Pakistan towards further aggravation of the conflict, pointing also to the grave responsibility they assumed thereby for their policy and actions.[6]

Both superpowers were thus giving China unambiguous warning against involvement in the Indo–Pak war. There remained the possibility that China would launch a limited attack at some point on the border, enough to bruise India's morale but not enough to invite a US reprisal. This was a danger which India had to contend with on its own. To deal with such an eventuality Shastri adopted a dual course. First he made regular and carefully worded responses—without innuendo or bravado but clear and firm in tone—denying Chinese allegations and expressing the hope that China would not take advantage of the current situation between India and Pakistan. Second, in consultation with his cabinet and the army and air force chiefs, it was decided that if China nevertheless attacked, India would fight back.

At about midnight on 16 September the Chinese government handed over a note to India's charge d'affaires in Peking, Jagat Mehta, demanding that the Government of India should demolish within three days the military structures which, according to the Chinese government, had been constructed by India on the Tibet side of the Tibet–Sikkim border or on the border itself, failing which India should be prepared to face 'grave consequences' arising from its refusal. On receiving this note Mehta asked the Chinese officials whether a neutral observer was not acceptable to China. The Chinese officials first evaded the question and then replied that there was no neutral observer in the world. Mehta asked whether the Chinese government note was an ultimatum of war. Again the official kept silent for a few moments and then replied: 'Yes, it is, and India should be prepared to face the consequences if she did not accept it.'[7]

Shastri saw the Chinese note and Mehta's forwarding comments on the morning of 17 September. News of the Chinese ultimatum had been flashed across the world and the question in New Delhi, London Washington and other capitals was: Is this getting to be a global war?

The situation was complex. There was no question of India succumbing to the Chinese threat: national honour was at stake. At the same time, responsible leaders everywhere were looking for a defusion of the crisis, not an escalation. Shastri convened an emergency meeting of the cabinet at which he discussed the implications of the Chinese ultimatum and secured support for the way in which he wanted to respond. The meeting over, he gave instructions for the immediate despatch of a reply on lines approved by the cabinet.

When parliament assembled that day (17 September), there was an atmosphere of excitement and crisis. The prime minister informed the speaker of the Lok Sabha that he would make a statement on the Chinese ultimatum in the afternoon. Meanwhile he gave concentrated attention to the preparation of his statement. By early afternoon he was ready. Just before 3.30 p.m. he entered the house. His manner was unexcited and reassuring.

> I want to inform the house that this morning we received a communication from the Chinese government demanding that within three days we should dismantle our defence installations which they allege are located on their side of the border in Tibet across the Sikkim border.

He then read out extracts from the Chinese note and portions of the Indian reply:

> Ever since the Sino–Indian border problem was raised by the Chinese government, the Government of India has made strenuous attempts to settle the question peacefully and with honour. Even after the unprovoked Chinese attack across the border in October/November 1962, the Government of India consistently followed the policy of seeking a peaceful settlement honourable to both parties concerned.
>
> As has been pointed out in various notes to the Chinese government in the past, the Government of India has given strict instructions to its armed forces and personnel not to cross the international boundary in the Eastern and Middle sectors and the so-called 'line of actual control' in the Western Sector. The Government of India are satisfied after careful and detailed investigations, that Indian personnel as well as aircraft have fully carried out their instructions and have not transgressed the international boundary and the 'line of actual control' in the Western Sector at any time at any place. The Government of India are, therefore, absolutely convinced that the allegations contained in the Chinese note under reply are completely groundless. . .

The prime minister then continued:

> The background of the matter is that in September 1962, some defence structures were constructed on the Sikkim side of the Sino–Indian frontier. These structures have not been in occupation since the cessation of hostilities in November, 1962. Since the Chinese government alleged that some of these structures were on their side of the border, India had in its note on 12 September, 1965 gone to the extent of suggesting that an independent observer be allowed to go to this border to see for himself the actual state of affairs. The Chinese government has not unfortunately accepted this reasonable proposal and has reiterated its proposal for joint inspection. In our reply which is being sent today, we are informing the Chinese government that their contention is entirely incorrect. Never-

theless, as an earnest of our desire for peace and to give no ground to the Chinese for making this a pretext for aggressive action, we are informing them that we have no objection to a joint inspection of those points of the Tibet–Sikkim border where Indian personnel are alleged to have set up military structures in Tibetan territory. The Government of India on their part are prepared to arrange such an inspection as early as possible, at an appropriate official level, on a mutually convenient date.

We have sent a reply to the Chinese note accordingly and hope that the Chinese government would agree to action being taken as proposed. Copies of the Chinese note and of our reply have been placed on the table of the House.

I know the House would feel concerned about the intentions of the Chinese government. We hope that China would not take advantage of the present situation and attack India. The house may rest assured that we are fully vigilant and that if we are attacked, we shall fight for our freedom with grim determination. The might of China will not deter us from defending our territorial integrity. I will keep the house informed of further developments.

Shastri's response to the Chinese went down very well. Newspapers everywhere conveyed the prime minister's assertion that the might of China would not deter India; statesmen of the world noted that Shastri had accepted an earlier proposal of the Chinese government for a joint inspection of the military structures in question, thereby taking away from the Chinese their *casus belli*. This did not mean that the war was averted, but it did mean that China could take back its threat of war without losing face if it wanted.

Harold Wilson, who was much concerned over the Chinese ultimatum and who had contacted Johnson on this development, sent a special message to Shastri complimenting him on his 'measured response' to the Chinese government. In the USA the state department said:

Prime Minister Shastri announced in Parliament today India's rejection of the allegations made in the Chinese Communist note of 16 September. He reaffirmed India's readiness to defend itself, but at the same time moved to undercut the basis of the Chinese ultimatum. Previously, India had offered to allow neutral observers to establish whether or not it was committing border violations in the Sikkim area, while the Chinese had pressed for a joint inspection. Shastri now has stated, however, that India would be willing to engage in a joint inspection 'as an earnest of our desire for peace and to give no grounds to the Chinese to make it a pretext for aggression'. The inspection could be arranged 'at an appropriate level and at a mutually convenient date'.

Shastri's move is designed to provide the Chinese with grounds for withdrawing their ultimatum should they so desire, and at the same time to cast Peking in a clearly untenable position in case it should resort to military action after the expiration of the ultimatum.[8]

Although the Chinese ultimatum was due to expire at midnight of Sunday, 19 September, the Chinese army began moving troops on Saturday, 18 September, closer to the Sikkim border in the east and the Demchok area. However, just before the expiry of their ultimatum, the Chinese issued another note, extending the time limit by three days. They went back in this new note on their proposal for a joint inspection of the so-called illegal military structures, saying that there was no need for any inspection as, in the Chinese view, military structures did exist on the Chinese side of the Tibet–Sikkim border. The Chinese now demanded the dismantling of the military structures in question within the extended time limit. The UN Security Council was due to meet on 20 September to consider the adoption of a resolution demanding a ceasefire by India and Pakistan and, clearly, the Chinese wanted to wait and see the result of the Security Council debate. Their purpose was also to bolster up the Pakistani position in regard to certain conditions which Ayub wanted fulfilled before agreeing to a ceasefire.

Shastri's response to the Chinese note of 19 September was explained in the following strongly worded statement which he made on 20 September:

> The house will recall that we had taken an attitude calculated to maintain peace when replying to the last note which we had received from the Chinese government. It is clear from the kind of response which China has sent that what China is looking for is not redress of grievances, real or imaginary, but some excuse to start its aggressive activities again, this time acting in collusion with its ally, Pakistan. The extension of the time limit for the ultimatum was, in our view, no more than a device to gain time to watch what comes out of the discussions in the Security Council.
>
> The allegations which China has been making in the series of notes that it has been sending to us, are such that they would hardly justify any civilized government in having recourse to force, even if the allegations were true. If there are any structures on the Chinese territory in areas where the border is delimited and not in dispute even according to the Chinese, surely there is nothing to prevent the Chinese government from having them removed instead of suggesting to us that we should have them removed, which would only be possible by our men going into their territory. Similarly no one can imagine that any government would threaten another on the ground that their cattle have been lifted or on the ground that out of the thousands of Tibetans who have sought asylum in this country, two or four are being detained here against their wishes.

To justify its aggressive attitude, China is pretending to be a guardian of Asian countries which, according to China, are being bullied by India. The basic objective of China, therefore, is to claim for itself a position of dominance in Asia which no self-respecting nation in Asia is prepared to recognize. Large or small, strong or weak, every country in Asia has the fullest right to preserve its independence and sovereignty on terms of equality. The dominance of the Chinese cannot be accepted by any of them. We reject China's claim to tell us anything about what we should or should not do about Kashmir, which is an integral part of India. Our offer of resolving the differences over these minor matters by peaceful means is still open.

However, China's aggressive intentions are clear from the fact that even while they have in their note extended the time limit by 72 hours, in actual fact, they have started firing at our border posts both in Sikkim and in Ladakh. If China persists in aggression, we shall defend ourselves by all means at our disposal.

A formal reply to the Chinese note will be sent later today.

After this statement, a senior member of the Lok Sabha asked for clarification: 'We want to know whether we are going to be just content with the sending of a note or that the orders to the Indian army are: "if they fire, you fire back".' Shastri replied: 'I would merely like to say that we will resist them and we will fight them.' The house was thus left in no doubt.

On 22 September Shastri had more news for the house on China:

We are still faced with the Chinese ultimatum. The house is aware that almost at the same time when the Chinese government announced the extension of the time limit of the ultimatum to India by 72 hours on 19 September, their troops started provocative activities at several points of the border. On the Sikkim border, about which the Chinese have been making baseless and threatening allegations, the Chinese troops crossed the well-known and delimited boundary at Dongchui La and Nathu La on 20 and 21 September respectively. They fired at our observation posts. They have tried also to intrude into our other territories. Our armed forces have clear instructions to repel the aggressor.

Yesterday, we sent a reply to the Chinese note of 20 September in which India was alleged to have intruded into Dum Chale and committed armed provocation. The Chinese charge was rejected as a fabrication and a cover-up for the intrusion and firing at Tsakur to which I have referred a little while ago. . .

Regarding the so-called military structures, we have already told the Chinese government that if after joint inspection, any structures are found on the Tibetan side of the border, there can be no objection to their being demolished. I have been told that China has announced that some of these so-called structures have been destroyed by our troops while withdrawing. All this is a product of their imagination.

I must tell the house that we view with grave concern the Chinese activities on the border and the armed intrusions into our territory. We have urged the Chinese government in our note of 21 September, replying to the Chinese note of 19 September, to forsake the path of belligerence and intimidation and to return to the path of peace and reason in its relations with India. I hope that even at this later hour, China will respond to this call and prevent a major crisis.

We do not know what the Chinese will do next. We have, however, to remain vigilant all along the frontier.

The Chinese were interested in the prolongation of the Indo–Pak war and had advised Ayub to carry on fighting. They were therefore disappointed when Pakistan accepted the United Nations Security Council Resolution of 20 September demanding an immediate ceasefire. They now saw no further point in maintaining their war of words against India and soon announced, not unexpectedly, that the 'offending structures' had already been demolished by 'retreating Indian soldiers'.

Shastri's diplomacy in this crisis was laced with humour. When he asked whether the Chinese realized that by asking the Indians to demolish structures 'on the Chinese side of the border' they were actually inviting the Indian army to enter Chinese territory, his riposte was reported all over the world to the amusement of newspaper readers. Minor though this incident might seem, it did help defuse a potentially international crisis.

During this critical period, Shastri had made every endeavour, consistent with national honour, to be conciliatory towards China because he recognized that, despite the serious differences which had arisen between the two countries in the recent past, India and China had eventually to live as peaceful and good neighbours. Besides, they had much in common in terms of culture and civilization which would help in reconciliation. However, he was also of the view that any initiative for the restoration of normal and friendly relations could appropriately be taken only after the passage of some more time to allow feelings on both sides to cool down.

I wish to digress here and record my own experience of the People's Republic of China. During the years 1974 to 1989, when I served as secretary-general of the International Maritime Organisation, UN, in London, my wife and I had the privilege of visiting China several times at the invitation of government authorities. We were received with overwhelming kindness and accorded the highest consideration and magnificent hospitality. We were received with great courtesy by some of the most eminent dignitaries of the state. We did not notice even the slightest anti-India bias. On the contrary, our gracious Chinese hosts talked of India respectfully and, on several occasions, proposed toasts to the India–China friendship. I responded by expressing my deep and abiding respect and admiration for the people and Government of China.

The Chinese are highly cultured, dignified, self-respecting, patriotic and humble. I found them most responsive to honest and frank approaches.

# Chapter 20

# India, Pakistan and the United Nations

Immediately on his return to the UN headquarters in New York on 16 September, U Thant submitted a preliminary report to the Security Council. Later the same day he submitted another report in which he gave his perception of the prevailing situation and his views as to the lines on which the Security Council might consider further action. This second report was a masterly diplomatic document. Some portions of it were:

> Each nation feels that it has been abused by the other, and each is convinced that the other has committed aggression.
>
> Inherent in this situation are all of the phenomena—the aroused emotions, misunderstandings, long pent-up resentments, suspicions, fears, frustrated aspirations and heightened national feelings—which throughout history have led to needless and futile wars. These are factors which also make it difficult for the leaders on both sides to respond to the unconditional ceasefire appeals of the Security Council. . .
>
> Both sides have expressed their desire for a ceasefire and a cessation of hostilities in the entire area of the current conflict. Nevertheless, up to now, I have not succeeded in securing an effective practical measure of compliance by the two sides with the Security Council's resolutions.

Stressing the threat to world peace, the secretary-general made the following proposal:

> The Security Council might now do what it has done once before, and successfully, in another dangerous conflict situation: it could order the two governments concerned, pursuant to Article 40 of the Charter of the United Nations, to desist from further hostile military action and to this end to issue ceasefire orders to their military forces. The Council might also declare that failure by the governments concerned to comply with this order would demonstrate the existence of a breach of the peace within the meaning of Article 39 of the Charter.[1]

The secretary-general thus recommended action by the Security Council under the 'mandatory' provisions of the United Nations charter. The consequences of non-compliance with these mandatory resolutions of the Security Council exist in Articles 39, 41 and 42. The latter two are particularly relevant:

Article 41—The Security Council may decide what measures not involving the use of armed force are to be employed to give effect to its decisions, and it may call upon the Members of the United Nations to comply with such measures. These may include complete or partial interruption of economic relations and of rail, sea, air, postal, telegraphic, radio, and other means of communication, and the severance of diplomatic relations.

Article 42—Should the Security Council consider that measures provided for in Article 41 would be inadequate or have proved to be inadequate, it may take such action by air, sea, or land forces as may be necessary to maintain or restore international peace and security. Such action may include demonstrations, blockade, and other operations by air, sea, or land forces of Members of the United Nations.

It was these same provisions which were invoked in the UN action against Iraq in the recent Iraq–Kuwait conflict.

The Security Council met on 17 September 1965. India was represented by Chagla, Jha and Parthasarathi. Shastri had had a long talk with Chagla before the latter's departure for New York.

At the Security Council session on 17 September, Chagla made a brilliant presentation of India's case. There were no histrionics, nor was this a marathon performance. Among other things, he said:

> This is a peculiar tragedy for our country. . . Our great leader, Mahatma Gandhi, gave the message of nonviolence and peace to the whole world, and it is sad that we should be involved in this war. But Mahatma Gandhi also said that a country must defend itself against aggression, that a country must have self-respect and dignity; if a country loses dignity and self-respect that country ceases to exist. I assure you that this particular conflict that is going on is a conflict not of our making. If we have to resist with arms Pakistan's aggression, it is purely for the purpose of self-defence. . . may I now point out that it was Pakistan which for the first time used field artillery; it was Pakistan that used tanks with air cover; it was Pakistan that started the bombing of cities; it was Pakistan that started the dropping of paratroops; it was Pakistan that used its navy to bomb one of our sea-ports, while we have not used our navy at all.
>
> The basic question which this Council faces and which it must answer and resolve is: Who is the aggressor? I ask the Council not to shirk giving a reply to that question. . . [I ask you] to respect the Secretary-General's report and if you are satisfied that aggression was committed by Pakistan on 5 August, I say that it is your duty to condemn this aggression. Otherwise, international law has no meaning and international society cannot exist.

Himself an Indian Muslim of impeccable secular credentials, Chagla devastated Pakistan's claim that this was a holy war:

Pakistan's other objective was to make this a religious war. We are living in the modern age. We have learned to understand that religion is something personal and intimate. . . There are two million Muslims in Kashmir but there are fifty million Muslims in India. India—some of the members do not realize this—is the third largest Muslim country in the world. These Muslim brothers of ours, fellow citizens of ours, live in perfect satisfaction with all the rights that the majority community enjoys under our Constitution. But Pakistan does not like this because it is a theocratic State; it is a religious State. To Pakistan religion is the basis of citizenship. To us religion is not the basis of citizenship. This argument will appeal to my friends from the Middle East and from other parts of the world where people of different religions live together as nationals.

There is one good thing about Bhutto: he lends himself to quotations. May I quote him again, on this question of religious war. This is what Bhutto said in his broadcast of 3 September 1965: 'Let India not be complacent in waging war in Kashmir. Let them not disregard the lessons of history. Let them not forget that if Pakistanis have hitherto shown the patience of a Solomon, they are also the descendants of the heroic soldiers of Islam who have never showed any hesitation in laying down their lives in defence of their honour and the pursuit of justice'.

Why 'heroic soldiers of Islam?' Are they fighting a war of Islam? It is an insult to Islam to suggest that Islam is intolerant or that Islam believes in wars and conflicts. Then Bhutto said the following at an Independence Day civic reception at Lahore on 14 August: 'India is known as a country believing in threats alone. . . I want to tell Shastri and India that after all justice is sure to prevail. We are not alone in this. Our religion is spreading all over the world.'

Again his appeal is a religious appeal. The Council will realize the danger of this. There are fifty million Muslims living in India in peace and amity, in friendship and concord, with other communities. The whole attempt of Pakistan was to disrupt this unity, to bring about communal discord and then to appeal to this Council, or to the world, by saying: You see, Indians treat their minorities badly.[2]

Closing his address, Chagla stressed the fact that Shastri had clearly accepted an unconditional ceasefire in his letters to the secretary-general dated 14 and 15 September. That was India's position even now. He added that India would not accept any of the conditions which had been laid down by President Ayub of Pakistan.[3]

During the debate which followed, the representative of Pakistan, their law minister, repeated Pakistan's contentions and reiterated Ayub Khan's conditions.

Among Security Council members there was strong support for the draft resolution which had been tabled already by the Netherlands' delegate on the basis of prior consultations with other members. This resolution 'demanded' an immediate ceasefire and a return of all armed personnel to pre-5 August positions. The political problem underlying the conflict was to be considered later. The representative of Malaysia strongly supported India's position and expressed total opposition to the conditions which Pakistan sought to attach to the proposed ceasefire. The USSR delegate gave support to the Indian position for an unconditional ceasefire. Only the Jordanian delegate supported the Pakistani position.

After a protracted debate lasting from 17 to 20 September 1965, the Security Council adopted the following resolution by ten votes in favour, with no vote against and with one abstention (Jordan):

> The Security Council
>
> Having considered the Reports of the Secretary-General on his consultations with the Governments of India and Pakistan,
>
> Commending the Secretary-General for his unrelenting efforts in furtherance of the objectives of the Security Council's resolutions of 4 and 6 September,
>
> Having heard the statements of the representatives of India and Pakistan,
>
> Noting the differing replies by the parties to an appeal for a ceasefire as set out in the Report of the Secretary-General (S/6683), but noting further with concern that no ceasefire has yet come into being,
>
> Convinced that an early cessation of hostilities is essential as a first step towards a peaceful settlement of the outstanding differences between the two countries on Kashmir and other related matters,
>
> (1) Demands that a ceasefire should take effect on Wednesday, 22 September 1965, at 0700 hours GMT and calls upon both governments to issue orders for a ceasefire at that moment and a subsequent withdrawal of all armed personnel back to the positions held by them before 5 August 1965;
>
> (2) Requests the Secretary-General to provide the necessary assistance to ensure supervision of the ceasefire and withdrawal of all armed personnel;
>
> (3) Calls on all States to refrain from any action which might aggravate the situation in the area;
>
> (4) Decides to consider as soon as operative paragraph 1 of the Council's resolution 210 of 6 September has been implemented, what steps could be taken to assist towards a settlement of the political problem underlying the present conflict, and in the meantime calls on the two governments to utilize all peaceful means, including those listed in Article 33 of the Charter, to this end;
>
> (5) Requests the Secretary-General to exert every possible effort to give effect to this resolution, to seek a peaceful solution, and to report to the Security Council thereon.[4]

For India, and particularly for Shastri, the adoption of this resolution was an exceptionally important political triumph for many reasons: not one of Pakistan's conditions had been accepted; there was no reference to any of the previous resolutions of UN on the subject of Kashmir and this amounted to a break from the past UN position; reference to 5 August was an indirect but clear acceptance of India's position that Pakistan was the aggressor; Pakistan's efforts to get India branded, directly or indirectly, as an aggressor had failed; both superpowers had taken the same stand, which was undoubtedly favourable to India. The USSR had maintained, both openly on the floor of the Security Council as well as behind the scenes, its support for India and was particularly pleased that Shastri had accepted an unconditional ceasefire. The USA had moved a long distance towards India and this was in part the result of Shastri's efforts with Johnson.

# Chapter 21

# Strength of Arms

The Indian army had 825,000 men and an additional 47,000 men in the Territorial Army, making a total of 872,000 men. This was the total land force, comprising twenty infantry divisions, one armoured division and one armoured brigade. Of these, only seven infantry divisions were available for deployment on the West Pakistan border, together with the armoured division and the armoured brigade.

Pakistan had a total of about 250,000 armed men, comprising 180,000 men in the Regular Army and 70,000 men in the Para Military Forces. It had six infantry divisions, of which one was stationed in East Pakistan and five in West Pakistan. In addition, Pakistan had two armoured divisions.

With regard to infantry divisions, in numerical terms India had some superiority. However, when one looks at the quality of equipment available to the two armies, the picture becomes significantly different.

On the Indian side, the artillery regiments were equipped with World War II vintage guns, while the Pakistani artillery regiments were equipped with modern US MAP supplied guns of high quality and calibre. Pakistan was equipped also with advanced anti-tank weapons, possessing high-grade tank-killing capability, such as 106 recoilless guns. The Pakistani infantry was equipped with the latest models of sophisticated American infantry weapons, especially automatic rifles, machine guns, guided missiles, long-range quick-firing artillery and amphibian personnel carriers. The Pakistani infantry divisions had formidable fire-power, both in range and volume, and had much greater mobility than the Indian infantry divisions.

As regards medium battle tanks, the table below gives the numbers.

| India | | Pakistan | |
|---|---|---|---|
| Centurians | 270 | Pattons | 594 |
| Shermans | 472 | Shermans | 330 |
| Total | 742 | Total | 924 |

India and Pakistan also had 424 and 144 light tanks respectively, but these did not figure prominently in the battles.

The significant fact for Ayub was that Pakistan had a distinct supe-riority in the number of medium tanks, which spearheaded Pakistan's thrust into India and which in effect were the battle tanks of the Indo–Pakistan War of 1965. All the tanks of the Indian army except the Cen-turians were of World War II vintage. The Centurians had been manufactured by Britain after World War II, but even they had become outdated by 1965. Pakistan's Patton tanks were the most advanced and sophisticated weapons of their type. Manufactured in the USA, Patton tanks (M-47 and M-48) were at that time among the front-line tanks of NATO forces in Europe. They were fitted with 90 mm guns with a firing range of 2000 yards, and were also fitted with infra-red equipment which provided deadly accurate 'eyes' for night operations. Pakistan had also a number of Patton M 36 B2 tanks, regarded as formidable tank destroyers because of their range and gun power.

Looking at the total picture at that time, Lt-General Harbaksh Singh made the following assessment of the relative army strength of India and Pakistan when the open war began:

> It is evident from the above that in terms of numbers and quality of equipment, Pak had a definite edge over us in armour. In artillery, her superiority was decisive in heavy guns, while the quality of her mediums was far above our own. Pak, therefore, possessed a formidable combina-tion of armour and artillery—a decisive factor both in offence and defence. Only in infantry did we enjoy a measure of numerical super-iority. This, as mentioned above, was offset by the large number of hastily trained recruits. Moreover, the automatic and anti-tank fire-power in a Pak infantry battalion was almost double compared to our own.

The General added that Pak's appreciation of her offensive poten-tialities *vis-à-vis* India's was mathematically correct. 'It was,' said the General, 'in assessing the human element that she faulted.'[1]

As regards the air force, the 1965 war was the first occasion since Independence that it had been called upon to join battle. According to an estimate put forward by Lewis A. Frank in his book *The Arms Trade and International Relations*, Pakistan possessed, before the 1965 war, 120 F-86 Sabres, 30 B-57 bombers and 20 F-104 Star Fighters.[2] John Fricker, in his book *Battle For Pakistan*, says that at that stage, the Pakistan air force had, additionally, 12 RT-33 Aircraft.[3] That brought the total strength of the Pakistan air force to 182 aircraft, of which 12 were positioned in East Pakistan, leaving altogether 170 for use in the west.

The Indian air force at that time had just over 450 combat aircraft of all types. Of these about 300 were distributed among its sixteen squadrons deployed in the West. In addition, the Indian air force had nine squadrons in the East which had been stationed there as a counter to possible Chinese move or the obvious Pakistani threat. Statistically, this gave the Indian Air Force (IAF) an approximately 1.8 to 1 superiority over the Pakistan air force (PAF). But numbers do not tell the whole story.

A large number of IAF aircraft consisted of Vampires, Mysteres and Toofanis. The Vampires were obsolete. Of these, the IAF had a little over one squadron in the West. Soon after the initial encounters, all the Vampires were withdrawn from active operations. Mysteres, which were somewhat better than Vampires, could, operate only under air cover provided by Gnats or Hunters. The IAF had four squadrons of Mysteres in the West. They were defenceless against the faster and more lethal Sabres and Star Fighters of the PAF. If these squadrons of obsolete Vampires and practically defenceless Mysteres are left out, the real and effective combat strength of the Indian and Pakistani air forces in the Western theatre of war was, according to knowledgeable observers, more or less equal.

In terms of sophistication and performance, the Indian air force had nothing comparable to Pakistan's Sabres or Star Fighters. The IAF did have a dozen MiG-21s, but they had been received too late—just before the war began—for any tactical significance and could not be used in missions except for some Combat Air Patrols (CAPs). Even the legendary Gnat—which after the war came to be called the 'Sabre-Slayer'—had obvious limitations. Sabres were fitted with six guns with a range of 1500 yards. The Gnats had two guns with a range of 800 yards. Sabres carried air-to-air heat-seeking Sidewinder missiles which could be lethal in aerial combats. Gnats had nothing approaching this kind of weaponry. The IAF had no match either for the F-104 Star Fighters in the Pakistan air force which, at that time, were the top frontline aircraft of the world.

In another crucial area the IAF had a clear disadvantage. After the debacle in 1962, it was decided by the government to raise the strength of the IAF to forty-five squadrons. By the time hostilities started in 1965, the IAF was far from having reached its optimum strength and was still only in the process of forming its thirtieth squadron. During the preceding three years there had been a rapid increase in the strength of the Indian air force, but this had been achieved at the cost of thorough training, and by 'bleeding' the regular squadrons of pilots and trained technicians.[4]

In October 1956 Air Chief Marshal P.C. Lal, then deputy secretary to the cabinet with the rank of Air Commodore, had gone abroad to survey the European market with a view to purchasing a suitable fighter aircraft for the Indian air force. On 15 October, while flying in a Supermarine Swift aircraft over the English Channel, he noticed a smart little fighter doing zig-zags in the sky. The aerobatics were, indeed, very impressive.

When the Supermarine deal fell through, Lal, remembering that impressive display of manoeuvrability over the Channel, approached its designer, W.E.W. Petter, to see if India could purchase the Gnat for her air force. Petter told Lal flatly that he could not agree to the sale of this invention to India. While Lal was ruminating over this blunt refusal in the midst of an ongoing working lunch session with Petter and his board members, the conversation somehow turned to cricket. This being a favourite subject of his, Lal cheered up again and gave a lively running commentary on cricket in India with particular reference to the recent encounter between the Indian President's Eleven and the Indian Prime Minister's Eleven. Petter and his board listened with rapt attention and an enjoyable lunch was had by all, but, sadly for Lal, no deal for the Indian air force.

A few days later, 'out of the blue', Lal got a call from Petter, advising that India could after all have the Gnat. To the bemused Lal's even greater surprise, Petter added that India would even be granted a licence to manufacture the plane herself. The deal was soon finalized and India thus acquired, in a most unexpected way, the legendary Gnat which was to play such a significant role in the Indo–Pakistan conflict.

The story has an interesting sequel. Years later, when both had become good friends, one day Petter suddenly made a clean breast of things: 'Pratap, I have a confession to make,' he confided to Lal, and added: 'When you first proposed buying the Gnat, I thought you chaps were Communists. So I refused to sell you my invention. But when you said that you played cricket—and I checked that out—I realized that you couldn't possibly be Communists. So I decided I would sell you the aircraft.'

As far as India was concerned, Pakistan's attack on 1 September 1965 came as a shock. There had been no intelligence reports which might have given a clue to the nature or extent of Operation Grand Slam. General P.P. Kumaramangalam, who was vice-chief of the army staff at that time, told me that General Chaudhuri was in Srinagar on the morning of 1 September when the Pakistanis launched their attack in Chhamb. The Indian ground forces were thrown back. General Chaudhuri returned to New Delhi in the afternoon and only then could he get the prime minister's approval for the deployment of the air force to counter the unexpected attack. These details of unreadiness and the absence of premeditated plans make it clear that India was reacting to a situation which had not been anticipated.

# Chapter 22

# War Operations

Between 6 and 8 September Indian armed forces had launched their counteroffensive against West Pakistan in three sectors: on 6 September in the Lahore sector; on 8 September in the Sialkot sector; and on 8 September in the Barmer Sector (Rajasthan–Sind border). Shastri explained to a massive gathering in New Delhi the circumstances in which India had no alternative:

> Although Pakistan's attack on India was first launched in Chhamb, they had an eye on our territory in Punjab also. As you know, they made a rocket attack on Amritsar and tried to destroy the airport near Wagah.
> President Ayub had been talking a great deal about the tanks and other military equipment Pakistan had acquired and had on many occasions boasted that if they decided to march on Delhi, it would be a walk-over. The military situation created by Pakistan was such that our forces had no choice but to advance in the Lahore Sector. Pakistan's attack was so formidable and so swift that we could not afford merely to talk of defending ourselves. We had to take decisive, effective action without losing time. The needs of the situation could no longer be answered by local action. We could not afford to endanger the freedom of our country. No country in the world would have allowed its freedom to be threatened as ours was. We have always held fast to the principle of peace, but in the situation that was created, not to act would have been cowardice and sloth. The display of armed might we saw within our territory could be resisted only with arms.[1]

The 'D' day was fixed for 7 September. 'However, on account of the unexpected turn of events in the Chhamb Sector,' says Lt-General Harbaksh Singh, ' "D" Day for XI Corps was advanced by 24 hours so as to relieve enemy pressure against the outer defences of Akhnoor. H-Hour was specified as 0400 hours.'[2]

The attack in the Lahore sector was launched in the early hours of 6 September and consisted of a three-pronged drive with the objective of securing the eastern bank of the Ichhogil Canal, inside Pakistani territory, at three different points, over a length of about thirty miles. The Ichhogil Canal had been built by Pakistan as a defensive moat close to the West Pakistan–India border at a distance varying from three to nine miles from

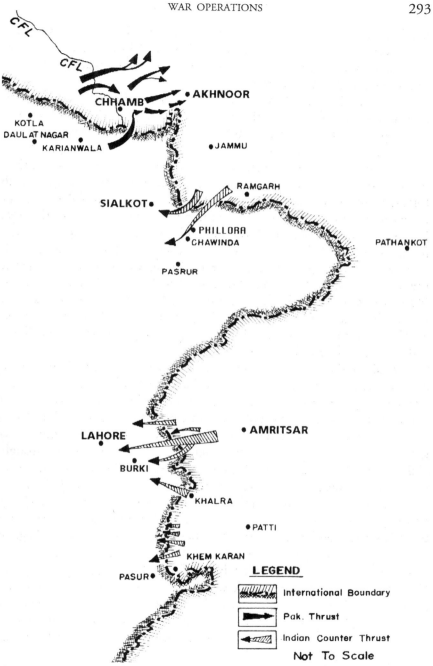

Map 3  Pakistani Thrust and India's Counter-thrust
(Western Sector)

the Indian border. This canal is forty-seven miles long, 140 ft wide and 15 ft deep. 'Built several years ago,' says Russell Brines, 'it serves as a tank trap facing eastward, and heavy fortifications and gun emplacements, many disguised as mud huts, reinforce it.'[3]

India needed to secure the eastern bank of the Ichhogil Canal to prevent a Pakistani attack with a view to capturing Amritsar and territory right up to the River Beas, 27 miles east of Amritsar. This was to be the final phase of Operation Grand Slam.

Of the three columns which moved towards the Ichhogil Canal on the morning of 6 September, the central column advanced towards the heavily fortified village of Burki close to the bank of the Ichhogil Canal and launched an attack at 8 pm on 10 September. The battle for Burki was a fiercely fought engagement involving tanks and heavy artillery. It lasted for an hour and a half. Indian jawans of the 4th Sikh Battalion took Burki by 9.30 p.m. Later the same day the Pakistanis were forced to retreat to the west bank of the Canal but they demolished the bridge over the Canal. From the Western bank, the Pakistanis tried to avenge their defeat by a massive barrage from their heavy artillery. 'But,' says Lt General Harbaksh Singh, 'the Punjabis and the Sikhs refused to budge.' This was 'a brilliant action executed with dash and determination.'[4]

Details of the battles are available in the documents of military history, but the area between the India–West Pakistan border and the Ichhogil Canal became a continuous battleground. For full four days, from 7 to 11 September, heavy fighting took place in which Pakistanis employed Pattons, Shermans and Chaffees and their heavy artillery. The Indians responded in strength and defeated Pakistani attempts to break through. This was vital because if the Pakistanis had been able to move ahead in this sector, they would have attempted a drive towards Amritsar. As it was, the battle honours alternated in this area and the crucially strategic village of Dograi changed hands three times. By 11 September the Pakistani offensive had been beaten back and it then petered out. But the village of Dograi was still in Pakistani hands and this had to be captured in order to secure possession of the eastern bank of the Ichhogil Canal. To capture Dograi, reconnaissance was made which showed that, it was defended by a series of pillboxes, 'merging with the configuration of the village and guarding the approaches to it. Extensive tunnelling within the village permitted safe and quick movement in the defensive position which was organised in depth.'[5]

An outflanking operation was launched by an Indian infantry brigade supported by divisional artillery. After rapid advance in the darkness of night, the Indian brigade attacked Dograi village from the flank and rear of Pakistani positions. 'The defenders were taken completely by surprise and though handicapped by the unexpected direction of attack, gave a very good account of themselves. But the Jats exploiting their brilliant outflanking manoeuvre, pressed home the attack with grim determination and after severe hand to hand fighting, captured Dograi at 0300 hours.'[6]

'The Wagah Sector,' says D.R. Mankekar, 'saw the fiercest fighting of the entire Lahore front. The Indian division in this sector inflicted maximum casualties on the enemy. Thirty three per cent (108, including 5 officers) of the total number of prisoners on the entire front were captured by this division. It also captured 21 tanks, one squadron of which it put to use.'[7]

In the southern Lahore segment the Indian armed forces won the most decisive battle of the war. In this segment 4 Mountain Division under the command of Major-General Gurbaksh Singh was assigned the task of proceeding from its base in Ferozepore/Khem Karan to the Ichhogil Canal and to capture on the way (1) the joint checkpost just across the border, (2) Ruhiwal, (3) the Bund junction, (4) Theh Pannunam and (5) Ballanwala. It was to secure the east bank of the canal between Bedian and Ballanwala and also between Ballanwala and Ganda Singh Wala. The division moved ahead at 5 am on 6 September and by 11.30 am succeeded in capturing four of the five positions listed above. But no further progress could be made as the Pakistan army launched a heavy offensive early in the afternoon. By the morning of 7 September, the Indians were back in Khem Karan from where they had started.

At this stage the Indian divisional commander realized that the Pakistani army which had thrown into the battle in this sector its crack armoured division and infantry division would not have done so unless it intended to launch a major offensive operation. This offensive had to be contained and broken because if it succeeded in breaking through Indian positions at Khem Karan, there was nothing to stop the Pakistani advance to Amritsar. The divisional commander of the Indian infantry division made a calm assessment of the situation, taking into account the available resources which now included an armoured brigade. He then decided to make a tactical retreat to a more defensible position in the rear of Khem Karan at a place called Assal Uttar. This move proved doubly advantageous because it gave an impression to the Pakistanis that the Indians were on the run.

Assal Uttar was ideally located for the purpose in view as it covered both the Khem Karan–Amritsar axis as well as the Khem Karan–Patti axis. The lie of the land lent itself to effective defence as compared to Khem Karan which could be bypassed. The divisional commander, acting with

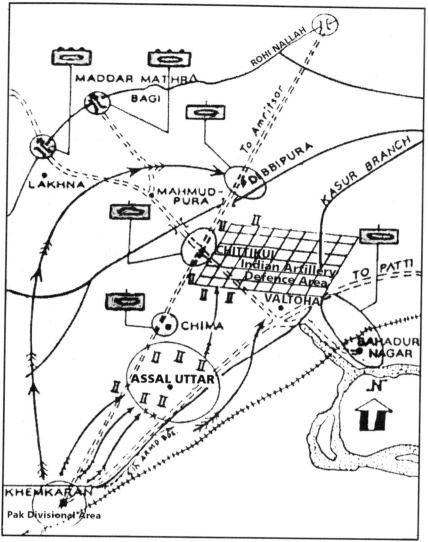

Blow-up of Battlefield Postion:
Assal Uttar

## LEGEND

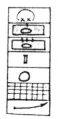

Indian Division
Tank Squadron
Tank Troop
Tanks
Defended Locality
Indian Artillery Area
Pak Armoured Thrust

Map 4   The Battle of Assal Uttar

speed and foresight, set up his defence with care. Fortunately, the Pakistani attack came a day later than anticipated and this provided invaluable time to the Indian divisional commander to position all his forces as well as those of the supporting armoured brigade under the command of Brigadier Theograj, on the edges of a strategic 'horseshoe', leaving the opening free for tempting the Pakistanis into this deathtrap.

As later events showed, Pakistan had prepared a detailed and audacious plan for the capture of Amritsar which was to be the final phase of Operation Grand Slam. The broad Pakistani strategy was to push its armoured division grouped with its infantry division to Khem Karan and, after establishing a lodgement there, to overtake in quick succession the bridge at Harike, Jandiala Guru to the east of Amritsar and finally the bridge over River Beas, about twenty-seven miles to the east of Amritsar. In this way Amritsar as well as considerable surrounding territory would have been a fabulous 'catch' in the Pakistani net. Furthermore, the Pakistanis had expected, through this bold stroke, to isolate Indian forces in the Punjab and the Jammu and Kashmir sectors and then possibly to roll down even to Delhi as, in their opinion, nothing could stop their heavy armour.

On the morning of 8 September, Pakistan attacked the Indian positions at Assal Uttar along Bhikhiwind axis with an armoured brigade. This was beaten back. The same night another Pakistani armoured brigade was launched along the Khem Karan–Patti axis. This Brigade also suffered considerable tank losses and could not break through the Indian defences. It seemed at this stage reasonably certain that Pak armour, in strength, would resort to a wide outflanking movement from the west between Rohi Nallah and Bhikhiwind Road. As a defence against this likely manoeuvre, a considerable number of tanks of the Indian armoured brigade under Brigadier Theograj were deployed around Lakhna–Mahmudpura–Chima area. As a master stroke, a portion of the approach area was deliberately flooded by breaching the Madhupur canal dykes, so as to impel the Pak tanks to the centre of the 'horseshoe' where Indian artillery and tanks lay in wait, effectively camouflaged in standing sugarcane crop.

As foreseen, the Pakistanis launched a massive attack on 10 September in the same area. Altaf Gauhar describes this operation as Pakistan's 'mailed fist'.[8] He goes on to assert that President Ayub Khan had personally approved this offensive, and further that Ayub himself was monitoring the developing military situation and 'was extremely optimistic about its outcome'.[9] It was a fierce and determined attack in two waves, first by Pakistan's 5th Armoured Brigade and second, in succession, by their 4th Armoured Brigade. The Pakistanis hurled into the battle all that they had in an effort to overrun the Indian positions but they soon walked into the elaborate trap which had been laid out for them by the Indian forces. Whichever way the Pakistanis turned, they received an Indian barrage from tanks and artillery. For the Pakistanis it was a complete rout: 97 Pakistani tanks were destroyed. 'The Khem Karan counteroffensive ran aground on 11 September,' acknowledges Altaf Gauhar, 'and with that collapsed Pakistan's entire military strategy. For Pakistan the war was over.'[10]

The Indian air force made a big contribution to this battle by destroying, on 8 and 9 September, two Pak trains laden with tanks, vehicles and artillery ammunition. Reportedly, a number of Pak tanks went into the battle with a limited supply of fuel and even of tank shells. Further, No. 1 Mystere Squadron gave ground support in the Khem Karan Sector during the Assal Uttar battle.[11]

But clearly, it was leadership failure in the higher levels of command in the Pakistan army which led to its defeat in the battle of Assal Uttar. This is what General Musa says to explain the failure: 'These frictions of war aggravated the confusion in the division caused mainly by ineffective leadership in its higher echelons of command . . . for inexplicable reasons, the Brigade Commander issued confusing orders . . . '[12] And this is how Musa describes the situation among Pakistani forces in that sector soon after the battle of Assal Uttar: 'Practically, the entire divisional command set-up had become paralysed due to the confusion that prevailed . . . '[13] Air Marshal Asghar Khan, who relinquished the post of commander-in-chief of the Pakistan air force on 23 July 1965, barely two weeks before the commencement of Operation Gibraltar in Kashmir, blames the failure of the Pakistani army, in his book *The First Round—Indo-Pakistan War 1965*, on the timid leadership of General Musa himself.

The war in the Sialkot sector is described by Russell Brines:

> What happened was . . . that General Chaudhuri daringly manoeuvred his armour to mount the Sialkot offensive. He left one force in the Lahore Sector and sent the other, mainly the newest equipment, into action around Sialkot. This required the movement of some 3,000 vehicles along a single road and into enemy terrain under potential aerial threat of considerable proportions. The gamble was twofold: first, the forces defending the road to Delhi would not be disproportionately weakened and, second that the movement toward Sialkot could be accomplished without devastating loss to enemy action. The gamble succeeded to the extent that the Indians were able to inflict heavy punishment on Pakistan's armoured striking force on two fronts.[14]

The battles in the Sialkot sector lasted for full two weeks from 7 September virtually until the hour of ceasefire in the morning of 23 September. India's only armoured division was now fully committed to this sector. So was Pakistan's recently formed second armoured division. Between them about 400 tanks were engaged in ferocious close range battles in flat land and in a choking atmosphere full of enormous dust raised by the movement of tanks and heavy artillery. This is how Brines describes the operations in this sector:

> In the north of the city, where the Indians launched their initial two-pronged attack on Sialkot, further heavy tank-infantry battles were fought. The Indians reported slow gains towards the heavily fortified city which, at the ceasefire, left them entrenched 4,000 yards away. They also cut a northern branch of the railway This position, however, meant that Sialkot was only partially encircled, and a main railway and road running due westward were apparently unaffected. When the fighting ended, the Indians claimed possession of 180 square miles of Pakistani territory in this area, most of it lying between the border and the principal battle zone of Phillora. Pakistan agreed generally with the depth of penetration claimed by India.[15]

Sialkot, the base from which Pakistan launched its offensive in the Chhamb area on 1 September, was like an armed fortress, girdled with a powerful ring of modern artillery, with long-range medium and heavy guns, in addition to the usual pillboxes, bunkers and gun emplacements. The Indian offensive in this sector took the form of a large pincer movement to attack Sialkot from north and south. Here the most crucial battle was fought for the town of Phillora as a part of the southern arm of the pincer movement. The major battle began on the night of 10 September when the Indian forces began to advance on the town of Phillora. By 12 September the Indian forces pierced through the defences of Phillora and captured the town.

After the battle of Phillora, there was some sort of a lull for about three days. Thereafter, fighting started again and the Indian forces made some further tactical gains. When the ceasefire came at 3.30 am on 23 September, the Indians forces were in control of about 180 square miles of Pakistani territory in the Sialkot sector. They were barely two miles from the city of Sialkot.

To complete the picture, I should also add that on 8 September the Indian army had opened a third front against Pakistan in the Rajasthan–Sind sector. The Indian army had moved across the border at Barmer and occupied Gadra town six miles inside the Pakistani border. Some fighting took place in that sector also but this was of a purely diversionary nature.

When in the second half of August 1965 the fighting escalated in Kashmir along the Ceasefire Line, India's air force chief, Air Marshal Arjan Singh decided to remain vigilant, just in case the need arose. It was thus that when called upon by Prime Minister Shastri on 1 September 1965 to join the military operations in Kashmir, the Indian air force was in combat within less than two hours. From then on until ceasefire on 23 September, the Indian air force participated effectively in achieving India's war objectives, the most immediate of which on 1 September was the stoppage of the advance of Pakistani army units on Akhnoor.

Thereafter, for the next three weeks until ceasefire, it was a saga of heroic aerial battles in which the Indian air force fought and got the better of far more sophisticated Pakistani planes such as Sabre jets and Star Fighters.

During the first two days of the war, the IAF discovered that its Vampires and Mysteres deployed for ground support over Chhamb–Jaurian area invariably attracted Sabres and Star Fighters, primarily because they were operating without fighter cover and were easily detected by Pak radars. On 2 September, a detachment of eight Gnats of 23 Sqn. located at Ambala, arrived at Pathankot, so also a few MiG-21s of 28 Sqn. On 3 September, the IAF appeared on the scene with a clever stratagem reportedly devised by Wg Cdr M.S.D. Wollen and Sqn Ldr J. Greene, both of whom rose to be Air Marshals later. This is what they planned. A formation of Mysteres led by Wg Cdr W.M. Goodman was to fly high and approach Chhamb–Jaurian so as to be clearly detected by Pak radars. On reaching the target area, they were to dive in a feint attack and disappear from the area. Eight Gnats in two formations were to follow at low level avoiding radar detection and then belt into the attacking Sabres after shedding the drop tanks and quickly gaining height. Two MiG-21s were to fly CAPs (Combat Air Patrols) over Pathankot airfield and join the fray if Star Fighters were spotted. The plan worked superbly. Sabres came for Mysteres as expected and IAF Gnats were efficiently directed to the marauding Sabres by IAF Fighter Controllers. In the aerial combat that followed, Sqn Ldr Trevor Keelor, flying the small Gnat, shot down the first Sabre.

He was promptly awarded the Vir Chakra, becoming the first IAF officer to win a gallantry award in the 1965 war. In fact, Sqn Ldr Trevor Keelor got a 'triple-first'—the first destroyer of a Sabre Jet, the first IAF officer to get the Vir Chakra, and the first member of the entire armed forces of India to win a gallantry award in the 1965 war.

I wish to digress here and refer to an interesting conversation I had with Trevor Keelor on 22 December 1992 when, accompanied by Sqn Ldr R.K. Pal, I met him at his residence in New Delhi. I asked him how he felt about his achievement in shooting down a Sabre jet: 'I was very lucky,' he said, 'I happened to be at the right place at the right time. Other colleagues of mine were equally well-trained and motivated. Any one of them could have got the first Sabre. I am profoundly grateful to my country for having made so much of me.'

About the merits of his combat aircraft—the Gnat, he was most eloquent: This was a revolutionary light aircraft with three important advantages: it had an extremely fast rate of climb, it could be manufactured in India, and it was economical.

'The Gnat was so small and fast, climbing up to 40,000 feet in under four minutes, that the enemy radars and pilots found it difficult to spot the aircraft. The plane had excellent manoeuvrability. And its two guns could shoot down anything within range.'

When India launched a major counteroffensive in the Lahore and Sialkot sectors, the role of the Indian air force widened greatly. Thereafter the chief of the army staff, General J.N. Chaudhuri, and the chief of the air staff, Air Marshal Arjan Singh, acted in concert to meet Pakistani aggression. The Indian air force provided excellent support to the Indian ground forces in both Lahore and Sialkot sectors.

On 7 September, the Indian air force launched a major attack on Sargodha, the largest and most important Pakistani air base. Altogether thirty-three sorties in six missions were flown by Mysteres and Hunters. This was a daring attack on the principal Pakistani air base. Sargodha was well in the interior of Pakistan and almost at the extreme end of the reach of Hunters. During this attack, the IAF destroyed three F-86 Sabres and one F-104 Star Fighter in the air battle against the loss of three Hunters and two Mysteres.

After a few days, IAF bombing missions went to fairly distant Pakistani air force bases such as those in Peshawar, Rawalpindi and Kohat. These missions involved long distance flying—about 600 miles, across hostile territory. Particularly daring was the night raid on 13/14 September by a squadron of Canberras over Peshawar, possibly the most extensively defended bastion of Pakistani air-power—its headquarters. For this mission, the IAF Canberras had to be flown to the extreme of their range without any margin for error or tactical deviation and without any fighter cover.

On 19 September, a Hunter squadron achieved a unique and important bombing success in the Sialkot sector. This squadron intercepted a column of Pakistani tanks in the morning of 19 September, moving through a defile in a single lane. The Indian squadron first attacked and immobilized the first and the last tanks in the convoy thereby bringing all intervening tanks to a halt. Thereafter all of them were destroyed in seven different passes.

The Indian Air Force played a crucial role in the entire theatre of war.

It successfully attained favourable air situation over various battle zones, it gave close support to the army in all major battles and it participated in the crippling of Pakistan's offensive war machine by the strategic bombing of military targets, supply depots, communications network and other defence installations.

This completes a necessarily brief description of the war operations during the Indo–Pak conflict of 1965. This book is not the place for a detailed account or analysis of the war: several others have been written on the subject.

# Chapter 23

# Assessment of the War

During World War II, the Allies had one objective—the total defeat of the Nazis and the Fascists. The Allies won the war and dictated the terms of peace. In the India–Pakistan war of 1965, neither India nor Pakistan had the objective of defeating the other country and then dictating terms of peace. Each country had limited objectives and the result of the war should be assessed with reference to those objectives.

Pakistan's objectives and their result are summarized with remarkable frankness by Altaf Gauhar: 'The fact could no longer be disputed that the war had been undertaken without proper planning and that the whole adventure was built on a series of false and fanciful assumptions. The government was now offering two reasons for its failure: the numerical superiority of the Indian armed forces, and the hostile attitude of the great powers. Surely both these factors were well-known before hostilities were provoked.'[1]

In contrast India's war objectives, as defined by Shastri, had been met. India's first objective was to defeat the Pakistani attempt to seize Kashmir by force. India's second objective was to destroy Pakistan's offensive armour and thus blunt Pakistan's war machine. An exact assessment of the extent of damage is hardly possible even now because authentic information has not yet been published by the governments concerned. From the accounts provided by numerous observers, it is clear that Pakistan's war machine was badly mauled. 'Militarily speaking,' says D.R. Mankekar, 'Pakistan lost the two most decisive battles of the war—the Battle of Assal Uttar in the Khem Karan sector and the 15-day tank battle in the Sialkot sector. Between the two of them, Pakistan lost nearly half of their American-gifted tanks. Their armoured corps, the very pride and spearhead of Pak army, today stands crippled and humbled. The psychological impact of it all upon the Pak army and the military leadership of the country cannot be underestimated.'[2]

*The Times* (London) defence correspondent, quoting 'first professional reports', commented: 'Though Pakistan originally claimed to have destroyed 500 Indian tanks, a more realistic figure is thought to be about 200 tank casualties for India, of which about half would be in Pakistani hands. . . Assuming a similar proportion of Pakistani tanks were lost to India, another 200 Pakistani tanks were probably hit but were recovered and should be repaired. . . Prospects for Pakistan in any future armoured battle are gloomy and will not improve as they must rely on further deliveries of American tanks, a doubtful contingency at present.'[3]

As regards damage caused to the Pakistani air force, this is what Selig Harrison, New Delhi correspondent of the *Washington Post*, reported:

> India's losses in aircraft have apparently not affected what was a four-to-two margin over Pakistan in the number of planes. It is possible that the effective balance may have been tipped even more sharply in India's favour. Pakistan' striking power has consisted mainly of 103 F-86 Sabre jets. Diplomatic sources estimate that at least 30 Sabre jets were shot down or bombed in the airfields (India claims 47).[4]

India's third objective was to occupy the minimum Pakistani territory for the first two objectives, it being the intention that such Pakistani territories would be vacated after the war. It was not intended that Lahore be taken over by India. While Lahore's capture would have thrilled India, it would at the same time have turned much of world opinion openly against India and might even have brought very close foreign intervention in support of Pakistan. Shastri's judgement was that India's political and military requirements had been met by the movement of the Indian army into Pakistan in the Lahore and Sialkot sectors. As far as Sialkot was concerned, its capture was neither sought nor forbidden by Shastri. Sialkot was a military bastion and the army was left totally free to decide its strategy. It is perfectly possible that if the war had continued, Sialkot might well have been occupied by the Indian army. But since ceasefire had become a serious possibility from 16 September, the capture of Sialkot, which would have definitely involved heavy loss of precious lives, was not seriously attempted. Shastri had left this matter to the judgement of General Chaudhuri. Even so, quite a large area of Pakistani territory had come under Indian occupation, especially in the Sialkot sector.

Lt-Gen Harbaksh Singh, Vr. C. (retd), provides an accurate overall assessment of the war:

> It would, however, be incorrect to compile a balance sheet of the conflict in mere materialistic terms, for there were other fields of achievements, which though less tangible had far-reaching consequences. The Pakistani myth that the Kashmiri brotherhood was impatiently waiting to be 'liberated' had been given the lie both at home and abroad. The illusion that she could steam-roll into India with the help of gifted American equipment had been replaced with a healthy respect for the Indian army. Ayub's conceited notion that a Pakistani soldier is the equivalent of three

Three teachers and five students of the Shastri degree course in philosophy, Kashi Vidya Peeth, Benares. *Left to right* : Janardan Pati Tripathy, Dularey Sahai, Pandit Gopal Shastri, Ram Sakhe Singh, Dr Bhagwan Das, Pandit Raja Ram Shastri, Dr Sampurnanand and Lal Bahadur Shastri (*the photo was taken in 1925*).

UP leaders' camp, Allahabad, 1939. Shastri is second from left in the first standing row. On the chairs, Nehru is third from right, Abul Kalam Azad is fifth from left, and Purshottam Das Tandon is fifth from right.

President Radhakrishnan, Prime Minister Nehru, Minister Shastri.

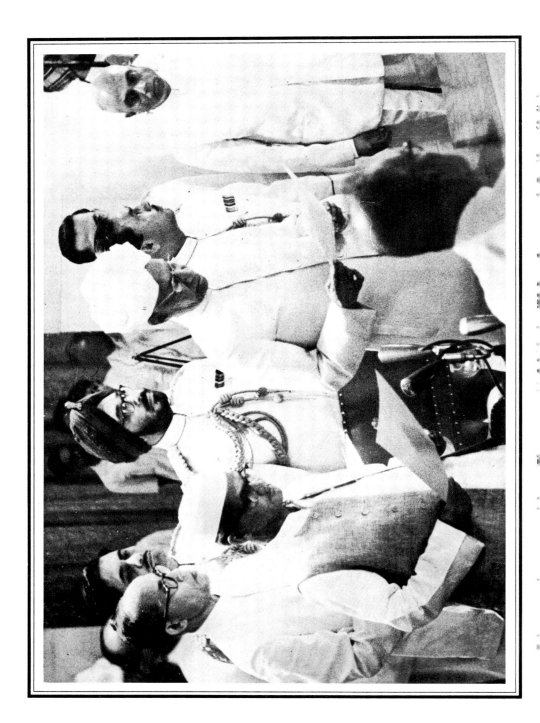

The new prime minister being embraced by Congress President Kamaraj. President Radhakrishnan looks on.

With his wife, Lalita Shastri.

Shastri with his mother, wife, and youngest son Ashok.

Shastri with his family.

Shastri with his daughter Suman (*to his right*) and two grandchildren. The author, his wife Nirmala (*to Shastri's left*), and his daughters Kalpana (*extreme left*) and Sadhana (*extreme right*) are calling on the Shastris on the occasion of Diwali

At a function in Bombay. The author's wife Nirmala introduces some guests to Shastri.

Being received by Wilson, London, December 1964.

With Nasser of Egypt, in Cairo.

With Tito of Yugoslavia and Makarios of Cyprus.

In conversation with the Canadian prime minister, Lester Pearson, Ottawa, 11 June 1965.

In conversation with Chester Bowles, the USA's
ambassador in New Delhi.

With the king of Nepal.

On the right, General J.N.Chaudhuri (*chief of the army staff*), with Air Marshal Arjan Singh (*chief of the air staff*).

Wartime discussions with Air Marshal Arjan Singh.

General P. P. Kumaramangalam,
vice- chief (later chief) of the
army staff.

The prime minister presents a
large sword to Lieutenant-General
Harbaksh Singh at the Gurdwara
Bangla Sahib, New Delhi.

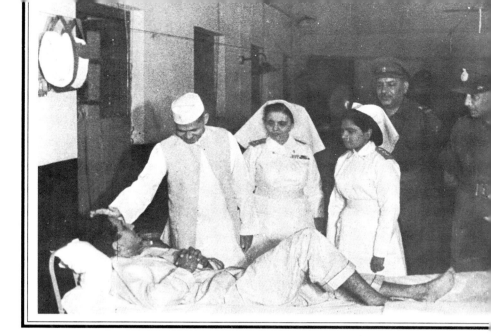

Talking to a wounded soldier.

Atop a captured Patton tank.

Squadron-Leader
Trevor Keelor, Vr. Ch.

Major Bhupinder
Singh, MVC.

Wing-Commander
P. P. Singh , MVC.

Lieutenant-Colonel
A. B. Tarapore,
PVC.

Squadron-Leader
P. Gautam, MVC.

Company Quarter-
Master Havildar
Abdul Hamid, PVC.

Indian jawans suffered a rude jolt. The Indian jawan forced his opponent to the knees in a straight contest. Our slow, simple and ponderous armour, contemptuously nicknamed 'Ancient Hulls' by the enemy, challenged and vanquished the ultra-modern tank, the Patton, to rub in the lesson that in the final test of battle it is the man behind the gun that counts. The Pak army was in short, cut to size.

Individually, each of these were commendable achievements; collectively they gave us moral ascendancy over an arrogant foe who had highly inflated notions of power and pride.

And there is yet another achievement which overshadows all. The humiliation heaped upon the Indian army at home and abroad, consequent upon the NEFA debacle in 1962 had always rankled deep in our minds and made us bend our heads in shame. This slur had been wiped out. In the eyes of the nation, the army enjoys a prestige rarely equalled before. To the world at large it has re-established its traditional fame. Within the army itself our faith has been restored. These are mighty gains, far greater than any stretch of enemy territory or the destruction of her military potential.[5]

Altaf Gauhar has recently claimed that there was one other factor which misled Ayub—his unawareness of the existence of a 'secret alliance' between America and India, forged in 1962 at the time of the Chinese invasion of India. According to Gauhar, the two letters which Jawaharlal Nehru had written to President Kennedy on 19 November 1962 asking for American military intervention to stem the Chinese advance, and Kennedy's reply to Nehru, constituted an Indo–US alliance against China. Now, Altaf Gauhar has not seen this correspondence, which is still classified but he has made the following observations on the basis of a conversation he had some time ago with an American presidential aide of those days—Carl Kaysen:[6]

> The Nehru letters remain classified. Why? The only answer is that these letters together with President Kennedy's response to them constitute an alliance between the US and the Government of India to take joint military action against China. The alliance would become operative in case India felt itself threatened by China. Pakistan was not aware of the terms of the alliance in 1965. That is why Ayub could never understand the reasons that compelled the US to come out in support of India during the Indo–Pakistan War of 1965. Pakistan had the support of China which made the US an ally of India. Had the terms of this alliance been known to Ayub he may never have authorized Operation Gibraltar.[7]

What terms? The only term of the 'alliance' which Gauhar mentions is joint Indo–US action if China threatened India. But surely America would have come to India's help in the event of any Chinese attack in

1965. And America would have done that in accordance with its declared policy of supporting the free world in the event of Communist aggression.

To suggest that Ayub did not know this and that therefore he went ahead with his war plans is to paint Ayub as politically naive. The truth is that Ayub knew the American position on the Chinese question perfectly well because he had been warned about this personally by Johnson, both through Bhutto and directly through a letter. Ayub therefore knew that America would support India if China threatened or attacked India. Clearly he had gone ahead with war despite this, because he overestimated his military might and had entertained the grand illusion of delivering one or two hard blows to knock down India. He had at the same time underestimated India's forces. Gauhar's thesis of a secret Indo–US alliance against China is not based on any available evidence. When, in 1965, the Chinese threatened India with a war ultimatum, neither Shastri nor Johnson referred in their correspondence, which I have seen, to any 'secret alliance' of 1962—obviously because none existed.

# Chapter 24

# Ceasefire

At the meeting of the Security Council on 20 September, when its resolution demanding ceasefire was adopted, Chagla had emphasized that India had already accepted an unconditional ceasefire and was ready to implement it as soon as Pakistan agreed to do the same. In this connection, he had read out relevant paragraphs from the letters dated 14 and 15 September which Shastri had written to the UN secretary-general. Pakistan, however, had still not conveyed its acceptance of unconditional ceasefire. The UN secretary-general was thereafter continuously in touch with Shastri and Ayub.

In India the atmosphere on 21 September was one of expectation of peace, though fighting was still continuing in full fury, especially in the Sialkot sector. No message about Pakistan's position was, however, received from the UN secretary-general.

Early on 22 September, U Thant sent an urgent request to Shastri to order a unilateral ceasefire with effect from the appointed time and ask the Indian forces to fire back only if attacked. This, of course, was entirely unacceptable. Shastri promptly rejected that suggestion. Just after midday on 22 September another message was received from the secretary-general confirming that Pakistan also had accepted ceasefire, and that to allow adequate time for orders to be conveyed to the field commanders the ceasefire time would now be 2200 hours GMT on Wednesday 22 September (0300 hours West Pakistan time on 23 September and 0330 hours New Delhi time on 23 September). Immediately after the receipt of this message, Shastri had a talk with Chavan and Sardar Swaran Singh. Then followed a memorable moment: Chaudhuri and Arjan Singh came to the office of the prime minister, Shastri received them with visible but controlled emotion, shook their hands warmly, formally conveyed orders for the ceasefire and expressed to both his profound gratitude and admiration. He expressed his admiration for their martial brilliance; on their part Chaudhuri and Arjan Singh expressed admiration for Shastri's leadership and guidance.

Shortly after 2 p.m. the necessary ceasefire orders were issued to commanders, instructing them to cease firing.

After meeting Chaudhuri and Arjan Singh, Shastri drove straight to parliament. Here he announced details of the ceasefire. He said at the conclusion of his speech:

There will now be cessation of hostilities. Peace is good. However, there is still a threat from the Foreign Minister of Pakistan, which he held out today, while speaking in the Security Council. We have, therefore, to be very watchful and vigilant.

The nation has recently been going through its greatest trial. The times have been difficult but they have served a great purpose. The whole world knows now that the people of India—Hindus, Muslims, Sikhs, Christians, Parsees and others, constitute a united nation with a determined common will and purpose. On the battle front, the supreme sacrifice has been made by members of all communities who have shown that they are Indians first and Indians last.

To our armed forces, I would like to pay on behalf of this parliament and the entire country, our warmest tributes. By their valour and heroism, they have given a new confidence to the people of India. Those who have lost their beloved on the battle front, have made a contribution to the preservation of our independence which will never be forgotten by a grateful nation. Their sorrow and their pride are shared by the whole country.

Mr Speaker, Sir, I would now seek your permission to express to all the members of this august house, to all the political parties in the country, to the leaders of public opinion, of labour organizations, of business and industry, and of many other voluntary associations, my feelings of the deepest gratitude. In the hour of trial each one of the 470 million people of this country stood up shoulder to shoulder to meet the challenge to our freedom.

I should like to inform the house that on 18 September 1965, I received a message from Mr Kosygin, Chairman of the Council of Ministers, USSR, offering his good offices for bringing about improved relations between India and Pakistan. Mr Kosygin is impelled by noble intentions. No one can even contest the view that ultimately India and Pakistan will have to live together as peaceful neighbours. We cannot, therefore, say no to any efforts, which may help to bring about such a situation, made by those who are sincere and genuine in their feelings of goodwill and friendship. I have, therefore, informed Mr Kosygin today that we would welcome his efforts and good offices.

I would also like to give the house some further details about the tragic accident in which the other day we suffered a grievous loss. Investigations conducted on the spot show that the aircraft in which Balvantray Mehta was travelling was shot down by a Pakistani plane. The marks on the fuselage establish that gun fire had been used. Preliminary investigations by the air force authorities who also have visited the scene confirm that the aircraft was shot down at a low height. The ammunition recovered at the site of the crash also proves that the attacking aircraft was a Pakistani plane. That a non-combatant civilian aircraft should have been shot down in this manner is one of the most inhuman acts which we must all deplore and condemn. Balvantrayji, his wife and the others who were travelling with him have laid down their lives at the altar of the freedom of the country. Their names will remain enshrined in our memory.[1]

Following the prime minister's statement, there was a major debate in parliament in which many members participated. The agreement to cease fire was supported but a great deal of disappointment was expressed over the fact that the Security Council had not branded Pakistan clearly as the aggressor. A number of members wanted India to retain possession of the posts across the Ceasefire Line, such as Haji Pir Pass, which India had occupied recently to prevent further infiltration. In other words, they wanted a new Ceasefire Line. Acharya J.B. Kripalani made an incisive speech. Referring to the existing Ceasefire Line which was agreed between India and Pakistan in July 1949, which he called the '5 August Line', he said:

I say that this line of 5th August was a line drawn ad hoc, I am afraid, by people who did not know geography. If they had known geography, they would not have allowed Haji Pir Pass to be in the hands of the Pakistanis. The Line has not been drawn scientifically and from the military point of view. It was drawn in a hurry to placate world opinion. I am afraid, today also what we have done, has been done in a hurry in order to placate world opinion. World opinion does not count and this United Nations Organization is only a little better than its predecessor, the League of Nations. It is dominated by power politics. It is dominated by a desire to keep balance of power. As long as this idea of balance of power continues, as long as there is power politics, truth can never have its way. It will only be compromised and that compromise will land us again and again into difficulties.

After a pause Acharya Kripalani added: 'If we fix a new line, then we will again be in difficulties.'

Another important participant in the debate was Vijay Lakshmi Pandit:

For the last few weeks we have passed through and faced the most serious threat since our Independence. The story of Pakistan's perfidy and deceit and the manner in which she aggressed for the third time on our country is a shameful one, but we are a proud people today, for we have given a reply in no uncertain terms. We have told those who sought to violate our territory and destroy the values on which our nation is built that they must keep their hands off, and not only keep their hand off, but keep their minds off certain concepts which belong to the mediaeval age and which they still choose to foster.

I would like, before I go on, to pay a respectful tribute to the bold leadership of the Prime Minister in this crisis . . .

Clearly, Mrs Pandit no longer thought Shastri a 'prisoner of indecision'.

An interesting speech was made by L.M. Singhvi, who pointed out that India's publicity and diplomatic effort was inadequate:

The UN Resolution shows a rare indifference to the proved fact of aggression by Pakistan. It shows that our case over the years has not been adequately explained in spite of the very eloquent exposition recently by Mr Chagla. What we are paying for is the accumulated indifference and neglect towards the projection and presentation of our case in an adequate and worthy manner over the years. It seems that the projection of our case has been altogether ineffective and unimaginative. I have been told times without number by responsible legislators in different countries of the World as well as by diplomats representing various countries that they have not been told the facts of the case in an adequate and persuasive manner. Obviously we find that, in the whole range of the United Nations, we have no country other than Malaysia and Singapore . . . to understand our point of view. While we cannot but deplore the situation, we must also do a bit of introspection in regard to our external publicity and our diplomacy.

Peter Alvares was interested in the Soviet Union: 'It has been a painful surprise that the Soviet government have shifted their attitude from one of the unconditional support to India in the Kashmir dispute and have now co-operated with the other great powers in de-freezing this issue at the United Nations level.'

Ansar Harvani spoke from his heart when he said: 'Sir, at the very outset let me congratulate the honourable prime minister for the bold and dynamic leadership that he gave to this country at this hour of crisis. This frail little man has proved the real successor and heir of the liberator of this country, Jawaharlal Nehru. When history will be written, the verdict of history will be that India was liberated by Jawaharlal Nehru, but India's liberty was defended bravely and heroically by Lal Bahadur Shastri.'

Chagla, who had led the Indian delegation at the Security Council meeting when the Resolution of 20 September was adopted, answered the various points which had been raised and explained most persuasively that the Security Council resolution was in no way pro-Pakistan. He said Pakistan was most unhappy about it and had initially rejected it. Chagla explained features of the resolution which favoured the Indian point of view.

Every section of the house expressed deep admiration for Shastri. What a remarkable transformation of the scene it was. Only a few weeks earlier, the opposition were pressing a motion of no-confidence. Now all of them expressed faith in Shastri's leadership.

In his response to the debate, Shastri said:

I must express my gratitude to all the Hon. Members who have participated in the debate today. There have been several speakers, and they have expressed themselves in words of their choice. But I have heard from every side of the house only one voice—the voice of patriotism, of national will to defend the sovereignty and territorial integrity of India no matter who the invader may be. This is the voice of the people of India expressed in unmistakable terms through their chosen representatives in parliament; this is the voice of the sovereign will of the people. Hon'ble Members would permit me to recall that, while speaking in this house in April last, I had appealed for the unity of heart amongst our people. That unity has been achieved in the fullest measure and has been demonstrated effectively in these critical days. In fact, it is this unity which has been the biggest source of strength to all of us in these testing times. . . About our State of Jammu and Kashmir, the house knows our stand which is firm and clear. This state is an integral part of India, a constituent unit of the federal union of India. There is hardly any case for the exercise of self-determination again. The people of Jammu and Kashmir have already exercised the right of self-determination through three general elections held on the basis of universal adult franchise . . . Shri Peter Alvares had expressed the opinion that the Soviet Union had apparently agreed to 'de-freezing' the Kashmir question. It would not be correct to say so. The Soviet Union is today an ardent champion of peace. They have known the horrors of war and they do want, in a friendly spirit, to endeavour to bring about improvement in the relationship between India and Pakistan. Their intentions are pure and we have therefore welcomed their initiative.

Some Hon'ble Members have referred to the work of our diplomatic missions abroad. I can tell the house with complete sincerity that on the present occasion each one of our missions has been alert and vigilant. They have done a good job in keeping the government to which they are accredited fully informed of the development and of the justness of our cause . . . To the tasks that lie ahead, we shall address ourselves in a realistic manner and in full awareness of the fact that self-reliance must be our watchword. I am grateful to this august house for the magnificent support which it has given in these historic times. Mr Speaker, Sir, I would appeal to the house to authorize you to convey, through our defence minister, the admiration and gratitude of this House to our armed forces for the splendid job they have done. I would also, with your permission, like to suggest that the house should rise and observe a minute's silence to honour the memory of those soldiers, airmen, policemen and civilians who have become martyrs in the defence of their motherland.

Shastri also, later that day, made a long broadcast to the nation, outlining the course of the war, the bravery of soldiers, and the people's ultimate victory.

# Chapter 25

# Pakistan's Attitude to the Ceasefire

The Ceasefire Line to which the Security Council Resolutions of 6 and 20 September 1965 had referred was established in July 1949 by a formal agreement between India and Pakistan. To ensure its observance by both countries, the United Nations had appointed a UN Military Observer Group stationed in Kashmir. The Head of the Group in August 1965 was General Nimmo who, as we saw, reported massive violations after 5 August 1965 by armed men from the Pakistan side. Subsequently, blame for violating the Ceasefire Line had been placed clearly on Pakistan which had been indirectly branded as the aggressor in the Indo–Pak conflict of 1965. The Security Council had demanded that the armed personnel of both sides should go back to positions occupied by them before 5 August 1965, which meant positions behind the Ceasefire Line. In other words, the Security Council had demanded that the old Ceasefire Line of 1949 be respected.

A number of important persons in the political field in India expressed to Shastri the view, immediately after the ceasefire on 23 September, that India should now regard the old Ceasefire Line as invalid in view of its massive violation by Pakistan.

Curiously, for their own reasons, Ayub and Bhutto were also of the view that the 1949 Ceasefire Line should not be regarded as sacrosanct. In fact they regarded the Ceasefire Line established in 1949 as a big barrier, standing in the way of their claims on Kashmir. In his letter dated 13 September 1965, addressed to the UN secretary-general, Ayub said:

> While you propose a 'ceasefire without condition' you go on to add that the Security Council would, soon after the ceasefire, proceed to implement its resolution of 6 September. The provisions of the Security Council Resolutions of 4 and 6 September that the ceasefire be followed immediately by withdrawal of all armed Pakistan personnel to the Pakistan side of the Ceasefire Line and the consolidation of the Ceasefire Line through the strengthening of the United Nations Observer Group would result in restoring India's military grip over Kashmir. We would thus merely revert to the same explosive position which triggered the present conflict.[1]

Bhutto, characteristically, was even more forthright, as reported in the *Morning News* of Karachi dated 20 August 1965: 'Bhutto told reporters that the Ceasefire Line, which India describes as an unshakable boundary, is a temporary arrangement. It could very well have been drawn further down inside occupied Kashmir.'

The UN secretary-general had this to say in his report, dated 3 September 1965, to the Security Council regarding Pakistan's attitude to the Ceasefire Line:

> I have not obtained from the Government of Pakistan any assurance that the Ceasefire and the Ceasefire Line will be respected henceforth or that efforts would be exerted to restore conditions to normal along the Line. I did receive assurance from the Government of India, conveyed orally by their representative at the United Nations, that India would act with restraint with regard to any retaliatory acts and will respect the Ceasefire Agreement and the Ceasefire Line if Pakistan does likewise.[2]

Obviously, Pakistan had no intention of respecting the 1949 Ceasefire Line: it did not serve Pakistan's interests. Whose interests did it serve then? This, as we shall see later, was one of the crucial points discussed between Shastri and Kosygin in Tashkent.

Leaving that aside, let us look at Ayub's quandary in 1965. On 18 September he had received a draft of the proposed Security Council resolution demanding immediate ceasefire, which was to be considered by the Security Council on 20 September. Ayub wanted to reject the proposed resolution. But the military situation was unfavourable to Pakistan. According to Gauhar, the army and air force chiefs were both against further prolongation of the conflict. 'General Musa was demoralised by the lack of ammunition and spare parts, and Air Marshal Nur Khan by the high attrition rate which was daily reducing the number of operational aircraft available to him.'[3] Western countries and the USSR were pressing Ayub to comply with the Security Council resolution. In this situation, Ayub turned to the Chinese. The ambassador of China, who had maintained close contact with Bhutto during the days of the war, was urging Pakistan to continue fighting. Ayub decided, however, that he should meet Chou En-lai personally before taking a final decision on the ceasefire resolution of the Security Council. Accompanied by Bhutto, Ayub flew to Beijing during the night of 19/20 September and returned the following night. The visit was kept a closely guarded secret. In Beijing Ayub and Bhutto had two long meetings with Chou En-lai and Marshal Chen Yi. According to Gauhar's version: 'Ayub explained the military situation and how the Indians, because of their superiority in numbers, were beginning to strengthen their hold, and how Western powers were giving full diplomatic support to India while persuading the Soviet Union to assume the role of a mediator.'[4]

Chou En-lai is reported to have urged Pakistan to fight on, promising to maintain China's pressure on India. When Ayub asked how long the Chinese would maintain that pressure, Chou En-lai is said to have replied: 'For as long as necessary, but you must keep fighting even if you have to withdraw to the hills.'[5] Chou En-lai is reported also to have cautioned Ayub against succumbing to American pressure or falling into the Russian trap. In brief the Chinese wanted the Pakistanis to reject the demand of the Security Council for ceasefire and engage in a long-drawn-out war with India. Quite obviously Ayub was in no position to do that. All he could do was reassure the Chinese about the permanence of his friendship. Having done that, he returned to Pakistan in a sombre mood.

Meanwhile the Security Council had adopted its resolution of 20 September demanding immediate ceasefire. Ayub now dispatched his foreign minister to New York to deal with the resulting critical situation.

Bhutto arrived in New York on 21 September and asked for an appointment to see Goldberg, the US delegate to the Security Council and its current president. This was arranged immediately. The following are excerpts from an official summary of conversation at that meeting between Goldberg and Bhutto:

> Bhutto opened by saying Pakistan favored cessation of hostilities and did not want to carry war to end. Wanted 'honorable' settlement' of Jammu and Kashmir question which had been pending for 18 years. Noted Pakistan had never resorted to military means in all that time, while India had slammed one door after another. Said Pakistan had studied res carefully and found 'basic weakness' in it. Res was discriminatory. It did not take account of Indian aggression or self-determination of people of Kashmir. As it stood res would not be acceptable to people of Pakistan.

In an effort to persuade Bhutto to accept the Security Council resolution of 20 September, Goldberg referred to those elements in it which were favourable to Pakistan, namely reference to Kashmir in the preamble and the contents of paragraph 4 which related to the future settlement of the dispute. Furthermore, pointed out Goldberg, the resolution now had unanimous support which was previously lacking. Here are some further excerpts from the same official summary:

> Asked Bhutto again what he wished him to convey to SC members. Bhutto said he did not think he wanted meeting right at that point. Said he wanted to talk to syg and would communicate Pakistani answer before

hour had expired. (Shortly before this point in conversation he had left room to take telephone call from Rawalpindi.) Said lack of reference to previous decisions and Aug 5 date were great difficulties and he doubted very much whether Pakistan would accept res.

Goldberg asked whether he should ask SC members to standby. Said if Bhutto wished to address SC immediately he would support that request.

Bhutto expressed thanks but said what he would have to say would depend upon decision in Rawalpindi and that it was not necessary for SC to meet at that point.

Goldberg asked what he should say to members about Pakistan attitude toward res. Should he say Pakistan thought Aug 5 date was effort to brand them with aggression and that failure to mention past reses prejudices Pakistani position. Bhutto replied he did not wish Goldberg to be so precise because it might create difficulties for him if Pakistan should accept res. Might be better to say they had frank discussion and that Bhutto had regretted India not branded as aggressor; had said res would 'have been better' if it had reaffirmed reses; and that he had asked for 'clarification' of Aug 5 date, and that Goldberg had replied this was reference to Ceasefire Line and international boundary.

Meeting broke up on this note with Goldberg and staff concluding as result of closing tenor of conversation that Bhutto had probably already received instructions from Rawalpindi during telecon to accept ceasefire.[6]

This summary of Goldberg's conversation with Bhutto was passed on to Secretary of State Dean Rusk and to the White House for Johnson by the midnight hour on 21/22 September.

It is evident from the conversation between Bhutto and Goldberg that Pakistan well understood the significance of the reference to 5 August in the Security Council resolution of 20 September, as also the implication of the fact that no reference had been made to previous resolutions. This was galling to Bhutto and, left to himself, he would have rejected the Security Council mandatory resolution. But he was under the firm control of Ayub who, by now had made up his mind to accept ceasefire.

Bhutto was obliged to convey the acceptance of ceasefire and for this purpose he sought another opportunity for a dramatic performance. The Security Council met at his request at about the midnight hour of 21 September and continued till early hours of 22 September. At this meeting, Bhutto made his usual attacks on India and held out the threat that Pakistan might leave the United Nations if no 'honourable' solution was found to the Kashmir problem soon. But he announced the acceptance of ceasefire. After this drama, the formal acceptance of ceasefire by the president of Pakistan was also conveyed to the UN secretary-general by the permanent representative of Pakistan, Syed Amjad Ali, who transmitted, in the early morning hours of 22 September, the following message from his president:

> Pakistan considers the Security Council Resolution No. 211 of 20th September as unsatisfactory. However, in the interest of international peace, and in order to enable the Security Council to evolve a self-executing procedure which will lead to an honourable settlement of the root cause of the present conflict, namely, the Jammu and Kashmir dispute, I have issued the following orders to the Pakistan armed forces:
>
> (1) They will stop fighting as from 1205 hours West Pakistan time today;
>
> (2) As from that time they will not fire on enemy forces unless fired upon; provided that the Indian government issues similar orders to its Armed Forces.[7]

The secretary-general of the United Nations then sent the following telegram to the prime minister of India and to the president of Pakistan on 22 September 1965:

> I have the honour to inform Your Excellency that the formal acceptance of the ceasefire demanded in the Security Council Resolution of 20 September has now been confirmed by both governments. The Security Council at its meeting in the early hours of the morning of 22 September has agreed that the President of the Council should inform the parties that the hour at which the ceasefire is to take effect is 2200 hours GMT on Wednesday 22 September (0300 hours West Pakistan time on 23 September and 0330 hours New Delhi time on 23 September). This postponement is in order to give time for the governments to issue the necessary ceasefire orders to the commanders in the field.[8]

The Government of Pakistan conveyed orders for ceasefire to its field commanders and the ceasefire became effective at 0300 hours, West Pakistan time, or 0330 New Delhi time, on 23 September 1965.

# Chapter 26

# The Post-war Period

The war had ended and, in the words of Prime Minister Shastri, 'an awakened' India had emerged. Pakistan had been defeated and the Chinese threat had been contained. Both Russia and the USA could now be said to have become friendly towards India, or at least 'positively neutral.' In the United States, political assessment after the cessation of hostilities was: 'With respect to India our stance was based on recognition that India had emerged from the conflict with strengthened unity, sense of national purpose, and status as the dominant power on the subcontinent.'[1]

By far the most important matter before Shastri during the weeks following the cessation of hostilities was still the many-faceted problem of relations with Pakistan. First, there was the question of the effective observance of ceasefire. Shastri had said in his broadcast to the nation on 23 September that, even after accepting the ceasefire, Pakistan had behaved in a 'most unworthy and atrocious manner' by deliberately bombing the civilian population of Amritsar and by shooting down an unarmed plane carrying the Gujarat chief minister. He told Chaudhuri that if the Pakistanis fired, violating the ceasefire, the Indian army should fire back.

The general assembly of the UN was due to meet, and anticipating that Pakistan would use the forum to raise the Kashmir question again, the prime minister sent a strong delegation led by Sardar Swaran Singh. Kashmiri cabinet minister Mir Qasim was included in the Indian delegation, which was briefed on the presentation of India's case in accordance with Shastri's policy announcements.

Another important task was the maintenance and strengthening of national unity and national consensus which had been forged so strongly during the days of the war. It was essential to maintain mass contact with people. With this in view, he addressed a series of public meetings in New Delhi, Bombay, Calcutta and other centres. His purpose was to establish a direct nexus with the people by explaining to them personally the policies which he had followed in the past and which he intended to follow in the future. He made a wide-ranging speech at the Ram Lila Grounds in New Delhi on 26 September 1965. He was in a confident and jovial mood and regaled his vast audience by giving the following reason for asking the Indian army to march towards Lahore:

*Sadar Ayub ne elan kiya tha ki woh Dilli tak chahal qadmi karte hue pahunch jaenge. Woh itne bare aadmi hain, laheem shaheem hain. Maine socha ki unko Dilli tak paidal safar karne ki takleef kyon dee jai. Hameen Lahore ki taraf barh kar unka istiqbal karen.* (President Ayub had declared he would soon walk through to Delhi. He is a great person, high and mighty of stature. I thought he should not undergo the travail of such a long walk. We should ourselves march towards Lahore to greet him.)

Pointing out that a portion of Kashmir was still held by Pakistan, Shastri refered to a B.B.C. broadcast from London suggesting that he had waged this war with Pakistan because he was a Hindu. 'There is no doubt,' said Shastri,

that I am a Hindu. Mir Mushtaq Sahib who is presiding over this meeting is a Muslim. Mr Frank Anthony who has also addressed you is a Christian. There are also Sikhs and Parsis here. The unique thing about our country is that we have Hindus, Muslims, Christians, Sikhs, Parsis and people of all other religions. We have temples and mosques, gurdwaras and churches. But we do not bring all this into politics. We are not working to make India a Hindu state or a Muslim state. This is the difference between India and Pakistan. Whereas Pakistan proclaims herself to be an Islamic state and uses religion as a political factor, we Indians have the freedom to follow whatever religion we may choose, to worship in any way we please. So far as politics is concerned, each one of us is as much an Indian as the other. It is a distortion of facts to accuse India of hostility to Pakistan on account of the narrow point of view of religion. After all, China is not an Islamic state. So far as the territorial integrity of India is concerned, we have taken the same stand with China as we have taken with Pakistan. . . The defence of the country has nothing to do with religion; it is a matter of the freedom and sovereignty of the Motherland.

Referring to the armed forces, he said:

Yesterday I visited some of our wounded jawans and officers in the military hospital. They have been badly hurt but I did not see a single tear or even a sad face. However serious the injury or wound was, each one of them was smiling and cheerful. An officer whose leg had been amputated told me with pride that he had shot down a Pakistani officer after his leg received the injury on the battlefield. I was very much moved to see another officer, Bhupinder Singh, whose whole body was covered with blood. Even now it is difficult to put a piece of cloth anywhere on his body. He was lying in bed with eyes closed. He apologized to me for not being able to stand up to show respect to the prime minister who was visiting him. He told me that he destroyed seven enemy tanks and that his unit had knocked out thirty-one. He also said that he was sure he would get well again, but even if he did not it did not matter because the country can now hold its head high. I told him how proud the country was of him, how deeply grateful the people of the country were for the way in which the Indian armed forces had faced the enemy. Every child, every man and woman in this country had the deepest respect for the men of the Indian army, for the air force pilots and other fighters.[2]

Meanwhile the Pakistanis continued sporadic firing. The situation began to deteriorate rapidly and, following reports of numerous violations of the ceasefire, the United Nations Security Council held an emergency meeting on 27 September and adopted a resolution demanding 'that the parties urgently honour their commitments to the Council to observe the ceasefire.'

Bhutto was not impressed. Speaking in London on 30 September he said that the Indo-Pakistani ceasefire was 'tenuous' and 'renewed fighting with India would set the world aflame.' He told a press conference: 'We are now mentally attuned to face a war of extermination.' The ceasefire would remain tenuous unless the Kashmir problem was equitably settled.[3] In effect, Bhutto was telling the world that there would be no effective ceasefire until the Kashmir issue was settled to Pakistan's satisfaction. He had flown in from New York after addressing the general assembly.

Bhutto's speech in the general assembly, which was a tirade against India, was called by Mir Qasim a mass of untruths and misrepresentations of fact and history, and an attempt to rely upon abuse and invective as substitutes for reason and hard facts. Qasim said to the assembly: 'Let me make one thing clear. Despite two aggressions against the Indian state of Jammu and Kashmir, Pakistan has not been able to annex the state by force of arms. Having failed to do so, having failed to compel India to discuss this so-called question of Kashmir at the point of a gun, Pakistan now seeks to put international pressure on India to enter into discussions. Let there be no misunderstanding or doubt about India's attitude on this subject.' Charging Bhutto with coveting Kashmir not for securing any imaginary rights of people but for self-aggrandisement, Qasim said: 'If Pakistan was really interested in the people of Kashmir, Bhutto and his government would not have bartered away large chunks of our territory to the Chinese nor imposed a repressive rule on our brethren in Pakistan-occupied Kashmir, whom Pakistan holds in bondage to this day and whom we cannot forsake.'

Shastri was now availing of every opportunity and every forum of importance to reiterate India's determination to maintain its territorial integrity and to emphasize the fact that Jammu and Kashmir was part of India. He had already written on these lines specifically to Johnson and Kosygin. The purpose was to tell them in advance that in any future negotiations between India and Pakistan, India's sovereignty over Kashmir would not be negotiable. While both these leaders were promoting a meeting between Shastri and Ayub, neither had written back contesting India's stand. If they had, Shastri would have declined to join any meeting. Clarity on this point was essential to avoid the build-up of pressure.

On 2 October 1965, Shastri's sixty-second birthday (which was also Mahatma Gandhi's), Shastri went in the morning to Rajghat to pay homage to the Father of the Nation. C. Subramaniam presented the prime minister with seven ears of corn and five ears of maize as tribute. Some thoughtful people presented a giant birthday cake in the shape of a Patton tank with colour and markings, as in an actual tank. Symbolically, the prime minister destroyed the tank by putting a knife through it. He then asked that the cake be sent to jawans. This was altogether a very happy day.

On 3 October the prime minister addressed a mammoth Sikh congregation outside Gurdwara Bangla Sahib in New Delhi. As a tribute to the exceptional heroism displayed by the Sikh community during the war, he began his address with the traditional Sikh invocation: *'Jo bole so nihal.'* (Whosoever takes the name of God is blessed.) The congregation responded thunderously: *'Sat Sri Akal.'* (Truth is immortal.)[4]

*Saropas* comprising scarves and swords were presented to Prime Minister Shastri and to the chief of the army staff, General Chaudhuri. The sword presented to Shastri was the longest I have ever seen. When the prime minister stood it up on the ground, its upper end came almost to his own height (not that Shastri was tall). He then looked around and spotted Lt-General Harbaksh Singh, army commander, Western Command. Holding the large sword in one hand, Shastri went up to Harbaksh Singh, took him by the other hand, brought him to the front of the gathering and handed over the sword: 'General Sahib, this sword rightfully belongs to you because as the army commander, Western Command, you led the Indian army in the war theatre and won a resounding victory for India.'

On 4 October Y.B. Chavan visited Bombay for a number of public engagements. During the war days, Chavan had played a crucial role. He had given strong support to the prime minister and had become one of his most trusted and admired cabinet colleagues. Addressing a meeting of the Citizens' Defence Committee, Chavan said: 'The architect of the successful and triumphant policy in our present conflict with Pakistan is the prime minister of India and no one else.'[5]

Meanwhile, the border situation was getting worse every day and sizeable encounters were taking place. On 7 October Shastri told his cabinet colleagues that the situation in the India–Pakistan border was potentially dangerous, that Pakistan's reported attempts to secure arms from abroad were ominous, and that Pakistan was deliberately destabilizing the ceasefire.

Shastri was taking the precaution of maintaining regular correspondence with Johnson. In a letter delivered on 7 October, he conveyed to Johnson his wishes for 'a full and speedy recovery' from an operation which Johnson was to undergo on 8 October. In the same letter Shastri expressed the hope that he would meet Johnson at an early date. This set into motion bilateral exchanges through diplomatic channels, resulting eventually in a mutually agreed decision that Shastri would visit Washington during the first week of February 1966. This decision had the obvious advantage of ensuring that Johnson would make no change in his policy about military and economic aid to India and Pakistan before their meeting. The main objective was to prevent the resumption of military aid to Pakistan.

On 7 October the British foreign secretary, Michael Stewart, conceded for the first time at a press conference in New York that Indian arguments in the Kashmir dispute about Kashmir's formal and constitutional accession to India could not be dismissed as mere obstinacy or unreasonableness and that there was a case which sincere and intelligent people would have to bear in mind and listen to. He had also begun to appreciate the natural anxiety of India about the threat to the whole basis of the Indian state which embraced people of so many races and religions.[6]

At this time within India the most important item on the nation's agenda, besides defence, was food. Speaking on the national radio network on 10 October 1965, the prime minister appealed to the farmer to produce more, to the trader to market supplies at fair prices, and to the consumer to exercise greater restraint on consumption. He said self-sufficiency in food was no less important than an impregnable defence system for the preservation of freedom. He reminded the nation that dependence on food imports undermined the country's self-confidence and self-respect. This is when he gave the nation a new slogan—'Jai Jawan, Jai Kisan.'

On 11 October, at about midnight, when I was leaving my office at 10 Janpath in the prime minister's residence, he said to me: 'Tomorrow morning you have to come early in the morning—at 5 a.m. We are going out. We will come back in the afternoon.' I arrived next morning at the appointed time and we left for the airport. The prime minister was going to the forward areas in the Lahore sector, right up to the Ichhogil canal.

We first flew and then moved around in motor vehicles. It was a visit never to be forgotten. The prime minister was conducted on this tour by Lt-General J.S. Dhillon and other high ranking military officers. He visited the towns of Burki and Dograi and then proceeded to the bank of Ichhogil canal. On the way, he saw the defence structures, such as pillboxes, which the Pakistanis had built and which the Indian jawans had had to capture to secure the canal bank.

The prime minister also visited the Khem Karan area and saw a large number of destroyed and captured Pakistani Patton tanks strewn all over the fields. He stood on one of them.

At Pathankot the prime minister was delighted to meet Sqn-Leader Trevor Keelor who stood by the side of a Gnat fighter aircraft which, for a war plane, was incredibly tiny in size. Trevor Keelor was not tall either. It seemed a remarkable gathering of three pint-sized war heroes. As Shastri quipped: *'Achcha, hum teeno hi chhote qad ke hain.'* (All three of us are pretty small, aren't we!)

Apart from Shastri's own public statements and statements made in the UN Security Council and the UN general assembly by representatives of India, the prime minister sent personal emissaries to some important countries. Vijay Lakshmi Pandit was sent to France to meet de Gaulle, V.K. Krishna Menon was sent to Cairo to meet Nasser.

On 15 October Shastri asked India's permanent representative to the United Nations to secure the immediate stoppage of provocative intrusions by Pakistani aircraft, which had assumed grave proportions during the preceding fortnight. The UN secretary-general was to be informed that Pakistani military aircraft had committed forty-eight intrusions over India and Indian held territories between 1 and 14 October and that the Pakistani violations had been particularly numerous in the Akhnoor area of Jammu, in Amritsar, Wagah, Khalra, and Fazilka in Punjab and in Jaisalmer district of Rajasthan.

Shastri made his second visit to the forward areas on 15 October, touring the Pakistani territories in the Sialkot sector, which had been occupied by the Indian army during the war. This was another moving experience. The prime minister addressed jawans at several points and everywhere he conveyed to them the nation's feelings of admiration for their historic achievements. He asked them to remain vigilant as Pakistan's intentions were not clear.

In Bombay later that month Shastri met G.D. Birla, who had just returned to India from a foreign tour. Birla said that during his visit to the US, he had found 'unqualified sympathy and admiration' for the way in which Shastri had handled the critical situation of the Pakistani aggression in Kashmir and Kutch. He had found the people of the US still unable to appreciate the proper position regarding Kashmir, as questions were still being raised. But there was now no more talk of any plebiscite in Kashmir, only some vague remarks that 'something should be done to settle the problem.' Birla was convinced that it was now the task of India's diplomats to convince the world of India's true position in regard to Kashmir. He said that during the hostilities pictures sympathetic to India were shown over US television networks. A procession of Bombay Muslims was shown protesting against Turkey and Iran extending aid to Pakistan, thus demonstrating that India's whole Muslim community was behind the Indian government. This, Birla said, had made a tremendous impression in the US.[7]

On 18 October 1965 Shastri travelled to Aurangabad, where he addressed the Citizens Defence Committee of Aurangabad division. Y.B. Chavan was present at this meeting. After recounting the events of the war and expressing his admiration for the armed forces, he amused the audience by recalling Pakistani comments about India's 'dhoti-wearing' prime minister. 'I am not a Marshal and I wear a dhoti. That may be the reason why Pakistan considers India weak,' the prime minister observed. And he added: 'Defence Minister Chavan also wears a dhoti. Dhoti-clad people have defended their country and marched up to Lahore.'

During the preceding two or three weeks, Pakistan had tried desperately to secure arms, ammunition and spares for its damaged weapons. It was reported in the press at about this time that Pakistan had received sizeable quantities of arms from Iran and Turkey and further that Turkey had supplied at least one squadron of Sabre jets.[8] Shastri knew and said that 'the country had to stand on its own feet, not in some distant future, but here and now. ' The gospel of swadeshi was as valid today as when Gandhi preached it forty years earlier. There were three specific fields in which self-reliance was of the highest importance. The armed forces had to be adequately equipped; the defence industry had to be developed at top speed; and the economic base had to be strengthened, with particular emphasis on food self-sufficiency.

Meanwhile, on 21 October Kuldip Nayar published an article in *The Hindustan Times*, pointing out that it was entirely erroneous to believe that by holding on to the Haji Pir Pass, India could effectively close the door to infiltrators because there were several other routes which could be used and were in fact used by Pakistani infiltrators in August 1965.

The scene at this stage shifted once again to the United Nations headquarters. Pakistan made a formal request on 22 October that the Security Council should meet urgently to consider what it called 'the fast deteriorating situation inside Jammu and Kashmir.' The Pakistani representative to the UN alleged also that the ceasefire had virtually collapsed because of 'total disregard' by India of 'the letter and spirit', of the ceasefire resolution.

When the debate began, Bhutto ignored the agenda and launched a vitriolic attack on India for repression in Kashmir. He refused to listen to the plea of the president of the council that he should confine his remarks to the item on the agenda. At that point, Indian Foreign Minister Sardar Swaran Singh and all other members of the Indian delegation walked out of the Security Council meeting. Thereafter, Bhutto used vile and unprintable language. This was the first time that the Indian delegation had walked out of a Security Council meeting and it signalled a new development in India's Kashmir policy. Hereafter, as far as India was concerned, the internal administration of the state of Jammu and Kashmir, which was India's internal affair, was not a matter for the Security Council. In New Delhi, the prime minister reviewed this matter with two senior colleagues, G.L. Nanda and Indira Gandhi, then decided that the boycott of the Security Council meeting may not be continued if assurance was available that this forum would not be allowed to be misused by the Pakistani delegation. A strong letter was sent by the Indian foreign minister to the president of the Security Council, protesting against Bhutto's atrocious behaviour.

At home, Shastri reviewed the ongoing debate in the Security Council and came to the conclusion that India's main effort at that time must be concentrated on defeating Pakistani efforts to bring about an immediate coupling of the political issues relating to Kashmir with the military questions, namely the effective observance of ceasefire and the withdrawal of armed personnel. The Security Council resolution of 20 September had two principal operative paragraphs: Paragraph 1 demanding an unconditional ceasefire and the withdrawal of all armed personnel to the position occupied prior to 5 August (that is, respective withdrawal behind the 1949 Ceasefire Line), and paragraph 4 proposing a consideration of the political issue at a later but undetermined point in time. Pakistan wanted a change by proposing in effect that the two paragraphs should be implemented together. India was completely against any such change.

Shastri declared on 28 October at a massive public meeting attended by about 3,00,000 people at Ramnivas Bagh in Jaipur that India was prepared to participate in the Security Council discussions on ceasefire and troop withdrawals but not on any discussions regarding Kashmir. He declared that if Pakistan did not withdraw from Chhamb, India would also not withdraw from Lahore and Sialkot. He demanded further that every infiltrator be withdrawn from Kashmir. The prime minister had taken care not to mention the Haji Pir Pass or the Tithwal sector in his address because he realized that this would go against the demand of the Security Council for all withdrawals to the positions prior to 5 August. Any such assertion would have immediately caused general hostility against India in the Security Council, because even the Soviet Union and Malaysia—India's only staunch supporters in the Security Council—fully supported complete withdrawals by both India and Pakistan to positions prior to 5 August, that is to the 1949 Ceasefire Line.

This firm stand enabled India to defeat Pakistan's efforts to couple the political issue of Kashmir with the question of withdrawals. Even the UK representative made statements in the Security Council supportive of the position which India had taken—not an insignificant gain. On 27 October, Lord Caradon of the UK made, inter alia, the following comments in the Security Council: 'The task on which we should concentrate all our effort at this time is the task of taking every possible action to render effective the ceasefire between India and Pakistan which this Council demanded together with the withdrawal of all armed personnel . . . The ceasefire and the complete withdrawal are in effect the only door to a sound settlement.' This was a considerable shift away from the position which the UK prime minister, Harold Wilson, had taken in his impetuous statement dated 6 September castigating India.

The USA, via Goldberg, also took the unusual step of chiding the US press for 'misrepresenting' India's action and its walkout from the Security Council's current series of discussions. He also emphasized that the UN had been 'even-handed' in the September resolutions and would be so over the political issue also. So, at the UN things were moving ahead on the basis of a complete implementation of the demand of the Security Council for effective ceasefire and withdrawal of all armed personnel to the positions held before 5 August, which definitely meant withdrawal by Pakistan from Chhamb and by India from the Haji Pir Pass and other parts on the Pakistan side of the Ceasefire Line of 1949.

On the last day of October Shastri flew in an Indian air force plane to Calcutta where he was given a hero's welcome. At the airport, he was received by a large gathering headed by Chief Minister P.C. Sen. There were welcome arches all along the ten-mile route from Dum-Dum airport to Raj Bhavan, the most prominent among them being those erected in memory of Lt Tapan Choudhury and Havildar Abdul Hamid who had laid down their lives in defence of the country.

In the evening Shastri addressed a mammoth public meeting at the hundred-acre Calcutta Maidan. I have never seen a larger gathering than this one in Calcutta. Shastri was moved by this massive demonstration. He spoke at length here. No one, he said, knew more than him about poverty. He was determined to apply himself to the eradication of poverty and to the provision of relief to the people who were entitled to a new deal from the government of the country. This was the only occasion I ever heard him, in public or private, talk about the poverty of his early life. That remark established a communion with the common people, most of whom were poor themselves.

Next morning, on 1 November, Shastri met representatives of the press and confirmed he had been invited by Johnson to visit the United States as early as convenient, though no dates had yet been agreed. He added that he welcomed the recent softening in the US attitude on the question of Kashmir.

Shastri returned to New Delhi on 1 November by the afternoon. This was a Monday. Speaking in Jaipur on 28 October, he had appealed to the people of India to miss a meal every week as a mark of austerity, which was essentially needed in the current difficult food situation. This would also generate a sense of fellow feeling and national solidarity. He and his family decided to make a beginning themselves. All members of the Shastri family forewent the evening meal on 1 November, and on every Monday thereafter while the food shortage lasted. He wanted to persuade by example.

A ticklish question arose towards the end of October 1965, involving Indo–Pakistan relations not connected with war. Under the Indus Water Treaty between India and Pakistan negotiated under the auspices of the World Bank, when Nehru was prime minister, a sum of Rs 80 crores was payable to Pakistan by India in ten equal instalments. Of these, five had already been paid and the sixth instalment now fell due. There were some in the opposition and some in the Congress Party who were opposed to this payment in the current situation. Shastri decided, however, that as India had not regarded herself as being at war with Pakistan, nor had diplomatic relations with Pakistan been broken off, India must honour her treaty obligations and pay the sixth instalment of Rs 8 crores. It was, however, arranged with the approval of the World Bank, that this amount would be paid only in non-convertible rupees, not in sterling, and further that the amount should be paid to Pakistan only in January 1966, though it was to be deposited in a special account with the Reserve Bank of India right then. Despite opposition, Shastri maintained his principled stand and did not give in to hotheads. In his statement in parliament on 5 November he declared that India must honour its pledge.

On 5 November, hours before the UN Security Council was to meet in New York, Shastri made a statement in parliament chiding the United Nations for its refusal to identify Pakistan clearly as the aggressor and for not taking certain steps in time which might have prevented the conflagration. 'The world,' he said, 'would be saved much trouble and misery if aggression is not countenanced anywhere and objective efforts are made to identify the aggressor. This was particularly necessary because a new technique was being adopted under which invasions were launched in disguise and forces of destruction unleashed without the usual declaration of war.' The tragic events of the last few months should make the UN and the Council realize, said Shastri, 'that prevention is not only better but easier than cure.' If firm action had been taken when infiltration began and General Nimmo reported on it, perhaps much of the tragic loss of life and property which followed might have been avoided, he remarked.[9]

A few hours later, at the United Nations headquarters in New York, the Security Council concluded its recent round of debates by adopting a new resolution on 5 November calling upon India and Pakistan to ask their armed personnel to co-operate with the United Nations 'towards a full implementation' of the ceasefire and withdrawal call demanded by the Security Council on September 20. The resolution demanded the 'prompt and unconditional' execution of a proposal that India and Pakistan name representatives to meet with a representative of Secretary-General U Thant on a plan for withdrawal of troops to positions as of August 5. Pakistan failed once again to secure a coupling of this matter with the political issue. On the other hand, India's position was fully upheld.

Suddenly, the unpredictable Bhutto publicly apologized at the United Nations headquarters in New York on 6 November for his derogatory remarks about Indians on 26 October. He said that he was then speaking under 'grave provocation' and could not be held responsible for his 'forensic flow', but 'if Indians were hurt by my remarks, I am very sorry.'[10] Considering everything, this was a notable turnabout.

Back home, at a meeting of the Congress the prime minister emphasized India's right to push out Pakistanis from the areas they had taken after the ceasefire. As regards Haji Pir Pass, Tithwal, and other areas in Kashmir, the prime minister said that 'conditions have to be created which will remove any apprehension of further influx of infiltrators. No question of discussion arises till such a situation has been created.' He took great care in stating his position on this sensitive issue. He did not say that there would be no withdrawal from the Haji Pir Pass and other posts. What he said was that conditions would have to be created which would remove the apprehension of any further influx of infiltrators. In its resolution the Congress Working Committee made no reference to the question of the

Haji Pir Pass and other posts, for obviously this was a matter for the prime minister.

Within the country, new policies were initiated for enhanced food production at home. Subramaniam was to proceed to the United States. The existing arrangement of month-by-month approval of food shipments from the US needed to be replaced by a longer-term arrangement. Subramaniam was to prepare the ground for this so that a new agreement could be signed during the projected meeting between Shastri and Johnson early in 1966. Urgent steps were taken to enhance defence production and to push this effort, a new department of defence production within the ministry of defence had been recently established. A high-powered team led by Special Secretary, Defence Production, H.C. Sarin, was sent to the Soviet Union to explore the prospects of acquiring a wide range of defence equipment.

From early December 1965, Prime Minister Shastri began to devote much of his time to preparation for the coming mediation by Prime Minister Kosygin between India and Pakistan. Shastri was by now, fifteen months into his premiership, India's unquestioned leader. Ambassador J.K. Galbraith had observed perceptively: 'There is more iron in his soul than appears on the surface. He listens to every point of view, he makes up his mind firmly, and once he has made them, his decisions stick . . . He is the kind of man who is trusted.'[11]

# Chapter 27

# Preparing for Tashkent

In his statement made in parliament on 23 September, Shastri had included the following:

> I should like to inform the House that on 18th September 1965, I received a message from Mr Kosygin, Chairman of the Council of Ministers of the USSR, offering his good offices for bringing about improved relations between India and Pakistan. No one can ever contest the view that ultimately India and Pakistan will have to live together as peaceful neighbours. We cannot, therefore, say no to any efforts which may help to bring about such a situation, made by those who are sincere and genuine in their feelings of goodwill and friendship. I have, therefore, informed Mr Kosygin today that we would welcome his efforts and good offices.

Kosygin had in fact taken the initiative in regard to the settlement of the Indo–Pakistan conflict as early as 4 September. In a letter addressed to Shastri, Kosygin had said:

> We should not be frank if we did not say that the military conflict in Kashmir arouses the concern of the Soviet government also because it has occurred in an area directly adjacent to the borders of the Soviet Union.
>
> I think you will agree that in the present serious situation it is hardly appropriate to place the question of the causes of the origin of the conflict in the forefront or to seek to determine who is right and who is to blame. The principal efforts should be concentrated upon the immediate cessation of military operations, the halting of the tanks and the silencing of the guns.
>
> In our opinion, the first step after the immediate cessation of hostilities could be the withdrawal of troops to positions behind the Ceasefire Line established by agreement between India and Pakistan in July 1949.

The implications of the Security Council resolution with regard to the vacation of the Haji Pir Pass have already been referred to: it was undoubtedly going to be a major issue at Tashkent. What was the prime minister to do about the withdrawals? This was the question on which he had to concentrate as a part of his preparation for a possible future meeting with Pakistan, arranged through the mediatory efforts of Kosygin.

On 11 November, Bhutto announced in Rawalpindi that Pakistan had accepted the Soviet offer of mediation and that he would soon visit Moscow for important talks with the Soviet leaders. It was known by now that Kosygin's mediatory efforts were being supported by both Johnson and Wilson. Their overriding priority was peace in the Indian subcontinent, even if the credit for bringing this about were to go to the USSR. The only country unhappy about this diplomatic initiative by the Soviet Union was China. Suddenly on 13 November, the Chinese opened fire on two Indian posts in the Dongchui La area on the Sikkim–China border. The fire was returned and two Chinese soldiers and one Indian soldier were killed.

On 16 November the prime minister, intervening in the Lok Sabha debate on foreign affairs, announced that Kosygin had now formally proposed a meeting in Tashkent with Ayub, and although he felt the time was neither right nor proper for such a meeting, he could not say no to the Soviet suggestion because of the importance of improving India's relations with Pakistan. The Soviets had suggested a discussion of the totality of India–Pakistan relations, which was alright. But he stated that the position that Indo–Pak amity could be established by India parting with Kashmir 'was wholly impossible and absolutely unacceptable.'

Referring to China, Shastri said that what had happened the other day (the attack on Indian posts on the Sikkim border) was not a good omen. It was difficult to say what China and Pakistan were preparing for. 'If they launched a joint attack on India,' said Shastri, 'we will be faced with a serious situation. In this context a disquieting piece of news came on 18 November. According to the Institute of Strategic Studies in London, the Chinese had amassed up to fifteen divisions in Tibet, of which at least six were stationed near the borders with Sikkim, Bhutan and Nepal. The Chinese had also constructed twenty-five airfields or airstrips in Tibet, at least two of which were capable of taking light jet bombers. They had also completed two roads leading from China to the Indian border and a lateral road along the entire frontier from NEFA to Kashmir. This showed the mighty military strength which the Chinese had built along the India–China border, obviously *vis-à-vis* India.

In order to keep up tension, the Chinese intruded again on the Sikkim–Tibet border on 19 and 20 November and seemed determined to go on creating incidents. On 23 November, Shastri stated in the Rajya Sabha that he had accepted a renewed Soviet suggestion received a couple of days earlier that he should meet Ayub in Tashkent. Once again, he made it clear that he would not negotiate with Pakistan on Jammu and Kashmir.

Shastri received a communication from Kosygin on 29 November, proposing that the meeting with Ayub be held in Tashkent towards the end of December 1965 or early in January 1966. This communication confirmed Ayub would discuss the whole range of India–Pakistan problems and not insist, as he had done earlier, on discussing Kashmir only. This matter was taken up by the prime minister at the cabinet meeting on 2 December when he informed his colleagues that he had decided to accept the Soviet suggestion for a meeting in Tashkent and that he preferred the first week of January 1966 for the meeting. The same day the prime minister received the USSR ambassador, I.A. Benediktov, and indicated to him his preference for a meeting in Tashkent during the first week of January 1966. The stage was now set for the Tashkent conference.

From this point on, Prime Minister Shastri was engaged almost continuously in wide-ranging consultations about the issues likely to come up for discussion in Tashkent. In addition to his cabinet colleagues and other Congress Party leaders, he consulted leaders in the opposition. He had detailed personal talks with the editors of leading newspapers in New Delhi. He made assessments of the military situation by talks with Chaudhuri and Arjan Singh. He asked Chavan, the defence minister, and Sardar Swaran Singh, the foreign minister, to accompany him to Tashkent. At the official level, the prime minister decided the foreign secretary, C.S. Jha, the home secretary, L.P. Singh, and the vice-chief of the army staff, General P.P. Kumaramangalam were included. The Indian ambassador to the USSR, T.N. Kaul, and the Indian high commissioner to Pakistan, Kewal Singh were in as well. From the prime minister's secretariat, L.K. Jha and I were included in the party as members of the delegation. Several senior officers of the external affairs and defence ministries—K.S. Bajpai, R. Jaipal, D.R. Kohli and others completed the prime minister's team.

During the two weeks prior to his departure for Tashkent, Shastri made a number of public speeches in which he spelt out his likely approach. He emphasized again and again that peace was of crucial importance for the economic development of India. Speaking at Allahabad on 18 December, Shastri said that if the Tashkent talks between him and Ayub failed, the whole country would have to remain prepared to meet any eventuality. If the talks succeeded, he said, he would be the happiest man in the world. He was sorry to note, however, that a speech by Ayub to the United Nations delivered on 13 December did not augur well because Ayub had made no reference at all to the coming Tashkent conference. In his view, the best way of promoting good neighbourly relations was the signing of a no-war pact. Both nations could then sit together and try to resolve their differences peacefully.

Significantly, the All-India Jamiat-Ulema whose general council met in New Delhi on 19 December, declared that Kashmir was an integral part of India and said: 'If any external power attacks Kashmir or interferes in its internal affairs, the all-India Jamiat-Ulema would regard it as a national duty to defend it.' The general council, presided over by Maulana Fakhruddin Ahmad, congratulated Lal Bahadur Shastri and his colleagues for the foresight, courage and determination displayed by them in the war against Pakistan.

Shastri made a goodwill visit to Burma on 21 and 22 December. In Rangoon, he had talks with General Ne Win. About Tashkent, he said he was going with an open mind. He emphasized that despite bitter experiences, India was making a peaceful approach to end the Indo–Pak hostilities because 'war cannot go on forever and peace must be restored.'

Back in Delhi he said: 'If Pakistan made sincere and honest attempts at Tashkent to settle the problems, there is a chance that both countries can live as peaceful neighbours. But if President Ayub takes a rigid stand, I am afraid an excellent opportunity that has come our way will be lost and the consequences will be dangerous and disastrous.'[1] Sardar Swaran Singh, who had gone to Moscow on 23 December for urgent discussions, returned to New Delhi on 26 December. On arrival, he told newsmen that the Soviet leaders were genuinely desirous of good Indo–Pakistan relations and would be happy if the talks in Tashkent resulted in the establishment of peaceful conditions in the subcontinent. Significantly, he added that to be fruitful the talks would have to be conducted in a flexible manner. During the next two days, the foreign minister briefed Shastri about his talks with the Soviet leaders—President Podgorny, Kosygin, and Foreign Minister Gromyko. The message he had brought back was clear. The traditional stand of the Soviet Union about Kashmir being part of India had not changed but the Soviet leaders were of the firm view that peace between India and Pakistan must be established on the basis of the UN Security Council resolution of 20 September, which demanded the withdrawal of all armed personnel to positions held prior to 5 August 1965.

The question of troop withdrawals was becoming urgent. This was a matter on which the views of Chaudhuri were of crucial importance. Shastri had long talks with General Chaudhuri in which the pros and cons of various possibilities were discussed. On the question of withdrawal from the Haji Pir Pass and other posts in the Uri–Poonch bulge, Chaudhuri's views were clear. The armed forces of India had achieved their objectives;

they had regained their morale; the army chief said he was aware of the prime minister's reluctance to vacate the Haji Pir Pass and other posts because of the need to prevent further infiltration. He would be happy if these posts could be retained in India's possession without jeopardizing the prospects of peace, but if it was necessary to give them up for securing peace, there should be no hesitation in doing so. Arjan Singh gave the same advice. He said that the Haji Pir Pass had somehow become an emotional issue, but from the overall military point of view at that time a period of peace was immeasurably more important than holding on to posts, whatever their local importance.

On 31 December, General Marambio, the representative of the UN secretary-general, announced that he had convened a meeting for 3 January at Lahore and another for 4 January at Amritsar to discuss the withdrawal of armed personnel by India and Pakistan in compliance with the UN Security Council resolution of 5 November. The Government of India accepted this invitation and appointed Lt-General Harbaksh Singh to represent India at this meeting.

Shastri proceeded next with his final political consultations. He spent many hours on 1 January 1966 discussing Tashkent with important individuals and groups. Most important of all he addressed meetings of the Congress Parliamentary Party executive and opposition leaders. At these meetings, Shastri explained the important issues candidly. He said that the coming Tashkent summit could prove useful if it was possible to reach an agreement that India and Pakistan would never resort to arms in solving their problems.

On 2 January 1966, the day prior to his departure for Tashkent, the prime minister presided over a two-hour cabinet meeting at which he explained the possible lines of approach in his talks with Ayub. L.P. Singh has confirmed to me that, at this meeting, the question of possible withdrawal from the Haji Pir Pass was discussed and the consensus was that this could be accepted if it was necessary in the interests of peace. L.P. Singh was asked to consult two cabinet ministers of the Kashmir government—Mir Qasim and D.P. Dhar. He did that himself and both expressed the same view.

2 January was a very busy day for Shastri. Besides the long cabinet meeting, he had several other engagements to fulfil, including a call on President Radhakrishnan. The prime minister also received Johnson's special envoy, Averell Harriman, and exchanged views on the Vietnam situation in the context of US moves for peace negotiations. Ambassador B.K. Nehru and Ambassador Chester Bowles were present at this meeting. In the evening, he addressed members of the Indo–Soviet Cultural Society

at a reception on the eve of his departure for Tashkent. At this send-off function, Shastri expressed the hope that Ayub's 'anger' might have cooled with time and he would be amenable to agreeing that there should be no further trial of arms between India and Pakistan:

> If Ayub feels that a no-war declaration is too high-sounding a phrase, I shall seek a simple assurance from him that our armies would not bear arms against one another. What must be borne in mind during the meeting at Tashkent was that if the Indo–Pakistan conflict was not immediately contained, it was capable of escalation with the danger of developing into a world conflict.[2]

Late in the evening he called on the Kashmir chief minister, G.M. Sadiq, who was indisposed. Shastri was closeted with Sadiq for about half an hour for final consultations.

Next morning, 3 January 1966, Shastri left New Delhi for Tashkent in an Air India Boeing. He was seen off at Palam airport by a joyous gathering which included Lalita Shastri and members of his family, his cabinet colleagues, diplomatic envoys of foreign countries, military and civilian officials and leading citizens of the capital.

Later the same day, Radhakrishnan, while inaugurating the 53rd Indian Science Congress in Chandigarh, referred to the coming Tashkent conference and said he had advised Shastri to display at Tashkent an attitude 'of bringing the people together and not of breaking them apart.' The president said 'Shastri would be highlighting at the Tashkent meeting, the features that unite us rather than dilating on things that divide us . . . Shastri had gone to the meeting with an open mind without even a tinge of prejudice or fanaticism or with any presuppositions and rigid hypotheses in his mind . . . Shastri's entire effort would be bent towards the scientific pursuit of truth so as to sort out the realities which would be for the betterment of humanity.'[3]

# Chapter 28

# Ayub Prepares for Tashkent

Ayub of Pakistan was making his own preparations for Tashkent. He was determined to pursue the idea of a plebiscite in Kashmir within a specified period of time. Failing an immediate agreement on this question, he wanted some 'self-executing machinery' to be set up to resolve the Kashmir question. However, from Shastri's numerous pronouncements Ayub knew that India was equally determined to maintain its position that India's sovereignty over Kashmir was simply not negotiable.

US–Pakistan relations were at a low ebb. Nevertheless, Ayub wanted to make an effort to regain American support for his position on Kashmir. He had already accepted an invitation to visit the USA and was hoping he might still rekindle favourable feelings in Johnson. His primary purpose in going to Washington before Tashkent was to secure the president's personal support for a detailed discussion of the Kashmir question in Tashkent with a view to the establishment of a standing machinery to pursue this matter until its final resolution to Pakistan's satisfaction. His ostensible purpose in going to the USA was to secure a much needed improvement in US–Pakistan relations.

Ayub arrived in New York on 13 December. His party included Bhutto, Commerce Minister Ghulam Faruque, Foreign Secretary Aziz Ahmad and Information Secretary Altaf Gauhar. On his arrival at Kennedy Airport, Ayub was received on behalf of Johnson by an assistant chief of protocol. This was, then, by no means an effusive reception. Nor was the general atmosphere helped by the publication in *The New York Times* of a despatch from Karachi by its leading columnist James Reston:

> The political atmosphere here is absolutely poisonous . . . the government-controlled press here [in Pakistan] is showing a distinct bias in favour of Communist China and in opposition to the US. Very little is reported in the newspapers here about American aid which had been running at the rate of over a million dollars a day. And a great deal is being reported about the achievements of Communist China and the Viet Cong who are invariably described as the freedom fighters of South Vietnam.

All this seemed a far cry from the rousing statement Ayub had made to the US Congress during an earlier state visit in July 1961: 'Let me tell you that if there is real trouble, there is no other country in Asia on whom you will be able to count. The only people who will stand by you are the people of Pakistan.' Congressmen and senators who remembered those words were unhappy with Ayub's volteface since 1961. He had then held himself out as an ally and Pakistan as a bastion of anti-Communist crusade. However, because the USA had given large economic aid and some arms to India since the Chinese attack in 1962, Ayub had changed his tune. Ayub had reportedly told Chou En-lai that his heart was with China and that his friendship with the USA was for tactical purposes only. Finding himself, by force of circumstances, back in the United States, he was now anxious to retrieve the situation.

By this time Johnson had made up his mind that the USA must not get involved in the Kashmir dispute directly. He had also decided that the US would not work for any particular solution of the Kashmir issue—such as a plebiscite or arbitration. As far as the US was concerned, Kashmir was from now on a bilateral issue for peaceful settlement between India and Pakistan. The USA might help promote a dialogue, but nothing more.

Ayub addressed the UN general assembly the day after his arrival in New York, on 14 December. In his speech he maintained his usual belligerent anti-India stance and stated unequivocally that he would consider India's offer of no-war pact only after the Kashmir question had been settled.

He then flew to Washington the same day for talks and dinner with Johnson.

From the 'sanitized' official documents available in the Lyndon B. Johnson Library in Austin, Texas, it is apparent that Johnson had prepared himself carefully to deal with the issues which Ayub was likely to raise. Here are some interesting excerpts from the official brief ('Talking Points') submitted to President Johnson at 4 p.m. on Monday, 13 December 1965, by the Presidential Assistant, R.W. Komer:[1]

(1) *Let's talk about the future not the past.* Many changes have occurred since we last met—such as the Sino–Indian border war and the recent Pak/Indian fight. You don't like a lot of the things we've done and vice versa. But the important thing is to see if we can build a new and constructive relationship, based on what we can legitimately expect of each other and what we can't. There is still a lot of common ground on which to build if we can reason together.

(2) *Pakistan must understand how we see our role in Asia.* The US has

the thankless task of holding off the Soviets and Chicoms all
around the rim of Asia till free Asian countries can stand on their
own feet. This has been our consistent aim since 1945 and has
guided our policy in Korea, Vietnam, and Pakistan/India as well.

(3)   *We realize that Pakistan sees a different central problem—India.* We
don't think that India intends to do in Pakistan. But in any case
Pakistan must realize that we can't join Red China in squeezing
India over Kashmir or in anything else. We can neither become
tacit allies of China and Pakistan against India, nor let Pakistan
dictate our India policy. If Ayub were in our shoes, he'd feel exactly
the same.

(4)   *We see Chicom pressure on India in the same light as Chicom pressure
in Vietnam.* When we are shedding blood and treasure to defend
Southeast Asia (in a war we think is Ayub's war too), the American
people are not going to back massive aid to countries that play ball
with Peking.

(5)   . . . Our interest is in the basic integrity and well-being of both[2]. . .

(6)   *Pak security against India . . . it wants to destroy us.* We just don't
buy this . . . India doesn't want another 100 million Muslims.
Many of our experts say that Pakistan itself keeps building up this
threat to justify outside support. But whatever the causes, we
remain prepared to do our best to see that India doesn't swallow
up Pakistan so long as Pakistan itself takes the road of peace and
alignment with its real friends.

(7)   *If only Kashmir were solved, Pakistan could co-operate with India
and help freeze out the Chicoms.* We'll keep trying under the UN
Resolution which we fully support. Maybe the Soviets can help at
Tashkent. But Ayub must realize that we cannot force India out
of Kashmir. Nor can the Paks. To be brutally frank, we think that
only out of a process of reconciliation with India is any compromise
likely to emerge.

On Tuesday 14 December, Johnson and Ayub had their first meeting
during the day. Just after this meeting, R.W. Komer sent another memorandum to President Johnson at 4.30 p.m., briefing him on his further
talks with Ayub which were to begin prior to the state dinner,[3] containing
the following significant comments:

. . . It sounds to me as if the two of you have staked out your first
positions . . . Ayub has used all his charm to convince us that if only we
get Kashmir arbitration and cut back Indian arms all would be rosy. You
in turn have told him that we admire him but that we can't get in bed
with China. *Now the real bargaining will begin.*

The two words Ayub most wants to hear are *plebiscite* or at least
*arbitration.* He makes a good case, and we've always sympathized with
it, but the hard fact is that *these are the two things that will drive India*

*up the wall.* If Ayub goes to Tashkent thinking we'll back arbitration, he won't even begin to compromise and we'll be back in the middle of the very insoluble dispute out of which we have just skilfully manoeuvred. In fact, I wouldn't even let him at Goldberg tonight (Arthur hoped we'd stay off Kashmir) . . . Instead the trick is to stay away from Kashmir and on those Pak policies we don't like. What we must explain is that, no matter how much you admire him personally, the US Congress and people just won't let you resume massive aid to a country which seems to be misusing our arms and consorting with the very enemy we're fighting in Vietnam.

(1)   We can only give such help to countries which see a community of purpose with us, rather than China, and which show it.

(2)   So if Pakistan and India want our aid they must both take the road of peace.

These briefs were summaries of the thinking in the White House and were meant to assist the president in his talks. They provide an invaluable insight into US policies at that time *vis-à-vis* India and Pakistan, especially as regards Kashmir and the forthcoming Tashkent talks.

Ayub and Johnson had further animated meetings on 14 and 15 December. The record shows that Johnson made the following comment about Kashmir at his state dinner for Ayub on 14 December: 'We'll keep trying, but I have no illusion that the US can settle Kashmir; if this were possible we would have settled it already.'[4]

With regard to the Pakistani 'fear' of an attack by India, Johnson did not agree to resume arms aid. Instead he gave a 'guarantee' of protection, reassuring Ayub that if the Pakistani people were in danger of being 'gobbled up', the United States would be there just as they were in Vietnam.[5] There was nothing in this to trouble Shastri because India had no intention of gobbling up Pakistan.

On the question of India–Pakistan relations, Johnson 'had told President Ayub that we are not going to let Pakistan say that we cannot feed India. Nor were we going to let India think that we cannot protect Pakistan.'[6] This was Johnson's way of reassuring Ayub but making it abundantly clear that Pakistan would not be allowed to influence US policy towards India. However, for the forthcoming negotiations between India and Pakistan at Tashkent, Johnson gave his full and open support by declaring that he 'was praying that the upcoming Tashkent Conference would be successful.'[7]

Diplomacy of the highest level was displayed in the following 'farewell' observations of Johnson as recorded in the White House: 'The President said that President Ayub had come asking for nothing but was going away with everything . . . with our friendship, our confidence, and our trust. "Indeed, everything we have got".'[8]

Of these fine words India could begrudge nothing and say 'Amen' with full heart, for the truth was that Ayub was going back without the help he so desperately sought on Kashmir and without any indication of further arms assistance. He had been told of US displeasure at Pakistan's collusion with China and had been asked to make his choice between friendship with the USA and friendship with its enemy, Communist China. Even if he chose friendship with the USA, the latter would not allow interference with US policy towards India. It had also been made clear that Johnson wanted the Tashkent conference to succeed on the basis of the UN Security Council resolution of 20 September 1965. There was no reference anywhere to past Security Council resolutions nor to plebiscite or arbitration.

In his oral statement at the end of Ayub's visit, Johnson summed up unambiguously America's determination to pursue her chosen policy in Asia, and, referring to his talks with Ayub, said: 'I have explained fully to him the deep commitment of our country to help defend freedom in Asian nations, as we are now doing in Vietnam . . . I am also encouraged to look forward hopefully toward a process of reconciliation between Pakistan and India. President Ayub says that both India and Pakistan must take the road of peace, and I believe that he is fully prepared to do all he can toward this end. He and I have agreed to keep in close touch.'[9]

The joint communique on the visit issued on 15 December 1965 included the following paragraphs:

> The two Presidents discussed at length events in South Asia, including the tragic conflict between India and Pakistan. They reaffirmed their Governments' intention to support the UN Security Council Resolution of September 20, 1965, in all its parts, as well as the resolutions adopted on September 27 and November 5, 1965.
>
> The two Presidents agreed on the need for a peaceful resolution of all outstanding differences between India and Pakistan, so that energies and resources of the peoples of the subcontinent would not be wastefully diverted from their efforts to meet their vitally important social and economic problems.[10]

Ayub Khan left Washington on 16 December. In Karachi on 19 December Ayub, with the benefit of recent insights, announced to an expectant press that Pakistan and India could not afford the disastrous consequences that were inevitable if there were a fresh conflict between them. He reiterated his offer of a no-war pact with India but added the familiar proviso that India must first settle with Pakistan the dispute over the state of Jammu and Kashmir.

# Chapter 29

# Kosygin Prepares for Tashkent

The contents of this chapter are based on information provided to me by His Excellency Ambassador Leonid Mitrofanovich Zamiatin, who has held very high diplomatic positions in the USSR government and has participated in many summit meetings involving Brezhnev, Kosygin, Gorbachev, Reagan, Margaret Thatcher, and others. Mr Zamiatin was the USSR ambassador to the United Kingdom in the late nineteen eighties when I was secretary-general of the International Maritime Organisation of the UN, with its headquarters in London. I had the privilege of becoming acquainted with Ambassador Zamiatin at that time.

In 1965 Zamiatin was a senior advisor to Kosygin and was working very closely with him. When the Tashkent conference was convened, Zamiatin was associated with important preparatory work and participated in the Tashkent conference as a senior member of the USSR delegation. Kosygin appointed him as his official spokesman. In this capacity Zamiatin was in constant touch with Kosygin as well as with the huge press corps of about 2000 persons which had gathered in Tashkent from all parts of the world for this historic conference.

While in London in 1989, I broached the question of the Tashkent conference with Ambassador Zamiatin and enquired whether he would be willing to talk with me about the events of that conference in the context of my preparations and research for Shastri's biography. The ambassador agreed readily. However, because of his heavy preoccupations and my own in the last year of office, we decided to meet later, at a mutually convenient time and place. In 1993 I re-established contact with him. He had also by this time retired from government service and was living in Moscow. We found dates which suited us both and I eventually travelled to Moscow and met him on 28 July and 8 August 1993. Ambassador Zamiatin was gracious and forthcoming. He told me that as he had retired and was no longer bound by government rules and regulations, he would talk freely about his experiences of that time. The following narration of events, culminating in Kosygin's successful mediation between India and Pakistan in Tashkent in January 1966, conforms to what ambassador told me personally during our two informative and enjoyable meetings in Moscow.

Aleksei Nikolayevich Kosygin became prime minister of the USSR in 1964, succeeding Khrushchev. While Khrushchev was a flamboyant and volatile political leader, Kosygin was a serious minded, down-to-earth technocrat who inspired confidence and trust in those who worked with him. Zamiatin described Kosygin as one of the most outstanding scientists of the USSR in the realm of economy and finance, and as a public servant totally committed to the welfare of the people. Kosygin was not, according to Zamiatin, a 'smiling' prime minister, but he was undoubtedly one of the cleverest people in the USSR.

According to Zamiatin, the Government of the USSR first considered whether it would be useful to take some initiative through the United Nations: a letter might be sent to the secretary-general of the United Nations and some meetings of the Security Council might be organized. This would certainly show that the USSR was doing something and might satisfy public opinion. But would this actually help to achieve any positive and practical result? That was the question. Kosygin's own view was that in the rapidly deteriorating situation some immediate and effective intervention was necessary to avoid a war and that to work through the United Nations was unlikely to produce the desired results quickly. So Kosygin reached the conclusion that it was essential for the USSR to take a bold initiative. Zamiatin emphasized that this was entirely Kosygin's own idea. Considering that Kosygin had been prime minister for hardly a year, this was a courageous decision. In order to be able to set things in motion, however, he had to obtain the prior approval of Brezhnev, who was the repository of final power and therefore the real head of government in the USSR. When Brezhnev asked: 'But what can we suggest?' Kosygin was ready with his reply: 'Let us appoint a group of senior officials to prepare the sort of declaration of peace which both India and Pakistan could be invited to subscribe to. The objective would be to urge them to live as good neighbours.' Brezhnev nodded approval and subsequently gave Kosygin a free hand.

Soon a small high-powered group under Kosygin himself began to work on the issue. Zamiatin was a member of this group. 'We worked during the months of June, July and August 1965 and prepared a paper,' said Zamiatin, 'which clearly enunciated Kosygin's ideas.' When the paper was finalized, Kosygin said: 'No one can predict what the result will be. However, let us start consultations with India and Pakistan to ascertain at least whether they will accept the good offices of the USSR.' Consultations were thus initiated through the normal diplomatic channels as well as through special envoys. Kosygin had the advantage in this of having already met Ayub in April and Shastri in May of that year, and his judgement was that he could bring the two leaders to the negotiating table.

On 18 September 1965, when the battles were still raging, Kosygin had sent a message to Shastri and Ayub, offering his good offices for bringing about improved relations between India and Pakistan. Shastri accepted this offer on 23 September, immediately after the ceasefire had become effective. Ayub's reaction was lukewarm. According to Altaf Gauhar, Ayub was doubtful as to the usefulness of a meeting with Shastri as proposed by Kosygin. His initial comment was: 'What purpose will it serve? Shastri will state his case and I will state my case.'[1] For this reason, Ayub hesitated for quite a while, but on 11 November Bhutto announced in Rawalpindi that Pakistan had also accepted the Soviet offer of mediation.

According to Zamiatin, Kosygin then began to prepare for the conference with single-minded attention and meticulous care. He studied the pros and cons of every issue which was likely to come up for discussion in Tashkent. He took great pains to gather precise information about the position of Shastri and Ayub on these issues. For hours on end he studied every aspect of India–Pakistan relations and formulated his own ideas. He was determined to leave nothing to chance. Every point of relevance to the Conference was now stored in his brain which, according to Zamiatin, 'worked like a computer'.

Kosygin received Bhutto and Swaran Singh for preparatory consultations. He was determined to ensure that the conference was held in a calm atmosphere without any exhibition of hostility or rancour. Zamiatin listed Kosygin's objectives:

(1)  To prevent a resumption of hostilities and to promote Indo–Pak relations based on the concept of 'good neighbourhood'
(2)  To convince both leaders not to use force to settle differences, but to use only peaceful means in future
(3)  To ensure the withdrawal of all Pakistani and Indian armed personnel to positions held by them prior to 5 August 1965, in compliance with the Security Council demand
(4)  To normalize diplomatic relations between the two countries.

Kosygin even formulated some texts on each of these points for possible incorporation in a peace declaration to be adopted at the Tashkent conference.

Kosygin sent Ambassador Zamiatin as his representative to Tashkent fifteen days ahead of the opening of the Tashkent conference, to ensure appropriate administrative and protocol arrangements. Absolute equality of treatment was to be accorded to the Indian and Pakistani delegations.

Zamiatin told me that as the available time was short, local Soviet army units were commissioned to spruce up the villas where Shastri and Ayub would reside and which they would use as their headquarters.

Kosygin himself travelled to Tashkent three days in advance of the arrival of Shastri and Ayub. In fact he celebrated New Year's Eve, 31 December 1965, in Tashkent with local dignitaries. He visited the villas and the venue of the conference to satisfy himself that all the arrangements were satisfactory. He had brought his own doctor from Moscow and alerted local doctors to be on hand in case of need. Kosygin had also obtained information through the USSR ambassadors about the food preferences of Shastri and Ayub and had given instructions that cooks who could prepare the requisite dishes should be located in the respective villas. Zamiatin told me in particular that Kosygin knew about Shastri being a strict vegetarian and had made special arrangements accordingly. Flowers were arranged in abundance. In brief, Kosygin looked into every detail personally. He was now ready to receive Shastri and Ayub Khan, and to dedicate himself to the task of persuading them to end the days of conflict.

# Chapter 30

## T.T. Krishnamachari's Resignation on the Eve of Tashkent

On the eve of the Tashkent conference, a serious governmental problem arose in New Delhi, claiming Shastri's attention in the very midst of his heavy preoccupations over the conference. In November 1965 Shastri received a memorandum signed by eleven members of parliament making serious and specific allegations of nepotism and corruption against Finance Minister T.T. Krishnamachari. The signatories demanded the establishment of a commission of enquiry and undertook to produce evidence before such a commission to substantiate their charges.

Parliament was in session at that time and the memorandum against the finance minister became a matter of general concern and comment. T.T. Krishnamachari (TTK) naturally felt deeply disturbed. He met the prime minister and stated to him categorically that there was no substance whatsoever in the allegations which had been made against him. He requested Shastri to personally examine the contents of the memorandum and make his own assessment. If, said TTK, the prime minister found the allegations to be untrue, he should make a statement in parliament as soon as possible, clearing him of the charges.

This posed a delicate problem. Shastri was sensitive to the anguish of his finance minister and had a duty to defend him if, as TTK asserted, the allegations against him were ill motivated and untrue. On the other hand, the memorandum containing specific charges had been submitted by eleven elected members of parliament. The prime minister's first conclusion was that the question of the appointment of a Commission of Enquiry would arise only if preliminary examination disclosed a *prima facie* case. If there was no such case, the prime minister would make a statement clearing the finance minister.

TTK had no problem with this first step, but he wanted the determination of the existence or non-existence of a *prime facie* case to be made by the prime minister himself, without consultation with any other person. The prime minister was of the view that while he would eventually make a determination in this regard himself, he must first have the informal opinion of a person of unimpeachable integrity and of the highest possible competence. Such a person, in his view, was the chief justice of India, whose informal opinion would provide solid ground for the prime minister's final decision: it would then be abundantly clear that the prime minister had acted in a fair and unbiased manner. Otherwise, in the circumstances of the case, the prime minister's own verdict, if made without any independent scrutiny, might well lead to questions about the genuineness of his declaration that his own integrity and that of his ministers was the sheet-anchor of his government.

T.T. Krishnamachari was vehemently opposed to such a procedure. He felt strongly that the basic question involved was that of the prime minister's confidence in his finance minister. He felt that the prime minister should not find it too difficult to examine the memorandum himself and reach his own conclusion. Shastri did not regard this matter as one merely of confidence. Indeed, he had shown full confidence in T.T. Krishnamachari by retaining him in his cabinet with a key portfolio. To Shastri, the major issue was of people's confidence in the prime minister himself to deal fairly but firmly with allegations of corruption. He explained his position to the finance minister in the following letter:

Prime Minister's House,
New Delhi,
29–12–1965

My dear Krishnamachariji,
    I have given anxious thought to the matter we discussed the other day and today. The main problem is the manner in which the memorandum signed by some Members of Parliament is to be dealt with. The signatories have asked for the appointment of a commission of inquiry and have taken the responsibility of substantiating the allegations.
    I do not consider that this obliges me to set up an inquiry because it is only when there is a *prima facie* case would such a step be called for.
    Of course, the conclusion that there is no case for inquiry must be reached in such a manner as will carry conviction with the people and Parliament.
    This could be done by taking the preliminary opinion of a person who could be relied upon to be independent and objective. Such an opinion would help me in reaching a final decision as to the need for an enquiry.
    I propose, therefore, to request the Chief Justice of India to study the papers and give me an opinion confidentially. You are one of my

senior-most and closest colleagues and you can well understand how much anxiety and concern this matter must have caused me. But even after protracted deliberation I find that I have no other alternative.

Yours sincerely,
Lal Bahadur.

T.T. Krishnamachari responded by submitting his resignation in a rather impetuous manner. His resignation letter reads as follows:

New Delhi
Dec 30, 1965.

My dear Lal Bahadurji,
   Thank you for your letter of 29th inst.
   You are seized of the matter and, therefore, it is for you to decide the course of action to adopt. But that does not prevent me from holding the view that the procedure you propose to follow is wrong, which would also set up an unhealthy precedent for the future.
   I shall be relinquishing charge as Finance Minister on the afternoon of Dec 31, 1965 and shall ask my Secretaries to seek your directions for carrying on their work thereafter.

Yours sincerely,
T.T. Krishnamachari.

The contents of this letter of resignation were rather unusual, even unique. Normally when a minister wishes to demit office, he sends a letter to the prime minister and awaits his decision. The prime minister may decide that the resignation should be accepted or he may request the minister to reconsider his decision to resign. In any case, a minister who has been sworn in as a minister of government cannot decide by himself the date and time of his handing-over charge. T.T. Krishnamachari departed from the established convention in ministerial conduct. I do not know whether he intended this as an affront to the prime minister or whether he inadvertently overshot the mark in a huff.

When Shastri received TTK's letter of resignation, he concluded that in view of its contents he had no option except to comply with Krishnamachari's wishes and to let him leave the government on the afternoon of 31 December 1965. Accordingly, he despatched the following letter by a special messenger:

Prime Minister's House,
New Delhi.
31-12-1965

My dear Krishnamachariji,

I am pained to receive your letter. The reason why it is necessary for me to seek an independent and reliable opinion in this matter, I have already explained to you in considerable detail.

I am exceedingly sorry that you should have decided to relinquish charge. Naturally this causes me distress and anguish. It would undoubtedly be a serious loss. However, I have to accept your decision and I am, therefore, requesting the President to accept your resignation effective from this afternoon as desired by you.

Yours sincerely,
Lal Bahadur.


The last epistle in this drama was the following, sent by T.T. Krishnamachari to the prime minister:

Dec 31, 1965

My dear Lal Bahadurji,

Thank you for your letter of 31st inst. I am grateful to you for the manner in which you have worded it. I fully realize that I held all along a responsible position—responsible not only to you, to the party and to the country. But circumstances in which you have placed me left me no other alternative.

As you will appreciate I have to explain my action and my reactions to the petition submitted to the President and to the public through the Press. I hope I have your permission to release, along with my statement that I may make, the correspondence that has passed between us in this context.

I may express my gratitude to you for the co-operation shown to me during these eighteen months and odd that I served under you.

Yours sincerely,
T.T. Krishnamachari.


Events moved rapidly thereafter. The prime minister met President Radhakrishnan, recommended the acceptance of T.T. Krishnamachari's resignation and the appointment of Sachindra Chaudhuri as the new finance minister.

Like many others, TTK had overestimated his own strength and underestimated that of the prime minister. He probably thought that by pressing his resignation from the cabinet at a time when the prime minister was busy with his preparations for the Tashkent conference, due to begin just four days later, he might compel the prime minister to change his mind. But Shastri was not the man to be pressurized.

T.T. Krishnamachari was extremely able, indeed brilliant. His departure was therefore a distinct loss to government and to Shastri personally. I had myself known him well and he was extremely kind and gracious to me. The prime minister never wanted to lose such an esteemed colleague. However, it was well known at that time that TTK had an irascible personality and an acerbic tongue. He had friends and admirers; he also had opponents and detractors. His resignation was not therefore universally lamented. By accepting T.T. Krishnamachari's peremptory resignation so promptly, Shastri demonstrated that he simply could not be forced to succumb to any sort of pressure.

# Chapter 31

# The Tashkent Conference

In his invitations to Shastri and Ayub Kosygin had not indicated a specific agenda. Each participating delegation had, therefore, arrived in Tashkent with its own ideas as to what the coming meeting should consider.

The USSR attached the greatest importance to securing peace between India and Pakistan by the implementation of Security Council resolution 211 of 20 September 1965 and resolution 214 of 27 September 1965.

India wanted to ensure that peace should be agreed to on terms which would provide firm assurance that there would be no repetition of aggression, open or disguised, against India. To this end India wanted a 'no-war' pact with Pakistan.

Pakistan wanted a substantive discussion on the question of Kashmir in order to secure India's agreement to the establishment of a 'self-executing machinery' for any further progress on this matter. Ayub reiterated this in a broadcast on 1 January 1966. He wanted Kosygin to 'influence and persuade Mr Shastri to see the light of reason' and to cut the 'Gordian Knot of the problem of Jammu and Kashmir.'[1]

Kosygin decided wisely to be an active but cautious participant in the deliberations from the very beginning. To prevent the development of an impasse, he took up the role of an intermediary. To prepare the ground for the later 'summit meetings', he met Shastri and Ayub separately in the evening of 3 January, a few hours after they reached Tashkent.

Kosygin came to Shastri's villa at 8 p.m. and stayed with him for an hour and fifteen minutes. As mentioned earlier, during Shastri's state visit to the USSR in August 1965, Kosygin and Shastri had developed great mutual regard. This first meeting in Tashkent enabled both of them to resume their friendship. Kosygin reiterated his pleasure at receiving Shastri once again in the USSR. He explained the arrangements which had been made for negotiations and emphasized the imperative need for peace. He reiterated the USSR's warm friendship for India. He then referred to the next day's programme which included a meeting at 11 a.m., when Kosygin would receive Shastri and Ayub for a preliminary meeting together, followed by luncheon for both. The conference would be opened formally at 4 p.m. Shastri responded in similar vein, expressing gratitude.

Kosygin's meeting with Ayub the same evening was, initially, not of the same tenor. According to Zamiatin, Ayub created difficulties for Kosygin even at this first meeting. 'Ayub told Kosygin that he would not shake hands with Shastri, using some uncomplimentary words for the Indian prime minister,' said Zamiatin, and added: 'Kosygin reacted immediately with visible anger and reminded Ayub firmly that he had accepted the invitation to come to Tashkent to discuss peace with Shastri who, as head of the government of his country, had an equal status and was entitled to the highest courtesy and consideration.' This remonstration by Kosygin had the desired effect, and Ayub apparently cooled down. Kosygin spent quite some time advising the Pakistani president to adopt a co-operative attitude. Ayub promised to do this and accepted Kosygin's suggestion that, in order to get the conference started on the right note, no specific reference to Kashmir should be made in the opening speeches of the three participating leaders. This suggestion was also made to Shastri, who welcomed it.

Next morning, 4 January 1966, at 9.30 a.m., Shastri had a meeting in his villa with Swaran Singh, Y.B. Chavan and senior officials of the Indian delegation, during which he briefed them on his talks the previous evening with Kosygin.

At 11.30 a.m., Kosygin received Shastri and Ayub at the 'neutral' villa. The three had a meeting together for the first time since their arrival in Tashkent. Things boded well. Despite the background of conflict, the general atmosphere was reasonably affable. In no small measure was this due to the fact that Kosygin, the host, had prepared the ground with scrupulous care. Kosygin was himself very courteous and a gentleman, and he had won the confidence and esteem of both Shastri and Ayub. Both were obviously anxious to make sure that nothing was said or done which would not be in keeping with the dignity of the occasion and the atmosphere of mutual respect that Kosygin had so carefully fostered. The luncheon hosted at 1 p.m. was an equally pleasant affair. Serious issues were still not mentioned as the general idea was that they should be taken up only after the formal opening of the conference.

Shastri returned to his villa immediately after lunch. He rested for a while and then got ready to proceed to the venue of the conference. The prime minister, his cabinet colleagues and other members of the Indian delegation reached the conference building well in time. We found all the arrangements perfect. At 4 p.m. punctually, the three delegations entered

the conference hall simultaneously, from three different gates. They sat at
the appointed places at a circular table.

The first person to speak was Kosygin. He expressed equally warm and
friendly feelings for Pakistan and India, so much so that on the twenty-six
occasions that he mentioned the two countries in the course of his address,
he took care to refer to India first and Pakistan next on thirteen such
occasions and to Pakistan first and India next on the other thirteen occasions.

> India and Pakistan are our southern neighbours. We always came out
> not only for the strengthening of friendly relations between the Soviet
> Union and India and Pakistan, but also for the reign of peace and
> friendship between these countries themselves. The history of the peoples
> of India and Pakistan knows quite a few examples when they came out
> shoulder-to-shoulder in the historic struggle against foreign domination.
> Victory over colonialism was achieved by common efforts, and for it,
> they bore common sacrifices. Today, as in the past, only enemies of
> Pakistan and India may be interested in a clash between them.
>
> We regard this meeting in Tashkent as one which may mark a
> turning point in the relations between Pakistan and India. We believe
> that the leaders of these states came to Tashkent with the desire to seek
> that end. Naturally, during one meeting it may prove to be difficult to
> find solutions for all the existing problems. What is important is to chart
> the path leading towards their settlement, to create a climate of trust and
> mutual understanding and simultaneously to solve those questions which
> today constitute an obstacle to normalizing the relations.
>
> That would be an important step forward, and together with all
> people of goodwill we hope that President Ayub Khan and Prime Min-
> ister Shastri will make efforts to take this step. Facts show that when
> governments coolly and objectively consider outstanding issues, taking
> mutual interests into account, not only are conflicts ended but the sources
> from which they spring are largely eliminated. We believe that public
> opinion in both countries and representatives of the Press, guided by
> peace-loving motives, would contribute towards that end.
>
> All who cherish peace follow the meeting of the President of Pakistan
> and the Prime Minister of India with great attention and hope. They
> believe in the wise statesmanship of the leaders of Pakistan and India,
> wish success to the Tashkent meeting, and peace and prosperity to the
> Indian and Pakistani peoples. They await good news from Tashkent,
> and hope that this meeting will be fruitful and will reinforce all progres-
> sive-minded people in their conviction that peace between states can be
> ensured, and that even in the present difficult situation ways of settling
> conflicts can be found.

Shastri and Ayub followed Kosygin in addressing the conference. Both
speeches were dignified, warm and friendly. Both expressed feelings of

gratitude to their host for providing hospitality and an excellent opportunity to come together and resolve their differences. Both accepted and, indeed, emphasized that peace was vital. At the same time, in a restrained and courteous manner, Shastri and Ayub expressed their differing points of view as to how this could best be achieved. Shastri stressed that the first step must be the renunciation of force. To this, Shastri added:

> Our assurance to each other not to use force would mean, therefore, that each agrees to respect the territorial integrity of the other. We have always said, and I say it today also, that we unreservedly accept Pakistan's sovereignty and territorial integrity. Equally, we have to preserve our own territorial integrity and sovereignty. Respect for each other's sovereignty is essential for peace and good relations.

But Shastri said, he was not suggesting that 'we could or should shut our eyes to the many points of difference that exist between the two countries . . . What I do say, however, is that all these problems must be resolved through talks and negotiations and not by resort to force.' He elaborated this point more directly and specifically by saying:

> It would be a notable achievement if at this meeting which Chairman Kosygin has convened, an agreement could emerge for renouncing the use of force for settling our differences. This should pave the way for the kind of good neighbourly relations which both countries need and would also make the solution of many of our problems much easier. We could and should, of course, discuss other matters as well, but even if we differ on some of them and cannot see our way to an immediate agreement, we should still not forsake the path of peace.

Shastri concluded his address with the following exhortation:

> A heavy responsibility lies on our shoulders. The subcontinent has a population of 600 million—one-fifth of the human race. If India and Pakistan have to progress and prosper, they must learn to live in peace. If there is constant conflict and hostility, our peoples would suffer even greater hardships. Instead of fighting each other, let us start fighting poverty, disease and ignorance. The problems, the hopes and the aspirations of the common people of both the countries are the same. They want not conflict and war, but peace and progress. They need, not arms and ammunition, but food, clothing and shelter. If we are to fulfil this obligation to our peoples, we should, in this meeting, try to achieve something specific and positive.
>
> This is a momentous meeting. The eyes of the world are upon us. Let it not be said that the president of Pakistan and the prime minister of India met and failed to reach an agreement. Let us show by our actions that we are capable of seeing our own problems in the wider context of world events.

When Shastri finished his speech there was general applause, except from Bhutto, who did not join in the clapping until he was nudged by his president.

Ayub spoke next, and like the two previous speakers he was impressive. He specifically acknowledged, as Kosygin and Shastri had done before him, that the prosperity of the six hundred million people of India and Pakistan depended on peace. 'For us,' he said, 'peace is vital—it is indispensable.' With Kashmir in mind, Ayub stated his position on the question of peace in the following terms:

> But wishing peace is not enough to establish peace. One has to work for it. And one way is to face the problems which endanger peace. We have learnt that we can ignore them at our peril. Nor can nations be content with a simulation of peace while the undercurrents of tension still remain. A semblance of peace is no substitute for real peace . . . It is for us to face the problem and to create conditions which will provide a firm and lasting basis for peace between our two countries. In this context I recently made a sincere offer in the General Assembly of the United Nations to enter into a no-war pact with India once the basic problem confronting us was resolved according to the principles already accepted by both of us. A no-war agreement between nations can work only if it is adopted after taking concrete steps for resolving the disputes which divide them. And disputes can be resolved only in a spirit of conciliation.

In other words, a 'no-war' pact was possible, according to Ayub, only after a satisfactory solution of 'the problem', which meant Kashmir. Here then was already in evidence a seemingly unbridgeable chasm between the Indian and Pakistani positions. Although the two points of view had been stated courteously, Kosygin must have noted one of his most delicate tasks —a reconciliation on this fundamental issue.

Ayub concluded his address with a powerful plea for positive results:

> Let this conference become a harbinger of peace and let us issue from here a message of hope for our people. There is no problem between us which cannot be solved peacefully and honourably. We should address ourselves to them in all earnestness. This is how we must begin if peace is what we seek remembering always that no one nation can lay down the terms of peace. The terms of peace are equality and justice. These are the terms which nations must learn to respect and obey.

Shastri returned to his villa and, after a brief rest, began to prepare himself for the crucial meeting with Kosygin scheduled to commence at 8.30 that evening. The issues were quite clear. Shastri did not expect any surprises.

After the usual exchange of courtesies and some general conversation,

Kosygin took up the subject of compliance with the Security Council demand for the withdrawal of all armed personnel to positions held by them prior to 5 August 1965. Kosygin emphasized that the USSR was a party to the Security Council resolutions 211 and 214 and that his country supported the prompt implementation of these resolutions.

The following is the gist of further conversation between them:

*Prime Minister Shastri*: I am most grateful for your interest in peace. And we are well aware of your noble intentions. We also are totally peaceful people but when aggression is committed against us then we have to take all necessary action in self-defence.

The Security Council wants India to withdraw its armed personnel to the position occupied by them before 5 August 1965. As you know, Pakistan had sent thousands of armed infiltrators to Kashmir with a view to causing destruction of life and property. Many of them have been dealt with by our security forces, but there are many still to be apprehended. Pakistan must accept responsibility for their withdrawal.

Furthermore, Pakistan has a history of surreptitious and disguised armed activity against India. On this occasion Pakistan organized a disguised invasion of India from 5 August 1965. We were compelled in self-defence to occupy the Haji Pir Pass and some other strategic locations to prevent further infiltration. This was done at a heavy sacrifice on the part of our brave armed forces. What is the assurance that Pakistan will not resort to 'disguised' invasion again if we were to withdraw from these strategic places? I trust, Mr Prime Minister, that you will see our genuine and serious difficulty in vacating these positions. Elsewhere withdrawal can certainly be agreed to.

*Premier Kosygin*: I fully understand your difficulties about the vacation of the Haji Pir Pass and other strategic locations occupied by India to prevent further infiltration. There are, however, several other crucial aspects of the larger problem which need to be taken into account before you make such final decisions as you may deem best for India.

As a friend of India and as the representative of a country which has the most cordial relations with your country, I wish to invite your attention to the following consequences which would follow if you were to decide not to withdraw from the Haji Pir Pass and other similar places on the other side of the 1949 Ceasefire Line.

(1) If India does not withdraw from these locations, Pakistan will not withdraw from Chhamb and other Indian territories occupied by Pakistan. And then, of course, India will not withdraw from the Lahore and Sialkot sectors. There will then be no agreement here. You will return to India to deal with the resulting situation.

Even at present there are numerous violations of the 'ceasefire'. The present situation in which the armed forces of India and Pakistan are facing each other and frequently firing at each other will continue as it is. Any reasonable person would agree that in such a dangerous situation, hostilities are very likely to break out again. This is not a theoretical but a very real prospect.

The question for your consideration is whether the Haji Pir Pass is so crucial to India that you would wish to hold on to it despite the possibility of a resumption of war.

(2) If the talks break down here solely because India declines to comply with the Security Council demand for a return to positions held prior to 5 August 1965, by insisting on maintaining the possession of the Haji Pir Pass, India will bear the responsibility for the consequential threat to peace or the resumption of hostilities.

The Security Council will then have to consider further action to maintain peace and also to ensure compliance with its resolution. The Security Council has already indicated that it would keep the matter under 'urgent and continuous review', so that it might 'determine what further steps may be necessary to secure peace and security in the area.' Acting under Chapter VII of the United Nations Charter, the Security Council might well consider action under Articles 41 and 42 to maintain peace and security in the Indo–Pak subcontinent.[2] These articles empower the Security Council to decide upon the imposition of economic sanctions or, if necessary, the use of armed forces, against a country responsible for breach of the peace. Is the Haji Pir Pass so vital to India as to oblige you to hold on to it even if it means non-compliance with the Security Council resolution and the possibility of attendant consequences?

The USSR is a party to the Security Council resolution of 20 September 1965, and we sincerely believe that a return to the position prior to 5 August 1965, which in effect means reciprocal withdrawal to the 1949 Ceasefire Line, is the most appropriate solution to the present critical situation. We too cannot view with disinterest any possibility of resumption of war between India and Pakistan.

(3) India's bigger enemy is China. During the recent war between India and Pakistan, China was threatening India. No overt action was taken by China, because there was unanimous pressure from all governments that no other country should intervene in the Indo–Pak conflict. If later, India is held to be intransigent because of noncompliance with the Security Council resolution, China may be under no such pressure. Any movement by China would create the possibility of a wider conflict.

(4) Because of your resolute and wise leadership during the Indo–Pak war and the exceptional bravery of India's armed forces, India's prestige today is very high. If you were to decide now to comply with UN resolution, which will involve a return to the 1949 Ceasefire Line and giving up the Haji Pir Pass, India will not be giving in to pressure from any foreign country or group of countries. It will be acting in accordance with the UN Charter in the interest of peace. If, however, India now insists on maintaining the Haji Pir Pass but is compelled later

to give it up because of UN action or other external factors, imagine the loss to India's prestige.

(5) It also needs to be examined whether the continued occupation of the Haji Pir Pass would effectively enable India to prevent infiltration. There are other points of entry as well. And India has to be ready to defend itself against China also. In that context, the Haji Pir Pass, I would suggest, has no relevance.

(6) As friends of India, we are of the view that the only way India can defend itself is by building up its internal strength—its economy and industry—and by strengthening its defence capability. For this, India needs peace more than anything else. Only a peaceful period would enable India to modernize and strengthen its armed forces and its economy.

(7) Adherence to the 1949 Ceasefire Line has one other great advantage. This is a line of demarcation which was established more than 15 years ago. A return to that line now would resanctify and strengthen the Ceasefire Line and give it an enhanced status. Any future violation of the Ceasefire Line would have to be regarded as contravention of a disposition recognised and reaffirmed by the Security Council. Furthermore, by proposing a 'no-war' pact with Pakistan, and even otherwise, India has in effect announced to the world that it will not use force to recover that part of the state of Jammu and Kashmir which was de-facto in the possession of Pakistan, as demarcated by the Ceasefire Line. And it would be unrealistic to expect that Pakistan would at any future date give up that portion voluntarily or peacefully. Evidently then the only possibility of a peaceful and final settlement between India and Pakistan on this question would lie in the 1949 Ceasefire Line being accorded a more substantive status. The maintenance and strict observance of the Ceasefire Line is thus, in our view, extremely important in the interests of India. This Ceasefire Line has been reconfirmed by the Security Council and will thus be inviolable. Any disturbance of the 1949 Ceasefire Line will not be in India's interests at all.

(8) As regards infiltrators who entered Kashmir in August 1965 and who may still be around, India should feel free to deal with them as you deem fit, especially because Pakistan denies any linkage with them.

(9) Mr Prime Minister, you have asked me what assurance can there be that Pakistan will not repeat 'disguised' invasion by armed infiltrators in the future. First of all, the peace agreement in Tashkent must provide that the Ceasefire Line will be fully respected in future. In other words, the Ceasefire Line will be inviolable. Any member of the United Nations who violates a Ceasefire Line accepted by the United Nations would in effect violate the UN charter and run a grave risk as its action would involve or threaten breach of the peace. Furthermore, any agreement arrived at and signed in the USSR will obviously have a certain strength of its own.

I am sorry, Mr Prime Minister, that I have taken so much of your time in explaining different aspects of the situation as we see it. I am aware of your concerns and those of the people of India. Please believe me, we, as your friends, have given very detailed consideration to this fundamental question and the result of our study has been provided to you with complete objectivity and sincerity.

It is now for you, Mr Prime Minister, to make whatever decision you deem appropriate in the best interest of your great country.

*Prime Minister Shastri*: I am immensely grateful to you, Mr Kosygin, for your deep analysis of the situation. I have listened to every word with full attention. There is a great deal of strength in what you have said. India, as you know well, has been dedicated to peace. The last war was forced upon us. We had to defend our country. We want peace in the future, but we will not allow aggression on us to succeed. Our armed forces and our people will always be ready to defend our freedom and territorial integrity. Our own main objective is peace with honour. I thank you again for your friendly words. I would nevertheless like to think about this question tonight. It is quite clear to me that your analysis is objective and fair. And yet I must say that the vacation of the Haji Pir Pass would cause me considerable anguish. It was with my personal approval that this crucial position was captured by our armed forces. It was an act of great heroism. Precious lives were lost. But this sacrifice had to be made because it was necessary to cut off one of the major routes through which infiltrators had been coming in.

*Premier Kosygin*: I fully understand your feelings. Indeed India's armed forces have shown great heroism in capturing the Haji Pir Pass. They showed similar heroism in other sectors as well. But, Mr Prime Minister, when war is over and peace has to be secured, then statesmen have to make decisions taking into account all the relevant factors. Fighting bravely during the war is important but fighting for peace is no less important. Sacrifices have to be made both in war and also for securing peace in the best interests of the country and its peoples. That is the responsibility of the leader of the country.

*Prime Minister Shastri*: Many many thanks, Mr Kosygin. I would like to think about this matter tonight. I know that in such matters decisions have to be made not on emotional but on practical considerations. And decisions have to be made wisely in the best interests of the country. I accept fully that it is my duty to enhance the prospects of peace. I will let you know my final position on this issue tomorrow.

But it still seems to me to be essential that Pakistan should agree to a no-war pact in order to enable both countries to develop better mutual relations. This will demonstrate that hereafter Pakistan will not resort to the use of force and that our mutual problems would be resolved by peaceful means only. Otherwise it would be a very tenuous peace and there would be no basis for mutual confidence.

*Premier Kosygin*: Thank you, Mr Prime Minister. I know very well that you will give full consideration to my submission about the UN Security Council resolution regarding the withdrawal of all armed personnel to the position they occupied prior to 5 August 1965.

As regards a no-war pact, I personally think it is vital that both sides should renounce the use of force and agree to use only peaceful means for the settlement of their differences. I will sound President Ayub on this. And you will, of course, take this up yourself with President Ayub at your meeting tomorrow.

Before I finish, I would like to refer to the question of Kashmir. President Ayub is extremely keen on having an in-depth discussion and substantive negotiations with you, Mr Prime Minister.

*Prime Minister Shastri*: As you know, Mr Kosygin, the state of Jammu and Kashmir is an integral part of India and there is absolutely nothing to negotiate about. India's position on this matter is totally firm and clear.

*Premier Kosygin*: That position is well known to me. At tomorrow's meeting, President Ayub is bound to raise this matter and he will give you a comprehensive idea of what he has in his mind.

So, thank you again very much Mr Prime Minister. We have a heavy responsibility and a historic opportunity. Let us try to find the right path ahead. I will look forward to our talks tomorrow.

This completed the day's proceedings. There was nothing in his talks with Kosygin to cause Shastri surprise or anxiety. It was evident, however, that, as Shastri had publicly expressed in India his reluctance to vacate the Haji Pir Pass, Kosygin had prepared himself very thoroughly on this question and had presented serious and substantial arguments that would require very careful consideration by the Indian side.

It was also evident that Kosygin had made a conscious decision to secure, through his personal efforts, India's acceptance of the Security Council demand for the disengagement of armed forces and for the return of all armed personnel to the positions held by them prior to 5 August 1965. He did not regard this as an issue for negotiations between India and Pakistan. In fact, both India and Pakistan were required to accept this demand of the Security Council. In this he had the full backing of Johnson, Wilson, and other important Western leaders. Failure on this vital issue would mean a failure of the whole conference, with the probability of resumption of the war. Kosygin was determined to take no chances. Without hesitation or compunction, he had put at stake the prestige of the USSR on this issue. Kosygin's reasoned arguments and his closing appeal to Shastri did not, in my view, amount to pressure and there was of course no question of arm twisting. After the conclusion of these initial talks with Kosygin, I spent quite some time with Shastri and did not find him under mental pressure. In fact he appeared satisfied with the way things had gone that day. At the same time, it was clear to the prime minister that he was face-to-face with a crucial moment in his country's history. There could be no second chances.

Shastri was calm. He knew that withdrawal from the Haji Pir Pass would expose him to uninformed criticism. There could also be an emotional response. In the political arena, there was no dearth of people who would characterize this as a betrayal.

Next morning, 5 January, Shastri had a long conversation with Y.B. Chavan, who expressed the view very firmly that the prospects of peace must not be jeopardized on account of the Haji Pir Pass. The defence minister reiterated his view that in deference to the wishes of the United Nations Security Council, and more especially in India's national interest, Shastri should agree to a return to the 1949 Ceasefire Line. Shastri then spoke to the rest of the Indian delegation (except Swaran Singh, who was unwell); they concurred with Chavan.

It was known that the Pakistani delegation was insisting on an agenda for the conference. Prime Minister Shastri said that he did not see much objection if the agenda was broadly worded, without any specific reference to Kashmir. All present agreed with this as well and the meeting concluded. The prime minister then had a conversation with the foreign minister, who indicated complete agreement.

Shastri then got ready for his meeting with Ayub which was due to begin at 11 a.m. at the Neutral Villa. He had met the Pakistani leader briefly the previous day but had only exchanged a few general comments. This morning's meeting therefore was to be the first substantive encounter.

After the preliminary courtesies, Ayub referred to the question of an agenda for the meeting. Shastri did not express any objection but said he wanted its contents to refer to general objectives and not to any specific question. Both agreed that their foreign ministers and officials might deal with this question. Ayub then referred to the history of Indo–Pakistani relations which, in his view had been bedevilled by the Kashmir question. The primary aim of both countries should be to develop their economies and thus to promote the welfare of their peoples. He expressed the view that once the question of Kashmir's accession to India or Pakistan was settled on the basis of the right of the Kashmiri people to self-determination and in accordance with relevant UN resolutions, both countries would be able to develop friendly relations. He explained Pakistan's viewpoint in detail and proposed that a joint 'self-executing machinery' be established to deal with the Kashmir question as he saw it.

Shastri listened without interruption. He responded by agreeing that friendly relations between India and Pakistan were vital for the welfare of the people of both countries. As regards the accession of Jammu and Kashmir to India, there were certain incontrovertible facts which had to be stated and understood very clearly from the start. Prior to independence, a legal framework had been established with the willing and open consent of the political leaders of the time, Nehru and his colleagues on behalf of India, and Jinnah and his colleagues on behalf of Pakistan. It was under this same legal framework that the state of Jammu and Kashmir acceded to India on 27 October 1947. It was an unconditional and final accession as demonstrated by the Instrument of Accession and its acceptance by Mountbatten. In fact there was no provision in the applicable law for anything like temporary or provisional accession.

There was one other important consequence of this accession which also needed to be grasped. No prime minister of India had the authority to agree to any arrangement which might by itself result—in certain situations—in the alienation of any part of Jammu and Kashmir. Only the elected representatives of the people of India acting through parliament had that right. The United Nations had no power under its charter to decide that a sovereign state should part with any portion of its territory. Quite to the contrary, the first objective and purpose of the United Nations was to ensure that the sovereignty and territorial integrity of every member state was preserved. The prime minister of India, whoever he might be, simply could not look at, let alone consider or accept, any scheme for the establishment of a 'self-executing' mechanism in relation to Jammu and Kashmir, as suggested by Ayub. After a moment's pause, Shastri said disarmingly: 'Mr President, if you were in my position, you would take the same stand, wouldn't you?' Shastri then stated that it would be wholly unrealistic to expect the parliament of India to accept any proposal which might result in yet another partition of the country.

As regards the right of 'self-determination,' Shastri recalled to Ayub that Sheikh Abdullah had himself strongly pleaded with the Government of India that the accession of Jammu and Kashmir should be accepted forthwith. While Sheikh Abdullah's views had no legal relevance at that time, his voice was the voice of the people of Jammu and Kashmir. True, in 1948 the Government of India had offered to ascertain the wishes of the people of Jammu and Kashmir in an organized way and the UN had evolved a plan for a plebiscite. But under this plan, the first step was to be taken by Pakistan—that of the withdrawal of Pakistani troops which had illegally invaded Kashmir. Pakistan had not taken that essential first step. Thus it was Pakistan itself which had thwarted the whole scheme, which was now dead and gone. In any case, mediation by the UN was possible only with the continuing consent of the concerned parties. For the reasons just adduced, India was not agreeable to any further mediation by the UN.

Shastri then explained what in his view was the fundamental problem. He asked to be forgiven for non-customary and perhaps excessive frankness in the expression of his views, but the importance of the occasion demanded no less.

Pakistan, he began, was still insistent upon a new exercise of the right of self-determination not because of any deep conviction about human rights as such but quite obviously because of the belief that in any vote, the Muslim population of Jammu and Kashmir could be persuaded by Pakistan's communal propaganda which would present the choice before the people as one between 'Muslim' Pakistan and 'Hindu' India. The fact that the Indian nation consisted not just of Hindus but included many millions of Muslims, Sikhs, Christians, etc. was conveniently ignored.

In pursuance of its 'Muslim' nation theory, Pakistan had established itself as an Islamic country. India rejected the 'two-nation' theory. Any alienation of Kashmir in pursuance of the 'two nation' theory would be destructive of everything that India stood for.

Shastri had spoken at length but he had spoken from his heart and with evident sincerity. As long as Pakistan continued to base its relations with India on its 'two nation' or 'two hostile nations' theory, Shastri concluded, there could be no peace and no good neighbourly relations. This, he said, was the deep-seated malaise which had bedevilled relations between Pakistan and India. And this, he stressed, could be resolved only by Pakistan. All the other problems facing them were merely symptoms of this fundamental disease. He finally added that India wanted to enter into a 'no-war' pact with Pakistan. He invited President Ayub to reflect objectively on what had just been said. He apologized for the time he had taken but his intention and his profound desire was to find a new way to mutual understanding between the two nations.

Ayub had listened very patiently but his reaction was one of grave disappointment. He also wanted peace, he said, but peace on honourable terms. He felt that it would be unrealistic to think that the Kashmir question could be set aside. A mutually acceptable solution had to be found and that was why he had proposed the establishment of a 'self-executing machinery.' A 'no-war' pact was possible, he affirmed, only after the Kashmir question had been settled. Ayub on his part invited Shastri to give the matter further thought. The meeting ended on this note, with anxiety writ large on the faces of both leaders. A meeting of minds was clearly nowhere in sight.

In the afternoon of that day, 5 January, the foreign ministers of India and Pakistan accompanied by senior officials met to discuss the question of the agenda. Various formulations were tried, but none was found that was mutually acceptable. Pakistan's sole interest was the inscription of Kashmir as a separate and specific item on the agenda. The main purpose behind this demand was stated clearly by the Special Correspondent of the British newspaper *The Guardian*, in his report published on 9 January 1965. 'President Ayub knows,' stated the correspondent,

> that, having failed to annex Kashmir militarily, he cannot secure it in Tashkent, but it is important for him at least to get India to begin talks on the issue. If he succeeds, he can tell his people that he has compelled India to reopen an issue which is regarded as settled . . . Ultimately no agreement could be reached on an agenda. The Indian view was that no specific agenda was really required for the summit meeting.

In the evening of 5 January there was a marathon meeting between Shastri and Kosygin. The question uppermost in the mind of Kosygin was withdrawal of armed personnel to the 1949 Ceasefire Line. Kosygin looked tense. Shastri opened the proceedings by immediately referring to this question. 'After very careful thought and consultations with my cabinet colleagues who are in Tashkent, and keeping in view the weighty considerations you mentioned yourself, Mr Kosygin, I have come to the conclusion,' said Mr Shastri, 'that in the interest of peace, I would accept your view in regard to the reciprocal return of all armed personnel to the position prior to 5 August 1965, which in effect means a return to the 1949 Ceasefire Line.' These words transformed Kosygin, who began to beam with joy. A tremendous anxiety had obviously been taken off his mind. 'By this bold and wise decision, Mr Prime Minister,' said a smiling Premier Kosygin in reply, 'you have made a decisive contribution to securing the peace and have greatly enhanced the prospects of success at Tashkent.'

Thereafter Shastri gave a detailed account of his long conversation with Ayub. Both had patiently and courteously listened to each other, he said, but they had not succeeded in reaching any agreement. President Ayub had turned down the suggestion for a 'no-war' pact. There had also been no agreement on the question of an agenda.

Kosygin had not met Ayub after the formal opening of the Tashkent conference the previous day. He now heard for the first time the details of the talks between Ayub and Shastri. Once again Kosygin became somewhat grim, but he did not make any comment to indicate whether he agreed with Shastri or with Ayub or with neither. All he said was that he would meet Ayub the next morning and that he would keep Shastri fully informed. He also expressed the confidence that Shastri would continue to deal with further developments with his usual patience.

The agreement now reached between Shastri and Kosygin regarding withdrawal from the Haji Pir Pass and other areas to the positions held prior to 5 August 1965, was not made known to the press corps. Only Kuldip Nayar, Special Correspondent of the United News of India, was able to get considerable information about this important development during a conversation with Y.B. Chavan. On this basis, as Nayar told me, he flashed the following news item to India in the evening of 5 January:

> Tashkent, Jan. 5 (UNI)—Prime Minister Shastri is believed to have informed Prime Minister Kosygin that India was prepared to withdraw its armed forces from the Haji Pir Pass and Tithwal sectors only if there was an assurance from Pakistan on the question of infiltrators into Kashmir.
>
> He is also believed to have told the Soviet Prime Minister that India was prepared to withdraw its armed forces from the Lahore, Sialkot and Rajasthan sectors if Pakistan did the same in the Chhamb–Jaurian, Rajasthan and Khem Karan sectors.
>
> Mr Shastri conveyed his views to Mr Kosygin when the Soviet leader reportedly emphasized the Indian withdrawal from Haji Pir and Tithwal under the disengagement Plan envisaged in the Security Council resolution of Sept. 20 during their two-hour talk last night.
>
> According to details of the talks available today, Mr Kosygin is understood to have conceded that the implementation of this clause was linked with the 'withdrawal of armed personnel', including infiltrators in Kashmir.
>
> But he tended to place the responsibility of liquidating the infiltrators on India rather than on Pakistan. Mr Kosygin is believed to have said that since Pakistan was not admitting responsibility for sending infiltrators into Kashmir, India was at liberty to liquidate and otherwise deal with them as it deemed fit.
>
> During the talk, the Soviet leader renewed his offer of readiness to intervene in the talks, if they got bogged down.
>
> Mr Shastri, who gave Mr Kosygin the gist of the talks he had yesterday with Mr Ayub, reportedly told him there was no need for this at present.
>
> Mr Kosygin is believed to have emphasized that the talks between Mr Shastri and Mr Ayub should not be allowed to fail because the Soviet Union had also a stake in them.[3]

Kuldip Nayar's report was a good and accurate synopsis of the Shastri–Kosygin talks and of the agreement which the two leaders had reached on the question of withdrawals. However, it did not contain the detailed reasons which Kosygin had put forward to Shastri in support of his proposal that the demand of the Security Council for withdrawals, which had the backing of the entire world, be accepted by India in full. Chavan had apparently divulged to Kuldip Nayar only the basic elements of the Shastri–Kosygin talks, without going into details. Readers of this news in India got to know of the agreement regarding the sensitive question of withdrawals, but without any detailed explanation as to why this agreement had been reached.

On 6 January there was no meeting between Shastri and Ayub. In fact there was a provisional agreement that the two should meet but this was cancelled. The day was, however, full of hectic negotiations in which Kosygin was the central figure. He was shuttling throughout the day between the villas of Ayub and Shastri.

In the morning Kosygin and Foreign Minister Gromyko were closeted with Ayub and Bhutto for nearly three hours. I asked Ambassador Zamiatin whether he could enlighten me on these negotiations. Ambassador Zamiatin replied:

> Despite the disappointment of the opening round, Kosygin had eventually found Ayub to be decent and gentlemanly. But he talked only in generalities. He left the details to his foreign minister, Bhutto. In effect, therefore, there were two simultaneous channels from the Pakistani side speaking with different voices. This made negotiations with the Pakistanis rather complicated and difficult. Gromyko found Bhutto a really obstructive person. In fact Bhutto was a destroyer of all ideas. Sometimes he would accept a proposal and then telephone a little later asking for changes. He knew the English language well and would suggest, with innocent appearance, the insertion of a comma in a previously agreed text, which would have the effect of changing the whole meaning of the relevant phrase or sentence! When dealing with Bhutto, one had to be very much on one's guard. With Shastri things were different. He agreed to proposals only after deep thought and, once convinced, he stuck to whatever he said. He was always straightforward. Kosygin greatly respected Shastri for this.

Although Bhutto was extremely difficult, Gromyko was more than a match for him in toughness as well as in resilience. As regards matters of substance, Ayub was strongly against Pakistani forces withdrawing from their foothold in Chhamb and he gave in only at a late stage, after Kosygin had explained to him, time and again, the consequences which were likely to follow his refusal to abide by the Security Council resolution. Could he really face a hostile world opinion? I have no doubt, however, that Ayub's initial position on the question of the vacation of Chhamb was only a negotiating gambit. Ayub new perfectly well that if Pakistan did not vacate

Chhamb, Shastri would keep Indian troops in the precincts of Lahore and Sialkot, where they were well entrenched. The real sticking point from the Pakistani side was Kashmir, which took up a lot of time in discussions.

After completing his marathon meeting with Ayub in the morning, Kosygin spent another three hours in the afternoon with Shastri. In brief, Kosygin informed Shastri that Ayub was adamant on the question of Kashmir and continued to maintain that Kashmir was the basic problem in Indo–Pakistani relations and that it was absolutely essential to establish a 'self-executing machinery'. Ayub had also informed Kosygin that a 'no-war' pact could not be considered until the Kashmir issue had been resolved. The resulting situation, said Kosygin grimly, was acutely difficult and he enquired whether Shastri could provide some light on the manner in which this impasse could be resolved.

Shastri responded by expressing the view that a 'no-war' pact was in fact no more than a reaffirmation of the obligation of every member state of the United Nations to settle all disputes by peaceful means. If Pakistan had a genuine intention to use peace should there be any objection to the reaffirmation of that obligation in a 'no-war' pact? On Kashmir, Shastri was firm. Kosygin then referred to the question of a 'no-war' pact and enquired whether a reaffirmation by both sides of their obligation under the UN charter to use peaceful means only to settle disputes, without any recourse to the use of force, would in the current situation meet with Shastri's approval. Shastri thought for a while and then answered in the affirmative. This provided Kosygin with some room for manoeuvre in his further talks with Ayub. After exchanging the usual greetings, Kosygin left the villa. It was not clear what he intended to do in his talks with Ayub later that evening. But the Russian premier did not give the impression that the difficulties were insurmountable.

Immediately after Kosygin's departure, Shastri convened a meeting with his party. He gave them an account of his latest talks with Kosygin. He indicated his determination to stand firm on Kashmir even if the Tashkent conference was not to succeed in producing an agreement. He was satisfied that neither the UN nor the host country nor any other reasonable and right-thinking persons would or could blame India if unfortunately the Conference were to fail because of Pakistan's demand on the Kashmir question.

Late in the evening, Shastri was advised that Kosygin had had a long evening session with Ayub, lasting more than two hours. There was no word, however, about any change in Ayub's position on the Kashmir question.

On Tuesday 7 January, direct talks between Shastri and Ayub were resumed after an interlude of nearly forty-eight hours. One meeting was held in the morning for 50 minutes and another was held in the evening for 35 minutes, just prior to a dance performance by Uzbek artists. No aides were present at these meetings. Between these two meetings, Shastri entertained his hosts, Kosygin, Gromyko and Defence Minister Malinowsky to lunch.

In their bilateral talks, Shastri and Ayub, as the prime minister later told me, had both looked at some other important issues—apart from the questions of Kashmir and 'no-war' pact—which would have to be included in any agreement that might eventually be found acceptable. On none of them was there any major disagreement; he said Shastri and Ayub had then returned to the questions of Kashmir and of a 'no-war' pact. The old familiar ground was covered again, each trying to persuade the other to his point of view. The talks were conducted with a great deal of courtesy, in chaste Urdu, but neither side would give in, and towards the end of these talks the following sentences were exchanged:

President Ayub : *'Kashmir ke mamle men kuchh aisa kar deejiye ki main bhi apne mulk men munh dikhane ke qabil rahoon.'* (Please do agree to some arrangement about the Kashmir question so that I may be able to show my face to my people.)

Prime Minister Shastri : *'Sadar Saheb, main bahut muafi chaheta hoon ki main is mamle men apki koi khidmat nahin kar sakta.'* (Mr President, I apologize profusely that in this matter I cannot be of any service to you.)

This informal account clearly demonstrated that both leaders were far apart and that a deadlock had arisen. Shastri and Ayub parted company in a sober mood, but their personal equation was still courteous. At this time neither knew what would happen next.

Meanwhile, in the afternoon of the same day, 7 January, Jha and Kaul had a protracted meeting with Gromyko and other USSR officials. At this meeting the view gained strength that the question of a formal agenda should be set aside. Despite discouraging news on the summit talks that the two leaders had just held, the outlines of a possible joint agreement or communique were discussed. This was a fresh attempt to prepare a text which might provide a new basis for discussion. Some earlier drafts had been summarily rejected by the recipient delegation but this had not yet deterred the Indian delegation from preparing yet another draft, following extensive consultations with the USSR delegation, especially Gromyko.

At 10 p.m. Shastri and other members of the Indian delegation attended a ballet performance. On his return to his villa, Shastri was given the draft text of a possible agreement which had been prepared by Jha.

Shastri read the draft and then asked me to go through the text with particular attention to the first few paragraphs, which touched upon mutual relations between India and Pakistan at the political level. We then went on to discuss the entire text.

The prime minister found the 'political' paragraphs rather effusive and not quite in keeping with the hard realities of a situation in which Indian and Pakistani troops were still snapping at each other with ominous regularity. Shastri indicated to me the lines on which the proposed paragraphs or articles on the fundamental political issues were to be redrafted. These related to the following questions:

(1)    Restoration of peaceful and normal relations between India and Pakistan;

(2)    Unambiguous reaffirmation of obligations under the UN Charter for the settlement of disputes by peaceful means without recourse to force; and

(3)    A brief reference to Jammu and Kashmir, coupled with a restatement of the respective positions of India and Pakistan.

By this time it was well past midnight. I requested the prime minister to retire and undertook to prepare a redraft by early next morning. After the prime minister had retired, I continued to work for some time. The draft paragraphs or articles that had been prepared by me were then left in the sitting room to be handed over to the prime minister first thing in the morning.

When I returned fairly early next morning, I found the prime minister had already studied the draft and had made improvements. We had a brief discussion again and the revised text was typed out for consideration at a meeting of the Indian delegation which had been convened at 10 a.m. that day.

On the question of the restoration of peaceful and normal relations between India and Pakistan, the revised text, which was more down to earth, read as follows:

> The Prime Minister of India and the President of Pakistan, having met at Tashkent and having discussed the existing relations between India and Pakistan, hereby declare their firm resolve to restore normal and peaceful relations between their countries and to promote understanding and friendly relations between their peoples. They consider the attainment of these objective of vital importance for the welfare of the 600 million people of India and Pakistan.

The question of the renunciation of use of force in the settlement of disputes was dealt with in the following manner:

Being welcomed by Kosygin at Tashkent, 3 January 1966.

The author being received by Kosygin at Tashkent, 3 January 1966.

Addressing the opening session of the Tashkent conference, 4 January 1966.

Stepping out of the meeting with Ayub, 7 January 1966. No agreement. Tension on both faces.

Ayub ponders a point made by Shastri. A possible thaw?

Being welcomed by Kosygin at the conference venue, 10 January 1966, to sign the Tashkent Declaration.

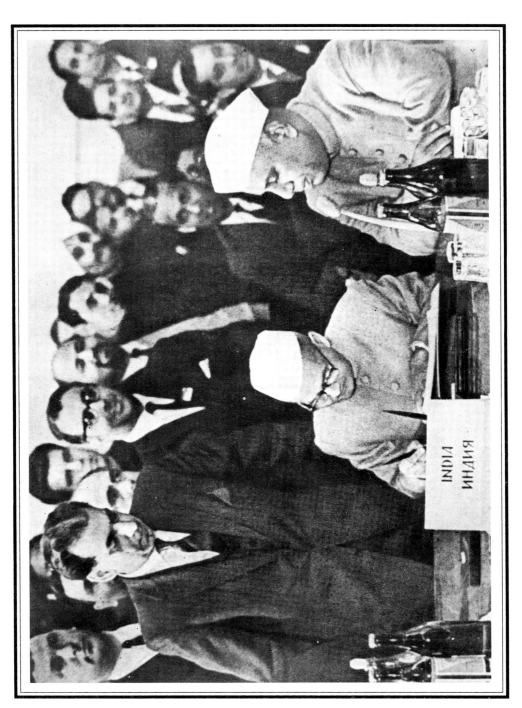

Signing the Tashkent Declaration on 10 January 1966.

Ayub signing the Tashkent Declaration, 10 January 1966. Bhutto continues to look less than happy.

Sharing a joke with Ayub before leaving Kosygin's reception, 9.45 p.m., 10 January 1966. The beaming figure is the Russian foreign minister. Mark the transformation from tension and distrust on 5 January to relaxed friendliness on 10 January.

Addressing the Indian press in Tashkent after signing the Declaration on 10 January 1966. Sitting, front row, alongside Shastri are Y.B.Chavan, Swaran Singh and C.S. Jha. Standing, back row, are L.P.Singh L.K.Jha, T.N.Kaul, General P.P.Kumaramangalam and others.

Y.B.Chavan, Swaran Singh and the author with Shastri at Tashkent. The prime minister looks at urgent papers.

The last photo taken of Shastri (*by Prem Vaidya and Narayanswami*), around midnight on 10 January 1966.

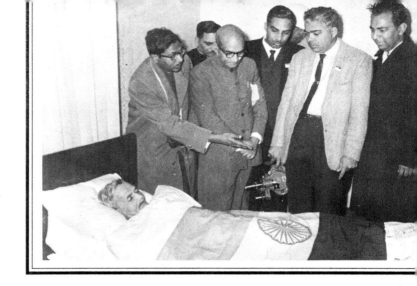

The tragedy of Tashkent. Shastri passes away
at 1.32 a.m. on 11 January 1966. His body is draped by the Indian flag.

Shastri's body upon a gun carriage, en route to Tashkent airport.

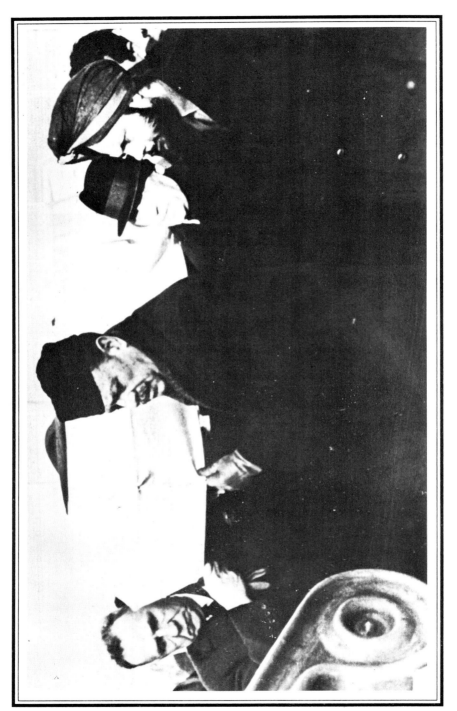

The anguish of the end: Ayub and Kosygin, pall-bearers of Shastri's coffin.

The Prime Minister of India and the President of Pakistan agree that both sides will exert all efforts to create good-neighbourly relations between India and Pakistan in accordance with the United Nations Charter. They reaffirm their obligation under the Charter not to have recourse to force and to settle their disputes through peaceful means.

The question of Jammu and Kashmir was circumscribed carefully in these words:

They considered that the interests of peace in their region and particularly in the Indo–Pakistan subcontinent and, indeed, the interests of the peoples of India and Pakistan, were not served by the continuance of tension between the two countries. It was against this background that Jammu and Kashmir was discussed, and each of the sides set forth its respective position.[4]

Immediately following the preceding texts was the article relating to the withdrawal of 'all armed personnel of the two countries' to the positions they held prior to 5 August 1965, with the commitment on both sides to observe the ceasefire terms on the Ceasefire Line.

Other articles referred to a mutual agreement on non-interference in the internal affairs of each other, the discouragement of hostile propaganda, the return of high commissioners to their respective posts, a consideration of measures that should be taken towards the restoration of economic and trade relations, the question of communications and cultural exchanges, the repatriation of prisoners of war, and related matters. In brief, the proposed text constituted a comprehensive agreement for the restoration of peace and for the promotion of normal relations between the two countries.

At 10 a.m. on 8 January, Shastri convened a meeting of the Indian delegation in his villa. Besides his cabinet colleagues, senior members of the delegation were present. After giving a brief resumé of his talks with Premier Kosygin and President Ayub, the prime minister referred to the draft text of a possible agreement. He explained the revised text of the first few paragraphs which reflected his own approach and the outer limit to which he was prepared to go for securing the success of the Tashkent conference. The delegation scrutinized the complete draft text as revised by the prime minister and accepted it as reflecting the final position of India on all issues referred to in the various articles. It was agreed further that this new text would be passed on to Ayub and Kosygin and Gromyko, who apparently were prepared and willing to pursue the matter further with Ayub and Bhutto. The new text was to be treated as strictly confidential in order to provide a fair chance to Kosygin and Gromyko to discuss its contents with Ayub and his foreign minister as they considered best.

The prime minister made it known that he intended to maintain his programme of leaving Tashkent on the morning of Tuesday, 11 January, and that if an agreement was to be reached at all it would have to be concluded before then. The atmosphere was tense, for although the Indian delegation had prepared a new draft agreement and had forwarded it to the USSR and Pakistani delegations by midday on 8 January, the overall situation was still one of deadlock. While there was no direct news, the signals going out to the large corps of foreign press correspondents indicated the existence of this deadlock and the probability of a breakdown of the talks. The perceptive Special Correspondent of *The Washington Post*, Warren Unna, sent the following dispatch on 8 January:

> The reported thaw between India and Pakistan . . . was in danger of freezing up again today. Kashmir and a proposed 'no-war' pact were the cold winds.
>
> At 2.30 p.m. a draft of the final Conference Communique was delivered from Indian Prime Minister Shastri to Pakistani President Ayub Khan. At 3 p.m., Shastri's headquarters had a call that Ayub's people wanted to come over. At 3.30 p.m., Ayub's answer was delivered—'Totally unacceptable.'[5]

*The New York Times* Special Correspondent, in his despatch dated 8 January, reported 'a virtual deadlock on all major issues.'[6] The Special Correspondent of UK's *Guardian* reported the same day:

> The breakdown might come at any moment because the positions as outlined by them on some vital issues reveal little meeting ground. Today this was emphasized by Pakistan's rejection of India's proposals for a 'no-war' pact. A spokesman here said that unless the Kashmir dispute was settled, such a pact would be irrelevant.
>
> Behind all the manifest divergence and hostility there is a latent desire to come to a settlement. If they wreck the talks they might earn much political acclaim in their respective countries, but they also realize that the economic and military consequences may be disastrous.
>
> Additionally, Mr Kosygin, the Russian prime minister, has set his heart on the success of the venture and has displayed remarkable energy as an honest broker.[7]

Indian correspondents in Tashkent filed similar reports. For example, Krishan Bhatia, Special Correspondent of *The Hindustan Times*, reported that Shastri and Ayub had been unable to find any meeting ground:

> Intermittent and slight contact between the Indian and Pakistani delegations was there today, but it was authoritatively admitted that on no basic issue had the two leaders—Prime Minister Shastri and Pakistan President Ayub—found any meeting ground yet.

The atmosphere of euphoria, which had persisted in Tashkent despite distinct indications of Pakistan's negative and unbending attitude, seemed to have evaporated this evening. Despite Soviet Foreign Minister Gromyko working strenuously as the proverbial honest broker throughout today, it was evident that Pakistan had refused to resile from its earlier stand that a no-war pact or declaration was irrelevant so long as there was no settlement on Kashmir.

At their meeting last evening, President Ayub reportedly told Prime Minister Shastri of his inability to respond for a joint declaration renouncing use of force in settlement of disputes.[8]

G.K. Reddy, Special Correspondent of *The Times of India*, also referred to the prevailing difficulties but did not feel that all was already lost:

India and Pakistan last night exchanged drafts of the proposed treaty for a declaration renouncing the use of force, but there is still no meeting ground for the divergent views held by the two countries on the subject.

The Tashkent talks have reached a very delicate and difficult stage, with Pakistan pressing hard for some agreed mechanism to settle the Kashmir issue as the inevitable price that India must pay for joint renunciation of force. India, on the other hand, is not budging from the position that Kashmir's sovereignty is not negotiable.

But the talks are not heading for a break, although no progress has been made in the last 48 hours after the two sides had tacitly agreed to bypass the agenda tangle. There is some lingering hope in Indian and Soviet circles here that common ground may still be found for a modicum of agreement at Tashkent.[9]

Pakistani press correspondents, reflecting the views which the Pakistani delegation wanted to propagate, emphasized that the settlement of the Kashmir issue must come first. Without any 'no-war' agreement, a pact would be irrelevant. Amjad Husain, Special Correspondent of *The Pakistan Times*, reported on 8 January:

Pakistan said today that unless the Kashmir dispute was settled in a just and honourable way or some mechanism for the resolution of the problem was established, a no-war agreement or pact would be irrelevant.[10]

Karachi's *Dawn*, came out on 9 January with a headline:

NO STABLE PEACE WITHOUT KASHMIR SOLUTION.

Its Special Correspondent, Nasim Ahmad, confirmed this:

As the Tashkent Conference on the Indo–Pakistan conflict entered its final phase today, Pakistan firmly told India that unless the Kashmir dispute and the basic cause of tension between India and Pakistan is removed, there is little likelihood of stable peace being established in the Indo–Pakistan subcontinent.[11]

These words were based on a statement by Altaf Gauhar, Pakistan's information secretary, who was also the spokesman of the Pakistan delegation.

By all accounts then it was clear that on the two fundamental issues, namely Kashmir and the 'no-war' pact, the two leaders had found no meeting ground. If these issues were not resolved, there would be no agreement.

To add to this sea of troubles came the news that China had just delivered a note to India alleging that Indians were engaged in 'frenzied efforts to create tension' and asserting that these were 'entirely prompted by the requirements of its present internal and external policies.' The note added ominously—'If the Indians continued their intrusions and provocations against China, the Chinese will strike back resolutely.' Both the content and the timing of this undisguised threat were reminiscent of a similar note which the Chinese had delivered to India on 17 September 1965, during the Indo–Pakistan war.

'The voice of the great outsider which has consistently supported Pakistan,' observed the Special Correspondent of the London newspaper *The Times*, 'and intervened with a similar Note during the three-week war last year may have heartened President Ayub for a tougher stand.'[12] Referring to this new development, J. Anthony Lukas, Special Correspondent of the *The New York Times*, commented: 'This immediately set off speculation that the Chinese Note had encouraged Pakistan to take an intransigent position at the Conference.'[13] *The Observer* of the United Kingdom reported this new development under the heading: *'Peking warning threat to Indo–Pakistani truce.' The Observer* Correspondent reported graphically:

> In the clean and peaceful air of the Uzbek capital, a violent political storm has suddenly blown up tonight destroying the so-called 'Tashkent spirit', which has never been very strong.
>
> The question which remains open is to what extent the origin of the storm has to be looked for in Peking.
>
> It was from that city that the Chinese Government addressed yesterday to India a strongly-worded warning whose effect could only be to stiffen Pakistan's intransigence in Tashkent or—more subtly perhaps—to embarrass President Ayub at the most difficult stage of the negotiations with India. Abandoning the usual reserve and the somewhat artificial politeness they had observed until now, the spokesmen of the Indian and Pakistani delegations tonight more or less buried the Conference. Everything is not completely lost as President Ayub and Prime Minister Shastri are going to meet once more tomorrow.

*Warning tremors*: But it becomes doubtful if, despite their wish not to offend the Soviet hosts, the two delegations will be able, before leaving Tashkent, to agree even on the most general statement of common aims.

Tashkent is famous not only for its roses but also for its earthquakes.

Tonight tremors were started by the Pakistani Secretary at the Ministry of Information, Altaf Gauhar. At the beginning of his Press briefing, he spent a few minutes thanking warmly the Soviet Government for the 'magnificent opportunity' it had offered in calling the conference, which already sounded like a funeral oration.[14]

Quite understandably, the Pakistani delegation ridiculed the suggestion that there was any link between the timing of the Chinese note and the delicate stage that the Tashkent negotiations had reached.

Western press correspondents were particularly interested in hearing the reaction of the Indian delegation to this new Chinese threat. In response, C.S. Jha described the note as 'pretty strongly worded even as Chinese notes go'.[15] He expressed the view that the timing of the Chinese note was rather 'odd'. Asked whether it was by chance that the publication of the note coincided with a slowdown in the conference, Jha replied that it had not affected India's attitude and added with diplomatic finesse—'we would not venture an opinion whether someone else had been influenced'.[16] Shastri thought the Chinese note was no worse than the note of 17 September 1965, during the thick of the Indo–Pakistan war. Shastri's judgement was that the Chinese were meddling just to show moral support for the Pakistanis without any serious intention to cause trouble on the border. And so it turned out. Shastri also felt that far from harming India's interests, the Chinese note might rebound to India's advantage *vis-à-vis* the USSR delegation and the wider world community.

At 4 p.m. that evening Shastri visited the Oriental Institute. At 5 p.m., he paid his respects at an important Muslim shrine. At 7 p.m. he went to see a performance of *Swan Lake* at the Ali Sher Navoi Uzbek Opera and Ballet Theatre. Meanwhile Gromyko had a series of meetings with the foreign ministers of India and Pakistan where the going was by no means good. Kosygin, even in these difficult circumstances, was fairly hopeful on the evening of 8 January that an agreement would be reached by 10 January. It was clear to him that whatever brinkmanship the Pakistani delegation might indulge in, ultimately the ground realities of the Pakistani military situation would oblige Ayub to go for peace. Ambassador Zamiatin, official spokesman of the USSR delegation at the conference, mentioned to me that Kosygin was quite concerned about the negative propaganda which the Pakistani delegation was conducting. The official spokesman of the Pakistani delegation was constantly telling the world press that the conference was 'meaningless' and that it would fail. He was also repeatedly saying that the 'optimistic' version put out by the USSR delegation did not present the true picture. 'One day,' said Zamiatin,

> I convened a press conference at 2 p.m. to explain the position of the USSR delegation. A little later the official spokesman of the Pakistani delegation telephoned me and asked that I should shift my press conference to 4 p.m. as he wanted to meet the press at 2 p.m. I asked him whether he had checked with the Indian delegation also. He replied brusquely that the Indian requirement was of no concern to him ... The Pakistanis were very aggressive about their propaganda. They always tried to meet the Press early everyday and to get their story out first, because as they knew, it would get circulated around the world quickly and thus influence public opinion.

In the evening of 8 January, Kosygin asked Zamiatin to contact Henry Shapiro, Principal Correspondent of the United Press of America and one of the most influential members of the press corps, and to tell him that the USSR prime minister was very hopeful that an agreement would be signed on 10 January. Zamiatin invited Shapiro forthwith and gave him this exciting and thoroughly unexpected message. Shapiro shook his head in disbelief but, with increasing excitement at the idea of a breakthrough, he asked: 'Can I quote you on that one, Mr Zamiatin?' 'No,' replied Zamiatin coolly, 'if I could say that in my own name, then I would have to speak to the entire press corps. You can attribute it to "the usually reliable and authoritative USSR Government sources".' Shapiro needed no second bidding and circulated the story. He was the only press correspondent to have put out a story indicating even the possibility of a successful outcome of the conference. Despite this note of optimism thus skilfully introduced by Kosygin himself, the fate of the conference, in reality, still hung in the balance.

The ninth of January dawned. It was to be a day of seemingly insurmountable crises, of endeavours by Kosygin to find a way through, of intensive persuasion, of some arm-twisting, and finally to everyone's intense relief, of breakthrough and, against all odds, final success at midnight. The day began in an atmosphere of general despair, bordering on the apprehension that the conference would break up without agreement or even a joint communiqué. Things seemed to be at a pretty low ebb.

But Kosygin, the indefatigable host, was not deterred. In fact, he returned in full force, raring to go. On 8 January, he had kept himself in reserve, allowing Gromyko to do all the talking. Now he seemed to have developed his own special strategy for breaking the deadlock. And I venture to think that the carefully timed Chinese intervention through their threatening note had the totally unintended side-effect of enhancing the firmness of Kosygin's resolve to snatch success from the jaws of failure.

Nothing could demonstrate better the intensity of his efforts than the following agenda:

| | | |
|---|---|---|
| 10.00 a.m. – | 12.30 p.m. | Talks with Prime Minister Shastri; |
| 2.00 p.m. – | 2.45 p.m. | Talks with President Ayub; |
| 4.45 p.m. – | 6.00 p.m. | Talks with President Ayub; |
| 6.40 p.m. – | 9.15 p.m. | Talks with Prime Minister Shastri; |
| 9.30 p.m. – | 11.30 p.m. | Talks and dinner with President Ayub; |
| 11.45 p.m. – | 00.45 a.m. | Talks with Prime Minister Shastri. |

At this stage, there were two and only two fundamental questions on which no agreement had been reached and on which none seemed possible. Shastri had gone as far as he possibly could on the question of Kashmir. He had agreed to a reference to this matter in the draft declaration, qualified and circumscribed by a reaffirmation of India's stand. Indeed he had agreed to a restatement of the respective position of each side. The only way open to Kosygin therefore was to persuade Ayub to accept the formulation on the Kashmir question which Shastri had already accepted and which represented an advance on his initial position that no discussion on Kashmir was possible. This was not an easy task.

The second question related to India's proposal for a 'no-war' pact. Ayub had turned that down. Shastri had already agreed that on this question a reaffirmation in the proposed agreement by both sides of their obligation under the United Nations Charter to settle their disputes by peaceful means without recourse to force would be acceptable. But an open, unambiguous and unqualified renunciation of the use of force in future was absolutely essential. Ayub had to be persuaded to see this point. This was Kosygin's second task.

Kosygin began his talks with Shastri by referring to the proposed draft agreement, of which he had a copy in his hand. Basically, it was the Indian draft, which covered the relevant issues. On the basis of Gromyko's talks with Bhutto, it could be assumed that the text as proposed for the different articles was acceptable, subject to certain minor modifications. In any case, no point of substance had been raised. As regards the Kashmir question and a clear renunciation of the use of force, Pakistan was adamant. Things were still decidedly unresolved.

Shastri reminded Kosygin that the Indian delegation had already made considerable adjustments in its position. Pakistan, on the other hand, had so far made no movement of that kind. It was now for them to give up their intransigence.

Kosygin said that he would try his best, though Bhutto and others were absolutely unbending. He would try nevertheless to persuade Ayub, who was more amenable to reason. In the afternoon Kosygin met Ayub twice for two hours. He left Ayub at 6 p.m. and, after spending about half an hour in his villa, accompanied by Gromyko, was back with Shastri. Ayub was still insistent that the Kashmir question had to be pursued further. On the question of a reaffirmation of the obligation under the UN charter not to use force, he was prepared, Kosygin reported, to reconsider his position provided that the Kashmir question was dealt with in a 'satisfactory' manner. This did not sound very encouraging, but Kosygin was cheered because this development was a definite, even if conditional, change in Ayub's position. On Kashmir, Kosygin said he had explained in detail Shastri's position again and had stressed that the Indian prime minister had changed his initial stand and had agreed to a reference to Kashmir in the proposed declaration in a limited manner. Kosygin then asked Shastri whether there was any way in which he could help further. This was the only moment during all his conversations with Kosygin in Tashkent when Shastri felt that there was a suggestion that he should make further accommodation on the Kashmir question. Or it might well have been part of Kosygin's special efforts to be as even-handed as possible. Shastri had anticipated a last-minute well-intentioned effort of this kind by Kosygin and he was ready with his answer. He replied:

> I want to make it totally clear that I do not agree and will never agree to any machinery for the discussion of India's sovereignty over the state of Jammu and Kashmir. India's sovereignty over Kashmir is non-negotiable. I am prepared to go back to India without an agreement, but I will not change my stand. And, on returning home, I will resign my post if necessary, but I will do nothing which I believe is contrary to the interests of India. And, of course, we will face the consequences.

Kosygin was taken aback, indeed shaken, by this response. He stood up from his chair, clasped Shastri's hands and said:

> Mr Prime Minister, it was not my intention to ask you to consider any proposal which is not in India's interests. I conveyed to you what President Ayub had said and I was merely exploring further possibilities without any specific idea in my mind. I fully understand your position which you have explained to me several times from various angles. Please be assured that I will never ask you to do anything which in your opinion is against the interests of India. We are your friends.

Kosygin was pensive, but still did not have the appearance of a defeated man. His usual smile had, however, disappeared.

At 9.15 p.m. Kosygin left Shastri's villa and went to Ayub for dinner and his last effort. Press correspondents had waited the whole day anxiously for some news. It was now time for them to send their despatches. The signals from both Indian and Pakistani delegations gave no hope of a settlement. The Pakistani spokesman, Gauhar, made a well considered and quotable comment that was intended to send them on their way: 'A communiqué is not a ticket home,' he said, 'you can leave a place without a communiqué.'[17]

So, when late in the evening of 9 January Indian and foreign press correspondents despatched their reports on the day's developments at the conference, the message was one of despair. Success was all but ruled out and Kosygin's herculean efforts (he was with Ayub at this time) were seen as an attempt to 'salvage' something from the wreckage.

Inder Malhotra, Special Correspondent of *The Statesman*, made his assessment of the latest situation in the following words:

> Tashkent, Jan 9—Mr Kosygin was trying desperately tonight to save the talks from total failure and collapse, but at the moment of writing, the outcome of his effort could not be known.
>
> Since all hopes of a no-war declaration or substantive agreement over specific issues have been given up, the Soviet Premier's current efforts are confined to getting the two sides to agree to a joint statement to be issued at the end of their talks tomorrow. But even this limited task is proving exceedingly difficult because of sharp differences between India and Pakistan over what is to be said in a communiqué, the main purpose of which is to record present disagreement as well as the resolve by the two countries to keep talking.[18]

Krishan Bhatia, Special Correspondent of *The Hindustan Times*, was equally despondent:

> Tashkent, Jan 9—Unless a miracle happens, the Tashkent conference should end tomorrow on an unmistakable note of disagreement between Prime Minister Shastri and President Ayub Khan of Pakistan. A detente on any basic issue is considered impossible.
>
> Even on the phrasing of a joint statement, the two leaders were known this evening to be in sharp disagreement.[19]

In similar mood, Dev Murarka, Special Correspondent of *The Indian Express*, reported:

> Tashkent, Jan 9—A joint statement by India and Pakistan is the most likely and the only outcome of the Tashkent talks now.

It will also depend on the success of the strenuous efforts made by the Soviet Prime Minister, Mr Kosygin, to reduce the differences between the Indian and Pakistani drafts.

Yesterday, the talks had virtually broken down and there was no meeting between Mr Shastri and Mr Ayub Khan today as planned. Instead, Mr Kosygin has been having a series of long meetings separately with both the delegations, accompanied by the Soviet Foreign Minister Mr Gromyko and other advisers.[20]

These reports were published in Indian newspapers on 10 January 1966, which was the last day of the Tashkent conference. It was known and confirmed that Shastri would leave Tashkent for Kabul on the morning of 11 January.

Pakistani press reports, despatched from Tashkent on the evening of 9 January and published in the newspapers of 10 January, gave a similarly gloomy account. *The Dawn* had the following front-page 8-column headline: TASHKENT TALKS MAY BREAK UP TODAY.

Amjad Husain of *The Pakistan Times* reported: TASHKENT SUMMIT MAY END TODAY.

The assessment of western press correspondents was no different. J. Anthony Lukas of *The New York Times* summed up his view thus:

Tashkent, USSR. Jan 9—The Soviet Premier, Aleksei Y. Kosygin, re-entered the Pakistani–Indian talks today in a last-minute effort to salvage something from an apparently hopeless stalemate . . . Altaf Gauhar, the Pakistani spokesman, hinted this afternoon that Pakistan was prepared to leave without any communiqué at all . . . This was interpreted as a warning that Pakistan would prefer no communiqué to one that did not make adequate mention of her views on the Kashmir issue.[21]

The Special Correspondent of *The Times* of London also referred to a 'deadlock over Kashmir' and added: 'The crisis seems to have arisen from a declaration that Pakistan is not prepared to accept what looks like agreement on peripheral questions unless there is some progress on the central issue of Kashmir.'[22]

Warren Unna of *The Washington Post* had come to the following conclusion: The best that seemed possible in the remaining 24 hours of the Conference was that the two leaders of the Indian subcontinent might be able at least to agree on a flowery, non-committal communiqué. 'Instead of differences diminishing since this Soviet sponsored conference began last Tuesday, the differences seem to be hardening . . . '[23]

Zamiatin told me a draft speech was prepared on 9 January for Kosygin's possible use the next day, announcing the failure of the conference and explaining the reasons and the likely consequences.

Kosygin had left to meet Ayub. For Shastri it had been a day-long battle of nerves. And the day was not over yet, as Kosygin had promised to return immediately after his talks and dinner with Ayub. I was watching the prime minister closely and was gratified to see how well he had withstood the pressure. We began talking and during the course of our conversation I asked what in his judgement was going to be the likely outcome of Kosygin's efforts with Ayub. Shastri replied:

Difficult to say. Mr Bhutto does not want an agreement. But I think President Ayub wants peace. He would not like to defy the Security Council, nor would he like to spoil Pakistan's relations with the USSR by breaking up the Conference. President Johnson also has, according to reports, made it clear to President Ayub that he wants compliance with the Security Council resolutions and the prompt withdrawal of all armed personnel to the 1949 Ceasefire Line. And then President Ayub himself would very much wish to see the withdrawal of Indian forces from the outskirts of Lahore and Sialkot as soon as possible. On Kashmir also, President Ayub probably realizes by now that he cannot force open the issue at this conference. If there is no agreement, there could be a resumption of hostilities. But, Pakistan's war machine has been badly damaged. Without outside help, Pakistan will not have the capacity to resume fighting. If Pakistan breaks up the conference now, the USSR and also the United States are not likely to provide any support or encouragement to Pakistan. Mr Bhutto is driven by passion and anger. He is smarting with rage because of the failure of his grand design on Kashmir. He now wants to retrieve something at this conference and hence he has made Kashmir the pivotal issue. But I have the impression that President Ayub understands the ground realities and very possibly he will opt for peace. And of course now the USSR will throw its full weight behind this approach . . . We will soon know what happens.

Kosygin was with Ayub from 9.30 p.m. to 11.30 p.m. for talks and dinner. From there Kosygin, accompanied by Gromyko, came straight to Shastri's villa. As Kosygin entered the villa, he had a spring in his step and his whole deportment indicated success. His face was beaming. Shaking Shastri's hands warmly, he said,

I have some good news. I have persuaded President Ayub to accept your texts on Kashmir and on the reaffirmation of the obligation under the UN Charter not to use force in the settlement of disputes.

This was everything that Shastri had hoped for. What seemed impossible even a few hours earlier had just been achieved within a hair's breadth of the final moment. Shastri was visibly moved and delighted. He congratulated Kosygin profusely. This was the longed for, the unexpected, moment of success—a moment never to be forgotten. Kosygin explained that he had reminded Ayub that the Security Council had demanded the restoration of peace and the return of all armed personnel to the positions occupied by them prior to 5 August 1965. This was a mandatory demand and had to be met by both India and Pakistan. India had already accepted this. If now there was no agreement because Pakistan wanted to go beyond the Security Council resolutions in insisting on an immediate reopening of the Kashmir question, the responsibility for the resulting situation, namely a breakdown of peace talks with the danger of resumption of war, would lie solely with Pakistan. As a permanent member of the Security Council, that would be the USSR's view and he had no doubt that all other members of the Security Council who wanted peace would agree with that view. World public opinion would be firmly against Pakistan.

According to Zamiatin, Kosygin had told President Ayub pointedly: 'If you leave without an agreement, what will be your prestige? What will be the future? Real war? What will be the reaction of the world public opinion? Heads of state come together to make peace.'

After a few more exchanges, Ayub had graciously given his assent to the proposed agreement. The situation was saved. Ayub had asked that the withdrawal of all armed personnel to the position prior to 5 August 1965 should be completed at the latest by 25 February 1966. After consultations with Chavan, this suggestion was accepted by Shastri. While this conversation was in progress at Shastri's villa, a message was received that Bhutto wanted to talk urgently with Gromyko. It was a chilling moment. What was he up to now?

Gromyko came to the telephone and began talking with Bhutto. We were all watching him with anxiety. For a while Gromyko listened patiently to Bhutto. Then his face began to show both surprise and anger. Suddenly, he exploded:

> No No No Mr Bhutto you are quite wrong. You had agreed to this and President Ayub had himself agreed to this. You cannot go back on it now. It will be very bad, very bad. Please convey this to your President immediately.

There was a pause. Obviously Bhutto was trying something even at this last moment. But the angry response from Gromyko seemed to have had its effect. A few moments later, Bhutto, probably after talking with Ayub, came back on the phone and withdrew whatever he had said.

Gromyko informed Kosygin and Shastri that Bhutto had raised an objection to the clause relating to a reaffirmation of the obligation under the UN charter not to use force for the settlement of disputes. He wanted the portion relating to non-use of force to be deleted. But Bhutto and

Ayub had already accepted the full text of the relevant clause and there was no question now of an important change of this kind. Fortunately the storm had blown over.

It was agreed then that Shastri and Ayub would give their formal nod of approval at the lunch on 10 January for Ayub hosted by Shastri. But that was to be just a formality. The entire text of the proposed Tashkent declaration had now been finally and firmly agreed. After an expression of mutual thanks and gratitude by the two leaders Kosygin left at 0045 hours. Shastri had gone through a gruelling day in which despair and hope had alternated from hour to hour. He was naturally very pleased with the final outcome.

On the morning of 10 January, all was quiet and peaceful. The days of hectic parleys, of anxious moments, of intense arguments, of despair and hope, were all over. The sun was shining and there was an atmosphere of cheer all round. Shastri looked rested and relaxed. In the first part of the morning, he had stayed on in bed, in a sitting posture, reclining against the pillows and reading some papers. Later he got ready and came to the sitting room. There was some brief, inconsequential conversation. He decided to go out into the garden for a stroll and some fresh air. I accompanied him, just as I had done on several occasions before. Whenever during the day there was an opportunity, he would go out for a breath of air. We would then talk, knowing that no one would be able to overhear us there. We soon returned to the sitting room of the villa. Shastri was looking forward to his luncheon with Ayub and began to collect his thoughts.

The Pakistani president arrived punctually at 1.30 p.m. He was received by Shastri with courtesy and respect. They were together for about an hour and a half. Their formal approval to the final text of the Tashkent declaration was accorded at that time.

After Ayub's departure, Shastri indicated that the lunch and the talks had gone extremely well. There was no time for me to have any detailed conversation with him as he had to get ready for the ceremony at 4 p.m. for signature on the Tashkent declaration. He set off well in time and reached the venue of the conference punctually. As on the occasion of the opening of the conference on 4 January, so also now, all arrangements had been made with punctilious care. The three leaders entered the cabinet room of the Uzbek council of ministers (the same room where the conference had opened on January 4) from three different doors. Shastri moved up to Ayub to shake hands, which both did with warmth. They shook hands later with Kosygin and everyone took his appointed seat.

The historic moment had arrived. The Tashkent declaration, in both

Russian and English, was placed before Shastri, and another set before Ayub. At the request of Kosygin, the text of the declaration was read out by Mr Benediktov, secretary-general of the USSR delegation, first in Russian and then in English. Shastri and Ayub then signed both copies of the Tashkent declaration. Peace had now been sealed and signed. There was loud and prolonged applause. Everyone joined in a standing ovation.

When the participants resumed their seats, Kosygin made the closing remarks:

> I would like to express my heartfelt gratitude to the president of Pakistan and the prime minister of India for the energy, patience and persistence displayed by them in the search for mutually acceptable decisions, the fulfilment of which will help the cause of strengthening peace and friendship between nations. I would like to express my wish that the document which you have confirmed today by your signatures might become the symbol of eternal friendship between India and Pakistan.

Kosygin walked up to Ayub, shook hands with him warmly and offered his congratulations; next to Shastri, shook his hands with warmth, and said: 'This event will further cement the eternal friendship between India and the Soviet Union and also friendship between India and Pakistan.' Shastri responded simply but with sincerity: 'I want to express my deep gratitude to you for the success of the conference and for the trouble you took to bring this about.' Shastri, Ayub and Kosygin then came together and clasped each other's hands, all smiling broadly. All three were, in equal measure, the heroes of this historic conference.

But how did it all happen at the last moment? Was there any secret offer of large economic or military aid? Was there a hidden threat? Was there some serious arm-twisting? These were the questions which bewildered press correspondents were asking on the evening of 10 January after the Tashkent agreement had been signed. The truth was simpler. This literally was an eleventh-hour decision—taken coincidentally at 11 p.m. Kosygin's 'magic' and Ayub's wisdom in accepting Shastri's conditions had turned despair and likely failure into success.

But how was it that a comprehensive declaration covering every conceivable aspect for the restoration of peace and good mutual relations between India and Pakistan was drafted overnight and agreed by the two sides? On this question, there was considerable speculation. Some correspondents thought that once the two central thorny issues had been resolved, all the remaining clauses had somehow been put together overnight. This, of course, was not the case. The fact was that the Indian delegation had arrived in Tashkent with the draft text of a comprehensive declaration based on India's own ideas. Kosygin's views had also been taken carefully into account. This text had been passed on to Kosygin and to Gromyko and became the basis of their detailed clause-by-clause talks with the Pakistanis. In his long conversations with Ayub, both Kosygin and Gromyko had used all their persuasive abilities to secure his agreement to most of the clauses. Whatever ideas had then emerged for some drafting modifications here and there were passed on by Kosygin and Gromyko to the Indian delegation, often through Ambassador Kaul, who was fluent in Russian. Taking all these comments and suggestions of Kosygin and Gromyko into account, a complete agreement was drafted by C.S. Jha and revised in some important respects by Shastri himself. This draft contained texts on the question of Kashmir and on the 'non-use' of force for the settlement of disputes which conformed to Shastri's views but which were, at that point in time, wholly unacceptable to Ayub. This comprehensive draft agreement had been passed on to Ayub and Kosygin. But as this text had been rejected by Pakistan within minutes of its receipt, it had then become just a piece of paper, as the Pakistani delegation described it. Nevertheless, the complete text was still there, ready at hand. It could be revived and used at any time. To the Pakistani delegation, everything contained in the text was 'peripheral' and of no great consequence for, in their view, if there was no agreement on the question of Kashmir, there would be no agreement at all. If, however, agreement was reached on the question of Kashmir and of the 'non-use' of force, the rest of the clauses could be accepted, as they ultimately were, without causing any problem. So the full text of the Tashkent declaration was not produced at the last moment as if by magic, nor was it 'hurriedly put together overnight', as some correspondents suggested. It was substantially the text prepared and circulated by the Indian delegation in the forenoon of 8 January which was 'buried' on 8/9 January after its rejection by the Pakistanis but resurrected at midnight between 9 and 10 January, after Premier Kosygin had secured Ayub's approval at the eleventh hour. The English text and its Russian version were then prepared by the USSR delegation in proper form and style for signature by Ayub and Shastri.

The full text of the declaration is reproduced below.

## THE TASHKENT DECLARATION

The Prime Minister of India and the President of Pakistan, having met at Tashkent and having discussed the existing relations between India and

Pakistan, hereby declare their firm resolve to restore normal and peaceful relations between their countries and to promote understanding and friendly relations between their peoples. They consider the attainment of these objectives of vital importance for the welfare of the 600 million people of India and Pakistan.

## I

The Prime Minister of India and the President of Pakistan agree that both sides will exert all efforts to create good-neighbourly relations between India and Pakistan in accordance with the United Nations Charter. They reaffirm their obligation under the Charter not to have recourse to force and to settle their disputes through peaceful means. They considered that the interests of peace in their region and particularly in the Indo–Pakistan Subcontinent and, indeed, the interests of the peoples of India and Pakistan were not served by the continuance of tension between the two countries. It was against this background that Jammu and Kashmir was discussed, and each of the sides set forth its respective position.

## II

The Prime Minister of India and the President of Pakistan have agreed that all armed personnel of the two countries shall be withdrawn not later than 25 February, 1966 to the positions they held prior to 5 August 1965, and both sides shall observe the ceasefire terms on the Ceasefire Line.

## III

The Prime Minister of India and the President of Pakistan have agreed that relations between India and Pakistan shall be based on the principle of non-interference in the internal affairs of each other.

## IV

The Prime Minister of India and the President of Pakistan have agreed that both sides will discourage any propaganda directed against the other country, and will encourage propaganda which promotes the development of friendly relations between the two countries.

## V

The Prime Minster of India and the President of Pakistan have agreed that the High Commissioner of India to Pakistan and the High Commissioner of Pakistan to India will return to their posts and that the normal functioning of diplomatic missions of both countries will be restored. Both Governments shall observe the Vienna Convention of 1961 on Diplomatic Intercourse.

## VI

The Prime Minister of India and the President of Pakistan have agreed to consider measures towards the restoration of economic and trade relations, communications, as well as cultural exchanges between India and Pakistan, and to take measures to implement the existing agreements between India and Pakistan.

## VII

The Prime Minister of India and the President of Pakistan have agreed that they will give instructions to their respective authorities to carry out the repatriation of prisoners of war.

## VIII

The Prime Minister of India and the President of Pakistan have agreed that the two sides will continue the discussion of questions relating to the problems of refugees and evictions/illegal immigrations. They also agreed that both sides will create conditions which will prevent the exodus of people. They further agreed to discuss the return of the property and assets taken over by either side in connection with the conflict.

## IX

The Prime Minister of India and the President of Pakistan have agreed that the two sides will continue meetings both at the highest and at other levels on matters of direct concern to both countries. Both sides have recognized the need to set up joint Indian–Pakistani bodies which will report to their Governments in order to decide what further steps should be taken.

## X

The Prime Minister of India and the President of Pakistan record their feelings of deep appreciation and gratitude to the leaders of the Soviet Union, the Soviet Government and personally to the Chairman of the Council of Ministers of the USSR for their constructive, friendly and noble part in bringing about the present meeting which has resulted in mutually satisfactory results. They also express to the Government and friendly people of Uzbekistan their sincere thankfulness for their overwhelming reception and generous hospitality.

They invite the Chairman of the Council of Ministers of the USSR to witness this Declaration.

PRIME MINISTER OF INDIA                PRESIDENT OF PAKISTAN

Lal Bahadur Shastri                   Mohammed Ayub Khan

Tashkent, 10 January 1966.

# Chapter 32

# A Historic Achievement

The success at Tashkent meant many things. First, peace had been restored between India and Pakistan and the danger of war had been eliminated. Peace had been achieved on an honourable basis, in accordance with the relevant resolution of the United Nations Security Council. Viewed dispassionately, this constituted the success of all three participants at the conference. Both sides agreed to withdraw their armed personnel to positions held by them prior to 5 August 1965, within six weeks from the date of the declaration, that is by 25 February 1966. The Ceasefire Line would be treated as inviolable. Both sides had reaffirmed their obligation not to have recourse to force and to settle their disputes through peaceful means. Zamiatin explained that in the opinion of Kosygin, this was one of the key provisions in the Tashkent declaration. As S.M. Yousuf, who later succeeded Aziz Ahmad as Pakistan's foreign secretary, said, Pakistan had 'conceded the substance of a "no-war" agreement' in Tashkent, the rest was 'a matter of words.'[1]

Second, both agreed to discourage hostile propaganda and encourage such propaganda as would promote friendly relations. Full diplomatic relations were to be restored and the high commissioners of the two countries were to be sent to their respective posts. Measures were to be considered towards the restoration of economic and trade relations as well as cultural exchanges. Existing agreements relating to these matters were to be implemented. Prisoners of war were to be repatriated. Both sides agreed to continue the discussion of questions relating to the problem of refugees and of illegal immigrants, the return of property, and other assets taken over by either side in connection with the conflict. Both sides agreed to meet periodically at the highest and other levels.

Taken together, all these points add up to an agreement far more comprehensive than many in Tashkent had expected. Shastri was particularly pleased with the contents of preambular paragraphs of the declaration under which both sides had gone much beyond the mere restoration of peace on the borders. During the luncheon on 10 January 1966, Ayub had suggested and Shastri had readily agreed that there should be a direct telephone link over which they could talk with each other, as frequently as necessary, without the intervention of intermediaries. 'Please call me on this hot line whenever you feel that something is going wrong or when you want me to do something and I will do the same myself,' Ayub told Shastri. Ayub had gone further and invited Shastri to stop at Rawalpindi on the way back home next day, for a cup of tea. This, Ayub had felt, would demonstrate that the two countries had already embarked upon a new chapter in their mutual relationship. Shastri would have agreed but could not because of the planned visit to Afghanistan the next day. He promised to visit Pakistan as soon as he could.

According to what Shastri told me, Ayub had not by any means given up Pakistani ambitions over Kashmir. He could not possibly have done that. What Shastri regarded as a breakthrough was, in his judgement, a genuine change of heart on the part of Ayub with regard to the basis on which he would conduct Pakistan's relations with India in future. By Shastri's transparent sincerity and humility as well as by his persuasive manner, which was remarkably effective in one-to-one conversations, Ayub seems to have been convinced that the Bhutto line of hatred, clandestine terrorism, use of force and the threat of a thousand years' war against India was not going to enable Pakistan to seize Kashmir. Ayub knew that the recent war had proved an unmitigated disaster. In this context, it is not difficult to understand why Ayub decided to make a new start on the basis of his unwritten but still genuine personal compact with Shastri. It must now remain a matter of speculation as to what would have actually happened in regard to India–Pakistan relations had Shastri not passed away. It can be reasonably assumed that if he had lived, he and Ayub would have provided strong support to each other in strengthening this new relationship.

At the international level, the Tashkent declaration was acclaimed as an act of courage and statesmanship. Johnson of the USA regarded it 'the result of statesmen reasoning together.'[2] *The Guardian* of the United Kingdom referred to the declaration as a 'brave attempt' and commented in its issue of 11 January 1966:

> The Tashkent talks—until the news of Mr Shastri's death—turned out better than most people dared to hope. The credit for this is due to the skill and persistence of Premier Kosygin, and to the good sense and goodwill of the two principals, Mr Lal Bahadur Shastri and President Ayub Khan. They certainly knew better than anybody else how ruinous to their two countries would be another outbreak of war between them, and there need be no doubt of the sincerity of their affirmation of the pledge demanded of members of the United Nations not to resort to force in the settlement of disputes. They must have been most conscious,

too, of the everyday, practical complications resulting from the cold war between them, and so they made use of the opportunity Tashkent offered to restore normality to diplomatic, commercial, and cultural intercourse. They made a fresh start; if nothing else comes of the meeting, that alone made it worthwhile.

The Delhi correspondent of the London *Times* sent the following perceptive despatch which was published on 11 January 1966:

In Delhi's morning newspapers today, Indian correspondents in Tashkent unanimously reported that the Conference was petering out into failure. Tonight, special editions are on the streets proclaiming the 'Tashkent Declaration' as the great diplomatic triumph it undoubtedly is.

Relief mixes with amazement and both with mystification—how was it done? The Declaration is seen here tonight as a victory for Mr Shastri, the Indian Prime Minister, as well as triumph for Mr Kosygin, the Soviet Prime Minister, but with gratification there is puzzlement as to how President Ayub of Pakistan was persuaded to sign the Declaration.

There is no hint of a concession from India's position that Kashmir is beyond negotiation, and the reaffirmation of both countries' obligation to abjure the use of force comes close to the Indian insistence on a 'no war' pact.

What has Pakistan got out of it? Under the commitment to withdraw all troops to their August 5 positions, India will have to relinquish her positions around the Haji Pir Pass in the Pakistan part of Kashmir, and there will be some protests here at that.

But such complaints will be drowned out in the general applause, and, anyway, it must be assumed that in Tashkent President Ayub went far to accepting responsibility for the guerillas who appeared in the valley last August. If he did that and was prepared to abjure the use of force, India could not have clung to Haji Pir.

While Mr Shastri's part is recognized, there is acknowledgement, too, that if the Tashkent Declaration fulfils its high promise as a point of new departure for this troubled subcontinent, President Ayub will deserve his full share of the credit.

The Tashkent Declaration appears to meet all the conditions so far articulated in Washington for a resumption of American economic assistance to India and Pakistan.

I have quoted this despatch in full because it sums up extremely well the reaction in New Delhi and indeed in India to the news received on the evening of 10 January 1966 about the signing of the Tashkent declaration.

In reply to a question about Haji Pir Pass and other posts, Shastri stated that as both sides had agreed to renounce the use of force and also to adhere in future to the Ceasefire Line and to observe the ceasefire terms, the conditions which he had outlined on this point in his letter to UN

Secretary-General U Thant had, in his judgement, been fulfilled. It was in this context that he had agreed to comply with the UN Security Council resolution of 20 September on the question of withdrawals. The prime minister stressed that the agreement had been reached keeping in mind the larger context of peace and amity in the subcontinent.

When on 10 January the special editions of newspapers and All India Radio gave details of the Tashkent declaration, the agreement to vacate the Haji Pir Pass was mentioned but the imperatives which had led to this decision were not explained because they were not known. Some opposition politicians made instant comments, as they got news of the Tashkent declaration. They had called the agreement a 'betrayal' and added: 'The politicians had lost what the soldiers had won.' The reference obviously was to the Haji Pir Pass. Shastri and his cabinet colleagues had taken into account the military and the political realities of the situation. Reluctantly, but entirely to serve national interests, they had to agree to abide by the Security Council resolution. There was no question of 'giving away' the Haji Pir Pass because of any weakness in negotiations. Nor was there any question of 'giving away' the Haji Pir Pass 'out of generosity', as some critics have suggested. Nor, again, was there any question of a disregard of the 'heroic feats' of the men of the armed forces who had captured Haji Pir Pass. But as advised by the army and the air force chiefs, peace was now essential.

To pursue this matter, I had a detailed conversation with General P.P. Kumaramangalam who was a member of the Indian delegation to the Tashkent conference and who, at the time, was vice-chief of the army staff. (General Kumaramangalam retired some years ago from the position of chief of the army staff.) Kumaramangalam confirmed to me his view that while naturally the army would have liked to retain possession of the Haji Pir Pass, on no account was this to be done by jeopardizing peace and risking a resumption of war. He said: 'I am well aware that initially Prime Minister Shastri was reluctant to agree to withdrawal from the Haji Pir Pass but he had had the courage to change his mind solely in the country's interests and with no other consideration in mind.' 'On this question,' said General Kumaramangalam, 'the reasoning of Premier Kosygin was absolutely right.'

To make things doubly sure about the views of Air Chief Marshal Arjan Singh on this sensitive issue, I had a talk with him. He expressed the view that the Haji Pir Pass had become an emotional issue quite out of proportion to it's strategic importance. He confirmed that he had advised Shastri to agree to the vacation of the pass because, in his view, peace was far more important than holding on to that pass.

# Chapter 33

# Shastri Dies On 11 January 1966

After a brief meeting with representatives of the Indian press, and a call on Kosygin, Shastri retired to his room to rest before leaving for Kosygin's reception on 10 January. He did not take long. By about 7.30 p.m., he left his villa. I accompanied him and sat by his side in the car. He was in good spirits. We arrived at the reception centre just after 8 p.m. The prime minister was received by a beaming Kosygin. There was the usual round of handshakes, much warmer now than before. The general atmosphere was one of jubilation and everyone was congratulating everyone else. Ayub looked pleased and relaxed, which is more than could be said of Bhutto and Asghar Khan.

By 9.45 p.m. Shastri started taking leave and his warm and prolonged handshake with Ayub conveyed the distinct impression of genuine mutual regard. Ayub said: *'Khuda Hafiz.'* (May God protect you.) Shastri replied: *'Khuda Hafiz.'* Shastri said: *'Achcha hi ho gaya.'* (It was all to the good.) Ayub said: *'Khuda achcha hi karega.'* (God will do only good.)

Shastri shook many more hands; finally, he had a few words with Kosygin. Thereafter he boarded his waiting car and I came back with him. On the way he expressed his satisfaction over the successful completion of his mission.

I still remember vividly the joyous scenes in the streets of Tashkent as we drove along. The people thronging the streets were delighted that this important conference in their city had been a success. They shouted 'Shastri, Shastri' and the prime minister responded by waving back to them.

We reached the villa at about 10.15 p.m. and we sat down in his study. He recounted his talks at the lunch with Ayub when both had agreed to the commencement of a new relationship. We had talked for about ten minutes when Shastri looked up and said: 'Every day so far we have been going to bed here after midnight. Let us retire early today. Tomorrow morning, we are going to Kabul. It is very cold there. You must wear adequate protective clothing.' I replied: 'I will take care but I have another engagement still. A few official members of the Indian delegation are due to meet the press representatives in a hotel located a few miles away and

I have been asked to join them. I have to go there right away.' Shastri said that this was important and that I should go. 'But how will you go?' he asked. I replied: 'There is a car waiting for me. It will take me there and bring me back.' Shastri said with concern: 'It is already very cold. I do not know whether the car which has been arranged for you is good enough. I would like you to go in my car, keep it there and come back in it.'

So saying, he came to the outer door with me, gave instructions to his driver and insisted that I go in his car. I was overwhelmed. I entered his car and as the car moved, I saw him waving to me with a broad smile, as if conveying his blessings. That, alas, was the last time I saw him alive.

I went to the hotel where meetings had been organized first with senior Indian press representatives and later with foreign press correspondents. When the press conference ended, I came back to my room in the Intourist Hotel where the Indian delegation was lodged. This place was about 250 yards away from the prime minister's villa and there was a direct path between the two places. I was about to get into bed when the telephone rang and Jagannath Sahai, in a broken voice, asked me to rush to the villa immediately as the prime minister had been taken seriously ill. I literally ran across and reached the villa within three or four minutes. The USSR military guard at the entrance was in a state of shock. Seeing me, he rushed forward and said: 'It is very bad with your prime minister. It is very bad.' My heart literally sank. I rushed to the bedroom and could not, for a few moments, believe what I was seeing. No, I told myself, it could not be true. How could it be? Barely three hours earlier, I had left him in excellent health and good cheer. There was no remaining engagement for the prime minister for that evening. For a moment, I prayed this might be a terrifying dream. But the terrible tragedy which I was witnessing was, alas, real. The prime minister was no more. For me, this was the most traumatic moment of my life. The body of the prime minister lay on the bed. His head was resting in the lap of his personal assistant, M.M.N. Sharma. Dr Chugh was still trying to revive the body and at the same time expressing his utter helplessness and despair incoherently. He told me with anguish that he could not save the life of the prime minister, and then he was overcome with grief. Everyone was in tears. Soon the USSR doctors arrived and they took over responsibility for the reanimation of the body.

One by one, others started coming: Sardar Swaran Singh, Y.B. Chavan, C.S. Jha, L.P. Singh, L.K. Jha, T.N. Kaul and other members of the Indian delegation. Within a few minutes came Kosygin, who was as distressed as any of us. He expressed his grief and consoled everybody. A little later Ayub Khan arrived. His sorrow was immense and transparently sincere. India's press representatives, who had been stunned by the news came in groups. Among them were Kuldip Nayar, Inder Malhotra, Krishan Bhatia, G.K. Reddy, Dev Murarka and others.

Kosygin who had gone back to his villa for a few minutes, returned with Gromyko and Malinovsky. Kosygin said: 'He did all he could for peace. He was a great man, a humanist of our time . . . a man who wanted to do much for his people.' Kosygin was the first to sign the Condolence Book which had just been placed before a photograph of the prime minister. He was followed by Gromyko. Warren Unna was next in line but he yielded place to Marshal Malinovsky, who wanted to sign just after the Soviet foreign minister.

Later they all went in single file, led by Swaran Singh, to the bedroom of the prime minister. His body lay on the bed in serene repose. His eyes were not fully closed. His mouth was slightly open. His grey hair was visible: the ubiquitous Gandhi cap was not there. The Indian tricolour had been spread over his body. Everyone stood there for a moment with bowed head and then moved away.

The president of India had been informed of the death of the prime minister. It was my lot to inform the prime minister's family. I conveyed the news of the unbelievable tragedy to Hari Krishna Shastri, the oldest son of the prime minister. It was heart-rending to hear the pain at the other end.

The team of USSR doctors led by Professor U.A. Aripov, Doctor of Medicine and Deputy Minister of Health, Uzbek SSR, assisted by Dr R.N. Chugh, had done what they could to reanimate the body but eventually they pronounced that Shastri had died of an acute attack of 'Infarkt Miocarda'. I reproduce below the concluding paragraph of their report:

'Taking into account the fact that Prime Minister L.B. Shastri had suffered even in the past from Infarkt Miocarda and the fact that during the night from 10th to 11th January 1966, there was an acute attack of the same disease it can be considered that death occurred because of an acute attack of Infarkt Miocarda.'

In order to prevent decomposition, the doctors had embalmed the body.

Since it was known that Shastriji had had two heart attacks earlier, one in 1959 and the other in June 1964, no one present in Tashkent at that time as a member of the Indian delegation had any reason to entertain any doubts about the report and the conclusion of the medical team that he had suffered yet another heart attack which had proved fatal.

Minute by minute the time passed by and the morning hour arrived. Arrangements were made to transport the body of the prime minister to the airport for the journey to New Delhi.

## THE LAST JOURNEY

The body of Prime Minister Shastri was placed in a casket and then mounted on a gun carriage. At about 9 a.m. Kosygin, accompanied by his daughter Ludmilla Grishiany and Madame Y. Nassiruddinova, president of the Uzbek Republic, walked up the drive to the main gate. They laid wreaths on the gun carriage on behalf of the Government of the USSR and the Government of Uzbekistan. Wreaths were also placed on behalf of other Soviet and Uzbek organizations. The procession then began to move towards the airport. The seventeen kilometre long route was lined all the way by the people of Tashkent, who stood motionless in sorrow. Many women were in tears. About a million people had thronged the route to bid final farewell to the Indian leader whom they had so lustily cheered the previous evening. Indian, Pakistani, USSR and Uzbek flags were flying half-mast, draped in black.

When the cortege reached the airport, Ayub was already waiting there to join the USSR leaders in paying final homage to Shastriji. When the casket was lowered from the gun carriage, Kosygin and Ayub Khan became the leading pall bearers, carrying the coffin on their shoulders to the gangway of the waiting Soviet aircraft. There would be very few instances in human history in which a war adversary of the day before became a warm friend and then a genuinely grieving pall bearer the next day. I saw for myself how deeply distressed and shocked President Ayub was.

As the body of Prime Minister Shastri was put aboard the USSR plane, a volley was fired as a salute to the departed leader. A band played funeral music and Soviet armed personnel stood with reversed arms. Among those present at the airport to pay their respects were Gromyko and Malinovsky. They, along with Kosygin and Ayub, stood at the airport, watching the Soviet plane take off for Delhi at 11 a.m.

## ARRIVAL IN NEW DELHI

The Soviet airliner arrived in New Delhi at about 1430 hours on 11 January. As the door was opened and the gangway brought to the aircraft, the large, grieving crowd shouted: 'Lal Bahadurji ki jai'. The first to alight were Y.B. Chavan and Sardar Swaran Singh. Chavan went first to Shastri's eldest son Hari Krishna Shastri, who was crying inconsolably. Chavan embraced him. Both were in tears. Then Chavan brought Hari Krishna into the aircraft to see the body of his father. Hari Krishna knelt and broke down. Chavan again held Hari Krishna and escorted him back to the tarmac.

The pall bearers then brought Shastriji's body out of the aircraft. His face was clearly visible and his head had been propped up on a pillow. His spotlessly clean cap was on his head. Led by the three defence chiefs, General Chaudhrui, Air Marshal Arjan Singh and Vice-Admiral Chatterjee, six pall bearers altogether, including one senior officer each from the army, air force and navy, carried Shastriji's body past rows of armed personnel with reversed arms, to the gun carriage decked with flowers. President Radhakrishnan, Vice-President Zakir Hussain, Prime Minister Nanda and his cabinet colleagues, state governors and chief ministers who had been able to reach New Delhi, and ambassadors and high commissioners stood in silence with bowed heads as the cortege moved past them.

My wife Nirmala had reached the airport and was doing all she could to console the members of Shastriji's family. Their loss was irreparable, so was ours.

The gun carriage began to move along slowly on its journey to the prime minister's official residence at 10 Janpath. On the way, more than a million people had gathered to pay their respects to the leader who had won their respect and affection and who had become the symbol of resurgent India. There was anguish on every face.

The most poignant moment came when the body reached 10 Janpath: Mrs Lalita Shastri collapsed as she touched her husband's body. There was no way that anyone could console her.

Shastriji's body was first taken to his bedroom in his nearby residence at 1 Motilal Nehru Place, and placed on the floor. The embalmed body, which had developed blue patches, was bathed, and Hindu rites were performed by priests who chanted the scriptures. In the early evening, Shastriji's body was brought to 10 Janpath and laid on a platform surrounded by a mass of flowers. Throughout that evening and the following night, members of the public filed past to glimpse their leader and pay homage.

Among the first foreign dignitaries to come to 10 Janpath to convey their condolences was Kosygin, who bowed down before Lalita Shastri as if to touch her feet, in the Indian way. His face showed deep pain and grief, though he maintained a dignified calm. Many world statesmen and dignitaries followed. Among them were the United States Vice-President Hubert Humphrey, Secretary of State Dean Rusk, and Ambassador Chester Bowles. The United Kingdom was represented by Lord Louis Mountbatten, George Brown, the deputy prime minister, and John Freeman, the British high commissioner. Among Indian leaders, I saw Morarji Desai, who was visibly moved.

At 9.30 a.m. on 12 January 1966 Shastriji's body was placed on a gun carriage for his last journey on this earth. The national flag was placed on top of layers of flowers. Slowly the funeral procession began to move, led by members of the armed forces with guns pointing downwards. They moved along Janpath, Curzon Road, Connaught Circus, and eventually arrived at the cremation ground, appropriately named Vijay Ghat, close to Raj Ghat and Shanti Van where Mahatma Gandhi and Jawaharlal Nehru had been cremated. All along the route hundreds of thousands of mourners had gathered, sobbing and shouting: *Lal Bahadur Shastri amar rahen* (Lal Bahadur Shastri will live forever.)

On arrival at the cremation ground, the body of Lal Bahadur Shastri was lifted from the gun carriage and placed on the funeral pyre. Priests chanted Hindu hymns. Then, one by one, national leaders, friends of Shastriji and relations climbed up the platform to pay their last homage.

For me also the moment of final parting had arrived. Following Shastriji's example, I had done my best to maintain my equanimity even at this time of immense sorrow. Slowly I climbed the steps, stood before his body, poured ghee on the pyre, folded my hands in prayer, and closed my eyes. In a flash, at that moment, I saw Shastriji standing at the outer door of his villa in Tashkent at 10.30 p.m. on 10 January 1966, waving his blessings to me with a smile on his face. That memory has remained ever since. I bowed to take leave, thus closing the most glorious and the most tragic chapter of my life. Moments later, Hari Krishna Shastri performed his holy duty to his father by igniting the funeral pyre. Within an hour the mortal remains of Lal Bahadur Shastri had been consumed by fire.

As the poet Kabir has said:

> *Das Kabir jatan se odhi,*
> *Jyon ki tyon dhar deeni chadariya.*

In essence this means: 'I have laid down my life as pure as I found it at my birth.'

One of the foreigners to witness this poignant and historic finale to Shastri's life was Warren Unna of *The Washington Post*. In his despatch from New Delhi which was published in *The Washington Post* on 13 January 1966, Unna said: 'Mankind historically has reserved its greatest occasions for the final journeys of its leaders—and India today made such an occasion.'

This ends my narration of the life of Lal Bahadur Shastri. It was a life of truth in politics.

# Epilogue

From humble origins, Lal Bahadur Shastri rose to the pinnacle of power as India's prime minister and achieved phenomenal success in national and world affairs entirely on the strength of his personal qualities. Of all great men it is Shastri who springs to my mind when I read Confucius's definition of the perfect gentleman. 'There are nine things,' said Confucius, 'the gentleman turns his thought to: to seeing clearly when he uses his eyes, to hearing acutely when he uses his ears, to looking cordial when it comes to his countenance, to appearing respectful when it comes to his demeanour, to being conscientious when he speaks, to being reverent when he performs his duties, to seeking advice when he is in doubt, to the consequences when he is enraged, and to what is right at the sight of gain.'[1]

As an individual Shastri had the moral and ethical attributes of a Mahatma, a great soul. He never swerved from the path of righteousness and truth. In his personal and professional relations, he was humble, considerate, self-respecting, dignified, benevolent, unselfish, cultured, un-hurried and soft-spoken.

As head of government and leader of his country, he was wise, far-seeing, firm of purpose and resolve, with an indomitable will. He was pragmatic and down to earth, dedicated to the welfare of the common man, and a person of impeccable integrity whom power could not corrupt. He acted with restraint or with boldness as the occasion demanded. He made his decisions after deep thought, never impulsively. He could not be pressurized by anyone against his will.

As an Indian he was deeply patriotic, having dedicated his life from the early age of sixteen to the service of his country. He was a firm believer in the fundamental unity of all world religions and was profoundly committed to secularism and to welding the people of his country into one united nation.

As a citizen of the world, he stood firmly for international amity and peace, but peace with honour. When India was invaded, this peace-loving and honourable man defended his country's sovereignty and territorial integrity with determination and carried the fight out into the invader's territory. And when he had achieved his war objective of defending the borders of his country, he staked his life to win peace and establish friendly relations with his erstwhile adversary. The world hailed him as a noble and exemplary statesman.

When he died, his life-sheet was spotlessly clean. He left no money, no house and no land. He did leave behind an example which will continue to inspire, fortify and encourage all those of every community and creed who believe that the only foundation for national life must be a dedication to truth and honesty. He never sought for himself any superlatives or fulsome praise. The epitaph that he might have liked would read:

**Lal Bahadur Shastri**

2 October 1904 –11 January 1966

In Deep Respect

for

**A Life of Truth in Politics**

# Postscript 1

# The Circumstances of Shastri's Death

Many in India as well as Indians living abroad have expressed to me their apprehension that there was something suspicious about the circumstances in which Shastri passed away suddenly during the night between 10 and 11 January 1966 at 1.32 a.m.

All those who were attending the Tashkent conference had seen Shastri in excellent health throughout that week. Despite incessant diplomatic negotiations, the stress of the developing situation and even the threat of a breakdown in the talks, Shastri had maintained complete equanimity, poise and dignity throughout the conference. At no time had he shown the slightest sign of stress, physical or mental, no adverse symptom with regard to his health.

On 10 January he seemed to be particularly pleased with everything that had happened. His luncheon meeting with Ayub had gone extremely well, opening the prospect of a new and friendly relationship with Pakistan. At 4 p.m. he had signed the Tashkent declaration. At Kosygin's reception in the evening, Shastri was literally beaming. He was moving around, shaking hands and exchanging greetings with members of the USSR and Pakistani delegations. When Shastri took leave of Ayub, the handshake was clearly warm and extended on both sides. Before leaving for his villa, Shastri had a few words with Kosygin when he expressed feelings of gratitude to Kosygin for his help. I can confirm all this, as I was with him throughout the day.

As I said, I had left Shastri at 10.30 p.m. to attend a press conference which had been convened by the Indian delegation to explain the Tashkent declaration to Indian and foreign press correspondents. After the press conference, I had just returned to my room when the call came from Jagannath Sahai informing me that the prime minister had been taken seriously ill. When I reached there, Shastri was already dead.

At this point I should mention that Shastri was rather private and reticent on the question of his health. He regarded this as a matter strictly between himself and his physician, Chugh. Knowing this, I had never referred to his health in my conversations with him, nor had he ever talked about it himself. Once my wife, Nirmala, urged him not to work so hard and for such long hours without respite. Shastriji's response was kind but clear and firm: 'I have to work like this. I cannot do otherwise. If something has to happen to me, it will happen.' That was his unshakeable stand. However, on that particular day, 10 January, as I have already indicated, I had not noticed any sign whatsoever in Shastriji's condition to cause even the slightest apprehension. Quite to the contrary.

In order to secure a first-hand version of what had happened in the prime minister's villa after my departure at 10.30 p.m. and his passing away at 1.32 am—that is, just three hours later—I have had long and detailed talks with Jagannath Sahai and M.M.N. Sharma, members of his personal staff, who were both present and were attending him until the moment of his death. I have known both of them for many years now and have full confidence in the truthfulness and accuracy of their account. They were also completely loyal and devoted to Shastri. Both Sahai and Sharma told me the following:

On returning from the USSR reception in the evening of 10 January, they began to pack up in preparation for the planned departure next morning for Kabul. Both of them had come away ahead of the prime minister. When Shastri and I had returned together, they were in the bedroom on the ground floor which had been allotted to Dr Chugh and other members of the prime minister's personal staff.

I had a brief conversation with the prime minister, and then left the villa, having been seen off at the outer door by the prime minister himself. Soon thereafter, the prime minister's personal attendant, Ram Nath, went to the prime minister and asked whether he should serve dinner. Jagannath Sahai was with the prime minister at that time. Shastri first said he was not very hungry, but after thinking for a moment he asked Ram Nath to bring a slice of bread, some *saag* and fruits. Ram Nath went to the kitchen and brought back a light meal prepared by the cook, Mohammad Jan, and the Russian cooks. Mohammad Jan was the cook of the Indian ambassador in Moscow, T.N. Kaul, and had been brought to Tashkent by Kaul, with the prior permission of the government, to cook Indian dishes for the prime minister and his guests. Shastri ate the food which had been brought by Ram Nath.

At about this time, V.S. Venkataraman, one of the prime minister's private secretaries, telephoned from New Delhi. Jagannath Sahai, who was then in Shastri's suite, received this call. Venkataraman asked whether the prime minister had any particular wishes with regard to the arrangements to be made for his reception at New Delhi airport on his return to India. Sahai asked Shastri who said: '*Wahan jo theek samjhen woh karen.*' (They should do whatever they consider appropriate). This was conveyed to Venkataraman by Sahai.

While Venkataraman was still on the telephone, the prime minister asked Sahai to find out from him what the general reaction to the Tashkent declaration was. Sahai put this question to Venkataraman, who replied that the declaration had been generally well received, except that A.B. Vajpayee (Jan Sangh) and S.N. Dwivedy (PSP) had been somewhat critical. Jagannath Sahai conveyed this to the prime minister, who then commented in his usual soft and unemotional tone: 'They are in the Opposition and it is their right to be critical.'

A little later, Jagannath Sahai connected a call with prime minister Shastri's residence in New Delhi. Shastriji wanted to speak with his wife but she could not hear the conversation properly. He then had a talk with some other members of his family who also had some feedback on the reaction in India to the Tashkent declaration. Shastri then requested V.N. Singh, his younger son-in-law, to send all the New Delhi papers of the next morning with the Indian plane which was to fly out to Kabul. V.N. Singh told me recently that during his conversation with Shastri, he had assured him that the reaction in India was good and that his success at Tashkent had been hailed all over the country, barring one or two inevitable critical comments.

When the telephone calls were over, Jagannath Sahai suggested to the prime minister that it might be a wise precaution to avoid overflying Pakistan when travelling from Kabul to New Delhi. He recalled how the Pakistanis had shot down the civilian plane in which Balvantray Mehta, chief minister of Gujarat, had lost his life. They might do something similar again. Shastri responded: 'Not really. President Ayub is a very good man. And now we have signed a peace agreement.'

Jagannath Sahai then conveyed to the prime minister a request from Prem Vaidya and Narayanswami—who were newsreel cameramen of the Government of India's ministry of information and broadcasting—for permission to take some photographs from outside his bedroom. The prime minister agreed and first appeared bareheaded. At Jagannath Sahai's request, he put on his Gandhi cap and his last photograph was then taken by Prem Vaidya and Narayanswami. During all this time, until 11.30 p.m., while Jagannath Sahai was still with him, the prime minister did not show any unusual symptoms.

Jagannath Sahai left Shastri's room at about 11.30 p.m. and then Ram Nath brought some milk which the prime minister drank. Ram Nath stayed on in Shastri's bedroom until half past midnight and left the room when the prime minister, who was already lying in bed, said that he should go and sleep. During all this time apparently the prime minister had not felt any discomfort.

Jagannath Sahai had returned to the staff bedroom at 11.30 p.m. and together with M.M.N. Sharma, Dr R.N. Chugh and Security Officer Kapur had completed the packing of the luggage. The heavy items for the hold were removed to the adjoining verandah. Dr Chugh went to bed and fell asleep. Jagannath Sahai, Sharma and Kapur were about to retire when, suddenly at 1.20 a.m., the prime minister appeared at the door of their bedroom. He was wearing his usual sleeping clothes. He was bareheaded but was wearing his chappals. His manner was quiet and unhurried. He paused for a few seconds at the door without entering the bedroom, looked around, and, seeing only the three of them, asked: 'Where is the Doctor?' Jagannath Sahai answered: 'Babuji, he is asleep right here. You may kindly return to your bedroom. I will bring the doctor immediately.'

Sharma and Kapur got up to accompany Shastri back to his room. They both held the prime minister's arms but the prime minister walked back on his own. When about half way there, he began to cough and thereafter went on coughing incessantly. When they got to his bed, Sharma and Kapur asked the prime minister to lie down, which he did. He was finding it difficult to speak but pointed to the flask. Sharma brought some water from it which Shastri sipped. According to Sharma, the prime minister was still fully conscious. Sharma then told him that as he had drunk water, he would soon feel better.

Dr Chugh and Sahai came running in, the doctor carrying his medicine cases. He checked the prime minister's pulse and gave him an injection. At the same time the doctor uttered the following words in deep anguish and despair: *'Babuji, aap ne mujhe mouka nahin diya.'* (Babuji, you did not give me a chance.)

The prime minister was still alive, but he was now in acute pain, coughing and breathless. During constant fits of coughing, he uttered the following words again and again: *'Arey baap, arey Ram.'* (O my father, O Lord Rama.)

Dr Chugh continued massaging his chest and gave him artificial respiration, but nothing proved of any avail. The prime minister passed away at 1.32 a.m.

Had Shastri a premonition of his death? On the morning of 10 January he had written the following couplet by the celebrated and venerated Urdu poet Saqib Lakhnavi on a piece of paper which Jagannath Sahai had picked up and kept with him for quite some time:

*Zamana bare shauq se sun raha tha*
*Hameen so gaye dastaan kahete kahete.*

(All the world was listening very intently,
Only I fell asleep while narrating the story.)

Many people in India continue to suspect that this was not a natural
death. It is their feeling that the heart attack to which Shastri succumbed
was induced by some substance which had been administered to him. It
seems that this view gained strength from the fact that Shastriji's face and
parts of his body had become blue in colour. Since the blue patches in
question led to widespread comments, the Soviet doctors who had attended
on Shastri on the fateful night subsequently issued a statement on 4
November 1970 to allay the suspicions in India. In their report they said:

> Since the body of the late prime minister was to be sent to his mother
> country, where, like in Tashkent, the climatic conditions cause quick
> decomposition, the embalming of the body of Mr L.B. Shastri was made
> in the presence of Dr R.N. Chugh.
> The embalming liquid, consisting of three litres of pure spirit, one
> litre of formalin and two hundred grammes of urotropine, was intro-
> duced through an incision into the femoral artery in the inguinal part
> of the body. So far as the references in the Indian press to the change
> in the colour of the face of the late L.B. Shastri are concerned, this is
> quite natural since such phenomena occurs in cases of embalming.

The colour of Shastri's face at the time of death was normal, without
any change. It was only after the embalming of the body that the face
became blue. At that time, Jagannath Sahai invited Dr Chugh's attention
to this change in colour and Dr Chugh stated that this was the direct result
of embalming.

Nevertheless, I wanted to obtain another specialist opinion on this
question. As I was living in London when I began work on this book, I
first discussed this matter with a highly qualified and reputed senior general
practitioner in London, Dr David M. Spiro, M.A. (Cambridge), M.B.,
B.CHIR., D.R.C.O.G., whom I have known for years and whose personal
advice I have always greatly valued. Dr Spiro felt it would be best to seek
the opinion of an internationally renowned pathologist and specialist in
forensic medicine, Dr Iain West, M.B., CH.B., F.R.C. PATH., D.M.J.,
head of the department of forensic medicine at Guy's Hospital, London.
Dr David Spiro and I met Dr West on 24 September 1992. I showed them
the medical reports, both of 1966 and 1970, narrated to them the
symptoms which were observed by the late prime minister's personal staff
during those twelve minutes of acute illness prior to his death, invited their

attention to the fact that a blue colour had developed on the face and other parts of the body, and asked their opinion on two specific questions:

(1)    What could have been the cause of the blue colour? Could it be the result of poisoning?

(2)    Could the symptoms—coughing, breathlessness and choking, leading to the diagnosis of an acute attack of myocardial infarction—have been induced also by the administration, through food or milk or water or otherwise, of some poisonous substance?

Dr Iain West listened to me with full attention and studied the documents which I presented to him. He then gave the following answers with which Dr Spiro fully agreed. With regard to the blue coloration, Dr West replied:

This blue colour is quite consistent with a death due to natural causes. It would be due to two factors, namely:

(1)    Cyanosis (a dark blue colour of the skin due to the removal of oxygen from the blood) and

(2)    the embalming process.

The embalming fluids may cause reduction (i.e. removal of the oxygen) of the haemoglobin, and perhaps this was the more important factor in this case.

It is relevant that the blood was not drained from the body (as is the usual practice) and that the embalming fluid used here was not the usual mixture. Both these factors might have caused a greater degree of blue discoloration than one would normally see. Although the fluid used (almost pure spirit) was quite adequate to delay decomposition of the body, a more conventional mixture might have produced a better cosmetic result. Probably the technique and materials used were the best that could be managed in Tashkent at that time.

When asked about the possibility of poison having been administered, Dr West again replied:

Without a postmortem examination and toxicological studies, it is impossible to say absolutely that no poison was administered. However, from the evidence available to me this seems most unlikely. The symptoms and Mr Shastri's behaviour as described by the witnesses are not suggestive of acute poisoning, but are much more suggestive of an acute myocardial infarction or of acute coronary insufficiency.

Then Dr West concluded:

Although poisoning could not be 100 per cent ruled out, there was no evidence that Mr Shastri had ingested any poison. On the other hand, all the available information was quite consistent with death from natural causes and so to suppose anything other than a natural death goes against the vast weight of the evidence.

This opinion by an eminent specialist speaks for itself. I would only add this information regards the circumstances of Prime Minister Shastri's death:

The events which took place on the evening of 10 January at the prime minister's villa have been narrated in this book fully and correctly. I was a witness to them myself until 10.30 p.m. Thereafter, the events as narrated are based upon the personal statements of two members of the prime minister's personal staff. They have read the relevant portions of this chapter and reconfirmed to me their veracity and accuracy.

During those twelve minutes of the late prime minister's acute illness prior to his death, or in the preceding hours, no other symptoms such as nausea or vomiting or giddiness were noticed by anyone present there.

No call bell had been installed at Shastri's bedside. Considering that he had a history of heart trouble, this was a serious omission in the arrangements. However, a buzzer telephone had been placed in the prime minister's suite. When the receiver was lifted, a loud buzzing sound was activated in the bedroom of the doctor and the personal staff. Shastri had used this on occasions to call the personal staff.

The buzzer telephone was kept in the sitting room attached to the prime minister's bedroom. Shastri spent most of his time till late in the evening in his sitting room. Although the buzzer telephone was located in the sitting room barely a few paces away from the prime minister's bed, there was no extension of that telephone just at the bedside. When the prime minister felt uneasy at about 1.20 a.m., he had therefore been obliged to get up from his bed. He could have used the buzzer telephone which was close by but, possibly because of the extreme kindness of his nature and the consideration he had for everyone, he may not have wished to use the buzzer's loud sound at that hour of the night, which would have awakened the entire staff. So, although he passed by the telephone, he decided to walk a few more paces up to the staff bedroom. Apparently at that time he was not feeling acute discomfort, because when he arrived at the door of the staff bedroom he was calm and collected and asked for the doctor in a clear, unfaltering voice. It was only when he was walking back that he began to cough and then went on coughing incessantly. This avoidable walk, short though it was, would, no doubt, have had an aggravating effect on his condition.

Certain persons advanced the view that Shastri was so upset by the news of the adverse reaction voiced by two opposition leaders to the Tashkent declaration, conveyed to him over the telephone, that a heart attack was instigated. Dr West also told me that the sudden conveyance of adverse or distressing news to a person who had suffered a heart attack previously, could, in some cases, trigger another such attack. As I was not with the prime minister when the two conversations with New Delhi took place, one between Jagannath Sahai and Venkataraman and the other between the prime minister himself and members of his family, I cannot give any personal assessment of the impact which the news or comments conveyed in these conversations might have had on him. However, I find it difficult to believe that this news would have upset him enough to induce a heart attack.

Some expressed the apprehension that Shastri was bullied and 'forced' by the Soviet leaders to sign the Tashkent declaration against his will. This is totally false. Shastri signed the Tashkent declaration freely and with a feeling of great achievement. The Soviet leaders never used any pressure tactics. And besides, Shastri was a person, who, as I know well, could not be pressurized.

In the face of the persisting suspicions, I have asked myself repeatedly who could have had a motive to assassinate Shastri in Tashkent. The possibility of any Russian agency or individual plotting such a cruel act is, in my view, absolutely ruled out. The Russians were extremely pleased with the prime minister. I was a witness to the obvious respect and admiration which Kosygin, Gromyko and other members of the Soviet delegation had for him. The truth is that the Russians were deeply saddened, because they genuinely believed that in the passing away of Lal Bahadur Shastri, they had lost a sincere and trustworthy friend.

It can be said that doubts have arisen because no postmortem examination was carried out. I asked L.P. Singh, then home secretary to the Government of India, who was a member of the Indian delegation in Tashkent and who was also an extremely close colleague and confidant of Shastri, whether this question had been considered. He told me that Ambassador T.N. Kaul had raised this subject with him, but as a team of USSR doctors, as well as the prime minister's own physician, Dr Chugh, had given a clear and categorical verdict as to the cause of death, as Shastri had a history of two previous heart attacks, and further as there was no other circumstance pointing to the need for a postmortem examination, they had both concluded that, as far as they were concerned, there was no need to pursue this matter further. Defence Minister Chavan and Foreign Minister Swaran Singh, who were both at the prime minister's villa and who were in charge of affairs after the death of Shastri, also did not ask for a postmortem examination for the same reasons.

It has also been pointed out that there was an opportunity for postmortem examination even after the late prime minister's body had arrived in India. Gulzari Lal Nanda, who had been sworn in as prime minister after Shastri's death, was himself present for quite a long time at No 10 Janpath where the late prime minister's body lay in state. Prime Minister Nanda, who had been briefed fully on the circumstances of Shastri's death in Tashkent, did not order a postmortem examination. Nor was such a suggestion made by anyone else, although the blue patches on the late prime minister's body had been noticed by all who saw the body. No one in the family of the late prime minister asked for a postmortem examination. In view of all the evidence, it is clear that Shastri died of a heart attack and, as there is nothing to indicate the intervention of any external factor, it would best serve his memory if the suspicions on this matter are laid to rest.

# Postscript 2

# World and National Comments
# and Tributes

Prime Minister Shastri's death only hours after he had signed a historic peace agreement with Pakistan, shocked and distressed the world.

The USSR prime minister, Kosygin, who was undoubtedly the most anguished world statesman at the time, having been the host of the Tashkent conference, expressed his feelings soon after arriving at the villa on hearing of Prime Minister Shastri's death, in the following words: 'It is a sad loss in which we all grieve with the Indian people. He was a great statesman, a great man with great wisdom and a man of great tact indeed. He did all he could for peace and for Indo-Pakistan friendship. All Soviet people bow their heads before the body of one who worked for lasting peace and friendship on earth.'

President Ayub Khan of Pakistan who arrived at Prime Minister Shastri's villa at about 3 a.m., was literally shaken by this traumatic development. Talking to Indian press representatives, he said: 'This is a very tragic occasion. I was really shocked when I heard about it this morning. I call it tragic for the sake of India as well as for the sake of the relationship between India and Pakistan because basically these are really matters of relationship between individuals in positions of responsibility.

He and I had established very good understanding with each other. I know he wanted peace and you can rest assured we also want peace. Mr Shastri died in the cause of peace.'[1]

Kuldip Nayar, who was also at Prime Minister Shastri's villa at this time, went up to President Ayub and exchanged a few words of grief at this tragedy. A pensive Ayub told Nayar: 'Through him we would have got durable peace in the subcontinent.' This remark confirms the comment of Prime Minister Shastri, made after his luncheon with President Ayub on 10 January 1966, that a real breakthrough had been secured by both of them in regard to India–Pakistan relations. Kuldip Nayar told me that he met Ayub again in 1972 after the Bangladesh War, when he was not in office. Nayar asked him why he had ordered the 'disguised' invasion of

Kashmir in 1965 by armed 'infiltrators' which had proved so disastrous for Pakistan. Ayub replied: 'Don't ask me. Ask Bhutto.' This confirms again that Bhutto was the man who had conceived and propelled that invasion. Kuldip Nayar asked Ayub whether he still retained the same faith in Shastri's dedication to peace. In reply Ayub repeated his words: 'Yes, I still maintain that through him we would have got durable peace.'

President Lyndon B. Johnson paid a very moving tribute: 'The world is smaller without him.' In a message to the president of India, President Johnson said:

> The sudden and tragic death of Prime Minister Lal Bahadur Shastri is a profound shock to me and to my countrymen. Our hearts go out to you, to his family, and to all Indians at this time of sadness. We had watched with admiration how Mr Shastri had calmly and courageously shouldered the heavy burdens of the high office he inherited under similar tragic circumstances not long ago. His star was bright, and his mark will be indelible. His steadfast devotion to the highest humanitarian ideals and to the improvement of the lot of his fellow-men was un-equalled. This rare quality singled him out as a man very much in tune with the hopes and aspirations of men everywhere. I am especially and deeply mindful that if Mr Shastri had lived, he would have been here with us next month and we mourn his death as if he were one of our own. To you, Mr President, and to all who were close to him, we express our deepest sympathy and assurances of our steadfast support in this dark moment of grief.[2]

The vice-president of the USA, Hubert Humphrey, said: 'A gallant apostle of peace is gone and all the world joins the people of India in mourning his passing.'[3]

The British high commissioner in India, John Freeman, conveyed his feelings in the following message to the president of India:

> I have heard of Lal Bahadur Shastri's death with an inexpressible sense of shock and personal grief. In his nineteen months as prime minister he had won the respect of the whole world for the strength and stature he manifested in his herculean task.
>
> More than that, he was above all a man of personal goodness. To his public life he brought the same standards of modesty, simplicity and decency which so noticeably infused his personal dealings. It is a tragedy for the world that his death should occur on the morrow of the success · at Tashkent, where patient statesmanship has opened what promises to be a new chapter in the history of Asia.
>
> For those of us who knew him and worked with him, our sense of loss is beyond words, and I offer to you and the people of India the deep and respectful sympathy of the whole staff of the British High Commission.[4]

The United States ambassador to India, Chester Bowles, said:

Prime Minister Shastri's tireless dedication to the cause of peace and to the task of improving the welfare of the Indian people is an inspiration to all men who look to the future with hope and confidence.

In another message, he added that the news of the death of Mr. Shastri

at the moment when his dedication to peace on the subcontinent and throughout the world was beginning to bear fruit was learnt with profound grief.[5]

In India, a state of mourning was declared for twelve days. President Radhakrishnan bestowed the nation's highest award, Bharat Ratna, post-humously on Lal Bahadur Shastri. Dr Zakir Hussain, Vice-President of India, expressed his feelings thus: 'I am stunned. My deep distress at the loss of a very dear friend fades into insignificance when one realizes what the nation has lost. Essentially a man of peace, he laid down his life at the altar of peace. A grateful nation is plunged in mourning at the loss of one it had not only respected but loved . . . The significance of his last act of statesmanship will reveal itself in the future and as his vision of a peaceful and friendly subcontinent realizes itself, his name will shine forth as one of the architects of peace in the world.'

Members of parliament belonging to different parties recorded their grief at a meeting held in the Central Hall of Parliament on the evening of 11 January 1966. Professor Hiren Mukherjee of the Communist Party of India said that Shastri had died in a trail of glory at a moment of triumph which would become a part of history. Atal Behari Vajpayee, leader of the Jan Sangh, paying a tribute, said that during Shastri's tenure a new India had been born. The nation had won back its self-respect and self-confidence and had accepted the fact that strength was necessary to protect peace. S.N. Dwivedy (PSP) said that Shastri's remarkable achievement was that he rose from the rank and file to occupy the highest post. He had done so because of the many eminent qualities he possessed and because of his organizational ability and statesmanship. Professor N.G. Ranga, leader of the Swatantra Party, said: 'This humble man became great and made other men feel great, greater than they were.'

C.N. Annadurai, leader of Dravida Munnetra Kazhagam, observed: 'After making history at Tashkent, Lal Bahadur himself has taken a sudden journey towards the valley of the immortal.' Frank Anthony, the Anglo-Indian leader, paid the following tribute: 'Mr Shastri by his transparent sincerity and his method of gentle persuasion rather than the bludgeon, of consensus rather than authoritarianism, had secured not only the trust but the affection of those of us who had the opportunity to work closely with him. The country will miss grievously his clear vision, fundamental good sense and statesmanship uninhibited by cliches and slogans.' Dr L.M. Singhvi, then a Member of Parliament and presently India's high commissioner in London, said: 'In the death of Mr Lal Bahadur Shastri, the country has lost a great leader whose practical wisdom and whose courageous statesmanship gave to the country a new national awareness, purposeful self-confidence and a sense of direction.'

G.N. Sahi, president of the Indian and Eastern Newspaper Society, commented: 'He provided stability to the country when it was needed most. He was a champion of the freedom of the press and a great believer in democratic values. The press of India has lost a great friend.'

Leaders of the Indian press paid their own tributes and, in doing so, provided their assessment of Shastri's performance as India's second prime minister.

Some of the most perceptive comments were made by one of the outstanding and respected figures in Indian journalism at that time—Frank Moraes, editor of *The Indian Express.* In an editorial, he observed:

> The drama of Tashkent has been cruelly heightened by its tragic denouement. The sudden death of Mr Lal Bahadur Shastri is a grievous loss to India for never were his qualities of patience and persistence, of flexibility and firmness, more needed than today. Following in the wake of the incandescent figure of Jawaharlal Nehru, Shastriji's homely, homespun personality suffered by comparison in the early days of his prime ministership but with each successive month, as crisis followed crisis, he grew in confidence and strength until the last confrontation with Pakistan found him the country's prime minister in his own right. Tashkent added more than a cubit to his stature as a statesman. It revealed him as a diplomat of considerable finesse and skill.
>
> Lal Bahadur had the wisdom which consists of commonsense in an uncommon degree, and this he revealed in growing measure in the brief nineteen months of his prime ministership. In that period he faced calmly and with resolution more successive crises than have come the way of most prime ministers. Foodgrain scarcity with rising prices posed the first menacing problem in his early days in office, and this was followed by growing tensions in Kashmir, culminating in the detention of Sheikh Abdullah. Then came the Pakistani incursion in Kutch and attack on Kashmir accompanied by Communist China's increasingly minatory postures on our northern frontier. Lal Bahadur had a rare capacity for remaining imperturbable but acutely vigilant through the most threatening times, and something of this calmness and confidence he was able to convey to his countrymen, more especially in the latter months of his prime ministership.
>
> Brought up on the teachings of The Servants of the People Society,

it was Lal Bahadur's great virtue that while conscious and proud of the finer traditions of Indian civilization, he was not unmindful of its lapses and sought to adjust the Indian picture within the larger framework and perspective of the world in which it had its being. This perspective gave him a sense of proportion in his handling not only of his own country's affairs but in his dealings with other countries, a trait which was noticeable in Tashkent . . .

He was a leader who because of his unusual attributes was ideally suited to guide his country in a time of crisis and fluidity, and it is no derogation of aspiring contestants to the prime ministership to observe that he will be difficult to replace. Although not unconscious of his own qualities, Lal Bahadur was a man of real humility in so far as he did not regard his own opinions as omnipotent and immutable but was prepared to listen to others and surprisingly often to defer to them. Politicians are notoriously prone to dot the capital I but nobody could accuse Shastriji of being self-centred. He was outgiving by temperament and training.[6]

This sympathetic and yet objective assessment was made by a person who had known Shastri closely for several years and who had maintained regular personal contact during the period of his prime ministership.

The following assessment was made by another leader of the Indian press, Pran Chopra, editor of *The Statesman* :

It has been rare in the history of this country or any other country that such a high office as that of prime minister has been adorned by a man so free of any flair for adornment, so untouched by the drama of his own elevation; it is rarer still that he not only filled the office to its full proportions, but in so short a time as nineteen months made it even greater force than he found it. I had glimpses of Mr Shastri in both phases, at the hesitant start and in his days of mastery, and the contrast fills me with admiration and amazement.

In the all too brief span of responsibility that fate gave him in the last and most creative spell of his life, Mr Shastri showed the qualities of mind which few people show if they are as deprived of advantages as he was in his early life, or if their youth and early manhood are as full of struggle as his, or if in their maturing years they are as much without liberalizing contact with other climes. He extracted from his experience not only humility but enlightened liberalism, and an understanding and tolerance of the other man's viewpoint.

Where others might have grown bigoted he only became firm; where others might have been infirm or vague, he was accommodating and flexible. Growing stronger with these qualities, he had made himself the man most suited both for preserving the honour of India and for winning peace with our neighbours. In search of that peace with honour, he met his end. Though his noblest years might still have been ahead of him, his accomplishments in a brief spell of office were indeed great.[7]

Much in the same strain, the third of this leading trio of press dignitaries, S. Mulgaonkar, editor of *The Hindustan Times* who, like Frank Moraes and Pran Chopra, had known Prime Minister Shastri well, made the following observations in an editorial on 12 January 1966:

> For when the greatest crisis after the attainment of freedom struck the country, a few months ago, it found the prime minister confident of himself, sure of his ground and able to provide the country with the determined leadership it needed. Whether he had grown with his office or had only rediscovered qualities always latent in himself is . . . a point of no great relevance except in this sense, that it is consistent with the picture his career presents of a man who does not seek out opportunities of playing a decisive part but who can be decisive if the part is thrust on him. Throughout the three-week war with Pakistan his voice rang strong and clear and his hand on the controls never wavered. But he also did not lose sight of the ultimate aim which was implied in the whole posture of this country in world affairs and in the image it had built up for itself of dedication to peace and good neighbourliness among nations. The meeting in Tashkent may therefore be said to mark the culmination of his effort and the agreement he reached there with President Ayub Khan as his real triumph.[8]

There were editorial comments in nearly all newspapers, journals and magazines throughout the country. Tributes were also paid by the organizations of men of business and industry, by trade unions and by many professional bodies in India. Leaders of foreign governments, editorial and column writers in the foreign press and political leaders of the right and the left—all had words of grief at Shastri's passing away and words of praise for his qualities and achievements.

I would wish to recall here the tribute paid, a few months earlier, to Prime Minister Shastri by the chief of the army staff, General J.N. Chaudhuri. On the occasion of Shastri's birthday, 2 October 1965, General Chaudhuri had conveyed his good wishes and had also expressed his feelings towards Prime Minister Shastri in the following words: 'Having worked so closely with you in the recent past, I can say with absolute sincerity that we have all been inspired by your courage and calmness.'

Air Chief Marshal Arjan Singh also expressed to me, when I met him recently, his deep admiration for Shastri's bold, clear, decisive and wise leadership during the period of the war. At that time the Air Chief Marshal used to meet Prime Minister Shastri every day. He referred to the great courtesy with which Prime Minister Shastri always received him. That, according to Air Chief Marshal Arjan Singh, was 'Lakhnavi tahzeeb' at its best.

General P.P. Kumaramangalam, former chief of the army staff, paid similar tributes to Prime Minister Shastri. In a recent conversation with me, he said: 'Shastri was never in a flap. He always listened carefully and then made up his mind firmly. This is what the armed forces wanted and admired.' The General became thoughtful for a moment and then added: 'When we lost him, we lost a great deal.'

Lt-General Harbaksh Singh expressed his abiding admiration for Prime Minister Shastri. Recalling Shastri's own decision, ordering the Indian army to launch a counterattack on Pakistan and to march towards Lahore on 6 September 1965, he commented: 'The tallest decision was made by the shortest man.'

When I met Wing Cdr Trevor Keelor on 22 December 1992, he recalled with pride his meeting with Prime Minister Shastri just after the cessation of hostilities in Pathankot and said:

> He was our prime minister in a very difficult period when the morale of the defence services needed a boost. He gave us that injection. He taught the Pakistanis a lesson. He demonstrated that we Indians did not just talk. We could act too. Even today, the high morale of the Indian air force must be attributed largely to his decision to use the air force in the 1965 war—an opportunity that had been denied to us in 1962 at the time of Chinese invasion.
>
> He was a soft spoken person. But the softer he spoke, the louder we heard him, for he was so inspiring.

Prem Vaidya, who was newsreel cameraman of the ministry of information and broadcasting in 1965, and who was present in Tashkent at the time of the conference, told me recently when I met him in Pune how deeply grieved he felt at the passing away of Shastri. He recalled that during his visits to the various theatres of war in 1965, he had invariably seen Prime Minister Shastri's photographs with soldiers in the barracks. He recalled also that on 11 January 1966 he had come back from Tashkent in the same plane which had brought Shastri's body. From the airport in Delhi he had taken a taxi to go to his residence. On the way, the taxi driver started talking. When he got to know that Prem Vaidya had come back with Shastri's body, he sobbed and said: *'Aap ne to mujhe yateem bana diya.'* (You have made me an orphan.)

After Prime Minister Shastri's death, some comment on record came from his successor—Indira Gandhi—in an interview she gave to Ved Mehta. Her remarks had two elements, first, her complaint about the treatment which, according to her, she had received from Shastri after he had become the prime minister, and second, her opinion of Shastri as prime minister. These remarks were recorded by Ved Mehta on pages 499 and 500 in his book *A Portrait of India*, which was published during the lifetime of Indira Gandhi.

Ved Mehta first asked her if press reports were true when they said that Nehru wanted her to succeed him as prime minister and that she could easily have done so. She replied:

> I was numbed by my father's death, and at that time I didn't want to think about holding any office. But I thought if I helped Shastri to become prime minister, then, when he got the office, he would consult with me, and in that way I would still have some influence on the future of our country. Shastri insisted that he needed to have me in the cabinet, so I consented to become minister of information and broadcasting. I did many things for Shastri, but once he got himself established as prime minister he didn't consult me on any of the major issues.

Before I refer to the second part of her remarks to Ved Mehta, I wish to comment on the first quoted above. Prime Minister Shastri had allocated to Indira Gandhi the portfolio which she had chosen herself. He had given her a very high place in the cabinet—at number 4, next after the prime minister, Home Minister Nanda, and Finance Minister T.T. Krishnamachari, and above very senior leaders such as Neelam Sanjiva Reddy, Y.B. Chavan and S.K. Patil. In fact her seniority in the Shastri cabinet was the same as that of Shastri himself in the preceding Nehru cabinet. Furthermore, Prime Minister Shastri had appointed Indira Gandhi as a member of all important committees of the cabinet. Every major issue was referred to the full cabinet or to one of its committees for consideration and decision. Even drafts of important letters, such as the one sent to the UN secretary-general on the question of ceasefire, were cleared by the appropriate cabinet body. Indira Gandhi thus had full opportunity of participating in the discussions and in the making of decisions. Once I asked Prime Minister Shastri as to the views of Mrs Gandhi about some matters. He replied briefly that she seldom expressed any view in the cabinet or in cabinet committees. We never talked again about Mrs Gandhi and he never made any comment about her to me or, as far as I know, to anyone else. Mrs Gandhi's complaint as expressed to Ved Mehta (and also to Inder Malhotra),[9] that she was not consulted on any major issue, must then mean that she expected Prime Minister Shastri to seek her advice outside the cabinet. But Prime Minister Shastri did not have an inner cabal or a kitchen cabinet because he believed in the institutional control of power. No other cabinet minister had any greater opportunity than had Mrs Gandhi to contribute to decisions on major issues. As far as Mrs Gandhi was concerned, he gave her a great deal of consideration because she was Nehru's daughter. He had told us that if Mrs Gandhi ever wanted to see him, he should be informed immediately and that he might himself go to meet her because she was passing through a period of grief.

The second part of Mrs Gandhi's comment came in answer to a question by Ved Mehta asking for her opinion on Shastri as prime minister. Her reply was very candid:

> Basically, he just didn't have a modern mind. He was an orthodox Hindu and full of superstitions. You can't lead the country out of poverty with superstition. You need a modern, scientific outlook for that. The orthodox say that we Indians are rich in our cultural heritage. Nowadays that just won't do—you must have a modern mind. But Shastri's dead, and it serves no purpose to dwell on our differences.

Shastri—an *orthodox* Hindu? True, he did not smoke, he did not drink, he was uncompromisingly vegetarian, he insisted on wearing his native dhoti, kurta and Jodhpuri coat in all climes and countries and he believed in the ancient values and culture of his country. But this is where his 'orthodoxy' ended. It would be entirely incorrect to suggest that Shastri had any religious prejudices or that he was ritualistic or superstitious or that he consulted astrologers or that he had any 'guru'. The truth is, as I know personally, that he had no such attributes at all. And secularism as well as great respect for all religions were articles of his faith.

Indira Gandhi said that Shastri did not have a 'modern mind' and suggested that he was not suitable to lead the country. About Shastri's mind, Frank Moraes made the following comments:

> Lal Bahadur was a reserved, reticent man, not given to imposing blanket bans or uttering absolute opinions, but if he knew anything he knew his mind. He also sensed and understood to an unusual degree the thoughts and needs of his countrymen. He was essentially a deshi product with no glittering, tinsel pretensions, and yet with a mind and outlook attuned to progress in the best sense of the term, unencumbered either by orthodox rigidities or by extravagantly modern notions or proclivities. He had, in the best sense of that much abused phrase, an open mind.[10]

What, then, were the reasons for Indira Gandhi's annoyance? I asked several persons who knew both of them whether they could shed some light on the Shastri–Indira relationship. Among them were Pandit Raja Ram Shastri, former Congress Party Member of Parliament, L.P. Singh, one of the most respected members of the Indian Civil Service, and Prem Bhatia, the present doyen of Indian journalism and a former ambassador of India. The view generally expressed was that during the later years of Pandit Jawaharlal Nehru's prime ministership, Mrs Gandhi had come to regard herself as the heir apparent and successor to her father as India's prime minister. She was therefore unhappy that Lal Bahadur Shastri had, as she thought, 'usurped' that position and her unhappiness had been aggravated by Shastri's performance as prime minister. Whatever her reasons, it is clear that Mrs Gandhi did not have a favourable opinion of Lal Bahadur Shastri.

To conclude, I would like to refer to some comments of a different kind made three years after Shastri's death by Chester Bowles contained in Bowles' Oral History (pages 41–2) deposited in the Lyndon B. Johnson Library, Austin, Texas, USA. On 11 November 1969, in an interview recorded by Joe B. Frantz, Chester Bowles talked of his years as ambassador and made the following observations about Shastri:

> Shastri was also an extraordinary man . . . I divide Indian leaders into two groups: One group I call the Adamses and the other is the Jacksonians. The Adamses are people educated in the UK or the US, therefore very anxious to prove to the Indians that they're not pro-American or pro-West and they go overboard the other way to prove they're not. They have one foot in Asia and one foot in Europe; charming, attractive and bright people, but they're not thoroughly Indian or deeply Indian. Now Shastri was a Jacksonian; his roots were in India. He'd never been out of India until after he became prime minister. And there are a lot of those. I have much more faith in that type of person for the future.

# References

## Chapter 1

1. *Congress Presidential Addresses 1885 – 1910* (Madras: Natesan & Co. 1935).
2. Jyotsana Srivastava, *Rashtra Ratna Shiv Prasad Gupta* (Varanasi: Gyan Mandal Ltd., 1989), p. 5.
3. Ibid., pp. 167–8.
4. Ibid., p. 168.

## Chapter 2

1. D.R. Mankekar, *Lal Bahadur – A Political Biography*, pp. 68–9.
2. Lala Lajpat Rai , Preamble to the *First Progress Report of The Servants of the People Society* (1927).

## Chapter 3

1. D.R. Mankekar, *Lal Bahadur Shastri – Builders of Modern India*, pp. 69–70.
2. D.R. Mankekar, *Lal Bahadur – A Political Biography*, p. 70.
3. Ibid., p. 78.
4. Ibid, p. 78.
5. D.R.Mankekar, *Lal Bahadur Shastri – Builders of Modern India*, p. 66.
6. Ibid., p. 84.
7. Ibid., p. 87.

## Chapter 4

1. Penderel Moon, *Wavell*, p. 120. Also quoted in Rajmohan Gandhi, *Patel, A Life*, p. 343.
2. *Harijansewak* and *Harijan*, 25 January 1942. Also quoted in Rajmohan Gandhi, *Patel, A Life*, p. 301.
3. D.R. Mankekar, *Lal Bahadur – A Political Biography*, p. 79.
4. A hilly tract in the Himalayas, from which Pant came.
5. Ibid., pp. 79–80.

## Chapter 5

1. D.R. Mankekar, *Lal Bahadur – A Political Biography*, pp. 91–2.
2. Ibid., p. 99.
3. Ibid., p. 97.
4. Ibid., p. 97.
5. Copy made available to me on 1 August 1991 by A.R. Bandyopadhyaya, IAS, additional secretary, Department of Administrative Reforms and Public Grievances, Government of India.
6. D.R. Mankekar, *Lal Bahadur – A Political Biography*, p. 108.
7. *Asian Recorder*, 22–28 January 1964, p. 5631. The following background information shows the great importance of this holy relic: 'The sacred relic had remained with the descendants of the Holy Prophet until it reached Sayyid Abdullah, the Mutawalli (administrator) of the Prophet's shrine in Medina. In 1634 the Sayyid left for India with his family and arrived at Bijapur (Deccan) where two years later he was granted jagir by the ruler there. The Sayyid stayed in Bijapur for 23 years and on his death his son, Sayyid Hamid, became the repository of the holy hair. Sayyid Hamid lived in Bijapur till the kingdom was conquered by Aurangzeb in AD 1692.

   Sayyid Hamid went to Jehanabad to get his jagir returned. Being in distress, he sought the help of a Kashmiri trader, named Khwaja Nur-ud-Din Ashwari, who was carrying on a prosperous business at Jehanabad. The Khwaja readily gave him the money but requested him to let him have the sacred relic. Hamid turned down this request, but the same night he was directed in a dream by the Prophet to hand over the hair relic to Khwaja Nur-ud-Din. According to *A History of Kashmir*, Khwaja Ashwari left for Kashmir with the relic but at Lahore, he was detained by Aurangzeb, who wanted to keep the sacred relic in Ajmer. The Khwaja was deeply shocked at being relieved of the relic by Aurangzeb and he died at Lahore, expressing his last wish to a friend, Khwaja Medanish, that should he succeed in getting back the relic, it should be taken to Kashmir. Aurangzeb too was directed in a dream by the Prophet to hand over the relic to Khwaja Medanish who later carried it to Kashmir. After being kept for some time in the Khangah of Naqshband, the holy hair was finally lodged in the Hazratbal Mosque which was originally built by Shah Jahan. The body of Khwaja Nur-ud-Din was also buried near the Ziarat (shrine).'
8. *The Telegraph*, London, 4 February 1964.
9. The home minister at this time was Gulzarilal Nanda.
10. *The Hindu*, Madras, 9 February 1964.
11. D.R. Mankekar, *Lal Bahadur – A Political Biography*, p. 113.

## Chapter 6

1. *The Hindustan Times*, New Delhi, 5 April 1958.

2. Ibid., New Delhi, 28 April 1958.
3. Ibid., New Delhi, 4 May 1958.
4. Frank Moraes, *India Today*, p. 226.
5. Welles Hangen, *After Nehru, Who?*, p. 129.
6. Ibid., p. 276.
7. Ibid., p. 129.
8. *The Hindustan Times*, New Delhi, 19 May 1964.
9. Ibid., New Delhi, 3 June 1964.
10. *The Philosophy of Mr Nehru, as revealed in a series of intimate talks with R.K. Karanjia*, p. 139.

## Chapter 7

1. *The Hindustan Times*, New Delhi, 4 May 1958.
2. Memorandum of the Planning Commission on Fourth Five Year Plan, p. 7.

## Chapter 8

1. *The Indian Express*, New Delhi, 3 June 1964.

## Chapter 9

No Notes.

## Chapter 10

1. Shanti Shankar Kumar, 'Father of the Green Revolution' (1987).
2. Shastri divested himself of this portfolio on 18 July 1964, when he appointed Sardar Swaran Singh as the foreign minister.
3. Michael Brecher, *Nehru's Mantle*, p. 117.
4. Ibid., p. 118.
5. Speech on the occasion of the foundation-stone laying ceremony of the Gandhi Smarak Nidhi at Trivandrum on 21 February 1965: *Selected Speeches of Lal Bahadur Shastri*, pp. 190–2.
6. Speech in Hyderabad on 21 March 1965: *Selected Speeches of Lal Bahadur Shastri*, p. 181.
7. Speech in New Delhi on 12 June 1964: *Selected Speeches of Lal Bahadur Shastri*, p. 192.
8. Memorandum: National Security File: National Security Action Memorandum: Box 7–NSAM 339, Critical Indian Food Situation: Lyndon B. Johnson Library, Austin, Texas, USA.
9. *The Hindustan Times*, New Delhi, 23 February 1965.

10. NSF Country Files, Mid-East India: Box 136; India-Shastri Correspondences 6/64 – 1/66, Doc 3 and 1168.NSF Country Files, Mid-East India: Box 136; India-Shastri Correspondences 6/64 –1/66, Docs 3 and 11b, Lyndon B. Johnson Library, Austin, Texas, USA.

## Chapter 11

1. Durga Das, ed., *Sardar Patel's Correspondence 1945–50*, vol. 1, p. 340.
2. Instrument of Accession of Jammu and Kashmir state. The following is the text of the actual Instrument of Accession executed by the Ruler of Jammu and Kashmir State on 26 October 1947:

Whereas, the Indian Independence Act, 1947, provides that as from the fifteenth day of August 1947, there shall, be set up an independent Dominion known as INDIA, and that the Government of India Act, 1935, shall, with such omissions, additions, adaptions and modifications as the Governor-General may by order specify, be applicable to the Dominion of India;

And whereas the Government of India Act, 1935, as so adapted by the Governor-General provides that an Indian State may accede to the Dominion of India by an Instrument of Accession executed by the Ruler thereof;

Now, therefore, I, Shriman Indar Mahindar Rajrajeshwar Maharajadhiraj Shri Hari Singhji, Jammu Kashmir Naresh Tatha Tibbet adi Deshadhipathi, Ruler of Jammu and Kashmir State, in the exercise of my sovereignty in and over my said State do hereby execute this my Instrument of Accession and;

1.   I hereby declare that I accede to the Dominion of India with the intent that the Governor-General of India, the Dominion Legislature, the Federal Court and any other Dominion authority established for the purposes of the Dominion shall, by virtue of this my Instrument of Accession but subject always to the terms thereof, and for the purposes only of the Dominion, exercise in relation to the State of Jammu and Kashmir (hereinafter referred to as 'this State') such functions as may be vested in them by or under the Government of India Act, 1935, as in force in the Dominion of India, on the 15th day of August 1947 (which Act as so in force is hereafter referred to as 'the Act').

2.   I hereby assume the obligation of ensuring that due effect is given to the provisions of the Act within this State so far as they are applicable therein by virtue of this my Instrument of Accession.

3.   I accept the matters specified in the Schedule hereto as the matters with respect to which the Dominion Legislature may make laws for this State.

4.    I hereby declare that I accede to the Dominion of India on the assurance that if an agreement is made between the Governor-General and the Ruler of this State whereby any functions in relation to the administration in this State of any law of the Dominion Legislature shall be exercised by the Ruler of this State, then any such agreement shall be deemed to form part of this Instrument and shall be construed and have effect accordingly.

5.    The terms of this my Instrument of Accession shall not be varied by any amendment of the Act or of the Indian Independence Act, 1947, unless such amendment is accepted by me by an Instrument supplementary to this Instrument.

6.    Nothing in this Instrument shall empower the Dominion Legislature to make any law for this State authorizing the compulsory acquisition of land for any purpose, but I hereby undertake that should the Dominion for the purposes of a Dominion law which applies in this State deem it necessary to acquire any land, I will at their request acquire the land at their expense or if the land belongs to me transfer it to them on such terms as may be agreed, or, in default of agreement, determined by an arbitrator to be appointed by the Chief Justice of India.

7.    Nothing in this Instrument shall be deemed to commit me in any way to acceptance of any future constitution of India or to fetter my discretion to enter into arrangements with the Government of India under any such future constitution.

8.    Nothing in this Instrument affects the continuance of my sovereignty in and over this State, or, save as provided by or under this Instrument, the exercise of any powers, authority and rights now enjoyed by me as Ruler of this State or the validity of any law at present in force in this State.

9.    I hereby declare that I execute this Instrument on behalf of this State and that any reference in this Instrument to me or to the Ruler of the State is to be construed as including a reference to my heirs and successors.

Given under my hand this 26th day of October, nineteen hundred and forty-seven.

(Sd.) Hari Singh
Maharajadhiraj of Jammu and Kashmir State

[From H.S. Gururaj Rao, *Legal Aspects of the Kashmir Problem* (Bombay: Asia Publishing House, 1967), pp. 212–13.]

3. S. Gopal, *Jawaharlal Nehru – A biography*, p. 185.
4. Ibid., p. 185.

## Chapter 12

1. Ved Vati Chaturshreni, *Indo–US Relations* (New Delhi: National Publishing House) p. 153.
2. Ibid., p. 153.
3. Ibid., p. 154.
4. DSB Volume xxvii (705), 29 December 1952, p. 1028.
5. Joint communiqué issued on 20 August 1953 in New Delhi at the end of Nehru–Mohammed Ali talks. See Ved Vati Chaturshreni, *Indo–US Relations*, pp. 176 and 181.
6. *The Dawn*, 13 June 1952.
7. *The Hindu*, 26 February 1954.
8. *Parliamentary Debates 1954*, vol. i, no.12, part ii, cols 963–74: Full text.
9. *Congressional Record*, vol. 100, 1954, p. 481. Also *The Hindu*, 5 March 1954.
10. Ved Vati Chaturshreni, *Indo–US Relations*, p. 220.
11. Ibid., p. 221.
12. *The Hindustan Times*, 22 October 1953 (overseas edition).
13. Ved Vati Chaturshreni, *Indo–US Relations*, p. 222.
14. Ibid., p. 222.
15. R.W. Komer and McGeorge Bundy were two top aides and advisers to President Kennedy in the White House
16. Container No. 24, Collection NSF NSC Histories, South Asia 1962–1966, Preface, Introduction, Narrative and Guides to Documents, Tab A, 1–7, Vol I, Doc 6b. Lyndon B. Johnson Library, Austin, Texas, USA.
17. Container No. 24, Collection NSF NSC Histories, South Asia 1962–66, Preface, Introduction, Narrative and Guide to Documents, Tab A, 1–7, Vol I, Doc 7e. Lyndon B. Johnson Library, Austin, Texas,USA.
18. Container No. 24, Collection NSF NSC Histories, South Asia 1962–66, Preface, Introduction, Narrative and Guide to Documents, Tab A, 1–7, Vol I, Doc 8d. Lyndon B. Johnson Library, Austin, Texas, USA.
19. Container No. 24, Collection NSF NSC Histories, South Asia 1962–66, Preface, Introduction, Narrative and Guide to Documents, Tab A, 1–7, Vol I, Doc 8u. Lyndon B. Johnson Library, Austin, Texas, USA.
20. Ibid., Doc 8v 1.
21. Ibid., Doc 9f.
22. Ved Vati Chaturshreni, *Indo–US Relations*, pp. 234–5. Also *The Dawn*, 2 July 1963.
23. Container No. 24, Collection NSF NSC Histories, South Asia 1962–66, Vol I, Preface, Introduction, Narrative and Guide to Documents, Tab A, 1–7, Vol I, Doc 10e. Lyndon B. Johnson Library, Austin, Texas, USA.
24. Ved Vati Chaturshreni, *Indo–US Relations*, p. 235.
25. Container No. 24, Collection NSF NSC Histories, South Asia 1962–66, Preface,

Introduction, Narrative and Guide to Documents, Tab A, 1–7, Vol I, Doc 10c – Record of White House Meeting on 12 August 1963. Sanitized does not mean altered or changed. It only means blacking out of sensitive portions. What remains is still original and authentic. Lyndon B. Johnson Library, Austin, Texas, USA.

26. Container No. 24, Collection NSF NSC Histories, South Asia 1962–66, Vol I, Tab B, 1–13, Doc 15a.

27. Ibid., Doc 15c.

28. Ibid., Doc 15e.

29. Ibid., Doc 15f: R.W. Komer's Memo of 13 December 1963 to McGeorge Bundy.

30. Container No. 128, Collection: NSF Country Files, Middle-East India, Department of State Telegram 1221 to Am. Embassy, New Delhi. Lyndon B. Johnson Library, Austin, Texas, USA.

31. Ambassador B.K. Nehru's letter dated 4 December 1963, forwarding Pandit Jawaharlal Nehru's letter dated 29 November 1963, Container No. 136, Folder – Nehru Correspondence, Doc # 1a Collection NSF Country Files, Middle East, India. Lyndon B. Johnson Library, Austin, Texas, USA.

32. Container No. 128, Collection NSF Country Files, Middle East, India, Vol I 12/63 – 3/64 Doc 93b. Lyndon B. Johnson Library, Austin, Texas, USA.

33. Ibid., Doc 93.

34. Ibid., Doc 92.

35. Container No. 24, Collection NSF NSC Histories, South Asia 1962–66,Vol I, Tab B, 1–13, Doc 16e. Lyndon B. Johnson Library, Austin, Texas, USA.

36. Ibid., Doc 17d.

37. Ibid., Doc 17f–1.

38. *Asian Recorder*, 18–24 March, 1964, p. 5726.

## Chapter 13

1. Bimal Prasad, *Indo–Soviet Relations 1947–1972*, p. 1.

2. Ibid., pp. 17–18.

3. Ibid., p. 22.

4. Ibid., p. 40.

5. Report of the Forty-Ninth Session of the Indian National Congress, p. 20.

6. Bimal Prasad, *Indo–Soviet Relations 1947–1972*, p. 57.

7. Ibid., p. 99.

8. SCOR Yr 12, mtg 799, pp. 1–4.

9. Bimal Prasad, *Indo–Soviet Relations 1947–1972*, p. 254.

## Chapter 14

1. *The Hindustan Times*, New Delhi, 13 October 1964.

2. General (retd) Mohammed Musa, H.J., *My Version – India-Pakistan War 1965*, pp. 4–5.
3. Ibid., p. 5.
4. Ibid., p. 7.
5. Ibid., pp. 5–6.
6. Ibid., p. 6.
7. Ibid., pp. 6–7.
8. USA, Collection Oral History – Bowles, pp. 61–2. Lyndon B. Johnson Library, Austin, Texas, USA.
9. Container No. 24, Collection NSF NSC Histories, South Asia 1962–66, Vol I, Tab A 1–13, Doc 10c. Lyndon B. Johnson Library, Austin, Texas, USA.
10. Collection Oral History – Bowles, pp. 60–1, Lyndon B. Johnson Library, Austin, Texas, USA.

## Chapter 15

1. Major Sita Ram Johri (retd), *The Indo–Pak Conflict of 1965*, p. 70.
2. Brines, *The Indo–Pakistani Conflict*, p. 287.
3. *The Hindustan Times*, New Delhi, 22 March 1965.
4. Major Sita Ram Johri (retd), *The Indo–Pak Conflict of 1965*, p. 74.
5. i.e. on Wednesday, 28 April 1965.
6. *The Hindustan Times*, New Delhi, 1 May 1965.
7. Ibid., New Delhi, 4 May 1965.
8. Brines, *The Indo–Pakistani Conflict*, p. 289.
9. Jayaprakash Narayan, 'Object Lesson in Peace-making', *The Hindustan Times*, New Delhi, 20 July 1965.
10. *The Hindustan Times*, New Delhi, 2 July 1965.
11. A Pakistani newspaper.
12. *The Dawn*, Karachi, 20 June 1965.
13. Brines, *The Indo–Pakistani Conflict*, p. 290.
14. Ibid., p. 301.

## Chapter 16

1. Brines, *The Indo–Pakistani Conflict*, pp. 301–2.
2. General (retd) Mohammad Musa, H.J., *My Version*, pp. 11–12.
3. Ibid., p. 36.
4. Ibid., p. 37.
5. Brines, *The Indo–Pakistani Conflict*, p. 302.
6. Ibid., p. 303.
7. General (retd) Mohammad Musa, *My Version*, pp. 35–6.
8. Ibid., p. 8.

9. Ibid., p. 44.
10. Gauhar, *Ayub Khan*, pp. 321–2.
11. Ibid., p. 55.
12. Gauhar, *Ayub Khan*, p. 323.
13. Ibid., p. 324.
14. Ibid., p. 318.
15. Ibid., p. 317.
16. General (retd) Mohammad Musa, *My Version*, p. 36.
17. Gauhar, *Ayub Khan*, p. 325.
18. Ibid., p. 329.
19. Ibid., pp. 331–2.
20. *The Hindustan Times*, New Delhi, 10 August 1965.
21. Ibid., New Delhi, 10 August 1965.
22. Ibid., New Delhi, 15 August 1965.
23. Ibid., New Delhi, 14 August 1965.
24. Ibid., New Delhi, 14 August 1965.
25. Ibid.
26. Ibid., New Delhi, 23 August 1965.
27. Ibid., New Delhi, 25 August 1965.
28. Gauhar, *Ayub Khan*, p. 326.
29. Ibid., p. 328.
30. Ibid., pp. 329–30.
31. *The Hindustan Times*, New Delhi, 1 September 1965.

# Chapter 17

1. Lt-Gen Harbaksh Singh VrC (retd), *War Despatches, Indo–Pak Conflict 1965*, p. 59.
2. Brines, *The Indo–Pakistani Conflict*, p. 320.
3. Also see *The Hindustan Times*, 4 September 1965.
4. *Indo–Pakistan Conflict, Security Council Documents, September 1965* (New Delhi: External Publicity Division, Government of India), pp. 13–14.
5. C.S. Jha, *From Bandung to Tashkent*, p. 211.
6. Obtained by me in Washington from a former US ambassador. Declassified document.
7. *Indo–Pakistan Conflict, Security Council Documents, September 1965* (New Delhi: External Publicity Division, Government of India), pp. 2–5.
8. USA: Memorandum – The Indo-Pakistan War and its Aftermath, Doc 41a, p. 6 – National Security File, NSC Histories, Box 24, South Asia, 1962–66, Vol 3, Indo Pak War, State Department History I. Lyndon B. Johnson Library, Austin, Texas, USA.
9. Ibid., p. 7.

10. Resolution 209 (1965) adopted by the Security Council at its 1237th Meeting on 4 September 1965.

11. *The Pakistan Times*, Lahore, 6 September 1965.

12. *The Hindustan Times*, New Delhi, 6 September 1965.

13. Harbaksh Singh, *War Despatches*, p. 63.

14. Mohammad Musa, *My Version*, p. 42.

15. Memo – Pakistan Memos Vol IV, Wilson to Shastri, Collection NSF Country File, Mid East, Container No.151, Doc 184a and 184b. Lyndon B. Johnson Library, Austin, Texas, USA.

16. *Indo–Pakistan Conflict, Security Council Documents, September 1965*, (New Delhi: External Publicity Division, Government of India), p. 19.

17. Memo – Pakistan Memos, Vol IV, Collection NSF Country, Mid-East, Container No. 151, Doc 184c. Lyndon B. Johnson Library, Austin, Texas, USA.

18. *From Bandung to Tashkent*, p. 213.

19. Ibid., pp. 216–17.

20. Resolution 210 (1965) adopted by the Security Council at its 1238th Meeting on 6 September 1965.

21. Letter dated 5 June 1965 from President Johnson to Prime Minister Shastri, India Shastri Correspondence, Collection NSF Country Files, Mid-East India, Container 136, Doc 37. Lyndon B. Johnson Library, Austin, Texas, USA.

22. Letter dated 9 July 1965 from Prime Minister Shastri to President Johnson, India Shastri Correspondence, Collection NSF Country Files, Mid-East India, Container 136, Doc 32. Lyndon B. Johnson Library, Austin, Texas, USA.

23. Prime Minister Shastri's letter dated 7 September 1965 to President Johnson, India Shastri Correspondence, Collection NSF Country Files, Mid-East India, Container 136, Doc 25a. Lyndon B. Johnson Library, Austin, Texas, USA.

24. Memo: The India–Pakistan War and its Aftermath, p. 9, Doc 41a: National Security File, NSC Histories, Box 24, South Asia 1962–66, Vol 3, Indo–Pak War: State Department History I. Lyndon B. Johnson Library, Austin, Texas, USA.

25. Memo dated 10 September 1965, Doc 41w, National Security File: NSC Histories, Box 24, South Asia, 1962–66, Vol 3, Indo–Pak War: State Department History I. Lyndon B. Johnson Library, Austin, Texas, USA.

26. Letter dated 4 September 1965 from President Johnson to President Ayub Khan NS File: NSC Histories, Box 24, South Asia, 1962–1966, Vol 3, Indo-Pak War, State Department History I, Doc 41k. Lyndon B. Johnson Library, Austin, Texas, USA.

27. Memo – Cable, Iran Cables Vol I, Collection: NSF Country File, Mid-East India: Container No. 136 (Cable from Tehran Embassy to Secretary of State, Washington dated 11 September 1965, Doc 18. Lyndon B. Johnson Library, Austin, Texas, USA.

28. *The Statesman*, 7 September 1965.

29. Ibid., 8 September 1965.

30. Ibid., 10 September 1965.

31. Cable dated 8 September 1965 from the Secretary of State to the US ambassador in New Delhi, NS File, NSC Histories, Box 24, South Asia, 1962–66, Vol 3, Indo-Pak War, State Department History I, Doc 41u. Lyndon B. Johnson Library, Austin, Texas, USA.

## Chapter 18

1. *The Dawn*, Karachi, 10 September 1965.
2. Ibid., 11 September 1965.
3. Ibid.
4. All correspondence between the UN Secretary-General and Prime Minister Shastri, as well as President Ayub Khan quoted from *Indo–Pakistan Conflict, Security Council Documents, September 1965*, pp. 31–8.
5. *The Hindustan Times*, New Delhi, 15 September 1965.
6. Letter dated 16 September 1965 from Prime Minister Shastri of India to President Johnson of USA – Collection NSF Country Files, India: Container No. 136, Doc 15a. Lyndon B. Johnson Library, Austin, Texas, USA.

## Chapter 19

1. *The Pakistan Times*, Lahore, 5 September 1965.
2. Ibid., 8 September 1965.
3. Ibid., 9 September 1965.
4. Ibid., 10 September 1965.
5. *The Hindustan Times*, New Delhi, 13 September 1965.
6. Ibid., 14 September 1965.
7. Ibid., 18 September 1965.
8. Memo dated 17 September 1965, Doc 41cc, from INR to Secretary of State, National Security File, NSC Histories, Box 24: South Asia, 1962–66; Vol 3; Indo-Pak War: State Department, History I. Lyndon B. Johnson Library, Austin, Texas, USA.

## Chapter 20

1. *Indo–Pakistan Conflict, Security Council Documents, September 1965*, p. 40.
2. *Kashmir – Text Of Speeches*, Mahomedali Currim Chagla, union minister of education and leader of the Indian Delegation, in the Security Council, on September 17, 18 and 20, 1965 (New Delhi: External Publicity Division), pp. 1–6.
3. Ibid., pp. 16–20.
4. *Indo–Pakistan Conflict, Security Council Documents, September 1965*, p. 47.

## Chapter 21

1. Harbaksh Singh, *War Despatches*, p. 7.
2. See *Fiza'ya*, by Singh, Rikhye and Steineman, p. 20.
3. Ibid., p. 42.
4. Air Chief Marshal P.C. Lal, *My Years with the IAF*, p. 115.

## Chapter 22

1. Quoted in Brines, p. 330.
2. *War Despatches*, pp. 86–7.
3. Brines, p. 328.
4. *War Despatches*, pp. 96, 98.
5. Ibid., p. 119.
6. Ibid., p. 120.
7. D.R. Mankekar, *Twenty-two Fateful Days*, pp. 109–10.
8. Gauhar, *Ayub Khan*, p. 339.
9. Ibid., p. 343.
10. Ibid., p. 343.
11. P.C. Lal, *My Years with the IAF*, p. 133.
12. Musa, *My Version*, p. 56.
13. Ibid., p. 58.
14. Brines, p. 342.
15. Ibid., p. 343.

## Chapter 23

1. Gauhar, *Ayub Khan*, p. 401.
2. *Twenty-two Fateful Days*, p. 154.
3. Ibid., p. 155.
4. Ibid., p. 156.
5. *War Despatches*, pp. 204–5.
6. *Ayub Khan*, p. 498.
7. Ibid., pp. 516–17.

## Chapter 24

1. The rest of the prime minister's statement related to the Chinese ultimatum and this part has been quoted elsewhere.

## Chapter 25

1. *Indo–Pakistan Conflict, Security Council Documents, September 1965,* p. 35.
2. Ibid., p. 4.
3. *Ayub Khan,* p. 353.
4. Ibid., p. 352.
5. Ibid., p. 352.
6. Telegram from Usun New York dated 22 September, 1965, – National Security File, NSC Histories, Box 24, South Asia, 1962–1966, State Department History II, Doc 58. Lyndon B. Johnson Library, Austin, Texas, USA.
7. *Indo–Pakistan Conflict, Security Council Documents, September 1965,* p. 51
8. Ibid., p. 51.

## Chapter 26

1. Memorandum, National Security File, NSC Histories, Box 24, South Asia, 1962–1966, Vol 3, Indo–Pak War, State Department History I, Doc 41a, p. 16.
2. *Selected Speeches of Lal Bahadur Shastri,* pp. 340–6.
3. *The Hindustan Times,* New Delhi, 1 October 1965.
4. Ibid., 4 October 1965.
5. Ibid., 5 October 1965.
6. Ibid., 9 October 1965.
7. Ibid., 18 October 1965.
8. UNI/PTI Report, *The Hindustan Times,* New Delhi, 20 October 1965.
9. *The Hindustan Times,* New Delhi, 6 November 1965.
10. Ibid., 7 November 1965.
11. *Lal Bahadur – A Political Biography,* p. 54.

## Chapter 27

1. *The Hindustan Times,* New Delhi, 26 December 1965.
2. Ibid., 3 January 1965.
3. Ibid., 4 January 1965.

## Chapter 28

1. Memorandum dated 13 December 1965 Monday, 4.00pm (Doc 37R) National Security File, NSC Histories, Box 24, South Asia, 1962–66, Vol 2, Tab B: 22–26. Lyndon B. Johnson Library, Austin, Texas, USA.
2. Meaning India and Pakistan.
3. Memorandum for the President, dated 14 December 1965, Tuesday, 4.30pm;

Doc # 37s National Security File, NSC Histories, Box 24, South Asia, 1962–66, Vol 2, Tab B: 22–26. Lyndon B. Johnson Library, Austin, Texas, USA.

4. Memorandum for the President: 2.15 p.m. Wednesday, 15 December 1965, Doc 37y; National Security File, NSC Histories, Box 24, South Asia; 1962–1966, Vol 2, Tab B: 22–26. Lyndon B. Johnson Library, Austin, Texas, USA.

5. Memorandum dated 15 December 1965 (5.30 p.m.) Doc 37f, p. 1, regarding meeting between President Johnson and President Ayub in Cabinet Room, White House, National Security File, NSC Histories, Box 24, South Asia, 1962–66, Vol. 2; Tab B: 22–26. Lyndon B. Johnson Library, Austin, Texas, USA.

6. Ibid., p. 2.

7. Memorandum dated 15 December 1965 (5.30 p.m.) Doc 37f, p. 1, regarding meeting between President Johnson and President Ayub in Cabinet Room, White House, National Security File, NSC Histories, Box 24, South Asia, 1962–66, Vol. 2; Tab B: 22–26. Lyndon B. Johnson Library, Austin, Texas, USA.

8. Ibid., p. 2.

9. Memorandum regarding President Johnson's Oral Statement made on 15 December 1965 at the end of President Ayub's visit, Doc 37w, National Security File NSC Histories, Box 24, South Asia, 1962–66, Vol 2, Tab B: 22–26. Lyndon B. Johnson Library, Austin, Texas, USA.

10. Memorandum/Joint Communiqué dated 15 December 1965, issued at the end of President Ayub's visit, Doc 37x, National Security File, NSC Histories, Box 24, South Asia, 1962–66, Vol 2, Tab B: 22–26. Lyndon B. Johnson Library, Austin, Texas, USA.

## Chapter 29

1. *Ayub Khan*, p. 354.

## Chapter 30

No Notes.

## Chapter 31

1. See editorial headed 'Tashkent' in *The Dawn*, 3 January 1966.

2. It was under these articles that the United Nations Security Council authorized armed action against Iraq in 1990.

Article 41 of the UN Charter:

The Security Council may decide what measures not involving the use of armed force are to be employed to give effect to its decisions, and it may call upon members of the United Nations to comply with such measures. These may include complete or partial interruption of economic relations and of rail, sea, air, postal, telegraphic, radio and other means of communication, and the severance of diplomatic relations.

Article 42 of the UN Charter:

Should the Security Council consider that measures provided for in Article 41 would be inadequate or have proved to be inadequate it may take such action by air, sea or land forces as may be necessary to maintain or restore international peace and security. Such action may include demonstrations, blockade, and other operations by air, sea, or land forces of Members of the United Nations.

3. *The Hindustan Times*, New Delhi, 6 January 1966.
4. i.e. the prime minister of India, and the president of Pakistan.
5. *The Washington Post*, Sunday, 9 January 1966.
6. *The New York Times*, 9 January 1966.
7. *The Guardian*, 9 January 1966. Emphasis by the author.
8. *The Hindustan Times*, New Delhi, 9 January 1966.
9. *Times of India*, New Delhi, 9 January 1966.
10. *The Pakistan Times*, 9 January 1966.
11. *The Dawn*, Karachi, 9 January 1966.
12. *The Times*, London, 9 January 1966.
13. *The New York Times*, 9 January, 1966.
14. *The Observer*, London, 9 January, 1966.
15. *The New York Times*, 9 January 1966.
16. *The Times*, London, 10 January 1966.
17. *The New York Times*, dated 10 January 1966.
18. *The Statesman*, New Delhi, 10 January 1966.
19. *The Hindustan Times*, New Delhi, 10 January 1966.
20. *The Indian Express*, 10 January 1966.
21. *The New York Times*, 10 January 1966.
22. *The Times*, London, 10 January 1966.
23. *The Washington Post*, 10 January 1966.

# Chapter 32

1. *Ayub Khan*, p. 400.
2. *The Washington Post*, 11 January 1966.

# Chapter 33

No Notes.

## Epilogue

1. *The Analects by Confucius* (Harmondsworth: Penguin Books), Book XVI, pp. 140–1.

## Postscript 1

No Notes.

## Postscript 2

1. *The Hindustan Times*, New Delhi, 2 January 1966.
2. Ibid., New Delhi, 13 January 1966.
3. Ibid., New Delhi, 12 January 1966.
4. Ibid., New Delhi, 12 January 1966.
5. Ibid., New Delhi, 12 January 1966.
6. *The Indian Express*, 12 January 1966.
7. *The Statesman*, 12 January 1966.
8. *The Hindustan Times*, New Delhi, 12 January 1966.
9. See Inder Malhotra, *Indira Gandhi: A Personal and Political Biography*, p. 83.
10. See Frank Moraes, 'A Grievous Loss', in *The Indian Express*, 12 January 1966.

# Select Bibliography

The published works on Lal Bahadur Shastri comprise a number of biographies and biographical sketches, generally somewhat limited in the range of coverage. There are also several Commemoration Volumes containing short articles by eminent political leaders and others who have recorded their own reminiscences and impressions and have recounted the various facets of Mr Shastri's virtue. All these provide excellent material.

Revealing information about Pakistan's preparation for and the conduct of Indo–Pak war of 1965 has been published in two books, by important and well-informed Pakistani authors, one by the then commander-in-chief of the Pakistan army, General (retd) Mohammed Musa, and the other by the then information secretary of the Pakistan Government, Altaf Gauhar. I have used this information to explain why the Indo–Pak war broke out and what the result was.

Declassified official documents about India–USA–UK–USSR–Pakistan–China relations were obtained by me from the Lyndon Baines Johnson Library in Austin, Texas, USA. These contain authentic and, as far as I know, hitherto unpublished information. I have quoted extensively from these documents to explain the attitudes of USA, USSR, UK and China towards India and Pakistan during Shastri's prime ministership, especially during the critical days of the Indo–Pak war.

Contemporary newspapers and journals of India, Pakistan, USA and UK were an exceedingly good source of day-to-day information and comments on important events in different parts of the world. The British Newspaper Library in Colindale, London, is a remarkable storehouse of all leading English language newspapers around the world, thanks to microchip technology. To me this newspaper library provided extremely absorbing information.

As the available material about Mr Shastri's early life was inadequate to explain the development of his personality and the vast array of his moral qualities, I travelled to Ramnagar, Mirzapur and Varanasi, where Shastri had spent his childhood days leading to his education in a High School and later Kashi Vidya Peeth, from where he obtained a First Class Degree. There I met some of his relations and friends. This was most rewarding in terms of the first-hand information I secured, especially from Shastri's classmate and lifelong friend Pandit Raja Ram Shastri. The chapters on Shastri's early life are based mainly on this primary source of authentic information.

All this was satisfactory but I was still concerned about the firm advice given to me by my well-wishers that I must discover some 'skeletons' about Mr Shastri and lay them bare, along with a narration of his qualities, in order to provide a 'balanced' picture and thus to establish my objectivity. Accordingly I asked all of Mr Shastri's relations and friends to give me some 'interesting' information. This was of no avail.

One day, while I was still in Varanasi, my nephew, Kailash Narain Srivastava, who lives there, suggested that I should talk to Mr Rohit Mehta, an internationally renowned Theosophist and humanist who was known for speaking the truth in all circumstances. We both saw Mr Mehta who was a contemporary of Mr Shastri and who was in remarkably good health, in his mid-eighties. Mr Mehta was delighted that I was writing Mr Shastri's biography. 'He was a great, good man,' said Mr Mehta. I then asked him straight: 'Did he have any flaw in his character, any weaknesses?' Mr Mehta did not obviously expect such a question about Shastri. He was taken aback. For quite a minute he pondered and then said: 'No, I do not know of any nor did I hear of any.' After pausing a moment he added emphatically: 'No, he had no weaknesses whatsoever.'

Finally, on returning to New Delhi, I explained my predicament to Mr L.P. Singh. He advised: 'Write the truth. Do not worry about the sceptics.' I accepted his advice.

And now to the bibliography. I have listed below the books and other published documents on which I have relied or which provide further reading material.

## Books

ADHIKARI, M., *Lal Bahadur Shastri* (Delhi: Rajpal and Sons, 1966).

AHLUWALIA, B.K., *Lal Bahadur Shastri* (New Delhi: New Light Publications, 1967).

ALEXANDER, Dr Mithrapuram K., *Lal Bahadur Shastri, An Illustrated Biography* (New Delhi: New Light Publishers, 1978).

ALI, Mir Najabat, *Lal Bahadur Shastri* (National Integration Series) (New Delhi: National Council of Educational Research and Training, 1969).

AMARNATH (ed.), *Shastri Smriti Granth* (Lucknow: Navyug Granthagar, 1966).

ASTHANA, Girja Rani, *Remembering Lal Bahadur Shastri* (New Delhi: Children's Book Trust, 1989).

BALODI, Ansuya Prasad, *Karmyogi Lal Bahadur Shastri* (New Delhi: Radha Publications, 1991).

BHATIA, Prem, *Of Many Pastures* (New Delhi: Allied Publishers Limited, 1989).

BHATNAGAR, B.B., *Shanti ke Pujari aur Yuddh ke Vijeta* (New Delhi: Shakun Prakashan, 1971).

BINDRA, Dr S.S., *Indo-Pak Relations Tashkent to Simla Agreement* (New Delhi: Deep and Deep Publications, 1981).

BOWLES, Chester, *Promises to Keep, My Years in Public Life 1941–1969* (New York: Harper and Row, Publishers, 1971).

BRECHER, Michael, *Nehru's Mantle, The Politics of Succession in India* (Westport, Connecticut: Greenwood Press, 1966).

BRINES, Russell, *The Indo–Pakistani Conflict* (London: Pall Mall Press Ltd., 1968).

CHANDER, Satish (ed.), *Shastri Memorial Souvenir,* SMS Committee (Delhi: Cultural Meet Publications, 1967).

CHATURSHRENI, Ved Vati, *Indo–US Relations* (New Delhi: National Publishing House; Delhi: K.L. Malik and Sons Pvt. Ltd., 1980).

*Congress Presidential Addresses, From the Foundation to the Silver Jubilee (1885–1910)* (Madras: G.A. Natesan and Co. Publishers, 1935).

*Congress Presidential Addresses, From the Silver to the Golden Jubilee (1911–1934)* (Madras: G.A. Natesan and Co. Publishers, 1934).

DURGA Das (ed.), *Sardar Patel's Correspondence 1945–50*, vol. I, *New Light on Kashmir* (The Navajivan Press, 1971).

DUTT, K. Iswara (ed.), *Shri Lal Bahadur Shastri—Purti Souvenir* (K. Jagannatha Rao, 1964).

FISCHER, Louis, *The Life of Mahatma Gandhi* (London: Grafton Books, 1982).

GANDHI, Rajmohan, *Patel, A Life* (Ahmedabad: Navajivan Publishing House, 1990).

GAUHAR, Altaf, *Ayub Khan, Pakistan's First Military Ruler* (Pakistan: Sang-e-Meel Publications, 1993).

GHOSE, Sankar, *Indian National Congress, its History and Heritage* (New Delhi: All India Congress Committee, 1975).

GOPAL, Sarvepalli, *Radhakrishnan: A Biography* (Delhi: Oxford University Press, 1989).

GOPAL, Sarvepalli, *Jawaharlal Nehru: A Biography,* Abridged Edition (Delhi: Oxford University Press, 1989).

GUJRATI, B.S., *A Study of Lal Bahadur Shastri* (Jullundur: Sterling Publishers Pvt. Ltd., 1965).

GUPTA, M.G., *The Prime Ministers of India* (Agra: 1989).

GUPTA, Ram Chandra, *Lal Bahadur Shastri: The Man and His Ideas (An Analysis of His Socio-Political and Economic Ideas)*, 1966.

GUPTA, Tansukhram, *Lal Bahadur Shastri Mahaprayan* (Delhi: Surya Prakashan, 1966).

HANGEN, Welles, *After Nehru, Who?* (London: Rupert Hart-Davis, 1963).

JHA, C.S., *From Bandung to Tashkent: Glimpses of India's Foreign Policy* (Sangam Books (India) Pvt. Ltd., 1983).

JOHRI, Major Sita Ram (retd), *The Indo-Pak Conflict of 1965* (Lucknow: Himalaya Publications, 1967).

KARANJIA, R.K., *The Philosophy of Mr Nehru* (London: George Allen and Unwin Ltd., 1966).

KARVE, D.G. and D.V. AMBEKAR (eds), *Speeches and Writings of Gopal Krishna Gokhale* (Bombay: Asia Publishing House; Poona: Servants of India Society, 1966).

KAUL, T.N., *Diplomacy in Peace and War, Recollections and Reflections* (New Delhi: Vikas Publishing House Pvt. Ltd., 1979).

KHAN, Air Marshal (retd) M. Asghar, *The First Round Indo–Pakistan War 1965* (Ghaziabad: Vikas Publishing House Pvt. Ltd.; London: Islamic Information Services Ltd., 1979).

KHAN, Mohammad Ayub, *Friends Not Masters: A Political Biography* (London: Oxford University Press, 1967).

LAJPAT Rai, *Young India, An Interpretation and a History of the Nationalist Movement from Within* (Lahore: Servants of the People Society, 1927).

LAL, Air Chief Marshal P.C., *My Years with the IAF* (New Delhi: Lancer International, 1986).

LLOYD, T.O., 'The Short Oxford History of the Modern World', *The British Empire 1558–1983* (Oxford: Oxford University Press, 1984).

Lok Sabha Secretariat, *Lal Bahadur Shastri and Parliament* (New Delhi: Allied Publishers Limited, 1993).

MAHAJAN, Mehr Chand, *Looking Back* (Bombay: Asia Publishing House, 1963).

MAJUMDAR, R.C. (gen. ed.), 'Struggle for Freedom', *The History and Culture of the Indian People* (Bombay: Bharatiya Vidya Bhavan, 1969).

MALHOTRA, Inder, *Indira Gandhi, A Personal and Political Biography* (UK: Hodder and Stoughton, 1989).

MANJULA, *Gudri ka Lal, Lal Bahadur* (Delhi: Umesh Prakashan, 1966).

MANKEKAR, D.R., *Lal Bahadur, A Political Biography* (Bombay: Popular Prakashan, 1964).

——, *Lal Bahadur Shastri, Builders of Modern India* (New Delhi: Publications

Division, Ministry of Information and Broadcasting, Government of India, 1973).

MANKEKAR, D.R., *Twenty-Two Fateful Days: Pakistan Cut to Size* (Bombay: P.C. Manaktala and Sons Pvt. Ltd., 1966).

MEHTA, Ved, *Portrait of India* (Delhi: Vikas Publications, 1971).

MORAES, Frank, *India Today* (New York: The Macmillan and Company, 1960).

MUSA, General (retd) Mohammad, H.J., *My Version: India–Pakistan War 1965* (Lahore: Wajidalis Limited, 1983).

NAQVI, Manzar Abbas, *Intakhab Ghazliat Saqib* (Lucknow: Uttar Pradesh Urdu Akademy, 1983).

National Council of Educational Research and Training (NCERT), *Lal Bahadur Shastri* (New Delhi: NCERT, 1969).

PANDE, B.N., *Indira Gandhi, Builders of Modern India* (New Delhi: Publications Division, Ministry of Information and Broadcasting, Government of India, 1989).

PANDEY, A.P., *Immortal Martyr of Peace: Shree Shastri* (Varanasi: Bhola Prakashan, 1966).

PATHAK, S.K., *Lal Bahadur Shastri, Jeevan Darshan aur Sansmaran* (Delhi: J.K. Book and Stationery Company, 1965).

PEREIRA, Arthur P., *Shastri, Man of Peace* (Bombay: Macmillan and Company Limited, 1966).

PRAKASH, Sumangal, *Wah Nanha sa Admi* (Varanasi: Bharatiya Jnanpith Publications, 1966).

PRAMANIK, Prahladkumar, *Our Lal Bahadur* (Bengali: Amader Lalbahadur) (Calcutta: Orient Book Company, 1966).

PRASAD, Bimal, *Indo–Soviet Relations 1947–1972, A Documentary Study* (New Delhi: Allied Publishers Pvt. Ltd., 1973).

PRASAD, Rajeshwar, *Days with Lal Bahadur Shastri, Glimpses From the Last Seven Years* (New Delhi: Allied Publishers Pvt. Ltd., 1991).

RAI, Lala Lajpat, 'Preamble to the First Progress Report of The Servants of the People Society', 1927.

RAJASHEKHAR, N., *The Great Little Man (A Short Biography of Lal Bahadur Shastri)* (Dehra Dun: E.B.D. Publishing and Distributing Company, 1967).

RAO, H.S. Gururaj, *Legal Aspects of the Kashmir Problem* (Bombay: Asia Publishing House, 1967), pp. 212–13.

RAU, M. Chalapathi, *Jawaharlal Nehru, Builders of Modern India* (New Delhi: Publications Division, Ministry of Information and Broadcasting, Government of India, 1973).

SAHAI, K.B. (ed.), *Lal Bahadur Shastri: Vyaktitva aur Vichar* (Jaipur: Chinmay Prakashan, 1967).

SAMPURNANAND, *Memories and Reflections* (New York: Asia Publishing House, 1962).

SAVARA, Sudershan K., *Champion of Peace, Tribute to Shastri* (New Delhi: Gyan Mandir, 1967).

SHAFFEE, C.M. (ed.), *Shri Lal Bahadur Shastri*, Birthday Abhinandan Granth (Souvenir) (New Delhi: 1964).

SHANKAR, Uma (ed.), *Mere Pati Mere Devta (Recollections and Reminiscences of Shrimati Lalita Shastri)* (Kanpur: Granth Bharati, 1967).

SHASTRI, Lal Bahadur, *Selected Speeches of Lal Bahadur Shastri* (11 June 1964 to 10 January 1966) (New Delhi: Publications Division, Ministry of Information and Broadcasting, Government of India, 1974).

SHASTRI, Sunil, *Lal Bahadur Shastri: Mere Babuji* (New Delhi: Purvoday Prakashan, 1988).

SHASTRI, Sunil (ed.), *Lal Bahadur Shastri* (Commemoration Volume) (New Delhi: 1970).

Shri Lal Bahadur Shastri Sewa Niketan, *Dharti ka Lal* (New Delhi: Lal Bahadur Shastri Smriti Granth, 1986).

Shri Lal Bahadur Shastri Sewa Niketan (Fatehpur Branch), *Saga of Lal Bahadur Shastri* (Commemoration Volume) (New Delhi: 1989).

SHRIVASTAVA, Harihar Lal, *Karmveer Lal Bahadur Shastri, Shri Lal Bahadur Shastri ki Jeevan Katha* (Varanasi: Archana Prakashan, 1985).

SINGH, Lt-Gen Harbaksh Vr.C. (retd), *War Despatches, Indo–Pak Conflict 1965* (New Delhi: Lancer International, 1991).

SINGH, Pushpindar, Ravi RIKHYE and Pieter STEINEMAN, *Fiza'ya: Psyche of the Pakistan Air Force* (New Delhi: The Society for Aerospace Studies, 1991).

SINGH, Sheobran and Mrs J.P. BANSAL, *Kashmir and Other Related Matters* (Agra: Oriental Publishing House, Educational Publishers, 1967).

SRIVASTAVA, Dr Mrs Jyotsana, *Rashtra Ratna Shiv Prasad Gupta* (Varanasi: Gyan Mandal Ltd., 1989).

TAHMANKAR, D.V., *Lokmanya Tilak, Father of Indian Unrest and Maker of Modern India* (London: John Murray, 1956).

THAPAR, Raj, *All These Years, A Memoir* (New Delhi: Seminar Publications, 1991).

VARMA, Ram Kumar, *Sansmark ke Suman* (Allahabad: Sahitya Bhavan, 1982).

YADAV, J.N.S., *Lal Bahadur Shastri, A Biography* (Delhi: Hariyana Prakashan, 1971).

## Booklets/Pamphlets

1. Indo–Pakistan Conflict, Security Council Documents, September 1965, External Publicity Division, Ministry of External Affairs, Government of India, New Delhi.
2. Kashmir, Text of Speeches by Mahomedali Currim Chagla, Union Minister of Education and Leader of the Indian Delegation, in the Security Council on 17, 18 and 20 September 1965, External Publicity Division, New Delhi.
3. Kashmir in Security Council, Text of Documents 2–7 September 1965, External Publicity Division, Ministry of External Affairs, New Delhi.
4. Kashmir, Text of Speeches by Mahomedali Currim Chagla, Union Minister of Education and Leader of the Indian Delegation, in the Security Council on 5 and 10 February and, 7, 12 and 18 May 1964, Information Service of India, New Delhi.
5. Memorandum of the Planning Commission on Fourth Five Year Plan, by the Planning Commission, Government of India.

## Archives

1. Lyndon B. Johnson Library, Austin, Texas, USA, White House Papers and Other Documents.
2. Yale University Library, Connecticut, USA, Chester Bowles Papers.
3. The British Library, Newspaper Library, Colindale, London.
Contemporary Newspapers of India, Pakistan, UK and USA.

## Contemporary Newspapers and Journals

### Indian Newspapers

*The Hindustan Times*
*The Hindu*
*The Indian Express*
*The Statesman*
*The Times of India*

### Pakistani Newspapers

*The Dawn*
*The Pakistan Times*

*U.K. Newspapers/Journals*

*The Times*
*The Telegraph*
*The Guardian*
*The Observer*
*The Economist*

*U.S.A. Newspapers*

*The New York Times*
*The Washington Post*

*Others*

*Asian Recorder*
*The People's Daily*

# Index